D1198967

*The Adams Papers*

L. H. BUTTERFIELD, EDITOR IN CHIEF

SERIES I

DIARIES

*Diary and Autobiography of John Adams*

# Diary and Autobiography of John Adams

L. H. BUTTERFIELD, *EDITOR*

LEONARD C. FABER AND WENDELL D. GARRETT

*ASSISTANT EDITORS*

———————— ☆ ————————

Volume 3 · *Diary* 1782–1804
*Autobiography*
*Part One* To October 1776

THE BELKNAP PRESS
OF HARVARD UNIVERSITY PRESS
CAMBRIDGE, MASSACHUSETTS

1961

Distributed in Great Britain by Oxford University Press · London

Funds for editing *The Adams Papers* have been provided by Time, Inc.,
on behalf of *Life*, to the Massachusetts Historical Society, under whose
supervision the editorial work is being done.

Library of Congress Catalog Card Number 60–5387 · Printed in the United States of America

# Contents

# Illustrations

of Foreign Affairs. (Photograph courtesy of the Netherlands Government Information Service.)

4. HUIS TEN BOSCH, THE STADHOLDER'S RESIDENCE NEAR THE
   HAGUE                                                                    33

The Huis ten Bosch or Maison du Bois was built between 1635 and 1652 by Pieter Post on the design of Jacob van Campen for Princess Amelia von Solms, widow of Prince Frederick Henry of Orange. The two wings were added before the middle of the 18th century by Daniel Marot. Here John Adams was received by Prince William V of Orange after Dutch recognition of American sovereignty in 1782, and was a frequent visitor thereafter during his sojourns at The Hague. See his Diary under 14 September 1782 and note, p. 5, 9.

In June 1784 Elkanah Watson, of Providence, Rhode Island, toured the Netherlands and provided the most detailed account we have of Adams' habits as American minister at The Hague. Of a visit with Adams to the Huis ten Bosch he wrote:

"Breakfasted with Mr. Adams — after which we visited *la Maison du Bois*, which is situated about a mile from the Hague, in the centre of the largest natural wood in Holland, and the only one, except the wood near Haerlem.

"This palace was built by the widow of prince Henry Frederick, for a house of mourning. It is an elegant structure and entirely sequestered from the gay world, being in a manner embosomed in a grove, cut into many romantick walks leading from the palace, which has a large garden behind it. Over the gate we saw the arms of Orange Nassau, and entered by a flight of steps.

"The grand saloon, with its exquisite paintings, are the principal objects of attention, and mostly executed by those great masters, Rubens and Van der Worf, representing in very large pieces, the brilliant triumphs of Frederick Henry, who finished the fabrick of independence for his country, which was founded by his immortal father, and vigorously carried on by his gallant brother Prince Maurice. . . .

"The floors are black walnut, covered with rich carpets. In one of the apartments we saw a valuable India japanned railing, enclosing the princess's bed; which is inlaid with the mother of pearl, and cost twenty eight thousand guilders. In another apartment was shewn us a flower piece, the work of a Flemish master, and valued at fifteen thousand florins. I was so enraptured with the paintings, that after a full hour's eager examination, I left them with regret.

"Mr. Adams then discharged his carriage, and we walked two hours more about the forest, which was very pleasing to me, notwithstanding the roads were heavy and sandy. The lofty oaks seemed to be so promiscuously thrown together, that it revived in my breast a lively picture of many such situations I had seen in the course of my tour through the United States of America, some years since. Our eyes were delighted with the fine plumage of the birds, whose sweet melody reechoed through the woods" (*A Tour in Holland, in*

MDCCLXXXIV, Worcester, 1790, p. 78–81). (Photograph courtesy of the Gemeente-Archief, The Hague.)

Now the Odeon Gebouw, Singel No. 460, this was the home and business headquarters of one of the principal banking houses that raised money for successive loans to the United States beginning in 1782. John Adams was in touch with Nicholas and Jacob van Staphorst, ardent supporters of the Patriot party and of the American cause, immediately upon his arrival in Amsterdam in 1780 and called on them often. See the List of Persons and Firms to be Consulted in the Netherlands, July–August 1780, vol. 2:444–445. (Photograph by George M. Cushing Jr.)

The Trèveszaal in the Binnenhof at The Hague where John Adams signed the Treaty of Commerce with the Dutch Republic on 8 October 1782. The room was built from designs by Daniel Marot in 1697. Portraits of the Stadholders, including William III of England, line the walls; the ceiling is painted with an allegorical representation of the union of the Seven Provinces by Theodorus van der Schuer. In a letter to the Secretary for Foreign Affairs, Robert R. Livingston, written on the day that the treaty was signed, Adams reported that he was "conducted into the Chamber of Business (Chambre de Besogne) an appartment adjoining to the Truce Chamber (Chambre de Treve) where were executed the Treaty of Commerce and the Convention concerning Recaptures, after an Exchange of Full Powers" (Adams Papers). The Trèveszaal is in that part of the Binnenhof now occupied by the Netherlands Ministry of Traffic and Waters. See the Diary entry of 8 October 1782 and note, p. 16–17. (Photograph courtesy of the Netherlands Government Information Service.)

Engraving, about 1830, of the "Velvet Makers' (or Merchants') Wall Street" and the canal that traversed it, the location of the first building acquired by the United States as a foreign legation. The structure, which was torn down between 1824 and 1830, stood on the site of the one-story wall and doorway to the left of the center of the engraving. When Elkanah Watson arrived at The Hague in 1784, he immediately sought out the American minister at "the grand hôtel belonging to the thirteen United States of America, lately purchased by Mr. Adams, for the residence of our future ambassadors. It is decently furnished, has a large library, and an elegant little garden" (*A Tour in Holland, in MDCCL-*

*XXXIV*, Worcester, 1790, p. 71–72). The site is now occupied by the Netherlands Government Printing Office. See the note under Adams' Memorandum of Visits Made and Received at The Hague following Dutch Recognition of American Independence, April 1782, p. 4–5. (From an engraving in the Adams Papers Editorial Files.)

8. MEDAL COMMEMORATING DUTCH RECOGNITION OF AMERICAN
   INDEPENDENCE, 19 APRIL 1782                                             65

Silver medal by the Amsterdam medalist, Joan George Holtzhey. The obverse side reads: "LIBERA SOROR / SOLEMNI DECR. AGN. / 19 APR. MDCCLXXXII" ("A free sister, acknowledged by solemn decree, 19 April 1782"). The reverse side reads: "TYRANNIS VIRTUTE REPULSA / SUB GALLIAE / AUSPICIIS" ("Tyranny repelled by valor under the auspices of France"). See C. Wyllys Betts, *American Colonial History Illustrated by Contemporary Medals*, New York, 1894, p. 290–291. Two allegorical figures, representing America and the Netherlands, grasp hands near a burning altar under the rays of the sun. America, in an Indian headdress, rests her foot on the head of a lion. On the reverse a unicorn, one of the supporters of the arms of England, lies wounded after breaking its horn against a precipitous rock.

On 2 November 1782 John Adams wrote Holtzhey to thank him for "the Present of a Medal, in Commemoration of the great Event of the 19th of April 1782," which he found "ingeniously devised and . . . very beautiful." He thought Holtzhey "would find a Sale for many of them at Boston and Philadelphia," and promised that upon his return to Holland "I shall be glad to purchase a few of them to give to my friends" (Adams Papers). On Adams' advice Holtzhey marketed a number of the medals through John Stockdale in London. When, on 24 March 1784, Adams sent a "Couple of Medals" to Charles Spener, a Prussian bookseller, he stated that "These Medals were not Struck by any publick Authority" but were "the Invention and Execution of the Medalist Holtzhey of Amsterdam solely" (Adams Papers). Concerning this and other medals associated with John Adams' mission to the Dutch Republic, see, further, Henry K. Pasma, "Dutch Fireworks — And Our Own," *National Historical Magazine* (a publication of the National Society of the D.A.R.), 73 (1939), No. 7, p. 8–11. (Courtesy of the Massachusetts Historical Society.)

9. THE AMERICAN COMMISSIONERS AT THE PRELIMINARY PEACE
   NEGOTIATION WITH GREAT BRITAIN, PARIS, 1782                           256

Unfinished painting (or more correctly, a sketch for a larger painting) by Benjamin West of the American commissioners and their secretary at the negotiation which resulted in the Preliminary Treaty with Great Britain which was signed on 30 November 1782. The painting was to have included the British representative, Richard Oswald, and his secretary, Caleb Whitefoord, but remains unfinished for reasons given by John Quincy Adams after a talk in London with the artist on 6 June 1817:

"Mr. West then told me that he had in the year 1783 made a sketch for a picture of the peace which terminated the war of the American Revolution, which he would send me to look at the next morning, as he accordingly did. I then recollected having seen it before, at the time when my father was sitting to him for his likeness in it. The most striking likeness in the picture is that of Mr. Jay. Those of Dr. Franklin, and his grandson, W. T. [William Temple Franklin], who was Secretary to the American Commission, are also excellent. Mr. Laurens and my father, though less perfect resemblances, are yet very good. Mr. Oswald, the British Plenipotentiary, was an ugly-looking man, blind of one eye, and he died without leaving any picture of him extant. This Mr. West alleged as the cause which prevented him from finishing the picture many years ago. Caleb Whitefoord, the Secretary of the British Commission, is also dead, but his portrait exists, from which a likeness may be taken. As I very strongly expressed my regret that this picture should be left unfinished, Mr. West said he thought he could finish it, and I must not be surprised if some day or other it should be received at Washington. I understand his intention to be to make a present of it to Congress" (*Memoirs*, ed. Charles Francis Adams, 3:559). (Courtesy of the Henry Francis du Pont Winterthur Museum.)

10. SIGNATURES AND SEALS ON THE DEFINITIVE TREATY OF PEACE WITH GREAT BRITAIN, SIGNED AT PARIS IN SEPTEMBER 1783                                                                    256

Last page of a duplicate original retained by John Adams; there are two originals of the Definitive Treaty in the Department of State Treaty File. See Hunter Miller, ed., *Treaties and Other International Acts of the United States of America*, Washington, 1931–1948, 2:151–157. On 5 September 1783 Adams reported to the President of Congress, Elias Boudinot: "On Wednesday, the third day of this Month, the American Ministers met the British Minister at his Lodgings at the Hotel de York and signed, sealed and delivered the definitive Treaty of Peace between the United States of America, and the King of Great Britain. Although it is but a Confirmation or Repetition of the Provisional Articles, I have the Honour to congratulate Congress upon it, as it is a Completion of the Work of Peace, and the best that We could obtain" (Adams Papers). John Thaxter, John Adams' secretary, returned to America shortly thereafter and brought one of the original copies of the Treaty to Congress. See the note under Adams' Diary entry of 7 September 1783, p. 142. (From the original in the Adams Papers.)

11. THE ADAMS FAMILY'S RESIDENCE IN AUTEUIL, 1784–1785  257

Photograph of Rue d'Auteuil Nos. 43–47, from Fernand Girardin, *Maisons de plaisances françaises, parcs et jardins*, Paris [1920].

This was the residence of John Adams during an illness in the fall of 1783 and of the Adams family from August 1784 to May 1785. See Adams' Diary under 14 September — 6 October 1783 and notes, p. 143–144; 17 August 1784, p. 171. For an illustrated description of the house, accompanied by richly detailed letters by Mrs. Adams about the family's life there, see Howard C. Rice Jr., *The Adams Family in Auteuil, 1784–1785*, Boston, 1956.

12. DU SIMITIÈRE'S DESIGNS FOR A MEDAL TO COMMEMORATE
THE EVACUATION OF BOSTON, 1776                                   257

Pierre Eugène Du Simitière's drawing of the obverse and sketch for the reverse of a gold medal to be presented by Congress to George Washington to commemorate his "wise and spirited conduct in the siege and acquisition of Boston." On 25 March 1776 John Adams was appointed to a committee "to prepare . . . a proper device for the medal." "I am put upon a Committee to prepare a Device for a Golden Medal to commemorate the Surrender of Boston to the American Arms," he wrote his wife on 14 August. "There is a Gentleman here of French Extraction, whose Name is Du Simitiere a Painter by Profession whose Designs are very ingenious, and his Drawings well executed. He has been applied to for his Advice. I waited on him yesterday, and saw his Sketches. For the Medal he proposes Liberty with her Spear and Pileus, leaning on General Washington. The British Fleet in Boston Harbour, with all their Sterns towards the Town, the American Troops, marching in" (Adams Papers). On the reverse, in pencil, an all-seeing eye casts rays over a naked sword, held upright by a hand, and the whole is surrounded by thirteen shields bearing the names of the states. These designs were superseded by those of a French medalist some years later. See Adams' Autobiography and note, p. 375–376. (Courtesy of the Library Company of Philadelphia.)

13. GROSVENOR SQUARE, LONDON, IN 1789                            288

Engraving of Grosvenor Square by Robert Pollard, 1789, after a drawing by Edward Dayes, the water colorist. This view from the northwest corner looks toward the earliest American legation building in London (see the following illustration), at Duke and Brook Streets in the northeast corner of the Square. (Courtesy of the British Museum.)

14. THE FIRST AMERICAN LEGATION BUILDING IN LONDON, COR-
NER OF DUKE AND BROOK STREETS, GROSVENOR SQUARE      288

The Adams family resided in this late 18th-century house from July 1785 until February 1788. "We shall live more as if we were a part of the World," Abigail Adams 2d informed her brother, John Quincy Adams, immediately after moving into the house, "than when in France and we already find ourselves better pleased" (letter of 4 July — 11 August 1785, Adams Papers). See the note

French colored engraving of a balloon flight in 1783. John Quincy Adams described the current enthusiasm for aerial navigation in a letter from Auteuil to his friend Peter Jay Munro, 10 November 1784 (Museum of the City of New York): "Messieurs Roberts made their third experiment, the 19th of September, and with more success than any aerostatic travellers have had before. They went up from the Thuileries, amidst a concourse of I suppose 10,000 persons. At noon, and at forty minutes past six in the Evening they descended at Beuory in Artois fifty leagues from Paris. This is expeditious travelling, and I heartily wish they would bring balloons to such a perfection, as that I might go to N. York, Philadelphia, or Boston in five days time. M.M. Roberts have publish'd a whole Volume of Observations upon their Voyage, or Journey or whatever it may be called, but I judge from the abstracts I have seen of it that they have taken a few traveller's Licenses, and have given some little play to their Imaginations. . . . They have established somewhere in Paris, a machine which they call *une tour aërostatique* where for a small price, any curious person may mount as high as he pleases, and so '*look down upon the pendent world.*'" (From an original in the Adams Papers.)

Titlepage of John Adams' copy of Edward Cocker's *Decimal Arithmetick*, 3d edition, London, 1703. This volume remains among his books in the Boston Public Library. "My School master neglected to put me into Arithmetick longer than I thought was right, and I resented it," Adams remembered in his Autobiography (p. 258). "I procured me Cockers I believe and applyd myself to it at home alone and went through the whole Course, overtook and passed by all the Schollars at School, without any master. I dared not ask my fathers Assistance because he would have disliked my Inattention to my Latin." Cocker's *Arithmetick* was published posthumously by John Hawkins in 1678 and attained a record of approximately a hundred English editions in the following century. Though often imported, the work appears never to have had an American printing. See Louis C. Karpinski, *Bibliography of Mathematical Works Printed in America through 1850*, Ann Arbor, 1940, p. 4–5. (Courtesy of the Boston Public Library.)

VOLUME 3

*Diary* 1782–1804

*Autobiography*

PART ONE

# Diary of John Adams

[MEMORANDUM OF VISITS MADE AND RECEIVED
AT THE HAGUE FOLLOWING DUTCH RECOGNITION
OF AMERICAN INDEPENDENCE, APRIL 1782.][1]

Liste des Visites faites le 22 May [*i.e.* April] 1782

Chez M[ess]rs.

De Pallandt ⎫
   Lohman ⎬ Korte Houtstraet chez Scheuer
De Schepper ⎭

Hekeren De Brantsenbourg  Heeregragt

Grand Pensionaire Van Blyswijk  Heeregragt

Van Citters—Princesse gr[acht] à coté de l'Amte. d'Amst. [l'Admiralité d'Amsterdam]

D'Aylva—ibid.

Bigot—Kl[eine] Voorhout, over York 't hoek

Hardenbroek ⎫
Bransen     ⎬ Heere Logement
De Clyver   ⎪
Hambroek  ⎭

Sloet tot de Haar  Voorhout

Snelle  à coté de Patras au Voorhout

Nordwyk  Voorhout à coté de M. Varel

Valkenburgh. Ibid à coté de Noordwyk

Van der Goes  Ibid. Maison de Rhoon

Nagel       Ibid à coté de Rosendaal

Tork de Rosendaal Pere ⎫ Le Coin du Voorhout &
  & le Fils      ⎭    Kneuterdyk

Twent  Noord Einde vis a vis la vieille cour

Cau  Ibid

G. De Randwyk. Ibid la 2e. m[aiso]n de la Vieille Cour

Greffier Fagel.[2]  Ibid

Boreel[3]  Ibid

Comte de Welderen  Oude Mol-Straet

Tromer. Papestraet [chez] le Kamer bewaar[d]er Mey

I

Sandheuvel Groenmarkt.
Linden de Hemmen  Beeste markt
De Schepper. Vlamingstraet, chez Villeneuve
Van der Lely. Logement de Delft au Hoogstraet
Bowens. Hoogstraet ibid.
D'Escury.  Sur la Place V[erte].
Changuyon ⎤
Kuffeler  ⎬  Buitenhof.
Alberda   ⎦
Rengers. Vyverberg, la 2d. m[aiso]n de Du Tour
Lynden de Swanenburg, près de Rengers  Ibid.
Ysselstein. chez Monsr. Champ Fleury, au Tournoy Veld.
De Lynden ⎤
De Brakel ⎦ Tournoy-Veld, au v[ieu]x Doelen
Hope—Plein, au Log[emen]t D'Amsterdam
Wieling ibid. à coté de M. Stein
Lynden de Blitterswyck. Ibid.
De Beere  chez D'Avans dans le L. Pooten.
Van der Haar. Spuy aux 7. Egl[ises] de R[ome].
Leenhof de L'Espierve, introuvable


Visites faites aux Villes D'Hollande.[4]

| | | |
|---|---|---|
| Dordrecht | Au long Vivier. | 8 |
| Haerlem | Au court Vivier. | 9 |
| Delft | Hoogstraet | 3. |
| Leyden | Buitenhof. | 4. |
| Amsterdam | Plein | 1. |
| Gouda | Voorhout. | 7. |
| Rotterdam | Plein | 10 |
| Gornichem ⎤ | | |
| Schiedam  ⎬ | Fluwele Burgwall | 11. |
| Schoonhoven ⎦ | | |
| Brielle | Spuystraet. | 2 |
| Alkmar ⎤ | | |
| Enkhuijsen ⎦ | Hof Cingel | 5. |
| Hoorn ⎤ | | |
| Edam | | |
| Monnikendam ⎬ | Voorhout | 6. |
| Medenblik | | |
| Purmerende ⎦ | | |

2

Visites Diplomatiques pour faire part de la Reception
de Mr. Adams, come Minister des E.U. pres de L.H.P.
faites le 24. May [*i.e.* April] 1782

S.E. Monsr. Le Duc de la Vauguyon Ambassadeur de S.M.T.C. Cette
Visite a été annoncee, et faite personellement et rendue de même,
selon l'Etiquette.
Monsr. De Liano, C. de Sanafé Min. Plenipo: D'Espne. Visite faite en
Personne le Dimanche 21. & rendue le Lundi 22. de meme.[5]

Les Suivants ont eu des cartes seulment
M[ess]rs. Cornet Env. Extr. de l'El[ecteur] de Col[ogne]
De St. Saphorin Env. Extr. du R. de Danmark
B. De Reischach, Env. Extr. & Min. Plenipo. de L'Emp.
D. Joas Theolonico de Almeida, Env. Extr. de Portug.
B. De Thulemeyer Env. Extr. du R. de Pr.—Lorrestraet
Prince de Gallitzin, Env. Extr. de L'Imp. de Russie. Voor-
hout
Markow              do.              Mar. de Turenne.[6]
Le Cte. Montagnini de Mirabel, Min. Plen. du R. de Sard.
Bn. D'Eeren Schwerd Env. Extr. de Swede. Westeinde
Magis Min. du P[rin]ce. de Liège. Houtweg.
Martens Min. Res. des Villes Hanseat.

[1] From Lb/JA/19 (Adams Papers, Microfilms, Reel No. 107), a letterbook bound in parchment-covered boards, on the front cover of which JA wrote: "Holland France England / 1782.3.4.5."

Though JA dated two of the headings in the present document in May 1782, the whole memorandum unquestionably belongs to April in that year, immediately after the States General of the United Netherlands voted, 19 April, to receive his credentials as minister plenipotentiary from the United States. On 23 April JA wrote to R. R. Livingston: "The greatest Part of my Time for several Days has been taken up in receiving and Paying of Visits, from all the Members and officers of Government, and of the Court, to the Amount of 150 and more" (LbC, Adams Papers). It is impossible to suppose that these ceremonial visits were repeated a month later, and there is other evidence (see note 5) indicating that the memorandum applies to April rather than May.

Soon after JA had left Amsterdam for Paris in July 1781, JQA had departed for St. Petersburg to serve as a companion, private secretary, and French interpreter for Francis Dana on his mission to the Russian court. See JA, *Corr. in the Boston Patriot*, p. 570–571; JQA, Diary, July–Aug. 1781. Early in August CA, who was miserably homesick and had been otherwise ill, sailed in the *South Carolina*, Capt. Alexander Gillon, supposedly for the United States, though he did not arrive there until late in Jan. 1782, and then in the *Cicero*, a privateer owned by the Cabots of Beverly, from Bilbao (letters of William Jackson to JA, Aug.–Nov. 1781; JA to AA, 2 Dec. 1781; Isaac Smith to JA, 23 Jan. 1782; all in Adams Papers). After his family broke up, JA himself fell ill with what he called "a nervous Fever," and during September maintained his correspondence only through John Thaxter (JA to Franklin, 4 Oct. 1781, LbC, Adams Papers).

In June 1781 Congress had revoked JA's powers to treat for peace with Great

Britain by appointing him first among five joint commissioners—the others being Franklin, Jay, Laurens, and Jefferson—to act in that capacity. Their instructions, later famous—or notorious—for the stipulation that the Commissioners were "to undertake nothing in the negotiations for peace or truce without [the] knowledge and concurrence" of the ministers of their "generous ally, the King of France," were dated the same day (*JCC,* 20:651–654). JA received these papers on 24 August. On 16 Aug. Congress had added to his other commissions "further powers . . . to form a treaty of alliance" among France, the United Provinces, and the United States, contingent on Dutch recognition of American independence (same, 21:876–880). These powers arrived late in November, together with news of Cornwallis' surrender at Yorktown. This event put a different face on American affairs, and by steady insistence JA obtained from the French government at the end of the year a rather guarded permission to press for recognition at The Hague. On 9 Jan. he presented a verbal address to Van den Santheuvel, current president of the States General, requesting "a categorical Answer" to his Memorial which had been under *ad referendum* consideration since the preceding May, and the President assured him that he would "make Report to their high Mightinesses" (JA to Congress, 14 Jan. 1782, incorporating the text of the address, LbC, Adams Papers; Wharton, ed., *Dipl. Corr. Amer. Rev.,* 5:97–100). In the following days JA reinforced his appeal for action by calling at the headquarters in The Hague of the eighteen cities of Holland represented in that province's assembly, and was cordially received (same; see also Dumas to Congress, 7, 15 Jan. 1782; same, 5:86, 102–103). In aid of his campaign JA's friends got up petitions in Leyden, Rotterdam, Amsterdam, and elsewhere, and compared with the way such affairs usually proceeded in the Netherlands, the results were surprisingly fast in coming in. On 26 Feb. the Provincial States of Friesland voted to instruct their deputies in the States General to recognize the United States. On 28 March the States of Holland voted likewise, and the other

five provinces fell rapidly into line during the next two to three weeks. At last on 19 April, one year precisely after JA had finished and signed his Memorial of 1781, the States General of the United Netherlands resolved "that Mr. Adams shall be admitted and acknowledged in Quality of Envoy of the United States of North America to their High Mightinesses, as he is admitted and acknowledged by the present" (JA to Livingston, 19 April 1782, LbC, Adams Papers; Wharton, ed., *Dipl. Corr. Amer. Rev.,* 5:315–319). Many of the petitions, together with all the provincial resolves and the final act of accreditation, were gathered and soon afterward printed by JA, in English, in an anonymous publication entitled *A Collection of State-Papers, Relative to the First Acknowledgment of the Sovereignty* [sic] *of the United States of America, and the Reception of Their Minister Plenipotentiary, by Their High Mightinesses the States-General of the United Netherlands,* The Hague, 1782. Three days after the States General's action JA was granted an audience by Willem V, Prince of Orange and Stadholder of the United Netherlands (JA to Livingston, 22 April, Lbc, Adams Papers; Wharton, ed., *Dipl. Corr. Amer. Rev.,* 5:319–320).

In anticipation of these events JA purchased, through Dumas and on behalf of the United States, "an house at the Hague, fit for the Hotel des Etats Unis, or if you will L'hotel de nouveau Monde. It is in a fine Situation and there is a noble Spot of Ground" (JA to Francis Dana, 15 March 1782, MHi: Dana Papers). Its cost was 15,207 guilders; it was bought from the Comtesse de Quadt Wykeradt née Baronne de Wyhe (according to her own signature, though the name is found in innumerable forms), and was situated on the Fluwelen Burgwal, on a site now occupied by the Netherlands Government Printing Office (Dumas to JA, 23 Feb., Adams Papers; JA to Livingston, 27 Feb., 7 Sept., both PCC, No. 84, IV; notarial record of agreement, 24 April, and bill of sale, 27 May, in The Hague Gemeente-Archief [photostats in Adams Papers Editorial Files]). JA moved in about mid-May. This, the first building acquired by the United States as a foreign legation, stood until sometime in the 1820's; a print of about 1830 of the Fluwelen Burgwal and the canal that then traversed it shows only a one-story wall and doorway on the site.

[2] Hendrik Fagel (1706–1790), *griffier* (secretary, "graphiary") of the States General from 1744 until his death (*Nieuw Ned. Biog. Woordenboek*, 3: 390–391). A strong supporter of the House of Orange and of what JA called the "Anglomane" party, Fagel nevertheless signed, as he was obliged to by his office, the States General's resolution recognizing the United States.

[3] Willem Boreel (1744–1796), of Amsterdam and later of The Hague, a deputy to the States General from the Province of Holland and holder of numerous civil and military offices (Johan E. Elias, *De vroedschap van Amsterdam, 1578–1795*, Haarlem, 1903–1905, 2: 945, 1188). As president of the week of the States General when the vote recognizing the United States was passed, Boreel signed, with Fagel, the text transmitted to JA (*Collection of State Papers*, 1782, p. 92). Boreel and his wife presided over a very hospitable household in The Hague; see numerous entries in JA's Diary during Sept.–Oct., below.

[4] That is, the houses or *hôtels* where the deputies from the cities of Holland to the "States of Holland" (the provincial assembly, which met at The Hague) had their respective headquarters. As for the numbers in the last column, Dr. H. M. Mensonides, Director of the Gemeente-Archief, The Hague, has made the following plausible suggestion: "The

figures . . . probably indicate the order in which the visits had to be made: first Amsterdam at the Plein (now Ministry of Foreign Affairs) as the most important; then through the Spuistraat (2), Brielle; the Hoogstraat (3), Delft; the Buitenhof (4), Leyden; the Hofsingel (5), Alkmaar and Enkhuizen; the Voorhout (6), Hoorn-Edam-Monnikendam-Medemblik-Purmerend; and (7), Gouda; the Lange Vijverberg (8), Dordrecht; the Korte Vijverberg (9), Haarlem; back to the Plein (10), Rotterdam (present War Ministry); and then to the outside of the town [and nearest his own establishment], the Fluwelen Burgwal (11), Gorinchem-Schiedam-Schoonhoven. If you will follow it on a modern map, you will see it is quite a logical itinerary" (letter to the editors, 29 Dec. 1959).

[5] Since Sunday and Monday fell on the 21st and 22d of April (and not of May) in 1782, this entry confirms the supposition that JA erred in dating these lists of ceremonial visits in May. It was Llano, the Spanish minister at The Hague, who at this time paid JA a compliment which he reported to various correspondents in bad French but with much satisfaction: "Vous avez frappé, Mo[n]sieur, (said he to me) le plus grand Coup de tout L'Europe. C'est le plus grand Coup, qui a jamais été frappé dans la Cause Americain. . . . C'est Vous qui a rempli cette nation d'Enthousiasme. C'est Vous qui a tournée leurs Tetes" (JA to Edmund Jenings, 28 April 1782, Adams Papers).

[6] Le Maréchal de Turenne—an inn.

---

## 1782 SEPTEMBER 14. SATURDAY.[1]

Supped last Night at Court in the Maison du Bois.[2] M. Boreel told me he had been to Paris which he quitted 8 days ago. That M. Franklin had been sick. It was at first reported that he had been struck with an Apoplexity. Then it was said he had a billious Cholick, and afterwards a Retention of Urine. But that he had got well before he left Paris.

Fell into Conversation naturally with Don Joas Theolonico de Almeida, Envoy Extraordinary of Portugal. . . .[3] He said to me, the Peace is yet a good Way off. There will be no Peace this Winter.

There will be another Campain, and no Peace untill the Winter following.... Spain will be the most difficult to satisfy, of all the Powers. Her Pretensions will be the hardest for England to agree to. As to the Independance of America, that is decided. I said to him, it is reported that Portugal is about to open her Ports to American Vessells.—I have not yet received says he any Intelligence of that.

The Comte Montagnini de Mirabel, Min. Plen. of the King of Sardinia, asked what was the Principle of the Indecision of G. Britain? Why dont they acknowledge your Independance? They must have some Intelligence, that is not publick.—I answered I dont believe there is any Principle, or System in it. It is merely owing to their Confusion. My Lord Shelburne, in complyance with the Will of his Master, refuses to do what all the World sees to be necessary.—Perhaps says the Comte they mean to annex certain Conditions, to the Acknowledgment of your Independance.—But says I, what if We should annex Conditions too? What if We should insist on an Acknowledgement of our Independence as a Preliminary Condition to entering into any Treaty or Conference?—Ay, says he, in that Case you may have work enough.

Mr. Magis said to me afterwards, I see you often in Conversation with Mr. de Mirabel. He is a great Politician. He is very well informed of all affairs in General, but particularly with the Affairs and political System of Germany.

Mr. De Llano, the Spanish Plenipo., said to me afterwards, do you know that Man, you have been in Conversation with this Evening so much, Mr. De Mirabel?—Very well says I.—The Baron de Thulemeyer, who was by, said Yes I see Mirabel often Attacks him.—I am told says I, that he is a great Politician.—Ay says Llano I see you know him—but he knows nothing else.

Mr. Boreel, The Baron de Linden de Hemmen, and the President of the grand Committee, all Members of the Assembly of their H[igh] M[ightinesses,] told me, that five Copies of the Treaties would be made out, according to my Desire, the English and Dutch Side by Side upon every Page, and the Treaty would be signed next Week.

The Baron de Thulemeyer chatted with me about riding on Horseback. Says he rides always in the Morning, at any Hour between 9 and Dinner, but never after Dinner.

They shewed me this Evening the Lady who holds at her House an Assembly every Evening, where the whole Corps Diplomatick assists. The Lady, who used to preside at Sir Joseph Yorks Table, and see that all was in order there.

The Comte de Welderen came as usual and made his Compliment to me. The Rhin Grave de Salm, Colonel Bentink, M. Van der Duesn,[4] and other Officers. In short I never spent so social an Evening at Court. My Party was stronger this Evening, Mirabel and Bentink never play, and there were several others in the same Case.

The Comte Sarsefield went with me and returned in my Carriage. The Duke de la Vauguion was not there.

Agreed with Lt. Gen. Van der Dussen to ride with him this Morning at 9.

Chatted at Supper with one of the Ladies of Honour, Madamoiselle Starembourg, in English, French and Dutch.

At 9 took my Ride with Mr. Vander Dussen Lt. General of Cavalry. He was mounted upon a noble English Horse, with an embroidered Housing and a white silk net, and with his sword. A servant behind him in Livery, upon another fine Horse with a white silk net. We made a long Ride, of three of four Leagues. In our Way We saw People digging Turfs out of Heaps of Sand. Upon observing more Attentively, I found that they dug away the sand hills to the Depth of 15 or 20 feet, and then came to bodies of Peat or Turf, which they cutt up to sell and to burn. The General says, at the Depth of 10, 15 or 20 feet, they find this layer of Turf which is also some times 10 or 15 feet deep and then come to a fine Soil, upon a Level nearly with the general surface of the Meadows. The Generals Hypothesis is this. —Before the Dykes were built, there were frequent Inundations in Consequence of storms which are still frequent. It is supposed that the whole Country was originally level and covered over with thick and heavy Forrests of Woods. In great Storms, the Waves of the Sea threw up vast Heaps of Sand, and carried them sometimes several Miles in upon the Land. By which means the Forrests of Trees were thrown down, or at least covered up, with Mountains of Sea Sand. That the Wood of these Trees in the Course of many hundreds perhaps some thousands of Years, has putrified and dissolved into Peat or Turfe. So that you have nothing to do, but to dig through the Sand Hills first, and the Turf Beds next to come to the original Surface of the Earth which is yet very fertile. Many fine Meadows have been made, in this Way.

In passing over the Spot of Downs between the Hague and Leyden, We saw three or four Hunters, Gunners, in search of Hares and Rabits and other Game, this being the Season of the Chase. The General seemed very apprehensive of these Sportsmen that they would not keep a good Look out but might be so eager for their Game, as to be inattentive to Travellers and fire upon our Bodies. This was a fear that never occurred to me, and I never felt it after it was mentioned.

The General was inquisitive after the American Savages and a great Part of our Conversation consisted in his Questions and my Answers concerning them. The Roads, the Woods, the Forests in America also, occasioned many Questions.—The General is a Relation as he told me, of the Minister of the same name at the Conferences of Gertruydenbourg.

Upon Inquiry to day I find that the Lady, who was so intimate at Sir Joseph Yorks, as to oversee his Entertainments, is named Madame de Boetzelaar. She holds an Assembly every Night, at her House, to which resort all the Corps diplomatique. There they Play. She paints but is horridly ugly.[5]

The Baron de Kruyningen holds an Office of Intelligence, where the Ministers or Secretaries meet of Mornings as at a Kind of Coffee house to exchange with each other the News, and compare Notes.

Mr. Magis holds such another. What these People get by their Assemblys and Offices, is a Question. Perhaps nothing more than a Reputation, an Acquaintance with foreign Ministers, and now and then an Invitation to dinner.

The Foreign Ministers here all herd together, and keep no other Company, but at Court and with a few in this Way.—It is not from Choice but necessity. There is no Family, but Mr. Boreel that ever invites any of them, to breakfast, dine or sup. Nor do any of the Members of the States General, the States of Holland, Bleiswick, Fagel, any of the Lords of the Admiralty, Gecommitteerde Raaden, Council of State, high Council of War, or any Body, ever invite Strangers or one Another.

Hospitality and Sociability are no Characteristicks here.

This Day Mr. Van Asp made me a Visit. This Gentleman is Chargé d'Affaires of Sweeden since the Departure of The Baron D'Ehrenswerd for Prussia. He is a solid prudent Man. He very much admired my House, and its Situation. I said smiling it was very well for a Beginning, and that I hoped We should have an House at Stockholm e'er long. He smiled in return, but said nothing. His Visit was not long. There is not a more sensible, manly, happy, or prudent Countenance in the whole Diplomatick Body. He has desired Mr. Dumas to inform him as soon as the Treaty is signed, that he may write itt to his Court before it arrives in the News papers.[6]

[1] First entry in D/JA/33, which consists of a few folded leaves containing

irregular entries through 3 Oct. 1782. On 23 April, the day following his first audience with the Stadholder, JA formally proposed to Van Citters, the current president of the States General, that negotiations be commenced for a treaty of amity and commerce between the Dutch Republic and the United States. Accordingly, "a grand Committee" of deputies from each of the Seven Provinces was appointed to confer with the American minister on this subject, and JA laid before them "a Project of a Treaty, which I had drawn up, conformable to the Instructions of Congress" (JA to Livingston, 23 April 1782, LbC, Adams Papers; JA, *Works*, 7:572–573). Under Dutch constitutional procedures the *projet* had to be taken *ad referendum* to the provincial assemblies before the States General could act, but at length on 22 Aug. JA could report to Livingston that "Their High Mightinesses have ... received their Instructions from all the Provinces, and I have this Day been in Conference with the grand Committee, who communicated to me the Remarks and Propositions in [on?] their Part. To this I shall soon give my Replication [on certain points not yet agreed on], and I hope the Affair will be soon ended" (LbC, Adams Papers; *Works*, 7:614). There were further delays, however, and the treaty was not signed and sealed until 8 Oct.; the final stages are reported in JA's Diary entries of 3–8 Oct., below.

Meanwhile, after some fumbling, "innumerable Vexations," and weeks of intense effort, JA had negotiated a loan for the United States with a syndicate of Dutch banking houses. On 11 June he signed five bonds in the amount of 1,000,000 guilders each for a loan to be raised by Wilhem & Jan Willink, Nicolaas & Jacob van Staphorst, and De la Lande & Fynje, at 5 per cent interest and with a 4 1/2 per cent commission to the bankers, repayment to begin after ten years and to be completed in fifteen years. See JA to Livingston, 9 June, 5 July, letterbook copies, Adams Papers; Wharton, ed., *Dipl. Corr. Amer. Rev.*, 5:482–483, 594–595; a printed copy of the contract, in Dutch, is in Adams Papers, 11 June 1782. Congress ratified the contract on 14 Sept. (JCC, 23:579–580). This was the first of four loans obtained by JA in the Netherlands (in

1782, 1784, 1787, and 1788), totalling 9,000,000 guilders, or more than $3,500,000 "which," as Samuel F. Bemis has observed, "at first were the sole effectual support to languishing American credit and which barely enabled the government of the Confederation to survive the peace, to function until the recognition of Washington's new national government under the Constitution of 1787" (*Diplomacy of the Amer. Revolution*, p. 169). By far the most authoritative and detailed account of these negotiations is that by P. J. van Winter, *Het aandeel van den Amsterdamschen handel aan den opbouw van het Amerikaansche gemeenebest*, The Hague, 1927–1933, especially vol. 1: chs. 3, 6.

[2] That is, at Court. The Huis ten Bosch, built in the mid-17th century and enlarged in the 1730's, is a small but charming palace in a wooded setting now in the eastern suburbs of The Hague. The woods surrounding it provided JA with one of his favorite walks. See illustration in this volume.

[3] Suspension points, here and below, in MS.

[4] Gen. Aegidius van der Dussen, who was, according to the bill of sale for the United States Legation building at The Hague, one of JA's next-door neighbors on the Fluwelen Burgwal.

[5] In the following year, however, the Baroness van den Boetzelaer, a widow, married Sir Joseph Yorke at Antwerp (*DNB*, article on Yorke).

[6] Though this is the first mention of C. W. F. Dumas in the text of the Diary, he has several times appeared in editorial notes above, because this remarkable man contributed in countless ways, large and small, to the success of JA's Dutch mission. A polyglot man of letters, born in Germany of French parents, Dumas lived for some years in Switzerland but settled at The Hague in 1756 and made a small living by his pen. Long before the Revolution broke out he had become a fervent admirer of America; in the 1760's he had considered emigrating to New England or Virginia and consulted Franklin in London to this end. On 19 Dec. 1775 Franklin addressed Dumas a letter on behalf of Congress' secret committee of correspondence, asking his

advice and aid in promoting the Colonies' interests in Europe (Wharton, ed., *Dipl. Corr. Amer. Rev.*, 2:64–67). This step opened up what eventually became a flood, for Dumas, as one student of his career has well said, was "animé de la manie épistolaire" (F. P. Renaut, *Les Provinces-Unies et la guerre d'Amérique* [1775–1784], Paris, 1924–1925, 5:37). After Franklin arrived in Paris Dumas was engaged on a small salary to serve as agent and correspondent at The Hague, and he worked hard and effectively in this capacity for years, though for reasons still not clear he never obtained a regular diplomatic appointment. Praised by JA as "indefatigable," "a walking Library," and "a Master of Languages ancient and modern," he made himself indispensable as adviser, gatherer of intelligence, translator, amanuensis, go-between with Dutch politicians, officials, and journalists, and general errand boy. JA liked and trusted Dumas so well that he invited him and his family to move into the Hôtel des Etats-Unis at The Hague (for which Dumas arranged the purchase) when JA moved there himself, and Madame Dumas served as a capable housekeeper in that establishment. Dumas remained American *chargé d'affaires*, in effect but not in title, for many years, dying in 1796 without fulfilling his ardent hope of visiting the United States. His papers are chiefly preserved in the Dumas Collection in the Rijksarchief at The Hague (the extensive American portions being available on microfilm in DLC:Dutch Reproductions), and in PCC, No. 93 (4 vols., 1776–1796). The best biographical sketch is one which precedes the printed inventory of his papers issued by the Algemeen Rijksarchief in its *Verslag*, or *Report*, for 1918, p. 379–401, which is also available in separate form. The fifth volume of Renaut's incomplete monograph, *Les Provinces-Unies et la guerre d'Amérique*, subtitled *La propagande insurgente: C. W. F. Dumas* (1775–1780), Paris, 1925, describes Dumas' labors for the American cause up to the point of JA's arrival in the Netherlands. JA's voluminous correspondence with Dumas, disregarding that which passed between Dumas and the joint commissioners in 1778–1779, extends from early 1780 to the end of 1795.

## 1782. SEPTR. 19.

Went to the Comedy. Saw the Sage dans sa Retrait, and Le Jugement du Midas—both well represented. The Musick was good, and the Show upon the Stage splendid. The Princess and all her Children were there. The foreign Ministers chiefly.

## OCT. 1.

Dined with Mr. Boreel a Deputy to the States General from the Province of Holland, with Lt. General Van derdussen, Mr. De Llano, Mr. Thulemeyer, Mr. Renovallis, Mr. Visher, Mr.                    of the Council of State for the City of Amsterdam, Mr.                    a Gentleman of the Court &c. The Dinner was elegant and a splendid Shew of Plate, as We see at the Tables of the rich Dutch Families.

A little Pleasantry with Mr. De Thulemeyer, about the Conduct of the Prussian Minister at Madrid in notifying to Mr. Charmichael, as Chargé des Affairs des Etats Unis de L'Amerique, his Presentation to the King and Royal Family.

Note. This is the Effect of the Step I took in notifying my Presentation, to all the foreign Ministers.

1782. OCT. 2.

Walked Yesterday to the House in the Woods in the rain. To day will dine with me Comte Sarsefield, Mr. Vischer and Mr. Gyselaer.— Received Yesterday a Volume of the Journals of Congress with some News papers by the Post from L'orient which cost me 37 Guilders.— The Comte, Mr. Vischer and Mr. Gyselaer, dined here. The Comte Sarsefield began as usual when We were alone to give me a Lesson of Etiquette. This is a Trait in his Character. No Man more attentive to the Rules of Ceremony, and Formality. No Man more precise. He says, that when I make an Entertainment, I should have placed the Ambassador of France, at my right Hand, and the Minister of Spain at my left, and have arranged the other Principal Personages. And when I rose from Table I should have said Messieurs, voudriez vous &c. or Monsieur Le Duc voudriez vous &c.—All this every one sees is a la Francaise. But it is very little regarded here. And it was because it is generally neglected here that I neglected it. But the Comte in every Affair of Dress, Billets, Rank &c. has from my first Acquaintance with him, ever discovered such a minute Attention to little Circumstances. How is it possible to reconcile these trifling Contemplations of a Master of Ceremonies, with the vast Knowledge of Arts, Sciences, History, Government &c. possessed by this Nobleman. An habit of living in the World, however, is necessary—a facility of living with Men. L'Habitude de vivre avec des hommes.

It is the Fashion among the Dutch, to arrange all the Company, by putting a Card with the Name of each Gentleman and Lady, upon the Napkin in the Plate. This I never saw practiced in France. Indeed, they Attend but to one Person in France. The Feast is made in honour of one Person. That is the Ton.

Mr. V. being told by the C[omte] that he and I were to dine tomorrow with General Vanderdussen, appeared surprized and said that the General, altho he had dined with me and rode with me, on horseback, would not have dared to have invited me, if he had not met me at Mr. Boreels.

I saw the other day Joachimi Hoppii [Hopperi] Commentatio Succincta, ad Institutiones Justinianas, at Mr. Luzacs.

Mr. Gyselaer informed me that the Committee, for examining the Administration of the Marine, were tomorrow to announce their Authority to the Prince. I told him he must make an harrangue, in order to give Dignity and Solemnity to his Commission. He said it was a delicate Thing to make a Speech upon the Occasion. This I agreed.

I I

I gave the Gentlemen an Account of the Practice of the Provincial Congress of Massachusetts when they first formed their Army. Dr. Warren, their President, made an Harrangue in the form of a Charge, in the Presence of the Assembly, to every Officer, upon the Delivery of his Commission, and that he never failed to make the Officer as well as all the Assembly shudder, upon those Occasions. C.S. appeared struck and affected with this Anecdote. I dare say he has it in his Journal.

C.S. told me the News of the Destruction of the Spanish floating Batteries, by the English red hot Bullets. He seemed much affected. Said all Europe would laugh at them and that they deserved it, for attempting a Thing so evidently impossible.—No Governments says he but Monarchies are subject to this kind of Misfortunes from Absurdity. In France a Madame Pompadour or de Barry may ruin a Kingdom. In Spain an absurd Priest, the Father Confessor of a superstitious King, may so far gain his Confidence, by working upon his conscience and superstitious Fears as to lead him into such foolish Councils.—How much Mischief says I, has Spain done in this just Cause.

### OCT. 3. THURSDAY.

Dined with Mr. Vanderdussen, Lt. General of the Cavalry, in Company with Mr. De Llano Minister of the King of Spain and Mr. De Renovalis, Secretary of his Legation, Mr. and Madame Boreel, Mr. and Madame Geelvink, Madam Dedel, the Rhinegrave de Salm, Mr. Saumase, a descendant of the famous Salmasius whom John Milton disputed with. Mr. Boreel is a Deputy to the States General for the Prov. of Holland. Mr. Geelvink is a Member of the Council of State for Amsterdam.

Gen. Vanderdussen told me he must ask me to take a Family Dinner with him one of these days in order to present me to a Couple of his Friends; one was his Brother and the other was Gen. Ponce; both zealous Americans he said.—I told him he would do me great Honour and give me much Pleasure.

Mr. Boreel desired me to send him the American Gazette which contains the Resolution of their High Mightinesses, acknowledging me as Minister, with his Name to it.

I forgot Mr. Magis, who said to me, entre Nous, Sir, if I were young I would endeavour to serve a great Power, because one has a Chance to be Something: but when one serves a small Power one is sure never to be any Thing.

Madame Boreel next to whom I sat at Table asked me if I understood the Dutch. I answered, very little, but that I began to learn it. That I had with me two ingenious young Gentlemen with whom at Breakfast, I every Morning attempted with the Aid of a Dictionary to read the Dutch Gazettes, and that We began to comprehend some Paragraphs.[1] Madame Boreel mentioned to the Company that I read the Dutch Gazettes. Mr. Geelvink called out to me, pleasantly enough, leese Mynheer de Diemer Meerche Courant.—Yea well, Mynheer says I, en de Hollandche Historische Courant oke.

The Dutch Part of this Company, were all high, in Office and Service, and therefore attached to the Court.

The Gen. Vanderdussen said laughing that he was ready to wish and to do any Thing to the English for they had almost ruined him. He was Governor of Ipres or Ypres one of the Barrier Towns, so that he has lost his Government, by the Demolition of the Barriers. I believe too they have done him some Damage in some Estates in the West Indies &c.

Mr. Boreel promised me to speak to Mr. Fagel and let him know that I wish to have the Treaty signed, that I might be able to send it by several Vessells now ready to sail at Amsterdam.

Somebody at Table said to C. Sarsfield that the Americans had laid aside the Use of Mr. Franklins Conductors. The C. appealed to me. I said by no means, on the Contrary the Use of them increased, and they were found very usefull.

Questions.—What are the Powers of the Council of State?—how many Members? who appoints them?—Are they for Life, or Years, or at Will? When do they sit? What Objects of Administration have they? Is their Power Legislative, Executive or Judiciary? Is the Council of State, the same Body, with the Gecommitteerde Raaden—[or][2] are they two.

Answer. The Council of State, and the Council of Commissioners, are two distinct Bodies.—De Raad van Staaten en de Gecommitteerde Raaden.—The 1. is for the 7 Prov[inces]—the last for the Province of Holland only.

---

[1] One of the young gentlemen was of course John Thaxter. The other was Charles Storer (1761–1829), of Boston, a relative of AA's and a Harvard graduate, 1779, who had recently arrived in Europe; he joined JA's household and served without pay for several years as his private secretary (Storer to AA, 17 Oct. 1782, Adams Papers; JA to Jay, 25 Aug. 1785, LbC, Adams Papers).

[2] MS: "are."

13

## THE HAGUE OCTOBER 5. 1782. SATURDAY.[1]

In conference with the G[rand] Pen[sionary] Bleiswick. He told me, it was determined to sign the Treaty of Commerce, on Monday next at Noon. That I should not find the Greffier Fagel for that being Saturday, he would spend it at his Country Seat and not come to Town. That the Revolution in the Crimea and the commotions among the Tartars would probably find Employment enough for Russia. That there were some Symptoms of Anglomanie, in Sweeden. That there was no News from Paris about Peace, that Mr. Brantzen had not, when the last Advices came away, had his first Audience, of the King.

I went next to Mr. Fagels house, but the Answer was that on Saturdays the Greffier never came to Town.

There is in the Rotterdamche Courant of to day the following Article from Philadelphia of the 7. August. Het is opmerklyk dat de Staaten Generaal, de Onafhanglykheit der Vereenigde Staaten, juist op den 19 April dezes Jaars erkend hebben, zynde die dag de zevende Verjaring van den Veldslag by Lexington, en dat deze zaak nog opmerklyker maakt is, dat de Eerste Memorie van den Heer Adams, die zulk een grooten Indruk op de Hollandsche Natie gemaakt heeft, gedagteekend is den 19 April 1781.[2]

### Money of the Low countries[3]

The Florin = 2 Scallings & 6. Sols
The Scalling = 7s. = 12s. 6d. of France.
Crown = 9 Scallings = 5£: 12s: 6d. of France.
17 Patars = 1 [l.t.][4] 12s. of France.
The Plaquette = 6s: 3d.
9 liards = 3s: 9d.

[1] First entry in D/JA/34, a gathering of leaves, quarto in size, the first in a series of twelve such booklets, some stitched and some unstitched but otherwise uniform in format and appearance, extending through July 1786 and virtually completing JA's Diary in Europe. In all of them JA wrote only on the right-hand half of the page, reserving the other half for additions.

[2] "It is remarkable that the States General have recognized the independence of the United States on exactly the 19th of April of this year, this day being the seventh anniversary of the battle at Lexington, and what makes the matter still more remarkable is that Mr. Adams' First Memorial, which has made such a deep impression on the Dutch nation, is dated 19 April 1781."

[3] This table is in the margin of the MS, opposite the beginning of the entry dated 5 October.

[4] In the MS appears a cryptic symbol which we conjecture stands for *livres tournois*. The *patar* or *patard*, a copper coin, was a Flemish stiver or sol.

### OCT. 7. MONDAY.

Mr. D[umas] has been out, upon the Discovery.—Neither Mr. V. nor Mr. G. could guess the Reason, why their H[igh] M[ightinesses] had sent their Agent De Spieringshoek to desire me to postpone the Signature of the Treaty untill tomorrow. Mr. B. whom he met in the Street explained it. He says the Prince had sent Word to their High M. that he desired a Conference with them to day, and as the Signature would take up some time they should be obliged to make the Prince or me wait. He learn'd afterwards from Mr. K. that the Council of War of the Navy Officers at the Texel, have sent an express to day, to inform the States, that it is impossible for the Fleet to go to Brest, according to the Resolution of their H.M. because they were not ready. They are in Want of Men, of Provisions, of Stores. Every Ship in the Fleet is in Want of Something essential. The Blame of this, will fall upon the Prince.[1]

The Prince, in his Conference, to day, has communicated his orders and Correspondence relative to the Navy.

[1] The initials standing for persons in this paragraph probably represent Messrs. Visscher, Gyselaar, Boreel, and Kruiningen. On the controversy over the unpreparedness of the Dutch fleet, a very warm issue at this time between the Patriots and the Stadholder, see Dumas to Livingston, 27 Sept.–22 Oct. 1782 (Wharton, ed., *Dipl. Corr. Amer. Rev.*, 5:776–778).

### OCT. 8. TUESDAY.

Mr. D. is indefatigable in his Way. He visits, every Day, the French Am[bassador], Mr. G., Mr. V.—and occasionally Mr. K. and sometimes the Prince de Gallitzin, Mr. D'Asp, &c.

No American Minister could do this. It would ruin his Character. I dont know whether it would do for a Secretary of Legation to do this. I can, however, make an excellent Use of him in this Way. I can get or communicate Intelligence this Way, better than any other, from and to various Persons and Places.

I have been indirectly put upon my Guard against "un Chien puant," made Use of as a Tool, in the Friesland Affair, which I read of, in C. S.s Journal.—He now makes his Court to both Sides. Llano the other day made a grand Eloge, of the Man and his Wife, of their peaceable amiable Character, and excellent Reputation. Thus it is when Parties run high. One Side crys crucify, and the other hozanna.

At Breakfast Comte Sarsefield came in, and put into my Hand, more of his Speculations.—I have read through his Journal of his Journeys into Holland in 1777 and in 1780 and he has promised me that of

1782. The Piece he lent me to day is on Slavery. He has assembled every Appearance of Argument in favour of the Slavery of the Glebe, (Villenage) or domestic Slavery, and has refuted them all.[1]

At twelve went to the State House, was received as usual, at the head of the Stairs by Mr. De Santheuvel, and Mr. De Linden, Deputies from Holland and Zealand, and conducted into the Truce Chamber where We signed and sealed the Treaty of Commerce and the Convention concerning Recaptures.[2]

Waited on the Duke de la Vauguion, to inform him, as I did, and also that I had received a Letter from Mr. Jay, 28 Septr., informing me that the Day before, Mr. Oswald received a Commission to treat of Peace with the Commissioners of the United States of America, and that I believed I should set out, according to Mr. Jays earnest desire, for Paris the latter End of next Week.[3] The Duke was pleased to say, and with a warmth that proved him sincere, that he rejoiced to hear it, for it seemed by it, that Mr. Jay and I were cordial, and he thought further it was absolutely necessary I should be there, for that the immoveable Firmness that Heaven had given me, would be usefull and necessary upon this Occasion. I could not help laughing at this and replying, that I had often occasion however for cooler Blood than had fallen to my Share, to regulate that same Firmness.

The Duke then entered into an History of his Negotiations with the States and the Prince to get the Fleet to Brest. He thinks there has been a secret Communication between Prince and Officers to represent the Fleet destitute of Sails, and Provisions &c.

While the Clerks were sealing the Treaties to day I cast an Eye on the Collection of Pictures of Claudius Civilis, and asked the Gentlemen who was the Painter. Secretary Fagel answered me that it was Otto Oevenius a Dutch Painter, Author of the Emblemata Horatiana. That each of those Pictures was formed upon some Passage of Tacitus. That his Father had been at the Pains to transcribe all those Passages and affix them to the back of the Picture. Upon this I turned one of them round, and found a Paragraph.[4]

[1] Sarsfield's essay on slavery, entitled "Quelques Considérations Sur L'Esclavage, La Servitude De La Glebe, L'Etat de Liberté qui leur a succedé Et les Effets qui Resultent des Uns Et des Autres," dated 28 Sept. 1782, remains among other MS essays by Sarsfield in the Adams Papers (filed at 1782–1783) and bears this notation in JA's hand on the cover page: "Aut Sarsefeildii aut Diaboli." Extracts from Sarsfield's jour-

nal of 1782 were copied by JA into his own Diary; see entry of 10 Oct., below.

[2] Copies of the Treaty of Amity and Commerce and of the Convention concerning Recaptures, in Dutch and English, are in Adams Papers under this date; the English copies are in JA's hand. For printings of the texts as signed, with essential notes on their transmission, ratification, and location, see Miller, ed., *Treaties*, 2:59–95. In a letter

of this day to Livingston JA furnished an illuminating history of the negotiation that produced the Treaty and Convention (PCC, No. 84, IV; Wharton, ed., *Dipl. Corr. Amer. Rev.*, 5:803–805). The Dutch Republic ratified them on 27 Dec. 1782; Congress did so on 23 Jan. 1783; and the ratifications were exchanged at The Hague on 23 June 1783, Dumas acting for JA, who was in Paris. On the day of this exchange the first minister from the Netherlands to the United States, Pieter Johan van Berckel, a burgomaster of Rotterdam and the brother of JA's friend E. F. van Berckel of Amsterdam, sailed for his post.

The "Truce Chamber" where the highly ceremonial signing took place is the magnificent room still known as the Trèveszaal, in a 17th-century building on the water side of the Binnenhof, now reached through Binnenhof 20 (offices of the Netherlands Ministry of Traffic and Waters). See illustration in this volume.

[3] Jay's note of 28 Sept., reporting that Richard Oswald, the British representative at Paris, had received a revised commission that acknowledged American sovereignty, and urging JA to come on "soon—very soon," is in Adams Papers (printed in JA, *Works*, 7:641–642).

[4] The painter was Jürgen, or Juriaan, Ovens, a Dutch artist of the 17th century, and his subject was the revolt of the Batavians against Roman rule, A.D. 69–70, led by Claudius, or more properly Julius, Civilis (*Nieuw Ned. Biog. Woordenboek*, 8:284–285; 10:698–699).

OCTOBER 9. WEDNESDAY.

Went this Morning to the Secretary Fagel and returned him the original Treaty, and the original Convention which was designed for their High Mightinesses. The others designed for Congress, I kept. We run over together the few litteral Variations, and corrected all, indeed all the Inaccuracies were found to be in my Copy which I kept to compare. Mr. Fagel said that one day this Week he would call upon me with the Copies, which he and I were to sign to be sent to Congress. That to day, the Committee would make report, their H.M. would thank them for the Pains they had taken, and each Province would take the Treaty and Convention ad Referendum, and lay them before their Constituents for Ratification.—He told me that his Intelligence from France, by the last Post, led him to expect Peace in the Course of this Winter. He asked me if mine did not? I answered, smiling, that I could not deny that there appeared some Symptoms of it.

About two O Clock, the Cte. de Sanafé made me a Visit, in Ceremony, to congratulate me, on the Signature of the Treaty. I told him I hoped by this Time the Cte. Daranda had signed a Treaty with Mr. Jay, with equal Advantage and Satisfaction. He enquired about the 22 and 23 Articles, and said he understood that I had met with Difficulty to get the States to agree with me upon a Substitute. I read to him in French, the Article as it now stands in the Treaty, which he was fully satisfied with. He enquired concerning the Prussian Minister at Madrid notifying to Mr. Jay his Presentation to the King and Royal Family—asked if it was true? Observed That Mr. Jay was not at Madrid but at Paris. I answered, the Visit was made to Mr. Charmichael, as Chargé des Affairs at Mr. Jays House. He asked me if I told it to Mr. Thulemeyer. I answered in the Affirmative. He asked me what I thought, of the late Behaviour, respecting the Dutch Fleet going to Brest—an Order of the States General and refusal of Obedience, on the Part of the Navy. I answered it was very extraordinary and very allarming. He said, he did not think this People would ever do any Thing. But the Requisition to send Ships to Brest was very well calculated to try them.

I shewed him the Paragraph in the London Evening Post which says that a Commission under the Royal Sign Manual has passed the great Seal of the Court of Chancery, authorizing Mr. Oswald of Philpot Lane, to treat of Peace with the United States of America....[1]

Mr. D. has learned, to day from our Friend, that the two Captains, Welderen and Van Hoey, did in Truth come with the Message that if the Fleet was ordered to Brest, all the Officers and Crews would resign, but finding that the States were likely to take Fire they were perswaded to soften it down to a Want of Sails, Provisions, Stores &c. This, all agree must have been a Plot. The Prince must be as daring in his System, as his Cousin has been.

The States of Holland have printed the Treaty, a Member has given one to Mr. D. who has sent it to day with his French Translation, to Leyden to be inserted in Mr. Luzacs Gazette.

Mr. Thaxter and Mr. Storer[2] have agreed to accompany me to Paris.

[1] Suspension points in MS.     [2] JA inadvertently wrote "Storey."

OCT. 10. THURSDAY.

The Comte de Sanafé wrote a Card to Mr. Dumas desiring a Copy in French of the 22d Article. Said that I had read it to him in french but his Memory had not retained it. I desired Mr. Dumas to send it. —Mr. D. at my desire had asked the Duke de la Vauguion what was the Usage in my Case, who am going to Paris. He brought me Answer, to take Leave of the President, Secretary Fagel and Grand Pensionary and after of the Prince and Princess. Mr. D. added that I should mention who I left as Charge des Affairs and present him. I told him there was none, and I had not Authority to constitute one.

Mr. Van heukelom has been here.—1400 Persons in Leyden have signed an Address of Thanks to the Regency, for their Proposition to enquire into the Administration of the Navy. Mr. John Luzac is now he says universally beloved. A Change of System, has made a Change of Circumstances. Mr. Elie Luzac was the most respected, and had the most Influence but his Anglomanie had brought him into Contempt. Elie Luzac's Father and Johns Father were Brothers. Elies Father is dead. He is called at Leyden een Agt en Veertiger. [These] [1] Nicknames of Agt en Veertiger and Twee en Agtiger, Eight and Fortyer and Two and Eightyer, are adopted as Party Distinctions instead of Whig and Tory, Anglomane and Republican &c.[2]

Received this day a Card, from the Baron de Linden de Blitterswyk, first Noble of Zealand, Brother of him who was Envoy in Sweeden, and his Lady to dine with them next Wednesday.

As the Commerce of Bruges and Ostend, have grown out of the American Revolution, and the Neutral Confederation, it may be worth while to make the following Extract.[3]

Extract from the Journal of C[omte] Sarsfield, 5 June 1782.

J'ay trouvé Bruges dans un grand Mouvement, par le Commerce qui y arrive. J'ai compté de 20 a 25 navires dans le Bassin, il en peut tenir beaucoup plus et on va l'agrandir. On abbat les fortifications, tous les magazins de la Ville sont remplis: on en construit de nouveaux, qui seront fort grands. La Journée d'un homme qui n'a que ses bras est de 16s. et nourri. 16s. du Pays font 1 [l.t.?] 10s. de France.

La Raison de cela est qu'Ostende est trop petit, pour toutes les affairs qui s'y font. Beaucoup de navires viennent a Bruges, ce qui est d'autant plus commode, qu'il faut toujous que les marchandizes y payent lors qu'on ne veut pas les expedier par mer. On m'a dit qu'en particulier les Espagnols expedioient toujous pour Bruges, ou ils n'ont point les memes lenteurs que le defaut de Emplacement occasionne a Ostende. On m'assure que le Canal a 21 Pieds de Profondeur. Tout ce que Je viens de dire se fait par les ordres qu'a donne, L'Empereur, lorsqu'il est venu ici. Il a declaré qu'on ne devoit regarder Ostende et Bruges que comme la meme Ville. L'Effect de cette Augmentation de Commerce, se fait sentir sur le Prix des Maisons, et s'etend surement sur tout.

6 Juin Ostende. Il y a deux Chemins pour y aller. L'Un suit le Canal. Il faut passer the Port en batteau pour entrer dans la ville. L'autre est plus long D[e] 2 1/2 Lieus a ce qu'on m'a dit. J'ay mis un peu moins de 4 1/2 heurs a le faire. Il est pave et pass par St. André,

Wassenaar, un autre Village, dont J'ay oublié le nom et Ghistele. Il
y a quelques barrieres a payer, excepté sur ce qui depend du Franc
de Bruges, que fait et entretient les Chemins a ses frais. On demolit
aussi les fortifications d'Ostende, pour y construire des Magazins. Le
nombre des Vaisseaux que J'y ai vus est tres considerable: le mouvement prodigieux.

On m'a dit a Middelbourg, que le Commerce se fait tres mal a
Ostende: les Commercans sont, dit on, tres negligens, quelquefois
meme infideles. Il m'a paru dans le detail, qu'il pouvoit bien n'y
avoir pas de leur faute, mais les affairs y sont si multipliees qu'ils ne
peuvent y satisfaire, et comme les Magazins leur manquent, ils ne
peuvent empecher bien des Marchandizes d'etre avariees. Ainsi les
reproches, qu'on leur fait pourront cesser d'etre merités, mais ceux
qu'on fait a leur Port ne se dissiperont pas de meme. On en dit
l'entree difficile, et effectivement la maniere dont on m'en a parlé a
Ostende meme, me le persuade.

It is an Observation in this Country, that the Wines of the Rhine
and Moselle, have in them the Principles both of the Stone and the
Gout, but that they loose these Principles, as they Advance in Age.

Extract from the Journal of C. Sarsefield,
1. July at the Hague.

Tout ce qui vient de se passer en Hollande, la Revolution qui s'y
est faite dans les Esprits en favour de la France, la maniere dont Le
Duc Louis de Brunswic a été ecarte des affairs, au moins en Apparence; enfin *cet ouvrage* de Mr. Le Duc de la Vauguion, merite
que J'en parle un peu. Je dis un peu, parce qu'il m'est impossible
d'en dire tout ce que l'on desireroit d'en savoir, M. de la Vauguion
n'en parlant Jamais, et etant d'un Secret impenetrable sur lequel
d'ailleurs J'ai été fort eloignee de vouloir l'attaquer. Tout Le monde
connoit les liaisons de ce pays cy avec L'Angleterre. On n'en connoit
pas moins le Principe, qui a été, si efficace que pendant long tems on
a cru que ces deux nations etoient necessairement attachées l'une a
l'autre, de maniere, a ne pouvoir s'en detacher. On eut dit que cette
Union etoit l'ouvrage de la nature même. Et Il y a peut etre encore
quelques gens chez lesquels ce Prejugé n'est pas entierement effacé.
Le Stathouder n'a suivant toutes les Apparences aucun autre motif
pour etre resté dans les Interets de L'Angleterre, au point ou Il l'est.
Les liens du Sang ne seroient pas suffisans, puis qu'il a les memes, et

plus intimes avec la Prusse dont le Sisteme est tout a fait opposé a celui de la prosperité de L'Angleterre. Son Abbaisement est essentiel a sa Sureté. Il faut donc que le Prince soit conduit par l'habitude de penser d'une certain maniere, et par le prejugé que Je viens de dire. Il se peut aussi, et cela est meme vraisemblable que la Crainte des Armes Angloises l'y ait engagé. Je remarquerai, a cette occasion, que ce Sentiment a operé certainement sur plusieurs des membres de la Republique.

Ainsi voicy, comme Je me la represente, au commencement de cette guerre cy. Le Chef decide en favour des Anglois, la plus grande Partie des Hollandois memes, ayant confusement dans la tete, L'Idee d'une Liaison avec L'Angleterre, necessaire, impossible a rompre ou tout au plus, pour des momens, effrayés d'ailleurs des Suites d'une conduite hardie, qui pourroit les entrainer dans une guerre, pour laquelle ils n'ont aucunes mesures prises. De grandes difficultés a vaincre, le danger de perdre les Juissance du moment, une tres ancienne habitude de Paresse, toute la nation semblant dans une sorte d'Etat de Lethargie, qui ne permet que difficilement d'en rien attendre, qui reponde a ce qu'elle a été autrefois.

Il n'est pas aussi facile de rendre raison de la Conduite de M. le Duc de Brunswic. Il est trop homme D'Etat, pour que les memes causes qui ont engourdi le Stathouder, et la nation, aient agi sur lui. On doit croire qu'il est trop eclairé, pour n'avoir pas senti des le premier moment, combien il etoit important pour elle de se montrer dans cette occasion; et, cependant il est toujours reste attache a L'Angleterre. Il a toujours agi pour elle. Il a meme maneuvré, suivant toute Apparence. Il y a, au moins, un fait, de ce genre qu'on ne peut nier, c'est la proposition fait en          d'augmenter l'armee de terre, au moment ou on alloit commencer, une Guerre de Mer. Quelques gens ont dit qu'il etoit payé, par l'Angleterre. J'en ai trouvé qui le defend sur ce point, et disent qu'il en est incapable. Et, quoiqu'ils ne l'aiment pas, rejettent cette Idee, avec une Sorte d'indignation. Il faut alors croire, que c'est l'attachment qu'il a pour son nom, qui le seduit, et lui fait penser qu'il est de l'interest de la Hollande de se soumettre a L'Angleterre de borner son commerce a la portion a laquelle elle jugera apropos de la reduire: d'etre, en un mot, aux terms d'une de ses Colonies, et de perdre sa place dans la Liste des Souverains d'Europe.

C'est en effet a quoi les decisions du Ministere Anglois, auroient conduit la Republique, si le Roy avoit envoyé un Ministre moins actif, moins penetrant, moins capable que Mr. de la Vauguion qui a sçu, au tres grand Etonnement des Hollandois meme, demonter tous les moyens de leur Administration, et ouvrir aux gens bien intentionnes, les Routes, pour faire parvenir leurs Sentiments a l'assemblee des Etats et la ramener a des Principes plus conformes a ses vrais Interets, on pourroit dire a la raison, et a leur honneur.

Quelques Gens pensent que malgré tous les Talens, et tout l'Art qu'il a develloppes, il auroit Eu beaucoup de peine a reussir, si l'Administration, n'avoit pas fait des fautes capitales. Je vais en exposer quelqu'unes. 1. Elle avoit poussé la Pusillanimité, jusqu'a defendre, aux commandans des Escortes de prendre, sous leur Protection, les navires, chargés pour la France, D'Effets utiles a la marine. Cette resolution secrette, fut sçu. M. de la V. presenta un memoire. On y repondit, et par lá, on avouoit le fait, qui auroit été bien difficile a prouver si on s'etoit contente de le nier.

2. Lorsque les Deputes d'Amsterdam vinrent presenter au Prince leur memoire, contre M. le Duc de Brunswic, ils annoncerent eux mêmes, que tout ce qu'ils alloient lui dire devoit etre renfermé sous un Secret impenetrable. On dit qu'ils paroissoient fort emus. Si le Prince avoit mis leur memoire dans sa poche, leur en avoit fait bien des Remerciemens, et les eut renvoyés en leur faisant sentir la necessité du Secret, que seroit devenue l'affaire? Rien probablement. Mais il leur rendit ce memoire, on les ranima, ils le publierent, ou plutot le rendirent public. Car Je ne sache pas qu'il y ait la de publication legale. 3. Alors M. Le Duc de Brunswic avoit un parti a prendre, qui etoit de laisser tomber, L'Affair, au moins Jusqu'au moment ou on feroit quelque Allegation speciale contre lui, ce qui auroit ete fort difficile. Au lieu de cela il se plaignit aux Etats Generaux, mit les formes contre lui tant parce qu'au lieu d'une requete ou d'un memoire, il fit une simple Lettre, que parce qu'il s'addressa, aux Etats Generaux pendant que c'etoient les seuls Etats de Hollande a qui il appartenoit de connoitre de cette affaire. On a vu les Suites qu'elle a eus, mais si le Duc, n'avoit rien dit, s'il avoit laissé aux Magistrats D'Amsterdam le Soin de donner le mouvement a cette affair, ils auroient pu se trouver fort embarrassés.

4. Avant le tems dont je viens de parler, l'Administration fit encore une grande faute contre ses vues. Elle vouloit que les Anglois fissent ce qui leur plairoit, et ce qui leur plaisoit, etoit de prendre tous les Vaisseaux charges pour la France, de matieres propres a L'Usage d'une flotte. Il falloit leur dire, de payer aux prix courant les effets qu'ils auroient saisis. Le Commerce n'auroit peut etre jamais remué. Alors les villes seroient probablement restees tranquilles par les raisons que J'ay

indiquées, au Commencement de cette note. Il est certain que ce ne sont que les Negotians qui les ont mis en Activite, ou au moins, Ils y ont bien contribues. Ceux qui parmi eux avoient le Sentiment de la Dignite de la Republique et qui souffroient de la voir aneantie, se sont fort appuyes sur les petitions des Negotians, mais quand les Negotians auroient été bien payés de leur Cargaisons, il auroit ete facile au parti anglois de les ecarter en leur repondant, qu'ils n'avoient aucun droit de se plaindre, aucun fondement legitime pour leurs representations. Etant payés suivant leurs factures, Ils ne pouvoient alors parler que du manque de respect pour le Pavillion, Chose qui ne les regardoit pas.

Cela auroit ete d'autant plus aise a etablir que les Regences, seroient fort fachees qu'on crut que c'est le Commerce qui les conduit, ou, si l'on veut qui les engage a telle ou telle demarche. Plus elles sentent que c'est au commerce que le Republique doit L'Existence qu'elle conserve, et plus elles veulent cacher cette Verite, afain de ne jamais dependre d'un corps qui leur est a quelques egards etranger. Les magistrats, surtout ceux D'Amsterdam, seroient bien fachés que l'on crut qu'ils font le Commerce, Ils veulent meme cacher que leurs Ancetres aient été commercans. Et Il y a tel homme, qui sauroit fort mauvais gré a celui qui lui diroit que son pere ou son grand Pere, avoit le premier Comptoir D'Amsterdam.

5. Une autre faute a été, dans la celebre affaire du pensionaire D'Amsterdam, de rendre aux Deputés de cette Ville la Sentence que la Cour de Hollande, avoit prononcé. C'etoit une Arme qu'il falloit conserver, quitte a ne jamais s'en servir. Des qu'on l'eut abandonnée, La Regence D'Amsterdam n'eut plus rien a craindre et se trouva en Liberte d'agir, comme elle l'a fait.

N[ot]a. On ne m'a pas bien expliqué comment cette Sentence, n'existoit que dans un seul papier, ce que les notaires appellent en Brevet. Les Tribunaux ont des registres, ou sont leurs Sentences, et la Public ne peut en avoir que des Expeditions. Quand J'ay fait cette question, on ne s'est pas trouvee en Etat, d'y repondre.

Voila une partie des fautes qu'on reproche a L'Administration. La premiere de toutes, fort anterieure a celles cy, a été, peut étre de se laisser voir de trop pres, mais certainement de ne s'etre pas attachée les gens les plus accredités dans les provinces pour en former son Conseil.

Le Duc scait tres mauvais gré a ceux qui vont a L'hotel de France. Il affecte le contraire, leur dit même non seulment qu'il y faut aller, mais qu'ils feront bien, et cherche ensuite de les desservir.

23

<sup></sup>¹ MS: "This."

² The 48'ers had supported the House of Orange upon the restoration of Willem IV as hereditary stadholder late in 1747, and the 82'ers were currently working to reduce (if not abolish) the power and influence of Willem V as stadholder.

³ The extracts that follow are given *literatim*, even though JA, as always when copying, was exceedingly careless in transcribing them.

### OCT. 11. FRYDAY.

C.S. came in familiarly at Breakfast, and I had a hours Conversation with him upon the foregoing Extract. I shew him some Papers. He thinks the American Cause ought to come in.

Walked to the House in the Wood.

Near 3 O Clock Mr. Fagel came in Person, and in Ceremony to make me a Visit, and delivered to me, the four other Copies of the Treaty attested by himself, to be sent to America. Complaisant as usual.

At 6 Mr. Van der Burg van Spieringshoek, the Agent of their H.M., came and delivered me their Resolution relative to Mr. Dubble de mutz's Vessell desiring me to transmitt it to Congress which I promised to do.

Spent most of the day in signing Obligations, for the United States. It is hard work to sign ones Name 1600 times after dinner.

### OCT. 12.

Spent the day in signing Obligations and packing the Treaties and dispatches.

### OCT. 13.

Sent 3 Copies of the Treaty of Commerce and as many of the Convention concerning Recaptures, by Mr. Storer to Amsterdam to go by three different Vessells.

Finished packing my Papers for my Journey to Paris. Mr. Storer is to prepare every Thing for Us to set off, from the Arms of Amsterdam, on Fryday Morning. Mr. Thaxter and I are to be there on Thursday night.

Walked the Tour of the Wood twice. Met the Court twice.

The Names of the Lords the Deputies of the Committee of foreign Affairs who signed with me, the Treaty of Commerce and the Convention concerning Recaptures, on the 8 of this Month are

| | |
|---|---|
| George Van Randwick | of Guelderland |
| Van den Santheuvel | of Holland |
| P. Van Bleiswyck | of Holland |

| | |
|---|---|
| W. C. H. Van Lynden | of Zeeland |
| D. S. [*i.e.* J.] Van Heeckeren | of Utrecht |
| Joan Van Kuffeler | of Friesland |
| H. Tjassens | of Groningen.[1] |

Vischer and Gyselaer have been pumping D. to get out of him my Secret. But luckily it was not in him. They insinuated to him that Fitzherbert had received Instructions to exchange full Powers with the American Ministers. That these were about to speak in a high Tone, "tenir une haute Langage." That there would be no Congress at Vienna nor Brussells, but the Peace would be made at Paris. This they learn I suppose from the Dispatches of their Ministers Berkenrode and Brantzen.

[1] Such committees were always composed of two members from the Province of Holland and one member from each of the six other provinces. JA inadvertently omitted the name of the member for Overyssel, F. G. van Dedem tot den Gelder (Miller, ed., *Treaties*, 2:85).

### 1782 OCT. 14. MONDAY.

Not long after my Reception here I was invited by Mr. Le Vaillant At Amsterdam, to dine with him in Company with Mr. Van Berckell, Mr. Bikker, and their Connections. When, according to the Ton in this Country, We came to that Period of the Feast, when the Toasts begin, Mr. Le Vaillant produced a beautifull Glass, round the Rim of which was engraved Aurea Libertas. He filled it, and first addressing himself to the Glass and then to me, pronounced these Words, with a profound Bow.

> Aurea Libertas gaude: Pars altera mundi
> Vindice te, renuit subdere colla jugo.
> Hæc tibi, Legatum quem consors Belga recipit,
> Pectore sincero pocula plena fero.
> Utraque Gens nectet, mox suspicienda Tyrannis
> Quæ Libertati vincula sacra precor.

Never was Bumper quaffed with more good Will.

The Duke de la Vauguion has invited me and my Family to dine with him to day. He advises me to present Mr. Dumas, to the President, Greffier and Grand Pensionary as my Chargé des Affairs in my absence. As Mr. D. has no Commission as Secretary to this Legation, nor any other Character than that of Correspondent of Mr. Franklin, or at most of an ancient Committee of Congress, which I suppose has ceased, I have some difficulty about this. Some members of Congress at least may think that I advance too fast.

At have after 9 I waited on Mr. Bleiswyck, to give him Notice that I intended to set off, on Thursday Morning for Paris. He cryes "C'est une bonne Augure, Monsieur."—"Oui Monsieur, Je m'en vais, avec la rameau d'olivier, dans la bouche, dans le Cœur et a la main."—He seemed to be very happy to learn it. I asked him, if their Ministers at Paris, had given them any late Information, concerning the Negotiations for Peace. He said Yes, they had informed him that the Court of Great Britain had fully acknowledged the Independence of America. That Mr. Fitzherbert was instructed to exchange Full Powers with the American Ministers.—I told him that I was invited and pressed by my Colleagues to go to Paris, and that I should be happy to take his Commands, on Wednesday.—I went next to Mr. Fagel, and informed him of my intended Journey. He seemed really overjoyed. Said "C'est un bon Mark" &c. He repeated to me, that their Ministers had written, that Mr. Fitzherbert had received such Instructions, and that the Comte de Vergennes had told them that he was now fully perswaded, that Great Britain, i.e. the British Ministry, were now sincerely disposed to Peace. Mr. Fagel said he did not expect that I should have gone so soon. I told him, that I was urged by my Colleague to come. That I had the Honour to be at the head of this Commission. That I was sent to Europe 3 Years ago, with a Commission as sole Minister Plenipotentiary, for Peace. But that last Year Congress had thought fit to change the Plan a little. They had sent me a Commission to this Republick, and had associated with me in the Commission for Peace, Mr. Franklin, Mr. Jay, Mr. Laurens and Mr. Jefferson. Mr. Laurens had resigned, or rather not accepted. Mr. Jefferson was in America, so that there remained only Mr. Franklin, Mr. Jay and myself. That Mr. Franklin was infirm—had the Gout and Gravel or Strangury and could not Sleep—so that it became more necessary for me to go. He asked how old Mr. Franklin was? I told him 76. That he was born in 1706.—He said that is my Age. I am of 1706, but I have no Disorders—no Pains or Uneasiness at all. In my Youth I was very infirm, had the Gravel and several Disorders, but they are all worn away with time.—I asked him if he took the Air much? He said Yes, a great deal, and he was very fond of Walking. He walked Yesterday four hours in the Downs from 10 to 2., and he was very well. He asked me when I should return? I answered, that if the Negotiations for Peace, should begin and go on, it was impossible to say: but that otherwise I should return in three Weeks....[1] He said he hoped, then, I should not return before next Spring.

This Gentleman has a very young Look—much younger than Mr.

Franklin. A Countenance, fresh and ruddy, clear, unclouded. A small, spare Man.

Dined with M. de la Vauguion, with M. De Llano, Renovalles, Sarsefield, Fenelon, Berenger, Dumas, Thaxter, Cremou, Creanci—very gay and social.

Fell into Conversation after Dinner with Sarsefield, Renovalles &c. about Biscay, Friesland &c. S. said the Genius of certain People had preserved them Priviledges.—What is the Genius of People? says I. It is a Manufacture, it is the Effect of Government and Education &c.—S. run on about the Panurge, Pantagruel &c. of Rabelais, the Romeo and Julliet of Shakespeare, the Mandragore of Machiavel, the Tartuff of Moliere, &c. &c.

¹ Suspension points in MS.

### OCT. 15. TUESDAY.

This Morning at 10 made my Visit to the President Van Randwick of Guelderland to take Leave of their H[igh] M[ightinesses] and presented Mr. Dumas as Chargé des Affairs in my Absence. Went next to the Hotel de Dordrecht to take Leave of Mr. Gyselaer, and next to that of Amsterdam, to take Leave of Mr. Vischer, who was more bold and open than ever I knew him. Said it was the Statholder who was the greatest; le plus g. t.¹ de ce Pays ci—entete come une Mule, &c. He shewed me a Letter from Mr. Brantzen at Paris, which contained that the C. de Vergennes told him, Mr. Fitzherbert had informed him that the Independence of America, would meet with no longer Difficulty. That he had received a special Commission to treat with the Ministers of the United States of America.

At 12 The Agent Vander Burg Van Spieringshoek enquired at the House If I could receive him at one. I answered in the affirmative. Accordingly at one he came, and said that he had it in Command from their High Mightinesses to inform me, that the President Mr. Van Randwyk had informed them of my Intention to take a Journey to France, that they had charged him to make me their Compliments, to wish me a good Journey, and a speedy Return in good Health.

At 3 I went to the House in the Wood and took Leave of the Princess and afterwards of the Prince. He asked me, several Questions. What were my Sentiments of the Negotiation at Paris? Whether I thought the King of Great Britain had taken upon himself, without an Act of Parliament to acknowledge the Independance of America? Who were the Ministers on the Part of America to treat of Peace.—Mr. Franklin,

Monsieur.—And who is the other.—Mr. Jay says I.—He who has been at Madrid? says he.—The same.

In the Evening, Mr. ⟨*Gyselaer*⟩ came in, and We had a long Conversation.[2] He told me, that a few Weeks ago, Mr. Thulemeyer visited the Duke de la Vauguion, and informed him that the King, (of Prussia) his Master, would not take it well that the Court of Versailles, or his Minister here, should intermeddle with the Interiour Parties and Disputes in the Republick. And at the same Time the Duke received a Letter from the C. De Vergennes, informing him that the Prussian Minister at Versailles had said the same Things to him: but that he had convinced him that all Jealousy of that kind was groundless.—He told me, that upon this Occasion He entered deep into Conversation, and said that he did not desire Versailles to intermeddle, unless as a Counterpoise to Prussias intermeddling.[3] There was an Affair of 1714 which had made the Prince absolute in Utrech, Guelderland and Overyssell. That if the Patriots should attempt to change that, and Prussia should interpose to prevent it, unless they should be supported by France, they must succumb and pass for the Dupes. That he[4] must be sensible, if they determined upon this Measure, and France should desert them, they must look out elsewhere.—Ay where?—Perhaps to the Emperor.—Furious.—Ay, but you[5] must be sensible that I ought [not][6] to quit your House, without Satisfaction upon this Point.

He[7] says the Prince has lately said that some Foreigner would soon interest himself in the Affairs of the Republick. He wished, if I could be usefull to them at Versailles, or here with the Duke that I would.

[1] Perhaps "le plus grand trouble" or "le plus grand tyran."

[2] The name in this sentence was heavily scratched out, apparently soon after it was written. The explanation of this can only be that JA thought the revelations of Gyselaar, a leading Patriot who suffered exile after the Prussian intervention of 1787, were too compromising to stand even in a private journal, and he therefore scratched out Gyselaar's name to prevent any possible disclosure. It is interesting and significant that the diplomats from other courts at The Hague were observing JA's conversations with leaders of the anti-Orange party at this critical moment. Baron von Thulemeier wrote his royal master Frederick II on 17 Sept.: "It is Adams whom they [the Orangists] accuse of being the leader of a lively intrigue against the Prince, but I do not perceive in the person of this American minister enough address or intelligence to lead any faction" (Marvin L. Brown Jr., ed., *American Independence through Prussian Eyes: . . . Selections from the Prussian Diplomatic Correspondence*, Durham, N.C., 1959, p. 70–71).

[3] Owing to JA's failure to use quotation marks or to supply clear antecedents for his pronouns, this remarkable conversation is far from easy to follow. The foregoing sentence should probably be interpreted as follows: He [Gyselaar] told me [JA] that upon this occasion [i.e. at an interview with La Vauguyon] he [Gyselaar] entered into deep conversation, and said that he did not desire Versailles to intermeddle unless as a counterpoise to Prussia's intermeddling.

[4-5] La Vauguyon.

[6] Inadvertently omitted by the diarist.

[7] Gyselaar.

### OCT. 16. WEDNESDAY.

Dined with the Baron De Linden de Blitterswick, the first Noble of Zealand. Llano, Almeida, Thulemeyer, Mirabel, Gallitzin and Markow, were all there. Geelwink, Sarsefield, Heyden, Boreel &c. 16 in all.

Mr. De Linden told me that their H.M. had lately consulted with all their Amirals and best Master Builders and had endeavoured to discover the best possible Model of a Ship, and that he would send it to me, as he did the next Morning. I have desired Mr. Dumas to send it to Congress.—Received an Invitation from Court to sup, tomorrow night. Sent an Excuse.

### OCT. 17. THURSDAY.

Began my Journey to Paris from the Hague, dined at Harlem and drank Tea at five O Clock at Amsterdam. Paid Mr. Bromfield 200 Ducats 1050 Guilders and took his Receipt upon Account....[1] Met Mr. Willink upon the Road, going to the Hague, with a Lady. He has left for me a Letter of Credit upon Paris, unlimited. He wished my Journey to Paris might have a Tendency towards Peace.

[1] Suspension points in MS.

### OCTOBER 18. FRYDAY.

Sat off, at ten from the Arms of Amsterdam with Mr. John Thaxter and Mr. Charles Storer. Refreshed our Horses at Loenen a Village, half Way to Utrecht, passed the Villages Bruykelen, Massen and Suylen.[1]

It is 8 hours, Stones, or Leagues from Amsterdam to Utrecht. The Village of Suylen and its Neighbourhood is full of Brick Killns. The Clay is found in that Neighborhood, and they burn the Bricks with Turf, Wood and Coal. Put up at Utrecht at the New Castle of Antwerp, which is now kept by Oblet, who speaks English very well, altho born at Leyden. The grand Canal, which runs through this Town is a great Curiosity. The paved Street upon each Side of it, is a covered Way, or rather, the Cover of a Cellar. The Cellars of the Houses are all continued out, under this Paved Street, to the Canal. And there are Doors through which Men pass from the Canal, under the Street into the Cellars of the Houses and e contra from the Cellars to the Canal and the Boats, Barks, or Schuits in it. The city maintains the Pavement but the Vaults underneath are maintained by the Proprietors. Oblet tells me, that the Spanish and Prussian Ambassadors were here, a few days ago. Came in an hired Carriage. That

Lord Stormont and his Lady were once here. Travelled only with 2 Men Servants. Very near. My Lady had not so much as a Maid, with her. Peterson is much hated. Oostergo makes a damned noise to day, about the fleets not going to Brest.

¹ Modern maps give the names of these villages as Breukelen, Maarssen, and Zuilen.

### OCTOBER 19. SATURDAY.

From Utrecht to Gorcum is 8 Leagues. Here we dined, at the Doele kept by Mr. Van Dongen. He told Us that as soon as We should get out of Town We should come to the River, near the Junction of the Maes with the Wahal, a Branch of the Rhine, that if We looked up the River We should have a full View of the Castle of Louvestein. We had accordingly a fair View of it. It stands upon an Island in the Middle of the River. There is an high and large square Tour of a Church at no great Distance from it. Gorinchem or Gorcum is one of the 18 Cities of the Province of Holland.

We dined at Gorcum, but as it was impossible to reach Breda before half after 6, when the Gates of that City are shut, my Servant rode forward on Horseback, and went to the Prince Cardinal a publick House, the Keeper of which applied to General Marsdam, the Governor, so that when We arrived at near 9 O Clock, We found an officer and a Guard at the Gate, who said he had orders to admit Mr. Adams the Ambassador of America. I gave the Guards 4 Guilders on the Spot and sent em 2 ducats afterwards.

The 4 last Leagues being Sand, were tolerable, but the former 4 being Clay were very bad—muddy, and deep.

### OCT. 20. SUNDAY.

Rising early this Morning and ringing for a Servant, was told that my Servant and most of those of the House were gone to Mass.—The Name of the Keeper of the Prince Cardinal is Van Opdorp.

Spent the whole day in travelling from Breda to Antwerp, without eating or drinking. The Distance is only ten Leagues. Put up at the grand Laboureur, opposite the Church with the Statue of the Prophet Elias upon it. The Coaches in great Numbers were driving backwards and forwards upon the Place Demier, as upon the Boulevards at Paris. It was Sunday Evening, and this March and Countermarch was for Pleasure and for Health.

Thus four days have been compleatly consumed in passing from the Hague to Antwerp, and We have seen nothing and conversed with

Nobody, so bad have been the Roads and so cold and rainy the Weather.—Reached Antwerp at Night and lodged at the Gran Laboureur upon the Place de Mier, where the Emperor lodged last Year and left his Portrait, which We saw, and an Inscription, in the Entry. Joseph 2d logé ici        day of        1781.

This Evening all the Carriages of the Town were parading in the Place de Mier, full of Ladies and Gentlemen as on the Boulvards at Paris.

### OCT. 21. MONDAY.

Went to the Cathedral Church, where We saw the Assumption of the Virgin Mary, the famous Altar Piece of Reubens, the Figures and Colouring are beautifull beyond description—and the Descent of Jesus from the Cross. Reubens has placed in this Piece his three Wives and Daughter, and his own head. The Colouring is all gloomy, accommodated to the Subject.

In this Church each Trade has its Altar. We remarked the Martyrdom of Crispin, Patron of the Shoemakers, in another Part the Martyrdom of St. Sebastian shot by Arrows. This Church is remarkably clean. No Dust upon any of the Figures.

Went next to the Church of St. James, principally To see the Tomb of Rubens. There is a Picture drawn by Rubens, containing in one Piece the Figures of his Grandfather, Father, two of his Wives and three of his Children. An Inscription at the Door, Ostium Monumenti Familiae Rubenianæ.

Rubens was born at Cologne, but removed at the Age of 10 Years, with his Family to Antwerp. He travelled into Italy. Mass is said 4 times a day at this Altar.

Went next to see the private Collection of Jaques Van Lancker. Here is an Head of his second Wife by Reubens and a larger Picture of the Saviour delivering the Keys to St. Peter. There is a Jealousy very remarkable in the face of one of the Apostles. A Christ by Reubens, a Magdalene by Paul Veronese, an Italian, A Man and his Wife by Rembrant, and several other Pieces by him, Vandyke &c.

We went in the last Place to see the private Collection of Pilaer and Beekmans, Negotiants en Dentelles, Diamans, Tableaux, Desseins, Estampes &c. Place de Mier.

The most remarkable Piece in this Collection is an old Woman, his Mother, with a Bible on the Table before her, by Rembrant. This is called his Master Piece. It is indeed an Admirable Picture.

The Son in Law of this house told me, there was a Society formed in this Town, which had begun to send Ventures to America.

After Dinner, We rode to Bruxelles, and put up, at the Hotel de belle Vue. Mr. Jennings came in, and We had a very agreable hour with him.

The Gate was shut before our Arrival. The Porter demanded my Name and Quality, in order to send them to a Burgomaster of the City, for a Billet du Porte. The Messenger returned with an order to admit Mr. Adams Minister Plenipotentiaire des Etats Unis &c. in stronger terms than usual. I did not know but the Burgomaster would have omitted the Quality in the order. But I am told that every body here is American.

OCTOBER 22. TUESDAY.

Visited Mr. William Lee, in the Place de St. Mitchell with Mr. Jennings. Mr. Lee said that the Swallow was a Sign of Summer. My Appearance denoted Peace.

Mr. Jennings let me into the Character of Mr. Fitsherbert. . . .[1] His Father was prevailed on by Ld. North to vote with him, but he was never easy in his mind about it, and finally cut his own Throat. The Gentleman at Paris is about 33, wholly dependent on Ld. Shelbourne. Has Parts but very conceited, and assuming. Not liked by the English while at Brussells, because he did not keep a Table. He was only Resident and his Appointment small, not more than 1500£.

He writes from Paris, that the C. de Vergennes has a Great Character, but that he sees nothing in him. . . . This is evidence of Vanity, for that Minister has at least a vast Experience, and too much reserve to give Proofs of Great or little Qualities so soon to this young Gentleman. . . . His Parts are quick and his Education has been good. . . . He has sometimes treated the English with cool Contempt and sometimes with hot Pride.

We set off on our Journey about Twelve but before We reached Halle, the Iron Axletree of our fore Weels snapped off like a Piece of Glass, our Carriage fell, and We were put to great difficulty to drag it, to the Porte Verde a Tavern in this Village. Being thus detained for the Reparation of our Carriage, after Dinner We walked about the Village and visited the Church of Notre Dame de Halle, but saw nothing but what is very common. The Village is dirty and poor. . . . What a Contrast to the Villages of Holland.

[1] Suspension points, here and below, in MS.

GESCHIEDENIS

VAN HET

GESCHIL

TUSSCHEN

GROOT-BRITANNIE

EN

A M E R I K A,

ZEDERT DESZELFS OORSPRONG, IN DEN
JAARE 1754, TOT OP DEN TEGEN-
WOORDIGEN TIJD.

DOOR ZIJNE EXCELLENTIE, DEN HEERE

JOHN ADAMS, Schildknaap,

GEVOLMAGTIGDEN STAATSDIENAAR DER DER-
TIEN VEREENIGDE STAATEN VAN NOORD-
AMERIKA, BIJ DE REPUBLIJK DER VER-
EENIGDE NEDERLANDEN.

Te AMSTERDAM
Bij W. HOLTROP, 1782.

1. JOHN ADAMS, MINISTER PLENIPOTENTIARY FROM THE
UNITED STATES TO THE DUTCH REPUBLIC, 1782

2. DUTCH TRANSLATION OF JOHN ADAMS'
"NOVANGLUS" LETTERS, 1782

3. HUIS VAN AMSTERDAM AT THE HAGUE

4. HUIS TEN BOSCH, THE STADHOLDER'S RESIDENCE NEAR THE HAGUE

OCT. 23. WEDNESDAY.

Rode to Mons in a great Rain, dined at the Couronne De L'Impereur, very well and very cheap, rode to Valenciennes and found our Axletree broken again. Put up at the Post house.

Walked about the Town, the Churches all shut, and nothing remarkable.

> The bright rosy morning, peeps over the Hills
> With blushes adorning, the Meadows and Fields.
>
> The merry, merry, merry horn, calls come, come away
> Awake from your Slumbers, and hail the new Day.
>
> The Stag rous'd before Us, away seems to fly
> And pants to the Chorus of Hounds in full Cry.
>
> The follow, follow, follow, follow, the musical Chase
> While Pleasure and Vigour each other embrace.
>
> The day Sports being over, makes blood circle right
> And gives the brisk Lover, fresh Charms for the night.
>
> Then Let Us, Let us now enjoy, all We can while We may
> Let Love crown the night Boys, as our Sports crown the day.

### The Banks of the Dee.

> T'was Summer, when softly the Breezes were blowing
> And sweetly the Nightingale sang from the Tree
> At the Foot of a Rock, where the River was flowing
> I sat myself down on the Banks of the Dee.
>
> Flow on lovely Dee! flow on thou sweet River
> Thy Bank's, purest Stream! shall be dear to me, ever
> For then I first gain'd the Affections and favour
> Of Jemmy, the Glory and Pride of the Dee.
>
> But now he is gone and has left me, thus mourning
> To quel the proud Tyrant, for valiant is he
> And Ah! there's nae hope of his speedy returning
> To stroll here again on the Banks of the Dee.
>
> He's gone hapless youth, o'er the wide roaring Billows
> The kindest the sweetest of all the young Fellows
> And has left me to wander among the green Willows
> The loneliest Lass, on the Banks of the Dee.

But time and my Prayers may perhaps yet restore him
Sweet Peace may return my dear Soldier to me
And when he returns, with such Care, I'll watch o'er him
He n'eer shall again leave the Banks of the Dee.

The Dee then shall flow all its Beauties displaying
The Lambs shall again on its Banks be seen playing
Whilst I with my Jemmy, am carelessly straying
And tasting afresh all the Sweets of the Dee.

All the Cities and Villages of Brabant are very different from those of Holland. The Streets very foul. The Houses very dirty, the Doors and Windows broken, Bricks and Glass wanting. The People, Men, Women and Children filthy and rag[g]ed.

### OCT. 24. THURSDAY.

Visited the Church at Valenciennes. Saw a notre Dame De Hall. She appears pregnant. A Collection of Portraits ancient and modern, and a Picture of the Virgin Mary in the Air, sending by Angels a Cord round the City with an Inscription importing, Valenciennes surrounded with a Cord by the blessed Virgin, and saved from the Plague Anno 1008.

Dined at Cambray, visited the Cathedral, saw the Tomb of Fenelon, his Statue, Picture &c. Saw the Chapter where the Chanoines meet twice a Week, and saw also the Room where are the Portraits of all the Archbishops and Bishops ancient and Modern, and Fenelon among the rest. There is also in this Church a curious Piece of Clock Work, which represents the whole Proscess with Jesus Christ like that in the 7 Chappells of Mount Calvare.—Lodged at Peronne.

### OCT. 25. FRYDAY.

Dined at Gourney. Carriage broke again. Arrived at Night, at Pont-Sainte-Maxence, two Posts from Chantilly and one and an half from Senlis.

### The Ecchoing horn

The ecchoing horn calls the Sportsmen abroad
To horse, my brave Boys, and away
The morning is up and the Cry of the hounds
Upbraids our too tedious Delay.

What Pleasure We find in pursuing the Fox
O'er hills and o'er Valleys he flies
Then follow, W'ell soon overtake him. Huzza
The Traitor is seized on and dies.

Tryumphant returning at night with our Spoils
Like Bacchanals shouting and gay
How Sweet with a Bottle and Lass to refresh
And loose the Fatigues of the Day.

With Sport, Love and Wine fickle Fortune defy
Dull Wisdom all Happiness sours
Since Life is no more than a Passage at best
Let's strew the Way over with Flowers.

### 1782 OCTOBER 26. SATURDAY.

Parted from Pont Sainte Maxence, for Chantilly. The distance is two Postes, and We found the Road very good. We went to see the Stables, and Horses. I had on my travelling Gloves, and one of the Grooms run up to Us, with 3 Whip Sticks, and presented them to Us. This is an Air which the Grooms give themselves, in order to get Something to drink. They do the same to the Prince of Condé himself, if he enters the Stables with Gloves on his hands. I gave them six Livres, but if I had been in a private Character, I should have thought 24s. or even half of it, enough.

We went round the Castle, and took a Look at the Statue of the grande Condé, in marble, half Way up the great Stair Case, and saw the Statue on Horseback in Bronze, of the grand Constable Montmorency. Walked round the Gardens, Fish Ponds, Grottoes and Waterspouts. And looked at the Carps and Swan that came up to Us for Bread. Nothing is more curious than this. Whistle or throw a Bit of Bread into the Water and hundreds of Carps large and fat as butter will be seen swimming near the Top of the Water towards you, and will assemble all in a huddle, before you. Some of them will thrust up their Mouths to the Surface, and gape at you like young Birds in a Nest to their Parents for Food.

While We were viewing the Statue of Montmorency Mademoiselle de Bourbon came out into the Round house at the Corner of the Castle dressed in beautifull White, her Hair uncombed hanging and flowing about her Showlders, with a Book in her Hand, and leaned over the Bar of Iron, but soon perceiving that she had caught my Eye, and that I viewed her more attentively than she fancied, she rose up with that Majesty and Grace, which Persons of her Birth affect, if they are not taught, turned her Hair off of both her Showlders, with her Hands, in a manner that I could not comprehend, and decently stepped back into the Chamber and was seen no more. The Book in her hand is consistent, with what I heard 4 Years ago at the Palais de Bourbon in Paris, that she was fond of Reading. . . .[1]

The Managery, where they exercise the Horses is near the end of the Stables and is a magnificent Piece of Architecture. The orangery appears large, but We did not look into it.

The Village of Chantilly, appears a small Thing. In the Forest or Park We saw Bucks, Hares, Pheasants, Partridges &c. but not in such Plenty as one would expect.

We took a Cutlet and glass of Wine, at ten at Chantilly, that We might not be tempted to stop again, accordingly We arrived, in very good Season at the Hotel de Valois, Rue de Richelieu, where the House however was so full that We found but bad Accommodations.

> Now the Hill Tops are burnished, with Azure and Gold
> And the Prospect around Us most bright to behold
> The hounds are all trying the Mazes to trace
> The Steeds are all neighing and pant for the Chase
> Then rouse each true Sportsman, and join at the Dawn
> The Song of the Huntsman, and Sound of the Horn.
>   The Horn, The Horn, the Song of the Huntsman
>       and Sound of the Horn.
>
> Wherever We go Pleasure waits on Us still
> If We sink in the Valley, or rise on the Hill
> See the Downs now we leave, and the Coverts appear
> As eager We follow, the Fox or the Hare.
>   The Horn, The Horn, the Song of the Huntsman
>       and Sound of the Horn.
>
> O'er Hedges and Ditches We valiantly fly
> For fearless of Death We ne'er think we shall die.
>   Chorus.
>
> From Ages long past by the Poets we are told
> That Hunting was lov'd by the Sages of old
> That the Soldier and Huntsman were both on a Par
> That the health giving Chase made them bold in the War.
>   Chorus.

The Chase being over away to the Bowl
The full flowing Bumper shall chear up our Soul
Whilst Jocund our Songs shall with Chorus's ring
A Toast to our Lasses, our Country and King.
  Chorus.

End.[2]

Arrived, at night at the Hotel de Valois, Rue de Richelieu, after a Journey of ten Days from the Hague, from whence We, Mr. John Thaxter, Mr. Charles Storer and I parted last Thursday was a Week.

The first Thing to be done, in Paris, is always to send for a Taylor, Peruke maker and Shoemaker, for this nation has established such a domination over the Fashion, that neither Cloaths, Wigs nor Shoes made in any other Place will do in Paris. This is one of the Ways, in which France taxes all Europe, and will tax America. It is a great Branch of the Policy of the Court, to preserve and increase this national Influence over the Mode, because it occasions an immense Commerce between France and all the other Parts of Europe. Paris furnishes the Materials and the manner, both to Men and Women, every where else.

Mr. Ridley lodges in the Ruë de Clairi [Cléry], No. 60.
Mr. Jay. Rue des petits Augustins, Hotel D'Orleans.

[1] Suspension points in MS. The romantic figure JA saw so fleetingly was Louise Adélaïde de Bourbon-Condé, later Princesse de Condé (1757–1824), who was born at Chantilly, fled to Brussels in 1789, entered a convent at Turin in 1795, and, largely owing to the vicissitudes of war, led a wandering life in Switzerland, Poland, England, and France; her letters to a lover she never married were published in 1834 (*La Grande Encyclopédie*, 12:341–342).

[2] At this point the present Diary booklet (D/JA/34) ends; the next sentence, continuing the record of 26 Oct. (though perhaps written on the 27th), begins a new booklet (D/JA/35) which is identical in format with its predecessor.

### 1782 OCT. 27. SUNDAY.

Went into the Bath, upon the Seine, not far from the Pont Royal, opposite the Tuilleries. You are shewn into a little Room, which has a large Window looking over the River into the Tuilleries. There is a Table, a Glass and two Chairs, and you are furnished with hot linnen, Towels &c. There is a Bell which you ring when you want any Thing.

Went in search of Ridley and found him.[1] He says F[ranklin] has broke up the Practice of inviting every Body to dine with him on

37

Sundays at Passy. That he is getting better. The Gout left him weak. But he begins to sit, at Table.

That J[ay] insists on having an exchange of full Powers, before he enters on Conference or Treaty. Refuses to treat with D'Aranda, untill he has a Copy of his Full Powers. Refused to treat with Oswald, untill he had a Commission to treat with the Commissioners of the United States of America.—F. was afraid to insist upon it. Was afraid We should be obliged to treat without. Differed with J. Refused to sign a Letter &c. Vergennes wanted him to treat with D'Aranda, without.[2]

The Ministry quarrel. De Fleury has attacked De Castries, upon the Expences of the Marine. Vergennes is supposed to be with De Fleury.—Talk of a Change of Ministry.—Talk of De Choiseul, &c.

F. wrote to Madrid, at the Time when he wrote his pretended Request to resign, and supposed that J. would succeed him at this Court and obtained a Promise that W. should be Sec[retary]. Jay did not know but he was well qualified for the Place.[3]

Went to the Hotel D'orleans, Rue des petites Augustins, to see my Colleage in the Commission for Peace, Mr. Jay, but he and his Lady were gone out.

Mr. R. dined with me, and after dinner We went to view the Appartements in the Hotel du Roi,[4] and then to Mr. J. and Mrs. Iz[ard], but none at home. R. returned, drank Tea and spent the Evening with me. Mr. Jeremiah Allen, our Fellow Passenger in the leaky Sensible, and our Fellow Traveller through Spain, came in and spent the Evening. He has been home since and returned.

R. is still full of Js. Firmness and Independance. Has taken upon himself, to act without asking Advice or even communicating with the C[omte] de V[ergennes]—and this even in opposition to an Instruction.[5] This Instruction, which is alluded to in a Letter I received at the Hague a few days before I left it, has never yet been communicated to me. It seems to have been concealed, designedly from me. The Commission to W. was urged to be filled up, as soon as the Commission came to O[swald] to treat with the Min[ister]s of the united States, and it is filled up and signed. W. has lately been very frequently with J. at his house, and has been very desirous of perswading F. to live in the same house with J.—Between two as subtle Spirits, as any in this World, the one malicious, the other I think honest, I shall have a delicate, a nice, a critical Part to Act. F.s cunning will be to divide Us. To this End he will provoke, he will insinuate, he will intrigue, he will maneuvre. My Curiosity will at least be employed, in observing his Invention and his Artifice. J. declares roundly, that he will never set his hand to a bad Peace. Congress may appoint another, but he will make a good Peace or none.

[1] In a letter to the *Boston Patriot,* published 24 July 1811, JA has more to say about why he sought out Matthew Ridley as soon as he reached Paris, and about what passed between them concerning the views of Franklin and Jay and other matters. Ridley had no official status (beyond his commission to borrow money for the State of Maryland), but he was a confidant of a surprising number and variety of Americans and others, and his journals for 1782–1783 (in MHi) are therefore a valuable source of information on persons and events connected with the peace negotiations.

[2] See Jay's own account of the negotiation, from the time of his arrival in Paris from Madrid late in June to the arrival of JA in Paris four months later, in a long and remarkable letter to Secretary Livingston, 17 Nov. 1782 (Wharton, ed., *Dipl. Corr. Amer. Rev.,* 6:11–49). See also JA's Diary entry of 3 Nov., below. The "first set" of articles for the preliminary treaty had been agreed on between Franklin and Jay on the one hand and the British Commissioner, Richard Oswald, on the other, 8 Oct.; a copy of these is in Lb/JA/21 (Adams Papers, Microfilms, Reel No. 109; Wharton, ed., *Dipl. Corr. Amer. Rev.,* 5:805–808). These were sent to London for the consideration of the British government.

[3] "W." is William Temple Franklin. His commission as secretary to the American peace commission, dated 1 Oct. 1782, is printed in same, p. 789–790. It was signed by Franklin and Jay on that date and by Laurens and JA retroactively in 1783. JA was nettled be-cause he had not been consulted about the appointment, but at Franklin's request Jay later categorically denied that he (Jay) had been solicited by Franklin in behalf of his grandson; see Jay to Franklin, 26 Jan. 1783 (same, 6:231). See also entry of 11 Jan. 1783, below.

[4] In the Place du Carrousel, between the Palais Royal and the Quai du Louvre, now in the courtyard of the (enlarged) Louvre. JA occupied apartments here from the end of Oct. 1782 until after the signing of the Definitive Treaty in Sept. 1783, though he found them both expensive and noisy. See his letter published in the *Boston Patriot,* 29 April 1812, and his Diary entry for 14 Sept. 1783, below.

[5] Of 15 June 1781: "... you are to make the most candid and confidential communications upon all subjects to the ministers of our generous ally, the King of France; to undertake nothing in the negotiations for peace or truce without their knowledge and concurrence; and ultimately to govern yourselves by their advice and opinion" (*JCC,* 20:651). JA received this instruction on 24 Aug. 1781, but, as he declared to Livingston on 31 Oct. 1782, he never supposed that it was intended to take "away from Us, all right of Judging for ourselves, and obliging Us to agree to whatever the french Ministers shall advise Us too [*sic*], and to [do] nothing without their Consent." If this was indeed Congress' intention, JA continued, "I hereby resign my Place in the Commission" (LbC, Adams Papers; JA, *Works,* 7:653; see also JA to Livingston, 18 Nov. 1782, LbC, Adams Papers, printed in same, 8:11–13).

1782. OCTOBER 28. MONDAY.

Dined with Mr. Allen.

OCT. 29. TUESDAY.

Dined at the Hotel du Roi. Mr. R. dined with Us. In the Evening, I went out to Passy to make my Visit to Franklin.[1]

[1] "Tuesday Oct. 29h: Called to see Mr. Adams. Dined with him. He is much pleased with Mr. Jay. Went in the Morning to see D: Franklin—did not know of Mr. Adams Arrival. Spoke to Mr. A. about making his visit to Dr. F. He told me it was time enough—represented to him the necessity of meeting. He replied there was no necessity—that after the usage he had received from him he could not bear to go near him. I told him whatever their differences were he would do wrong to discover any to the World and that it might have a bad effect on our Affairs at this time. He said the D: might come to him. I told him it was not [his] place—the last comer always paid the first visit. He replied the Dr. was to come to him [since] he was first in the Comm[issio]n. I ask[ed] him how the D: was to know he was here unless he went to him. He replied that was true, he did not think of that and would go. Afterwards when pulling on his Coat he said he would not, he could not bear to go where the D: was. With much persuasion I got him at length to go. He said he would do it, since I would have it so; but I was always making mischeif and so I should find" (Matthew Ridley, Diary, MHi).

### OCT. 30. WEDNESDAY.

## Dined with Mr. Jay.[1]

[1] "Wednesday Oct. 30h: Dined at Mr. Jays, Dr. Franklin, Mr. Adams, Mr. Oswald, Mr. Strachey there—also two Mr. Vaughans. All Things do not seem to go clever. Strachey insisting on changing the boundaries, a Mr. Roberts is with him" (Matthew Ridley, Diary, MHi).

### OCT. 31. THURSDAY.

## Dined with Mr. Oswald. Dr. F., Mr. Jay, Mr. Oswald, Mr. Stretchy,[1] Mr. Roberts[2] and Mr. Whitford.[3]

[1] Henry Strachey (whose name JA always had difficulty in spelling) was a British under-secretary of state who had been sent to Paris to stiffen what was thought to be a too pliant attitude on the part of Oswald; his instructions concerning the British right to Sagadahock (eastern Maine), western lands ("as a means of providing for the Refugees"), restraints on American fishing rights, and a provision for the payment of American debts to British merchants, are embodied in a Cabinet Minute of 17 Oct. (*Correspondence of King George the Third* . . . , ed. Sir John Fortescue, London, 1927–1928, 6:143–144). There is a sketch of Strachey in *DNB*.

[2] W. Roberts, according to JA's recollections, was "the oldest clerk in the board of trade and plantations, and a very respectable character. He was sent over by the British cabinet with huge volumes of . . . original records . . . in order to support their incontestible claim to the Province of Maine" (letter published in the *Boston Patriot*, 23 Oct. 1811). It was Roberts whom JA astonished by producing still more impressive records of Massachusetts' claim to Maine; see entry of 10 Nov., below, and note 1 there.

[3] Caleb Whitefoord, Oswald's secretary; he signed the Preliminary Articles of 30 Nov. as a witness (*DNB*). Some scanty correspondence and papers of Whitefoord relating to the peace negotiations are in W. A. S. Hewins, ed., *The Whitefoord Papers* . . . , Oxford, 1898.

### NOVEMBER 1. FRYDAY.

## Dined at Passy with Mr. F.

NOV. 2. SATURDAY.

Mr. Oswald, Mr. Franklin, Mr. Jay, Mr. Strechy, Mr. W. Franklin, dined with me at the Hotel du Roi, Rue du Carrousel.

Almost every Moment of this Week has been employed in Negotiation, with the English Gentlemen, concerning Peace. We have made two Propositions. One the Line of forty five degrees. The other a Line thro the Middles of the Lakes. And for the Bound between Mass. and Nova Scotia—a Line from the Mouth of St. Croix to its Source, and from its Source to the high Lands.[1]

[1] The foregoing paragraph is the first in JA's "Peace Journal," extending (with omissions) from this point through 13 Dec. 1782, which has a curious and still partly obscure history and which acquired much contemporary notoriety. It is the only portion of JA's Diary that became publicly known while he was still in public life, and he had cause to regret that it did.

The long-standing and never-questioned explanation of how the "Peace Journal" got into circulation is that given by CFA in a note in JA's *Works*, 3:349:

"Here ends that portion of the Diary, beginning at the place marked with an asterisk on page 300, from which extracts were made by Mr. Adams, and sent home to one of the delegates of Massachusetts in the Congress of the Confederation, Mr. Jonathan Jackson, for the sake of furnishing unofficial, but interesting information, respecting the negotiation. By some mistake in sealing up the packages, these went with the despatches to Mr. Livingston, and not with the letter to Mr. Jackson; and they were deemed so valuable that they were not given up to that gentleman when he went to claim them, and thus became official papers. This statement is necessary to explain the facts which were eighteen years afterwards made the ground of a political and personal attack upon the author, involving an insinuation even against his veracity, by Mr. Hamilton."

This is a highly inaccurate and misleading explanation, though the fault lies by no means entirely with the conscientious editor of JA's *Works*. CFA was simply summarizing the diarist's own garbled explanation of this affair, in a letter dated 18 June 1811 which was published in the *Boston Patriot* the following 7 Sept.—one of the long series of communications in which JA tried to answer all the detractions uttered against him throughout his career that he could remember, and especially those of Alexander Hamilton. In short, this letter to the *Boston Patriot* is a conspicuous example of how JA's memory played tricks on him when he described political battles in which he had fought long ago. CFA's paragraph being on the whole an acceptable condensation of JA's several columns, no more needs to be said of the latter here. The task is to try to discover, from strictly contemporary evidence, how "that obnoxious Journal" (JA's own phrase) was prepared, transmitted, and received in 1782–1783.

The "Peace Journal" itself is a paper, or series of papers, totaling 55 pages of text, of which portions are alternately in the hands of John Thaxter and Charles Storer, on file among JA's dispatches to R. R. Livingston in the Papers of the Continental Congress, No. 84, IV, 242–296, between dispatches dated from Paris 11 and 21 Nov. 1782, respectively. (This may have been where Livingston himself placed it after it was read to Congress, although it could not have been received in its entirety with either of those dispatches, and its present location was more likely fixed by William A. Weaver, the State Department clerk who in the 1830's arranged the Papers of the Continental Congress in the order that they have ever since retained. See Carl L. Lokke, "The Continental Congress Papers: Their History, 1789–1952," *National Archives Accessions,*

No. 51 [June 1954], especially, p. 9–10.) The Thaxter-Storer transcript contains most of the contents of JA's Diary as found in the MS (and as printed in the present edition), 2 Nov.–13 Dec. 1782, but with frequent and sometimes substantial omissions, which have been indicated in our edition; see entry of 3 Nov., below, and note 3 there. The text was first printed from the MS in PCC by Jared Sparks in his *Diplomatic Correspondence of the American Revolution*, Boston, 1829–1830, 6:465–512, with at least one further omission prompted by Sparks' extreme discretion; see entry of 10 Nov., below, and note 2 there. It was printed again by Wharton, but distributed under its dates, and docked, apparently inadvertently, of its last two entries (*Dipl. Corr. Amer. Rev.*, vols. 5–6).

The Thaxter-Storer transcript was prepared *in parts*, and the first part was ready by 17 Nov., when JA concluded a confidential letter to Jonathan Jackson as follows:

"When We see the French intriguing with the English against Us, We have no Way to oppose it, but by Reasoning with the English to shew that they are intended to be the Dupes. Inclosed are a few broken Minutes of Conversations, which were much more extended and particular, than they appear upon Paper. I submit them to your Discretion" (RC, MHi:Misc. Coll.; LbC, Adams Papers, has the direction at foot of text: "Jonathan Jackson Esqr. Member of Congress or in his Absence to any Delegate of Massachusetts").

But in spite of the lack of any explanation about a missing or an unexpected enclosure, either to Jackson or to Livingston, these "broken Minutes" were sent to Livingston rather than to Jackson—and (as will be seen) not by any "mistake" on JA's part. Two further installments followed (or accompanied) them, extending in date a fortnight beyond the signing of the Preliminary Articles at the end of November, without any (recorded) explanation by JA to Livingston or acknowledgment by the latter. Livingston's Despatch Book, however, contains an entry under 12 March 1783 recording his receipt, by Capt. Joshua Barney of the packet *Washington*,

of JA's letters dated 4, 6, 11, 18 Nov., and 14 Dec. 1782, together with "Extracts from Mr. Adam's Journal"—presumably *all* the installments (PCC, No. 126). No doubt, then, the "Extracts" were read in Congress as soon as the Preliminary Articles and the numerous letters from the Commissioners, also brought by Barney, had been read. This seems to be confirmed by an entry in Charles Thomson's Despatch Book dated 14 and 15 March: "Extract of a Journal [by JA] from Nov. 2 to 9 Dec." (PCC, No. 185, II).

On 7 Dec. 1783 Samuel Osgood, a Massachusetts delegate to Congress, which was then sitting at Annapolis, wrote a very long letter to JA, ventilating his embittered feelings about American subservience to French policy and explaining what had happened to JA's "Peace Journal":

"You will pardon me in candidly mentioning to you the Effects of your long Journal, forwarded after the signing of the provisional Treaty. It was read by the Secretary in Congress. It was too minute for the Delicacy of several of the Gentlemen. They appeared overmuch disposed to make it appear as ridiculous as possible; several ungenerous Remarks were made upon it, as being unfit to be read in Congress, and not worth the Time expended in reading it. The Day after it was read, the Delegates of Masstts. found on the Table of Congress your Letter addressd to J. Jackson or the Delegates. A Passage in that Letter led them to conclude that your Journal was not intended for Congress, as you mention that you had enclosed for his Perusal a Journal; and there was none enclosed. They therefore agreed to move that the Journal might be delivered to them. This Motion soon found Opponents. It was then said that it contained Matters of great Importance, which you had not mentioned in your other Letters—but we examined your other Letters, and found all the great Matters touch'd upon, and the smaller ones omitted. The Secretary for foreign Affairs, was sent for to know whether it came address'd to him; he produced three several Covers with your Seal, all directed to him, and the foldings corresponded to those of the Journal: after this, we let the Matter subside, as we found we should loose the Question; and also, that a Number of the Members were convinced, that there was some Mistake: nothing was said against it afterwards. Whatever your Intentions were respecting your Journal, it was necessary for us to take the Measure we did; and it had a very happy Effect" (NN).

This tells much, but JA's answer tells more. On 30 June 1784 he replied to Osgood from Paris:

"The Journal which caused such Wonder, was intended to be sent to Mr. Jackson. But recollecting the frequent Injunctions of your Secretary [Livingston], to be minute: to send him even the Looks of Ministers to be sure, Conversations, and considering that in the Conferences for the Peace, I had been very free, which I had Reason to expect would be misrepresented by Franklin, I suddenly determined to throw into the Packet for Livingston, what was intended for another.—Let them make the most and the worst of it" (LbC, Adams Papers).

If the "most" was made of it when it was read in Congress in 1783 amid warm debates on the conduct of the American Commissioners in violating their instruction to defer to the French ministry, the "worst" was made of JA's "Peace Journal" seventeen years later, by Alexander Hamilton; see entry of 10 Nov., below, note 2.

It is clear that JA caused still another copy of his journal of the negotiations of 1782 to be prepared, though where it is now is unknown to the editors. On 28 Dec. JA wrote AA: "I dare say there is not a Lady in America treated with a more curious dish of Politicks, than is contained in the inclosed Papers. You may shew them to discrete Friends, but by no means let them go out of your hands or be copied. Preserve them in Safety against Accidents" (Adams Papers). This is cryptic enough, but AA certainly referred to this budget of material in replying on 28 April 1783: "Your journal has afforded me and your Friends much pleasure and amusement. You will learn, perhaps from Congress that the journal, you meant for Mr. Jackson, was by some mistake enclosed to the Minister for foreign affairs; and consequently came before Congress with other publick papers. The Massachusetts Delegates applied for it, but were refused it. Mr. Jackson was kind enough to wait upon me, and shew me your Letter to him, and the other papers inclosed, and I communicated the journal to him" (same). If by "communicated" AA meant she gave the journal to Jackson, this would explain its disappearance from the family papers; and though she would thus have violated the letter of JA's injunction to her, she might well have thought that Jackson was entitled to this copy since his own was irrecoverable. All this, however, is conjectural. Even though it is now lost, we can say with some confidence that the copy sent to AA was fuller than that sent to Livingston, for the markings ("C") in the original Diary MS that indicate what was to be copied (or possibly what had been copied) include more than one substantial passage edited out of the "Peace Journal" now in the Papers of the Continental Congress; these markings in the MS extend in fact through the entry of 26 Dec. 1782. It would be impossible to make sense of them without supposing that another transcript of the journal once existed—in all likelihood the one first begun and continued longest, from which the shorter transcript in PCC, No. 84, IV, was taken.

## 1782. NOVEMBER 3. SUNDAY.

In my first Conversation with Franklin on Tuesday Evening last, he told me of Mr. Oswalds Demand of the Payment of Debts and Compensation to the Tories. He said their Answer had been, that We had not Power, nor had Congress. I told him I had no Notion of cheating any Body. The Question of paying Debts, and that of compensating Tories were two.—I had made the same Observation, that forenoon to Mr. Oswald and Mr. Stretchy, in Company with Mr. Jay at his House....¹ I saw it struck Mr. Stretchy with peculiar Pleasure, I saw it instantly smiling in every Line of his Face. Mr. O. was apparently pleased with it too.

In a subsequent Conversation with my Colleagues, I proposed to them that We should agree that Congress should recommend it to the States to open their Courts of Justice for the Recovery of all just Debts. They gradually fell in to this Opinion, and We all expressed these Sentiments to the English Gentlemen, who were much pleased with it, and with Reason, because it silences the Clamours of all the British Creditors, against the Peace, and prevents them from making common Cause with the Refugees.

Mr. J. came in and spent two hours, in Conversation, upon our Affairs, and We attempted an Answer to Mr. Oswalds Letter.² He is perfectly of my Opinion or I am of his respecting Mr. Dana's true Line of Conduct as well as his with Spain, and ours with France, Spain and England.

†I learn from him that there has not been an Harmony, between him and C[armichael]. The latter aimed at founding himself upon a French Interest, and was more supple to the french Ambassador at Madrid, and to Mr. G[érard] than was approved by the former. G. endeavoured to perswade him to shew him, his Instructions, which he refused at which offence was taken.† ³

V[ergennes] has endeavoured to perswade him to treat with D'Aranda, without exchanging Powers. He refuses. V. also pronounced Oswalds first Commission sufficient, and was for making the Acknowledgement of American Independance the first Article of the Treaty. J. would not treat. The Consequence was, a compleat Acknowledgment of our Independence by Oswalds new Commission under the great Seal of G.B. to treat with the Commissioners of the United States of America.—Thus a temperate Firmness has succeeded every where, but the base System nowhere.

†R[idley] says that Jennings is in easy Circumstances, and as he always lives within his Income, is one of the most independent Men in the World. He remitted him 3000£. St. when he came over to France. His Father left him Ten Thousand Pounds. He kept great Company in England and no other. He is related to several principal Families in America, and to several great Families in England. Was bred to the Law in the Temple, and practised as Chamber Council, but no otherwise.†

44

D'Estaing has set off for Madrid and Cadix. Reste a Scavoir, what his Object is. Whether to take the Command of a Squadron, and in that Case where to go—whether to R. Island to join Vaudreul, and go vs. N. York, or to the W. Indies. Will they take N. York, or only prevent the English from evacuating it.—O. proposed solemnly to all 3 of Us, Yesterday, at his House, to agree not to molest the British Troops in the Evacuation, but We did not. This however shews they have it in Contemplation. Suppose they are going against W. Florida —how far are We bound to favour the Spaniards? Our Treaty with France must and shall be sacredly fulfilled, and We must admit Spain to acceed when She will, but untill She does our Treaty does not bind Us to France to assist Spain.

The present Conduct of England and America resembles that of the Eagle and Cat. An Eagle scaling over a Farmers Yard espied a Creature, that he thought an Hair. He pounced upon him and took him up. In the Air the Cat seized him by the Neck with her Teeth and round the Body with her fore and hind Claws. The Eagle finding Herself scratched and pressed, bids the Cat let go and fall down.— No says the Cat: I wont let go and fall, you shall stoop and set me down.[4]

[1] Suspension points in MS.
[2] There is no letter from Oswald to the American Commissioners on record to which this could pertain except one dated 4 Nov. concerning the compensation of loyalists (Tr, Adams Papers), which was answered by JA, Franklin, and Jay on the 7th (RC, Public Record Office, London) after several conferences. These letters are printed in Wharton, ed., *Dipl. Corr. Amer. Rev.*, 5:848, 849–850 (the answer under date of 5 Nov.).
[3] Passages preceded and followed by dagger signs were not included in the transcript of his Diary furnished by JA to Secretary Livingston; see note on preceding entry. In view of JA's purpose and of the noise made by his "Peace Journal" when it was read in Congress, JA's "editing" of the text is of some interest.
[4] JA later told this fable in more detail and in a different context but with the same point, and attributed it to Franklin (*Corr. in the Boston Patriot*, p. 45–46).

### NOVEMBER 4. MONDAY.

†Called on J. and went to Oswalds and spent with him and Stretchy from 11. to 3. in drawing up the Articles respecting Debts and Tories and Fishery.[1]

I drew up the Article anew in this form—"That the Subjects of his Britannic Majesty, and the People of the said United States, shall continue to enjoy unmolested, the Right to take fish of every kind, on all the Banks of Newfoundland, in the Gulph of St. Laurence and all other Places, where the Inhabitants of both Countries used, at any time heretofore, to fish: and also to dry and cure their Fish, on the

Shores of Nova Scotia, Cape Sable, the Isle of Sable, and on the Shores of any of the unsettled Bays, Harbours or Creeks of Nova Scotia, and the Magdalene Islands, and his Britannic Majesty and the said United States will extend equal Priviledges and Hospitality to each others Fishermen as to his own." [2]

Dined with the Marquis de la Fayette, with the Prince du Poix, the Viscount de Noailles and his Lady, Mr. Jay, Mr. Price and his Lady, Mrs. Izard and her two Daughters, Dr. Bancroft, Mr. W. Franklin.

The Marquis proposed to me in Confidence his going out with D'Estaing, to the W. Indies. But he is to go a Month hence in a Frigate.—Mem.†

All the forenoon from 11 to 3 at Mr. Oswalds, Mr. Jay and I. In the Evening there again, untill near 11.

Stretchy is as artfull and insinuating a Man as they could send. He pushes and presses every Point as far as it can possibly go. He is the most eager, earnest, pointed Spirit.

†We agreed last night to this.

Whereas certain of the united States, excited thereto by the unnecessary Destruction of private Property, have confiscated all Debts due from their Citizens to British Subjects and also in certain Instances Lands belonging to the latter. And Whereas it is *just* that private Contracts made between Individuals of the two Countries before the War, should be faithfully executed, and as the Confiscation of the said Lands may have a Latitude not justifiable by the Law of Nations, it is agreed that british Creditors shall notwithstanding, meet with no lawfull Impediment, to recovering the full value, or Sterling Amount of such bonâ fide Debts as were contracted before the Year 1775, and also that Congress will recommend to the said States, so to correct, if necessary, their said Acts respecting the Confiscation of Lands in America belonging to real british Subjects as to render their said Acts consistent with perfect Justice and Equity. [3]

[1] This conference resulted in a "second set" of provisional articles, which were taken by Strachey to London for consideration by the British ministry; they are printed in Wharton, ed., *Dipl. Corr. Amer. Rev.*, 5:851–853.

[2] For a later draft by JA of this article, see entry of 28 Nov., below.

[3] Copied from a draft in Jay's hand now in Adams Papers under the assigned date of Nov. 1782.

NOVEMBER 5. TUESDAY.

Mr. Jay likes Frenchmen as little as Mr. Lee and Mr. Izard did. He says they are not a Moral People. They know not what it is. He dont like any Frenchman.—The Marquis de la Fayette is clever, but he is a Frenchman.†—Our Allies dont play fair, he told me.[1] They were endeavouring to deprive Us of the Fishery, the Western Lands, and the Navigation of the Missisippi. They would even bargain with the English to deprive us of them. They want to play the Western Lands, Missisippi and whole Gulph of Mexico into the Hands of Spain.

Oswald talks of Pultney, and a Plott to divide America between France and England. France to have N. England. They tell a Story about Vergennes and his agreeing that the English might propose such a division, but reserving a Right to deny it all. These Whispers ought not to be credited by Us.[2]

[1] Because of the omission of preceding matter, this sentence in JA's "Peace Journal" furnished to Congress reads: "Mr. Jay told me our Allies did not play fair."

[2] Oswald had told this highly improbable "Story" earlier to Jay in greater detail; see John Jay, *Diary during the Peace Negotiations of 1782*, ed. Frank Monaghan, New Haven, 1934, p. 12. For a related story see entry of 24 Dec. and note, below.

Though he made no entries in his Diary during the next three days, JA summarized the state of the negotiation in a long letter to Livingston, 6 Nov. (PCC, No. 84, IV; Wharton, ed., *Dipl. Corr. Amer. Rev.*, 5:854–858).

NOVEMBER 9. SATURDAY.

The M. de la Fayette came in, and told me he had been to Versailles and in Consultation with him [Vergennes] about the Affair of Money as he and I had agreed he should.—He said he found that the C. de Vergennes and their Ministry were of the same Opinion with me. That the English were determined to evacuate New York. —After Sometime he told me in a great Air of Confidence, that he was afraid the Comte took it amiss that I had not been to Versailles to see him. The C. told him that he had not been officially informed, of my Arrival, he had only learn'd it from the Returns of the Police.

I went out to Passy to dine with Mr. F. who had been to Versailles and presented his Memorial and the Papers accompanying it.[1] The C. said he would have the Papers translated to lay them before the King, but the Affair would meet with many Difficulties. F. brought the same Message, to me from the C. and said he believed it would be taken kindly if I went. I told both the Marquis and the Dr. that I would go tomorrow Morning.[2]

[1] Concerning a further loan to the United States; see Franklin to Vergennes, 8 Nov. (*Writings*, ed. Smyth, 8:619–620).

[2] In 1811, after quoting the foregoing paragraph in one of his letters to the *Boston Patriot*, JA added this remark: "Though I hinted nothing to either, yet Dr. Franklin, if he recollected his own, and the Comte's complaints to Congress against me, and the declaration of the letter [latter?], that he would have noth-

ing to do with me, could be at no loss for the motives of my want of assiduity in paying my court to Versailles" (*Boston Patriot*, 31 Aug. 1811). Thus when he went to Versailles the next day JA could hardly help wondering whether he was going "to hear an expostulation? a reproof? an admonition? or in plain vulgar English, a scolding? or was there any disposition to forget and forgive? and say, all malice depart?" (same, 4 Sept. 1811). It is in this context that the following entry, which became notorious because it recorded so many compliments to himself, should be read.

### NOVEMBER 10. SUNDAY.

Accordingly at 8 this Morning I went and waited on the Comte. He asked me, how We went on with the English? I told him We divided upon two Points the Tories and Penobscot, two ostensible Points, for it was impossible to believe that My Lord Shelburne or the Nation cared much about such Points. I took out of my Pocket and shewed him the Record of Governour Pownals solemn Act of burying a Leaden Plate with this Inscription, May 23. 1759. Province of Massachusetts Bay. Penobscot. Dominions of Great Britain. Possession confirmed by Thomas Pownal Governor.

This was planted on the East Side of the River of Penobscot, 3 miles above Marine Navigation. I shew him also all the other Records —the Laying out of Mount Desert, Machias and all the other Towns to the East of the River Penobscot, and told him that the Grant of Nova Scotia by James the first to Sir William Alexander, bounded it on the River St. Croix. And that I was possessed of the Authorities of four of the greatest Governors the King of England ever had, Shirley, Pownal, Bernard and Hutchinson, in favour of our Claim and of Learned Writings of Shirley and Hutchinson in support of it. —The Comte said that Mr. Fitzherbert told him they wanted it for the Masts: but the C. said that Canada had an immense quantity. I told him I thought there were few Masts there, but that I fancied it was not Masts but Tories that again made the Difficulty. Some of them claimed Lands in that Territory and others hoped for Grants there.[1]

The Comte said it was not astonishing that the British Ministry should insist upon Compensation to them, For that all the Precedents were in favour of it. That there had been no Example of an Affair like this terminated by a Treaty, without reestablishing those who had adhered to the old Government in all their Possessions. I begged his Pardon in this, and said that in Ireland at least their had been a Multitude of Confiscations without Restitution.—Here We ran into some Conversation concerning Ireland, &c. Mr. Rayneval, who was present talked about the national honour and the obligation they were under to support their Adherents.—Here I thought I might indulge a little more Latitude of Expression, than I had done with Oswald and Stratchey, and I answered, if the Nation thought itself bound in honour to compensate those People it might easily do it, for it cost the Nation more Money to carry on this War, one Month, than it would cost it to compensate them all. But I could not comprehend this Doctrine of national honour. Those People by their Misrepresentations, had deceived the Nation, who had followed the Impulsion of their devouring Ambition, untill it had brought an indelible Stain on the British Name, and almost irretrievable Ruin on the Nation, and now that very Nation was thought to be bound in honour to compensate its Dishonourers and Destroyers. Rayneval said it was very true.

The Comte invited me to dine. I accepted. When I came I found the M. de la Fayette in Conference with him. When they came out the M. took me aside and told me he had been talking with the C. upon the Affair of Money. He had represented to him, Mr. Morris's Arguments and the Things I had said to him, as from himself &c. That he feared the Arts of the English, that our Army would disbande, and our Governments relax &c. That the C. feared many difficulties. That France had expended two hundred and fifty Millions in this War &c. That he talked of allowing six millions and my going to Holland with the Scheme I had projected, and having the Kings Warranty &c. to get the rest. That he had already spoken to some of Mr. De Fleury's Friends and intended to speak to him &c.

We went up to Dinner. I went up with the C. alone. He shewed me into the Room where were the Ladies and the Company. I singled out the Comtesse and went up to her, to make her my Compliment. The Comtess and all the Ladies rose up, I made my Respects to them all and turned round and bowed to the reste of the Company. The Comte who came in after me, made his Bows to the Ladies and to the Comtesse last. When he came to her, he turned round and called out Monsieur Adams venez ici. Voila la Comtesse de Vergennes. A Nobleman in Company said Mr. Adams has already made his Court to Madame la Comtess. I went up again however and spoke again to the Comtess and she to me.—When Dinner was served, the Comte led Madame de Montmorin, and left me to conduct the Comtesse who gave me her hand with extraordinary Condescention, and I conducted her to Table. She made me sit next her on her right hand and was remarkably attentive to me the whole Time. The Comte who sat opposite was constantly calling out to me, to know what I would eat and to offer me petits Gateaux, Claret and Madeira &c. &c.—In

short I was never treated with half the Respect at Versailles in my Life.

In the Antichamber before Dinner some French Gentlemen came to me, and said they had seen me two Years ago. Said that I had shewn in Holland that the Americans understand Negotiation, as well as War.

The Compliments that have been made me since my Arrival in France upon my Success in Holland, would be considered as a Curiosity, if committed to Writing. Je vous felicite sur votre Success, is common to all. One adds, Monsieur, Ma Foi, vous avez reussi, bien merveilleusement. Vous avez fait reconnoitre votre Independance. Vous avez fait un Traité, et vous avez procuré de l'Argent. Voila un Succés parfait.—Another says, vous avez fait des Merveilles en Hollande. Vous avez culbuté le Stathouder, et la Partie angloise. Vous avez donné bien de Mou[ve]ment. Vous avez remué tout le Monde.— Another said Monsieur vous etes le Washington de la Negotiation.— This is the finishing Stroke. It is impossible to exceed this.

Compliments are the Study of this People and there is no other so ingenious at them.[2]

[1] JA was well prepared for his call on the French minister of foreign affairs. The documents he carried with him or was prepared to show when wanted were attested copies of the Massachusetts charters and attested extracts from the records of the General Court relative to the boundaries of Massachusetts. These had been made at JA's request by the clerk of the General Court when JA had sailed for Europe late in 1779 as sole commissioner to treat for peace with Great Britain; they survive in the JA Miscellany (Adams Papers, Microfilms, Reel No. 191). In four long communications to the *Boston Patriot*, 23, 26 Oct., 6, 9 Nov. 1811, JA later told how they proved useful in establishing the northeastern boundary of the United States in the preliminary negotiations of 1782; these letters are partly reprinted in an appendix to JA's *Works*, 1:665–669.

[2] The several foregoing paragraphs were clearly those that evoked amusement at JA's expense when his "Peace Journal" was read in Congress in 1783; see note on entry of 2 Nov., above. Alexander Hamilton was a delegate to Congress at the time, and in 1800,

when assembling all the evidence he could gather to discredit JA as a Federalist candidate for the Presidency, he cited the "Peace Journal" as proof of JA's boundless vanity and jealousy.

"The reading of this Journal [Hamilton went on], extremely embarrassed his friends, especially the delegates of Massachusetts; who, more than once, interrupted it, and at last, succeeded in putting a stop to it, on the suggestion that it bore the marks of a private and confidential paper, which, by some mistake, had gotten into its present situation, and never could have been designed as a public document for the inspection of Congress. The good humor of that body yielded to the suggestion" (*Letter from Alexander Hamilton, concerning the Public Conduct and Character of John Adams, Esq., President of the United States*, N.Y., 1800, p. 7–8).

JA's reply to this passage in Hamilton's tract is in a letter published in the *Boston Patriot*, 4, 7 Sept. 1811.

It is worth noting that when Jared Sparks printed the "Peace Journal" from the Papers of the Continental Congress he silently omitted the whole paragraph recording the French comparison of JA with Washington, thus cutting the ground from under Hamilton's charge (*Diplomatic Correspondence of the American Revolution*, Boston, 1829–1830, 6:471). It may also be worth noting that Matthew Ridley reported in his Diary (MHi), 10 Nov. 1782, that "Some time ago he [JA] was told that Mr. Washington was the greatest General in the World and that he Mr. A. was the General Washington in politics. —All this makes no Impression on him."

### 1782 NOVEMBER 11. MONDAY.

Mr. Whitefoord the Secretary of Mr. Oswald came a second Time, not having found me at home Yesterday, when he left a Card, with a Copy of Mr. Oswalds Commission attested by himself (Mr. Oswald).[1] He delivered the Copy and said Mr. Oswald was ready [to] compare it to the original with me. I said Mr. Oswalds Attestation was sufficient as he had already shewn me his original. He sat down and We fell into Conversation, about the Weather and the Vapours and Exhalations from Tartary which had been brought here last Spring by the Winds and given Us all the Influenza. Thence to french Fashions and the Punctuality with which they insist upon Peoples wearing thin Cloaths in Spring and fall, tho the Weather is ever so cold, &c. I said it was often carried to ridiculous Lengths, but that it was at Bottom an admirable Policy, as it rendered all Europe tributary to the City of Paris, for its Manufactures.

We fell soon into Politicks. I told him, that there was something in the Minds of the English and French, which impelled them irresistably to War every Ten or fifteen Years. He said the ensuing Peace would he believed be a long one. I said it would provided it was well made, and nothing left in it to give future Discontents. But if any Thing was done which the Americans should think hard and unjust, both the English and French would be continually blowing it up and inflaming the American Minds with it, in order to make them join one Side or the other in a future War. He might well think, that the French would be very glad to have the Americans join them in future War. Suppose for Example they should think the Tories Men of monarchical Principles, or Men of more Ambition than Principle, or Men corrupted and of no Principle, and should therefore think them more easily seduced to their Purposes than virtuous Republicans, is it not easy to see the Policy of a French Minister in wishing them Amnesty and Compensation? Suppose, a french Minister foresees that the Presence of the Tories in America will keep up perpetually two Parties, a French Party and an English Party, and that this will compel the patriotic and independant Party to join the French Party is it not natural for him to wish them

51

restored? 3. Is it not easy to see, that a French Minister cannot wish to have the English and Americans perfectly agreed upon all Points before they themselves, the Spaniards and Dutch, are agreed too. Can they be sorry then to see us split upon such a Point as the Tories? What can be their Motives to become the Advocates of the Tories? The french Minister at Philadelphia has made some Representations to Congress in favour of a Compensation to the Royalists, and the C. de Vergennes no longer than Yesterday, said much to Me in their favour. The Comte probably knows, that We are instructed against it, that Congress are instructed against it, or rather have not constitutional Authority to do it. That We can only write about it to Congress, and they to the States, who may and probably will deliberate upon it 18 Months, before they all decide and then every one of them will determine against it.—In this Way, there is an insuperable Obstacle to any Agreement between the English and Americans, even upon Terms to be inserted in the general Peace, before all are ready.—It was the constant Practice of The French to have some of their Subjects in London during the Conferences for Peace, in order to propagate such Sentiments there as they wished to prevail. I doubted not such were there now. Mr. Rayneval had been there. Mr. Gerard I had heard is there now and probably others. They can easily perswade the Tories to set up their Demands, and tell them and the Ministers that the Kings Dignity and Nations honour are compromised in it.

For my own Part I thought America had been long enough involved in the Wars of Europe. She had been a Football between contending Nations from the Beginning, and it was easy to foresee that France and England both would endeavour to involve Us in their future Wars. I thought [it] our Interest and Duty to avoid [them] as much as possible and to be compleatly independent and have nothing to do but in Commerce with either of them. That my Thoughts had been from the Beginning constantly employed to arrange all our European Connections to this End, and that they would be continued to be so employed and I thought it so important to Us, that if my poor labours, my little Estate or (smiling) sizy blood could effect it, it should be done. But I had many fears.

I said the King of France might think it consistent with his Station to favour People who had contended for a Crown, tho it was the Crown of his Ennemy. Whitefoord said, they seem to be, through the whole of this,[2] fighting for Reputation. I said they had acquired it and more. They had raised themselves high from a low Estate by it, and they were our good Friends and Allies, and had conducted generously and nobly and We should be just and gratefull, but they might have political Wishes, which We were not bound by Treaty nor in Justice or Gratitude to favour, and these We ought to be cautious off. He agreed that they had raised themselves very suddenly and surprisingly by it.

†We had more Conversation on the State of Manners in France, England, Scotland and in other Parts of Europe, but I have not Time to record this.

[1] Oswald's second commission, dated 21 Sept. 1782, empowering him to treat with "any Commissioners or Persons vested with equal Powers, by and on the part of the Thirteen United States of America"—fhe recognition that Jay had insisted on before treating with a British commissioner. A copy is in the Adams Papers under date of 9 Nov. 1782, the day it was attested by Oswald for presentation to JA; a printed text is in Wharton, ed., *Dipl. Corr. Amer. Rev.*, 5:748–750.

[2] Comma supplied for clarity, but the passage is obscure in the MS, and a word may have been omitted by JA.

### 1782 NOVEMBER 12. TUESDAY.

Dined with the Abby Chalut and Arnoux. The Farmer General, and his Daughter, Dr. Franklin and his Grand Son, Mr. Grand and his Lady and Neice, Mr. Ridley and I with one young French Gentleman made the Company. The Farmers Daughter is about 12 Years old and is I suppose an Enfant trouvee. He made her sing at Table, and she bids fair to be an accomplished Opera Girl, though she has not a delicate Ear....† [1]

The Compliment of "Monsieur vous etes le Washington de la Negotiation" was repeated to me, by more than one Person. I answered Monsieur vous me faites le plus grand honour et la Compliment le plus sublime possible.—Eh Monsieur, en Verite vous l'avez bien merité.—†A few of these Compliments would kill Franklin if they should come to his Ears.

This Evening I went to the Hotel des treize Etats Unis to see the Baron de Linden, to the Hotel de York to see the Messrs. Vaughans,[2] and to the Hotel D'orleans to see Mr. Jay, but found neither. Returned through the Rue St. Honorée to see the decorated Shops, which are pretty enough. This is the gayest Street in Paris, in point of ornamented Shops, but Paris does not excell in this respect.

The old Farmer General was very lively at dinner. Told Stories and seemed ready to join the little Girl in Songs like a Boy.—Pleasures dont wear Men out in Paris as in other Places.

The Abby Arnoux asked me at Table, Monsieur ou est votre Fils Cadet qui chant, come Orphée.—Il est du retour en Amerique.—To

Mademoiselle Labhard, he said Connoissez vous que Monsieur Adams a une Demoiselle tres aimable en Amerique?

[1] Suspension points in MS.

[2] Benjamin Vaughan and probably his brother Samuel (see 25 Feb. 1783, below). Benjamin (1751–1835), a political liberal and a devoted admirer of Franklin, served as Lord Shelburne's confidential observer at the peace negotiations and, shuttling between Paris and London, worked hard to obtain the concessions that the American Commissioners felt they must have from Great Britain. He later settled at Hallowell, Maine, and maintained an extensive correspondence for many years. A large collection of his papers is now in the American Philosophical Society; see its *Procs.*, 95 (1951):209–216; but no adequate biography of him exists. In 1828 Vaughan commenced a correspondence with JQA on the peace negotiations of 1782–1783, and in the course of it sent a voluminous mass of copies of his own papers relating thereto, which remain among the Adams Papers (Microfilms, Reel Nos. 256, 488).

### NOVEMBER 13. WEDNESDAY.

This is the Anniversary of my quitting home. Three Years are compleated. Oh when shall I return?—Ridley dined with me. Captain Barney called in the Evening and took my dispatches. One set he is to deliver to Capt. Hill, another to Capt.        and the 3d he takes himself.[1]

[1] "According to Your request I have to inform You, that the letters intrusted to my care to go by the Ships Cicero and Buccaneir I have Deliver'd to the Captns. Hill and Phearson.... their Sailing is still Very uncertain" (Joshua Barney to JA, Lorient, 18 Dec. 1782, Adams Papers). Hugh Hill commanded the *Cicero* (in which CA had sailed home from Bilbao the year before), and Jesse Fearson the *Buccanier*; both vessels belonged to the Cabots of Beverly (L. Vernon Briggs, *History and Genealogy of the Cabot Family*, Boston, 1927, 1:77, 83–84, 95–98).

### NOVEMBER 14. THURSDAY.

### NOVEMBER 17. SUNDAY.

Have spent several Days in copying Mr. Jays dispatches.†[1]

On Fryday the 15, Mr. Oswald came to Visit me, and entered with some Freedom into Conversation. I said many Things to him to convince him that it was the Policy of my Lord Shelburne and the Interest of the Nation to agree with Us upon the advantageous Terms which Mr. Stratchey carried away on the 5th. Shewed him the Advantages of the Boundary, the vast Extent of Land, and the equitable Provision for the Payment of Debts and even the great Benefits stipulated for the Tories.

He said he had been reading Mr. Paines Answer to the Abby Raynal, and had found there an excellent Argument in favour of the Tories.[2] Mr. Paine says that before the Battle of Lexington We were so blindly prejudiced in favour of the English and so closely attached to them, that We went to war at any time and for any Object, when they bid Us. Now this being habitual to the Americans, it was excuseable in the Tories to behave upon this Occasion as all of Us had ever done upon all the others. He said if he were a Member of Congress he would shew a Magnanimity upon this Occasion, and would say to the Refugees, take your Property. We scorn to make any Use of it, in building up our System.

I replied, that We had no Power and Congress had no Power, and therefore We must consider how it would be reasoned upon in the several Legislatures of the separate States, if, after being sent by Us to Congress and by them to the several States in the Course of twelve or fifteen Months, it should be there, debated. You must carry on the War, Six or Nine months certainly, for this Compensation, and consequently spend in the Prosecution of it, Six or Nine times the Sum necessary to make the Compensation for I presume, this War costs every Month to Great Britain, a larger Sum than would be necessary to pay for the forfeited Estates.

How says I will an independant Man in one of our Assemblies consider this. We will take a Man, who is no Partisan of England or France, one who wishes to do Justice to both and to all Nations, but is the Partisan only of his own.[3]

Have you seen says he, a certain Letter written to the C. de V. wherein Mr. S.A. is treated pretty freely.[4] —Yes says I and several other Papers in which Mr. J. Adams has been treated so too. I dont know, what you may of heard in England of Mr. S.A. You may have been taught to believe, for what I know, that he eats little Children. But I assure you he is a Man of Humanity and Candour as well [as] Integrity, and further that he is devoted to the Interest of his Country and I believe wishes never to be, after a Peace, the Partisan to France or England, but to do Justice and all the good he can to both. I thank you for mentioning him for I will make him my orator. What will he say, when the Question of Amnesty and Compensation to the Tories, comes before the Senate of Massachusetts. And when he is informed that England makes a Point of it and that France favours her. He will say here are two old, sagacious Courts, both endeavouring to sow the Seeds of Discord among Us, each endeavouring to keep Us in hot Water, to keep up continual Broils between an English Party and a french Party, in hopes of obliging the Independent and patriotic Party, to lean to its Side. England wishes them here and compensated, not merely to get rid of them and to save them selves the Money, but to plant among Us Instruments of their own, to make divisions among Us and between Us and France, to be continually crying down the Religion, the Government, the Manners of France, and crying up the Language, the Fashions, the Blood &c. of England. England also means by insisting on our compensating these worst of Ennemies to obtain from Us, a tacit Acknowledgment of the Right of the War—an implicit Acknowledgment, that the Tories have been justifiable or at least excuseable, and that We, only by a fortunate Coincidence of Events, have carried a wicked Rebellion into a compleat Revolution.

At the very Time when Britain professes to desire Peace, Reconciliation, perpetual Oblivion of all past Unkindnesses, can She wish to send in among Us, a Number of Persons, whose very Countenances will bring fresh to our Remembrance the whole History of the Rise, and Progress of the War, and of all its Atrocitys? Can she think it conciliatory, to oblige Us, to lay Taxes upon those whose Habitations have been consumed, to reward those who have burn'd them? upon those whose Property has been stolen, to reward the Thieves? upon those whose Relations have been cruelly destroyed, to compensate the Murtherers?

What can be the design of France on the other hand, by espousing the Cause of these Men? Indeed her Motives may be guessed at. She may wish to keep up in our Minds a Terror of England, and a fresh Remembrance of all We have suffered. Or She may wish to prevent our Ministers in Europe from agreeing with the British Ministers, untill She shall say that She and Spain are satisfyed in all Points.

I entered largely with Mr. Oswald, into the Consideration of the Influence this Question would have upon the Councils of the British Cabinet and the Debates in Parliament. The King and the old Ministry might think their personal Reputations concerned, in supporting Men who had gone such Lengths, and suffered so much in their Attachment to them.—The K. may say I have other dominions abroad, Canada, Nova Scotia, Florida, the West India Islands, the East Indies, Ireland. It will be a bad Example to abandon these Men. Others will loose their Encouragement to adhere to my Government. But the shortest Answer to this is the best, let the King by a Message recommend it to Parliament to compensate them.

But how will My Lord Shelburne sustain the shock of Opposition? When Mr. Fox and Mr. Burke shall demand a Reason why the Essential Interests of the Nation, are sacrificed to the unreasonable demands of those very Men, who have done this great Mischief to the Empire. Should these Orators indulge themselves in Philippicks against the

Refugees, shew their false Representations, their outragious Cruelties, their innumerable demerits against the Nation, and then attack the first Lord of the Treasury for continuing to spend the Blood and Treasure of the Nation for their Sakes.

Mr. Vaughan came to me Yesterday, and said that Mr. Oswald had that morning called upon Mr. Jay, and told him, if he had known as much the day before as he had since learned, he would have written to go home. Mr. V. said Mr. Fitzherbert had received a Letter from Ld. Townsend,[5] that the Compensation would be insisted on. Mr. Oswald wanted Mr. Jay to go to England. Thought he could convince the Ministry. Mr. Jay said he must go, with or without the Knowledge and Advice of this Court, and in either Case it would give rise to jealousies. He could not go. Mr. Vaughan said he had determined to go, on Account of the critical State of his Family, his Wife being probably abed. He should be glad to converse freely with me, and obtain from me, all the Lights and arguments against the Tories, even the History of their worst Actions, that in Case it should be necessary to run them down it might be done or at least expose them, for their true History was little known in England.—I told him that I must be excused. It was a Subject that I had never been desirous of obtaining Information upon. That I pitied those People too much to be willing to aggravate their Sorrows and Sufferings, even of those who had deserved the Worst. It might not be amiss to reprint the Letters of G[overnor] Bernard, Hutchinson and Oliver, to shew the rise. It might not be amiss to read the History of Wyoming in the Annual Register for 1778 or 9, to recollect the Prison Ships, and the Churches at New York, where the Garrisons of Fort Washington were starved in order to make them inlist into Refugee Corps. It might not be amiss to recollect the Burning of Cities, and The Thefts of Plate, Negroes and Tobacco.

I entered into the same Arguments with him that I had used with Mr. Oswald, to shew that We could do nothing, Congress nothing. The Time it would take to consult the States, and the Reasons to believe that all of them would at last decide against it. I shewed him that it would be a Religious Question with some, a moral one with others, and a political one with more, an Economical one with very few. I shewed him the ill Effect which would be produced upon the American Mind, by this Measure, how much it would contribute to perpetuate Alienation against England, and how french Emmissaries might by means of these Men blow up the flames of Animosity and

War. I shewed him how the Whig Interest and the Opposition might avail themselves of this Subject in Parliament, and how they might embarrass the Minister.

He went out to Passy, for a Passport, and in the Evening called upon me again. Said he found Dr. Franklins Sentiments to be the same with Mr. Jays and mine, and hoped he should be able to convince Lord Shelburne. He was pretty confident that it would work right.—The Ministry and Nation were not informed upon the Subject. Ld. Shelburne had told him that no Part of his office gave him so much Paine as the Levy he held for these People, and hearing their Stories of their Families and Estates, their Losses, Sufferings and Distresses. Mr. V. said he had picked up here, a good deal of Information, about those People, from Mr. Allen and other Americans.

†Ridley, Allen and Mason, dined with me, and in the Evening Capt. Barney came in, and told me that Mr. Vaughan went off to day at noon. I delivered to Barney, Mr. Jays long Dispatches, and the other Letters.†

In the Evening the Marquis de la Fayette came in and told me, he had been to see Mr. de Fleuri, on the Subject of a Loan. He told him that he must afford America this Year a Subsidy of 20 millions. Mr. de Fleuri said France had already spent 250 millions in the American War, and that they could not allow any more Money to her. That there was a great deal of Money in America. That the Kings Troops had been subsisted and paid there. That the British Army had been subsisted and paid there, &c. The Marquis said that little of the Subsistance or pay of the British had gone into any hands but those of the Tories within their Lines. I said that more Money went in for their Goods than came out for Provisions or any Thing. The Marquis added to Mr. Fleury that Mr. Adams had a Plan for going to the States General, for a Loan or a Subsidy. Mr. Fleury said he did not want the Assistance of Mr. Adams to get Money in Holland, he could have what he would. The M. said Mr. A. would be glad of it. He did not want to go, but was willing to take the Trouble, if necessary.

The Marquis said he should dine with the Queen tomorrow and would give her a hint, to favour Us. That he should take Leave in a few days and should go in the fleet that was to sail from Brest. That he wanted the Advice of Mr. F., Mr. J. and me before he went, &c. Said there was a Report that Mr. Gerard had been in England, and that Mr. de Rayneval was gone. I told him I saw Mr. Gerard at Mr. Jays a few Evenings ago.

He said he did not believe Mr. Gerard had been. That he had mentioned it to C. de V. and he did not appear confused at all, but said Mr. Gerard was here about the Limits of Alsace.

The Marquis said that he believed, the Reason why C. de Vergennes said so little about the Progress of Mr. Fitsherbert with him, was because the difficulty about Peace was made by the Spaniards and he was afraid of making the Americans still more angry with Spain....[6] He knew the Americans [were] [7] very angry with the Spaniards.

[1] That is, Jay's long memoir, including copies of his correspondence, relative to the negotiations from the time that he had arrived in Paris late in June to the time JA arrived in October; dated 17 Nov. 1782, it is printed in Wharton, ed., *Dipl. Corr. Amer. Rev.*, 6:11–49. It is a severe indictment of the motives and conduct of the French ministry toward America on the eve of the peace settlement, and by implication a defense of the Commissioners' breach of their instructions to do nothing without French concurrence; see especially its last dozen paragraphs. JA's copy is in Adams Papers under the present date.

[2] Thomas Paine, *Letter Addressed to the Abbe Raynal on the Affairs of North-America ...*, Philadelphia, printed; Boston, reprinted, 1782; see p. 44–45.

[3] The present Diary booklet (D/JA/ 35) ends here, and JA's conversation with Oswald this day continues without break in the next booklet (D/JA/ 36), identical in format with its predecessor.

[4] Marbois to Vergennes, No. 225, Philadelphia, 13 March 1782, in which Marbois reported that Samuel Adams, who "delights in trouble," was the leader of an anti-French party opposed to any peace which excluded New Englanders from the Newfoundland and other North

Atlantic fisheries. The writer went on to give suggestions how such "enthusiasts" could be quieted by a statement from the King of France disapproving their stand. See the text in Wharton, ed., *Dipl. Corr. Amer. Rev.*, 5:238–241. This dispatch was intercepted by the British and a copy placed in Jay's hands with the intent of splitting the Franco-American alliance. For its effect on Jay, see his letter to Livingston transmitting a copy, 18 Sept. 1782 (same, p. 740). In Congress it led to a reconsideration of the instructions of 15 June 1781, though the effort to revise them did not succeed; see Madison's Notes of Debates, 24, 30 Dec. 1782, 1 Jan. 1783 (JCC, 23:870–874; 25:845). When imparted to JA (enclosed in a letter from Jay of 1 Sept., Adams Papers), it confirmed his worst suspicions of French policy; see entries of 20 Nov. 1782 and 2 May 1783, below. Several copies of the offending dispatch, in English translation, are among his papers, and in old age he devoted to it a whole series of his communications to the *Boston Patriot*, 14–24 Aug. 1811 (partly printed in *Works*, 1:669–674).

[5] Thomas Townshend, later 1st Viscount Sydney, home secretary in Shelburne's ministry (*DNB*).

[6] Suspension points in MS.

[7] MS: "very."

NOVEMBER 18. MONDAY.

Returned Mr. Oswalds Visit. He says Mr. Stratchey who sat out the 5 did not reach London untill the 10....[1] Couriers are 3, 4, or 5 days in going according as the Winds are.

We went over the old ground, concerning the Tories. He began to use Arguments with me to relax. I told him he must not think of that, but must bend all his Thoughts to convince and perswade his Court to give it up. That if the Terms now before his Court, were not accepted, the whole negotiation would be broken off, and this Court would probably be so angry with Mr. Jay and me, that they would set their Engines to work upon Congress, get us recalled and some others sent, who would do exactly as this Court would have them. He said, he thought that very probable....

In another Part of his Conversation He said We should all have Gold Snuff Boxes set with Diamonds. You will certainly have the Picture.[2] I told him no. I had dealt too freely with this Court. I had not concealed from them any usefull and necessary Truth, although it was disagreable. Indeed I neither expected nor desired any favours from them nor would I accept any. I should not refuse any customary Compliment of that Sort, but it never had been nor would be offered me.... My fixed Principle never to be the Tool, of any Man, nor the Partisan of any Nation, would forever exclude me from the Smiles and favours of Courts.

In another Part of the Conversation, I said that when I was young and addicted to reading I had heard about dancing on the Points of metaphisical Needles. But by mixing in the World, I had found the Points of political Needles finer and sharper than the metaphisical ones.

I told him the Story of Josiah Quincys Conversations with Lord Shelburne in 1774, in which he pointed out to him, the Plan of carrying on the War, which has been pursued this Year, by remaining inactive at Land and cruising upon the Coast to distress our Trade.

He said he had been contriving an artificial Truce since he found we were bound by Treaty not to agree to a separate Truce. He had proposed to the Ministry, to give Orders to their Men of War and Privateers, not to take any unarmed American Vessells.

I said to him, supposing the armed Neutrality should acknowledge American Independence, by admitting Mr. Dana who is now at Petersbourg with a Commission for that Purpose in his Pocket, to subscribe the Principles of their marine Treaty? The K. of G.B. could find no fault with it. He could never hereafter say, it was an Affront or Hostility. He had done it himself. Would not all Newtral Vessells have a right to go to America?—and could not all American Trade be carried on in Neutral Bottoms.

I said to him that England would always be a Country which would deserve much of the Attention of America, independently of all Considerations of Blood, Origin, Language, Morals &c. Merely as a commercial Country, She would forever claim the Respect of America, because a great Part of our Commerce would be with her provided She came to her Senses and made Peace with Us without any Points in the Treaty that should ferment in the Minds of the People. If the People should think themselves unjustly treated, they would never be easy, and they were so situated as to be able to hurt any Power. The Fisheries, the Mississippi, the Tories were points that would rankle. And that Nation that should offend our People in any of them, would sooner or later feel the Consequences.

Mr. Jay, Mr. Le Couteulx and Mr. Grand came in. Mr. Grand says there is a great Fermentation in England, and that they talk of uniting Lord North and Mr. Fox in Administration. D. of Portland to come in and Keppel go out.—But this is wild.

You are afraid says Mr. Oswald to day of being made the Tools of the Powers of Europe.—Indeed I am says I.—What Powers says he.— All of them says I. It is obvious that all the Powers of Europe will be continually maneuvring with Us, to work us into their real or imaginary Ballances of Power. They will all wish to make of Us a Make Weight Candle, when they are weighing out their Pounds. Indeed it is not surprizing for We shall very often if not always be able to turn the Scale. But I think it ought to be our Rule not to meddle, and that of all the Powers of Europe not to desire Us, or perhaps even to permit Us to interfere, if they can help it.

I beg of you, says he, to get out of your head the Idea that We shall disturb you.—What says I do you yourself believe that your Ministers, Governors and even Nation will not wish to get Us of your Side in any future War?—Damn the Governors says he. No. We will take off their Heads if they do an improper thing towards you.

Thank you for your good Will says I, which I feel to be sincere. But Nations dont feel as you and I do, and your nation when it gets a little refreshed from the fatigues of the War, when Men and Money are become plenty and Allies at hand, will not feel as it does now.— We never can be such damned Sots says he as to think of differing again with you.—Why says I, in truth I have never been able to comprehend the Reason why you ever thought of differing with Us.[3]

[1] Suspension points, here and below, are in MS.

[2] Of the King. See JA's conversation with Lynden van Blitterswyck, former Dutch minister to Sweden, 21 Dec., below.

[3] Below the last line in this entry JA wrote the words "thus far," which CFA attached to the last sentence of this paragraph, where they make perfectly good sense. But from the position of the phrase in the MS and from its not being copied in the "Peace Journal" sent to Livingston, it seems much more likely to have been a direction to the copyists than a part of the Diary text.

†1782. NOVEMBER 19. TUESDAY.

In the Morning Mr. Jay called and took me with him in his Carriage to Versailles. We waited on the C. de Vergennes and dined with him, in Company with all the Foreign Ministers, and others to the Number of forty four or five.

Mr. Berkenrode the Dutch Ambassador, told me, that he thought We should see something very singular in England. The Conflicts of Parties and contentions for the Ministry were such, that he did not know where it would end. It was thought that Lord Shelburne could not support himself without an Union with Ld. North or Mr. Fox, and that the Choice of either would determine the Intentions of the Court and Parliament.

Mr. Brantzen told me, that they had begun the Negotiations on their Part, but were as yet very far asunder, but hoped they should approach nearer in a little Time. Both he and Berkenrode asked me how We advanced? I told him Mr. Oswald was waiting for a Courier, in answer to his of the 5. which arrived the 10th. I told them both that We should not be behind hand of them. That if it was once said that France, Spain and Holland were ready, the British Ministry would not hesitate upon any Points between Us that remained. They both said they believed We should find less difficulty to arrange our affairs with England, than any of the others would.

The Sweedish Minister went to a Gentleman and asked him to introduce him to Mr. Jay and me which he did. The Minister told us he had been here since 1766.[1]

The same Ministers are here from Russia, Denmark and Sardinia, whom I knew here, formerly.

Mr. Jay made his Compliment to Count D'Aranda, who invited him to come and see him and dine with him.

I see, by a long Conversation at Table with the Baron de Linden, that he has an Inclination to go to America, Yet he modestly gives Place to Mr. Vanberckel.

The Marquis de la Fayette took leave of the King to day in his American Uniform and Sword. He told me, that the C. de Vergennes told him the day before that, Mr. de Rayneval was gone to England again. That he did not think the English so sincere, as he wished, for a speedy Peace. He wished it himself, but could not see a Prospect of it, suddenly, &c.

In returning I asked Mr. Jay what he thought of the K. of Great Britains sending an Ambassador to Congress. After Mr. Oswalds Commission, he might do it, and Congress must receive him.—Jay said do you think with me upon that Point too? If I were the K. of G.B. I would send a Minister in the highest Character, he should be Ambassador Extraordinary, and I would accredit him, to our dear and beloved Friends. And I would instruct that Minister to treat Congress with as high Respect as any crowned head in Europe.

But says I, he ought to be well instructed too in other Points—vizt. never to hint or to suffer an hint against the Treaties with France and Holland, never to admit the Idea of our failing in our public faith or national Honour—and farther never to interfere in our Parties, general or particular, with our internal Policy, or particular Governments, and to warn our People not to let the French Ministers do it.

If the Britons should strike with Us, I would agree with you after the terms are signed to advise to the Measure. If I were the King of G. Britain, I would give Orders to all my Ambassadors at the Neutral Courts, to announce to those Courts the Independence of America, that I had acknowledged it, and given a Commission under the Great Seal to treat with the Ministers of the United States of America. That I recommended to these Courts to follow the Example, and open Negotiations with the said United States. That I recommended to those neutral States to send their Vessels freely to and receive Vessels freely from, all the Ports of the United States. I would send the Earl of Effingham Ambassador to Congress, instructed to assure them that I would do them my best Offices, to secure to them the Fisheries, their Extent to the Missisippi and the Navigation of that River. That I would favour all their Negotiations in Europe, upon their own Plan of making commercial Treaties with all Nations. That I would interpose my good offices with the Barbary States, to procure them Mediterranean Passes, &c.

[1] Gustaf Philip, Count Creutz, whose character JA praised in a letter to Edmund Jenings, 14 Feb. 1783 (Adams Papers), and who shortly afterward signed on behalf of Sweden a treaty of amity and commerce with the United States (Miller, ed., *Treaties*, 2:123 ff.).

### NOV. 20 WEDNESDAY.

Dr. Franklin came in, and We fell into Conversation. From one Thing to another, We came to Politicks. I told him, that it seemed uncertain whether Shelburne could hold his Ground without leaning Upon Ld. North on one hand or Fox on the other. That if he joined North, or North & Co. should come in, they would go upon a contracted System, and would join People at this Court to deprive Us of

the Missisippi and the Fisheries &c. If Fox came in or joined Shelburne they would go upon a liberal and manly System, and this was
the only Choice they had. No Nation had ever brought itself into such
a Labyrinth perplexed with the demands of Holland, Spain, France
and America. Their Funds were failing and the Money undertaken to
be furnished was not found. Franklin said, that the Bank came in
Aid, and he learned that large Sums of Scrip were lodged there.—In
this Situation says I they have no Chance but to set up America very
high—and if I were King of G.B. I would take that Tone. I would send
the first Duke of the Kingdom Ambassador to Congress, and would
negotiate in their favour at all the Neutral Courts &c. I would give the
strongest Assurances to Congress of Support in the Fisheries, the
Missisippi &c. and would compensate the Tories myself.

I asked what could be the Policy of this Court in wishing to deprive
Us of the Fisheries? and Missisippi? I could see no possible Motive for
it, but to plant Seeds of Contention for a future War. If they pursued
this Policy they would be as fatally blinded to their true Interests as
ever the English were.

Franklin said, they would be every bit as blind. That the Fisheries
and Missisippi could not be given up. That nothing was clearer to him
than that the Fisheries were essential to the northern States, and the
Missisippi to the Southern and indeed both to all. I told him that Mr.
Gerard had certainly appeared to America, to negotiate to these Ends,
vizt. to perswade Congress to give up both. This was the Reason of his
being so unpopular in America, and this was the Cause of their dislike
to Sam Adams, who had spoken very freely both to Gerard and [in?] [1]
Congress on these heads. That Marbois appeared now to be pursuing
the same Objects. Franklin said he had seen his Letter. [2] I said I was
the more surprized at this, as Mr. Marbois, on our Passage to America,
had often said to me, that he thought the Fisheries our natural Right
and our essential Interest, and that We ought to maintain it and be
supported in it. Yet that he appeared now to be maneuvring against it.

I told him that I always considered their extraordinary Attack upon
me, not as arising from any Offence or any Thing personal, but as an
Attack upon the Fishery. There had been great debates in Congress
upon issuing the first Commission for Peace, and in Setting my Instructions—that I was instructed not to make any Treaty of Commerce
with Britain, without an express Clause acknowledging our Right to
the Fishery. This Court knew that this would be, when communicated
to the English, a strong Motive with them to acknowledge our Right,
and to take away this they had directed their Intrigues against me,

6. TRUCE CHAMBER AT THE HAGUE WHERE JOHN ADAMS
SIGNED THE DUTCH-AMERICAN TREATY OF 1782

5. RESIDENCE AND OFFICE OF THE VAN STAPHORST BANKING
FIRM IN AMSTERDAM

7. FLUWELEN BURGWAL, SITE OF THE HÔTEL DES ÉTATS-UNIS AT THE HAGUE, THE FIRST AMERICAN FOREIGN LEGATION BUILDING

8. MEDAL COMMEMORATING DUTCH RECOGNITION OF AMERICAN INDEPENDENCE, 19 APRIL 1782

to get my Commission annulled, and had succeeded.³ They hoped also to gain some Advantage in these Points by associating others with me in the Commission for Peace. But they had failed in this for the Missisippi and Fishery were now much securer than if I had been alone. That Debates had run very high in Congress. That Mr. Drayton and Governieur Morris had openly espoused their Plan and argued against the Fishery.⁴ That Mr. Laurens and others of the Southern Gentlemen, had been staunch for them, and contended that as Nurseries of Seamen and Sources of Trade the Southern States were as much interested as the Northern. That Debates had run so high that the Eastern States had been obliged to give in their Ultimatum in Writing and to say they would withdraw, if any more was done, and that this Point was so tender and important that if not secured it would be the Cause of a Breach of the Union of the States—and their Politicks might for what I knew be so profound as to mean to lay a foundation for a rupture between the States, when in a few Years they should think them grown too big. I could see no possible Motive they had, to wish to negotiate the Missisippi into the Hands of Spain, but this. Knowing the fine Country in the Neighbourhood, and the rapidity with which it would fill with Inhabitants, they might force their Way down the Missisipi and occasion another War. They had certainly Sense enough to know too that We could not and would not be restrained from the Fishery. That our People would be constantly pushing for it, and thus plunge themselves into another War, in which We should stand in need of France.

If the old Ministry in England should come in again, they would probably join this Court in attempting to deprive Us. But all would not succeed. We must be firm and steady, and should do very well. —Yes he said he believed We should do very well, and carry the Points.

I told him I could not think that the K. and Council here had formed any digested Plan against Us upon these Points. I hoped it was only the Speculation of Individuals.

I told him, that if Fox should know that Shelburne refused to agree with Us merely because We would not compensate the Tories, that he would attack the Minister upon this Ground and pelt him so with Tories as to make him uncomfortable. I thought it would be very well to give Fox an hint.—He said he would write him a Letter upon it. He had sometimes corresponded with him, and Fox had been in Conversation with him here, before I arrived.

I walked before Dinner to Mr. Jays, and told him, I thought there was danger, that the old Ministry would come in, or Shelburne unite with North. That the King did not love Us, and the old Ministry did not love Us: but they loved the Refugees, and thought probably their personal Characters concerned to support them. Rayneval was gone to England, and I wanted to have him watched to see, if he was ever in Company with North, Germain, Stormont, Hillsborough, Sandwich, Bute or Mansfield. If the wing clipping System and the Support of the Tories should be suggested by this Court to any of them it would fall in with their Passions and Opinions, for several of the old Ministry, had often dropped Expressions in the Debates in Parliament, that it was the Interest of England to prevent our Growth to Wealth and Power.

It was very possible, that a Part of the old Ministry might come in, and Richmond, Keppel, Townsend and Cambden go out, and in this Case, tho they could not revoke the Acknowledgment of our Independence, they would certainly go upon the contracted plan of clypping our Wings. In this Case it is true, England would be finally the Dupe, and it would be the most malicious Policy possible against her. It is agreed that if the Whigs go out, and Richmond, Keppell, Townsend, Cambden &c. join Fox and Burke in Opposition, there will be great Probability of a national Commotion and Confusion.

Mr. Jay agreed with me, in all I had said, and Added that six days would produce the Kings Speech. If that Speech should inform Parliament that he had issued a Commission to treat with the United States, and the two Houses should thank him for it, it would look as if a good Plan was to prevail: but if not, We should then take Measures to communicate it far, and wide.

I told him I thought, in that Case We should aid Opposition as much as We could, by suggesting Arguments, to those who would transmit them in favour of America, and in favour of those who had the most liberal Sentiments towards America, to convince them that the Wing clipping Plan was ruinous to England, and the most generous and noble Part they could Act towards America, the only one that could be beneficial to the Nation, and to enable them to attack a contracted Ministry with every Advantage, that could be.

I thought it was now a Crisis, in which good Will or Ill will towards America would be carried very far in England, a time perhaps when the American Ministers may have more Weight in turning the Tide of Sentiment, or influencing the Changes of Administration than they ever had before and perhaps than they would have again. That I thought it our Duty, Upon this Occasion to say every Thing We could, to the Englishmen here, in order that just Sentiments might prevail in England at this Moment, to countenance every Man well disposed, and to disabuse and undeceive every body.

To drive out of Countenance and into Infamy, every narrow Thought of cramping, stinting, impoverishing or enfeebling Us. To shew that it is their only Interest to shew themselves our Friends, to wear away, if possible, the Memory of past Unkindnesses. To strike with Us now upon our own Terms, because tho We had neither Power nor Inclination to make Peace, without our Allies, yet the very report that We had got over all our difficulties would naturally make all Europe expect Peace, would tend to make Spain less exorbitant in her demands, and would make Holland more ardent for Peace, and dispose France to be more serious in her Importunities with Spain and Holland, and even render France herself easier, tho I did not imagine she would be extravagant in her Pretentions. To shew them the ruinous Tendency of the War if continued another Year or two. —Where would England be if the War continued 2 Years longer? What the State of her Finances? What her Condition in the E. and W. Indies, in N. America, Ireland, Scotland and even in England? What hopes have they of saving themselves from a civil War? If our Terms are not now accepted, they will never again have such offers from America. They will never have so advantageous a Line—never their Debts—never so much for the Tories, and perhaps a rigorous demand of Compensation for the Devastations they have committed.

Mr. Jay agreed with me in Sentiment, and indeed they are the Principles he has uniformly pursued thro the whole Negotiation before my Arrival. I think they cannot be misunderstood or disapproved in Congress.

There never was a Blunder in Politicks more egregious than will be committed by the present Ministry, if they attempt to save the Honour of the old Ministry and of the Tories. Shelburne may be too weak to combat them: but the true Policy would be to throw all the Odium of the War, and all the Blame of the Dismemberment of the Empire upon the old Ministers and the Tories. To run them down, tarnish them with Votes, envey against them in Speeches and Pamphlets, even strip them of the Pensions and make them both ridiculous, insignificant and contemptible, in short make them as wretched as their Crimes deserve. Never think of sending them to America.—But Shelburne is not strong enough. The old Party with the King at their Head, is too powerful, and popular yet.

I really pitty these People, as little as they deserve it. For surely no Men ever deserved worse of Society.

If Fox was in, and had Weight enough, and should take this decided Part which is consistent enough with the Tenor of his Speeches, which have been constant Phillippicks against the old Ministry and frequent Sallies against the Refugees, and should adopt a noble Line of Conduct towards America, grant her all She asks, do her honnour and promote her Prosperity, he would disarm the hostile Mind, and soften the resentful heart, recover much of the Affection of America, much of her Commerce, and perhaps equal Consideration and Profit and Power from her as ever. She would have no Governors nor Armies there and no Taxes, but She would have Profit, Reputation and Power.

Today I received a Letter from my Excellent Friend Mr. Laurens 12 Nov. London in answer to mine of the 6. agreeing as speedily as possible to join his Colleagues. "Thank God, I had a Son, who dared to die for his Country!" [5]

[1] MS: "his"—which scarcely makes sense.

[2] See entry of 17 Nov., above, and note 4 there.

[3] For Vergennes' efforts in 1780–1781 to obtain JA's recall, or at least to restrict his powers, see William E. O'Donnell, *The Chevalier de La Luzerne . . .*, Bruges and Louvain, 1938, p. 124–137, with notes citing Vergennes' instructions and La Luzerne's dispatches in reply. One result was the joining of JA with other commissioners and the highly restrictive instructions from Congress of 15 June 1781. See also Bemis, *Diplomacy of the Amer. Revolution*, p. 176–177, 189–190.

[4] A note added by JA in the margin of the MS opposite this sentence reads: "A mistake, as Mr. J[ay] tells me."

[5] Approximately quoted from Henry Laurens' letter to JA, 12 Nov. 1782 (Adams Papers), in answer to JA's note of 6 Nov., enclosing an order of Congress for Laurens to attend the peace conference in Paris (LbC, Adams Papers). Col. John Laurens had been killed in an obscure action in South Carolina, Aug. 1782.

## 1782 NOV. 21. THURSDAY.

Paid a Visit to Mr. Brantzen, and then to the Comte de Linden; spent 2 hours with him.

He says the King of Sweden has overwhelmed him with his Goodness, is perpetually writing to his Ministers to compliment and applaud him for the Part he has acted in refusing to go to Vienna and for the Reason he gave for it.

Says the Revolution in Sweeden, was advantageous to France, in Point of Œconomy, for France used to pay very dear, for Partisans, in Pensions. That Russia too, used to have a Party there and pay Pensions. Now by means of the Court, France predominates, more easily.

He said that on Tuesday he prayed the Introductor of Ambassadors to speak to the Prince de Tingry to put him upon the List to go to the Comedy, with the King, Queen and Royal Family, in the little Salle de Spectacle. That the K. and Q. eyed him the whole Evening, and as they came out the Introductor told the K. that it was the Comte de Linden, a Man very zealous for the patriotic System. The K. said Oui, Je scais son Affair.

He says that there is no Man in the Republic who receives any Thing, from any foreign Prince or State. That the Law is very strict against it, and obliges every Man to take an Oath that he has not and will not—and no Man dares. He dont believe that the Duke[1] ever did. It would be a blunder in the English to offer it, for he is by his Name and Family enough attached without it.

He says, that he has followed the Principles which were given him by his Uncle, Boerslaer [Boetzelaer], who was high in favour at Court and in great Power thro the Rep[ublic]. That his Age and Family would be an Objection against his going to America, but after Affairs shall be a little settled, he expects that his Friends will ask him what will be agreable to him, but if not, he shall take his Place in the States General and retire to his Estate in Zealand.

Ridley and Bancroft came in and spent the Evening. B. says that Mr. Oswald dont feel very well, that he thinks of going home. That the K. will bring in some of the old Minsters, &c.

[1] The Duke of Brunswick, for many years the principal adviser of Willem V, Stadholder of the Dutch Republic.

### NOV. 22. FRYDAY.

Made a Visit to Dr. Bancroft, and spent an hour or two with him. Mr. Walpole he says is a Correspondent of Mr. Fox. I told him I wished I could have two hours Time with Fox.—Visited Mr. Mayo, Livingston, Vaughan, Rogers and Lady and Mr. Jay.

Mr. Jay says that Oswald received a Courier from London last Evening. That his Letters were brought in while he was there. That Oswald read one of them and said, that "the Tories stick." That Stratchey is coming again, and may be expected today. Oswald call'd upon him this morning, but young Franklin was there: so he said nothing, as he would not speak before him. Jay says We had now to consider, whether We should state the question in writing to the Comte de Vergennes, and ask his Answer.

I said to him We must be more dry and reserved and short with him (Oswald) than We had been. He said We must endeavour to discover, whether they agree to all the other Points. I asked what he thought of agreeing to some Compensation to the Tories, if this Court advised to it. He said they would be very mad if We did. He said that a Tract of Land, with a Pompous Preamble, would satisfy the English. But he would call upon Oswald this Afternoon, and endeavour to know more, and call upon me in the Evening.

Bancroft said to day, that Fitsherbert was sensible but conceited, that the Englishmen who were acquainted with him however said he was reserved about the Secrets of his Negotiation: But he expressed openly his Feelings, when Rayneval went over to England, as it implied or seemed to imply a Want of Confidence in him. He was displeased. . . .[1] That he had dined with him and Mr. Jay, at Mr. Oswalds. He said he found that the Englishmen here, were prepared with their Quibbles, about the Acknowledgment of American Independence. That the enabling Act did not impower the King, to grant such a Commission. It enabled him to make Peace with the Colonies, and to treat and conclude with any Discription of Men, but not expressly to acknowledge them independent States. So that it might be cast upon the Crown or Ministry as an illegal Act. Ld. Cambden had given his Opinion that the Act did not authorize the K. to acknowledge the Independence of America.

To this it may be answered that the King or Crown cannot go back. That an Act of Parliament only can annul it. The K. would make himself ridiculous in the Eyes of all Men, Souvereigns especially, if he should consent to such an Act. That a Vote of either House of Parliament, declaring the Commission illegal and null, would never pass. It would break off all Negotiations, allarm America and raise a Rebellion in England.

But the Truth is, the Crown of England is absolute in War and Peace. There is not even a fundamental Law, as there is, in France, that the King can not allienate the domains of the Crown. On the contrary by the British Constitution, the King has Power to cede and Alienate Parts and indeed all his Dominions, i.e. there is no Limitation.

Bancroft said there is an Act of Parliament that the King shall never alienate Gibraltar. So that Gibraltar cannot be ceded to Spain without an Act of Parliament.

B. says that Mr. Garnier is in Burgundy upon his Estate, where he passes the Summers, and comes only to Paris in the Winter.

B. said if the K. in his Speech should not announce Mr. Oswalds Commission, you Gentlemen Commissioners would do well to take some measures for the Publication of it, in England and abroad.

I said I wondered, that Mr. Fox had not sent over some Friend here, during the Conferences, to pick up what he could of Intelligence. But upon Recollection, I said his Friends, Richmond, Keppell, Townsend, Cambden &c. were in the Council and Cabinet, and therefore no doubt informed him, of all Intelligence, and let him into all the Secret of Affairs.[2]

Dr. Franklin, upon my saying, the other day, that I fancied he did not exercise so much as he was wont, answered, "Yes, I walk a League every day in my Chamber. I walk quick and for an hour, so that I go a League. I make a Point of Religion of it." I replied, that as the Commandment Thou shalt not kill, forbid a Man to kill himself as well as his Neighbor, it was manifestly a Breach of the 6. Commandment not to exercise. So that he might easily prove it to be a religious Point.

Bancroft said to day, That it was often said among the French People, that M. de Vergennes loved Spain too well, and was too complaisant to the Spanish Court. That he was ambitious of being made a Grandee of Spain, in order to cover his Want of Birth, for that he was not nobly born.—This I fancy is a Mistake. But such are the Objects, which Men pursue. Titles, Ribbons, Stars, Garters, Crosses, Keys, are the important Springs that move the Ambition of Men in high Life.—How poor! how mean! how low! Yet how true.—A low Ambition indeed! The Pride of Nobles and of Kings.

> Let us, since Life can little more supply
> Than just to look about Us and to die,
> Expatiate free.

[1] Suspension points in MS.

[2] The present Diary booklet (D/JA/36) ends here, and the record of this day continues without break in the next booklet (D/JA/37), identical in format with its predecessor.

### 1782 NOVEMBER 23. SATURDAY.

Mr. Jay called at 10 and went out with me to Passy to meet the Marquis de la Fayette, at the Invitation of Dr. F. The Marquis's Business was to shew Us a Letter he had written, to the C. de V. on the Subject of Money.[1] This I saw nettled F. as it seemed an Attempt to take to himself the Merit of obtaining the Loan if one should be procured. He gave Us also a Letter to Us 3, for our Approbation of his going out, with the C. D'Estaing. He recites in it that he had remained here by our Advice, as necessary to the Negotiations.[2] This nettled both F. and J. I knew nothing of it, not having been here, and they both denied it.

This unlimited Ambition will obstruct his Rise. He grasps at all civil, political and military, and would be thought the Unum necessarium in every Thing. He has so much real Merit, such Family Supports, and so much favour at Court, that he need not recur to Artifice.

—He said that C. de V. told him as the Chev. de la Luzernes Dispatches were not arrived, the Ct.³ could do nothing in the affair of Money, without Something french to go upon. His Letter therefore was to supply the Something French.—He told us that the C. D'Aranda had desired him to tell Mr. Jay, as the Lands upon the Missi[ssi]ppi, were not yet determined, whether they were to belong to England or Spain, he could not yet settle that matter. So that probably the Attempt will be to negotiate them into the Hands of the Spaniards, from the English. D'Aranda, Rayneval, Grantham, &c. may conduct this without Fitzherbert.

Spent part of the Evening at Mrs. Izards. Mr. Oswald sent for Mr. Jay, desired to meet him at either house. Mr. Jay went and I came off.†⁴

¹ To Vergennes, 22 Nov. 1782 (Wharton, ed., *Dipl. Corr. Amer. Rev.*, 6:67–70).
² This letter has not been found; perhaps it was withdrawn.
³ "Count" or "Court"? JA's usual abbreviation for Count was "C."; when written out, "Comte."
⁴ "Saturday Novr. 23d.... Mr. Strachey is returned from England. I

find the Ministers here Mr. Oswald and Fitzherbert are very doubtful about Peace and are indeed doubtful of Ld. Shelburne keeping his Ground.—Mr. Vaughan went to England in consequence of Reneval's going that he might be at hand to prompt Ld. Shelburne to the Peace—his pretence was going to see Mrs. Vaughan" (Matthew Ridley, Diary, MHi).

### 1782 NOVEMBER 25. MONDAY.

Dr. F., Mr. J. and myself at 11. met at Mr. Oswalds Lodgings.¹

Mr. Stratchey told Us, he had been to London and waited personally on every one of the Kings Cabinet Council, and had communicated the last Propositions to them. They every one of them, unanimously condemned that respecting the Tories, so that that unhappy Affair stuck as he foresaw and foretold that it would.

The Affair of the Fishery too was somewhat altered. They could not admit Us to dry, on the Shores of Nova Scotia, nor to fish within three Leagues of the Coast, nor within fifteen Leagues of the Coast of Cape Breton.

The Boundary they did not approve. They thought it too extended, too vast a Country, but they would not make a difficulty.

That if these Terms were not admitted, the whole Affair must be thrown into Parliament, where every Man would be for insisting on Restitution, to the Refugees.

He talked about excepting a few by Name of the most obnoxious of the Refugees.

I could not help observing that the Ideas respecting the Fishery appeared to me to come piping hot from Versailles. I quoted to them the Words of our Treaty with France, in which the indefinite and exclusive Right, to the Fishery on the Western Side of Newfoundland, was secured against Us, According to the true Construction of the Treaties of Utrecht and Paris. I shewed them the 12 and 13 Articles of the Treaty of Utrecht, by which the French were admitted to Fish from Cape Bona Vista to Cape Rich.[2]

I related to them the manner in which the Cod and Haddock come into the Rivers, Harbours, Creeks, and up to the very Wharfs on all the northern Coast of America, in the Spring in the month of April, so that you have nothing to do, but step into a Boat, and bring in a parcel of Fish in a few Hours. But that in May, they begin to withdraw. We have a saying at Boston that when the Blossoms fall the Haddock begin to crawl, i.e. to move out into deep Water, so that in Summer you must go out some distance to fish. At Newfoundland it was the same. The fish in March or April, were inshore, in all the Creeks, Bays, and Harbours, i.e. within 3 Leagues of the Coasts or Shores of Newfoundland and Nova Scotia. That neither French nor English could go from Europe and arrive early enough for the first Fare. That our Vessells could, being so much nearer, an Advantage which God and Nature had put into our hands. But that this Advantage of ours, had ever been an Advantage to England, because our fish had been sold in Spain and Portugal for Gold and Silver, and that Gold and Silver sent to London for Manufactures. That this would be the Course again. That France foresaw it, and wished to deprive England of it, by perswading her, to deprive Us of it. That it would be a Master Stroke of Policy, if She could succeed, but England must be compleatly the Dupe, before She could succeed.

There were 3 Lights in which it might be viewed. 1. as a Nursery of Seamen. 2 as a Source of Profit. 3. as a Source of Contention. As a Nursery of Seamen, did England consider Us as worse Ennemies than France. Had She rather France should have the Seamen than America. The French Marine was nearer and more menacing than ours. As a Source of Profit, had England rather France should supply the Marketts of Lisbon and Cadiz, with Fish and take the Gold And Silver than We. France would never spend any of that Money in London, We should spend it all very nearly. As a Source of Contention, how could We restrain our Fishermen, the boldest Men alive, from fishing in prohibited Places. How could our Men see the French admitted to fish and themselves excluded by the English; it would then be a Cause of Disputes, and such Seeds France might wish to sow.

—That I wished for 2 hours Conversation on the Subject with one of the Kings Council, if I did not convince him he was undesignedly betraying the Interest of his Sovereign, I was mistaken. Stratchey said perhaps I would put down some Observations in Writing upon it. I said, with all my heart, provided I had the Approbation of my Colleagues. But I could do nothing of the Kind, without submitting it, to their Judgments, and that whatever I had said or should say, upon the Subject however strongly I might express myself, was always to be understood with Submission to my Colleagues. I shewed them Capt. Coffins Letter and gave them his Character. His Words are,

"Our Fishermen from Boston, Salem, Newbury, Marblehead, Cape Ann, Cape Cod and Nantucket, have frequently gone out on the Fisheries, to the Streights of Bell Isle, North Part of Newfoundland, and the banks adjacent thereto, there to continue the whole Season, and have made Use of the North Part of Newfoundland, the Bradore [Labrador] Coast in the Streights of Bell Isle, to cure their Fish, which they have taken in and about those Coasts. I have known several Instances of Vessells going there to load in the Fall of the Year, with the Fish taken and cured at those Places for Spain, Portugal and &c. I was once concerned in a Voyage of that kind myself and speak from my own Knowledge.

"From Cape Sable, to the Isle of Sable and so on to the Banks of Newfoundland, are a Chain of Banks, extending all along the Coast, and almost adjoining each other, and are those Banks where our Fishermen go for the first Fare, in the early Part of the Season. Their second Fare is on the Banks of Newfoundland, where they continue to Fish till prevented by the tempestuous and boisterous Winds, which prevail in the Fall of the Year on that Coast. Their third and last Fare is generally made near the Coast of Cape Sables or Banks adjoining thereto, where they are not only relieved from those boisterous Gales, but have an Asylum to fly to in Case of Emergency, as that Coast is lined, from the head of Cape Sable to Hallifax, with most excellent Harbours.

"The Sea Cow Fishery was before the present War, carried on to Great Advantage, particularly from Nantucket and Cape Cod, in and about the River St. Laurence, at the Islands of St. Johns and Anticoste, Bay of Shalers [Chaleurs] and the Magdalene Islands, which were the most noted of all for that Fishery. This Oil has the Preference to all other except Sperma Cœti." [3]

Mr. Jay desired to know, whether Mr. Oswald had now Power to conclude and sign with Us?

Stratchey said he had absolutely.

Mr. Jay desired to know if the Propositions now delivered Us were their Ultimatum. Stratchey seemed loth to answer, but at last said No. —We agreed these were good Signs of Sincerity.

Bancroft came in this Evening and said, it was reported that a Courier had arrived from Mr. Rayneval in London, and that after it, the C. de Vergennes told the King, that he had the Peace in his Pocket. That he was now Master of the Peace.

[1] At this conference the Commissioners of both powers took up the "third set" of provisional articles, formulated by the British ministry and brought to Paris by Strachey. A copy of these in JA's hand is in Lb/JA/21 (Adams Papers, Microfilms, Reel No. 109); a printed text is in Wharton, ed., *Dipl. Corr. Amer. Rev.*, 6:74–77. A summary of Oswald's new instructions brought by Strachey is in Thomas Townshend to the King, 19 Nov. (*Correspondence of King George the Third . . .*, ed. Sir John Fortescue, London, 1927–1928, 6:156–157).

[2] JA means Point Riche, but there was much dispute about its location (and consequently about control over the western coast of Newfoundland) for nearly two centuries after the Treaty of Utrecht, 1713. See entry of 26 Nov., below; also Ralph G. Lounsbury, *The British Fishery at Newfoundland, 1634–1763*, New Haven, 1934, p. 240 and *passim*, especially the map following the index.

[3] Quoted (with omissions and insignificant alterations) from Alexander Coffin to Charles Storer, Amsterdam, 12 Nov. 1782 (Adams Papers); see also entry of 30 Nov., below. The "Sea Cow" is the walrus.

### NOV. 26. TUESDAY.

Breakfasted at Mr. Jays, with Dr. Franklin, in Consultation upon the Propositions made to Us Yesterday by Mr. Oswald. We agreed unanimously, to answer him, that We could not consent to the Article, respecting the Refugees as it now stands. Dr. F. read a Letter upon the Subject which he had prepared to Mr. Oswald, upon the Subject of the Tories, which We had agreed with him that he should read as containing his private Sentiments.[1] —We had a vast deal of Conversation upon the Subject. My Colleagues opened themselves, and made many Observations concerning the Conduct, Crimes and Demerits of those People.

Before Dinner Mr. Fitsherbert came in, whom I had never seen before. A Gentleman of about 33, seems pretty discreet and judicious, and did not discover those Airs of Vanity which are imputed to him.

He came in Consequence of the desire, which I expressed Yesterday of knowing the State of the Negotiation between him and the C. de Vergennes, respecting the Fishery. He told Us that the C. was for fixing the Boundaries, where each Nation should fish. He must confess he thought the Idea plausible, for that there had been great dissentions between the Fishermen of the two nations. That the french

Marine Office had an whole Appartment full of Complaints and Representations of disputes. That the French pretended that Cape Ray was the Point Riche.

I asked him if the French demanded of him an exclusive [Right] [2] to fish and dry between Cape Bona Vista and the Point riche. He said they had not expressly, and he intended to follow the Words of the Treaty of Utrecht and Paris without stirring the Point.

I shewed him an Extract of a Letter from the Earl of Egremont to the Duke of Bedford, March 1. 1763, in which it is said that by the 13 Art[icle] of the Treaty of Utrecht, a Liberty was left to the French to fish, and to dry their fish on Shore; and for that Purpose to erect the Necessary Stages and Buildings, but with an express Stipulation de ne pas sejourner dans la dite Isle, au dela du tems necessaire pour pêcher et sêcher le Poisson.—That it is a received Law among the Fishermen, that whoever arrives first, shall have the Choice of the Stations. That the Duke de Nivernois insisted, that by the Treaty of Utrecht the French had an exclusive Right to the Fishery from Cape Bona Vista to Point Riche. That the King gave to his Grace the D. of Bedford express Instructions to come to an Ecclaircissement upon the Point with the French Ministry, and to refuse the Exclusive Construction of the Treaty of Utrech &c.

I also shew him a Letter, from Sir Stanier Porteen, Lord Weymouths Secretary, to Ld. Weymouth, inclosing an Extract of Ld. Egremonts Letter to the Duke of Bedford, by which it appears that the Duke of Nivernois insisted

"That the French had an exclusive right to the Fishery from Cape Bona Vista to Point Riche, and that they had, on ceding the Island of Newfoundland to G. Britain by the 13 Article of the Treaty of Utrecht, expressly reserved to themselves such an exclusive Right, which they had constantly been in Possession of, till they were entirely driven from North America in the last War."

For these Papers I am obliged to Mr. Izard.[3] Mr. Fitsherbert said it was the same Thing now Word for Word: but he should endeavour to have the Treaty conformable to those of Utrecht and Paris. But he said We had given it up, by admitting the Word "exclusive" into our Treaty.—I said perhaps not, for the whole was to be conformable to the true Construction of the Treaties of Utrecht and Paris, and that if the English did not now admit the exclusive Construction they could not contend for it vs. Us. We had only contracted not to disturb them, &c.

I said it was the Opinion of all the Fishermen in America that England could not prevent our Catching a fish without preventing themselves from getting a Dollar. That the 1st. Fare was our only Advantage. That neither the English nor French could have it. It must be lost if We had it not.

He said, he did not think much of the Fishery as a Source of Profit, but as a Nursery of Seamen. I told him the English could not catch a fish the more, or make a Sailor the more, for restrain[in]g Us. Even the French would rival them in the Markets of Spain and Portugal. It was our Fish which they ought to call their own, because We should spend the Profit with them. That the southern States had Staple Commodities, but N. England had no other Remittance but the Fishery. No other Way to pay for their Cloathing. That it entered into our Distilleries and West India Trade as well as our European Trade, in such a manner that it could not be taken out or diminished, without tearing and rending. That if it should be left to its natural Course We could hire or purchase Spots of Ground on which to erect Stages, and Buildings, but if We were straightened by Treaty, that Treaty would be given in Instructions to Governors and Commodores whose duty it would be to execute it. That it would be very difficult to restrain our Fishermen, they would be frequently transgressing, and making disputes and Troubles.

He said his principal Object was to avoid sowing Seeds of future Wars.—I said it was equally my Object, and that I was perswaded, that if the Germ of a War was left any where, there was the greatest danger of its being left in the Article respecting the Fishery.

The rest of the Day, was spent in endless Discussions about the Tories. Dr. F. is very staunch against the Tories, more decided a great deal on this Point than Mr. Jay or my self.[4]

[1] Article V in the "third set" of provisional articles read: "It is agreed that restitution shall be made of all estates, rights, and properties in America which have been confiscated" (Wharton, ed., *Dipl. Corr. Amer. Rev.*, 6:76). Franklin's famous letter to Oswald, 26 Nov., proposing to balance American losses against loyalist losses, is in Franklin's *Writings*, ed. Smyth, 8:621–627. See, further, 29 Nov. below, and note 1 there.

[2] MS: "Rich."

[3] Copies of the letters quoted are in Adams Papers under the assigned date of Nov. 1782. They are printed in the Autobiography, below, following the record of Congress' instructions to JA for negotiating a commercial treaty with Great Britain, 16 Oct. 1779.

[4] "Tuesday Novemr. 26h. Dined at Mr. Adams's. Mr. Strachey who is arrived from England insists much on the Affair of the Refugees. It seems however to be inadmissible and unless he has Instructions to get over this the Negotiations will probably break off" (Matthew Ridley, Diary, MHi).

### 1782 NOV. 27. WEDNESDAY.

Mr. Benjamin Vaughan came in, returned from London where he had seen Lord Shelburne.

He says he finds the Ministry much embarrassed with the Tories, and exceedingly desirous of saving their Honour and Reputation in this Point. That it is Reputation more than Money &c.

Dined with Mr. Jay and spent some time before Dinner with him and Dr. Franklin, and all the Afternoon and Evening with them and Mr. Oswald, endeavouring to come together, concerning the Fisheries and Tories.[1]

[1] "Wednesday Novr. 27h. Dined at Mr. Jay's. Mr. Franklin Mr. Adams and many others there. Mr. Vaughan is returned from England. At the same time another Courier came from there supposed to bring more conciliating propositions with respect to the Tories. It is said the French Negotiation is in great forwardness.—Called upon Vaughan in the Evening—says there are no signs of a change of Ministry. . . . It is said the French Negotiation is not so forward as reported. The Dutch Minister knows not of it. Mr. Strachey pretends it is very nigh—says that if America will consent to give liberty to the Refugees to purchase in their property at the last sum sold at it would be assented to, but that something was necessary to save the Kings Honor in respect to those who had adhered to him. His former language was, nothing short of a restoration of property would do—and had even said the King would admit of exceptions to six or Seven of the most Obnoxious.—He is working to do all he can but our principal will not be departed from" (Matthew Ridley, Diary, MHi).

### NOV. 28. THURSDAY.

This Morning I have drawn up, the following Project

### Art. 3.

That the Subjects of his Britannic Majesty, and the People of the said United States, shall continue to enjoy, unmolested, the Right to take Fish of every kind, on the Grand Bank and on all the other Banks of Newfoundland: also in the Gulph of St. Laurence, and in all other Places, where the Inhabitants of both Countries, used at any time heretofore to fish; and the Citizens of the said United States shall have Liberty to cure and dry their Fish, on the Shores of Cape Sables, and of any of the unsettled Bays, Harbours or Creeks of Nova Scotia, or any of the Shores of the Magdalene Islands, and of the Labradore Coast: And they shall be permitted in Time of Peace to hire Pieces of Land, for Terms of Years, of the legal Proprietors in any of the Dominions of his said Majesty, whereon to erect the necessary Stages and Buildings and to cure and dry their Fish.[1]

[1] Compare the earlier draft in the entry of 4 Nov., above; also Article III in the "third set" of propositions (Wharton, ed., *Dipl. Corr. Amer. Rev.*, 6:75–76); and that in the Preliminary Articles as signed on 30 Nov. (Miller, ed., *Treaties*, 2:98).

"Thursday Novemr. 28h. . . . In the Evening called again on Mr. Adams. He had dined at Passy, was to meet the Commrs. again this Evening, desired to see us at 1/2 past Nine. . . . He said he had laid down a Line and beyond that he would not go let who would be ready.—At 1/2 past Nine he returned from the meeting—was in Spirits and said all was going well—but some difficulties had been started which he was sure had been in Consequence of Renevals going to England. Had a pretty long Conversa-

tion with him. He says Dr. F is the most Violent of the three for not admitting the Tories—but speaks very well of him in the course of the Negotiation" (Matthew Ridley, Diary, MHi).

### 1782 NOVEMBER 29. FRYDAY.

Met Mr. Fitsherbert, Mr. Oswald, Mr. Franklin, Mr. Jay, Mr. Laurens and Mr. Stratchey at Mr. Jays, Hotel D'Orleans, and spent the whole Day in Discussions about the Fishery and the Tories. I proposed a new Article concerning the Fishery. It was discussed and turned in every Light, and multitudes of Amendments proposed on each Side, and at last the Article drawn as it was finally agreed to. The other English Gentlemen being withdrawn upon some Occasion, I asked Mr. Oswald if he could consent to leave out the Limitation of 3 Leagues from all their Shores and the 15 from those of Louisbourg. He said in his own Opinion he was for it, but his Instructions were such, that he could not do it. I perceived by this, and by several Incidents and little Circumstances before, which I had remarked to my Colleagues, who were much of the same opinion, that Mr. Oswald had an Instruction, not to settle the Articles of the Fishery and Refugees, without the Concurrence of Mr. Fitsherbert and Mr. Stratchey.

Upon the Return of the other Gentlemen, Mr. Stratchey proposed to leave out the Word Right of Fishing and make it Liberty. Mr. Fitsherbert said the Word Right was an obnoxious Expression.

Upon this I rose up and said, Gentlemen, is there or can there be a clearer Right? In former Treaties, that of Utrecht and that of Paris, France and England have claimed the Right and used the Word. When God Almighty made the Banks of Newfoundland at 300 Leagues Distance from the People of America and at 600 Leagues distance from those of France and England, did he not give as good a Right to the former as to the latter. If Heaven in the Creation gave a Right, it is ours at least as much as yours. If Occupation, Use, and Possession give a Right, We have it as clearly as you. If War and Blood and Treasure give a Right, ours is as good as yours. We have been constantly fighting in Canada, Cape Breton and Nova Scotia for the Defense of this Fishery, and have expended beyond all Proportion more than you. If then the Right cannot be denied, Why should it not be acknowledged? and put out of Dispute? Why should We leave Room for illiterate Fishermen to wrangle and chicane?

Mr. Fitsherbert said, the Argument is in your Favour. I must confess your Reasons appear to be good, but Mr. Oswalds Instructions were such that he did not see how he could agree with Us. And for my Part, I have not the Honour and Felicity, to be a Man of that Weight and Authority, in my Country, that you Gentlemen are in yours (this was very genteelly said), I have the Accidental Advantage of a little favour with the present Minister, but I cannot depend upon the Influence of my own Opinion to reconcile a Measure to my Countrymen. We can consider our selves as little more than Pens in the hands of Government at home, and Mr. Oswalds Instructions are so particular.

I replied to this, The Time is not so pressing upon Us, but that We can wait, till a Courier goes to London, with your Representations upon this Subject and others that remain between Us, and I think the Ministers must be convinced.

Mr. Fitsherbert said, to send again to London and have all laid loose before Parliament was so uncertain a Measure—it was going to Sea again.

Upon this Dr. Franklin said, that if another Messenger was to be sent to London, he ought to carry Something more respecting a Compensation to the Sufferers in America. He produced a Paper from his Pocket, in which he had drawn up a Claim, and He said the first Principle of the Treaty was Equality and Reciprocity. Now they demanded of Us Payment of Debts and Restitution or Compensation to the Refugees. If a Draper had sold a Piece of Cloth to a Man upon Credit and then sent a servant to take it from him by Force, and after bring his Action for the Debt, would any Court of Law or Equity give him his Demand, without obliging him to restore the Cloth? Then he stated the carrying off of Goods from Boston, Philadelphia, and the Carolinas, Georgia, Virginia &c. and the burning of the Towns, &c. and desired that this might be sent with the rest.[1]

Upon this I recounted the History of G[eneral] Gages Agreement with the Inhabitants of Boston, that they should remove with their Effects upon Condition, that they would surrender their Arms. But as soon as the Arms were secured, the Goods were forbid to be carried out and were finally carried off in large Quantities to Hallifax.

Dr. Franklin mentioned the Case of Philadelphia, and the carrying off of Effects there, even his own Library.

Mr. Jay mentioned several other Things and Mr. Laurens added the Plunders in Carolina of Negroes, Plate &c.

After hearing all this, Mr. Fitsherbert, Mr. Oswald and Mr. Stratchey, retired for some time, and returning Mr. Fitsherbert said that upon consulting together and weighing every Thing as maturely as possible, Mr. Stratchey and himself had determined to advise Mr. Oswald, to strike with Us, according to the Terms We had proposed as our Ultimatum respecting the Fishery and the Loyalists.—Accordingly We all sat down and read over the whole Treaty and corrected it and agreed to meet tomorrow at Mr. Oswalds House, to sign and seal the Treaties which the Secretaries were to copy fair in the mean time.

I forgot to mention, that when We were upon the Fishery, and Mr. Stratchey and Mr. Fitsherbert were urging Us to leave out the Word Right and substitute Liberty, I told them at last In Answer to their Proposal, to agree upon all other Articles, and leave that of the Fishery to be adjusted, at the definitive Treaty. I said, I never could put my hand to any Articles, without Satisfaction about the Fishery. That Congress had, 3 or 4 Years ago, when they did me the Honour to give me a Commission, to make a Treaty of Commerce with G. Britain, given me a positive Instruction, not to make any such Treaty, without an Article in the Treaty of Peace, acknowledging our Right to the Fishery, that I was happy that Mr. Laurens was now present who I believed was in Congress at the Time, and must remember it.[2]

Mr. Laurens upon this said, with great Firmness, that he was in the same Case, and could never give his Voice for any Articles without this.

Mr. Jay spoke up and said, it could not be a Peace, it would only be an insidious Truce without it.[3]

[1] A copy of Franklin's counter-proposal is in Adams Papers, Nov. 1782, docketed "An Article proposed & read to the Commissioners before signing the preliminary Articles, with a state of facts"; a printed text is in Franklin's *Writings*, ed. Smyth, 8:632, note. In reporting the end of the preliminary negotiation, Franklin said that "Apparently . . . to avoid the discussion" of his proposed new article, the British Commissioners "suddenly changed their minds, dropped the design of recurring to London, and agreed [also] to allow the fishery as demanded" (to Livingston, 5 Dec. 1782; same, p. 632–633). For the tame compromise on the question of restoring loyalist property (a recommendation by Congress to the state legislatures), see Miller, ed., *Treaties*, 2:98–99.

[2] Instructions of 16 Oct. 1779, q.v. in JA's Autobiography. Those for negotiating peace had of course been super-seded by fresh instructions to the joint commissioners, 15 June 1781, prepared under the eye of La Luzerne (JCC, 20:651–654); and JA's instructions to negotiate a treaty of commerce had been revoked by a resolution of Congress, 12 July 1781 (same, p. 746).

[3] "Friday Novemr. 29.... Dined at Mr. Adams—in good Spirits. Said he on being asked if he would fish at Dinner, No laughingly—'he had had a pretty good Meal of them today.' I told [him] 'I was glad to hear it as I knew a small Quantity would not satisfy him.'

"In the Evening I learned every thing was going right and that in all probability the whole would be finished tomorrow off or on. I am well satisfied it will be on. All goes well and we have all that can be wished. Mr. A is well satisfied with Dr. F's Conduct and says he has behaved well and Nobly; particularly this day" (Matthew Ridley, Diary, MHi).

NOVEMBER 30. SATURDAY. ST. ANDREWS DAY.

We met first at Mr. Jays, then at Mr. Oswalds, examined and compared the Treaties. Mr. Stratchey had left out the limitation of Time, the 12 Months, that the Refugees were allowed to reside in America, in order to recover their Estates if they could. Dr. Franklin said this was a Surprize upon Us. Mr. Jay said so too. We never had consented to leave it out, and they insisted upon putting it in, which was done.

Mr. Laurens said there ought to be a Stipulation that the British Troops should carry off no Negroes or other American Property. We all agreed. Mr. Oswald consented.

Then The Treaties were signed, sealed and delivered, and We all went out to Passy to dine with Dr. Franklin.[1] Thus far has proceeded this great Affair. The Unravelling of the Plott, has been to me, the most affecting and astonishing Part of the whole Piece.—

As soon as I arrived in Paris I waited on Mr. Jay and learned from him, the rise and Progress of the Negotiation. Nothing that has happened since the Beginning of the Controversy in 1761 has ever struck me more forcibly or affected me more intimately, than that entire Coincidence of Principles and Opinions, between him and me. In about 3 days I went out to Passy, and spent the Evening with Dr. Franklin, and entered largely into Conversation with him upon the Course and present State of our foreign affairs. I told him without Reserve my Opinion of the Policy of this Court, and of the Principles, Wisdom and Firmness with which Mr. Jay had conducted the Negotiation in his Sickness and my Absence, and that I was determined to support Mr. Jay to the Utmost of my Power in the pursuit of the same System. The Dr. heard me patiently but said nothing.

The first Conference We had afterwards with Mr. Oswald, in considering one Point and another, Dr. Franklin turned to Mr. Jay and said, I am of your Opinion and will go on with these Gentlemen in the Business without consulting this Court. He has accordingly met Us in most of our Conferences and has gone on with Us, in entire Harmony and Unanimity, throughout, and has been able and usefull, both by his Sagacity and his Reputation in the whole Negotiation.

I was very happy, that Mr. Laurence came in, although it was the last day of the Conferences, and wish he could have been sooner. His Apprehension, notwithstanding his deplorable Affliction under the recent Loss of so excellent a Son, is as quick, his Judgment as sound, and his heart as firm as ever. He had an opportunity of examining the whole, and judging, and approving, and the Article which he caused to be inserted at the very last that no Property should be carried off, which would most probably in the Multiplicity and hurry of Affairs have escaped Us, was worth a longer Journey, if that had been all. But his Name and Weight is added which is of much greater Consequence.

These miserable Minutes may help me to recollect, but I have not found time amidst the hurry of Business and Crowd of Visits, to make a detail.

I should have before noted, that at our first Conference about the Fishery, I related the Facts as well as I understood them, but knowing nothing Myself but as an Hearsay Witness, I found it had not the Weight of occular Testimony, to supply which defect, I asked Dr. Franklin if Mr. Williams of Nantes could not give Us Light. He said Mr. Williams was on the Road to Paris and as soon as he arrived he would ask him. In a few days Mr. Williams called on me, and said Dr. Franklin had as I desired him enquired of him about the Fishery, but he was not able to speak particularly upon that Subject, but there was at Nantes a Gentleman of Marblehead, Mr. Sam White, Son in Law to Mr. Hooper, who was Master of the Subject and to him, he would write.

Mr. Jeremiah Allen a Merchant of Boston, called on me, about the same time. I enquired of him. He was able only to give such an hearsay Account as I could give myself, but I desired him to write to Mr. White at Nantes, which he undertook to do and did. Mr. White answered Mr. Allens Letter by referring him to his Answer to Mr. Williams, which Mr. Williams received and delivered to Dr. Franklin, who communicated it to Us, and it contained a good Account.

I desired Mr. Thaxter to write to Messrs. Ingraham and Bromfield, and Mr. Storer to write to Captn. Coffin at Amsterdam. They delivered me the Answers.[2] Both contained Information, but Coffins was the most particular, and of the most importance, as he spoke as a Witness. We made the best Use of these Letters, with the English Gentlemen and they appeared to have a good deal of Weight with them.

From first to last, I ever insisted upon it, with the English Gentlemen, that the Fisheries and the Missisippi, if America was not satisfied in those Points, would be the sure and certain Sources of a future War. Shewed them the indispensible Necessity of both to our Affairs, and that no Treaty We could make, which should be unsatisfactory to our People upon these Points, could be observed.

That the Population near the Missisippi would be so rapid and the

Necessities of the People for its navigation so rapid, that nothing could restrain them from going down, and if the Force of Arms should be necessary it would not be wanting. That the Fishery entered into our Distilleries, our coasting Trade, our Trade with the Southern States, with the West India Islands, with the Coast of Affrica and with every Part of Europe in such a manner, and especially with England, that it could not be taken from Us, or granted Us stingily, without tearing and rending. That the other States had Staples. We had none but fish. No other Means of remittances to London or paying those very Debts they had insisted upon so seriously. That if We were forced off, at 3 Leagues Distance, We should smuggle eternally. That their Men of War might have the Glory of sinking now and then a fishing Schooner but this would not prevent a repetition of the Crime, it would only inflame and irritate and inkindle a new War. That in 7 Years We should break through all restrain[ts] and conquer from them the Island of Newfoundland itself and Nova Scotia too.

Mr. Fitsherbert always smiled and said, it was very extraordinary that the British Ministry and We should see it, in so different a Light. That they meant the Restriction, in order to prevent disputes and kill the Seeds of War, and We should think it so certain a Source of disputes, and so strong a Seed of War. But that our Reasons were such that he thought the Probability of our Side.

I have not time to minute the Conversations about the Sea Cow Fishery, the Whale Fishery, the Magdalene Islands and the Labradore Coasts and the Coasts of Nova Scotia. It is sufficient to say they were explained to the Utmost of our Knowledge and finally conceeded.

I should have noted before the various deliberations, between the English Gentlemen and Us, relative to the Words "indefinite and exclusive" Right, which the C. de Vergennes and Mr. Gerard had the Precaution to insert in our Treaty with France.[3] I observed often to the English Gentlemen that aiming at excluding Us, from Fishing upon the North Side of Newfoundland, it was natural for them to wish that the English would exclude Us from the South Side. This would be making both alike, and take away an odious Distinction. French Statesmen must see the Tendency of our Fishermen being treated kindly, and hospitably like Friends by the English on their Side of the Island, and unkindly, inhospitably and like Ennemies on the French Side. I added, farther, that it was my Opinion, neither our Treaty with the French, nor any Treaty or Clause to the same Purpose which the English could make, would be punctually observed. Fishermen both from England and America would smuggle, especially the Americans in the early Part of the Spring before the Europeans could arrive. This therefore must be connived at by the French, or odious Measures must be recurred to, by them or Us, to suppress it, and in either Case it was easy to see what would be the Effect upon the American Mind. They no doubt therefore wished the English to put themselves upon as odious a footing, at least as they had done.

Dr. Franklin said there was a great deal of Weight in this Observation, and the Englishmen shewed plainly enough that they felt it.

I have not attempted in these Notes to do Justice to the Arguments of my Colleagues ⟨both⟩ all of whom were, throughout the whole Business when they attended, very attentive, and very able, especially Mr. Jays, to whom the French, if they knew as much of his negotiations as they do of mine, would very justly give the Title with which they have inconsiderately decorated me, that of Le Washington de la Negotiation, a very flattering Compliment indeed, to which I have not a Right, but sincerely think it belongs to Mr. Jay.

[1] JA made a copy in his own hand of the Preliminary Articles, including the separate and secret article (concerning the boundary between the United States and Florida if England recovered Florida in the general peace settlement), which is in Lb/JA/21 (Adams Papers, Microfilms, Reel No. 109). The single known original text, as signed by the Commissioners of both powers, is in the Public Record Office, London. This is printed in Miller, ed., *Treaties*, 2:96–107, with notes on the tangled history of the transmission of the two signed originals (one of which is lost) and the certified copies, with their textual variations and present locations. After lengthy debate Congress ratified and proclaimed the Preliminary Articles (not including the secret article, which never went into effect because Spain retained Florida) on 15 April 1783; see JCC, 24:241–251, and Madison's Notes on Debates, same, 25:924–926, 928–936, 938–945, 957–960. The British ratification, under the King's seal, took place on 6 Aug., and exactly a week later, the ratifications were exchanged between Hartley and the three American ministers in Paris (Wharton, ed., *Dipl. Corr. Amer. Rev.*, 6:633, 645).

[2] See entry of 25 Nov., above. The letter from Ingraham & Bromfield to Thaxter, Amsterdam, 14 Nov., is in Adams Papers.

[3] In Article X of the Franco-American Treaty of Amity and Commerce of 1778; see Miller, ed., *Treaties*, 2:10.

### †1782 DECEMBER 1. SUNDAY, AND 2. MONDAY.[1]

Made many Visits &c.†

[1] First entry in D/JA/38, which is identical in format with the Diary booklets that immediately precede it.

### DECEMBER 3. TUESDAY.

Visited Mr. Brantzen Hotel de la Chine. Mr. Brantzen asked me, how We went on. I told him We had come to a full Stop, by signing and sealing the Preliminaries, on the 30. of November. I told him that

We had been very industrious, having been at it, forenoon, Afternoon and Evening, ever since my Arrival, either with one another or with the English Gentlemen.

He asked if it was definitive and seperate? I said by no Means. They were only Articles to be inserted in the definitive Treaty. He asked if there was to be any Truce, or Armistice in the mean time? I said again by no means.

He then said that he believed, France and England had agreed too. That the C. de Vergennes's Son was gone to England with Mr. De Rayneval; but he believed the Spaniards had not yet agreed. And the Dutch were yet a great Way off, and had agreed upon Nothing. They had had several Conferences. At the first, he had informed Mr. Fitsherbert, that their H. Mightinesses insisted upon the Freedom of Navigation as a Preliminary and a Sine qua non. Mr. Fitsherbert had communicated this to his Court, but the Answer received was that his Court did not approve of conceeding this as a Sine qua non, but choose to have all the Demands of their H.M. stated together. Mr. Brantzen answered that his Instructions were, not to enter into any Conferences, upon other Points untill this was agreed to. That it was the Intention of the British Court to agree to this. That he could not consider any Changes in the Ministry as making any Alteration, they were all Ministers of the same King and Servants of the same Nation. That Mr. Fox when he was Secretary of State, by his Letter to the Russian Minister, had declared the Intention of the King to consent to the Freedom of Navigation &c.

Mr. Brantzen said, however, that he had in his private Capacity and without compromising his Ministerial Character, entered into Explanations with Mr. Fitsherbert, and had told him that he should insist upon 3 Points, the Freedom of Navigation, the Restitution of Territories in the East and West Indies, and Compensation for Damages. The two first Points could not be disputed, and the 3d. ought not, for the War against them had been unjust, the Pretences for it were groundless, their Accession to the armed Neutrality must now be admitted, even by Britains Accession to it, to have been an illegitimate Cause of War, and the Project of a Treaty with America, could not be seriously pretended to be a just Cause of War. And Many Members of Parliament, had in the time of it, declared the War unjust, and some of those Members were now Ministers. Even the Prime Minister, My Lord Shelburne himself had freely declared the War unjust in the House of Peers, and if the War was unjust, the Damages and Injustice ought to be repaired.

Mr. Fitsherbert said, that there was no Precedent of Compensation for Damages in a Treaty of Peace.

Mr. Brantzen begged his Pardon and thought there had been Instances. One Example in particular which the English themselves had set against the Dutch which just then came into his Head. Cromwell had demanded Compensation of them, and they had agreed, as now appears by the Treaty, to pay an hundred thousand Pounds Sterling as a Compensation.

Mr. Brantzen was not furnished with a full Account of all the Losses of Individuals and therefore could not precisely say, what the Amount would be. That perhaps they might not insist upon prompt Payment, nor upon a stated Sum, but might leave both the Sum and Time of Payment to be ascertained by Commissioners at their Leisure after the Peace.

I observed to him that We intended to write to Mr. Dana and send him a Copy of our Preliminaries that he might commence his Negotiations with the neutral Powers, and if he succeeded We could then make common Cause with Holland, and insist on an Article to secure the Freedom of Navigation. This Idea he received with great Pleasure, and said he would write about it to the States. Upon this I asked him, with whom, he and the other Dutch Ministers abroad, held their Correspondence? He answered that the Secretary Fagel was properly speaking the Minister of foreign Affairs. That their principal Correspondence was with him: but that they had a Correspondence with the Grand Pensionary Bleiswick too. That the Letters received by the Secretary, were laid before the Besogne Secrete, or Committee of Secrecy. This Committee consisted of so many Members, one at least for each Province, that it was very difficult to keep any Thing secret. Foreign Ministers were very inquisitive, and the Duke de la Vauguion would be likely to get at it. So that if they had any Thing to write which they wished Secreeted, they wrote it to the G. Pensionary who is not obliged to lay before the States Letters entire. He selects such Parts as he judges proper and prints them to be taken ad Referendum, and laid before the Regencies of the Cities. That they had sometimes a little Diffidence of this Court, (quelque Mefiance) for this Court was very fine, (diablement fin) and when this happened, they wrote to the G. Pensionary, that it might not be communicated to the french Minister and consequently to his Court. These People are vastly profound. They will not favour the Spaniards in obtaining the Floridas. They will play England against Spain and Spain against England, England against you and you against England, and all of you against Us and Us against all of you, according to their own Schemes and Interests. They are closely buttoned up about Gibraltar, and as to Jamaica, they wont favour Spain in that View. I expect they will get their own affair arranged, and then advise England to agree to the Freedom of Navigation and a Restitution of Territory and then advise Us to be easy about Compensation. Thus Mr. Brantzen.

I next visited Mr. Jay to talk about writing to Mr. Dana and communicating to the neutral Powers the Preliminary Articles. Mr. Jay says that Mr. Oswald is very anxious, that his Court should do that —and he has been writing to the Ministry to perswade them to it.

Had a long Conversation with Mr. Jay about the manner of settling the Western Lands. This I cannot now detail.

Went next to Mr. Lawrens, upon the Subject of writing to Mr. Dana, and found him full in my Sentiments. And at my return found answers from Dr. Franklin and Mr. Laurens to the Letters I wrote them, both agreeing, that this is the critical Moment for Dana to commence his Negotiations. Dr. Franklin promises to have an authentic Copy made to send to Mr. Dana.[1]

In the Evening many Gentlemen came in, among the rest Mr. Bourse, the Agent of the Dutch East India Company, who expressed a good deal of Anxiety about their Negotiation and feared they should not have Justice in the East Indies.

[1] See JA to Franklin and to Laurens, 3 Dec. (letterbook copies in Adams Papers; the former is printed in JA's *Works*, 8:15–16); Franklin to JA, 3 Nov. [i.e. Dec.], and Laurens to JA, 4 Dec. (Adams Papers; Franklin's letter is printed in JA's *Works*, 7:656, with the mistaken date Franklin gave it). See also entry of 12 Dec., below.

DECEMBER 4. WEDNESDAY.

It is proper that I should note here, that in the Beginning of the Year 1780, soon after my Arrival at Paris Mr. Galloways Pamphlets fell into my Hands. I wrote a long Series of Letters to a Friend in Answer to them. That Friend sent them to England: But the Printers dared not to publish them. They remained there untill the last Summer, when they were begun to be printed, and are continued to this day, not being yet quite finished, in Parkers General Advertiser, but with false dates, being dated in the Months of January and February last, under the Title of Letters from a distinguished American. They appear to have been well received and to have contributed somewhat, to unite the Nation in accellerating the Acknowledgment of American Independance, and to convince the nation of the Necessity, of respecting our Alliances and of making Peace.[1]

I hope it will be permitted to me or to some other who can do it better, some Ten or fifteen Years hence, to collect together in one View, my little Negotiations in Europe. Fifty Years hence it may be published, perhaps 20. I will venture to say, however feebly I may have acted my Part or whatever Mistakes I may have committed, yet the Situations I have been in between angry Nations and more angry Factions, have been some of the most singular and interesting that ever happened to any Man. The Fury of Ennemies as well as of Elements, the Subtilty and Arrogance of Allies, and what has been worse than all, the Jealousy, Envy, and little Pranks of Friends and CoPatriots, would form one of the most instructive Lessons in Morals and Politicks, that ever was committed to Paper.[2]

[1] In June 1780 JA acknowledged to Thomas Digges, his secret correspondent in London, the receipt of several parcels of English newspapers, pamphlets, and books; among them were copies of Joseph Galloway's *Cool Thoughts on the Consequences to Great Britain of American Independence*, London, 1780, and other tracts recently published by the Pennsylvania loyalist in London (JA to Digges, 22 June 1780, LbC, Adams Papers; JA, *Works*, 7:203–204, under date of 24 June). Galloway's thesis was that the loss of America would mean the eclipse of Great Britain as a great power, and therefore that the British government and public could not for a moment entertain the idea of a peace with American independence. JA, who then held an exclusive commission to treat for peace and believed that these able pamphlets might influence British policy, at once set himself the task of answering them, particularly the *Cool Thoughts*. His view was that the conclusion to be drawn from Galloway's arguments was the opposite of what the writer intended: if England stood to lose so much by the separation of America, as Galloway maintained, she would lose vastly more by *continuing* the war; her best course would be to make a good peace before England and America were both exhausted. See JA to the President of Congress, 16 and 17 June 1780, PCC, No. 84, II; Wharton, ed., *Dipl. Corr. Amer. Rev.*, 3:787–793, 794–798. The answers that he prepared for publication he sent to Edmund Jenings at Brussels, who transmitted them to a friend in England, but nothing happened concerning them for two years. When peace became imminent, however, the letters began to appear, to JA's surprise, in *Parker's* [London] *General Advertiser and Morning Intelligencer*, as "from a Distinguished American," running from 23 Aug. to 26 Dec. 1782 and with false dates affixed to them, as if they had been written in the first two months of that year instead of nearly two years earlier (photostats in Adams Papers Editorial Files from the British Museum file of the *General Advertiser*). Some part of the series was reprinted in the Amsterdam *Politique Hollandais*, but no separate and complete publication of them, such as JA hoped for, has been found, and JA apparently never recovered the originals that would have made such a publication possible. See JA to Jenings, 16, 27 Sept. 1782 (Adams Papers), and JA to Cerisier, 9 June 1783 (LbC, Adams Papers).

JA's own copies of two and possibly three of Galloway's pamphlets of 1780, including the *Cool Thoughts*, with marginal summaries and other markings in JA's hand, have been identified among the bound tracts in the Boston Athenæum while the present volume was in the press.

[2] On this day JA wrote a letter to Livingston resigning "all my Employments in Europe"; he proposed that Laurens be appointed minister at The Hague and that Dana be joined to the commission to complete and sign the Definitive Treaty (LbC, Adams Papers; *Works*, 8:16).

†DECEMBER 5. 1782.

The Duke de la Vauguion came in. He says that France and England are agreed, and that there is but one Point between England and Spain. England and Holland are not yet so near. I shewed him our preliminary Treaty, and had some difficulty to prevent his seeing the seperate Article, but I did prevent him, from seeing any Thing of it, but the Words "Seperate Article."

Dined at Mr. Jays with Mr. Fitsherbert, Oswald, Franklin, Laurens, and their Secretaries, Ellis, Whitefoord, Franklin and Laurens.[1] Mr. Jennings was there too, he came home and spent the Evening with me.

[1] Henry Laurens Jr.

DECEMBER 6. 1782.

Spent the Evening with Mr. Laurens, at his own Lodgings hotel de York and on a Visit to Mr. Curson, hotel de York.

Mr. Laurens said, that We should very soon raise Figs and Olives and make Oil in America. That he had raised great Quantities of Figs in his own Garden in Carolina and that the Figs in Carolina and Georgia were the most delicious, he had ever tasted. That he had raised in one Year in his own Garden in Carolina, between fifty and an hundred Bushells of Olives. That there were large Quantities and a great Variety of wild Grapes in Carolina and Georgia, of some of which very good Wine had been made.

As Mr. Curson talked of going to Marsailles, Mr. Laurens advised him to send to America some Barbary Sheep. He says he had one in Carolina, but never could make the American Rams go to that Sheep.

He gives a beautifull description of Marsailles. Says it will rival Bourdeaux, in the Wine Trade with America. The Levant Trade furnishes it with Carpets, Cottons, Silks, Raw Silk, and Drugs, and it has a large Manufactory of Castile Soap.

Mr. Laurens's Appartments at the hotel de York are better than mine, at the hotel du Roi, au Carrousel. Yet he gives but twelve Louis and I am obliged to give Eighteen. He has two large Rooms, besides a large commodious Bed Chamber, and a large Antichamber for Servants.

He says there will be an outrageous Clamour in England, on Account of the Fisheries and the Loyalists.—But what is done, is irrevocable.

DECEMBER 7. SATURDAY.

Dined with my Family, at the Place Vendome the Abby Chaluts. An Abby there crys voila la Semence d'une autre Guerre.

DECEMBER 8. SUNDAY.

At home all Day. Mr. Jennings, Mr. Grand Pere et Fils, Mr. Mason and Mr. Hoops called upon me.

1782. DECEMBER 9. MONDAY.

Visited C. Sarsfield who lent me his Notes upon America.† [1] Visited Mr. Jay, Mr. Oswald came in. We slided, from one Thing to another into a very lively Conversation upon Politicks.—He asked me what the Conduct of his Court and Nation ought to be, in Relation to America. I answered the Alpha and Omega of British Policy, towards America, was summed up in this one Maxim—See that American Independence is independent, independant of all the World, independent of yourselves as well as of France, and independent of both as well as of the rest of Europe. Depend upon it, you have no Chance for Salvation but by setting up America very high. Take care to remove from the American Mind all Cause of Fear of you. No other Motive but Fear of you, will ever produce in the Americans any unreasonable Attachment to the house of Bourbon.—Is it possible, says he that the People of America should be afraid of Us, or hate Us? —One would think Mr. Oswald says I, that you had been out of the World for these 20 Years past. Yes there are 3 millions of People in America who hate and dread you more than any Thing in the World. —What says he now We are come to our Senses?—Your Change of System, is not yet known in America, says I.— Well says he what shall We do to remove these Fears, and Jealousies?

In one Word says I, favour and promote the Interest, Reputation and Dignity of the United States in every Thing that is consistent with your own. If you pursue the Plan of cramping, clipping and weakening America, on the Supposition that She will be a Rival to you, you will make her really so, you will make her the natural and perpetual Ally of your natural and perpetual Ennemies.—But in what Instance says he have We discovered such a disposition?—In the 3 Leagues from your Shores and the 15 Leagues from Cape Breton, says I to which your Ministry insisted so earnestly to exclude our Fishermen. Here was a Point that would have done Us great harm and you no good, on the contrary harm. So that you would have hurt yourselves to hurt

Us. This disposition must be guarded against.—I am fully of your Mind about that, says he. But what else can We do?—Send a Minister to Congress, says I, at the Peace, a clever Fellow, who Understands himself, and will neither set Us bad Examples, nor intermeddle in our Parties. This will shew that you are consistent with yourselves, that you are sincere in your Acknowledgment of American Independence, and that you dont entertain hopes and designs of overturning it. Such a Minister will dissipate many fears, and will be of more Service to the least obnoxious Refugees than any other Measure could be. Let the King send a Minister to Congress and receive one from that Body. This will be acting consistently and with Dignity, in the Face of the Universe.

Well what else shall We do says he?—I have more than once already says I, advised you to put your Ministers upon negotiating the Acknowledgment of our Independence by the Neutral Powers.—True says he and I have written about it, and in my Answers, says he, laughing, I find myself charged with Speculation. But I dont care, I will write them my Sentiments. I wont take any of their Money. I have spent already twelve or thirteen hundred Pounds, and all the Reward I will have for it shall be the Pleasure of writing as I think. My opinion is that our Court should sign the armed Neutrality, and announce to them what they have done with you, and negotiate to have you admitted to sign too. But I want to write more fully upon the Subject, and I want you to give me your Thoughts upon it, for I dont understand it so fully as I wish. What Motives can be thrown out to the Empress of Russia? or what Motives may she be supposed to have to acknowledge your Independence? and what Motives can our Court have to interfere, or interceed with the Newtral Powers to receive you into their Confederation?

I will answer all these Questions says I, to the best of my Knowledge and with the Utmost Candour. In the first Place, there has been with very little Interruption a Jealousy, between the Courts of Petersbourg and Versailles for many Years. France is the old Friend and Ally of the Sublime Port the natural Ennemy of Russia. France not long since negotiated a Peace between Russia and the Turk, but upon the Empresses late Offers of Mediation, and especially her Endeavours to negotiate Holland out of the War, France appears to have been piqued, and as the last Revolution in the Crimea happened soon after, there is Reason to suspect that French Emmissaries excited the Revolt against the new independent Government which the Empress had taken so much Pains to establish. Poland has been long a Scæne of

Competition between Russian and French Politicks, both Parties having spent great Sums in Pensions to Partisans untill they have laid all Virtue and public Spirit prostrate in that Country.

Sweeden is another Region of Rivalry between France and Russia, where both Parties spent such Sums in Pensions, as to destroy the Principles of Liberty and prepare the Way for that Revolution which France favoured from a Principle of Œconomy rather than any other. These hints were sufficient to shew the opposition of Views and Interests between France and Russia, and We see the Consequence of it, that England has more Influence at Petersbourg than France. The Empress therefore would have two Motives, one to oblige England, if they should interceed for an Acknowledgment of American Independence, and another to render America less dependent upon France. The Empress moreover loves Reputation, and it would be no small Addition to her Glory, to undertake a Negotiation with all the neutral Courts to induce them to admit America into their Confederacy. The Empress might be further tempted. She was bent upon extending her Commerce and the Commerce of America, if it were only in Hemp and Duck, would be no small Object to her.

As to the Motives to your Court. Princes often think themselves warranted if not bound to fight for their Glory. Surely they may lawfully negotiate for Reputation. If the Neutral Powers should ⟨receive⟩ acknowledge our Independence now, France will have the Reputation, very unjustly, of having negotiated it. But if your Court now takes a decided Part in favour of it, your Court will have the Glory of it, in Europe and America, and this will have a good Effect upon American Gratitude.

But says he, this would be negotiating for the Honour and Interest of France, for no doubt France wishes all the World to acknowledge your Independence.

Give me leave to tell you, Sir, says I, you are mistaken. If I have not been mistaken in the Policy of France from my first Observation of it to this hour, they have been as averse to other Powers acknowledging our Independence as you have been.—Mr. Jay joined me in the same Declaration.—God! says he I understand it now. There is a Gentleman going to London this day. I will go home and write upon the Subject by him.

[1] These are regrettably not among the papers by Sarsfield retained by JA; see note 4 on entry of 12 June 1779, above.

### DECEMBER 10. TUESDAY.

Visited Mr. Oswald, to enquire what News from England. He had the Courier de L'Europe in which is Mr. Secretary Townsends Letter to the Lord Mayor of London dated the 3d. of this Month in which he announces the Signature of Preliminaries on the thirtieth of November, between the Commissioner of his Majesty and the Commissioners of the U. States of America.

He had also received the Kings Speech, announcing the same Thing.

Mr. Oswald said that France would not seperate her Affairs from Spain. That he had hoped that America would have assisted them, somewhat, in compromising Affairs with France &c. Dr. Franklin, who was present, said he did not know any Thing of the other Negotiations. He said that neither Mr. Fitsherbert, nor the C. de Vergennes, nor the C. D'Aranda communicated any Thing to him. That he understood, the Dutch were the farthest from an Agreement.

Upon this I said, Mr. Oswald, Mr. Fitsherbert cant, I think, have any difficulty, to agree with Mr. Brantzen. There are 3 Points. 1. The Liberty of Navigation. 2. Restitution of Possessions. 3. Compensation for Damages. The Liberty of Navigation I suppose, is the Point that sticks. But why should it stick? When all Nations are agreed in the Principle, why should England stand out? England must agree to it! She has already in Effect agreed to it, as it affects all Nations but Holland and America, and if She were disposed, She could not prevent them from having the Benefit.

Upon this Dr. Franklin said the Dutch would be able in any future War, to carry on their Commerce even of naval Stores, in the Bottoms of other neutral Powers.

Yes says Mr. Oswald, and I am of Opinion that England ought to subscribe the armed Neutrality.

Very well, says I, then let Mr. Fitsherbert agree this Point with Mr. Brantzen, and let Mr. Harris at Petersbourg, take Mr. Dana in his hand, and go to the Prince Potempkin or the C. D'osterman, and say the K[ing] my Master has authorized me to subscribe the Principles of the armed Neutrality, and instructed me to introduce to you Mr. Dana, Minister from the United States of America, to do the same; let him subscribe his Name under mine.—At this they all laughed very heartily. Mr. Oswald however recollecting himself, and the Conversation between him and me Yesterday on the same Subject, very gravely turned it off, by saying he did not see a necessity to be in a hurry about that. America was well enough.

I said, as to Restitution of the Dutch Territories, I suppose your Court wont make much difficulty about that if this Court does not, as it is not probable she Will. And as to Compensation for damages, the Dutch will probably be as easy as they can about that.

Dr. Franklin said he was for beginning early to think about the Articles of the difinitive Treaty. We had been so happy as to be the first in the Preliminaries, and he wished to be so in the definitive Articles.—Thus We parted.

†It may be proper for me to minute here some Points to propose in the difinitive Treaty.

1. The Liberty of Navigation. 2. That no Forts shall be built or Garrisons maintained upon any of the Frontiers in America, nor upon any of the Land Boundaries. 3. That the Island of Bermudas be ceeded to Us—or independent, or not fortified, or that no Privateers be fitted or sent out from thence or permitted to enter there, or prizes carried in. 4. That the Isle of Sables remain the Property of its present owner, and under the Jurisdiction of the United States or Massachusetts. 5. That the Account of Prisoners be ballanced, and the Sums due for their subsistence &c. be paid, and the Ballance of Prisoners paid for according to the Usages of Nations.[1]

[1] This list of proposals is interestingly amplified by a separate list in JA's hand of "Articles to be proposed in the definitive Treaty," without date but filed (with related drafts) in the Adams Papers under Dec. 1782–June 1783.

### DEC. 11. WEDNESDAY.

Dined with Mr. Laurens.†

### 12. THURSDAY.

Met at Mr. Laurens's, and signed the Letter, I had drawn up to Mr. Dana, which I sent off inclosed with a Copy of the Preliminaries[1]— and consulted about Articles to be inserted in the definitive Treaty. Agreed that Mr. Jay and I should prepare a joint Letter to Congress.

At 7. I met Mr. Jay at his House and We drew a Letter.[2]

[1] Signed by the four American Commissioners and dated this day, this letter is in MHi:Dana Papers; a facsimile is in Cresson, *Francis Dana*, facing p. 278.

[2] The version finally agreed upon, dated 14 Dec., signed by the four Commissioners, and sent to Secretary Livingston, is in PCC, No. 85; printed in Wharton, ed., *Dipl. Corr. Amer. Rev.*, 6:131–133. In the Adams Papers is JA's "rough draught of a common [i.e. joint] Letter," dated one day earlier. See also the following entry in this Diary. This dispatch and its enclosure, a certi-

fied copy of the Preliminary Articles, were carried to Philadelphia by Capt. Joshua Barney in the packet *Washington*. Barney did not sail from Lorient, however, until mid-January and did not arrive until 12 March (Pres. Boudinot to George Washington, 12 March 1783; Burnett, ed., *Letters of Members*, 7:71).

## 1782 DECEMBER 13. FRYDAY.

I went first to Mr. Jay, and made some Additions to the joint Letter, which I carried first to Mr. Laurens, who made some Corrections and Additions, and then to Passy to Dr. Franklin who proposed a few other Corrections, and shewed me an Article he has drawn up for the definitive Treaty to exempt Fishermen, Husbandmen and Merchants as much as possible from the Evils of future Wars. This is a good Lesson to Mankind at least. All agreed to meet at my House at 11 tomorrow to finish the joint Letter.[1]

[1] See the preceding entry and note 2 there. With the present entry the extracts copied by Thaxter and Storer from JA's Diary of the preliminary peace negotiation and sent to Livingston come to an end, at least so far as they are found in PCC, No. 84, IV; see note on entry of 2 Nov., above.

## DECEMBER 14. SATURDAY.

## 15 SUNDAY.

## DEC. 16. MONDAY.

Mr. Fitsherbert and Mr. Oswald, Mr. Laurens &c. dined with me.

## DECR. 16 [*i.e.* 17]. TUESDAY.

The 4 Commissioners dined with Mr. Fitsherbert. Ld. Mountnorris a celebrated Speaker in the Irish house of Lords dined there, and several English Gentlemen.

The Rock Salt is taken out of the Salt Pits in England, Ld. Mountnorris said. He gave me a Description of the Caverns, and the kind of Architecture with which they support them, like the Pillars of a Temple.

We met at Mr. Laurens's at Dr. Franklins Summons or Invitation at 11 O Clock. He produced a Letter to him from the Comte de Vergennes, and a Project of an Answer which he had drawn up which We advised him unanimously to send.[1]

[1] Vergennes' letter to Franklin, 15 Dec., complaining of the American Commissioners' failure to consult with him before concluding their negotiation with the British, and Franklin's famous reply thereto, 17 Dec., are both printed in Franklin's *Writings*, ed. Smyth, 8:641–643.

### 1782 DECEMBER 19. THURSDAY.

Visited M. Louis Secretary of the Royal Colledge of Surgery, in order to form a Correspondance, between it and the medical Society at Boston. Was very politely received, and promised every Thing that the Colledge could do. Mr. Louis talked a great deal, and very ingeniously and entertainingly.[1]

Spent the Evening, at the Abby Chalut's with the Abby de Mably, two other Abbys and two Accademicians. The Abby de Mably has just published a new Work, Sur la maniere d'ecrire L'histoire. He is very agreable in Conversation, polite, good humoured and sensible. Spoke with great Indignation against the practice of lying, chicaning and finessing, in Negotiations. Frankness, Candour, and Probity, were the only means of gaining Confidence. He is 74 or 75 Years old.

Mr. L.[2] told me this Morning that the Salt Pits in England are directly under the River Dee and that Ships sail over the Heads of the Workmen. Bay Salt is such as is made in France and Spain, round the Bay of Biscay. Rock Salt from Saltertudas.[3]

[1] In a letter from Weymouth, 26 Sept. 1782, announcing the formation of the Massachusetts Medical Society, Cotton Tufts had requested JA to solicit "the Aid and Communications of the Gentlemen of the Faculty in Europe" for the new organization (Adams Papers). Hence JA's visit to the Académie Royale de Chirurgie and apparently other similar visits, from which a flurry of somewhat ceremonial communications resulted in the following months; see entry of 23 Dec. and note, below.

[2] Presumably Henry Laurens.

[3] That is, Salt Tortuga, an uninhabited island off the coast of Venezuela. The name was spelled with wild variety by American traders who loaded salt there; see Richard Pares, *Yankees and Creoles: The Trade between North America and the West Indies before the American Revolution*, London, &c., 1956, p. 103–104 and notes.

### 1782 DECR. 20. FRYDAY.

Dined with Mr. Laurens.

### DECR. 21. SATURDAY.

Visited Mr. Jay and then went out to Passy to shew Dr. Franklin, Mr. Dana's Letter.[1] The Dr. and I agreed to remit Mr. Dana the Money, to pay the Fees to the Russian Ministers according to the Usage, upon the Signature of a Treaty. Six Thousand Roubles to each Minister who signs the Treaty.

The C. de Lynden told me the other Day that the King of Sweeden was the first Inventer and Suggester of the Plan of the armed Neutrality. That his Minister first proposed it to the C. Panin, where it slept some time. Lynden says that the King of Sweeden has Penetration and Ambition, and that his Ambition to be the first Power, to propose an Alliance with Us, is perfectly in Character. This Step, however I conjecture, was suggested to his Minister here, in order to support Dr. Franklin, by the C. de Vergennes.

The C. de Lynden shewed me his gold Snuff Box set with Diamonds, with the Miniature of the King of Sweeden, presented to him, on taking leave of that Court. The King is like Mr. Hancock.

Dr. Franklin went to Versailles Yesterday, and was assured of the Six millions, and all is fair Weather—all friendly and good humoured. So may it remain. I suspect however, and have Reason, but will say nothing. Our Country is safe.

Mr. Jay is uneasy, about the French Troops in America— afraid that more are going, and that they will overawe our Councils. That France is agreed with England upon her Points, and that the War will be continued for Spanish Objects only. In that Case We are not obliged to continue it.

[1] Dana to JA, St. Petersburg, 14/25 Nov. 1782 (Adams Papers).

#### 22 SUNDAY.

Made several Visits &c.

#### 23 MONDAY.

Received from Monsieur Geoffroy, Docteur Regent de la Faculté de Medicine de Paris, a Letter of Thanks from the Societe Royale de Medecine, for my Letter to him proposing a Correspondence between that Society and the Medical Society at Boston.[1]

Made several Visits. &c. Went to the Italian Comedy, saw Les Troqueurs, the two Harlequins &c.

[1] Geoffroy's letter, together with others of the same character addressed to JA by French medical men and institutions, 1782–1783, are now in the Boston Medical Library (MBM). Copies are in Adams Papers, Lb/JA/22 (Microfilms, Reel No. 110). See entry of 19 Dec. and note, above; also JA to Edward Augustus Holyoke, President of the Massachusetts Medical Society, 10 June 1783, 3 April 1786 (letterbook copies, Adams Papers).

#### DECEMBER 24. TUESDAY.

There are Men who carry the Countenance and Air of Boys through Life.

This Evening Mr. Jay told me an extraordinary Story of Lord Mount Steuart, the British Minister at Turin, which he had from Mr. Oswald.[1]

[1] Of a rumored plan to divide America between England and France. See John Jay, *Diary during the Peace Negotiations of 1782*, ed. Frank Monaghan, New Haven, 1934, p. 15–17; also entry of 5 Nov. and note, above.

### DECR. 25. WEDNESDAY. CHRISTMAS.

Lady Lucans Verses on Ireland[1]

Hear this, Ye Great, as from the Feast Ye rise
Which every Plundered Element supplies!
Hear, when fatigued, not nourish'd Ye have din'd
The Food of Thousands is to roots confin'd.

Eternal Fasts that know no Taste of Bread:
Nor where who sows the Corn by Corn is fed.
Throughout the Year, no feast e'er crowns his board
Four Pence a day, ah! what can that afford? &c.

Open our Ports at once with generous Minds,
Let Commerce be as free as Waves and Winds.
Seize quick the Time, for now, consider well
Whole Quarters of the World, at once rebel.

[1] Margaret (Smyth) Bingham, wife of an Irish peer, the first Baron Lucan, was better known for her paintings than for her verse (*DNB*).

### DEC. 26. THURSDAY.

Mr. Brantzen call'd upon me, at one. He says that Mr. Fitzherbert and he are yet a great Way asunder. The first Point of the Freedom of Navigation sticks. The other Points they have agreed on, or may agree on, not being far off. Mr. F. has no Answer from London to the Dutch Propositions.

I told him he might make himself very easy about the Freedom of navigation, for that the English must come into it. I suspected My Lord Shelburne was maneuvring, to save a little Pride. That he thought, it would be less humiliating to the English and less flattering to the Dutch, to conceed that Point, to the armed Neutrality, first. I knew it had been recommended to his Lordship by Mr. Oswald and other English Gentlemen here, and I had seen in the English Papers, that Couriers had been sent off, from the Secretary of States Office, to all the foreign Courts. Combining these Circumstances together I suspected, that they had given orders to their Minister at Petersbourg to sign the Treaty of armed Neutrality as France and Spain have done, and after this negotiation shall be accomplished they will have no difficulty to agree with the Dutch, for they demand no more than the Principle of the armed Neutrality.

Mr. Brantzen said this never had occurred to him, but [that he] [1] thought it possible and natural. [2]

I gave him Mr. Higginsons Letter and Papers [3] and a Copy of our Treaty, in Confidence, all but the Sep[arate] Art[icle]. He says Mr. Bourse will not do for Minister to America. He is of the wrong Side and will not be gouté du tout.

The Duke de la Rochefoucault made me a Visit to day, and desired me to explain to him some Passages in the Connecticut Constitution, which were obscure to him, which I did.

Sir James Jay too came in from the Hague, full of Projects of burning Towns and making fifty Gun Ships equal to 110 Guns Ships. I told him that this Country abounded so much with Projects and Projectors, that there would be a Presumption and Prejudice against him, at first blush: but he is going to the Marquis de Castries.

Mr. Vaughan and Mr. Brantzen both told me today that the C[omte] de V[ergennes] sent off a Courier to London the night before Christmas. Mr. Brantzen told me, that he had twice seen Dr. Franklin, once at Versailles and once at Mr. Grands. That he appeared to him heavy and inactive and that if he had been alone, America would not have obtained such good Terms. I said he was right, for if he had been alone, We should not at this Moment have had any Terms at all. That our Negotiation would have trained on as heavily and confusedly as all the rest. That if his Advice and that of the C. de V. had been followed We should now have been treating under Mr. Oswalds first Commission. It was the Refusal of Mr. Jay and me to treat under that Commission, against the Opinion and Advice of V. and F. that produced Mr. Oswalds new Commission, acknowledging our Independence.

That was a noble Tryumph for You, says Mr. Brantzen.

Mr. Vaughan shew'd me, to day, a parcel of new French Books. Le Systeme naturelle, Le Systeme moral, Le Systeme Social, Le Systeme Politique. There is one Shop tolerated in selling forbidden Books. —Vaughan has a Brother in Philadelphia, who has written him a long Letter about the Constitutionists and the Republicans. They have chosen Mr. Dickinson Governor, and Mr. Mifflin into Congress.

[1] MS: "the."

[2] On the contrary, Great Britain refused the Dutch *sine qua non* and contrived altogether to avoid subscribing to the principle of free navigation as laid down by the Armed Neutrality. Owing to the indifference of France and the intransigence of England, to mention no other circumstance, the preliminaries between England and the Netherlands were not concluded until 2 Sept. 1783, the day before the definitive treaties between the other powers at war were signed. The definitive Anglo-Dutch settlement was delayed until the following May, and its terms were humiliating to the Republic. See entry of 20 Jan. 1783, below, and, for the peace settlement

generally, Friederich Edler, *The Dutch Republic and the American Revolution*, Baltimore, 1911, ch. 9. JA was greatly distressed by all this, as his correspondence during 1783–1784 shows, but he found himself powerless to help his Dutch friends.

[8] Not found and probably not addressed to JA. In 1785 Stephen Higginson, Boston shipmaster, merchant, and partner of JA's friend Jonathan Jackson, commenced a correspondence with JA on Massachusetts' foreign trade; see "Letters of Stephen Higginson, 1783–1804," Amer. Hist. Assoc., *Ann. Rpt. for 1896*, 1:704–841.

### 1783. PARIS JANUARY 1.[1]

Went to Versailles, made my Visit and Compliments of the Season to M. Le C. de Vergennes and delivered him a Copy of our Treaty and Convention with the States General. He received me with Politeness, made me the Compliments of the Season, tres sincerement, and was sensibly obliged to me for the Copies and invited me to dine.

I went to see the Ceremony of the Knights of the St. Esprit, in the Chappell, where the Queen shone in great Splendour, dined with an immense Company at the Comtes and returned to Paris.

One of these first days of January I had a Conversation with Mr. Benjamin Vaughan, upon the Liberty of Navigation as claimed by the confederated neutral Powers and the Dutch. Shewed him the Necessity England was in, of acceeding to it, and the Importance of doing it soon that they might have it to say, that they had arranged their Affairs with the Dutch, as well as with the United States.

He said he saw the Importance, of pulling at the hairs one by one, when you could not pull out the whole Tail at once. That he had written and would write again to my Lord Shelburne upon the Subject: but says he you can not blame us for endeavouring, to cary this point to Market, and get Something by it. We can not prevent the French from getting some Territory in the East Indies more than they had and perhaps We may buy this of the Dutch for this Point.

The same day I called upon Mr. Jay, and asked him to speak with Mr. Oswald upon the same Subject, called next upon Mr. Laurens and mentioned the same Idea to him, called at Mr. Oswalds to talk with him upon it, but he was gone out.

[1] First entry in D/JA/39, which is identical in format with the several preceding Diary booklets.

### JANUARY 5. SUNDAY.

Dined with M. Vaughan, in Company with the Abbys de Mably, Chalut, Arnoux and Ter Saint [Tersan].—Had more Conversation with de Mably than at any Time before. He meditates a Work upon our American Constitutions.[1] He says the Character he gives of Herodian in his last Work, Sur la maniere d'ecrire L'histoire, has procured to his Bookseller, Purchases, for all the Copies of that Historian which he had in his Shop.—Arnoux said that Rousseau, by his Character of Robinson Crusoe, helped his Bookseller to the Sale of an whole Edition of that Romance in a few days.

[1] As a result of this conversation, and at the request of those present, JA on 15 Jan. addressed a long letter to Mably listing the chief sources from which a comprehensive history of the American Revolution would have to be drawn, together with advice on the subjects to be treated, including those in what would today be called social and institutional as well as political history (LbC, Adams Papers; printed in *Works*, 5:492–496, with an approximate date, "1782," supplied by JA from memory). Two days later JA prepared a second letter to Mably listing his own political writings from 1761 to 1779, which he had earlier excluded; but at the foot of his retained copy he wrote: "This Letter was never sent, but the Original was burned by me. It may remain here, without Imputation of Vanity" (Lb/JA/20, Adams Papers, Microfilms, Reel No. 108).

JA arranged with Cerisier for the publication at Amsterdam of Mably's *Observations sur le gouvernement et les loix des Etats-Unis d'Amérique*, 1784 (JA to Cerisier, 16 Oct. 1783, LbC, Adams Papers). An English translation, *Remarks concerning the Government and the Laws of the United States of America: In Four Letters, Addressed to Mr. Adams*, appeared in London later the same year. Copies of both are among JA's books in the Boston Public Library.

### JANUARY 11. SATURDAY.

Mr. W. T. Franklin came in to talk with me, about a Subject which he said he did not often talk about, and that was himself. He produced a Commission, drawn up, for Messrs. Franklin and Jay to sign, when they only were here, before I arrived, and in fact signed by them. I took the Commission and read it. He asked me to sign it. I told him, that I considered myself as directly affronted in this Affair. That considering that I came out to Europe without any Solicitation of mine, single in the Commission for Peace, and considering that Congress had done me the Honour to place me at the head of the new Commission, I had a right to be consulted in the Appointment of a Secretary to the Commission. But that without saying or writing a Word to me, Dr. Franklin had wrote to Mr. Jay at Madrid and obtained a Promise from him. That considering the Relation to me in which Mr. Thaxter came out, and his Services and Sufferings in the Cause and the small Allowance he had received, I thought he had a better right to it. That I thought my self ill treated in this as in many other Things. That it was not from any disrespect to him, Mr. W.T.F., that I declined it. That I should not, if my Opinion had been asked, have named Mr. Thaxter but another Gentleman.[1]

He told me, how his Grandfather was weary, that he had renewed his Solicitation to Congress, to be relieved. That he wanted to be with his Family at Philadelphia &c. &c. &c.

I told him I was weary too, and had written an unconditional Resignation of all my Employments in Europe.[2] That an Attack had been made upon me by the C. de Vergennes, and Congress had been induced to disgrace me. That I would not bear this disgrace if I could help it. That I would wear no Livery with a Spot upon it. The Stain should be taken out or I would not wear the Coat. That Congress had placed me now in a Situation, that I could do nothing without being suspected of a sinister Motive, that of aiming at being restored to the Mission to Great Britain. The Conduct of the American Cause in Europe had been a constant Scramble for Offices and was now likely to be a new and more passionate Scæne of Factions for Places. That I would have nothing to do with it, had not been used to it.

He said that Congress would have now a Number of Places and would provide for Mr. Thaxter. That they would undoubtedly give me full Satisfaction &c.

I told him that the first Wish of my Heart was to return to my Wife and Children &c.

He shewed me, Extract of a Letter of Dr. F. to Congress concerning him, containing a studied and long Eulogium—Sagacity beyond his Years, Diligence, Activity, Fidelity, genteel Address, Facility in speaking French. Recommends him to be Secretary of some Mission, thinks he would make an excellent Minister, but does not propose him for it as yet.[3]

This Letter and other Circumstances convince me, that the Plan is laid between the C. de Vergennes and the Dr., to get Billy made Minister to this Court and not improbably the Dr. to London. Time will shew.

[1] See entry of 27 Oct. 1782, above, and note 3 there. JA's candidate, if Thaxter was not to be chosen, was Edmund Jenings; see JA to Laurens, 15 Aug. 1782 (LbC, Adams Papers; *Works*, 7:611), and JA's letter in the *Boston Patriot*, 24 July 1811.

[2] JA to Livingston, 4 Dec. 1782 (LbC, Adams Papers; *Works*, 8:16).

[3] Franklin to Pres. Huntington, 12 March 1781; for the passage shown to JA, see Franklin, *Writings*, ed. Smyth, 8:221–223.

### JANUARY 12. SUNDAY.

Mr. B. Vaughan came in. I told him, I had some Facts to communicate to him in Confidence. They affected my personal Interest, Character, and Feelings so intimately, that it was impossible for me to speak of them without being suspected of personal Resentments and sinister Motives. But that these Facts were at the same time so connected, with public Affairs, with the Interests of the House of Bourbon, and with the essential Interests of Great Britain and America and the true System of Policy, which the two last ought in future to pursue towards each other, that it was my indispensable Duty to communicate them to some English Gentleman who might put their Government upon their Guard.

The two Facts I should now mention were two Instances of the Policy of the C. de Vergennes to defeat the good Intentions of Congress, towards G. Britain. I then shewed him my two original Commissions—one as Minister Plenipotentiary for making Peace, the other as Minister Plenipotentiary to make a Treaty of Commerce with the Ambassador or Plenipotentiary of his Britannic Majesty, vested with equal Powers, and whatever shall be so agreed and concluded for Us and in our Name to sign and thereupon make a Treaty of Commerce, and to transact every Thing that may be necessary for compleating, securing and strengthening the same, in as ample Form and with the same Effect, as if We were personally present and acted therein, 29. Sept. 1779.

Mr. Vaughan said he was astonished at my Secrecy and Patience, in never communicating this before. That they never had any Idea of this in London. I told him the C. de Vergennes had required me in the name of the King not to communicate it.

I then shew him the Resolution of Congress of 12 July 1781, by which the Commission and Instructions for negotiating a Treaty of Commerce between the U. States and G. Britain given me on the 29. day of Sept. 1779, were revoked.[1]

I then read to him the following Part of my Instructions of the 16. Oct. 1779, vizt. That the common Right of Fishing shall in no Case be given up. That it is essential to the Welfare of all these United States, that the Inhabitants there of, at the Expiration of the War should continue to enjoy the free and undisturbed Exercise of their common Right to fish on the banks of Newfoundland and the other fishing Banks and Seas of North America. That our Faith be pledged to the Several States, that without their unanimous Consent no Treaty of Commerce shall be entered into nor any Trade or Commerce whatever carried on with G. Britain without the Explicit Stipulation herein after mentioned. You are therefore not to consent to any Treaty of Commerce with G. Britain, without an explicit Stipulation on her Part not to molest or disturb the Inhabitants of the United States of

America in taking fish on the Banks of Newfoundland and other Fisheries in the American Seas &c.—Here I stopped.

You see here says I Mr. Vaughan, a proof of a great Confidence in me. And what was the Cause of it? No other than this, My Sentiments were known in Congress, to be unalterable for Independence, our Alliance, Fisheries and Boundaries. But it was known also to be a fixed Principle with me, to hurt G. Britain no farther than should be necessary to secure our Independence, Alliance and other Rights.

The C. de Vergennes knew my Character, both from his Intelligences in America and from my Conversation and Correspondence with him. He knew me to be a Man who would not yield to some of the designs he had in View. He accordingly sets his Confidential Friend Mr. Marbois, to negotiating very artfully with Congress. They could not get me removed or recalled, and the next Scheme was to get the Power of the Commission for Peace into the hands of Dr. Franklin.

To this End the Choice was made to fall upon him, and four other Gentlemen who could not attend.[2] They have been however mistaken, and no Wrestler was ever so compleatly thrown upon his Back as the C. de Vergennes.

But their Policy did not stop here. I had still a Parchment, to make a Treaty of Commerce with G. Britain, and an Instruction annexed to it, which would be a powerfull Motive with G.B. to acknowledge our Right to the Fisheries. This Commission and these Instructions were to be and were revoked.

Mr. Vaughan said this was very important Information and entirely new. That he was much enlightened and had Sentiments upon the Occasion. That he would write it to the E. of Shelburne, and his Lordship would make great Use of it, without naming me, &c.

---

[1] This resolution, which JA long considered the most humiliating stroke he had sustained in the course of his public life, was entered on the Secret Journal of Congress in the following terse form: "A motion was made by Mr. [James] Madison, seconded by Mr. [John] Mathews, That the commission and instructions for negotiating a treaty of commerce between these United States and Great Britain, given to the honourable John Adams on the 29 day of September, 1779, be and they are hereby revoked" (JCC, 20:746). JA expressed his long pent-up feelings concerning this action in a letter he addressed to Robert R. Livingston on 5 Feb. 1783 (LbC, Adams Papers; *Works*, 8:33–34). In his Diary for 30 April 1783 he attributed it to the baleful influence of Vergennes. Still later James Madison, who had moved the resolution of 12 July 1781, alluded to the circumstances of both the grant and the withdrawal of JA's commission, but he failed to give an explanation of either of them that is at all helpful to students of JA's career (Madison to Jefferson, 16 March 1784; Jefferson, *Papers*, ed. Boyd, 7:34).

[2] Insert after the word "who" in this sentence a parenthetical phrase, "it was supposed," or some equivalent. Of the five appointees only Thomas Jefferson, as things turned out, "could not attend."

### JANUARY. 13. MONDAY.

Mr. Oswald came to take Leave and shewed me a Letter from the Secretary of State for him to come home. He goes off, on Wednesday.

I told him if he was going home, I would communicate to him, what I had not intended.

I told him what I told Yesterday to Vaughan and gave him some short Account of my Correspondence with the C. de Vergennes, upon the Question whether I should communicate to Lord G. Germain, my Commissions, and his Requisition from the King, not to do it, &c.

### 1783. JANUARY 19. SUNDAY.

Received a Note from Mr. Franklin, that the C. de Vergennes had written to him to desire me, to meet him at his office, tomorrow at ten.[1] Went out to Passy, told Mr. Franklin that I had been informed last night, that the Comte was uneasy at Mr. Oswalds going away, because he expected to sign the Preliminaries in a day or two.

[1] Vergennes' note and Franklin's reply, both dated 18 Jan., and Franklin's note to JA, 19 Jan., are all printed in Franklin, *Writings*, ed. Smyth, 9:8–9.

### JANUARY 20. MONDAY.

Mr. Franklin and I met the Comte de Vergennes at his office at Ten. He told us, he was going to sign Preliminaries and an Armistice. At Eleven the C. D'Aranda came in, and Mr. Fitsherbert. After examining the Papers, D'Aranda and Fitsherbert signed the Preliminary Treaty, between the Crowns of G. Britain and Spain. De Vergennes and Fitsherbert that between Britain and France. Then Fitsherbert on one Part and Adams and Franklin on the other, signed, sealed and exchanged Declarations of an Armistice between the Crown of Great Britain and the United States of America.[1]

Previous to the Signature all the original Commissions were shewn. The C. D'Aranda shewed his. The C. de Vergennes his. Mr. Fitsherbert his—and Adams and Franklin theirs. Fitsherbert agreed to exchange Copies with Us.—Thus was this mighty System terminated with as little Ceremony, and in as short a Time as a Marriage Settlement.

Before the British and Spanish Ministers came in I asked the C. de Vergennes what was to become of Holland. He smiled and said, that We had nothing to do with that. I answered, with a Smile too, it was very true We had nothing to do with it, but that I interested myself very much, in the Welfare and Safety of that People. He then assumed an affected Air of Seriousness and said he interested himself in it too a good deal, and then told me, that the English had first wished to retain Demerary and Essquibo, but the King would not hear to that. Then they wanted Trincamale in the East Indies. But the King would not agree to that. Then they wanted Negapatnam. This the King left them to settle with the Dutch, but insisted on a Declaration from the King of G. Britain that he would restore all the other Possessions.

Fitsherbert told me afterwards it was the Severity of the Spaniards, that obliged his Court to be so hard with the Dutch. The Spaniards would do nothing without Minorca and the Floridas.

Returned to Paris and dined with the Duchess D'Anville and the Duke de la Rochefaucault.

[1] Copies, in French, of the declarations of cessation of hostilities, as agreed upon and exchanged by the American Commissioners (JA and Franklin) and the British Commissioner (Alleyne Fitzherbert), are in the Adams Papers under this date; English translations are printed in Wharton, ed., *Dipl. Corr. Amer. Rev.*, 6:223–224. John Jay had "gone upon a little Excursion to Normandie and Mr. Laurens was gone to Bath, both for their health. . . . Thus drops the Curtain upon this mighty Trajedy . . . and Heaven be praised. . . . I hope to receive the Acceptance of my Resignation so as to come home in the Spring Ships" (JA to AA, 22 Jan. 1783, Adams Papers).

### JANUARY 21. TUESDAY.

Went to Versailles to pay my Respects to the King and Royal Family, upon the Event of Yesterday. Dined with the foreign Ambassadors at the C. de Vergennes's.

The King appeared in high Health and in gay Spirits: so did the Queen. M[adam]e Elizabeth is grown very fat. The C. D'Artois seems very well. Mr. Fitsherbert had his first Audience of the King and Royal Family and dined for the first time with the Corps Diplomatique.

### 1783. JANUARY 23. THURSDAY.

Mr. Whitefoord made me a Visit. He said it was the fatal Policy of the Earl of Chatham, in supporting the K. of Prussia against the House of Austria, that had given an Austrian Queen to France. That the French had contrived too to marry the Kings two Brothers to Princesses of Savoy, by which they had damped the Zeal of another of the Allies of England the King of Sardinia.

I told him the Story of my Correspondence with the C. de Vergennes in 1780, about communicating my Mission to Lord G. Germain. He said if I had followed my own Opinion, and written to his Lordship and published the Letter, it would have turned out the old

Ministry. I told him I was restrained by a Requisition from the King. Besides the Defeat of D'Estaing and Langara, had turned the Heads of the People of England at that time.

### 1783 TUESDAY. FEB. 18.

Received a Letter from my Son John, dated at Gottenburgh the 1. of Feb. This Letter gave me great Joy, it is the first I have received from him since he left Petersbourg, and the first News I have had of him since the Beginning of December, when he was at Stockholm.— I have suffered extream Anxiety on his Account.[1]

I have omitted my Journal, and several Things of some Consequence, but I am weary, disgusted, affronted and disappointed. This State of Mind I must alter—and work while the day lasts.

I have been injured, and my Country has joined in the Injury. It has basely prostituted its own honour by sacrificing mine. But the Sacrifice of me for my Virtues, was not so servile, and intollerable as putting Us all under Guardianship. Congress surrendered their own Sovereignty into the Hands of a French Minister. Blush blush! Ye guilty Records! blush and perish! It is Glory, to have broken such infamous orders. Infamous I say, for so they will be to all Posterity. How can such a Stain be washed out? Can We cast a veil over it, and forget it?

[1] JQA's letter is in Adams Papers. He had left St. Petersburg in company with a Count Greco, 30 Oct. 1782, and traveled via Helsingfors (Helsinki) to Stockholm, which he reached on 22 Nov.; he and his companion left there on 31 Dec. and arrived at Göteborg on 16 Jan. after a tedious delay on account of bad weather; from there, traveling for the most part alone, he proceeded on 11 Feb. to Copenhagen and thereafter to Hamburg, Bremen, Amsterdam, and The Hague, arriving at the Hôtel des Etats-Unis on 21 April (JQA, Diary). JA's correspondence during the first several months of 1783 shows that officers of the Dutch and French diplomatic and consular services were constantly scouring the Baltic and North Sea ports looking for the fifteen-year-old boy. "My Younker ought to think himself highly honoured, by the Notice that has been taken of him by so many respectable Personages" (JA to Dumas, 19 March 1783, LbC, Adams Papers).

### 1783 FEB. 24. MONDAY.

Dined in Company with Mr. Malesherbes, the famous first President of the Court of Aids, Uncle of the Chevalier de la Luzerne, and Son of the Chancellor de la Moignon. He is about half Way in Appearance, between Mr. Otis and Mr. A. Oliver.

F[ranklin] this Morning mentioned to me the Voyage de la Fonté, who mentions a Captain Chapley, and a Seymour Gibbons. F. thinks it is translated from the Spanish, and that the Translator or Printer has put Seymour for Seignor. He had once a Correspondence about this Voyage, and Mr. Prince found there had been a Captain Chapelet at Charlestown and a Gibbons but not named Seymour.[1]

[1] This "Voyage" was supposed to have taken place in 1640; an account of it was first published in a London periodical in 1708. The purported leader and narrator, Admiral Bartholomew de Fonte, claimed to have sailed from Lima in Peru up the west coast of North America and to have found a water route to Hudson Bay, since he encountered a Boston ship which must have entered the Bay from the northeast. These claims were disputed with some warmth on both sides of the question during the middle decades of the 18th century, and French and English maps showing the discoveries in detail were published by those who believed a northwest passage existed. By the end of the century they were totally discredited; modern geographers consider Admiral de Fonte an entirely fictitious person. See Henry R. Wagner, "Apocryphal Voyages to the Northwest Coast of America," Amer. Antiq. Soc., *Procs.*, 41 (1931):179–234, which includes a reprint of the De Fonte "Letter" and facsimiles of several pertinent maps.

In his Diary entries for 17, 19 June, below, JA records more speculation and conversation on the controversy over the northwest passage.

### FEB. 25. TUESDAY.

Mr. Samuel Vaughan says that Cooks Voyage will be 3 Volumes 60 Plates, and will not be out these 12 Months. The Plates are of Islands discovered &c.

He mentions a new Sort of Bark, much redder and much stronger, than any known before.

### FEB. 27. THURSDAY.

Dined at the Farmer Generals, in Company with the Comte de Polastron, Father of the Duchesse de Polignac. No Friend of D'Estaing.

Spent the Evening in Company with the Abby de Mably, some other Abbys and Accademicians. De Mably says There are in France Three Orders of Citizens. The first Order is of the Clergy. 2. The Second of the Nobility. 3. And the third is called Le Tiers Etat.— There are several Classes in the Order of the Clergy, 7 or 8 Classes in the Order of Nobles, and Thirty Classes in the Tiers Etat. The Nobles all believe that their Nobility is from God. And therefore, the Nobles are all equal, and that the King cannot confer Nobility.

### FRYDAY MARCH 7.

In the Morning Chronicle of Saturday February 22, Mr. Secretary Townsend in the Debate upon the five Propositions of Lord John Cavendish, is represented to have said "He was willing to give his full Assent to the first Proposition, because such a Declaration from Parliament was, after the Address voted on Monday last, indispensably necessary. To the second, and to the third Resolutions, likewise he had no Objections. The fourth he certainly should resist, because it conveyed a direct Censure upon Ministers, reprobated and condemned the Peace, would give Alarm and Umbrage to the foreign Powers, with whom the Peace had been made, and be attended with a Variety of bad Consequences.

"With Regard to the fifth, that respecting the Loyalists, it would produce much Evil. It would totally defeat the Recommendations which Congress were pledged to make in favour of the Loyalists, and put them in a worse Predicament than that they already stood in, by the Treaty. In order to support this Assertion Mr. Townsend reasoned a good deal on the great danger arising at all times from creating Jealousies and Suspicions in Parties negotiating; but if there was any Party more prone to Jealousy, any State more liable to catch Suspicion sooner than another, it must be the United States of America, on Account of their having been little accustomed to the Business of negotiating, and *being obliged to trust their first and dearest Interests in the hands of Persons of whose Fidelity they had scarcely any pledge of Security*. Mr. Townsend concluded with saying, that for these Reasons he should resist the fifth Resolution as well as the fourth." [1]

[1] Lord John Cavendish's resolutions of censure on the provisional peace settlements were debated in the House of Commons on 21 Feb.; the debate resulted in a vote of 207 to 190 against the Shelburne ministry on the ground of its having made greater "concessions . . . to the adversaries of Great Britain . . . than they were entitled to" (*Parliamentary Hist.*, 23:498–571). On 24 Feb., as a direct upshot, Shelburne resigned, and an "inter-ministerium" of seven weeks followed, postponing negotiations for the Definitive Peace which JA had expected in January would be completed within a few weeks. See Horace Walpole, *Last Journals* . . . , *1771–1783*, ed. A. Francis Steuart, London, 1910, 2:487, 508.

MARCH 9 [*i.e.* 8]. SATURDAY.

Dined at Passy, the Spanish Ambassador, the Comte de Rochambeau, the Chevalier de Chatelux [Chastellux], Mr. Jay &c. present.

Chatelux said to the Abby Morlaix that I was the Author of the Massachusetts Constitution, and that it was the best of em all, and that the People were very contented with it.

MARCH 9. 1783 SUNDAY.

Mercure de France 1. Feb. 1783, p. 26

Academie Royale de Musique.

Lorsqu'un homme entre dans la carriere des Arts, n'ayant pour guide et pour Appui que son Genie; lorsque L'Intrigue et la Charlatanerie, ces deux grandes Ressources des petits talens, lui sont etrangères, il doit s'attendre à être long tems persecuté, méconnu, arrêté à chaque pas. Mais qu'il ne perde point courage; tous les Obstacles s'applanissent peu-a-peu devant lui; ses Ennemis se lassent ou deviennent odieux et suspects; et le public, éclairé par ces memes productions qu'il n'avoit pas d'abord appreciees, rend enfin Justice à leur Auteur.

Il est vrai qu'un Artiste qui se presente apres vingt-cinq ans de gloire et de Succès ne devroit pas eprouver les mêmes degouts; son nom fameux dans l'Empire des Arts, paroitroit fait pour en imposer à ses détracteurs; mais si dans le nouveau pays ou il arrive, son Art est encore ignoré; s'il y règne un faux Savoir, pire que L'Ignorance; si l'on y a la manie des Preferences, des *Preferences exclusives*, et que l'on ait dejà choisi l'Objet de ces Preferences, son nom lui devient inutile ou meme dangereux; et la Reputation qui le précède, en éveillant l'Envie, n'est pour lui qu'un Obstacle de plus.

On se rappelle aujourd hui, avec une espece de honte, les excès où l'on se porta d'abord contre l'Auteur de Roland. Les quolibets, les plattes Epigrammes, les comparaisons injurieuses, rien ne fut épargné.

Mr. Picini [Piccinni] is the Author of Roland.

In this Country, the Demon of Monarchy haunts all the Scænes of Life. It appears in every Conversation, at every Table and upon every Theatre. This People can attend to no more than one Person at a Time. They can esteem but one, and to that one their Homage is Adulation and Idolatry.

I once heard the Baron Van der Capellen de Poll say that the Dæmon of Aristocracy appeared every where in that Republick. That he had collected together a Number of Merchants to sign a Requête. They agreed upon the Measure but insisted upon appointing a Committee to sign it. Many of them declared they would not sign it, with a Crowd, avec une foule.

Thus it is that the human Mind contracts habits of thinking from the Example of the Gouvernment. Accustomed to look up to a few as all in an Aristocracy, they imitate the same practice in private Life, and in common Things. Accustomed in monarchies to look up to one Man in great Affairs, they contract a similar disposition in little ones.

In the same manner in Democracies We contract an habit of deciding every Thing by a Majority of Votes. We put it to vote whether the Company will sing a Song or tell a Story. In an Aristocracy they ask 2 or 3 of the better Sort. In a Monarchy they ask the Lady or the Gentleman, in whose honour the feast was made.

I dined with the Comte de Pilo, under the Incognito name of Mr. D'Olavide, heretofore Intendant of Seville who established the Colony of Sierra Morena in Spain, Mr. Boystel Consul General of France in Spain, the Comte de Jaucourt Marechal de Camp, the C. de Lusignem M. de Camp and the C. de Langeron M. de Camp, Commandant a Brest, at C. Sarsefields.

Ephemerides du Cytoyen par L'Abbe Baudau.
Memoire sur les Administrations provincials par Mr. Throne.
Dialogue sur les Bleds par L'Abbe Galliany.[1]

[1] These are books JA purchased or intended to purchase. The *Ephémérides du citoyen* was a French periodical devoted to the ideas of the Physiocrats, of which scattered volumes are among JA's books in the Boston Public Library; he also obtained a copy of G. F. Le Trosne's tract, *De l'administration provinciale, et de la réforme de l'impôt*, Basle, 1779 (*Catalogue of JA's Library*, p. 84, 144). But no copy of Ferdinand Galiani's *Dialogues sur les blés*, 1770, has been found among his books.

### 1783 PARIS APRIL 27. 1783.

Mr. Hartley met Mr. Franklin, Laurens, Jay and me, at my Lodgings, and shewed Us an Instruction under the Kings Privy Seal, and signed George Rex, in which his Majesty recites that he had appointed Mr. Hartley his Minister Plenipotentiary to treat with Us &c.[1]

The American Ministers unanimously required a Commission under the great Seal, and promising to ratify what he should do.—Mr. Hartley was chagrin'd.[2]

Much Conversation passed, which might as well have been spared. Mr. Hartley was as copious as usual. I called on Mr. Jay in the Evening and We agreed to meet at my House next Morning at 10.

[1] The weeks that followed the signing of the provisional treaties between Great Britain and France, and Great Britain and Spain, made "a very dull Pause," as JA wrote Arthur Lee (12 April, Adams Papers), during which JA worried about his health and in long letters to intimate correspondents poured out his suspicions of "French and Franklinian Politicks" (to AA, 16 April, Adams Papers). After what seemed interminable delays the Coalition government of Fox and North was at length formed, and on 18 April David Hartley received his instructions, as successor to Richard Oswald, to treat with the American Commissioners for a definitive peace settlement. Hartley, an old friend of Franklin's whom JA had first encountered, without being favorably impressed, five years earlier (see 19 April 1778, above), arrived in Paris on 24 April. JA was to change his estimate

of Hartley and eventually to recognize his intense sincerity in endeavoring to obtain a liberal settlement, especially in respect to trade relations, but the negotiations in Paris from April to September proved perfectly fruitless. They are well summarized in a single sentence in the Commissioners' letter to Pres. Boudinot of Congress, 10 Sept. 1783: "We had many conferences and received long memorials from Mr. Hartley on the subject [of new commercial regulations]; but his zeal for systems friendly to us constantly exceeded his authority to concert and agree to them" (Wharton, ed., *Dipl. Corr. Amer. Rev.*, 6:688). The best secondary account of this negotiation, which has been little studied but was not unimportant in spite of its failure, is in George H. Guttridge, *David Hartley, M.P., an Advocate of Conciliation*, Berkeley, 1926, ch. 4. There is need for a more detailed and comprehensive study.

[2] For Hartley's new commission see entries of 19, 22 May, below.

### APRIL 28. MONDAY.

At 10 Mr. Jay came in, and I shewed him a Variety of Projects, which I had drawn up last night, concerning the Removal of the Troops, opening the Ports, tranquilizing the Tories now within the Lines, Articles for Commerce, in Explanation of the provisional Treaty &c.

We drew together a Proposition, for withdrawing the Troops, opening the Ports and quieting the Tories, and went with it in my Carriage to Mr. Laurens, who thought it might do.[1] I said to my Brothers, I shall be very ductile about Commerce. I would agree at once to a mutual Naturalization, or to the Article as first agreed on by Dr. F. and Mr. Jay with Mr. Oswald, or I would agree to Mr. Hartleys Propositions, to let the Trade go on as before the War or as with Nova Scotia. I could agree to any of these Things because that Time and the natural Course of Things will produce a good Treaty of Commerce. G.B. will soon see and feel the Necessity of alluring American Commerce to her Ports, by Facilities and Encouragements of every kind. We called at Mr. Hartleys Hotel de York. He was out.—At Mr. Jays, Mr. Hartley came in. We told him, We thought of making him a Proposition, tomorrow, and would meet him at Mr. Laurens's at one. Wrote to Dr. Franklin and W. T. Franklin, desiring their Attendance at Mr. Laurens's Hotel de L'Empereur at 11. tomorrow. Received an Answer that they would attend.[2] Mr. Hartley desired of me Letters of Introduction for Il Comte di Fermé a Cousin of the Neapolitan Ambassader in London, who is going to America, which I promised him and wrote in the Evening.[3]

[1] As presented to Hartley on 29 April, these *projets* will be found in the next entry of this Diary.

[2] The note to the Franklins, in JA's hand, is in DeHi; the answer has not been found.

[3] The letters of introduction, addressed to John Hancock, James Bowdoin, and Benjamin Lincoln, are dated this day in Lb/JA/20 (Adams Papers, Microfilms, Reel No. 108). Conte Francisco dal Verme, of Milan, visited the United

States and traveled from New Hampshire to South Carolina later this year; in 1787 he extended kindnesses to Jefferson during the latter's brief visit to Italy (Wash- ington, *Writings*, ed. Fitzpatrick, 27:79 and note, 165–166 and note; Jefferson, *Papers*, ed. Boyd, 11:437; 12:38–39, 42–43, 587–589).

### APRIL 29. TUESDAY.

At 11, We all met at Mr. Laurens's near the new French Comedy, and agreed upon a Proposition to open the Ports as soon as the U. States should be evacuated. At one Mr. Hartley came and We shewed it to him, and after some Conversation with him, We agreed upon 3 Propositions. 1. To open the Ports as soon as the States should be evacuated. 2. To set all confined Tories at Liberty at the same time and 3. To set all Prisoners of War at Liberty, upon the same terms respecting the Accounts of their Expences as those between France and England.

Three Articles proposed by the American Ministers and delivered to Mr. David Hartley, 29. April 1783.[1]

### Article

No. 1.

It is agreed, that so soon, as his Britannick Majesty shall have withdrawn all his Armies, Garrisons and Fleets, from the United States of America, and from every Port, Post, Place and Harbour within the same, as stipulated by the 7 Article of the Provisional Treaty of 30. Nov. 1782, Then and from thenceforth, for and during the Term of          Years, all Rivers, Harbours, Lakes, Ports and Places, belonging to the United States, or any of them, shall be open and free, to the Merchants and other Subjects of the Crown of Great Britain, and their trading Vessells; who shall be received, treated and protected, like the Merchants and trading Vessells of the State in which they may be, and be liable to no other Charges or Duties.

And reciprocally all Rivers, Harbours, Lakes, Ports and Places under the Dominion of his Britannic Majesty, shall, thenceforth be open and free to the Merchants and trading Vessells of the said United States, and of each and every of them, who shall be received, treated and protected, like the Merchants and trading Vessells of Great Britain, and be liable to no other Charges or Duties: saving Always to the Chartered Trading Companies of Great Britain, such exclusive Use, and Trade of their respective Ports and Establishments, as neither the other Subjects of Great Britain, or any the most favoured Nation, participate in.

### Article

No. 2.

It is agreed that such Persons as may be in Confinement, in the United States of America for or by Reason of the Part which they may have taken in the late war, shall be set, at Liberty, immediately on the Evacuation of the said States by the Troops and Fleets of his Britannic Majesty.

And it is likewise agreed, that all such Persons who may be in confinement in any Parts under the Dominion of his Britannic Majesty for and by Reason of the Part which they may have taken in the late War, shall at the same time be also immediately set at Liberty.

### Article

No. 3.

The Prisoners made respectively by the Arms of his Britannick Majesty, and those of the United States of America, both by Land and Sea, shall be immediately set at Liberty, without Ransom, on paying the Debts they may have contracted during their Captivity: And each contracting Party shall respectively reimburse the Sums which shall have been advanced for the Subsistence and Maintenance of their Prisoners, by the Sovereign of the Country, where they shall have been detained, according to the Receipts and attested Accounts and other authentic Titles, which shall be produced on each Side.

[1] The text of the three proposed articles appears, not in the present Diary booklet, but in that which follows (D/JA/40), in the left-hand margin across from entries beginning 3 May. For Hartley's answer, 21 May, to the first and principal proposition, see entry of 22 May, below.

### 1783. APRIL 30. WEDNESDAY.

Mr. Hartley did me the Honour of a Visit to assure me, as he said of the Satisfaction he had in reflecting, upon what passed Yesterday, and upon what We had agreed upon. He thought it was exactly as it should be. I was glad to hear of his Satisfaction and expressed my own. I told him that I was so convinced, that Great Britain and America would soon feel the Necessity and Convenience of a right Plan of Commerce that I was not anxious about it. That it was simply from a pure regard to Great Britain, and to give them an opportunity of alluring to themselves as much of our Commerce, as in the present State of Things would be possible, that I should give myself any Trouble about it. That I had never had but one Principle and one System, concerning this Subject, before, during or since the War, and that had generally been the System of Congress viz. That it was not our Interest to hurt Great Britain any further than was necessary to support our Independence and our Alliances. That the French Court had sometimes endeavoured to warp us from this System, in some degrees and particulars, that they had sometimes succeeded with some American Ministers and Agents, Mr. Deane particularly, and I must add that Dr. Franklin had not adhered to it at all times with so much Firmness as I could have wished, and indeed Congress itself from the Fluctuation of its Members, or some other Cause had sometimes appeared to loose Sight of it. That I had constantly endeavoured to adhere to it, but this Inflexibility had been called Stubbornness, Obstinacy, Vanity &c. and had exposed me to many Attacks, and disagreable Circumstances. That it had been to damp the Ardour of returning Friendship as I supposed, which had induced the French Minister, to use his Influence to get the Commission to make a Treaty of Commerce with Great Britain, revoked without appointing another. That I did not care a Farthing for a Commission to Great Britain, and wished that the one to me had never existed, but that I was very sorry it was revoked without appointing another. That the Policy of this Court he might well think would be, to lay every stumbling Block between G. Britain and America. They Wished to deprive Us of the Fisheries and Western Lands for this Reason. They espoused the Cause of the Tories for this Reason.

I told him the Comte de Vergennes and I were pursuing different Objects. He was endeavouring to make my Countrymen meek and humble and I was labouring to make them proud. I avowed it was my Object, to make them hold up their Heads, and look down upon any Nation that refused to do them Justice. That in my Opinion Americans had nothing to fear, but from the Meekness of their own Hearts. As Christians I wished them Meek, as Statesmen I wished them proud, and I thought the Pride and the Meekness very consistent. Providence had put into our hands such Advantages, that We had a just Right and it was our Duty to insist upon Justice from all Courts, Ministers and Nations.

That I wished him to get his Commission as soon as possible and that We might discuss every Point and be perfectly ready to sign the definitive Treaty.

He said his Commission would come as soon as the Courier could go and return, and that he would prepare his Propositions for the definitive Treaty, immediately. He said he had not imagined that We had been so *stout* as he found Us.—But he was very silent and attentive. He has had hints I suppose, from Laurens and Jay, and Franklin too.

He never before discovered a Capacity to hearken. He ever before took all the Talk to himself. I am not fond of talking, but I wanted to convey into his Mind a few Things, for him to think upon. None of the English Gentlemen have come here apprized of the Place where their danger lay.

### 1783 MAY 1. THURSDAY.

Dined with the Marquis de la Fayette, with the other American Ministers and others.

Visited the Duke and Dutchesse de la Vauguion at the petite Luxembourg. The Duke is to stay here some time.

I told him he and I were in the same Case, and explained to him my Situation and gave him my frank Sentiments of a certain Minister. He said he was veritablement touché.

### FRYDAY. MAY 2.

Mr. Hartley came in to introduce to me his Secretary Mr. Hammond, whom he introduced also to mine, Mr. Thaxter and Storer.

He told me that the C. de Vergennes had been treating with Mr. Fitsherbert about the Post of Panmure at the Natches, which is within the Limits which England has acknowledged to be the Bounds of the United States. The Spaniards want to keep it, and the C. de Vergennes wants to make a Merit of procuring it for them with a few Leagues round it.—I told Mr. Hartley that this Subject was within the exclusive Jurisdiction of Mr. Jay. That the Minister for Peace had nothing to say in it.

I told Mr. Hartley the Story of my Negotiations with the C. de Vergennes about communicating my Mission to Ld. G. Germaine 3 Years ago and the subsequent Intrigues and Disputes &c. It is necessary to let the English Ministers know where their danger lies, and the Arts used to damp the Ardour of returning friendship.

Mr. Jay came, with several Pieces of Intelligence. 1. The Story of Panmure. 2. The Marquis de la Fayette told him that no Instructions were ever sent by the C. de Vergennes to the C. Montmorrin to favour Mr. Jays Negotiations at Madrid and that Montmorrin told la Fayette so.

Mr. Jay added that the Marquis told him, that the C. de Vergennes desired him to ask Mr. Jay why he did not come and see him? Mr. Jay says he answered how can he expect it? when he knows he has endeavoured to play Us out of the Fisheries and vacant Lands? Mr.

Jay added that he thought it would be best to let out by degrees, and to communicate to some French Gentlemen, the Truth and shew them Marbois's Letter. Particularly he mentioned C. Sarsefield.

Mr. Jay added, every Day produces some fresh Proof and Example of their vile Schemes. He had applied to Montmorin, to assist him, countenance him, support him, in his Negotiation at Madrid, and shewed him a Resolution of Congress by which the King of France was requested to Aid him. Montmorin said he could not do it, without Instructions from his Court, that he would write for Instructions, but Mr. Jay says he never heard any farther about it. But Yesterday La Fayette told him that Montmorin told him, no such Instruction had ever been sent him.

In Truth Congress and their Ministers have been plaid upon like Children, trifled with, imposed upon, deceived. Franklin's Servility and insidious faithless Selfishness is the true and only Cause why this Game has succeeded. He has aided Vergennes with all his Weight, and his great Reputation, in both Worlds, has supported this ignominious System and blasted every Man and every Effort to shake it off. I only have had a little Success against him.[1]

[1] The foregoing paragraph was omitted by CFA in his edition of JA's Diary.

### 1783 MAY 3. SATURDAY.[1]

When We met Mr. Hartley on Tuesday last at Mr. Laurens's, I first saw and first heard of Mr. Livingstons Letter to Dr. Franklin upon the Subject of Peace dated Jany. 7. 1781, but indorsed by Dr. F. Jany. 7. 1782.[2] The Peace is made, and the Negotiations all passed before I knew of this Letter and at last by Accident.—Such is Dr. Franklin.

Visited Mr. Jay. Found him, his Lady, Miss Laurens and Marquis de la Fayette at Breakfast going out of Town. Visited Mr. Laurens— not at home. Duke de la Vauguion—not at home. Mr. Hartley at home, Mr. Laurens came in soon after. I agreed to make a Visit to the Duke of Manchester this Evening. His Rank, as Duke and as Ambassador, and the Superiority of the State he represents, make it unnecessary to attend to the Rule in this Town, which is that the last comer make the first Visit, or to enquire very nicely what the sublime Science of Etiquette dictates upon this Occasion.

Mr. Hartley proposes that We should agree that the English should continue their Garrisons in Detroit, Niagara and Michillimachinac for a limited Time, or that Congress should put Garrisons into those Places, to protect their People, Traders and Troops from the Insults of the Indians. The Indians will be enraged to find themselves betrayed into the hands of those People against whom they have been excited to War.

Mr. Hartley proposes allso that We should agree that all the Carrying Places should be in Common. This is a great Point. These Carrying Places command the Fur Trade.—Mr. Laurens hinted to me, between Us, that this was the Complaint in England against the Ministry who made the Peace. That they had thrown the whole Fur Trade, into the Hands of the United States by ceeding all the Carrying Places, and that the Lakes and Waters were made useless to them by this means.

Mr. Laurens quoted a Creek King, who said he would not be for quarrelling with either Side, especially with Us Americans for We were all born of the same Mother and sucked at the same Breast. But turning to his young Men he said with Tears in his Eyes, *whichever Side prevails I see that We must be cutt off.*

Mr. Hartley talked about Passamaquaddi, and the Islands at the Mouth of the River St. Croix. He is for settling this matter, so as to prevent Questions.

Between 5 and 6 I made my Visit to the Duke of Manchester the British Ambassador upon his Arrival. Not at home. Left my Card.

The next day or next but one, the Duke returned my Visit. Came up to my Appartement and spent an half hour in familiar Conversation. He is between 50 and 60. A composed Man—plain Englishman.

One day this Week I visited the Duke de la Vauguion, upon his Arrival [from] [3] the Hague, who returned my Visit in a day or two.

[1] With this entry JA began a new Diary booklet (D/JA/40), identical in format with those preceding. The marks "C" (standing for "To be copied" or "Copied") run throughout this booklet at the foot of the pages, as they do also in D/JA/41–42, ending with the entry of 27 Oct. 1783. No transcript of this portion of his Diary has, however, been found. Perhaps the sensation stirred up by his earlier "Peace Journal" (see note on entry of 2 Nov. 1782, above) dissuaded him from sending any more such papers home.

[2] The correct date was certainly 7 Jan. 1782, since Livingston was not appointed secretary for foreign affairs until Aug. 1781. Livingston's letter embodied American arguments for claiming all territory to the Mississippi and undisturbed rights in the Newfoundland fishery, and arguments against the restitution of loyalist property (Wharton, ed., *Dipl. Corr. Amer. Rev.*, 5:87–94).

[3] MS: "at."

### 1783 MONDAY MAY 5.

Dined with my Family at C. Sarsefields. The Dukes de la Vauguion and de la Rochefaucault, Mr. Jay &c. of the Party.

### TUESDAY MAY 6.

Dined at Mr. Jays. Lt. General Mellville, who is here to solicit for the Inhabitants of Tobago, the Continuance of their Assembly and Tryals by Jury, was there.

### WEDNESDAY MAY 7.

Dined at Mr. Caluns [Calonne's].

### THURSDAY MAY 8.

The Duke de la Vauguion and Mr. Hartley, Mr. Laurens and Jay, Mr. Barclay[1] and Ridley, dined with me.

[1] Thomas Barclay (1728–1793), a Philadelphia merchant, had been elected by Congress United States consul in France, 5 Oct. 1781; on 2 Jan. 1783 he was named consul general. He had business interests at Lorient, but JA first encountered him in Amsterdam, and before long Barclay rented a large house in semirural Auteuil on the outskirts of Paris. Here JA was to be his guest during a period of illness in the fall of 1783, and afterward JA rented the house for the use of himself and family. In 1782 Barclay was given a commission to settle the accounts of all American ministers and agents in Europe; from 1785 he served as United States agent in protracted and futile negotiations with Morocco. See JCC, 21:1036; 23:730; 24:3; Barclay's letters in PCC, Nos. 91, 118; JA-Barclay correspondence in Adams Papers; Jefferson, *Papers*, ed. Boyd, vols. 7–12, *passim*; VMHB, 8:19, 21 (July 1900); scattered references in PMHB; Diary entries of 14 Sept., 7 Oct. 1783, 17 Aug. 1784, below.

### FRYDAY MAY 9.

Dined with Mr. Laurens, with a large Company. The M. de la Fayette shewed me, the Beginning of an Attack upon the Chancellor &c. &c.

### SATURDAY. MAY. 10.

Dined with the M. de la Fayette, with a large American Company.

### MONDAY MAY. 19.

The American Ministers met Mr. Hartley at my House, and he shewed Us his Commission and We shewed him ours. His Commission is very magnificent, the Great Seal in a Silver Box with the Kings Arms engraven on it, with two large gold Tassells &c. as usual.[1]

[*In the margin*: The Commissions of the Comtes de Vergennes and D'Aranda, on the 20. of January, were plainer than ours, and upon Paper. The French reserve their Silver Boxes to the Exchange of Ratifications.]

Dined with Mr. Laurens and Mr. Jay at Mr. Hartleys, Hotel de York.

We are to meet of Evenings at 6 O Clock, De Die, in Diem, at my House.

Mr. Hartley informed Us to day that the Kings Council had not agreed to our Proposition, of putting Britons upon the Footing of Americans in all American Ports, Rivers &c. and Americans on the Footing of Britons in all British Ports, Rivers &c. He says he is very sorry for this because he thinks it just and politick And that he shall ever be in Parliament for bringing Things to that point.

¹ Hartley's full power under the Great Seal, as required by the American Commissioners (see 27 April, above), was dated 14 May 1783; of the several copies in the Adams Papers, one forms a part of JA's Diary record for 22 May, below.

### TUESDAY MAY 20.

Saw Philadelphia Papers to the 12 of April. The Corvette dispatched from Cadiz by the Comte D'Estaing, carried the first News of the Preliminaries of the 20 of January. Mr. Livingston wrote it to Carlton and Digby, but they thought it, however respectable, not authentic for them. Soon after the February Packet arrived, at New York, from whence English News Papers were sent out and the Provisional and Preliminary Treaties all published in the Philadelphia Papers.

Visited Mr. Hartley. He said he thought the Dutch Negotiation in a bad Way, and that there would be a civil Contest in Holland; a Struggle between the Statholder and the States.

Mr. Hartley said, that some Dutch Friends he had in London, had told him there would be a civil dissention in Holland, and he was now more convinced of it. He said the K. of Prussia and the King of England would take the Part of the Statholder. I answered they would do well to consider whether in that Case, France and the Emperor would not assist the Republicans, and thus throw all Europe into a Flame. I told him I thought the English Policy towards the Republick, all wrong. They were wrong to make themselves Partisans of the Statholder vs. the Republicans. That they ought to be impartial. That they were interested in the Conservation of the Liberties of that Country. If that Spot should be annexed to the Empire or to France it would be fatal to Great Britain. That without its Liberty it could not maintain its Independency. Human Life, in that Country, struggling against the Sea, and in danger from so many Quarters, would be too painfull and discouraging without Liberty. That the K. of England and the Statholder would make a fatal Mistake, if they thought of making the lat[t]er Sovereign, or of increasing his Power. The Country would not be worth the Governing. That the Families of Orange and Brunswick owed their Grandeur to the Cause of Liberty, and if they now engaged in a Conspiracy against it they must go to Italy after the Stewarts.

I added that Sir Joseph York had been wrong to attach himself so closely to the Court, and declare War so decidedly against the Patriots. That he should have kept upon good Terms with the Capellens, Vanberckel, Gyzelaer, Visher &c.

I had reflected much upon this Subject. I had always been ready to acknowledge that I could not distinctly foresee, what would be the Consequence of our Independence in Europe. It might depress England too much and elevate the House of Bourbon too high. If this should be the Case, neither England nor America could depend upon the Moderation of such absolute Monarchies and such ambitious Nations. America might find France and Spain demanding of her Things which she could not grant. So might England. Both might find it necessary to their Safety to join, and in such a Case it would be of great Importance to both to have Holland join them. Whereas the Policy of the British Court if pursued would drive the Dutch into the Arms of France and fix them there. That I hoped the Case put would never happen, but England would have a stronger reason than ever now, to cultivate the Friendship of Holland. That in my Opinion she ought to give up Negapatnam and the Liberty of Navigation, give Satisfaction to the Duch, and carry an even hand in future between the Court and the States. That the British Minister ought to seek the Acquaintance and Friendship of the principal Patriots in all the Provinces and give them the Assurances of his Court that nothing should be attempted against their Constitution.

Mr. Hartley said he was of my Mind and had said as much to Mr. Fox before he left London. But the King would stand by the Statholder. The King, says he, will go wrong in Holland and in Ireland and Scotland too, but it will all work against himself. There are discontents in Scotland, as well as Ireland. We shall have Struggles, but I dont dread these. We shall have settled with America, and the American War was all that I dreaded.

### WEDNESDAY. MAY 21.

What is it, in the Air, which burns? When We blow a Spark with the Bellows, it spreads. We force a current of Air to the Fire, by this machine, and in this Air, are inflammable Particles. Can it be in the same manner that Life is continued by the Breath. Are there any Particles conveyed into the Blood of Animals through the Lungs, which increase the heat of it, or is the Pulse caused by rarifying the Blood or any Part of it, into Vapour, like the Experiment made with Spirits of Wine in a Glass Tube, with a globule at each End. If one End, or Globule, is placed in a Position a little Warmer, than the other, you see a Pulsation, caused by repeated rarefactions of the Spirits of Wine into Vapour at one End, which flows to the other and then reflows Again to its former Position where it is again rarified, and protruded.

The external Air, drawn into the Lungs in Breathing, through the Mouth or Nostrils, either Leaves some Particles behind, in the Lungs, or in the Blood, or carries some Particles off with it. It may do both, i.e. carry in some Particles that are salubrious, and carry out others which are noxious. The Air once breathed is certainly altered. It is unfit to be breathed again. The Body is said to render unfit for Respiration a Gallon of Air in a Minute. 4 Persons in a Coach would render unfit, 4 Hogsheads of Air in an Hour, which is more than the Coach would hold, which shews the Necessity of keeping the Windows open, and of frequently airing your dining Rooms, keeping Rooms and Bed Chambers. I suspect that the Health of Mankind is much injured by their Inattention to this Subject.[1]

Mr. Hartley, Mr. Franklin, Mr. Jay, Mr. Laurens, met me, at my House, Hotel du Roi, Au Carrousel, this Evening, and We exchanged with Mr. Hartley Full Powers, and entered into Conferences.

Mr. Hartley made Us the following Proposition in writing, viz.

"Whereas it is highly necessary that an Intercourse of Trade and Commerce should be opened, between the People and Territories, belonging to the Crown of Great Britain, and the People and Territories of the United States of America, and whereas it is highly expedient, that the Intercourse between Great Britain and the said United States, should be established, on the most enlarged Principles of reciprocal Benefit to both Countries; but from the Distance between Great Britain and America, it must be a considerable Time, before any Convention or Treaty for establishing and regulating the Trade and Intercourse between Great Britain and the said United States of America, upon a permanent Foundation can be concluded: Now, for the Purpose of making a temporary Regulation of the Commerce and Intercourse between Great Britain and the said United States of America

"It is agreed, that all the Citizens of the United States of America, shall be permitted to import into, and export from any Part of his Britannick Majestys Dominions in American Ships, any Goods, Wares and Merchandises, which have been so imported or exported by the Inhabitants of the British American Colonies, before the Commencement of the War, upon payment of the same Duties and Charges, as the like sort of Goods or Merchandize, are now or may be subject and liable to, if imported by British subjects, in British Ships, from any British Island or Plantation in America. And that all the Subjects of his Britannick Majesty shall be permitted to import and to export from any Part of the Territories of the thirteen United States of America, in British Ships, any Goods, Wares and Merchandizes, which might have been so imported or exported by the Subjects of his Britannic Majesty, before the Commencement of the War, upon Payment of the same Duties and Charges, as the like Sort of Goods, Wares and Merchandizes are now or may be subject and liable to if imported in American Ships, by any of the Citizens of the United States of America.

"This Agreement to continue in Force untill—

"Provided always that nothing contained in this Agreement, shall at any Time hereafter, be argued, on either Side, in Support of any future demand or Claim." [2]

Mr. Hartley withdrew and We entered into Consultation, upon his Proposition.

We agreed to write a Line to Mr. Hartley to enquire if he thought himself authorized to sign that Agreement without further orders from St. James's. The Gentlemen proposed that I [should write it] [3] as first in the Commission. I answered that in that Case I must have their Sanction to the Letter. They desired me to draw one. I sat down to the Table and wrote

Sir

The American Ministers have done me the Honour to direct me, to present you their Compliments, and desire to be informed whether you think yourself sufficiently authorized to agree and subscribe to the Proposition you have made them this Evening, without further Instructions or Information from your Court.

Dr. Franklin moved that the Secretary should sign and send it, which was agreed, the Letter being approved in the foregoing Words.

The Gentlemen desired me to draw an Answer to Mr. Grands Letter, and a Letter to the Bankers in Amsterdam which I agreed to do and lay it before them at their next Meeting.

---

<sup>1</sup> This passage shows some advance in JA's views on fresh air since his dispute with Franklin over open or closed windows when they lodged together on their way to the conference with Lord Howe on Staten Island; see JA's Autobiography under date of 9 Sept. 1776.

<sup>2</sup> Quotation marks have been regularized by the editors in the foregoing *projet* by Hartley.

<sup>3</sup> Words in brackets have been supplied by the editors. In the MS JA inserted a caret at this point but did not fill the gap in sense.

### MAY 22. THURSDAY.

This Morning I drew the following Letters to be laid before the Ministers this Evening.

Sir                                                          Paris May 22. 1783

We have received the Letter you did Us the Honour to write Us on the          day of this Month, containing a brief State of the Affairs of the United States in your hands. We see the Difficulties you are in, and are sorry to say that it is not in our Power to afford you any Relief.

We have &c.

Mr. Grand<sup>1</sup>

Gentlemen

Mr. Grand has laid before Us, a State of the Affairs of the United States, under his Care, and the Demands upon him for Money to discharge the Bills drawn upon him, are such as to require some Assistance from you, if the Demands upon you will admit of it.

If therefore, the State of the Cash in your Hands compared with the Draughts made upon you, will allow of it, We advise you to remit to Mr. Grand, on Account of the United States, the Amount of five Millions of Livres Tournois, and We doubt not that Congress and their Minister of Finances will approve of it, although We have not in Strictness Authority to give orders for it.

We have &c.

Messrs. Wilhem and Jan Willink
   Nicholas and Jacob Van Staphorst
     and
   Dela Lande and Fynje, Bankers of the United States of America, at Amsterdam.

This Morning I also drew the following to be laid before the Gentlemen this Evening.

Articles

Agreed upon by and between David Hartley Esq., Minister Plenipotentiary of his Britannic Majesty for [*line and a half left blank in MS*] in behalf of his said Majesty, on the one part and J.A. B.F. J.J. and H.L. Ministers Plenipotentiary of the United States of America, for treating of Peace with the Minister Plenipotentiary of his said Majesty, on their behalf on the other Part

in Addition

to those agreed upon, on the 30th day of November 1782, by and between Richard Oswald Esq., the Commissioner of his Britannic Majesty for treating of Peace, with the Commissioners of the United States of America, in behalf of his said Majesty, on the one Part, and the said J.A. B.F. J.J. and H.L. Commissioners of the said States for treating of Peace, with the Commissioner of his said Majesty, on their Behalf, on the other Part.

Whereas it is expedient, that an Intercourse and Commerce should be opened, between the People and Territories subject to the Crown of Great Britain, and those of the United States of America, and that this Intercourse and Commerce, should be established, on the most enlarged Principles of reciprocal Benefit to both Countries

1. It is agreed that Ministers shall be forthwith nominated and vested with full Powers to treat, agree and conclude upon a permanent Treaty of Commerce, between the two Powers and their respective Citizens, Subjects and Countries.

2. For the Purpose of a temporary Regulation of such Intercourse and Commerce it is agreed, that the Citizens of the United States shall import into and export from, any part of the Dominions subject to the Crown of Great Britain, in American Ships, any Goods, Wares, and Merchandises, which have been so imported or exported, by the Inhabitants of the British American Colonies before the Commencement of the late War, paying only the same Duties and Charges, as the like Sort of Goods or Merchandises, are now, or may be subject to, if imported by British Subjects in British Ships, from any British Island or Plantation in America: And that the Subjects of his Britannick Majesty, shall import to and export from any Part of the Territories of the United States of America, in British Ships, any Goods, Wares and Merchandize, which might have been so imported or exported, by the Subjects of his Britannick Majesty, before the Commencement of the War, paying the same Duties and Charges, as the like Sort of Goods, Wares and Merchandizes, are now or may be sub-

ject to, if imported in American Ships, by any of the Citizens of the said United States.

This Agreement to continue in force for all Vessells which shall sail from any Port of either Party, on or before the      day of      and no longer.

Provided Always that nothing in this Agreement shall at any time hereafter be argued on either Side, in support of any Proposition which may be made, in the future negotiation of a permanent Treaty of Commerce.

It was observed last Evening that all the Laws of Great Britain, for the Regulation of the Plantation Trade, were contrived solely for the Benefit of Great Britain.

These Laws therefore ought not now to be *the* Regulation, which ought now to be for the reciprocal Benefit of both. The new System of Commerce, the permanent Treaty ought to be framed for the Benefit of the United States, as much as for that of G. Britain. Will not this temporary Revival of the old partial System, encour[a]ge British Merchants and Statesmen to aim at the perpetuation of it in the Treaty? Will not our making such a Convention, be a temptation to the British Court to postpone the definitive Treaty? perhaps to be indifferent about ever signing a definitive Treaty.

By this Project of Mr. Hartleys, American Manufactures are excluded from the British Dominions, but British Manufactures are not excluded from the United States. Americans are excluded from carrying the Productions of other Countries to the British Dominions: But Britains are not excluded, from carrying the Productions of other Countries to America.—Two Instances of Partiality, and Inequality, which may be Seeds of discord. Mens Minds cannot be contented, under Partiality, among Equals. They think it as it is Injustice. It is humiliating. It is thought disgracefull.

The Dutch will allow Americans to bring their Manufactures, and those of other Countries to Amsterdam, and this Attraction will draw our ships to that Market. We may carry hatts, Sperma Cœti Candles, &c. from America, Wines from Portugal, Spain or France to Holland, Sugars &c. from the W. India Islands, to Holland &c.

If other Nations allow Americans, to carry any Thing to them which Britain forbids, this will allure them to foreign Ports, and drive them from those of Britain.

At 10 this morning Mr. Hartley called upon me. Said he had received our Note of last night, and had reflected upon our Question, reviewed his Instructions and called upon the Duke of Manchester to consult with him, and upon the whole he thought he must wait the Return of a Courier which he should send off tomorrow.

I told him that his Court must be sensible, if the Trade was renewed upon the old System, it must be upon that System entire, and even then it would be a Reciprocity all on one Side, all in favour of Great Britain. That if they thought of excluding Us from the West India Trade, they must think, it would obstruct our Agreement, and I was afraid if he mentioned it, and thus put it into the Heads of the Council, they would embarrass him with some wrong orders about it. He said he should support what was right as We wished it in his Dispatches, and so would the Duke of Manchester, but they thought it most prudent to send to London for orders.

He then said he had heard a Story, in which the Marquis de la Fayette was named, that the French Court had applied to the American Ministers to know if they would come into the definitive Treaty, under the Mediation of the two Imperial Courts. That We answered that such a Thing might be very well, but We could not help observing, that those Courts had not acknowledged our Independence as yet. The Reply was that accepting the Mediation would be acknowledging our Independance.—Whence came this Story? Secrets will always be thus kept, while Negotiations are carried on by such circuitous Messages.[2]

At Eleven returned Visits to Mr. Fitch and Mr. Boylstone, and then to the Baron de Waltersdorf, Chamberlain of the King of Denmark, who remarked to me, that he was surprized that his Court had never been informed, that Mr. Dana had Powers to treat with Denmark. I told him that Mr. Dana had been advised against communicating it. But that his Court might send a Full Power to their Minister at Petersbourg, to treat and conclude with any Minister of the United States vested with equal Powers. And the Conferences might begin as soon as they please. He said that he hoped the Dutch would not regain all their Trade but that the Northern Nations would retain some of it. That he thought St. Eustatia would be of no Value in future, as the King had made St. Thomas's a free Port. That Vessells might lie in Safety at St. Thomas's in the hurricane Months but not at St. Eustatia. He said that some Danish Vessells had gone to America loaded with Linnens, Duck, Sail Cloth, &c.

The following is a Copy of the order in Council of 14 May 1783, delivered to Us last night by Mr. Hartley.

At the Court of St. James 14 May 1783
Present
The Kings most excellent Majesty in Council.

Whereas by an Act of Parliament passed this Session, intituled, "an Act for preventing certain Instruments from being required, from Ships belonging to the United States of America, and to give to his Majesty for a limited Time certain Powers for the better carrying on Trade and Commerce between the Subjects of his Majestys Dominions and the Inhabitants of the said States," it is among other Things enacted that during the Continuance of the said Act, it shall and may be lawful for his Majesty, in Council, by order or orders to be issued and published, from Time to Time, to give such Directions, and to make such Regulations, with Respect to Duties, Drawbacks or otherwise for carrying on the Trade and Commerce between the People and Territories belonging to the Crown of Great Britain, and the People and Territories of the said United States, as to his Majesty in Council shall appear most expedient and salutary, any Law, Usage or Custom to the contrary notwithstanding:

His Majesty doth therefore, by and with the Advice of his Privy Council, hereby order, and direct, that any Oil, or any unmanufactured Goods or Merchandizes, being the Growth or Production of any of the Territories of the said United States of America, may untill further order, be imported directly from thence into any of the Ports of this Kingdom, either in British or American Ships, by British Subjects, or by any of the People inhabiting in and belonging to the said United States, or any of them, and such Goods or Merchandizes shall and may be entered and landed in any Port in this Kingdom, upon Payment of the same Duties as the like Sort of Goods, are, or may be subject and liable to, if imported by British Subjects, in British Ships, from any British Island or Plantation in America and no other, notwithstanding such Goods or Merchandizes, or the Ships in which the same may be brought, may not be accompanied with the Certificates or Documents heretofore required by Law. And it is hereby further ordered and directed that there shall be the same Drawbacks, Exemptions and Bounties on Merchandizes and Goods exported from Great Britain into the Territories of the said United States of America, or any of them, as are allowed upon the Exportation of the like Goods or Merchandizes, to any of the Islands, Plantations or Colonies, belonging to the Crown of Great Britain in America; and it is hereby farther ordered and directed, that all American Ships and Vessells which shall have voluntarily come into any Port of Great Britain since the 20th. of January 1783, shall be admitted to an Entry and after such Entry made, shall be entitled together with the Goods and Merchandizes on board the same Ships and Vessells, to the full Benefit of this order. And the Right Honourable the Lords Commissioners of his Majestys Treasury and the Lords Commissioners of the Admiralty, are to give the necessary Directions herein, as to them may respectively appertain.   Signed  Wm. Fawkener.[3]

Copy of Mr. Hartleys Full Power, exchanged with that of the American Ministers 19 May 1783.

George R.

George the Third, by the Grace of God, King of Great Britain, France, and Ireland, Defender of the Faith, Duke of Brunswick and Lunenbourgh, Arch Treasurer and Prince Elector of the Holy Roman Empire &c. To all to whom these Presents shall come, Greeting.

Whereas for the perfecting and establishing the Peace, Friendship, and good Understanding, so happily commenced by the Provisional Articles signed at Paris the thirtieth Day of November last by the Commissioners of Us and our good Friends, the United States of America, vizt., New-Hampshire, Massachusetts-Bay, Rhode Island, Connecticut, New York, New Jersey, Pensylvania, the Three lower Counties on Delaware, Maryland, Virginia, North Carolina, South Carolina and Georgia, in North America, and for opening, promoting and rendering perpetual, the mutual Intercourse of Trade, and Commerce, between our Kingdoms and the Dominions of the said United States, We have thought proper to invest some fit Person with full Powers, on our Part, to meet and confer, with the Ministers of the said United States now residing at Paris, duly authorized for the accomplishing of such laudable and salutary Purposes. Now know Ye, that We, reposing special Trust and Confidence, in the Wisdom, Loyalty, Diligence and Circumspection of our Trusty and Welbeloved, David Hartley Esquire (on whom We have therefore conferred the Rank of our Minister Plenipotentiary), have nominated, constituted and appointed, and by these Presents do nominate, constitute and appoint our true, certain and undoubted Commissioner, Procurator and Plenipotentiary; giving and granting to him all and all manner of Faculty, Power and Authority, together with General as well as Special order (so as the General do not derogate from the Special, nor the Contrary) for Us and in our Name, to meet, confer, treat and conclude, with the Minister or Ministers furnished with sufficient Powers, on the Part of our said Good Friends, the United States of America, of and concerning all such Matters and Things as may be requisite and necessary for accomplishing and compleating the several Ends and Purposes, herein before mentioned, and also for Us and in our Name to sign such Treaty or Treaties, Convention or Conventions, or other Instruments whatsoever as may be agreed upon in the Premisses, and mutually to deliver and receive the same in Exchange, and to do and perform all such other Acts, matters and Things as may be any Ways proper and conducive to the Purposes abovementioned, in as full and ample Form and manner, and with the like Validity and Effect as We Ourself, if We were present, could do and perform the same: Engaging and promising our Royal Word, that We will accept, ratify and confirm in the most effectual manner, all such Acts, matter and Things, as shall be so transacted and concluded by our aforesaid Commissioner, Procurator and Plenipotentiary, and that We will never suffer any Person to violate the same, in the whole or in Part, or to act contrary hereto.

In Testimony and Confirmation of all which, We have caused our Great Seal of Great Britain to be affixed to these Presents signed with our Royal Hand. Given at our Palace at St. James's, the fourteenth Day of May in the Year of our Lord one Thousand seven hundred and Eighty three and in the Twenty third Year of our Reign.

I David Hartley the Minister above named certify the foregoing to be a true Copy, from my original Commission; delivered to the American Ministers this 19 Day of May 1783.   Signed  D. Hartley.

Mr. Hartleys Observations and Propositions left with the American Ministers the 21. May 1783.[4]

A Proposition having been offered by the American Ministers for the Consideration of his Britannick Majestys Ministers, and of the British Nation, for an entire and reciprocal Freedom of Intercourse and Commerce between Great Britain and the American United States, in the following Words, viz.

"That all Rivers, Harbours, Lakes, Ports and Places belonging to the United States or any of them, shall be open and free to the Merchants and other Subjects of the Crown of Great Britain, and their trading Vessells, who shall be received, treated and protected, like the Merchants and trading Vessells of the State in which they may be, and be liable to no other Charges or Duties.—And reciprocally, that all Rivers, Harbours, Lakes, Ports and Places under the Dominion of his

131

Britannic Majesty, shall be open and free to the Merchants and trading Vessells of the said United States, and of each and every of them, who shall be received, treated and protected, like the Merchants and trading Vessells of Great Britain, and be liable to no other Charges and Duties, saving always to the Chartered Trading Companies of Great Britain, such exclusive Use and Trade of their respective Ports and Establishments, as neither the other Subjects of Great Britain, or any the most Favoured Nation participate in."

It is to be observed that this Proposition implies a more ample Participation of British Commerce than the American States possessed, even under their former Connection of dependence upon Great Britain, so as to amount to an entire Abolition of the British Act of Navigation, in respect of the thirteen United States of America; and although Proceeding on their Part, from the most conciliatory and liberal Principles of Amity and Reciprocity, nevertheless, it comes from them as newly established States and who in Consequence of their former Condition of Dependence, have never yet had any established System of national Commercial Laws, or of commercial Connections by Treaties with other nations, free and unembarrassed of many weighty Considerations which require the most scrupulous Attention and Investigation on the Part of Great Britain, whose antient System of national and commercial Policy, is thus suddenly called upon to take a new Principle for its Foundation, and whose Commercial Engagements with other ancient States may be most materially affected thereby. For the Purpose therefore of giving sufficient Time, for the Consideration and discussion of so important a Proposition, respecting the present established System of the commercial Policy and Laws of Great Britain, and their subsisting commercial Engagements with foreign Powers, it is proposed that a temporary Intercourse of Commerce shall be established between Great Britain and the American States, previously to the Conclusion of any final and perpetual Compact. In this intervening Period, as the strict Line and Measure of Reciprocity from various Circumstances, cannot be absolutely and compleatly adhered to, it may be agreed, that the Commerce between the two Countries shall revive, as nearly as can be, upon the same Footing and Terms as formerly subsisted, between them; provided always that no Concession on either Side, in the proposed temporary Convention, shall be argued hereafter, in support of any future Demand or Claim. In the mean time, the Proposition above stated may be transmitted to London, requesting with his Majestys Consent that it may be laid before Parliament for their Consideration.

It is proposed therefore, that the unmanufactured Produce of the United States should be admitted into Great Britain, without any other Duties, those imposed during the War excepted, than those to which they were formerly liable. And it is expected in return that the Produce and Manufactures of Great Britain, should be admitted into the United States in like manner. If there should appear any Want of Reciprocity in this Proposal, upon the Grounds of asking Admission for British Manufactures into America, while no such Indulgence is given to American Manufactures in Great Britain; the Answer is obvious, that the Admission of British Manufactures into America, is an Object of Great Importance, and equally productive of Advantages to both Countries; while on the other hand, the Introduction of American Manufactures into Great Britain, can be of no Service to either, and may be productive of innumerable Frauds, by enabling Persons so disposed, to pass foreign European Goods, either prohibited or liable to great Duties, by the British Laws, for American Manufactures.

With regard to the West Indies, there is no Objection to the most free Intercourse between them and the United States. The only Restriction proposed to be laid upon that Intercourse is prohibiting American Ships carrying to those Colonies any other Merchandize than the Produce of their own Country. The same Observation may be made upon this Restriction as upon the former. It is not meant to affect the Interest of the United States, but it is highly necessary, least foreign Ships should make Use of the American Flagg to carry on a Trade with the British West Indian Islands.

It is also proposed upon the same Principle to restrain the Ships that may trade to Great Britain from America, from bringing foreign Merchandize into Great Britain. The Necessity of this Restriction is likewise evident, unless Great Britain meant to give up her whole Navigation Act. There is no Necessity of any similar Restrictions, on the Part of the American States; those States not having as yet, any Acts of Navigation.

[1] Ferdinand Grand's letter to the Commissioners, 10 May, to which the foregoing is a reply, is printed in Wharton, ed., *Dipl. Corr. Amer. Rev.*, 6:420–421.

[2] See Lafayette to the Commissioners, 12 May (same, p. 424).

[3] After quoting this document in his "second autobiography," JA added the following comment:

"*Quincy. Dec.* 15, 1811.—This Order in Council is the first link in that great chain of Orders in Council, which has been since stretched and extended, till it has shackled the commerce of the whole globe; that of Great Britain herself, as much as any other. Poor unfortunate commerce! Universal commerce! The commerce of the world! Thou art become, like the author of all our calamities, an object of commiseration to every humane and feeling mind! Bound with strong cords and bandages, by the head and shoulders, arms and hands, thighs, legs, and feet, like the unhappy patient in Dr. Rush's tranquilizing chair.

"I have before observed that this moment in English and American history, appeared to me of great importance. That coalition administration, which afterwards subverted the British constitution by the India bill, in one point now subverted it in another by making the thing [i.e. king] absolute in all commercial matters. The law of nature and nations was a part, of the common law of England, and a part an essential part of the constitutional law of the British empire. The maratime and naval law of nations was also a part of the constitutional law of England. Parliament itself had no more authority over it than the king, and the king no more than Zingis Can, or the king of Otaheite. Yet this combination of nobles of all parties undertook by an act of parliament, to divest themselves and the nation of all authority in matters of commerce and navigation, and to make the thing [king] absolute over commerce and the seas, that he might have the power to deprive America of the rights he had so recently acknowledged by the preliminary and provisional treaty. I mean the rights of an independent maratime power" (*Boston Patriot*, 4 Jan. 1811).

⁴ In answer to the proposal for complete commercial reciprocity, the first of the three American *projets* of 29 April, q.v. in the entry of that date, above. This memorial by Hartley is dated 19 May in the Hartley Papers (MiU-C).

## 1783 MAY 23. FRYDAY.[1]

Last Evening, the American Ministers and Secretary met, again at my House, and signed the Letters to Mr. Grand and to the Bankers at Amsterdam.

Mr. Laurens gave it as his Opinion that the Ballance of Trade, for the future between Great Britain and America would be in favour of the latter. I asked him what in that Case would become of the former? He replied She must be humble. . . .[2] She has hitherto avoided trading with any Nation when the Ballance was against her. This is the Reason why She would not trade with France.

This Morning Mr. Laurens called upon me to introduce to me a West India Gentleman from Jamaica, a Mr.         .[3]

Mr. Laurens says the English are convinced that the Method of coppering Ships is hurtfull. The Copper corrodes all the Iron, all the Bolts, Spikes and Nails, which it touches. The Vessell falls to Pieces all at once. They attribute the late Losses of so many Ships to this. That Mr. Oswald made an experiment 20 Years ago, which convinced him that Copper was fatal. He lost a Ship by it.

Mr. Laurens, Mr. Jay, and Mr. Jarret and Mr. Fitch, two West India Gentlemen said to be very rich, dined with me. Mr. Fitch is a Native of Boston, holds an office of Receiver General, I think in Jamaica. Ward Nicholas Boylston was to have dined with me but was taken sick.

Mr. J. told me that the C. de Vergennes turned to him and Mr. Franklin and asked "Ou est Mr. Adams?" Franklin answered "Il est a Paris."—Then turning to Jay he said Ce Monsieur a Beaucoup de

L'Esprit, et beaucoup de Tête aussi.—Jay answered, Ouy Monsieur, Monsieur Adams a beaucoup D'Esprit.[4]

[1] First entry in D/JA/41, which is identical in format with the Diary booklets that precede it.

[2] Suspension points in MS.

[3] Probably the "Mr. Jarret" mentioned below in this entry.

[4] "NOTE—The word tête was an equivoke. It might mean, resolution, or judgment, or obstinacy. This was the first and the last trait which escaped the comte of any pique against me, on account of our former disputes. From my arrival from Holland, in October 1782, to my final departure from France to England in the month of May 1785, I lived on terms of entire civility with the comte de Vergennes, as if no asperity had ever passed between us on either side" (JA in the *Boston Patriot*, 25 Jan. 1812).

## 1783 SUNDAY MAY 25.

Mr. Hartley came in, and shew me a Letter concerning his Beloved Sister whose Case is very dangerous and keeps him in deep Affliction. She is his Housekeeper and Friend. She examines his Writings, and proposes Corrections. She has transcribed his Papers, his American Letters &c. She has laboured much for America, &c.

I made a Transition, and asked what News from England? He said none. I told him I had heard that it was expected by some, that Shelburne would come in. He said No.—I asked him why cant you coalesse with Shelburne as well as North? He said Shelburne is an Irishman, and has all the Impudence of his Nation. He is a Parlaverer beyond all description. He parlavers every Body, and has no Sincerity.[1]

Mr. Barclay dined with me, after having been out to see Dr. Franklin. The Doctor he says is greatly disappointed in not having received Letters from Congress, containing his Dismission. He wants to get out of this, and to be at home with his Family. He dont expect to live long.

[1] "Note, in 1812.—I said nothing to Mr. Hartley, but I had not known and I have never known any proofs of insincerity in Shelburne, more than in Fox and Burke. He was certainly a better friend to America than either of them. I could see nothing in all these attractions and repulsions, these dissolutions and coalitions, these conjunctions and oppositions in London, but national prejudices and family feuds between England, Scotland and Ireland" (JA in the *Boston Patriot*, 25 Jan. 1812).

## MONDAY MAY 26.

I hope for News to day, from the Hague.[1]

[1] Probably concerning the sailing date of P. J. van Berckel, who had been appointed minister from the Dutch Republic to the United States. JA had for some time entertained the hope that the negotiation in Paris would be completed in time for him to accompany Van Berckel. In a letter of 23 May Dumas informed JA that the Dutch minister would sail about 15 June, and also that

he (Dumas) had received Congress' instrument ratifying the Dutch treaty (Adams Papers). On 29 May JA answered that he could not leave Paris and ordered Dumas to exchange ratifications with the Dutch government (LbC, Adams Papers).

### 1783 JUNE 1. SUNDAY.

The Loadstone is in Possession of the most remarkable, wonderfull and misterious Property in Nature. This Substance is in the Secret of the whole Globe. It must have a Sympathy with the whole Globe. It is governed by a Law and influenced by some active Principle that pervades and operates from Pole to pole, and from the Surface to the Center and the Antipodes. It is found in all Parts of the Earth. Break the Stone to Pieces, and each Morcel retains two Poles, a north and a south Pole, and does not loose its Virtue. The Magnetic Effluvia are too subtle, to be seen by a Microscope, yet they have great Activity and Strength. Iron has a Sympathy with Magnatism and Electricity, which should be examined by every Experiment, which Ingenuity can devise.

Has it been tryed whether the Magnet looses any of its Force in Vacuo? in a Bottle charged with Electrical Fire? &c. This Metal called Iron may one day reveal the Secrets of Nature. The primary Springs of Nature may be too subtle for all our Senses and Faculties. I should think however that no Subject deserved more the Attention of Philosophers or was more proper for Experiments than the Sympathy between Iron and the magnetical and Electrical Fluid.

It would be worth while to grind the Magnet to Powder and see if the Dust still retained the Virtue. Steep the Stone or the Dust in Wine, Spirits, Oyl and other fluids to see if the Virtue is affected, increased or diminished.

Is there no Chimical Proscess, that can be formed upon the Stone or the Dust to discover, what it is that the magnetic Virtue resides in.

Whether boiling or burning the Stone destroys or diminishes the Virtue.

See whether Earth, Air, Water or Fire any wise applied affects it, and how.[1]

Mr. Laurens came in, in the Morning and We had a long Conversation upon his proposed Journey to England to borrow some Money. I explained to him the Manner and Conditions of my Loan in Holland.

Dined at the Spanish Ambassadors with the Corps Diplomatick. Mr. Markoff was there, and was very civil.

D'Aranda lives now in the End of the New Buildings which compose the Façade de la Place de Louis 15. From the Windows at the End you look into the grand Chemin, the Champs eliseés, and the

Road to Versailles. From the Windows and Gallery in the Front you see the Place de Louis 15, the Gardens of the Tuilleries, the River and the fine Rowe of Houses beyond it, particularly the Palais du Bourbon and the Dome of the Invalids. It is the finest Situation in Paris.

Mr. Fitzherbert told me, I might depend upon it the present Ministry would continue, at least untill the next Meeting of Parliament. He says there is little to be got in the Company of the Corps Diplomatick. They play deep, but there is no Conversation.

He says he is acquainted with half a Dozen of the Women of the Town, who live in houses which with their Furniture could not have cost less than twenty five Thousand Pounds. They live in a style he says which cannot be supported for less than two Thousand a Year. These are kept by grave People, Men of the Robe, &c. He says there is nothing like this in London. That the Corruption of manners, is much greater here, than there.[2]

Mr. De Stutterheim the Minister from Saxony came to me and said, he had received orders from his Court to propose a Treaty of Commerce with the United States. He said he had spoken to Mr. Franklin about it. I asked him if Mr. Franklin had written to Congress upon it. He said he did not know. I told him that I thought Mr. Dana at Petersbourg had Power to treat tho not to conclude. He said he would call upon me, some Morning at My House, to consult about it.

Herreria dined there and the Duke of Berwick.

[1] "NOTE—If anyone should ask how it happened that I should amuse myself with subjects and questions so entirely out of my sphere, my answer is, that Mr. Hartley's communications had convinced us that the coalition had determined to do nothing by treaty, but determined all things ex parte, by their orders in Council. I was there[fore] idle as well as ignorant" (JA in the *Boston Patriot*, 25 Jan. 1812).

[2] This paragraph was omitted by CFA in editing JA's Diary.

### 1783 JUNE [8].

Went to Versailles on the Day of Pentecôte.

#### JUNE 17. TUESDAY.[1]

Went to Versailles, had a Conference with the C[omte] de V[ergennes].—Made my Court with the Corps Diplomatick, to the King, Queen, Monsieur, Madame, the C. D'Artois, Madame Elizabeth, Madames Victoire and Adelaide.[2] Dined with the Ambassadors. Had much Conversation with the Ambassadors of Spain, Sardinia, Mr. Markoff, from Russia, the Dutch Ambassadors, &c.—It was to me, notwithstanding the Cold and Rain, the Equinoxial Storm at the Time of the Solstice, when all the Rooms had Fires like Winter, the most agreable Day I ever saw at Versailles. I had much Conversation too with the Duke of Manchester and Mr. Hartley, Dr. Franklin and his Son, Mr. Waltersdorf &c. Mr. Maddison and Mr. Shirley &c.

The C. de. V. observed, that Mr. Fox was startled at every Clamour of a few Merchants. I answered C'est exactement vrai—and it is so. The C. recommended to Us to discuss and compleat the definitive Treaty, and Leave Commerce to a future Negotiation.—Shall We gain by Delay? I ask myself. Will not French Politicks be employed, to stimulate the English to refuse Us, in future, Things that they would agree to now? The C. observed, that to insist on sending British Manufactures to America, and to refuse to admit American Manufactures in England was the Convention Leonine.[3]

The Duke of Manchester told me, that the Dutch had offered them Sumatra and Surinam, for Negapatnam. But We know says the Duke that both those Settlements are a charge, a Loss.

Brantzen told me he had not desplayed his Character of Ambassador, because, it would be concluded from it, that he was upon the Point of concluding the Peace.

The C. D'Aranda told me he would come and see me. He said Tout, en ce monde, a été Revolution.—I said true—universal History was but a Series of Revolutions.[4] Nature delighted in Changes, and the World was but a String of them. But one Revolution was quite enough for the Life of a Man. I hoped, never to have to do with another.— Upon this he laughed very hartily, and said he believed me.

The Sardinian Ambassador said to me, it was curious to remark the Progress of Commerce. The Furs which the Hudsons Bay Company sent to London from the most northern Regions of America, were sent to Siberia, within 150 Leagues of the Place where they were hunted. He began to speak of La Fonte's Voyage and of the Boston Story of Seymour or Seinior Gibbons, but other Company came in, and interrupted the Conversation.

[1] JA does not mention in his Diary that on 14 June Hartley addressed a long letter, enclosing an equally long memorial (of 1 June), to the Commissioners, the burden of which was that the British navigation acts were not likely to be suddenly altered in favor of the United States, and that the working out of mutually agreeable trade regulations would take considerable time (Wharton, ed., *Dipl. Corr. Amer. Rev.*, 6:465–469, 483–487). From London Henry Laurens wrote his fellow Commissioners on 17 June that Secretary Fox had told him: "The navigation act is the vital of Great Britain, too delicate to bear a touch" (same, p. 493).

[2] "Monsieur" was the Comte de Provence, afterward Louis XVIII; "Madame" was the Comtesse de Provence. The Comte d'Artois, another brother of the King, was afterward Charles X. Madame Elisabèth was the King's sister, and Mesdames Victoire and Adélaïde his

aunts. Madame Campan (*née* Genet), daughter of Edmé Jacques Genet, JA's friend in the French foreign office, gives intimate views of all these royal personages in her *Mémoires sur la vie privée de Marie-Antoinette* ..., Paris, 1823; 3 vols. Further reflections on court life inspired by this visit to Versailles were recorded in a letter from JA to AA, 19 June (Adams Papers; JA, *Letters*, ed. CFA, 2:96–99).

³ A term in Roman law: "a contract in which the advantage is, in the judgement of the Court, manifestly and unfairly one-sided" (*OED*).

⁴ Dash supplied in this sentence.

### WEDNESDAY. JUNE 18.

Visited the Duke de la Vauguion, and had a long Conversation with him. He was glad to hear I had been plusieurs fois a Versailles dernierement. The Duke said he had conversed with the C. de V. and had told him, he thought it would be for the Good of the common Cause, if there were more Communication between him and me. I told him that I had expressed to the C. a desire to be informed of the Intentions of the King concerning the Communication between the U.S. and his Islands, and that the C. had answered, that if I would give him a Note, he would consult with the Marquis de Castries and give me an Answer. He added smiling, you will leave to Us, the Regulation of that, and let Us take a little Care of our Marine, and our Nurseries of Seamen, because We cannot go to your Assistance (Secours) without a Marine.

The Duke said it would be very difficult to regulate this Matter. They could not let Us bring their Sugars to Europe, neither to France nor any other Part. This would lessen the Number of French Ships and Seamen. But he thought We should be allowed to purchase Sugars for our own Consumption. (How they will estimate the quantity, and prevent our exceeding it, I know not.) He said there were Provinces in France, as Guienne and Provence, which depended much upon supplying their Islands with Provisions, as Wheat and Flour &c. I asked him if We should be allowed to import into their Islands, Wheat, Flour, Horses, Live Stock, Lumber of all Sorts, Salt Fish &c. He said it would be bien difficile for Wheat and Flour &c.

### 1783. JUNE 19. THURSDAY. FETE DIEU.

The Processions were less brillant than ordinary on Account of the Storm.

Went with Mr. Hartley in his Carriage to Passy where he made his Propositions for the Definitive Treaty.¹ We had a long Conversation about De Fonte's Voyage from Peru to Hudsons Bay.² He says he found an Inlet and a River which he entered, and navigated untill he came to a Lake in which he left his Ship and followed the Course of a River, which descended, with Falls in it, or rather Rapides, in his Boats untill he came to Hudsons Bay where he found Seimor Gibbons or Sennor Gibbons, Major General Edward Gibbons of Boston as Dr. Franklin supposes. Dr. Franklin had once a Correspondence with Mr. Prince upon this Voyage, and perhaps Mr. Gill in the Journal of Mr. Prince, has some Information about it. The Trade to Hudsons Bay was carried on, by Boston People from its first discovery, untill after the Restoration of Charles the 2d., from whom the Hudsons Bay Company obtained their Charter, and there are several Families in New England descended from Persons who used that Trade, vizt. The Aldens.[3] De Fonte's Voyage was printed in English in a Collection called Miscellanea Curiosa in 1708 and has been lately printed in French in a large Collection of Voyages in 20 Volumes. Dr. Franklin once gave to Lord Bute his Reasons in Writing for believing this a genuine Voyage. De Fonte was either a Spaniard or Portuguese. Enquiry has been made at Madrid, but no Traces could be discovered there of De Fonte or his Voyage.

Cook in one of his Voyages, anchored in the Latitude of Philadelphia 40, on the West Side of the Continent of America and ascertained the Longitude, from whence Dr. F. computes the Distance from Philadelphia to the South Sea to be 2000 Miles. Cook saw several Inlets and he entered that between America and Asia, Kamskatska, where the Passage is not wider than that between Calais and Dover.

The Seperation of America from Asia is between the 60th. and 70th. degree of North Latitude, precisely at the Arctick polar Circle. It is called in the French Maps Detroit du Nord. The northern Streight or Streight of the North. It is near the Archipel du Nord or northern Archipelago. The Point of Land in Asia is under the Dominion of Russia, and is called Russian Tartary. The Streight forms the Communication between the Eastern and the frozen Oceans, the Mer Orientale and the Mer Glaciale. There is a Number of Islands in the Archipelago, and one in the Streight itself called on the Map, Alaschka Island. There is a Sea and a Promontory called Kamskatska situated on the Eastern Ocean within 10 or 12 degrees of the Streight. The 3 Tartarys, Independent Tartary, Chinese Tartary and Russian Tartary form a vast Country, extending from Persia, Indostan and China, to the Point of Asia at the Streights of the North, which divide Asia from America.

What should hinder the Empress of Russia, from establishing a trading City on the Sea of Kamskatska, and opening a Commerce with

Pekin, Nankin and Canton, the Cities of China? It is so near the Islands of Japan, the Phillippines, the Moluccas, that a great Scæne may one day be opened here.

Lima the Capital of Peru is in 10 degrees of S. Lat. So that De Fonte must have sailed by the Istmus of Panama, Mexico, California, New Mexico, C[ape] Mendocin, Canal du Roi George, and entered the River at the Mouth of which is the Isle San Carlos. About half Way between the South Sea and Hudsons Bay is a great Lake. Here it is to search for a North West Passage to the East Indies.

Baffins Bay, Baffins Streight, Davis's Streight, Hudsons Bay, Hudsons Streight, are all one great Inlet of Water, the Entrance of which is a Streight formed by Greenland on one Side and Labradore, on the other.

[1] These are presumably "Mr. Hartley's Six Propositions–June 1783," found, together with the Commissioners' "Answers" (of 29 June), in Lb/JA/15 (Adams Papers, Microfilms, Reel No. 103). Both the propositions and the answers are printed under the arbitrary date 1 June 1783 in Wharton, ed., *Dipl. Corr. Amer. Rev.*, 6:469–470.

[2] See entry of 24 Feb., above, and note there.

[3] The three preceding words were added by JA in the margin of the MS.

### THE HAGUE JULY 23 1783.[1]

I satt off in October for Paris where I arrived on the 26th of Oct. 1782, where the Peace has been made, and I returned here last Night.

[1] This memorandum appears in a letterbook entitled by JA "Holland Vol. 3" (Lb/JA/18, Adams Papers, Microfilms, Reel No. 106).

Before the end of June JA was convinced that there was no hope of obtaining any commercial concessions from Great Britain, and an order in council of 2 July that excluded American vessels from British West Indies ports confirmed his conviction (text of order in JA's letter to Livingston, 14 July, LbC, Adams Papers; Wharton, ed., *Dipl. Corr. Amer. Rev.*, 6:540–542). Since this action came as a complete surprise to Hartley and undermined all his proposals for liberalizing trade relations between the two countries, JA surmised that "Mr. Hartley ... is probably kept here if he was not sent at first merely to amuse Us, and to keep him out of the Way of Embarrassing the Coalition" (to Livingston, 18 July, LbC, Adams Papers; same, p. 560). Bored with the listless and fruitless negotiation in Paris and believing that the Dutch would be quick to take advantage of British restrictions on American trade, JA decided, as he told Livingston in the same letter, to pay a visit to the Netherlands in order "to assist the Loan and to turn the Speculations of the Dutch Merchants, Capitalists and Statesmen, towards America." He also hoped to mend his own health by travel and a change of scene, and he planned to bring JQA back with him to Paris.

### PARIS SEPTR. 7. 1783.[1]

This Morning, I went out to Passy, and Dr. Franklin put into my hand the following Resolution of Congress, which he received last night, vizt.,

By the United States in Congress assembled, May 1. 1783. on the Report of a Committee, to whom was referred a Letter of Feb. 5 from the Honble. J. Adams.

Ordered that a Commission be prepared to Mess[rs]. John Adams, Benjamin Franklin, and John Jay, authorizing them, or either of them in the Absence of the others, to enter into a Treaty of Commerce, between the United States of America, and Great Britain, subject to the Revisal of the contracting Parties, previous to its final Conclusion, and in the meantime, to enter into a Commercial Convention, to continue in Force, one Year.

That the Secretary for Foreign Affairs, lay before Congress, without Delay, a Plan of a Treaty of Commerce and Instructions, relative to the same, to be transmitted to the said Commissioners.    Signed Cha's. Thomson Secy.[2]

[1] This memorandum appears in Lb/ JA/20 (Adams Papers, Microfilms, Reel No. 108).

JA spent a busy fortnight in the Netherlands conversing with his Patriot friends at The Hague and with bankers and merchants in Amsterdam, paying his respects to the Stadholder, and writing lengthy letters to Livingston on the sugar trade, on American commercial opportunities generally, and on European politics. With JQA he left The Hague on 6 Aug. and was back at the Hôtel du Roi on the 9th (JA to Livingston, 10 Aug., LbC, Adams Papers; Wharton, ed., *Dipl. Corr. Amer. Rev.*, 6:641; see also JQA, Diary, 6–9 Aug. 1783).

He found that no appreciable progress had been made in the negotiation at Paris, and on the very day of his return the real explanation of the British ministry's tactics was set down in a letter from London by Henry Laurens to his fellow commissioners. Laurens had seen Secretary Fox, who conceded that the Preliminary Articles left much to be desired but was unwilling to negotiate new terms "under the eye of, or in concert with, the court of France"; it would be much better to start over again by the appointment of an American minister to London, a measure that Fox said would be very acceptable to the British government (Wharton, ed., *Dipl., Corr. Amer. Rev.*, 6:637–640). It was therefore agreed in Paris that the Preliminary Articles would be ratified without change

except for a preamble declaring them to be the Definitive Treaty (JA to Livingston, 13 Aug., LbC, Adams Papers; same, p. 645). On 3 Sept. this was done, at Hartley's lodgings in the Hôtel d'York (now 56 Rue Jacob in the 6th Arrondissement, a building occupied by the publishing firm of Firmin Didot). In the Adams Papers are copies of the exchange of full powers and a text of the Definitive Treaty as signed and sealed. For a printed text (from one of the two originals in the State Department Treaty File), see Miller, ed., *Treaties*, 2:151–157, with notes on the transmittal and ratification of the Definitive Treaty. John Thaxter brought one of the originals to Congress; see entry of 14 Sept., below. The Commissioners' final report on the five-month negotiation was dated 10 Sept. 1783 (LbC, Adams Papers; Wharton, ed., *Dipl. Corr. Amer. Rev.*, 6:687–691); for some reason the original report sent to Congress is not in place among the Commissioners' dispatches in PCC, No. 85, though a long series of the proposals exchanged by Hartley and the American Commissioners, selected in a somewhat hit-or-miss fashion and not carefully dated, originally enclosed in that dispatch, is present in that volume.

[2] JA's letter to the President of Congress, 5 Feb. 1783, was a protest over the unexplained revocation in July 1781 of JA's commission to negotiate a treaty of commerce with Great Britain, together with a strong plea for the appointment

of an American minister to London in order to perform this and other tasks (LbC, Adams Papers; Wharton, ed., *Dipl. Corr. Amer. Rev.*, 6:242–247). On 1 May a committee of Congress of which Alexander Hamilton was chairman brought in a report on JA's letter which led to the foregoing vote (JCC, 24:320–321). For James Madison's sarcastic observations on JA's letter see his letter to Jefferson, 6 May (Jefferson, *Papers*, ed. Boyd, 6:265). Secretary

Livingston resigned early in June before carrying out Congress' order of 1 May; new instructions were not agreed upon until 29 Oct., and then in terms that omitted Great Britain (JCC, 25:753–757). No commissions were issued under this order, and the new arrangement of the United States foreign service was not settled until the following May; see note 1 on JA's Diary entry of 22 June 1784, below.

## PARIS SEPTR. 14[–6 OCTOBER] 1783.[1]

Septr. 14. Mr. Thaxter took his Leave of me to return to America, with the definitive Treaty of Peace and the original Treaty with the States General.—I had been some days unwell, but soon fell down in a Fever. Sir James Jay, who was my Physician, gave me a vomit, &c. &c.

On the 22d of September, I removed from the grand Hotel du Roi, to Mr. Barclays at Auteuil, where I have continued to this Sixth day of October 1783.[2]

Mr. Thaxter sailed in the Packet, from L'Orient, or rather from the Island of Groa [Groix], on the 26 of Septr. with a good Wind.[3]

At first I rode twice a day in my Carriage, in the Bois de Boulogne: but afterwards I borrowed Mr. Jays Horse, and have generally ridden twice a day, untill I have made my self Master of this curious Forest.

The Pavillon of Bagatelle, built by Mgsr. Comte D'Artois. The Castle of Madrid. The Outlet of the Forest near Pont Neuilly, the Porte which opens into the Grand Chemin, the Castle of Muet [La Muette] at Passy. The Porte which opens to the great Road to Versailles. The other Porte which opens into a large Village, nearly opposite to St. Cleod [Cloud], are the most remarkable Objects in this Forest.[4]

[1] First entry in D/JA/42, a booklet identical in format with those preceding.

[2] See Howard C. Rice Jr., *The Adams Family in Auteuil, 1784–1785 ...*, Boston, 1956. Since the publication of this admirably illustrated brochure on the Hôtel de Rouault and its spacious garden pleasantly dotted with antique statuary, the garden has been filled with a complex of towering metal-and-glass office buildings, the headquarters of La Compagnie Française Pétrole.

[3] He reached Philadelphia, where Pres. Mifflin then was, on 22 Nov. 1783

(Thaxter to JA, 19 Jan. 1784, Adams Papers).

[4] In one of the last of his autobiographical communications to the *Boston Patriot* JA had more to say about his illness in Paris, his move to Auteuil, and his life there than appears in his Diary:

"Mr. Thaxter was gone, and I soon fell down in a fever, not much less violent than that I had suffered two years before at Amsterdam. Sir James Jay who had been sometime in Paris, and had often visited at my house, became

143

my physician, and I desired no better. The grand hotel du Roi, place du Carrousel, where I had apartments, was situated at the confluence of so many streets, that it was a kind of thoroughfare. A constant stream of carriages was rolling by it over the pavements for one and twenty hours out of the twenty-four. From two o'clock to five in the morning there was something like stillness and silence, but all the other one and twenty hours was a constant roar, like incessant rolls of thunder. When I was in my best health I sometimes thought it would kill me. But now reduced to extreme weakness and burning with a violent fever, sleep was impossible. In this forlorn condition, Mr. Thaxter, who had been to me a nurse, a physician and a comforter at Amsterdam, was now separated from me forever. . . . With none but French servants about me, of whom however I cannot complain, for their kindness, attention and tenderness surprised me, I was in a deplorable condition, hopeless of life, in that situation.

"In this critical and desperate moment, my friends all despairing of my recovery in that thoroughfare, Mr. Barclay offered me apartments in his hotel at Auteul, and sir James Jay thought I might be removed and advised it. With much difficulty it was accomplished.

"On the 22d of September I was removed, and the silence of Auteul exchanged for the roar of the carousal, the pure air of a country garden in place of the tainted atmosphere of Paris, procured me some sleep and with the skill of my physician gradually dissipated the fever, though it left me extremely emaciated and weak. . . .

"Lost health is not easily recovered.— Neither medicine nor diet nor any thing would ever succeed with me, without exercise in open air: and although riding in a carriage, has been found of some

use, and on horseback still more; yet none of these have been found effectual with me in the last resort, but walking.— Walking four or five miles a day, sometimes for years together, with a patience, resolution and perseverance, at the price of which, many persons would think, and I have been sometimes inclined to think, life itself was scarcely worth purchasing. Not all the skill and kind assiduity of my physician, nor all the scrupulous care of my regimen, nor all my exercise in carriage and on the saddle was found effectual for the restoration of my health. Still remaining feeble, emaciated, languid to a great degree, my physican and all my friends advised me to go to England, and to Bath, to drink the waters and to bath[e] in them. The English gentlemen politely invited me with apparent kindness to undertake the journey.

"But before I set out I ought not to forget my Phisician. Gratitude demands that I should remember his benevolence. His attendance had been voluntarily assiduous, punctual, and uniformly kind and obliging; and his success had been equal to his skill in breaking the force of the distemper and giving me a chance of a complete recovery in time. I endeavored to put twenty guineas into his hand, but he positively refused to accept them. He said the pleasure of assisting a friend and countryman in distress in a foreign country, was reward enough for him, and he would have no other. I employed all the arguments and persuasions with him in my power at least to receive the purchase of his medicines. He said he had used no medicines but such as he had found in my house among my little stores, and peremptorily and finally refused to receive a farthing for any thing" (*Boston Patriot*, 29 April, 2 May 1812).

AUTEUIL OCTOBER 7. 1783. TUESDAY.

I am now lodged in Mr. Barclays House, which he hires of the Comte de [Rouault].

There is a large Garden, full of all Vegetables and Fruits as Grapes, Pears, Peaches. There is besides a large Flower Garden.

From the Windows in my Chamber and more distinctly, from those of the Chambers, one Story higher, you have a View of the Village of Isis [Issy], of the Castle Royal of Muydon [Meudon], of the Pallace of Belle Vuë, of the Castle of the Duke of Orleans at St. Cleod and of Mont Calvare. Upon the Bank of the River Seine, at the Foot of the Hill, on which stands the Palace of Belle Vuë, is a Glass House, which smoakes night and Day. But in the Night, it blazes at every Window and exhibits a very gay appearance.

Opposite to St. Cleod, is the Village of Boulogne, from whence the Grove or Forest takes its Name. This Wood merits a particular Description.

From Mr. Barclays House, where I now am, I go to the Gate, by which you enter the Bois de Boulogne, from the Village of Auteuil. I turn to the left and follow the Path, which runs in sight of the Stone Wall of 12 feet high which bounds the Forrest, untill I come to a Gate which they call Porte Royal, out of which you go to Versailles. From this Gate I follow the Path which runs near the Boundary Stone Wall, untill I come to the Gate which opens into the Village of Boulogne. I pursue to this Path by the Wall untill I come to the Pavillon of Bagatelle, belonging to the Comte D'Artois. The Estate of the Comte is seperated from the Forest only by a Treillage or a kind of Picketted Wooden Fence. Having passed the Bagatelle you come to the Royal Castle of Madrid, passing this you go out of the Wood into the Grand Chemin, by the Gate called Porte Neuilly, near the new Bridge of that Name. But by following the Path in Sight of the Stone Wall which seperates the Forrest from the Grand Chemin, you come to the Gate, which is called Porte Maillot, at the Plain de Sablons. By following the Grand Road from this Gate, you come to the Royal Castle of Muet, at Passy, near which is the Gate by which you enter the Forest from Passy. By following the Path near the Stone Wall, which bounds the Wood, You come to the Gate, at Auteuil, by which We first entered the Forest.[1]

Near the Center of the Forest, is a Circle, of clear Ground, on which are no Trees or Shrubbs. From the Center of this Circle, proceed Avenues in all Directions. One goes to the Porte Royale, another to the Village of Boulogne, another to the Castle of Madrid, another to the Castle of Muet at Passy, and another to the Gate of Auteuil.

In riding over this Forrest, you see some neat Cattle, some Horses, a few Sheep, and a few Deers, Bucks, Does and Fawns, now and then a Hare and sometimes a few Patridges. But Game is not plenty in this Wood.

145

In this Village of Auteuil, is the Seat of the famous Boileau. It is in the Rue des Garrennes. I have been twice to see it. The Gardener has not the Keys of the Appartements, so that I could not see the Inside of the House: But the Gardiner shew me the Stables, Coach House, and all the Outhouses, and the Garden, which is very large, containing perhaps five or six Acres. It is full of Flowers and of Roots and Vegetables of all Kinds, and of Fruits. Grapes of several sorts and of excellent Quality. Pears, Peaches &c. But every Thing suffers for want of Manure. There is an Acre or two of Ground, without the Garden Fence which belongs to the Estate, which affords Pasture for a Cow, but the Land is poor.

There is an Head of Boileau over the Door, behind the House, and the Heads of two Children, one on each Side of the Door, which are said to be the heads of two Children of his Gardiner, that he was fond of, and ordered to be placed there near him.

The Estate now belongs to Madame Binet, who advertises it for Sale, and it is said asks forty five Thousand Livres for it. She declines letting it, or I should have hired it.

The Principal People in this Village of Auteuil, are Madam Helvetius, who lives but a few Doors from this House, Madame Boufleurs, who lives opposite, &c.

[1] JA's circuit may be traced quite readily on a detail of Jean Rocque's map of 1792, reproduced in Rice, *The Adams Family in Auteuil*, pl. 3.

### 1783. OCTOBER 20. MONDAY.

Set out with my Son and one Servant, Levêque, on a Journey to London. We went from Auteuil, thro the Bois de Boulogne, and went out at the Port de Maillot to St. Dennis, where We took Post Horses. We dined at Chantilly, and lodged at Night at St. Just.

### OCTOBER 21. TUESDAY.

Dined at Amiens, and put up, at night, at Abbeville. The Roads are the best I have ever seen in France. They are not paved, or if they are, the Pavement is covered, with Flynt Stones. They Pick up in the neighbouring Fields, a Species of small Flynt Stones, which they lay along in heaps on the Side of the Road, and with these they mend the high Ways from time to time. The Wheels of the Carriages crushes them to Dust, and they made admirable Roads.

There are no Vines, on this Road. The Country is all sown with Wheat. They are every where, cutting up by the Roots the Elms and other Forest Trees, which formerly ⟨grew⟩ were planted on the Sides of the Roads and introducing Apple Trees in their stead. We found Tea Apparatus's generally in the publick houses, and the hand Irons, Tongs &c. and several other Things more in the English Style than you find in other Parts of France.

1783. OCTR. 22. WEDNESDAY.

Went to Calais. Dined at Boulogne sur mer. Put up at Mr. Dessins.[1]

[1] "When we arrived at Calais, as soon as we had set down in our Chamber, up comes the master of the House, and with a low bow says, *Messieurs je suis vôtre trés humble serviteur; Je suis Dessein* (Yorick's man) *et je viens vous rendre mes devoirs; savoir si vous vouléz de l'argent &c.*" (JQA to Peter Jay Munro, 19 Nov. 1783, NNMC). Pierre Dessin kept the Hôtel d'Angleterre and had been considerably enriched and in some degree immortalized by Laurence Sterne's entertaining portrait of him in *A Sentimental Journey*, 1768. In Aug. 1784 the whole Adams family stopped at the Hôtel d'Angleterre when traveling from London to Paris, and AA2 playfully supposed she saw Yorick's "very Monk" passing her window on his way "to present himself to papa" (AA2, *Jour. and Corr.*, 1:8). They were there again in 1785 when returning to London; see JA to Jefferson, 23 May 1785 (Jefferson, *Papers*, ed. Boyd, 8:161). Dessin proved useful to Jefferson in the troublesome business of importing purchases from England to France; see their correspondence (which establishes Dessin's name, spelled in a great variety of ways by travelers), in same, 9:438, 542; 10:206, 292, 333.

OCT. 23. THURSDAY.

Went on board the Packet at Nine, put off from the wharf at Ten, but had such contrary Winds and Calms, that We did not arrive at Dover untill 3 O'Clock next Morning. I was 18 hours on the Passage. The Packet was 17. She could not come in to the Harbour, made Signals for a Boat, which carried Us ashore for five shillings a head.

I was never before so Sea sick, nor was my Son. My Servant was very bad. Allmost all the Passengers were sick. It is a remarkable Place for it. We are told that many Persons Masters of Vessells and others who were never Sea sick before have been very bad in making this Passage.

OCT. 24. FRIDAY.

We are lodged at Dover, at the Royal Hotel Inn, kept by Charles Mariee. On the Backside of his house is one of the Dover Cliffs; it is an high Mountain, and at this Place is perpendicular, and there is an Appearance of Danger that the Rocks at Top, might split off by their own Weight, and dash to Pieces some of the small brick Houses at its Foot.—White Stone.

I walked round with my Son to the Coach road, and ascended to the

147

Top of this Mountain. It is very steep. It is covered with a thick Sward, and with a Verdure quite to the Top. Upon the Top of the Mountain, there is a plowed Field, sown with Turnips, which look very vigorous. I went into the ploughed ground to examine its Composition, and found it full of Flynt Stones, such as the Road from Chantilly to Calais is made of, and all the Fields on that road are full of. In short the White Stone of the Cliffs, and the Flynt Stone of the Fields, convince me that the Lands here are the same with those on the other Side of the Channell and but a Continuation of the same Soil. From this Mountain, We saw the whole Channel, the whole Town and harbour of Dover. The Harbour is but a Basin and the Town, but a little Village. We saw three small Vessells on the Stocks, building or repairing, and fifteen or twenty small Craft, Fishing Sloops and schooners chiefly in the harbour. It has not the Appearance of a Place of any Business at all. No Manufacture, No Commerce, and no Fishery of any Consequence, here.

The Sheep here are very large, and the Country all around has a Face of Verdure and Fertility beyond that of France in general: but this is owing no doubt to the difference of Cultivation. The Valleys only in France look rich, Plains and Mountains look meagre. Here the Mountain is rich.

The Channell between this and Calais, is full of Vessells, french and English, fishing for Herrings. The Sardine are not caught here.

### SATURDAY OCT. 25.

Went in a Post Chaise, from Dover through Canterbury, Rochester, &c. to Dartford, where We lodged.

### SUNDAY OCTR. 26.

Went to London and the Post Boy carried Us to the Adelphi Buildings in the Strand, to John's Street.[1]

We are at Osbornes Adelphi hotel. I am obliged here to give Thirteen Shillings a day, for a Parler, a bed Chamber, and another Bed Chamber over it for my Son, without any dining Room or Antichamber. This is dearer than my Lodgings at the Hotel du Roi in Paris—half a Guinea for my bed Chamber and Parlour, and half a Crown for my Sons bed Chamber. My Servants Lodging is included in the half Guinea. The Rooms and Furniture are more to my Taste than in Paris, because they are more like what I have been used to in America.

[1] "1783. Sunday, October 26—Went to London; and the post-boy (who upon asking where I would be carried, was answered, to the best inn in London, for

all are alike unknown to me) carried us to the Adelphi Buildings in the Strand. Whether it was the boy's cunning, or whether it was mere chance, I know not; but I found myself in a street which was marked 'John's-street,' the postilion turned a corner, and I was in 'Adams-street.' He turned another corner, and I was in 'John Adams-street.' I thought surely we are arrived in fairy land. How

can all this be?" (JA in the *Boston Patriot*, 6 May 1812).

The Adelphi Buildings had been erected in 1768 by the Adam brothers on arches thrown over the slope below the Strand to the Thames, and handsome streets, some of them named for the builders, were laid out around them (Wheatley, *London Past and Present*, 1:4–7).

## 1783. OCTOBER 27. MONDAY.

Went to see Mr. Jay who is lodged with Mr. Bingham, in Harley Street, Cavendish Square, No. 30.[1] And in the Afternoon went to see Mr. Johnson, Great Tower Hill,[2] who informed me that a Vessell with 1000 Hogsheads of Tobacco is passed by, in the Channel, from Congress to Messrs. Willinks. I gave Mr. Johnson his Letter, as I had left Mr. Hartleys for him at his House, who is gone into the Country, to Bath as he says.

These Adelphi Buildings are well situated on the Thames. In sight of the Terrace is Westminster Bridge one Way, and Black Fryars Bridge on the other. St. Pauls is by Black Fryars Bridge.[3]

[1] William Bingham (1752–1804), Philadelphia financier, land speculator, and (later) U.S. senator, had recently brought his young wife, the former Ann Willing, to Europe on a combined business and pleasure trip; in 1784–1786 the Adamses were to see much of the Binghams at The Hague, Paris, and in London again (*DAB*, under both husband's and wife's names; Margaret L. Brown, "Mr. and Mrs. William Bingham of Philadelphia," *PMHB*, 61:286–324 [July 1937], which quotes relevant material from published Adams correspondence and journals).

[2] Joshua Johnson, who had now returned with his family from Nantes to London and was living in Cooper's Row, Great Tower Hill, which the Adamses used as a mailing address during this visit to England.

[3] There being no further entries in JA's Diary for nearly eight months, this is a fitting place to insert his last autobiographical communication to the *Boston Patriot*, dated at Quincy, 17 Feb. 1812. This extraordinary letter covers the rest of his sojourn in England (to the end of 1783) and his heroic January

crossing of the North Sea, with JQA, in order to save the credit of the United States in Amsterdam. For vivid detail there is perhaps nothing in all of JA's writings that surpasses the latter part of this narrative, and it therefore made an appropriate, though apparently unexpected, finale to his "second autobiography" as published in the *Patriot*. (Precise dates for some of the occurrences recorded in the letter have been editorially supplied, in brackets, from JA's correspondence and JQA's Diary and correspondence.)

"To the Printers of the Boston Patriot

"I was not long at the Adelphi, but soon removed to private lodgings, which by the way were ten times more public, and took apartments at Mr. Stokdale's, in Piccadilly [29 Oct.], where Mr. Laurens had lately lodged before me.— Here I had a great opportunity of learning, for Dr. Bret [typographical error for John Debrett, London bookseller] was at the next door, the state of the current literature of London. I will not enlarge upon this subject at present, if ever. . . .

"Curiosity prompted me to trot about London as fast as good horses in a decent carriage could carry me. I was introduced by Mr. Hartley, on a merely ceremonious visit [15 Nov.], to the Duke of Portland, Mr. Burke, and Mr. Fox; but finding nothing but ceremony there, I did not ask favours or receive any thing but cold formalities from ministers of state or ambassadors. I found that our American painters had more influence at court to procure all the favors I wanted, than all of them. Mr. West asked of their majesties permission to shew me and Mr. Jay, the originals of the great productions of his pencil, such as Wolf, Bayard, Epaminondas, Regulus, &c. &c. &c. which were all displayed in the Queen's Palace, called Buckingham House. The gracious answer of the king and queen was, that he might shew us 'the whole house.' Accordingly, in the absence of the royal family at Windsor, we had an opportunity at leisure [8 Nov.], to see all the apartments, even to the queen's bedchamber, with all its furniture, even to her majesty's German bible, which attracted my attention as much as any thing else. The king's library struck me with admiration; I wished for a weeks time, but had but a few hours. The books were in perfect order, elegant in their editions, paper, binding, &c. but gaudy and extrava[ga]nt in nothing. They were chosen with perfect taste and judgment; every book that a king ought to have always at hand, and as far as I could examine, and could be supposed capable of judging, none other. Maps, charts, &c. of all his dominions in the four quarters of the world, and models of every fortress in his empire.

"In every apartment of the whole house, the same taste, the same judgment, the same elegance, the same simplicity, without the smallest affectation, ostentation, profusion or meanness. I could not but compare it, in my own mind, with Versailles, and not at all to the advantage of the latter. I could not help comparing it with many of the gentlemen's seats which I had seen in France, England, and even Holland. The interior of this palace was perfect; the exterior, both in extent, cost and appearance, was far inferior not only to Versailles, and the seats of the princes

in France, but to the country houses of many of the nobility and gentry of Great Britain. The truth is, a minister can at any time obtain from parliament an hundred millions to support any war, just or unjust, in which he chooses to involve the nation, much more easily than he can procure one million for the decent accommodation of the court. We gazed at the great original paintings of our immortal countryman, West, with more delight than on the very celebrated pieces of Vandyke and Reubens; and with admiration not less than that inspired by the cartoons of Raphaeel.

"Mr. Copely, another of my countrymen, with whom I had been much longer acquainted, and who had obtained without so much royal protection, a reputation not less glorious; and that by studies and labours not less masterly in his art, procured me, and that from the great Lord Mansfield, a place in the house of lords, to hear the king's speech at the opening of parliament [11 Nov.], and to witness the introduction of the Prince of Wales, then arrived at the age of twenty one. One circumstance, a striking example of the vicissitudes of life, and the whimsical antithesis of politics, is too precious for its moral, to be forgotten. Standing in the lobby of the house of lords, surrounded by a hundred of the first people of the kingdom, Sir Francis Molineux, the gentlemen usher of the black rod, appeared suddenly in the room with his long staff, and roared out with a very loud voice—'Where is Mr. Adams, Lord Mansfield's friend!' I frankly avowed myself Lord Mansfield's friend, and was politely conducted by Sir Francis to my place. A gentleman said to me the next day, 'how short a time has passed, since I heard that same Lord Mansfield say in that same house of lords, "My Lords, if you do not kill him, he will kill you."' Mr. West said to me, that this was one of the finest finishings in the picture of American Independence.

"Pope had given me, when a boy, an affection for Murray. When in the study and practice of the law, my admiration of the learning, talents and eloquence of Mansfield had been constantly increasing, though some of his opinions I could not approve. His politics in American

150

affairs I had always detested.—But now I found more politeness and good humor in him than in Richmond, Cambden, Burke or Fox.

"If my business had been travels I might write a book. But I must be as brief as possible.

"I visited Sir Ashton Lever's museum [4 Nov.], where was a wonderful collection of natural and artificial curiosities from all parts and quarters of the globe. Here I saw again that collection of American birds, insects and other rarities, which I had so often seen before at Norwalk, in Connecticut, collected and preserved by Mr. Arnold, and sold by him to Governor Tryon for Sir Ashton. [See JA to Waterhouse, 7 Aug. 1805 (MHi: Adams-Waterhouse Coll.; Ford, ed., *Statesman and Friend*, p. 22–29).] Here also I saw Sir Ashton and some other knights, his friends, practising the ancient but as I thought long forgotten art of archery. In his garden, with their bows and arrows, they hit as small a mark and at as great a distance as any of our sharpshooters could have done with their rifles.

"I visited also Mr. Wedgwood's manufactory, and was not less delighted with the elegance of his substitute for porcelain, than with his rich collection of utensils and furniture from the ruins of Herculaneum, bearing incontestible evidence in their forms and figures of the taste of the Greeks, a nation that seems to have existed for the purpose of teaching the arts and furnishing models to all mankind of grace and beauty, in the mechanic arts no less than in statuary, architecture, history, oratory and poetry.

"The manufactory of cut glass, to which some gentlemen introduced me, did as much honor to the English as the mirrors, the seve China, or the gobeline tapestry of France. It seemed to be the art of transmitting glass into diamonds.

"Westminster Abbey, St. Pauls, the Exchange and other public buildings, did not escape my attention. I made an excursion to Richmond Hill [29 Nov.] to visit Gov. Pownal and Mr. Penn, but had not time to visit Twickenham. The grotto and the quin cunœ [quincunx], the rendezvous of Swift, Bolinbroke, Arbuthnot, Gay, Prior, and even the surly Johnson and the haughty War-burton, will never be seen by me, though I ardently desired it.

"I went to Windsor and saw the castle and its apartments, and enjoyed its vast prospect. I was anxiously shewn the boasted chambers where Count Tallard, the captive of the Duke of Marlborough, had been confined. I visited the terrace and the environs, and what is of more importance I visited the Eaton school; and if I had been prudent enough to negotiate with my friend West, I doubt not I might have obtained permission to see the queen's lodge. But as the solicitation of these little favors requires a great deal of delicacy and many prudent precautions, I did not think it proper to ask the favor of any body. I must confess that all the pomps and pride of Windsor did not occupy my thoughts so much as the forest, and comparing it with what I remembered of Pope's Windsor forest.

"My health was very little improved by the exercise I had taken in and about London; nor did the entertainments and delights assist me much more. The change of air and of diet from which I had entertained some hopes, had produced little effect. I continued feeble, low and drooping. The waters of Bath were still represented to me as an almost certain resource. I shall take no notice of men nor things on the road. I had not been twenty minutes at the hotel in Bath [24 Dec.] before my ancient friend and relation, Mr. John Boylston called upon me and dined with me. After dinner he was polite enough to walk with me, about the town, shewed me the crescent, the public buildings, the card rooms, the assembly rooms, the dancing rooms, &c. objects about which I had little more curiosity than about the bricks and pavements. The baths and the accommodations for using the waters were reserved for another day. But before that day arrived, I received dispatches from America, from London, and from Amsterdam, informing me that the drafts of congress by Mr. Morris, for money to be transmitted, in silver, through the house of Le Couteux, at Paris, and through the Havana to Philadelphia; together with the bills drawn in favor of individuals in France, England and Holland, had exhausted all my loan of the last summer which had cost me so much fatigue and ill health; and that an immense flock of new bills had arrived, drawn in favour of Sir George Baring, or Sir Francis Baring, I forget which, of London, and many other persons; that these bills had been already presented, and protested for non-acceptance; and that they must be protested in their time for non-payment, unless I returned immediately to Amsterdam, and could be fortunate enough to obtain a new loan, of which my bankers gave me very faint hopes. [See Willinks, Van Staphorsts, and De la Lande & Fynje to JA, 2, 23 Dec. (Adams Papers; JA, *Works*, 8:161–164, 166–168), and JA's reply, 29 Dec. 1783 (LbC, Adams Papers).] It was winter; my health was very delicate, a journey and voyage to Holland at that season would very probably put an end to my labours. I scarcely saw a possibility of surviving it. Nevertheless no man knows what he can bear till he tries. A few moments reflection determined me, for although I had little hope of getting the money, having experienced so many difficulties before, yet making the attempt and doing all in my power would discharge my own conscience, and ought to satisfy my responsibility to the public. I returned to London [28 Dec.], and from thence repaired to Harwich [3 Jan. 1784]. Here we found the packet detained by contrary winds and a violent storm. For three days detained, in a very uncomfortable inn, ill accommodated and worse provided, myself and my son, without society and without books, wore away three days of ennui, not a little chagrined with the unexpected interruption of our visit to England, and the disappointment of our journey to Bath; and not less anxious on account of our gloomy prospects for the future.

"On the fourth day [5 Jan.] the wind having veered a little, we were summoned on board the packet. With great difficulty she turned the point and gained the open sea. In this channel, on both sides the island of Great-Britain, there is in bad weather a tremulous, undulating, turbulent kind of irregular tumbling sea that disposes men more to the mal de mer than even the surges of the gulph stream, which are more majestic. The passengers were all at extremities for almost the whole of the three days that we were struggling with stormy weather and beating against contrary winds. The captain and his men, worn out with fatigue and want of sleep, despaired of reaching Helvoet Sluice, and determined to land us on the island of Goree [Goeree, Province of Zeeland]. We found ourselves, upon landing [8 Jan.], on a desolate shore, we knew not where. A fisherman's hut was all the building we could see. There we were told it was five or six miles from the town of Goree. The man was not certain of the distance; but it was not less than four miles nor more than six. No kind of conveyance could be had. In my weak state of health, rendered more impotent by bad nourishment, want of sleep, and wasting sickness on board the packet, I thought it almost impossible, that in that severe weather, I could walk through ice and snow, four miles before I could find rest. As has been said before, human nature never knows what it can endure before it tries the experiment. My young companion was in fine spirits; his gaiety, activity, and attention to me increased as difficulties multiplied, and I was determined not to despair. I walked on, with caution and moderation, and survived much better than could have been expected, till we reached the town of Goree. When we had rested and refreshed ourselves at the inn, we made enquiries concerning our future rout. It was pointed out to us, and we found we must cross over the whole island of Goree, then cross the arm of the sea to the island of Over Flackee, and run the whole length of that island to the point from whence the boats pass a very wide arm of the sea, to the continent, five or six miles from Helvoet Sluice. But we were told that the rivers and arms of the sea were all frozen over, so that we could not pass them but upon the ice, or in ice boats. Inquiring for a carriage of some kind or other, we were told that the place afforded none better, and indeed none other than boor's waggons. That this word boor may not give offence to any one, it is necessary to say, that it signifies no more in Dutch, than peasant in France, or countryman, husbandman or farmer in America. Finding no easier vehicle, we ordered a waggon, horses and driver to be engaged for us, and departed on our journey. Our carriage had no springs to support, nor cushions to soften the seats. On hard benches, in a waggon fixed to the axle-tree, we were trotted and jolted over the roughest road you can well imagine. The soil upon these islands is a stiff clay, and in rainy weather becomes as soft and miry as mortar. In this state they have been trodden by horses, and cut into deep ruts by waggon wheels, when a sudden change of the weather had frozen them as hard as rocks. Over this bowling green, we rolled, or rather hopped and skipped, twelve miles in the island of Goree, and I know not how many more in Over-flackee, till we arrived at the inn at the ferry, where we again put up. Here we were obliged to wait several days, because the boats were all on the other side. The pains of waiting for a passage were much alleviated here by the inexpressible delight of rest after such violent agitations by sea and land, by good fires, warm rooms, comfortable beds, and wholesome Dutch cheer. And all these were made more agreeable by the society of a young English gentleman, not more than twenty, who happening to come to the inn, and finding we had the best room and the best fire, came in, and very modestly and respectfully requested to sit with us. We readily consented and soon found ourselves very happy in his company. He was cheerful, gay, witty, perfectly well bred, and the best acquainted with English literature of any youth of his age I ever knew. The English classics, English history, and all the English poets were familiar to him. He breakfasted, dined, supped, and in short lived with us, and we could not be dull, and never wanted conversation while we staid. As I never asked his name, or his history, I cannot mention either.

"We were obliged to bid high for a passage, and promise them whatever they demanded. Signals were made and at last an ice-boat appeared. An ice-boat is a large ferry boat placed and fastened on runners. We embarked early in the morning. The passage is very wide over this arm of the sea. We were rowed in the water till we came to the ice, when the skipper and his men, to the number of eight or ten perhaps, leaped out upon the ice and hauled the boat up after them, when the passengers were required to get out of the boat and walk upon the ice, while the boatmen dragged the boat upon her runners. Presently they would come to a spot where the ice was thin and brittle, when all would give way and down went the boat into the water. The men were so habituated to this service that they very dexterously laid hold of the sides and leaped into the boat—then they broke away the thin ice till the boat came to a part thick enough for the passengers to leap in, when the men broke away the thin ice forward and rowed the boat in the water till she came to a place again strong enough to bear, when all must disembark again and march men and boat upon the ice. How many times we were obliged to embark and disembark in the course of the voyage I know not, but we were all day and till quite night in making the passage. The weather was cold—we were all frequently wet—I was chilled to the heart, and looked I suppose, as I felt, like a withered old worn out carcase. Our polite skipper frequently eyed me and said he pitied the old man. When we got ashore he said he must come and take the old man by the hand and wish him a safe journey to the Hague. He was sorry to see that I was in such bad health and suffered so much as he had observed upon the passage. He had done every thing in his power and so had his men, to make it easy and expeditious; but they could do no better. This I knew to be true. We parted very good friends, well satisfied with each other. I had given them what they very well loved and they had done their best for me.

"I am weary of my journey and shall hasten to its close. No carriage was to be had and no person to be seen; but by accident a boor came along with an empty waggon. We offered him any thing he would ask to take us to the Briel. Arrived there [10 Jan.] we obtained a more convenient carriage; but the weather was so severe and the roads so rough that we had a very uncomfortable journey to the Hague. Here [12 Jan.] I was at home in the Hotel Des Etats Unis, but could not indulge myself. My duty lay at Amsterdam among undertakers and brokers, with very faint hopes of success. I was however successful beyond my most sanguine expectations, and obtained a loan of millions enough to prevent all the bills of congress from being protested for non-payment and to preserve our credit in Europe for two or three years longer, after which another desperate draft of bills from congress obliged me once more to go over from England to Holland to borrow money. I succeeded also in that which preserved our credit till my return to America, in 1788, and till the new government came into operation and found itself rich enough.

"In the course of my correspondence with you I might have related many anecdotes and made many sketches of characters and drawn many portraits at full length, but I have avoided such things as much as I could. I was never a traveller, nor a book-maker, by profession, and shall never be likely to make profit by making a book.

"Here ends the very rough and uncouth detail of my voyages, journies, labors, perils and sufferings under my commissions for making peace with Great-Britain" (*Boston Patriot*, 9, 13, 16 May 1812).

This was not the end of the present letter, nor did JA intend this letter to be the last installment of his apologia for his public life, for at the end he added a parenthetical paragraph: "As it is not my intention, Messrs. Printers, that my correspondence with you shall be eternal, I have hastened over every thing but documents; and shall continue to be in future, as brief as possible." But no more of his autobiographical letters were printed in the *Patriot*. Perhaps no more were written.

## Abigail Adams' Diary of her Voyage from Boston to Deal, 20 June–20 July 1784[1]

### SUNDAY JUNE 20 1784.

Embarked on Board the ship Active Capt. Lyde commander, with my daughter and 2 servants for London.[2] To go back to the painfull Scenes I endured in taking leave of my Friends and Neighbours will but excite them over again. Suffice it to say that I left my own House the 18 of june. Truly a house of mourning; full of my Neighbours. Not of unmeaning complimenters, but the Honest yeomanary, their wifes and daughters like a funeral procession, all come to wish me well and to pray for a speedy return.—Good Heaven, what were my sensations? Heitherto I had fortified my mind. Knowing I had to act my little part alone, I had possessd myself with calmness, but this was too much for me, so I shook them by the hand mingling my tears with theirs, and left them. I had after this to bid my neices, adieu. And then another scene still more afflictive, an aged Parent from whom I had kept the day of my departure a secret knowing the agony she would be in.[3] I calld at her door. As soon as the good old Lady beheld me, the tears rolled down her aged cheek, and she cried out O! why did you not tell me you was going so soon? Fatal day! I take my last leave; I shall never see you again. Carry my last blessing to my son.—I was obliged to leave her in an agony of distress, myself in no less. My good

Sister Cranch who accompanied me to Town endeavourd to amuse me and to console me. I was glad to shut myself up the remainder of the day and to be denied to company. Saturday I had recoverd some from my fatigue and employed the day in writing to several of my Friends and in getting my baggage on Board. Several of the Passengers calld upon me, amongst whom was a Col. Norton from Marthas Vinyard a Member of our Senate, a grave sedate Man about 50 Years of age. A Mr. Green an english Gentleman who was Seceretary to Admiral Arbuthnot when he was at Charlestown, a high monarckacal man you may easily discover but he behaves like a Gentleman. A Dr. Clark and Mr. Foster, Mr. Spear and a Capt. Mellicot make up the number of our male passengers. We have one Lady a name sake of mine, Mrs. Adams Daughter of the late Revd. Mr. Laurence of Lincoln whose Husband has been absent ever since the War, is a physician and setled abroad. A modest, amiable woman well educated with whom I had a passing acquaintance before I came on Board. Sund[ay] at 12 oclock Mr. Foster sent his carriage for myself and daughter. We bid adieu to our Friends and were drove to Rows Wharf, from whence we allighted amidst an 100 Gentlemen who were upon the Wharf, to receive us. Mr. Smith handed me from the Carriage and I hastned into the ship from amidst the throng. The ship was soon under sail and we went of with a fine wind. About 2 oclock we reachd the light when the Capt. sent word to all the Ladies to put on their Sea cloaths and prepare for sickness. We had only time to follow his directions before we found ourselves all sick. To those who have never been at Sea or experienced this disspiriting malady tis impossible to discribe it, the Nausia arising from the smell of the Ship, the continual rolling, tossing and tumbling contribute to keep up this Disorder, and when once it seazeis a person it levels Sex and condition. My Servant Man was very attentive the first day, not sick at all, made our beds and did what I should not have put him upon in any other Situation for my maid was wholy useless and the sickest of either.[4] Monday mor[nin]g very fogy every Body on Board Sick except the Dr. and 3 or 4 old sea men. My Servant as bad as any. I was obliged to send a petition to the Capt. to release to me Jobe Feild whose place on board the ship I had procured for him.[5] He came and amply supplied the others place. Handy, attentive, obligeing and kind, an excellent Nurse, we all prized him. He continued untill tuesday when we had a fine mor'g. Our sickness abated and we went upon Deck, beheld the vast and boundless ocean before us with astonishment, and wonder. How great, how Excellent, how stupendous He who formed, governs, and directs it.

155

¹ This record of the voyage of AA and AA2 to Europe is inserted here from a duodecimo volume bound in brown boards (M/AA/1, Adams Papers, Microfilms, Reel No. 197) that contains three brief journals kept by AA. The others (20–28 July 1787, 30 March–1 May 1788), since they help to fill large gaps in JA's own Diary, are inserted in their chronological places below. These are the only three diaries known to have been kept by AA.

As far back as 1782 AA had proposed joining her husband in Europe, and had even begged to do so. At first JA gave her qualified encouragement, but on 28 Dec. of that year he informed her that, having resigned all his commissions, he was waiting only for word from Congress to come home himself (Adams Papers). Expecting that the the Definitive Treaty would be settled and signed early in 1783, he was determined to sail home in one of the spring ships from the Texel. The delay in Hartley's arrival in Paris rendered this impossible, and upon receipt of Congress' vote of 1 May approving in principle (though not yet fully authorizing) a negotiation for a commercial treaty with Great Britain, he at once wrote to urge his wife to come over with their daughter, either immediately or in the spring (7 Sept. 1783, Adams Papers). He wrote still more urgently on 14 Oct., adding that "The Family affair which has been mentioned in Several of your Letters, may be managed very well.—The Lady comes to Europe with you.—If the Parties preserve their Regard untill they meet again and continue to behave as they ought, they will be still young enough" (Adams Papers). These allusions are to AA2 and Royall Tyler, a young Harvard graduate (Class of 1776) and lawyer who had recently settled in Braintree and laid siege to AA2's affections; see AA to JA, 23 Dec. 1782, and JA's apprehensive reply, 22 Jan. 1783 (Adams Papers). On Tyler, who later gained celebrity as the first American playwright and distinction as a scholarly judge in Vermont, see DAB. His eventually unsuccessful suit of AA2 is fully documented in letters to be printed in the Adams Family Correspondence, Series II of the present edition. See

also JA's Diary, 1 July 1786, below, and note there.

Despite trepidation about the rigors of the voyage itself and about her responsibilities as an American diplomat's wife in European capitals, AA began preparations late in 1783, but she did not sail until she received absolute assurance that JA was appointed one of the commissioners to negotiate commercial treaties; because of Congress' divided and vacillating mood, this was long in coming (AA to JA, 20 Nov. 1783, 3 Jan. 1784; Elbridge Gerry to AA, 16 April, 7 May 1784; all in Adams Papers). Thomas Jefferson, who on 7 May had been joined with JA and Franklin in the commission, replacing John Jay, hastened to Boston, as he wrote JA, 19 June, "in hopes of having the pleasure of attending Mrs. Adams to Paris and of lessening some of the difficulties to which she may be exposed" (Adams Papers; Jefferson, *Papers*, ed. Boyd, 7:309). But he was too late to forestall her sailing in the *Active*, which was "much crowded" with passengers, as he reported the day after she sailed (to David Humphreys, 21 June; printed in same, p. 311).

² The *Active* was owned, in part, by Joseph Foster of Boston, a fellow passenger on the voyage, as AA notes below; see also her Diary entry of 6 July. The master was Nathaniel Byfield Lyde, also of Boston. The activities of both owner and master may be traced to some extent in the Thwing Catalogue, MHi.

³ JA's mother, Susannah (Boylston) Adams Hall.

⁴ AA reported to JA, 11 Feb. 1784, that she had found "an honest faithfull Man Servant," one John Briesler, "who was brought up in the family of Genll. Palmer, has since lived with Col. Quincy and is recommended by both families" (Adams Papers). Briesler later married Esther Field, the daughter of a Braintree neighbor of the Adamses, who accompanied AA on this voyage, and the two remained fixtures in the households of the Adams family in Europe and America for many years. See AA to Mrs. Cranch, 10 Feb. 1788 (MWA).

⁵ Probably the Job Field who had been confined in Mill Prison, Plymouth, England, as a prisoner of war and to

whom JA had sent two guineas, 24 Oct. 1781, signing himself "your affectionate Friend and Neighbour" (LbC, Adams Papers).

### WEDENSDAY [23 JUNE].

Our ship dirty, ourselves sick. Went upon deck and sent the servants down to clean her up: very little attention is paid on Board this Ship to that first of virtues cleanliness. I wonder this necessary virtue was not ranked amongst those which are called Cardinel and Deified. I have often reflected upon the observation of my best Friend, that of all Beings a Lady at Sea was the most dissagreable. To which I will add an other. That I cannot conceive any inducement sufficient to carry a Lady upon the ocean, but that of going to a Good Husband and kind parent. With the best accommodations it will be dreadfull, to a Lady of any delicacy. All the Gentlemen endeavour to make every thing agreable as possible. But we are but poor company, so sick, and so tosst with the motion of the Ship, which is excessive dissagreable from being too tight, loaded partly with oil which leaks and adds to the *flavour*. You who have never tried the Sea can form no Idea of it. Our *state* room is about 8 foot square with a small grated window. In this room were 3 cabbins for 3 persons, between which one chair could stand. The door opened into the cabbin where the Gentlemen slept. We were obliged to keep open our Door or be suffocated and poisoned so that we only closed it, to undress, and dress and sometimes so sick that we fell from side, to side, in doing it. The first days *Jobe* was obliged to put on and take of our shoes as moveing a finger would set us going. He layd himself down by the side of our door and slept upon the trunks two nights. He is the favorite of the whole Ship. Poor Brisler is not yet come to himself.

### THURSDAY [24 JUNE].

A fine wind and clear air but the Ship going before the wind rolls sadly. Dr. Clark has been well through the whole, and kindly attentive to us. If he had been our Brother he could not have been more so. I know not what we should have done without him. No airs, but a pleasent, Benevolent, friendly kindness, as tho he was rewarded by the disposition alone of doing good. Our Captain an exelent Sea man, but little attention to any thing besides his Sails and his ropes. The Stores on Board good, but the cook misirable. Not a Quarter part utensials enough for the passengers. I regret that I did not know what my Situation was to be. My silver poringer of vast Service, it being the only bowl, poringer or cup belonging to the Ship. I should not have been in this condition if I had not been assured that the Ship supplied every thing. I think the price we paid intitled us to better accommodations. In short I have been obliged to turn cook myself and have made two puddings, the only thing I have seen fit to eat. I have been obliged to order and direct sick as I have been to the cleaning out of the cabbin every day. It is a great misfortune that Ester is so sick. I have been obliged to see to the cleaning of the milk pail which has been enough to poison any body. If we do not die of Dirt now we shall at least eat our peck.

SUNDAY JUNE 27.

I have been so sick that I could not be regular in my journal. We have had two days calm since we came to Sea. The rest of the time good winds which have brought us on our Way rejoiceing, for we have not had any bad weather except rain, thunder and lightning one evening which was not severe. I have been surprized at myself to find that I can sleep notwithstanding the lasshing of the waves; and the tumbling of the vessel. This is the 8th day of our imprisonment. We are now about 200 and 50 leagues from Boston. Our Gentleman all civil and polite. This Mr. G——n mentiond in the former part of this journal as an englishman, I rather think is Scotch, and appears to have inflamibility enough to furnish a Waggon load of Baloons. He talks much. His countanance planly speaks the ruleing passions of his mind. He governs himself as he appears to know what belongs to a Gentleman. Our Captain appears more amiable at sea than on shore, his men all still and quiet, nothing severe towards them has yet appear'd. The mate a droll being; swears for all the rest of the Ship. A Good deal in his manners like Captn. Newcombe, has been several time[s] taken during the war, and has many a sad as well as diverting Story to tell which he does with a countanance as droll as you please. He is a right Tar in his manners.

MONDAY MOR'G 28 JUNE.

A very dissagreeable Night. Wind at the southard near the Banks of Newfoundland. The morning damp. A most voilent Headack. Sick every one of us. Our Ship goes at about nine and 8 knots an hour. No going upon deck. Their is so much confinement on Board a Ship and such a Sameness that one knows not what to do. I have been reading since I came on Board Buchan Domestick Medicine. He appears a sensible, judicious and rational writer.[1]

158

I endeavour to bear my voyage with patience. It was at the request of my dear long absent Friend that I undertook it. I expected it would be dissagreable to be at sea. I can bear every thing I meet with better than the Nausias Smells: it is utterly impossible to keep nice and clean. I strive for Decency, and that can hardly be obtained. How flattering is attention and how agreeable does it render a person when it appears the result of a good Heart, disposed to make every one happy. This Dr. Clark is a very agreable Man. His kindness is of that Benevolent nature which extends to all: to the Servant as well as the Master. He has renderd our passage much pleasenter than it could have been without him, and we have been so sick, that his advise has been of great use to us. By tomorrow we hope to make a quarter part of our passage. When may I begin to look forward to the joyfull day of meeting my long absent partner. Heaven grant it may be a joy, without alloy.

[1] William Buchan, *Domestic Medicine; or, the Family Physician*, Edinburgh, 1769, which went through 21 editions in English by 1813 (BM, *Catalogue*). Among JA's books in the Boston Public Library is listed an edition in French published at Geneva, 1781–1782, in 7 vols., 12mo (*Catalogue of JA's Library*).

### THURSDAY JULY 1 1784.

"And thou, Majestick, Main,
A Secret World of Wonders in thyself
Sound his stupendous praise; whose greater voice
Or bids you roar, or bids your roarings fall."

I have not been able to write a line since Monday when a North east Storm came on and held till Wednesday Mor'g. It was with the utmost difficulty that we could set or lie only by holding by each other with our feet against a table braced with ropes, that we could keep up; and when in bed I was obliged to hold fast by the sides till my hands and wrists aked to keep in: only conceive a great cradle rocking with amaizing force from side, to side, whilst a continual creek from every part of the Ship responded to the roll: not a wink of Sleep to be had, bottles, mugs, plates, every thing crashing to peices.

The Sailors call it a Breize only. But if it was only of that kind: good heaven defend me from a storm. Tho they all allow that it is very unusual at this Season of the year to meet with such a *Breize* there is no time when the vessel does not roll like the moderate rocking of a cradle; it is easily accounted for. The writing shews the constant motion of the Vessel when not one letter in ten, can be made in its proper Shape.[1]

I am more and more of the mind that a Lady ought not to go to sea. It is impossible to preserve that Decency and Cleanliness which ought to be an inherint principal in every female. Even those times which by Gentlemen are Esteemed fine and pleasent cannot fail to be dissagreable to a Lady. I have reflected upon Mrs. Hayley['s] observation to me, that altho she was surrounded with every accommodation that could be obtained on Board a fine large Ship, with agreable company, yet it was a terrible thing for a Lady to attempt, and nothing but the ardent desire she had to visit a Country so distinguished for its noble and ardent defence of the rights of Mankind, could have tempted her at her advanced age to have undertaken a sea voyage.[2] What ever curiosity might prompt, I think I should content myself with the page of the Historian if I had no superiour inducement to visit foreign climes, but when I reflect that for ten years past I have been cut of from a large Share of Domestick happiness by a Seperation from my partner, I think my Sufferings small when I look forward to the recompence and the reward.

> Unutterable happiness! which Love
> alone bestows, and on a *favourd few*
> those sacred feelings of the Heart, informed
> by reasons purest ray.

We have on Board a Mr. Spear, the only single Gentleman of all the passengers. He is a droll mortal and keeps us in good Spirits, which is very necessary on board a Ship. Change of Ideas, says the medical writer, is as necessary for Health, as change of posture. Learned Men often contract a contempt for what they call trifling company. They are ashamed to be seen with any but philosophers. This however is no proof of their being philosophers themselves. No Man deserves that Name who is ashamed to unbend his mind, by associating with the cheerfull and gay. Even the Society of children will relieve the mind, and expell the Gloom which application to study is too apt to occasion.

I transcribe this passage because I think the Health of my best Friend has sufferd from too intense application to study and the perplexing Science of politicks in which he has been constantly engaged. I believe he has sufferd greatly; for Want of his family and a thousand little attentions which sooth the mind and warm the heart. Of all happiness domestick is the sweetest. It is the sun shine of the Heart.

I have great satisfaction in the behaviour of my daughter. The

Struggle of her mind was great, her passions strong, never before calld into opposition; the parting of two persons strongly attached to each other is only to be felt; discription fails.

Yet when once the struggle was over, she has obtaind a Calmness and a degree of cheerfulness which I feard she would not be able to acquire. To this the kindness and attention of Dr. Clark has contributed, tho he knew not that there was more than ordinary occasion for them. His manners are soothing and cheerfull. I do not however esteem him as a Man of superiour parts but he has the art of making Men happy and keeping them so. Says Buchan all that is necessary for Man to know in order to be happy, is easily obtaind and the rest like the forbiden fruit serves only to encrease his misiry.

This if true is no great compliment to Learning, but it is certain that your deep thinkers seldom enjoy Health, or Spirits.

[1] In the two foregoing paragraphs AA's punctuation, unsystematic at best, is unusually difficult to interpret and may not have been rendered exactly according to her intentions, especially in respect to breaks between sentences.

[2] Mrs. Hayley was Mary, sister of the radical politician John Wilkes and the widow of George Hayley, an alderman of London who had had mercantile connections with the Hancock firm in Boston. Renowned for her eccentricities, the Widow Hayley had come to Boston toward the close of the Revolution not merely because she was a devotee of "the rights of Mankind" but because she intended to collect debts due her late husband. The best account of her is that by George Lyman Kittredge in *The Old Farmer and His Almanack ...*, Boston, 1904, p. 9–14, which cites, corrects, and amplifies numerous earlier accounts of a figure who has become part of Boston folklore.

FRYDAY 2 OF JULY.

A fine wind and a pleasent day. Our sea sickness has left us in a great measure. Went all of us upon Deck to enjoy the fresh air, had our rooms cleaned out, begin to feel a little more reconciled to our confinement. Hemd a hankerchief upon Deck. Yesterday mor'g the Capt. sent an embassy to the Ladies representing the distressed state of our poor cow, who by the late Storm had been disabled from standing for several days and tho several attempts had been made to raise her, they had proved unsuccessfull, but as she was particularly devoted to the Ladies, he thought himself under obligation to consult them whether she should be put out of her misiry; or die a lingering Death. Col. Norton was charged with the message and deliverd it in form— upon which Sentance of Death was pronounced upon her; and she was accordingly consigned to a watery grave; but not without mourning for we feel her loss most essentially.—This Day fortnight I left my habitation! Dear Cottage how often do I look back to your peacefull Walls, and Breath a Sigh to your memory. Where is my next abode?

No matter where: so that it only be, in the arms of my dearest, best of Friends. I hardly dare trust my immagination or anticipate the day. Cruel sleep how have you tormented me?

SATURDAY 3 JULY.

A fine morning. Rose by six o clock. Went upon deck. None of the Gentlemen up; our Second Mate, a grand son of the Revd. Dr. Chauncy of Boston. He was upon deck and handed me out. A likely young fellow whose countanance is a good Letter of recommendation. We were all prejudiced in his favour as soon as we saw him; he told me to day that he was taken a prisoner during the War, and carried to Plimouth jail in England where after being confined a Year he made his escape and got to Holland, where he saw Mr. Adams, who gave him money and a letter to Commodore Gillion but that he had sailed for America before he reached the Vessel. He said there were several other prisoners with him at that time who received Money from Mr. Adams. It always give me pleasure when I hear of the kindness of my best Friend to the poor and the needy. The Blessing of him that is ready to perish come upon him. By this said our Blessed saviour shall all Men know that ye are my diciples, if ye have Love to one an other; how many inducements does the Christian Religion offer to excite us to universal Benevolence and Good will towards each other, and yet how often do we suffer the vilest of passions to Dominer over us and extinguish from our Bosoms every generous principal.

This afternoon saw a sail. She bore down to speak with us. Said she was from Abberdeen bound to Novia Scotia, was full of Emigrants —men, women and children. Capt. Cullen in the brigg John, designd afterward for Philadelphia, wanted to put some Letters on Board of us. Our Capt. offerd to lay too, if she would higst out her Boat, but instead of that they attempted to come so near as to throw them on Board, and by that means were in danger of running on Board of us. The Capt. was allarmed, and gave them a hearty broad side: obliged to croud all our sails to keep clear; and tho I was first pleased with the sight of her, I was so much allarmed by our danger, that I wished her many leagues of. We put away as fast as possible without her Letters. —We suppose ourselves in Latitude 42.

SUNDAY JULY 4TH 1784.

This is the Anniversary of our Glorious Independance.

O thou! by whose Almighty Nod the Scale,
of Empires rises, or alternate falls,

Send forth the Saveing virtues round our land
In bright patrol; white peace, and social Love,
The tender looking Charity, intent
on Gentle Deeds, and sheding tears through Smiles,
Undaunted Truth, and Dignity of mind
Courage composed and keen; sound temperance
Healthfull in Heart and look; Clear Chastity
with blushes reddening as she moves along
Disordered at the deep regard she draws;
Rough Industery; Activity untir'd,
With copious Life informed and all awake;
While in the Radient front, superiour shines
That first parental virtue, publick Zeal;
Who throws o'er all an equal wide survey;
And ever museing on the common Weal,
Still Labours glorious with some great design;

Whilst the Nations of Europe are enveloped in Luxery and dissipation; and a universal venality prevails throughout Britain, may the new empire, Gracious Heaven, become the Guardian and protector of Religion and Liberty, of universal Benevolence and Phylanthropy. May those virtues which are banished from the land of our Nativity, find a safe Assylum with the inhabitants of this new world.

We have a fine wind and a clear sky. We go at 7 knots an hour; I hope two Sundays more, will bring us safe to land but we have all conquerd our Sea Sickness, and are able to do much better than for the first ten days. It is said of Cato, that one of the three things which he regreted at the close of Life; was that he had once gone by sea when he might have made his journey by land; alass poor Cato! I fancy thy Philosophy was not proof against this dispiritting disease.

#### TUESDAY JULY 6TH.

I was not able to write yesterday the wind blew so fresh; and not very fair, so that there was too much motion of the Ship. In the afternoon it came on rainy, and continued so through the night, this morning a small north east wind cloudy and unpleasent. Whilst our Friends on shore are melting under a mid Summer Sun; there has been no day so warm at Sea; but what I could wear a double calico Gown, a Green Baize over that a cloth Cloak; and a camblet cloak; lined with Baize; wraped round me, when ever I went up upon Deck.[1] I had no Idea of the difference before I came on Board; this morning before I rose the Dr. came down into the Cabbin and invited us to come up upon Deck and see a porpoise which the mate had killd with a harpoon; this creature has a fine smooth skin; a head resembling a Hog, two fins which he throughs out of water when he swims and rolls over as we often see them; a tail like an anchor and cross way of his Body, a very small Eye, in proportion to its Body; his inwards resemble those of a Humane Body.

We have so few objects to take up our attention on Board that we hardly know how to amuse ourselves. There is no great pleasure in working. I read as much as possible, but sometimes I feel unfit even for that, my Head swims and my sight leaves me. In the evening we generally make a party at Cards. This Mr. Foster who is a passenger with us, is the youngest son of Deacon Foster of Boston; lately married to a daughter of Mr. John Cutlers of Boston; he is in partnership with his Brother William and part owner of this ship. He is a Gentleman of soft and delicate manners, natural good understanding, a merchant, not much acquainted with Books, appears to have a taste for domestick Life, and speaks of his wife as I love to hear every married man speak; with tenderness and affection.

We shall make but small progress to day; our ship moves but slowly.

¹ Thus punctuated in MS. It is not easy to say how many layers of clothing AA is here enumerating.

### THURSDAY JULY 8TH.

If I did not write I should lose the Days of the Weeks. Yesterday a cold wet day. Could not go upon deck. Spent a large part of the day in writing to Mrs. Cranch.¹ Any thing for amusement is agreeable, where there is such an unavoidable sameness.

> "Were e'en paridice my prison,
> I should long to leap, the cristal walls."

The Ship itself is a partial prison, and much more so, when we are confined to our cabbin; we work, read; write; play; calculate our Distance; and amuse ourselves with conjectures of our arriving in port. Some say 28 days, some 30, and some 33, which to me is most likely; if we meet with no worse weather than we have already; we may set it down for an excellent passage tho it should amount to 33 days. To day is wet and fogy, but a fine fair wind, which must reconcile us to the weather. Last evening Mr. Foster came and invited me upon deck; to see what he had heard me express a wish for, the sparkling of the Water, and its firery appearence; this is a phenominan in Nature hitherto unaccounted for; the ocean looks in a light flame, with millions of sparkling Stars, which resemble the fire flies in a dark Night.

This morning saw a large Ship a stern; scarcly a day but what we have seen Birds. The Sailors call them Mother Carys Chickens, and that they portend wind. They have an other adage. That there is no want of wind, when they have women on Board.

[1] On 6 July AA had begun an epistolary journal of her voyage addressed to her sister Mrs. Cranch; this amplifies the present journal at some points, and it continues well beyond it (through 30 July). The original is now in MWA; it was printed by CFA in AA's *Letters*, 1848, p. 157–186.

### FRYDAY JULY 9.

A fine day; but little wind; have been upon Deck the chief of the Day, engaged in reading Campbles political Survey of Great Britain.[1] None of the advantages which he has enumerated belonging to Britain of Soil, climate, water; &c. but what America possesses in an equal if not superiour degree. As our Country becomes more populous, we shall be daily makeing new discoveries and vie in some future day, with the most celebrated European Nation; for as yet; we may say, with the Queen of Sheby, the one half has not been told. We are in the infancy of Science, and have but just begun to form Societies for the propagation and encouragement of the fine Arts. The ⟨3⟩ 2 most celebrated painters now in Britain are Americans ⟨Mrs. Wright⟩ Mr. Copely and Mr. West.[2]

[1] John Campbell, *A Political Survey of Britain; Being a Series of Reflections on the Situation, Lands, Inhabitants, Revenues, Colonies and Commerce of This Island*, London, 1774; 2 vols.
[2] AA very properly struck Mrs. Wright's name from this list, but it is not determinable whether she did so immediately or after her visit to Patience Wright's "repository" or museum of wax portraits in Cockspur Street, London, later this month; see her journal-letter to Mrs. Cranch, 6–30 July 1784 (MWA; AA, *Letters*, ed. CFA, 1848, p. 177–178). The present journal being otherwise uncorrected, it is likely that she did so at once, feeling that she had overstated American claims to artistic eminence. On the eccentric Quaker artist and supposed American spy Patience (Lovell) Wright, see *DAB*; also Lewis Einstein, *Divided Loyalties* . . . , Boston and N.Y., 1933, p. 390–395. There is a lively and amusing characterization of her by AA2 in her journal-letter to JQA, 4 July–11 Aug. 1785 (Adams Papers).

### SATURDAY 17 OF JULY.

I have neglected my journal for a week. During that time we have had 3 calm days, some wet weather but nothing worth remarking has occur'd. I have been several days sick of the Rheumatisim, occasiond I suppose by the dampness of the Ship, which made my Bed so too. I had the precaution to take some medicine on Board proper for the Disease, which the Dr. administerd, and I have in a great measure got the better of it. This day makes 27 since we came to Sea. From observation to day we were in Latitude 49 and a half,[1] Long[itude] 6. We have seen a great Number of Vessels to day which lead us to think we are not far from the Channel. A small Sail Boat spoke with us out 3 days from Morlay, told us we were nearer the channel than we imagind, upon which the Capt. sounded and found bottom 55 fathom.

We have a head wind, but go at about 4 knots an hour. Hope to make land to morrow. Can it be that I have past this great ocean with no more inconvenience, with such favourable weather upon the whole. Am I so near the land of my fore Fathers? And am I Gracious Heaven; there to meet, the Dear long absent partner of my Heart? How many how various how complicated my Sensations! Be it unto me according to my wishes.

[1] MS reads: ". . . in Latitude in 49 and half."

### SUNDAY JULY 18TH.

This Day about 2 oclock made land. It is almost a Calm, so that we shall gain but little. We hope to land at Portsmouth a tuesday; this is doing very well; I have great reason to be thankfull for so favourable a passage. The mate caught a shark this morning but he got away, after receiving several wounds with a harpoon. I believe I could continue on Board this Ship 8 or ten days more, and find it less urksome than the first 8 or ten hours, so strong is habit and so easily do we become reconciled to the most dissagreeable Situation.

### MONDAY MORNING JULY 19TH.

A calm. The vessel rolling: the wind freshning towards Night. We hope for a speedy passage up the Channel. Tuesday a fine wind but squally.[1] We have seen land supposed to be Dover cliffs.

[1] AA's chronology here and in the next entry is confused, which is perhaps not surprising in view of her having slept only four hours between Saturday the 17th and Tuesday the 20th (which was in fact the day she landed), as she told her sister Cranch in her journal-letter of 6–30 July (MWA; AA, *Letters*, ed. CFA, 1848, p. 168).

### WEDENSDAY [*i.e.* TUESDAY, 20 JULY].

Early in the morning a pilot Boat came of to us from Deal. The wind blew very high and the Sea ran with a great Swell.[1]

[1] In her journal-letter of 6–30 July AA gives a colorful account of the landing of the *Active's* passengers in the surf at Deal and of their trip through Canterbury, Rochester, Chatham, and Black- heath (where a highwayman had just been apprehended) to London. They arrived at 8 in the evening of the 21st, and mother and daughter were "set down at Lows Hotel in Covent Gardens"

(MWA; AA, *Letters*, ed. CFA, 1848, p. 169–172). On the 23d, having been discovered and advised by solicitous American friends, AA wrote JA from "Osbornes new family Hotel—Adelphi at Mrs. Sheffields No. 6" (Adams Papers).

JA had confidently expected the arrival of his wife and daughter by an earlier vessel and had sent JQA from The Hague to London to meet them in mid-May; after awaiting them there for more than a month, JQA had returned to the Netherlands. On receipt of AA's letter of 23 July, JA replied that it had made him "the happiest Man upon Earth. I am twenty Years younger than I was Yesterday. It is a cruel Mortification to me that I cannot go to meet you

in London, but there are a Variety of Reasons decisive against it, which I will communicate to you here. Meantime I send you a son who is the greatest Traveller, of his Age" (26 July, Adams Papers). On 30 July both mother and son announced to JA their reunion in London, JQA reporting also his negotiation for the purchase of a coach that would accommodate the whole family (both letters in Adams Papers). Two days later JA canceled all previous plans. "Stay where you are," he told his wife, "untill you see me" (1 Aug., Adams Papers). What followed is recorded in the brief entries in JA's own Diary (see 4, 7 Aug., below), which must now be resumed at a slightly earlier date.

## [*John Adams' Diary resumes.*]

### THE HAGUE JUNE 22. 1784. TUESDAY.[1]

Last night at Court one of the Ladies of Honour, told me, that the Supper was given, in a great Measure, for Mrs. Bingham. Cette Super a été donne, en grande Partie, pour elle. There was great Enquiry after her, and much Admiration expressed by all who had seen her, of her Beauty. As the Princess of Orange was enquiring of me concerning her, and her Journey to Spa, Paris, Italy, the Spanish Minister said "She would form herself at Paris." I replied very quick but smiling "J'espere qu'elle ne se formera a Paris qu'elle est deja formée." This produced as hearty a laugh as is permitted at Court both from the Princess and the Comte. The Princess asked me immediately, if I had not been pleased at Paris? I answered that I had: that there was something there for every Taste [*added in the margin*: but that such great Cities as Paris and London were not good Schools for American young Ladies at present]. The Princess replied that Mrs. B. might learn there the French Language.

I made Acquaintance with Mr. Kempar of Friesland, once a Professor, at Franaker, who says there are but two Millions of People in the 7 Provinces. He quoted to me two Authors who have written upon the Subject, one 20 Years ago, and the other 10, and that they have decided this Subject. Stated the Numbers in each Province, City, Village. Accurate Accounts are kept of Births and Deaths, Baptisms and Funerals. The Midwives and Undertakers are obliged to make returns of all they bring in or carry out of the World.—This last fact I had from Linden de Blitterswick the first Noble of Zealand.

Mirabel repeated what he had said often before, as well as Reichack and Calischef, that their Courts expected a Letter from Congress, according to the Rules and Precedents, to inform them of their Independence.[2] —Mem. I think Congress should inform them that on the 4. July 1776 they assumed their Sovereignty, that on the     day of France made a Treaty, on the 7 of Oct. 1782, Holland—on the G.B.—on the     day of          Sweeden.[3]

[1] First entry in D/JA/43, a stitched gathering of leaves identical in format with its predecessors but containing only very scattered entries from the present date through May 1785.

After a day or two of rest at The Hague following his hazardous trip from London in January, JA went on to Amsterdam and applied, as his bankers had suggested, to the Regency of that city for emergency aid to the languishing American loan so that Robert Morris' heavy overdrafts for the United States would not be protested. But on 24 Jan. he reported to Franklin that all such efforts were in vain: "I am here only to be a Witness that American Credit in this Republick is dead, never to rise again" (LbC, Adams Papers; JA, *Works*, 8:171). Nevertheless, when he proposed a few days later that a separate loan be raised at a higher premium, the bankers responded eagerly, and after numerous exchanges between them JA signed a contract on 9 March for a new loan of 2,000,000 guilders, to be repaid by 1807, on terms that JA declared "exorbitant" but was in no position to refuse since fresh drafts from Morris continued to come in. See correspondence between JA and the Willinks, Van Staphorsts, and De la Lande & Fynje, 29 Jan.–9 March 1784, Adams Papers; partly printed in JA, *Works*, 8:172–183. Copies of the contract, in Dutch and English, with Congress' instrument of ratification, 1 Feb. 1785, are also in Adams Papers. The extraordinarily complicated terms of this loan are set forth in P. J. van Winter, *Het aandeel van den Amsterdamschen handel aan den opbouw van het Amerikaansche gemeenebest*, The Hague, 1927–1933, 1:80–85.

Meanwhile JA remained ignorant of Congress' intentions respecting the foreign establishment of the United States in general and how Congress meant to

dispose of him in particular. The reason was that Congress did not know its own intentions; see note 2 on entry of 7 Sept. 1783, above. On 15 Dec. 1783 a committee consisting of Jefferson, Gerry, and Hugh Williamson was appointed to report on letters from JA, Franklin, Dana, Dumas, and Barclay; on the 20th the committee reported a draft, largely the work of Jefferson, which pointed out that the instructions to JA, Franklin, and Jay of 29 Oct., for negotiating treaties "with the commercial powers of Europe," had not yet been implemented with commissions but that such treaties would be advantageous to the United States, and it went on to frame detailed instructions for this purpose (JCC, 25: 813, note, 821–828; Jefferson, *Papers*, ed. Boyd, 6:393–400). The complex history of this report, which was frequently debated and three times recommitted during the next six months, is given by Mr. Boyd in an editorial note (same, p. 400–402) and therefore need not be repeated here. On 7 and 11 May 1784 the report as finally amended was adopted, authorizing the negotiation of treaties of amity and commerce with sixteen nations (JCC, 26:357–362; 27: 369–374). On the same day that the first part of the report was agreed to, Thomas Jefferson was elected to succeed John Jay as a minister plenipotentiary and joint commissioner in Europe, and Jay was elected secretary for foreign affairs to succeed Robert R. Livingston, who had resigned almost a year earlier (same, 26:355–357). A few days later Jefferson left Annapolis for the north, hoping to accompany AA to Europe (see note 1 on entry in AA's Diary of 20 June, above). On 16 May Secretary Thomson sent him commissions accrediting the three plenipotentiaries jointly to twenty nations, four of the Barbary Powers having been added to the list (Thomson to Jefferson, 16 May, with enclosures; Jefferson, *Papers*, ed. Boyd, 7:261–271). The commissions, dated 12 May, were to the following powers: Russia, Austria, Prussia, Denmark, Saxony, Hamburg, Great Britain, Spain, Portugal, Naples, Sardinia, Rome, Venice, Genoa, Tuscany, the Ottoman Porte, Morocco, Algiers, Tunis, and Tripoli. To these Congress added on 3 June three further commissions, for supplementary treaties of commerce with France, the Netherlands, and Sweden, sent by Thomson to the ministers in a letter of 18 June (JCC, 27:529–530; Jefferson, *Papers*, ed. Boyd, 7:308–309).

All this explains the long delay in AA's departure for Europe and the longer uncertainty in JA's mind where he should establish himself in Europe or whether he should sail home without being recalled. On 16 April Elbridge Gerry wrote AA from Annapolis that "probably" Congress would "make their Arrangements, for negotiating commercial Treaties this Week. The Subject has several Months been prepared, for Deliberation, but this has been prevented by the Want of a full Representation; untill of late, there being eleven States on the Floor,

the Matter has been much discussed" (Adams Papers). In a letter to JA after this involved affair had been settled, Gerry furnished more of its inner history: Congress' indecision, he explained, was in considerable part owing to disagreement between supporters of JA and supporters of Franklin; the placing of JA at the head of the new commission and the replacement of William Temple Franklin as secretary by David Humphreys signalized a victory for the former (16 June, Adams Papers; extract printed in Burnett, ed., *Letters of Members*, 7:554). See further on this contest Stephen Higginson to Jonathan Jackson, April 1784 (Tr in JQA's hand, Adams Papers; Amer. Hist. Assoc., *Ann. Rpt. for 1896*, 1:717–719).

[2] Reischach and Kalicheff were ministers at The Hague from Austria and Russia respectively.

[3] The omitted dates of the treaties are as follows: with France, 6 Feb. 1778; with Great Britain, 3 Sept. 1783; with Sweden, 3 April 1783, although there is some confusion about the date of the last of these (Miller, ed., *Treaties*, 2:3, 151, 123, 149).

### JULY 10. 1784 SATURDAY.

May not the Ascent of Vapours be explained, or rather accounted for upon the Principle of the Air Balloon? Is not every Bubble of Vapour, that rises, an Air Balloon? Bubbles are formed at the Bottoms of Canals, Rivers, Ponds, rise to the Top, and mount up. These Bubbles are particles, or small quantities of inflammable Air, surrounded with a thin film of Water.

Champaign Wine, Bottled Porter &c. are full of Air Bubbles or Balloons. Set a Decanter or Tumbler of Water in the Sun, and thousands of Air Balloons are formed in the Water at the Bottom and on the Sides of the Glass. Turn the Glass aside so as to expose these Bubbles to the Air, many of them burst in an Instant, others do not, but continue sometime covered with a thin film of Water. Inflammable Air being lighter, than common Air, rises in it.

In the common Experiment with which Boys amuse them selves, the Air which is blown through the Tobacco Pipe, into the Soap Suds, is common Air, of equal Weight with that which surrounds the Bubble and therefore will not ascend very high. But if inflammable Air were blown thro the Pipe instead of common Air, we should have a Series of Ballons aerostatiques, which would ascend like those of Montgolphier.[1]

[1] The earliest "aerostatic experiments" (balloon flights), by the Montgolfier brothers and others in France, 1783–1784, attracted world-wide attention and are frequently alluded to in the correspondence of JA, Franklin, and Jefferson at this period. Among the Adams Papers is a colored drawing entitled "Bon Voyage," reproduced in this volume, showing the "Nouveau Globe Aérostatique inventée par M[essieu]rs. Charles et Robert; enlevé devant la Famille Royale le lundi 1er. Décembre 1783, à 1. heure 40. minutes." On 19 Sept. 1784 the Adams family watched a balloon ascension from the Tuileries Gardens (AA2, *Jour. and Corr.*, 1:18–19).

## 1784. AUGUST. 3.

### AUG. 4.

Sett off, for London, had a tedious Passage from Helvoet, of near two days. Obliged to put in at Leostoff [Lowestoft], and ride from thence 24 miles in a Cart.[1]

[1] JA's sudden decision to go to London himself and take his family directly to Paris without a pause of some weeks at The Hague, was prompted by the news of Jefferson's arrival in Europe a month or so before JA expected him; see JA to AA, 1 Aug. (Adams Papers), and Jefferson to JA, "On board the Ceres off Scilly," 24 July (Adams Papers; Jefferson, *Papers*, ed. Boyd, 7:382–383, with note quoting JA's expressions of pleasure in the appointment of Jefferson as a fellow commissioner).

In JA's accounts as settled by Congress there appears the following entry: "Expences of his Removal with his Family from the Hague & London to Auteuil in August 1784 including extra Expences of Carriages, Post Horses, Passages by Sea from Helvoet to Harwich & from Dover to Calais &c. £100.... Purchase of a Carriage in London. £120" (DNA: RG 39, Foreign Ledgers, Public Agents in Europe, 1776–1787, p. 267).

### AUG. 7.

Arrived at the Adelphi Buildings and met my Wife and Daughter after a seperation of four Years and an half. Indeed after a Seperation of ten Years, excepting a few Visits. Set off the next Day for Paris.[1]

[1] On this date the Diary of AA2, so far as it is known (no MS has been found), begins. The first entry reads: "London, Aug. 7th, 1784. At 12, returned to our own apartments; when I entered, I saw upon the table a hat with two books in it; every thing around appeared altered, without my knowing in what particular. I went into my own room, the things were moved; I looked around—'Has mamma received letters, that have determined her departure?— When does she go?—Why are these things moved?' All in a breath to Esther. 'No, ma'm, she has received no letter, but goes to-morrow morning.' 'Why is all this appearance of strangeness?—Whose hat is that in the other room?—Whose trunk is this?—Whose sword and cane?— It is my father's,' said I. 'Where is he?'

'In the room above.' Up I flew, and to his chamber, where he was lying down, he raised himself upon my knocking softly at the door, and received me with all the tenderness of an affectionate parent after so long an absence. Sure I am, I never felt more agitation of spirits in my life; it will not do to describe" (*Jour. and Corr.*, 1:viii).

AA2's Diary is quite full for the family's journey to Paris, which was by way of Dover, Calais, Boulogne, Montreuil, Amiens, and Chantilly (same, p. 7–14).

### AUG. 13.

Arrived at Paris, at the Hotel de York on the             .[1]

[1] In the present entry and the next, the blank space (which is in the MS) is meant to be filled up with the date at the head of the entry.

### AUG. 17.

Removed to Auteuil the          at the House of the Comte de Rouault, opposite the Conduit. The House, the Garden, the Situation near the Bois de Boulogne, elevated above the River Seine and the low Grounds, and distant from the putrid Streets of Paris, is the best I could wish for.[1]

[1] The arrangements with the Comte de Rouault had been made at JA's request by Thomas Barclay, who had formerly rented the house; see JA-Barclay correspondence, 23 April–9 Aug. 1784 (Adams Papers). The reader is again referred to the detailed and colorful letters of AA describing the Hôtel de Rouault and the Adamses' life there during the following eight months, a selection of which appears in Howard C. Rice Jr., *The Adams Family in Auteuil, 1784–1785*, Boston, 1956, and more of which will be included in Series II of the present edition. The journal kept by AA2 at Auteuil from Aug. 1784 through May 1785 is also valuable despite its rather girlish concentration on the guests present at social affairs given or attended by the family; see AA2, *Jour. and Corr.*, 1:14–78. This portion of her journal contains numerous glimpses of Jefferson, Franklin, the Binghams, David Humphreys, William Short, the Lafayettes, Mme. Helvétius, and the Adamses' friends among the *corps diplomatique*, as well as sometimes entertaining and illuminating passages on Paris fashionable life and amusements, religious ceremonies, balloon ascensions, and the like. If the MS were available, the entries for this period would have been printed here to help fill in a long gap in JA's Diary, but as edited by AA2's daughter, Caroline Amelia (Smith) de Windt, in 1841, the text is far from dependable: there are obvious mistakes in transcription, names are given as blanks and initials, and editorial cuts have probably been made.

[ORDERS DRAWN ON MESSRS. VAN DEN YVER FOR PERSONAL AND FAMILY EXPENSES, SEPTEMBER 1784–MAY 1785.][1]

| | £ | s | d |
|---|---|---|---|
| Auteuil Sept. 10. 1784. Drew an order on M.M. Van den Yvers in favour of my son J.Q.A. for two hundred Louis D'ors or 4800 Livres | 4800: | 0: | 0 |
| Oct. 11. drew an Order on M. Van den Yver in favour of my son J.Q.A. for 4800 Livres | 4800: | 0: | 0 |

Nov: 15. drew an order on Mr. Van den Yver in favour
of my son J.Q.A. for 4800 Livres                    4800: 0: 0
Decr. 23. drew an order on M[ess]rs. Van den Yver in
favour of my son J. Q. Adams for 4800 Livres        4800: 0: 0
1785. Feb. 11. drew an order on Messrs. Van den Yver
in favour of My son J.Q.A. for 4800 Liv.            4800: 0: 0
March 5. Accepted a Bill of Dr. Tufts for £50, payable
at the House of Messrs. Richard and Charles
Puller No. 10 Broadstreet Buildings London, to
be paid at Sight                                    1200: 0: 0
March 26 drew an order on Messrs. Van den Yver in
favour of my son J.Q.A. for 4800 Liv.               4800: 0: 0
May 4. drew an Order on Messrs. Van den Yver in
favour of my son J.Q.A. for 4800£.                  4800: 0: 0
May 18 drew an Order on Messrs. Van den Yver in
favour of the Bearer Mrs. Adams for                 4800: 0: 0

[1] Taken from Lb/JA/19 (Adams Papers, Microfilms, Reel No. 107). The firm of Van den Yver Frères acted as agents in Paris for the Amsterdam banking house of W. & J. Willink. JA had drawn his salary through the Van den Yvers during the peace negotiations.

JANUARY 31. 1785. MONDAY.[1]

Last Evening the Marquis de la Fayette, lately returned from America, called upon me, in his Way home from Versailles. He gave me, a very pleasing Account of the Commerce, the Union &c. in America, and then began to discourse of another Subject. He interrogated me, whether I had any Correspondents in Holland, whether I received Letters, from Week to Week and from Post to Post from thence? Who were the Heads of the Republican Party? Whether I knew any Thing of the Intentions of the States Gen[eral] to place Mr. de Maillbois at the Head of their Armies. He then talk'd of Mailbois, said he had great Abilities, and that he had heard him justify himself very well in the Affair of D'Etrees. Said that M. de Vergennes was his Friend.— I said that I knew it, for that I had once in 1778 heard the Comte wish [that][2] Mr. de Mailbois had the Command of our Army in America.[3] He said that the Cte. de Broglie wished for the Command in America at the same time.

As he went out he took me aside and whispered, that altho he would not serve a foreign Prince, he would serve a Republick, and although he should hurt himself with the Queen and her Party to a great degree, yet if the States General would invite him, without his soliciting or appearing to desire it, he would accept the Command. Mailbois loved Money, and demanded splendid Appointments. He did not regard Money so much and would be easy about that. I was the first Mortal to whom he had suggested the Idea, he wished I would think of it, and he would call and see me again in a few days.[4]

[1] The first formal meeting of the American Commissioners to negotiate treaties of amity and commerce took place at Passy on 30 Aug., David Humphreys, secretary to the mission, being present and beginning that day a record of its proceedings. This record, preserved in a volume sometimes called "Minutes of the Commissioners" (PCC, No. 116), contains, besides actual minutes of their meetings, copies of the Commissioners' commissions and instructions, of their correspondence with the diplomatic agents of the powers to which they were accredited (with the accompanying treaty *projets*, &c.), and of their joint "Reports" or dispatches to the President of Congress and Secretary Jay, numbered "First" through "Ninth" (11 Nov. 1784 to 2–11 Oct. 1785), thus extending beyond the time when Franklin left for home and JA and Jefferson were appointed ministers plenipotentiary at London and Paris respectively, while retaining their joint commission to negotiate commercial treaties (see note on entry of 3 May, below). The original letters received by the Commissioners (with enclosures), together with drafts and originals of most of their reports to Congress, are filed in PCC, No. 86. All this documentation for JA's last joint commission in Europe is printed in a single sequence in *Dipl. Corr.*, 1783–1789, 1:499–600, but much more reliable texts and indispensable annotation are provided in Jefferson, *Papers*, ed. Boyd, vols. 7–8, where these letters and

papers are distributed under their dates. The best way to follow the Commissioners' work, which was arduous but only very partially successful, is to read their reports. Those that are germane to the present gap in JA's Diary are the First, Second, and Third, dated 11 Nov., 15 Dec. 1784, and [9] Feb. 1785 (same, 7:493–500, 573–574, 646–647).

[2] MS: "the."

[3] The Comte de Maillebois, a marshal of France, assumed the command of the Dutch army, but, as JA later remarked, with little credit to himself; see JA's Autobiography under date of 29 April 1778. CFA has a learned note on Maillebois' notorious quarrel with the Maréchal d'Estrées, alluded to above (JA, *Works*, 3:389).

[4] "Last Night, I had a visit from the Marquis, whom I was glad to see, for a variety of Reasons.... His views are now opening, at least in confidence to me, and his aspiring Soul aims at Objects in Europe, as grand and glorious as those he has obtained in America.... From these Hints you may guess the whole matter. His Plan, I must say, is as laudable, as it is sublime; but I doubt the possibility of his Success" (JA to Jay, 31 Jan., LbC, Adams Papers). On Lafayette's interest in the situation of the Dutch Republic, which was in the midst of a crisis with the Austrian Empire over the issue of opening the navigation of the Scheldt, see Gottschalk, *Lafayette*, 4:152–153.

#### 1785. MARCH 19. SATURDAY.

Saturday. Met Mr. F[ranklin] and Mr. J[efferson] at Passy, read the Letter from Mr. Carm[ichael] at Madrid, with the Letters from C. de Florida Blanca, the Letters from Morocco to Mr. Harrison at Cadiz, and the Letters from Morocco to Dr. F. concerning the Vessell of Mr. Fitzsimmons of Philadelphia, taken by a Morrocco Frigate.

I asked for Books and Collections of Treaties. They were brought. I looked for and read the Treaty between Louis 14. and Algiers, and the Treaties between Holland and Algiers, and found a Multitude of Treaties between Algiers and Morrocco and the Christian States as France, Holland, England, &c. with the Passes, in the Corps Diplomatique.

We came to no Resolution, but that I should go, Tomorrow to Versailles and ask the Advice of the C[omte] de V[ergennes].—Dr. F. being confined by his Stone, could not go, and Mr. Jefferson, being worse with his Disorder cannot go. I was for writing a Letter to the C. —but my Colleagues were not.[1]—F. and J. are confident that England has no right to appoint a Consul, without a Treaty or Convention for that Purpose. I think, they have a Right by the Law of Nations.[2]

[1] This and the following entry mark the beginning of prolonged efforts by the Commissioners to reach an accord, on behalf of the United States, with several of the piratical Barbary States in order to protect American shipping in the Mediterranean. The efforts were prompted by seizures of American vessels reported in the letters mentioned in the first paragraph of the present entry; extracts from these were handed by JA to Vergennes next day, and copies were forwarded by the Commissioners to Jay in their Fifth Report, 13 April 1785 (PCC, No. 86); a list of them, with their dates and locations, is given in a note on JA's report to his colleagues on his interview with Vergennes, 20 March (Jefferson, *Papers*, ed. Boyd, 8:46–48,

q.v.). For a connected narrative of early American negotiations with the Barbary Powers, see Ray W. Irwin, *The Diplomatic Relations of the United States with the Barbary Powers, 1776–1816*, Chapel Hill, 1931, chs. 2–3. The correspondence and other documents are printed under their dates in Jefferson, *Papers*, ed. Boyd, vols. 7–10.

[2] This doubtless alludes to the appointment in February of John Temple as British consul general in the United States; see JA to James Warren, 26 April 1785 (LbC, Adams Papers; *Warren-Adams Letters*, 2:250–261). Though the sentiments of Congress were divided on whether or not to recognize Temple, a vote of that body did so on 2 Dec. 1785 (JCC, 29:897–898).

AUTEUIL NEAR PARIS MARCH 20. 1785.

Sunday. Went early to Versailles, and found the C. De V.—communicated to him my Errand and Papers. He read those in Italian, Spanish and French, and Mr. Charmichaels Letter in English. I asked him, whether the French Treaty with Algiers, was renewed? He said it was upon the Point of expiring, but he could not tell me whether it was renewed as it was not in his Department but in that of the M. de Castries. I asked him if he would be so good as to inform me, what Presents were sent annually to the several Barbary Powers, by the King, in what they consisted, and to what they amounted? He said He did not know, but if We would make an Office of it, he would communicate it to the Minister of Marine, and obtain for Us all the Information he could. I told him, I had obtained Information, authentically from Holland, from Mr. Bisdom and Mr. Van der Hope.[1] I asked him if he would be so good as to convey a Letter from Us to the Emperor of Morocco, by means of the French Consull. He said that I might depend upon it whenever We made an Office, it should be punctually attended to. But he said that Cadiz would be the best Place from whence to send Presents. That the Emperor of Morocco was the most interested Man in the World and the most greedy of Money.

He asked if We had written to Congress and obtained their Instructions. I told him We had received Full Powers to treat with Morocco, Algiers, Tunis, Tripoli and all the Rest and had written for Instructions upon the Article of Money and Presents. He said that there was a frequent Communication between Marseilles and the Coast of Barbary, but that as these Things were not in his Department, We must state our Desires in Writing, which I agreed to do. I asked him if he thought it adviseable for Us to send any one to Morro[cco]. He said yes, but as We could neither go nor were authorized to substitute, We should write to the Emperor untill Congress could send a Consull. I asked what he thought of our leaving it by our Letter in the Option of the Emperor, to send a Minister here to treat with Us, or to wait untill We could write to Congress and recommend to them to send him a Consull. He said by no means, for the Expence of receiving his Minister here would be much greater, for We must maintain him and pay all his Expences. He said that the King of France never sent them any naval Stores. He sent them Glaces[2] and other Things of rich Value, but never any military stores.

[1] JA's views on American policy toward the piratical states of Barbary are embodied in a letter to John Jay, 15 Dec. 1784 (LbC, Adams Papers; *Dipl. Corr., 1783–1789*, 1:470–472). On 22 Dec. he had addressed a letter to Dumas at The Hague asking the latter to inquire what tribute in the form of gifts was paid by the Dutch Republic to the Barbary Powers for the protection of its commerce (LbC, Adams Papers). Dumas' answer, 25 Feb. 1785, enclosed a copy of the written information obtained from J. C. van der Hoop, "Conseiller Fiscal du College de l'Amirauté d'Amsterdam," and D. R. W. Bisdom, "Conseiller Fiscal de l'Amirauté de la Meuse" (Adams Papers; text of questions and answers printed in a note on the American Commissioners' Fourth Report, 18 March, Jefferson, *Papers*, ed. Boyd, 8:38).

[2] Thus in MS, but JA's report to Franklin and Jefferson on this interview has "glasses," i.e., doubtless, looking-glasses (20 March, LbC, Adams Papers, in JQA's hand; printed in same, p. 46–47).

AUTEUIL MAY 3. 1785.

Tuesday. At Versailles, the C. de Vergennes said he had many Felicitations to give me upon my apointment to England. I Answered that I did not know but it merited Compassion more than felicitation.—Ay why?—Because, as you know it is a Species of Degradation in the Eyes of Europe, after having been accredited to the King of France to be sent to any other Court.—But permit me to say, replies the Comte it is a great Thing to be the first Ambassador from your Country to the Country you sprung from. It is a Mark.—I told him that these Points would not weigh much with me. It was the difficulty of the service, &c.

I said to him, as I would not fail in any Point of Respect or Duty to the King, nor any of our Obligations to this Country, I wished to be advised, whether an Audience in particular of Congé, was indispensable. He said he would inform himself.

The Duke of Dorsett said to me, that if he could be of any Service to me by Writing either to publick or private Persons he would do it with Pleasure. I told his Grace that I should be glad of half an hours Conversation with him, in private.—I will call upon you at Auteuil says he, any Morning this Week.—I answered that any Morning and any hour, agreable to him, should be so to me.—Saturday says he at 12 O Clock.—I shall be happy to receive you, says I.—He repeated that if he could be of any Service, he would be glad. I said it may probably be in your Graces Power to do great service to me, and what was of infinitely more importance to his Country as well as mine, if he thought as I did upon certain Points, and therefore I thought it was proper We should compare Notes. He said he believed We did think alike and would call on Saturday. He said that Lord Carmaerthen was their Minister of foreign Affairs, that I must first wait upon him, and he would introduce me to his Majesty. But that I should do Business with Mr. Pitt very often. I asked him Lord Caermaerthens Age. He said 33. He said I should be stared at a good deal. I told him I trembled at the Thoughts of going there, I was afraid they would gaze with evil Eyes. He said no he believed not.

One of the foreign Ambassadors said to me, You have been often in England.—Never but once in November and December 1783.— You have Relations in England no doubt.—None at all.—None how can that be? You are of English Extraction?—Neither my Father or Mother, Grandfather or Grandmother, Great Grandfather or Great Grandmother nor any other Relation that I know of or care a farthing for have been in England these 150 Years. So that you see, I have not one drop of Blood in my Veins, but what is American.—Ay We have seen says he proofs enough of that.—This flattered me no doubt, and I was vain enough to be pleased with it.[1]

¹ In their First Report to the President of Congress, 11 Nov. 1784, the Commissioners stated that on 31 Aug. they had notified David Hartley and on 28 Oct. the Duke of Dorset (the British ambassador who had succeeded the Duke of Manchester in Paris) that they had powers for entering into a treaty of amity and commerce with Great Britain; but Hartley had been ordered to England and Dorset had replied that he could only notify his government (Jefferson, *Papers*, ed. Boyd, 7:494–495; see also p. 456–457). On 24 Nov. Dorset informed the Commissioners of his government's view "that the United States should send a Person properly authorized and invested with the necessary powers to London, as more suitable to the dignity of either Power, than would be the carrying on at any third Place a negotiation of so great importance" (same, p. 547). Dorset's letter was transmitted to Congress in the Commissioners' Second Report, 15 Dec. (same, p. 573–574). Before this report was received, presumably, Secretary Jay submitted to Congress a draft of "Instructions for the Ministers to be sent by the United States to the Court of London," which was read in Congress on 7 Feb., debated from time to time, and exactly a month later was adopted with some omissions and the highly significant alteration of the word "Ministers" in the title to "Minister" (JCC, 28:45–46, 123). In the meanwhile a tussle had taken place over who should be the first American minister accredited to the Court of St. James's. It turned out to be JA, who was elected on 24 Feb., but the bare result recorded in the journal (same, p. 98) conveys no idea of the length of the struggle or the views of the members who were for and against his appointment. Fortunately Elbridge Gerry, in a letter written on the day the contest ended, supplied what is wanting elsewhere. The other nominees, he told JA, were Robert R. Livingston and John Rutledge; some southern members opposed JA on the ground that he was "totally averse to the Slave Trade" and would not exert himself "to obtain Restitution of the Negroes taken and detained from them in Violation of the Treaty"; other members thought he would not be as firm as he should be

on the issue of American debts; and finally some of JA's communications to Congress, notably his "Peace Journal" of 1782 (see note on entry of 2 Nov. 1782, above), were cited as evidence of his vanity, "a weak passion, to which a Minister ought never to be subject" because it would make him vulnerable to flattery by "an artful Negotiator" (Gerry to JA, 24 Feb. 1785, Adams Papers; Burnett, ed., *Letters of Members*, 8:39–40).

JA's commission to Great Britain is in the Adams Papers, 24 Feb.; it was brought to him, with his instructions and other papers, by Col. William Stephens Smith (subsequently JA's son-in-law and referred to in this work as WSS), whom Congress had appointed on 1 March "Secretary to our legation to his Britannic Majesty" (JCC, 28:111, 149–150). On 7 March Congress gave leave to Benjamin Franklin "to return to America as soon as convenient," and on the 10th Thomas Jefferson "was unanimously elected" to succeed Franklin at the Court of Versailles (same, p. 122, 134). JA and Jefferson retained their joint commission to negotiate commercial treaties with European and African nations.

JA learned of these new arrangements toward the close of April, and on the 28th of that month he addressed a letter to Gerry expressing profound thanks for his confidential account of the election contest and commenting in a temperate manner on the objections Gerry had reported as having been raised against his appointment (LbC, Adams Papers). On the day before the present Diary entry was written JA wrote a second answer to Gerry which is one of the most remarkable letters he ever composed. It is an historical and analytical discourse on the "various kinds of Vanity" to which men have been subject—the dangerous kinds that JA had had to contend with, as he explained, in his adversaries and even among his colleagues, and his own kind, which he conceded was a marked trait of his character but which was innocent and harmless. Since what appears to be the copy intended for the recipient remains among the Adams Papers, since no letterbook copy was made, and since, finally, no acknowledgment by Gerry of such a letter has been found, JA evidently decided against sending it; but happily he did not destroy it, and it will be published in its place among his papers in Series III of the present edition. The state of Anglo-American relations on the eve of JA's mission to London is well summarized and documented in an editorial note on the Duke of Dorset's letter to the American Commissioners, 26 March 1785, in Jefferson, *Papers*, ed. Boyd, 8:56–59.

AUTEUIL MAY [9 *or* 16] 1785.

Monday. The Posts within the Limits of the United States, not yet surrendered by the English, are

Oswegatchy in the River St. Lawrence

Oswego  Lake Ontario

Niagara and its dependencies

Presqu'Isle  East Side of Lake Erie.

Sandusky  Ditto.

Detroit.

Michilimakinac.

St. Mary's. South Side of the Streight between Lakes Superiour and Huron.

Bottom of the Bay des Puantz

St. Joseph. bottom of Lake Michigan.

Ouitanon.

Miamis.[1]

[1] This memorandum, the last entry in D/JA/43 and the last written by JA in his Diary for a period of more than ten months, must have been made on either 9 or 16 May, since it was written at Auteuil on a Monday and follows an entry dated there on 3 May, and since on 20 May JA set out with his wife and daughter for London (JA to Jefferson, 22 May, NNP; Jefferson, *Papers*, ed. Boyd, 8:159–160). Congress' instructions of 7 March required JA to "insist, that the United States be put without further delay in possession of all the posts and territories within their limits which are now held by British Garrisons" (JCC, 28:123). On 1 May JA had a conversation with Daniel Hailes, secretary of the British embassy in Paris, and he had another with Dorset on the same subject, apparently on 10 May (AA to Cotton Tufts, 2 May, Adams Papers; JA to Jay, 13 May, LbC, Adams Papers, printed in *Dipl. Corr.*, *1783–1789*, 1: 495–498). He was to make the question of British occupation of posts on the northern lakes the first and indeed a standing order of business during his London mission, but, for reasons that were hinted at by David Hartley two years earlier and that have been very fully set forth by Mr. Bemis, the British did not evacuate them for a decade; see entry of 3 May 1783, above, and Samuel F. Bemis, *Jay's Treaty*, N.Y., 1923, ch. 1.

[LIST OF VISITS PAID AND RETURNED
IN LONDON, JUNE–JULY? 1785.][1]

Le Comte de Lusi. Minister            of Prussia. Great Pultney Street.
    r

De Tribolet Hardy. Secretaire de Legation de S.M. Prussienne.  r

Mr. De Jeanneret de Dunilac late Chargé D'Affairs of his Prussian Majesty at the British Court. South Moulton Street Oxford Street. No. 49. r

Lord Mahon. Downing Street. r

The Earl of Abbington. r.

The Earl of Effingham. r.

Mr. Cottrell Assistant Master of the Ceremonies Berners Street. r

Mr. Grand. Great Marlborough Street No. 54. r

Mr. Horn and Tooke. r

Mr. Brand Hollis. Bruton Street Berkley Square. 1st House on the right.

Mr. Bridgen. r.

Mr. R. Penn. Queen Ann Street, West Cavendish Square. r.

Mr. Strachy. Portman Square. No. 18. r

Lt. General Melvill  Brower Street No. 30. r

Mr. Nicholls  Queen Ann Street West. No. 42. r.

Sir Clement Cottrell Dormer. r. Wimpole Street. r.

Le Comte de Pollon, Lincolns Inn Fields. Brother of the Chevalier. Min[ister] of Sardinia. r.

Mr. Winchcomber Hartley. Golden Square. r.

Mr. Chamberlain  Palsgrave Place Strand. No. 5. r

Mr. Chew. Charles Street St. James's Square No. 23. r

Mr. Granville Penn.

Count Woronzow Envoy Extr. & M.P. from the Empress of Russia. r

Mr. Frances, at Ray's Saddler Piccadilly No. 83. r.

Mr. Martin  New Street. Bishops Gate Street. r.

Mr. Middleton  Bryanston Street.

General Stewart. Norfolk Street Strand No. 33

Mr. Cunningham  Dto.

Mr. Lane, Nicholas lane.

⟨*Mr. Martin. New Street. Bishopsgate Street.*⟩

Jos. & Isaac Saportas. Great Crescent Minories. No. 5.

Mr. Wallace  Bedford Street.

Mr. Bordieu.

Jos. & Isaac Saportas. Great Crescent Minories No. 5.

Brigr. General Forbes, in the Service of Portugal  George Street. York Buildings No. 17. r

Sir James Harris. Park Street. Westminster. r

Mr. Wallace  Bedford Street.

I. Heard  Garter. r

Lord Hood. r
Mr. Jennings. Soho. Wrights Hotel.

¹ A loose, folded sheet, without date, in JA's hand and docketed by him: "List"; filed in Adams Papers under the assigned date 1785?. This sheet was afterward used as a cover for other papers, for on its blank fourth page appears a docketing notation in the hand of WSS: "Illegal Captures & Complaints of Injuries receiv'd."

From scattered allusions in JA's and AA's correspondence during June–July 1785 there can be little doubt that this is a list of some (though by no means all) of the visitors received by the Adamses during their first weeks in London. The calls they returned are indicated by the abbreviation "r." Only a few of the calls recorded were of the ceremonial, diplomatic kind, the explanation of which may be that, as the Dutch minister in London, D. W. Lynden van Blitterswyck, told JA, "Here the New Minister receives the first Visit, from all the foreign Ministers, whereas in France and Holland the New Minister makes the first visit to all the foreign Ministers and notifies formally to them his reception. This saves me," JA went on to say, "from an Embarrassment, and we shall now see who will and who will not" (to Jefferson, 27 May, LbC, Adams Papers; Jefferson, *Papers*, ed. Boyd, 8:167). Other visits were from persons like the Penns who had American connections (though it should be noted that there are no loyalist refugees on the list) or who were favorably disposed toward America (e.g. the Earls of Effingham and Abingdon, Lord Mahon [later 3d Earl Stanhope], John Horne Tooke, Thomas Brand Hollis, and David Hartley's brother Winchcombe). Still others were old friends or former acquaintances (e.g. Edward Bridgen, Henry Strachey, Gen. Robert Melville, and Edmund Jenings). The purpose of Admiral Lord Hood's very unexpected visit is interestingly detailed in a letter JA wrote to John Jay, 26 June, a few days after it occurred (LbC, Adams Papers; *Dipl. Corr., 1783–1789*, 2:387).

The new minister's family had been reduced by one before leaving Auteuil. In the preceding fall JA and AA had decided that their eldest son should re-turn to America to take a degree at Harvard and prepare himself for the bar. JA accordingly wrote President Joseph Willard of Harvard, 8 Sept. (MH), and Willard replied on 14 Dec. enclosing a vote of the President and Fellows to admit JQA to whatever class an examination showed him qualified to enter (Adams Papers). JA's letters to Willard and to Professor Benjamin Waterhouse, dated 22 and 24 April respectively, describing the studies his son had pursued while in Europe are of the highest interest (letterbook copies, Adams Papers; the letter to Willard is printed in Col. Soc. Mass., *Pubns.*, 13 [1910–1911]:115–116; that to Waterhouse in Ford, ed., *Statesman and Friend*, p. 5–8, under date of 23 April). JQA left Auteuil for Lorient on 12 May, went on board the French packet *Courier de l'Amérique* on the 18th (where he found seven dogs being sent by Lafayette to George Washington, which JQA was charged to see were "well fed" during the voyage), sailed on the 21st, kept a careful journal of the passage to send to his sister, and arrived in New York on 17 July (JQA to AA2, 11 May, 25 May–17 July; JQA to JA, 18 May; Lafayette to JQA, 18 May; all in Adams Papers; see also JQA's Diary, which is very regular and full for the period concerned).

On 20 May the three remaining Adamses left Auteuil by carriage and traveled via Montreuil to Calais, where they put up again at "Dessin's," beguiling a dusty journey by reading a copy of Jefferson's *Notes on the State of Virginia* presented to them by the author; they reached London on the 26th and stopped at the Bath Hotel in Piccadilly, where Charles Storer had engaged rooms for them (JA to Jefferson, 22, 23, 27 May, and AA to Jefferson, 6 June; Jefferson, *Papers*, ed. Boyd, 8:159–161, 167, 178–181). On the very night of his arrival JA announced his presence in London to Foreign Secretary Lord Carmarthen, who received him the following day. On 1 June he was formally received by George III; both men were deeply moved by the circumstances in which they found themselves, and both distinguished themselves by their words and conduct (JA to Carmarthen, 26 May, LbC, Adams Papers; Carmarthen to JA, 27 May, Adams Papers; JA to Jay, 2 June, reporting verbatim what the King and he had said to each other, LbC, Adams Papers, printed in *Works*, 8:255–259).

As a result of AA's house-hunting efforts, JA signed on 9 June a lease for a house "in the North East Angle of Grosvenor Square in the Parish of Saint George Hanover Square," owned by the Hon. John Byron of Purbright, for the term of 21 months at an annual rental of £160 (Lease in Adams Papers; see also AA to Mrs. Cranch, [22]–28 June, MWA, printed in AA, *Letters*, ed. CFA, 1848, p. 252). This, the first United States legation in London, is still standing, unoccupied in 1959, at the junction of Duke and Brook Streets, overshadowed by the immense new American Embassy building on the west side of Grosvenor Square. Into it the Adamses moved their furnishings and books, just

arrived from the Hôtel des Etats Unis at The Hague, during the first day or two of July; and in a remarkable journal-letter begun on 2 July AA2 provided her brother with a chatty description of the "appartments" in the house, their furnishings, the servants, the neighbors in Grosvenor Square (one of whom was Lord North), visitors and visits, &c., &c. (to JQA, 2 July–11 Aug. 1785, Adams Papers). Subsequent installments of her journal-letters—carefully numbered, each of them running to many pages, and none of them published—furnish by far the fullest account of the Adamses' domestic and social life in London, 1785–1788, compensating in some measure for JA's near-abandonment of his Diary during this period.

On 17 June JA had begun his conferences with Secretary Carmarthen concerning the principal points to be adjusted between the United States and Great Britain; see his letter to Jay of that date (LbC, Adams Papers; *Dipl. Corr., 1783–1789*, 2:378–382).

GROSVENOR SQUARE WESTMINSTER MARCH 27. 1786.[1]

March 26. Sunday, dined in Bolton Street Piccadilly, at the Bishop of St. Asaphs.[2] Mr. and Mrs. Sloper, the Son in Law and Daughter of the Bishop; Mrs. and Miss Shipley the Wife and Daughter; Mr. and Mrs. Vaughan, Mr. Alexander and Mrs. Williams, Mr. Richard Peters and myself, were the Company. In the Evening other Company came in, according to the Fashion, in this Country. Mrs. Shipley at Table asked many Questions about the Expence of living in Philadelphia and Boston. Said she had a Daughter, who had married, less prudently than they wished, and they thought of sending them to America.

[1] First entry in D/JA/44, a stitched gathering of leaves identical in format with the preceding booklets and containing scattered entries through 21 July 1786; more than half of this booklet consists of blank leaves.

It is not possible in a paragraph or two to fill the preceding gap of some ten months in JA's Diary with any adequacy. During his first months in England the new American minister wrote often to Carmarthen on the subjects at issue between the two powers, and late in August

he sought and obtained an interview with William Pitt, but on 15 Oct. he told Jay that he could "obtain no Answer from the Ministry to any one demand, Proposal or Inquiry" (LbC, Adams Papers; *Dipl. Corr., 1783–1789*, 2:479). Five days later he had a long conversation with Carmarthen covering ground well trod before—the western posts, British trade restrictions, the slaves carried off during the war, American debts to British creditors, &c. Carmarthen was civil but not really responsive, and JA characterized the discussion as "useless" (to Jay, 21 Oct., LbC, Adams Papers; same, p. 483–491). At length in an interview on 8 Dec. JA submitted a memorial (dated 30 Nov.) requesting that in accordance with the seventh article of the Definitive Treaty the British garrisons in the Northwest be withdrawn (LbC, Adams Papers; same, p. 542–543; see also p. 543–544). Carmarthen took nearly three months to answer, and when he did he counterbalanced the British retention of the posts in violation of the seventh article against impediments erected by most of the American states in the way of collecting debts due to British creditors, in violation of the fourth article of the Treaty (Carmarthen to JA, 28 Feb. 1786, Adams Papers; printed as an enclosure, together with supporting papers, in JA to Jay, 4 March, in same, p. 580–591). These issues were to remain thus poised until the Jay Treaty of 1794.

The discussions begun at The Hague between JA and Baron von Thulemeier in March 1784 had finally been brought to an end, after a lengthy and many-sided correspondence and much maneu-vering about protocol, in a treaty of amity and commerce between Prussia and the United States which was signed by Franklin at Passy on 9 July, by Jefferson at Paris on 28 July, by JA at London on 5 Aug., and by Thulemeier at The Hague on 10 Sept. 1785 (see facsimile in Jefferson, *Papers*, ed. Boyd, vol. 8: facing p. 566). The treaty was transmitted to Congress in a joint letter from JA and Jefferson, London and Paris, 2–11 Oct., being the Commissioners' "Ninth Report" (PCC, No. 86; same, p. 606). The treaty itself is printed in Miller, ed., *Treaties*, 2:162–183. In Aug. 1786 JA decided to go himself to The Hague to exchange the ratifications.

Concerning other negotiations of 1785–1786 for which Jefferson was jointly responsible with JA, see note 2 on entry of 29 March, below.

[2] Jonathan Shipley, Bishop of St. Asaph and an intimate friend of Franklin, had long been a popular figure in America because of his early and vigorous criticism in the House of Lords of the British ministry's American policy (*DNB*). In June Shipley was to officiate at the wedding of AA2.

## WEDNESDAY [29 MARCH].

Dined at Mr. Blakes.[1] Mr. Middleton and Wife, Mr. Alexander and Mrs. Williams, Mr. Jefferson.[2] Coll. Smith[3] and my Family.

[1] William Blake (1739–1803), a wealthy and well-connected South Carolina planter, lived much of his life in England but contrived to save most of his property in America; his wife was the former Anne Izard (*S.C. Hist. and Geneal. Mag.*, 2:231–232 [July 1901]; 9:81–82 [April 1908]; 34:199 [Oct. 1933]).

[2] The joint commission to negotiate commercial treaties held by JA and Jefferson (Franklin having returned to Philadelphia) was due to expire on 12 May of this year. Much of the Commissioners' correspondence between London and Paris during the past ten months had dealt with arrangements for the complicated negotiations with Morocco and Algiers which they were authorized to depute to Thomas Barclay and John Lamb respectively, who were exasperat-ingly deliberate in their movements. See the documents prepared for these agents by JA and Jefferson in Sept.–Oct. 1785, which are printed in Jefferson, *Papers*, ed. Boyd, 8:610–624. The advent of an envoy from Tripoli in London, one Abdrahaman, gave JA an opportunity to discover whether that piratical power would offer terms that the United States would or could accept; and on 17 Feb. 1786 he sent Jefferson a famous and inimitable account of his first discussion with "the Tripoline Ambassador," during which JA smoked a pipe which reached to the floor and exchanged "in aweful pomp . . . Wiff for Wiff" with his host (LbC, Adams Papers; same, 9:285–288). A further interview prompted JA to urge his colleague to come at once to London, not only in order to try to conclude a treaty with Tripoli but to finish

a negotiation begun in November with the Chevalier de Pinto, the minister from Portugal in London (to Jefferson, 21 Feb., LbC, Adams Papers; same, p. 295). They were also to make one last effort to interest the British government in a commercial treaty with the United States. On 13 March JA announced in a note to Carmarthen the arrival of Jefferson and requested an interview on behalf of both Commissioners (LbC, Adams Papers; same, p. 327). This first and sole visit of Jefferson to London lasted until 26 April. In respect to treaty-making it accomplished nothing. See the Commissioners' reports to Jay of 28 March and 25 April and the documents (mainly from the Adams Papers) relative to the commercial treaty with Portugal, which was signed by the American ministers on 25 April but which the Portuguese government allowed to lapse unratified (same, p. 357–359, 406–409, 410–433); also Jefferson's account of his English sojourn in his Autobiography (*Writings*, ed. Ford, 1:88–90).

³ William Stephens Smith (1755–1816), JA's secretary of legation and soon to be his son-in-law; he is designated in the present work as WSS. He was the son of John Smith, a merchant in New York City, was graduated from Princeton in 1774, studied law briefly, and served as an officer in the Continental Army, beginning in Aug. 1776, throughout the war, under the command or on the staff, successively, of Sullivan, Lee, Lafayette, and Washington. The best summary and appraisal of his service to June 1782 is in a certificate from Washington himself, stating that WSS in all his "several Military Stations" had "behaved with great fidelity, bravery, and good conduct" (Washington, *Writings*, ed. Fitzpatrick, 24:377). His last assignment was overseeing the British evacuation of New York City, and he left the army in Dec. 1783 with the rank of lieutenant colonel. Appointed by Congress secretary to the legation in London, he arrived just ahead of the Adamses and quickly overcame their doubts about him on the score of his being "a Knight of Cincinnatus" (JA to Gerry, 28 April 1785, and to Lafayette, 3 June 1785, letterbook copies, Adams Papers). Before long he also made a

deep impression on AA2, and on 12 June 1786 they were married; see note on entry of 1 July, below. WSS's dispatches as secretary of legation, 1785–1787, are in PCC, No. 92; they have more autobiographical than historical value. In 1788 the Smiths returned to America and settled in New York City. WSS held a succession of civil and military appointments but in 1806 virtually wrecked his career by complicity in the scheme of his old friend Francisco de Miranda to liberate Venezuela from Spanish rule. (He furnished a vessel for the expedition, and his son William Steuben Smith, to the infinite distress of JA, who profoundly disapproved of the whole enterprise, was captured by the Spanish authorities.) Having won an acquittal in a federal court on charges of violating the neutrality of the United States, but having also lost his post as surveyor of the Port of New York, WSS retired to "Smith's Valley," Lebanon, Hamilton co., N.Y., emerging only to serve a term in Congress 1813–1815, before his death. According to JQA, he left his worldly affairs "in inextricable confusion" (JQA, Diary, 4 May 1819). A memoir of WSS was prepared by his daughter Caroline Amelia (Smith) de Windt and published, together with some of his correspondence, in AA2's *Jour. and Corr.*, 1841–1842; the memoir, which is highly filial, is at 1:99–117. Katharine Metcalf Roof's *Colonel William Smith and Lady*, published in 1929, is based on both printed and MS sources (including some family papers which cannot currently be traced), but is excessively romantic and chatty in tone and is not documented. An earlier and briefer account is still useful, especially respecting WSS's family: Marcius D. Raymond, "Colonel William Stephens Smith," *N.Y. Geneal. and Biog. Record*, 25:153–161 (Oct. 1894). In 1795 WSS purchased an estate on the East River, built an elegant seat there which he called Mount Vernon, and planned a great stone stable which still survives at 421 East 61st Street, almost under the Queensboro Bridge in New York City. The history of the estate and the buildings on it has been related and illustrated by Joseph Warren Greene in "Mount Vernon on the East River and Colonel William Stephens

Smith," *NYHS Quart.*, 10:115–130 (Jan. 1927). Because he had greatly overreached himself financially, WSS was obliged to sell this property in 1796, and in 1826 the mansion was destroyed by fire. But the stone stable, after many vicissitudes, was acquired in 1924 by the Colonial Dames of America, which

uses it as a national headquarters under the name of the Abigail Adams Smith House; see a pamphlet by Katharine Metcalf Roof, *The Story of the Abigail Adams Smith Mansion and the Mount Vernon Estate*, issued by the Colonial Dames of America in 1949.

LONDON THURSDAY MARCH 30.

Presented Mr. Hamilton to the Queen at the Drawing Room.[1]

Dined at Mr. Paradices.[2] Count Warranzow [Woronzow] and his Gentleman and Chaplain, M. Sodorini the Venetian Minister, Mr. Jefferson, Dr. Bancroft, Coll. Smith and my Family.

Went at Nine O Clock to the French Ambassadors Ball, where were two or three hundred People, chiefly Ladies.[3] Here I met the Marquis of Landsdown and the Earl of Harcourt. These two Noblemen ventured to enter into Conversation with me. So did Sir George Young [Yonge]. But there is an Aukward Timidity, in General. This People cannot look me in the Face: there is conscious Guilt and Shame in their Countenances, when they look at me. They feel that they have behaved ill, and that I am sensible of it.

[1] William Hamilton (1745–1813), Pennsylvania land magnate and patron of landscape gardening, whose house called Bush Hill on the outskirts of Philadelphia the Adamses were to occupy when the government moved to that city in 1790; his niece Ann Hamilton was a great favorite in the Adams household in Grosvenor Square (Charles P. Keith, *The Provincial Councillors of Pennsylvania . . .*, Phila., 1883, p. 135–136; AA to Charles Storer, 22 May 1786, Adams Papers; AA to Mrs. Cranch, 12 Dec. 1790, MWA, printed in AA, *New Letters*, p. 65–67).

[2] John Paradise (1743–1795), a scholarly and eccentric Englishman of partly Greek descent, who had married the Virginia heiress Lucy Ludwell (1751–1814) in London in 1769; they lived and kept a salon in Charles Street, Cavendish Square. This dinner may have been the occasion on which Jefferson met the Paradises, whose adviser and protector during their endless personal and financial difficulties he became. See Archibald B. Shepperson, *John Paradise and Lucy Ludwell of London and Williamsburg*, Richmond, 1942.

[3] On 2 April AA wrote her nieces Elizabeth and Lucy Cranch a letter apiece on the Comte d'Adhémar's supper and ball, dwelling at length on what the ladies wore (in MHi:Norton Papers, and MWA, respectively; both printed in AA, *Letters*, ed. CFA, 1848, p. 278–286).

[NOTES ON A TOUR OF ENGLISH COUNTRY SEATS, &C., WITH THOMAS JEFFERSON, 4–10? APRIL 1786.][1]

Mr. Jefferson and myself, went in a Post Chaise to Woburn Farm,[2] Caversham, Wotton, Stowe, Edghill, Stratford upon Avon, Birmingham, the Leasowes, Hagley, Stourbridge, Worcester, Woodstock, Blenheim, Oxford, High Wycomb, and back to Grosvenor Square.

Edgehill and Worcester were curious and interesting to us, as Scænes where Freemen had fought for their Rights. The People in the Neighbourhood, appeared so ignorant and careless at Worcester that I was provoked and asked, "And do Englishmen so soon forget the Ground where Liberty was fought for? Tell your Neighbours and your Children that this is holy Ground, much holier than that on which your Churches stand. All England should come in Pilgrimage to this Hill, once a Year." This animated them, and they seemed much pleased with it. Perhaps their Aukwardness before might arise from their Uncertainty of our Sentiments concerning the Civil Wars.

Stratford upon Avon is interesting as it is the Scæne of the Birth, Death and Sepulture of Shakespear. Three Doors from the Inn, is the House where he was born, as small and mean, as you can conceive. They shew Us an old Wooden Chair in the Chimney Corner, where He sat. We cutt off a Chip according to the Custom. A Mulberry Tree that he planted has been cutt down, and is carefully preserved for Sale. The House where he died has been taken down and the Spot is now only Yard or Garden. The Curse upon him who should remove his Bones, which is written on his Grave Stone, alludes to a Pile of some Thousands of human Bones, which lie exposed in that Church. There is nothing preserved of this great Genius which is worth know-ing—nothing which might inform Us what Education, what Company, what Accident turned his Mind to Letters and the Drama. His name is not even on his Grave Stone. An ill sculptured Head is sett up by his Wife, by the Side of his Grave in the Church. But paintings and Sculpture would be thrown away upon his Fame. His Wit, and Fancy, his Taste and Judgment, His Knowledge of Nature, of Life and Charac-ter, are immortal.

At Birmingham, We only walked round the Town and viewed a manufactory of Paintings upon Paper.

The Gentlemens Seats were the highest Entertainment, We met with. Stowe, Hagley and Blenheim, are superb. Woburn, Caversham and the Leasowes are beautifull. Wotton is both great and elegant tho neglected. Architecture, Painting, Statuary, Poetry are all em-ployed in the Embellishment of these Residences of Greatness and Luxury. A national Debt of 274 millions sterling accumulated by Jobs, Contracts, Salaries and Pensions in the Course of a Century might easily produce all this Magnificence. The Pillars, Obelisks &c. erected in honour of Kings, Queens and Princesses, might procure the means. The Temples to Bacchus and Venus, are quite unnecessary as Mankind have no need of artificial Incitements, to such Amuzements.[3] The Temples of ancient Virtue, of the British Worthies, of Friendship, of Concord and Victory, are in a higher Taste. I mounted Ld. Cobhams Pillar 120 feet high, with pleasure, as his Lordships Name was familiar to me, from Popes Works.

Ld. Littletons Seat interested me, from a recollection of his Works, as well as the Grandeur and Beauty of the Scænes. Popes Pavillion and Thompsons [Thomson's] Seat, made the Excursion poetical. Shenstones Leasowes is the simplest and plainest, but the most rural of all. I saw no Spot so small, that exhibited such a Variety of Beauties.

It will be long, I hope before Ridings, Parks, Pleasure Grounds, Gardens and ornamented Farms grow so much in fashion in America. But Nature has done greater Things and furnished nobler Materials there. The Oceans, Islands, Rivers, Mountains, Valleys are all laid out upon a larger Scale.—If any Man should hereafter arise, to embellish the rugged Grandeur of Pens Hill, he might make some thing to boast of, although there are many Situations capable of better Improvement.

Since my Return[4] I have been over Black Fryars Bridge to see Viny's Manufacture of Patent Wheels made of bent Timber.

Viny values himself much upon his mechanical Invention. Is loud in praise of Franklin who first suggested to him the Hint of a bent Wheel. Franklin once told me, he had seen such a Wheel in Holland, before he set Viny to work. Viny says that Franklin said to him, "Mankind are very superficial and very dastardly. They begin upon a Thing but meeting with a difficulty they fly from it, discouraged. But they have Capacities if they would but employ them." "I," says Viny, "make it a Rule to do nothing as others do it. My first Question is how do others do this? and when I have found out, I resolve to do it, another Way, and a better Way. I take my Pipe and Smoke like a Limburners Kiln, and I find a Pipe is the best Aid to thinking." This Man has Genius, but has Genius always as much Vanity? It is not always so open. It is really modest and humble sometimes. But in Viny it is very vain. His Inventions for boiling and bending his Timber, and for drilling his Irons, are very ingenious. The force requisite for bending a Stick of Ash into a hoop, suitable for a large Wheel, or a small one, is prodigious.[5]

[1] In the MS the present entry has the bare caption "London April," indicating, as does the substance of the entry itself, that it was written after the tourists had returned from their circuit from London to scenic and historic sites in Surrey, Berks, Bucks, and Warwick, as far as The Leasowes in Shropshire, and back through Worcester and Oxford to London. The dates of the tour have been

well worked out by Julian P. Boyd in his editorial notes on Jefferson's "Memorandums" taken on the tour, the entries in Jefferson's Account Book being especially helpful for that purpose (Jefferson, *Papers*, 9:374). Readers comparing JA's and Jefferson's records of this pleasure jaunt should take note that the latter began his tour two days earlier (visiting Twickenham, Hampton Court, Woburn Farm, and other nearby points) and returned to London where he was joined by JA on 4 April, and also that Jefferson's notes have an addendum for his separate trip or trips to Moor Park, Enfield Chace, and Kew, which took place after he and JA had finished their tour together. They will further notice that while Jefferson mentions only those sites they visited that are dealt with in Thomas Whately's *Observations on Modern Gardening, Illustrated by Descriptions*, London, 1770, JA by no means confined himself to famous gardens, though he entered in the margins of his own copy of Whately's book (4th edn., 1777, in MB) every garden he visited with Jefferson.

² This was a return visit for Jefferson to Woburn Farm, near Weybridge, Surrey; see his Account Book, 1783–1790 (MHi), under both 3 and 4 April 1786.

³ Contrast Jefferson's memorandum at Hagley, Lord Lyttelton's seat near Stourbridge, Worcester: "From one of these [ponds] there is a fine cascade; but it can only be occasionally, by opening the sluice. This is in a small, dark, deep hollow, with recesses of stone in the banks on every side. In one of these is a Venus pudique, turned half round as if inviting you with her into the recess" (*Papers*, ed. Boyd, 9:372).

⁴ The evidence is indeterminate on the exact date of the return to London. When the two friends started they did not know how far they would go. "We have seen Magnificence, Elegance and Taste enough to excite an Inclination to see more," JA wrote his wife from the village of Buckingham, 5 April (NhD). "We conclude to go to Birmingham, perhaps to the Leasowes, and in that Case shall not have the Pleasure to see you, till Sunday

or Monday" (i.e. till the 9th or 10th). From entries in Jefferson's Account Book it is clear that on the 9th they visited Blenheim and Oxford and came on to Tatsworth and High Wycombe (where Jefferson paid for "ent[ertainmen]t" 10s. 10d.), which seems to indicate that they lodged there for the night. But he also recorded paying that day for horses as far as Uxbridge, which is closer to London than High Wycombe. Considering the distance and the stops, it is most likely that the travelers spent the night of the 9th on the road and came on to London next day.

On the 9th Jefferson also recorded in his Account Book: "received of Mr. Adams £9–9 in part towards preceding expences from our leaving London Apr. 4. which are joint." A later, separate account (DLC:Jefferson Papers, under date of Aug. 1786) is fuller:

"Whole expences of

| | |
|---|---|
| our journey | £35–16–9 |
| One half is | 17–18–4 1/2 |
| Mr. Adams furnished | 9– 9 |
| | £ 8– 9–4 1/2" |

⁵ The date of the visit to the works of John Viney, "Timber-bender, Great Surry-Str. Blackfri[ars]" (*The Universal British Directory of Trade, Commerce, and Manufacture*, 3d edn., London, 1797, 1:319), is also indeterminate, but it must have occurred between 10 and 15 April, since the next entry in the Diary bears the latter date. Jefferson was also in the party, and if JA was inclined to belittle Viney's bent-timber wheels because the proprietor admired both himself and Franklin too highly to suit JA's taste, Jefferson was later indignant on patriotic grounds. In a letter to St. John de Crèvecoeur about published claims for Viney's process, Jefferson recalled his visit to Viney's works and pointed out that farmers in New Jersey had long made cartwheels by bending saplings into circles and had probably learned the process from Book IV of the *Iliad*, "because ours are the only farmers who can read Homer" (15 Jan. 1787; Jefferson, *Papers*, ed. Boyd, 11:43–45).

SATURDAY AP. 15.

Dined with Mr. Brand Hollis in Chesterfield Street.[1] His Mantle Trees are ornamented with Antiques. Penates. Little brazen Images of the Gods. Venus, Ceres, Apollo, Minerva &c. Hollis is a Member of the Antiquarian Society. Our Company were Price,[2] Kippis, Bridgen, Romilly, and another besides Jefferson, Smith and myself.

[1] Thomas Brand (1719–1804), who had in 1774 assumed the name Hollis upon inheriting the estate of Thomas Hollis, the well-known benefactor of Harvard College. Brand Hollis was a wealthy dissenter, political radical, and antiquarian. In July the Adamses were to visit his country seat in Essex (see entries of 24–27 July, below), and for some years thereafter they corresponded with him. Some of their letters are printed in John Disney's *Memoirs of Thomas Brand-Hollis, Esq.*, London, 1808, p. 30–40. See also Caroline Robbins, "Thomas Brand Hollis (1719–1804), English Admirer of Franklin and Intimate of John Adams," Amer. Philos. Soc., *Procs.*, 97 (1953):239–247.

[2] Richard Price (1723–1791), of Newington Green, dissenting minister, writer on government and finance, and friend of America (*DNB*). JA and Price had been correspondents for some years and continued to be so until the latter's death. During their stay in London the Adamses regularly attended Price's religious meeting at Hackney.

AP. 18. TUESDAY.

Yesterday dined here, Mr. Jefferson, Sir John Sinclair, Mr. Heard, Garter King at Arms, Dr. Price, Mr. Brand Hollis, Mr. Henry Loyd of Boston, Mr. Jennings, Mr. Bridgen, Mr. Vaughan, Mr. Murray,[1] Coll. Smith.

[1] William Vans Murray (1760–1803), a young Marylander studying at the Middle Temple. He had formed a close friendship with JQA, was liked by all the Adamses, and became a valued political disciple of JA. A Federalist member of Congress, 1791–1797, he was appointed by Washington successor to JQA as minister at The Hague, and it was largely through his efforts, concluding in the Franco-American Convention of Mortefontaine, Sept.–Oct. 1800, that JA as President was able to end the quasi-war with France. See *DAB*; JQA's anonymous obituary of Murray in the *Port Folio*, 1st ser., 4:5–6 (7 Jan. 1804); articles by Alexander DeConde on Murray's diplomacy, *Md. Hist. Mag.*, 48:1–26 (March 1953), and on his *Political Sketches*, London, 1787 (a work dedicated to JA), MVHR, 41:623–640 (March 1955); and "Letters of William Vans Murray," ed. W. C. Ford, Amer. Hist. Assoc., *Ann. Rpt. for 1912*, p. 341–715 (mainly letters to JQA, from the Adams Papers).

LONDON APRIL 19. 1786. WEDNESDAY.

This is the Anniversary of the Battle of Lexington, and of my Reception at the Hague, by their High Mightinesses. This last Event is considered by the Historians, and other Writers and Politicians of England and France as of no Consequence: and Congress and the Citizens of the United States in General concur with them in Sentiment.

I walked to the Booksellers, Stockdale, Cadel, Dilly, Almon, and met Dr. Priestly for the first Time.[1]—The Conquest of Canaan, the Vision of Columbus, and the History of the Revolution in S. Carolina, were the Subject. I wrote a Letter to Jn. Luzac, for Dilly.[2]

This Day I met Dr. Priestly and Mr. Jennings, with the latter of whom I had a long Walk. I spent the Day upon the whole agreably enough. Seeds were sown, this Day, which will grow.[3]

[1] Joseph Priestley (1732–1804), dissenting clergyman, discoverer of oxygen, political radical, and voluminous writer on theology and other subjects (*DNB*). This was the beginning of a long but not untroubled relationship, for Priestley fled from Birmingham to Pennsylvania in 1794 and his political views and utterances during JA's Presidency led to suggestions that he be deported under the Alien Act—suggestions which JA refused to act on (JA, *Works*, 9:5–6, 13–14). There is an excellent brief account of their relationship in Haraszti, *JA and the Prophets of Progress*, ch. 14, which includes JA's marginalia in his own copies of some of Priestley's theological writings.

[2] Not found.

[3] This must pertain, at least in part, to JA's efforts to arrange for publication in London of the works of the American authors mentioned in the preceding paragraph. On 5 March David Humphreys, a poet himself and a member of the Connecticut circle that included Timothy Dwight and Joel Barlow, had written JA from Paris to say that WSS was bringing to London a printed copy of Dwight's *Conquest of Canaan* (which had been published at Hartford, 1785) and a MS copy of Barlow's *Vision of Columbus* (eventually published at Hartford, 1787), which their authors hoped could be published in London (Adams Papers). JA wrote Dwight on 4 April that he knew "of no heroick Poem superior to [*The Conquest of Canaan*], in any modern Language, excepting always Paradise lost," but after consulting with Dr. Price and others about the poems he predicted "a cold reception" for them from British publishers and readers (LbC, Adams Papers). On the same day he wrote Barlow in more or less similar terms (LbC, Adams Papers). By one means or another, however, both poems were eventually published in London, Barlow's by Dilly and Stockdale in 1787, and Dwight's by J. Johnson the next year. See Blanck, *Bibliog. Amer. Lit.*, 865, 5040; Sabin 3435, 21548.

At the end of 1785 David Ramsay, a literary physician and a delegate to the Continental Congress from South Carolina, had published at Trenton his two-volume *History of the Revolution of South-Carolina* and optimistically sent 1600 copies to Charles Dilly for sale in England. See Ramsay to JA, 23 Dec. 1785 (DSI), and JA's characteristic reply, 9 Feb. 1786 (LbC, Adams Papers). Ramsay later informed JA that Dilly had "declined publishing my history from an apprehension that it would expose him to prosecutions" (14 May 1786, Adams Papers). There were proposals to cut out passages that would give offense in England, but as JA told Ramsay, "your Friends have expressed so much Indignation at them that I hope and believe they will be laid aside, and that by degrees the American Edition may be sold" (1 Aug., LbC, Adams Papers). See, further, Robert L. Brunhouse, "David Ramsay's Publication Problems, 1784–1808," Bibliog. Soc. Amer., *Papers*, 39 (1945):51–67.

LONDON APRIL 20 1786 THURSDAY.

Went with Mr. Jefferson and my Family to Osterly, to view the Seat of the late Banker Child.[1] The House is very large. It is Three Houses, fronting as many Ways—between two is a double row of Six

Pillars, which you rise to by a flight of Steps. Within is a Square, a Court, a Terrace, paved with large Slate. The Green House and Hot House were curious. Blowing Roses, ripe Strawberries, Cherries, Plumbs &c. in the Hot House. The Pleasure Grounds were only an undulating Gravel Walk, between two Borders of Trees and Shrubs. All the Evergreens, Trees and Shrubbs were here. There is a Water, for Fish Ponds and for Farm Uses, collected from the Springs and wet Places in the farm and neighbourhood. Fine flocks of Deer and Sheep, Wood Doves, Guinea Hens, Peacocks &c.

The Verdure is charming, the Music of the Birds pleasant. But the Ground is too level.—We could not see the Apartments in the House, because We had no Tickett. Mrs. Child is gone to New Markett it seems to the Races.

The beauty, Convenience, and Utility of these Country Seats, are not enjoyed by the owners. They are mere Ostentations of Vanity. Races, Cocking, Gambling draw away their attention.

On our Return We called to see Sion House belonging to the Duke of Northumberland. This Farm is watered, by a rivulet drawn by an artificial Canal from the Thames. A Repetition of winding Walks, gloomy Evergreens, Sheets of Water, Clumps of Trees, Green Houses, Hot Houses &c. The Gate, which lets you into this Farm from the Brentford Road, is a beautifull Thing, and lays open to the View of the Traveller, a very beautifull green Lawn interspersed with Clumps and scattered Trees.

The Duke of Marlborough owns a House upon Sion Hill, which is only over the Way.

Osterly, Sion Place and Sion Hill are all in Brentford, within Ten Miles of Hide Park Corner. We went through Hide Park and Kensington to Brentford. We passed in going and returning, by Lord Hollands House, which is a Modern Building in the gothic manner.

[1] Osterley Park, Heston, Middlesex, the seat of Robert Child (d. 1782), of the Child banking dynasty, a 16th-century mansion that had been remodeled by Robert Adam; see Walpole, *Letters,* ed. Mrs. Toynbee, 8:291–292; 12:306; Walpole, *Corr.,* ed. W. S. Lewis, 28: 413–414.

### SUNDAY. AP. 23.

Heard Dr. Priestley at Mr. Linseys in Essex Street.[1]

[1] Theophilus Lindsey (1723–1808), minister of the Essex Street Chapel; the first avowedly Unitarian place of worship in London (*DNB*; Thomas Belsham, *Memoirs of the Late Reverend Theophilus Lindsey* ..., London, 1812).

MONDAY [24 APRIL].

Viewed the British Musæum. Dr. Grey who attended Us spoke very slightly of Buffon. Said "he was full of mauvais Fois. No Dependence upon him. Three out of four of his Quotations not to be found. That he had been obliged to make it his Business to examine the Quotations. That he had not found a quarter of them. That Linnæus was quoted from early Editions long after the last Edition was public of 1766 the 12th, which was inexcuseable. He did not think Buffon superiour to Dr. Hill. Both had Imagination &c."—This is partly national Prejudice and Malignity, no doubt.[1]

[1] This visit was arranged by Benjamin Vaughan. "Dr. Gray makes a private party for Mr. V:, and of course will be happy to see Mrs. and Miss Adams, with Col. Jefferson and Col. Smith" (Vaughan to JA, 20 April 1786, Adams Papers). Their guide was Edward Whitaker Gray, botanist and keeper of the collections of natural history and antiquities at the British Museum (*DNB*).

LONDON JUNE 26. 1786.

On Saturday night returned from a Tour to Portsmouth, in which We viewed Paines Hill in Surry, as We went out; and Windsor as We returned. We were absent four days. Paines Hill is the most striking Piece of Art, that I have yet seen. The Soil is an heap of Sand, and the Situation is nothing extraordinary. It is a new Creation of Mr. Hamilton. All made within 35 Years. It belongs to Mr. Hopkins, who rides by it, but never stops. The owners of these enchanting Seats are very indifferent to their Beauties.—The Country from Guilford to Portsmouth, is a barren heath, a dreary Waste.[1]

[1] "Painshill" (as spelled by Whately) was formerly "The seat of Mr. [Charles] Hamilton, near Cobham in Surry" (*Observations on Modern Gardening*, 4th edn., London, 1777, p. 184 and note). According to a marginal note in JA's copy of Whately, the Adamses' visit took place on 21 June, so that their excursion began on the 20th and ended on the 24th. In a letter to Lucy Cranch, 20 July, AA gave her impressions of Windsor at length (MHi:Misc. Bound Coll.; AA, *Letters*, ed. CFA, 1848, p. 297–298).

LONDON JULY 1. 1786.

Last night, Coll. Smith and his Lady, took their Leave of Us, and went to their House in Wimpole Street.[1]

Yesterday visited Desenfans's Collection of Pictures. A Port in Italy by Claude Lorraine, is the best Piece that remains. A Sampson sleeping in the Lap of Dalilah, while the Philistines cutt of his Locks, is said to be by Rubens, but Mr. Copely who was present doubts it.

Supposes it to be by some one of Reubens's School. Fine Colours and the Air of one of Reubens's Wives, is given to Dalilah.

This Art shews Us Examples of all the various Sorts of Genius which appear in Poetry. The Epic Poet, the Trajedian, the Comedian, The Writer of Pastorals, Elegies, Epigrams, Farces, and Songs. The Pleasure, which arises from Imitation, We have in looking at a Picture of a Lanscape, a Port, a Street, a Temple, or a Portrait. But there must be Action, Passion, Sentiment and Moral to engage my Attention very much. The Story of the Prince, who lost his own Life in a bold attempt to save some of his Subjects from a flood of Water is worth all the Paintings that have been exhibited this Year.

Copleys Fall of Chatham or Pierson, Wests Wolf, Epaminondas, Bayard &c. Trumbulls Warren and Montgomery, are interesting Subjects, and useful. But a Million Pictures of Flours, Game, Cities, Landscapes, with whatever Industry and Skill executed, would be seen with much Indifference. The Sky, the Earth, Hills and Valleys, Rivers and Oceans, Forrests and Groves, Towns and Cities, may be seen at any Time.

¹ The severing of the engagement between AA2 and Royall Tyler (see note 1 on entry of 20 June 1784 in AA's Diary, above), and the engagement and marriage of AA2 and WSS make a long story that is told in abundant detail in the family correspondence and can only be summarized here, with a general reference to the years 1784–1786 in Series II of the present edition. For a time after the Adams ladies' departure for Europe all went well enough with the engaged couple. AA2 commenced a correspondence with Tyler, and they exchanged miniature portraits. By the spring of 1785, however, AA2 became convinced that Tyler was not writing her, and after much silent suffering she complained to him on this score. This letter of hers, written soon after her arrival in London, has not been found, nor has his reply, which in her own opinion and that of her mother was a prevarication rather than a justification. Late in the summer of 1785, therefore, she returned him his few letters and his picture and requested him to deliver hers to her uncle, Richard Cranch (*Grandmother Tyler's Book: The Recollections of Mary Palmer Tyler . . .*, ed. Frederick Tupper and Helen Tyler

Brown, N.Y. and London, 1925, p. 76). In imparting this news to Mrs. Cranch (in whose house in Braintree Tyler boarded), AA quoted the maxim that "a woman may forgive the man she loves an indiscretion, but never a neglect" (15–16 Aug. 1785, MWA). During the following months Mrs. Cranch wrote long and gossipy letters saying that Tyler refused to admit that he had been dismissed, was otherwise uncandid with the Cranches, continued to wear AA2's miniature, and was in general behaving badly. When he could no longer conceal a situation that everyone in Braintree knew and discussed, Tyler declared, said Mrs. Cranch, that he would go to London and settle the little "misunderstanding" between himself and AA2, which he attributed to the prejudice and malice of her relatives at home (to AA, 10 Dec. 1785, 9 Feb. 1786, Adams Papers).

Meanwhile in London AA2 and WSS had of course been thrown much together, and by Aug. 1785 the secretary of legation had learned enough about the young lady's situation to conclude that, from motives of delicacy, he ought to step out of the scene for a time. He therefore requested and obtained a leave of absence to tour the Continent and was gone for several months. Returning toward the end of the year, he composed, in properly gallant and circumlocutory language, a formal request to AA for the hand of her daughter (29 Dec., Adams Papers). His suit, at least, was approved by both AA and JA, who had a very favorable opinion of his character and conduct, and in January and February AA dropped hints to JQA, her sister Cranch, and other family connections in America that AA2's marriage to a very worthy partner might be expected before long, though AA herself wished that there might be a longer interval in view of the broken engagement. The wedding took place on 12 June, and, by special license from the Archbishop of Canterbury, at the Legation in Grosvenor Square, with only the Copley family and a few other American friends present. The Bishop of St. Asaph officiated, because, as JA explained to Richard Cranch, "Dissenting Ministers have not authority to marry" (4 July, MWA).

### JULY [6] THURSDAY.

Dined at Clapham, at Mr. Smiths. Dr. Kippis, Dr. Reese, Dr. Harris, Mr. Pais, Mr. Towgood and his two Sons, Mr. Channing were the Company.[1]

Mr. Pais told a Story, admirably well of a Philosopher, and a Scotsman. The Wit attempted to divert himself, by asking the Scot if he knew the immense Distance to Heaven? It was so many Millions of Diameters of the Solar System, and a Cannon Ball would be so many Thousand Years in running there. I dont know the Distance nor the Time says the Scot, but I know it will not take you a Millionth part of the Time to go to Hell.—The Scottish Dialect, and Accent was admirably imitated. The Conversation was uniformly agreable. Nothing to interrupt it.

[1] The host was William Smith (1756–1835), M.P. for Sudbury, Suffolk, and a noted advocate of parliamentary reform, the repeal of religious tests, the abolition of the slave trade, and other liberal causes. The guests were mainly if not entirely dissenting clergymen and laymen. For Rev. Andrew Kippis and the encyclopedist Abraham Rees see *DNB*. Joseph Paice, who told the story that follows, was a patron and trustee of dissenting academies (Thomas Belsham, *Memoirs of the Late Reverend Theophilus Lindsey*, London, 1812, p. 291 and note).

### LONDON JULY 8. SATURDAY.

In one of my common Walks, along the Edgeware Road, there are fine Meadows, or Squares of grass Land belonging to a noted Cow keeper. These Plotts are plentifully manured. There are on the Side of the Way, several heaps of Manure, an hundred Loads perhaps in each heap. I have carefully examined them and find them composed of Straw, and dung from the Stables and Streets of London, mud, Clay, or Marl, dug out of the Ditch, along the Hedge, and Turf, Sward cutt up, with Spades, hoes, and shovels in the Road. This is laid in vast heaps to mix. With narrow hoes they cutt it down at each End, and with shovels throw it into a new heap, in order to divide it and mix it more effectually. I have attended to the Operation, as I walked, for some time. This may be good manure, but is not equal to mine, which I composed in similar heaps upon my own Farm, of Horse Dung from Bracketts stable in Boston, Marsh Mud from the sea shore and Street Dust, from the Plain at the Foot of Pens hill, in which is a Mixture of Marl.

### LONDON JULY 16, 1786. SUNDAY.

At Hackney, heard a Nephew of Dr. Price, who is settled at Yarmouth.

It may be of Use to minute miscellaneous Thoughts like Selden, Swift &c.

It is an Observation of one of the profoundest Inquirers into human Affairs, that a Revolution of Government, successfully conducted and compleated, is the strongest Proof, that can be given, by a People of their Virtue and good Sense. An Interprize of so much difficulty can never be planned and carried on without Abilities, and a People without Principle cannot have confidence enough in each other.

Mr. Langbourne of Virginia, who dined with Us on Fryday at Col. Smiths, dined here Yesterday. This Gentleman who is rich, has taken the Whim of walking all over Europe, after having walked over most of America. His Observations are sensible and judicious. He walks forty five or fifty miles a day. He says he has seen nothing superiour to the Country from N. York to Boston. He is in Love with N. England, admires the Country and its Inhabitants. He kept Company with the King of Frances Retinue, in his late Journey to Cherbourg. He says the Virginians have learned much in Agriculture as well as in Humanity to their Slaves, in the late War.[1]

[1] William Langborn (d. 1814), of King William co., Va., who had served as aide-de-camp to Lafayette in America and was in 1783 breveted lieutenant colonel. According to family tradition he wandered for many years on his walking tours. He had just arrived in England from France, where on 15 June Jefferson had issued him a passport. See Heitman, *Register Continental Army*; Jefferson, *Papers*, ed. Boyd, 5:637–638; 9:643–644; *WMQ*, 1st ser., 4:184 (Jan. 1896); 11:257–260 (April 1903); also entry of 21 July and note, below.

### LONDON JULY 20. THURSDAY.

"Every Act of Authority, of one Man over another for which there is not an absolute Necessity, is tyrannical."

"Le Pene che oltre passano la necessita di conservare il deposito della Salute pubblica, sono ingiuste di lor natura." Beccaria.[1]

The Sovereign Power is constituted, to defend Individuals against the Tyranny of others. Crimes are acts of Tyranny of one or more on another or more. A Murderer, a Thief, a Robber, a Burglar, is a Tyrant.

Perjury, Slander, are tyranny too, when they hurt any one.

[1] "All punishments that go beyond the requirements of public safety are by their very nature unjust"—Beccaria, *Dei delitti e delle pene*, ch. 2. JA is quoting from his own copy of the Italian text (new edn., Haarlem and Paris, 1780, p. 10), which he had acquired in July 1780. This passage is near the end of ch. 2. The quotation in English in the preceding paragraph of this entry is also from Beccaria, ch. 2 (near the beginning of that chapter), but is taken from JA's copy of the English translation (*An Essay on Crimes and Punishments*, London, 1775, p. 7). This shows that JA used the original and the translation together, but the new Italian edition of 1780 varies markedly in its text from the version on which the earlier translation was based. Both volumes are among JA's books in the Boston Public Library; JA presented the English translation to his son TBA in 1800.

LONDON JULY 21. FRYDAY.

Maj. Langbourne dined with Us again. He was lamenting the difference of Character between Virginia and N. England. I offered to give him a Receipt for making a New England in Virginia. He desired it and I recommended to him Town meetings, Training Days, Town Schools, and Ministers, giving him a short Explanation of each Article. The Meeting house, and Schoolhouse and Training Field are the Scænes where New England men were formed. Col. Trumbul, who was present agreed, that these are the Ingredients.[1]

In all Countries, and in all Companies for several Years, I have in Conversation and in Writing, enumerated The Towns, Militia, Schools and Churches as the four Causes of the Grouth and Defence of N. England. The Virtues and Talents of the People are there formed. Their Temperance, Patience, Fortitude, Prudence, and Justice, as well as their Sagacity, Knowledge, Judgment, Taste, Skill, Ingenuity, Dexterity, and Industry.—Can it be now ascertained whether Norton, Cotton, Wilson, Winthrop, Winslow, Saltonstall, or who, was the Author of the Plan of Town Schools, Townships, Militia Laws, Meeting houses and Ministers &c.

[1] Many years later Richard Rush, while serving as American minister in England, wrote JA that "An old Scotch woman, in North-Shields, signing herself Ann Hewison," had sent him (Rush) "a manuscript Quarto" of extracts from the diary of William Langborn "during his travels through several parts of Europe." No trace of Langborn's diary has been found, but Rush copied into his letter the following passage from it: "London July 18. 1786. Saturday— Did myself the pleasure, agreeably to yesterdays invitation, of dining with Mr. Adams and his family. We had but one stranger, he remarkable for his American attachments. Our dinner was plain, neat, and good. Mrs. Adams's accomplish-

ments and agreeableness would have apologized for any thing otherwise; after dinner took an airing in the park.

"Thursday the 23. Dined again with Mr. Adams. Mr. Trumball, a student of Mr. Wests was there. The English custom although bad still exists; we set to our bottle; I not for wine, but for the conversation of the Minister, which was very interesting, honest and instructive. He informed us that the Portuguese Minister had by order of his Queen a pleasing piece of intelligence, which was, that

her fleet in the Mediterranean had her orders to give the same protection to all American vessels as to her own. I must not forget Mr. Adams's requisites to make citizens like those republicans of New England; they were, that we should form ourselves into townships, encourage instruction by establishing in each public schools, and thirdly to elevate as much the common people by example and advice to a principle of virtue and religion" (Rush to JA, 2 May 1818, Adams Papers).

JULY 24. 1786. MONDAY.[1]

Went with Mr. Bridgen, Col. Smith, Mrs. Smith, to The Hide in Essex, the Country Seat of Brand Hollis Esqr.[2] We breakfasted at Rumford, and turned out of the Way to see the Seat of Lord Petre at Thorndon. Mr. Hollis prefers the Architecture of this House to that at Stow, because it is more conformable to Paladio, his Bible for this kind of Knowledge. There are in the back Front six noble Corinthian Pillars. There is a grand Saloon unfinished in which are many ancient Pictures, one of Sir Thomas More, his Wife and two Daughters, with a Group of other Figures. There is in another Appartment, a Picture of the Cornaro Family by Titian. This House is vast, and the Appartements are grand and the Prospects from the Windows are extensive and agreable. The furniture is rich and elegant. The Pictures of King James the 2d, of Lord Derwentwater who was beheaded in 1715, as well as many others besides that of Sir Thomas More, shew that the Family is Catholick. The Library shews this more fully as the Books are generally of that kind, but the Chapel furnishes full proof. The Library is semicircular, with Windows and Mahogany Collonades, very elegant, but contrived more as an ornamented Passage to the Chappell, than for Study. There are two Stoves, but at neither of them could a Student be comfortable in cold Weather. I might talk of Glades and Forrests, Groves and Clumps, with which this House is surrounded like all other Palaces of the kind.

We dined at the Hide, with Mr. Brand Hollis and his Sister Miss Brand. This is a curious Place. The House is the Residence of an Antiquarian, as most of the Apartments as well as the great Hall, sufficiently shew. I will perhaps take a List of all the Antiques in this Hall. The most interesting to me is the Bust of my Friend as well as Mr. Brands Friend, the late Thomas Hollis Esq., in beautifull white Marble.

This House which is a decent handsome one was the Seat of Mr. Brands Father, and the Chamber where We lodge, is hung round with the Portraits of the Family. It is at the End of the House, and from two Windows in front and two others at the End, We have a pleasant View of Lawns and Glades, Trees and Clumps and a Piece of Water, full of Fish. The Borders, by the Walks, in the Pleasure Grounds, are full of rare Shrubbs and Trees, to which Collection America has furnished her full Share. I shall here have a good Opportunity to take a List of these Trees, Shrubbs and Flours. Larches, Cypruses, Laurells are here as they are every where. Mr. Brand Hollis has, planted near the Walk from his Door to the Road, a large and beautifull Furr, in Honour of the late Dr. Jebb his Friend. A Tall Cyprus in his Pleasure Grounds he calls General Washington, and another his Aid du Camp Col. Smith.

[1] First entry in D/JA/45, an un-stitched gathering of leaves identical in format with the preceding booklets and containing entries only through 29 [i.e. 28] July 1786; most of the leaves are blank.

[2] Near Ingatestone. Brand Hollis him-self used the spelling "The Hide," but his heir and biographer, John Disney, whose *Memoirs of Thomas Brand-Hollis, Esq.*, London, 1808, contains a number of views of the house and grounds, used the presumably more elegant form, "The Hyde."

### THE HIDE JULY 25 1786 TUESDAY.

Mr. Brand Hollis and Mr.[1] Brand, Mr. and Mrs. Smith, and Mr. and Mrs. Adams, took a ride to Chelmsford, stopped at a Booksellers, the Printer of a Newspaper in which Mr. B. Hollis had printed the late Act of Virginia in favour of equal religious Liberty. We then went to Moulsham Hall, built originally by Lord Fitzwalter, but lately owned by Sir William Mildmay, one of the Commissaries[2] with Governor Shirley at Paris in 1754, for settling the Boundaries between the French and English in America. Lady Mildmay owns it, at present, but is not yet come down from London. Mr. B. Hollis admires the Architecture of this House, because it is according to the Principles of Palladio. The Apartments are all well proportioned in Length, Breadth and Height. There is here a Landscape of Rembrandt. The Words Halls, Parlours, Saloons and Drawing Rooms occur upon these Occasions, but to describe them would be endless. We returned by another road through the race grounds, to the Hide and after Dinner, made a Visit to the Gardiners House to see his Bees. He is Bee mad, Mr. B. Hollis says. He has a number of Glass Hives, and has a curious Invention to shut out the Drones. He has nailed thin and narrow Laths at the Mouth of the Hive, and has left Spaces between them barely wide enough for the small Bees to creep through. Here and there he has made a Notch in the lath large enough for a Drone to pass, but this Notch he has covered with a thin light clapper which turns easily upwards upon a Pivot. The Drone easily lifts up the Clapper and comes out, but as soon as he is out, the Clapper falls and excludes the Drone, who has neither Skill nor Strength to raise it on the outside. Thus shut out from the Hive the Gardiner destroys them because he says they do nothing but eat Honey. The Gardiner who is a Son of Liberty, and was always a Friend to America, was delighted with this Visit. Dame says he to his Wife, you have had the greatest honour done you to day that you ever had in your Life.—Mr. B. Hollis says he is a proud Scotchman, but a very honest Man and faithfull Servant.—After Tea Mr. B. Hollis and I took a circular Walk, round the Farm. He shew Us a kind of Medallion, on which was curiously wrought a Feast of all the Heathen Gods and Goddesses sitting round a Table. Jupiter throws down upon the Middle of it, one of his Thunder bolts, flaming at each End with Lightning, and lights his own Pipe at it, and all the others follow his Example. Venus is whiffing like a Dutchman, so is Diana and Minerva, as well as Mars, Bachus and Apollo.

Mr. B. Hollis is a great Admirer of Marcus Aurelius. He has him in Busts, and many other Shapes. He observed to me, that all the Painters of Italy, and from them most others, have taken the Face of Marcus Aurelius, for a Model in painting Jesus Christ. He admires Julian too, and has a great veneration for Dr. Hutchinson, the Moral Writer who was his Tutor, or Instructor.[3] He has a Number of Heads of Hutchinson, of whom he always speaks with Affection and Veneration. Ld. Shaftesbury too is another favourite of his.

In the dining room are two Views of that Estate in Dorsetshire, which the late Mr. Hollis gave to Mr. Brand. There is only a Farm House upon it. Here are to be seen Hollis Mede and Brand Pasture. In Hollis Mede, Mr. Hollis was buried, ten feet deep, and then ploughed over, a Whim to be sure. But Singularity was his Characteristic. He was benevolent and beneficient, however, throughout.—In the Boudoir is a Dagger, made of the Sword which killed Sir Edmunbury Godfrey. An Inscription—Memento Godfrey, Protomartyr, pro Religione Protestantium.

Mr. Hollis's Owl, Cap of Liberty and Dagger are to be seen every where. In the Boudoir, a Silver cup with a Cover, all in the shape of an Owl, with two rubies for Eyes. This piece of Antiquity was dug up, at Canterbury, from ten feet depth. It was some monkish conceit.

[1] Doubtless a slip of the pen for "Miss."

² JA probably meant to write "Commissioners."
³ Francis Hutcheson (1694–1746), professor of moral philosophy at Glasgow, where Brand Hollis had studied.

### JULY 26. WEDNESDAY.

Mr. B. Hollis, Miss Brand, Mrs. Adams, Mrs. Smith, and I walked to Mill Green, or Mill Hill the Seat of a Mr. Allen a Banker of London.¹ We walked over the Pleasure Grounds and Kitchen Garden and down to Cocytus, a canal or Pond of Water surrounded with Wood in such a Manner as to make the Place gloomy enough for the Name. This is a good Spot, but Mr. Allen has, for want of Taste, spoiled it by new Pickett Fences at a great Expence. He has filled up the Ditches and dug up the Hedges and erected wooden Fences and brick Walls, a folly that I believe in these days is unique. They are very good, civil People, but have no Taste.

¹ According to AA2, who in a journal-letter to JQA, 27 July–22 Aug., adds many details about this excursion to Essex that are not found elsewhere, Allen was a retired wine merchant (Adams Papers).

### THE HIDE JULY 28 [*i.e.* 27]. 1786. THURSDAY.

Went with Mrs. Adams to Braintree about Eighteen miles from the Hide. As our Objects were fresh Air, Exercise and the Gratification of Curiosity, I thought We ought to make a little Excursion to the Town after which the Town in New England where I was born and shall die was originally named. The Country between Chelmsford and Braintree, is pleasant and fertile, tho less magnificent in Buildings and Improvements than many other Parts of England: but it is generally tillage Land and covered with good Crops of Barley, Oats, Rye,¹ Wheat and Buckwheat.

Braintree is a Markett Town, and Fairs are held here at certain Seasons. I went to the Church, which stands in the Middle of a triangular Piece of Ground, and there are parallell to each Side of the Tryangle, double Rows of handsome Lime Trees, which form the Walks and Avenues to the Church. The Church is a very old Building of Flint Stones. Workmen were repairing it, and I went all over it. It is not much larger than [Mr?]² Cleverleys Church at Braintree in New England. I examined all the Monuments and Grave Stones in the Church and in the Church Yard, and found no one Name of Person or Family of any Consequence, nor did I find any Name of any of our New England Families except Wilson and Joslyn, Hawkins, Griggs and Webb. I am convinced that none of our Braintree Families came from this Village, and that the Name was given it by Mr. Coddington in Compliment to the Earl of Warwick, who in the Begginning and Middle of the Seventeenth Century had a Manor here, which however at his death about 1665 went out of his Family. The Parish of Bocking has now more good Houses. Braintre is at present the Residence only of very ordinary People, manufacturers only of Bays's.[3]

Chelmsford was probably named in Compliment to Mr. Hooker who was once Minister of that Town in Essex, but afterwards in Holland, and after that Minister at "Newtown" (Cambridge) and after that at ⟨New Haven⟩ Hartford in New England. We returned to Dinner, and spent the Evening in examining the Curiosities of Mr. Thomas Brand Hollis's House. His Library, his Miltonian Cabinet, his Pictures, Busts, Medals, Coins, Greek, Roman, Carthaginian and Egyptian Gods and Goddesses, are a Selection of the most rare, and valuable. It would be endless to go over the whole in Description.

We have had, with Alderman Bridgen, an agreable Tour and an exquisite Entertainment.

I should not omit Alderman Bridgens Nuns, and Verses. About 30 Years ago Mr. Bridgen in the Austrian Netherlands purchased a compleat Collection of the Portraits of all the orders of Nuns, in small duodecimo Prints. These he lately sent as a Present to the Hide, and Mr. Hollis has placed them in what he calls his Boudoir, a little room between his Library and Drawing Room. Mr. Bridgen carried down with him a Copy of Verses of his own Composition, to be hung up with them. The Idea is that banished from Germany by the Emperor they were taking an Asylum at the Hide, in sight of the Druid, the Portico of Athens and the verable[4] Remains of Egyptian, Greek, Roman and Carthaginian Antiquities.[5]

[1] MS: "Rue"—clearly an inadvertence.

[2] Overwritten, possibly with an initial letter, and not clear. At any rate, Joseph Cleverly, JA's old schoolmaster, is meant; he conducted services at Christ Church, Braintree, during the Revolution while no Anglican clergyman resided there (Pattee, *Old Braintree and Quincy*, p. 255).

[3] "At 2 Pappa and Mamma returnd not much pleased with the appearance of the Town they had been to visit. Mr. H. told us it was a Poor, dirty, miserable village and such they found it" (AA2 to JQA, 27 July–22 Aug., Adams Papers).

[4] Thus in MS.

[5] A large broadside printed text of Alderman Bridgen's verses, "On sending some Pictures of Nuns and Fryers to Thomas Brand Hollis, Esq. at the Hyde in Essex, supposed to be Real Personages turned out of the Convents and Monasteries in Flanders by the Emperor," without author's name, imprint, or date, is in the Adams Papers under the assigned date of July 1786.

JULY 29 [*i.e.* 28]. 1786. FRYDAY.

Returned to Grosvenor Square to Dinner.[1]

[1] The Adams party's return to London on Friday, 28 July, is verified by a passage in AA2's letter to JQA, 27 July–22 Aug. (Adams Papers).

Here ensues a gap in JA's Diary of a full year, his next (and last European) entries being the fragmentary notes of his tour with AA and AA2 to the west of England in July–Aug. 1787.

American relations with Great Britain during this year remained *in statu quo*, no new issues of any magnitude arising and no standing issues being settled. During the spring and early summer of 1786 JA had reiterated to both official and private correspondents that no diplomatic progress would be made in London until the various state acts impeding payment to British creditors were repealed, for, as he observed to Samuel Adams, "When We have done Equity We may with a good Grace, demand Equity" (2 June 1786, NN; see also JA to Jay, 25 May, 16 June, letterbook copies, Adams Papers, printed in *Dipl. Corr., 1783–1789*, 2:659–661, 668–670). Ten months after JA had made his first recommendation on this point to Congress as urgently as he knew how to do, that body unanimously adopted a report by Foreign Secretary Jay that had long been on its table, the heart of which was "That all such acts or parts of Acts as may be now existing in any of the States repugnant to the treaty of Peace ought to be forthwith repealed" (21 March 1787; JCC, 32:124–125); this was to be embodied in a circular letter to the states, adopted 13 April (same, p. 177–184).

On 25 Jan. 1787 JA had the satisfaction of signing, at last, the treaty, or rather the "unilaterally executed grant" of protection for American shipping, which the gifts conveyed by Thomas Barclay to the Emperor of Morocco had purchased. Jefferson had signed this document in Paris on 1 Jan.; an English text is printed as an enclosure in Barclay's letter to the Commissioners, Cadiz, 2 Oct. 1786, together with valuable editorial notes, in Jefferson, *Papers*, ed. Boyd, 10:418–427; see also Miller, ed., *Treaties*, 2:185–227.

More important than any of the occurrences mentioned above was the Adamses' visit during Aug.–Sept. 1786 to the Netherlands. Its importance is owing to a consequence that was unexpected and has been too often overlooked. On his return from the family excursion to Essex at the end of July, JA found Congress' tardy ratification, dated 17 May 1786, of the commercial treaty with Prussia (see note 1 on entry of 27 March, above). Since by its Article 27 an exchange of ratifications was required within one year of the signing of the treaty, that is to say by 10 Sept. 1786, since there was no Prussian minister residing at either London or Paris, and since time was short, JA felt obliged to go himself to The Hague for that purpose. This would also enable him to pay his respects to officials and friends in the republic to which he was still the accredited United States minister and, by taking AA with him, to show her the country she had expected to but did not visit three years earlier. Leaving London on 3 Aug., JA and AA traveled by way of Harwich, Hellevoetsluis, and Rotterdam to The Hague, where they arrived on the 8th. On that very day JA signed and exchanged ratifications with the Prussian minister Thulemeier. The Adamses were now free for diversions, and AA characteristically provided in her letters a full and colorful record of Dutch modes of travel, social activities, and sightseeing during their stay of nearly a month; her letters to her daughter are in AA2, *Jour. and Corr.*, 2:53–64; see also AA to Mrs. Cranch, 12 Sept., MWA, printed in AA, *Letters*, ed. CFA, 1848, p. 300–305.

Among other places, they visited Utrecht, where they happened to be present when the new magistrates of that city, which had undergone a constitutional reform at the hands of the Patriot party, were sworn into office. The incident had a profound effect on JA. "In no Instance, of ancient or modern History," he wrote Jefferson, 11 Sept., "have the People ever asserted more unequivocally their own inherent and unalienable Sovereignty" (LbC, Adams Papers; Jefferson, *Papers*, ed. Boyd, 10:348). And in a letter to Jay he represented this event, which was a high-water mark in the efforts of the Dutch Patriots, as the first visible fructification in Europe of the principles of the American Revolution (3 Oct., LbC, Adams Papers; *Dipl. Corr.*, *1783–1789*, 2:676–677). His discussions with Dutch friends and his reflections on the significance of what was happening in their country became one of JA's principal motives in undertaking the most ambitious literary work of his life, *A Defence of the Constitutions of Government of the United States of America.* The root of this treatise lay, as is well known, in JA's objections to Turgot's critique of the American state constitutions, embodied in Turgot's letter to Price written in 1778 but first published in 1784 (see note on Turgot and JA under the entry of 9 April 1778, above). But its other immediate inspiration (besides the events occurring in the Dutch Republic) was the disturbing news he read in London about "the Seditious Meetings in the Massachusetts" that were to lead to Shays' Rebellion; see JA to Richard Cranch, 15 Jan. 1787 (NN; JA, *Works*, 1:432–433), and also Letter I in the *Defence* itself, which seriously suggested that the discontented people in Massachusetts wished to depose the governor and senate of that state "as useless and expensive branches of the constitution" because they had been reading Turgot's letter to Price (JA, *Defence* [vol. 1], London, 1787, p. 4).

Upon his return from the Netherlands JA began with almost feverish haste and concentration to read for and compose his treatise on the dangers of republican government and the means of averting them. The first volume, an octavo of 392 pages, was published before the middle of Jan. 1787. A second followed in September, and a third in 1788. He was so absorbed in the task that he abandoned his Diary altogether; and his letterbooks during the fall, winter, and spring of 1786–1787 are more meager than at any other period of his decade in Europe. AA took up part of the burden he dropped, writing with greater frequency to American correspondents and explaining that "Mr. Adams ... says his friends must not expect any letters but printed ones from him" (to Cotton Tufts, 29 April 1787, Adams Papers). (The *Defence* was composed in the form of letters, nominally addressed to JA's son-in-law, WSS.)

JA recognized that the *Defence* was a "strange" and faulty book, but it was his chief political testament, and its composition, the complex bibliography of its successive editions, and its reception and influence in Europe and America, as well as upon his own career, deserve closer study than they have yet had—indeed could have had until his papers bearing on the subject, including a mass of notes and drafts still only partially arranged, were made available. Pending such a comprehensive study, the reader may be referred to three especially pertinent chapters in Zoltán Haraszti's *JA and the Prophets of Progress* (chs. 3, 8, 9), and to the excellent analysis of JA's political theory in a world context which will be found in Robert R. Palmer's *Age of the Democratic Revolution* ... : *The Challenge*, Princeton, 1959, p. 269 ff.

JA was obliged to interrupt work on Volume 2, dealing with the history of Italian republics, by another and quite unexpected trip to the Netherlands in May–June 1787. He went in order to execute a contract for a third American loan in Amsterdam, essential to meeting a large interest payment for which the measures of the Board of Treasury in New York had proved inadequate. Leaving London on 25 May with John Brown Cutting as a traveling companion and temporary secretary, he arrived just in time to save American credit in the Netherlands once more. Despite the serious civil disturbances then going on (there was rioting in Amsterdam during his first two nights there that presaged the extinction of the Patriot party), the bankers had prepared a contract for a loan of a million guilders at 5 per cent interest, to be redeemed in 1798–1802; JA signed it on 1 June, and during the following days signed 2,000 obligations on behalf of the United States. By 9 June he was back in London. (See JA's correspondence with the Willinks and Van Staphorsts, May–June 1787; J. B. Cutting to AA, 25, 28 May; JA to AA, 1, 2 June; all in Adams Papers; P. J. van Winter, *Het aandeel van den Amsterdamschen handel aan den opbouw van het Amerikaansche gemeenebest*, The Hague, 1927–1933, 1:175–178.) JA had some qualms about this transaction, since he had acted in the financial emergency without specific authorization from Congress; see his report to Jay, 16 June, enclosing the contract (LbC, Adams Papers; *Dipl. Corr.*, 1783–1789, 2:787–792). Congress, however, promptly ratified the contract, 11 Oct. (*JCC*, 33:649); an English translation of the contract, with the ratification signed by Pres. Arthur St. Clair and Secretary Thomson, is in Adams Papers.

In March 1787 the Smiths moved from Wimpole Street to the Legation in Grosvenor Square because AA2 was expectant. On 2 April, with Dr. John Jeffries, a former Bostonian and loyalist, in attendance, JA's first grandchild was born; it was a boy and was christened, by Dr. Price, William Steuben Smith (AA to Mrs. Cranch, 20 Jan., 25–27 Feb.; to Lucy Cranch, 26 April; all in MWA). In announcing this news to C. W. F. Dumas, 3 April, JA said he now expected to have "some Amusement" (LbC, Adams Papers).

# Abigail Adams' Diary of a Tour from London to Plymouth, 20–28 July 1787 [1]

### FRYDAY JULY 20 1787 LONDON.

This day three years I landed at Deal. Since that time I have travelld to France, to Holland and several parts of England but have never kept any journal, or record except what my Letters to my Friends may furnish nor have I ever perused this Book since it was first written till this Day when looking into the first page, it excited all my former emotions and made the Tears flow affresh. I have now determined on this journey to keep a journal. This Day we set out from Grosvenour Square on a Tour to Plimouth. Mr. Adams, myself, Mrs. Smith and Son about 3 months old, her Nursery maid, Esther my own maid and Edward Farmer a footman, our own Coachman and a postilion. Our first Stage was to Epsom in the county of Surry where we dinned. This place is famous for the races which are held there. From Epsom we proceeded to Guilford where we put up for the Night. This is an agreeable road and a highly cultivated Country.

[1] From a MS designated as M/AA/1 (Adams Papers, Microfilms, Reel No. 197), described in note 1 on the entry of 20 June 1784 in AA's Diary, above. Though AA, JA, and AA2 all kept journals at times during their excursion to the west of England, the results, even when combined, are meager and leave numerous gaps. JA's few fragmentary notes have been placed after AA's journal entries, which cover only the first nine days of a month's trip of some 600 miles. AA2's record is longer than either her mother's or her father's, but since the MS has not been found and the text as published (AA2, *Jour. and Corr.*, 1:84–94) is not trustworthy, it has not been included in the present edition, though it has been occasionally quoted or cited in editorial notes.

The excursion had been recommended by the Adamses' physician, Dr. John Jeffries, because AA's health had been poor throughout the winter and spring (AA to Mrs. Cranch, 16 July 1787, owned by Dr. Eugene F. DuBois, N.Y. City, 1957). JA and AA had also been warmly and repeatedly urged by John Cranch of Axminster, nephew of AA's brother-in-law, Richard Cranch, to visit Devon, the county from which the Cranches and Palmers of Braintree, Mass., had emigrated. JA having completed the second volume of his *Defence* for the printer (though only just in time), and WSS being absent on a mission for Congress to the Queen of Portugal, the moment was opportune for a family excursion. (On WSS's mission to Portugal, April–Aug. 1787, see his report to Jay, 12 Sept., with enclosures; *Dipl. Corr.*, *1783–1789*, 3:69–84.)

## 21.

We set out about 9 in the morning, stoped and baited at Farnham, dinned at Alton and reached Winchester about 8 oclock. Robert Quincy Earl of Winchester formerly resided here and was I presume an ancestor of my mothers, bearing the same arms. There is a Cathedral Church here, it being a Bishops See. The present Bishop of Winchester is Brother to Lord North whose Seat and park is in Farnham. There is a remarkable high Hill calld Catharine Hill just after you quit Guilford near two miles long from which one has a good view of the Town which seems to be placed between 2 Hills. The Houses are very old. In further examining respecting this earl of Winchester, I find that Saar de Quincy was created first Earl of Winchester by King John in 1224 and signed Magna Charta. In 1321 the title is said to be extinct, but this I do not believe as my Ancestors who went to America bore the same Name and Arms. And I well remember seeing when I was a child a parchment containing the Descent of the families in the possession of my Grandfather and that it was traced back to William the conquerer who came from Normandy. Saer de Quincy was a French Marquiss. Mr. Edmund Quincy borrowed this Genealogicall Table of my Grandmother for some purpose and lost it as he says.[1] If the Tittle had been extinct for want of Male Heirs, it is not probable that an illegitimate ospring would have taken pains to have preserved the Geneoligy. These matters have heitherto been of so little consideration in America that scarcly any person traces their desent beyond the third Generation by which means the Britains sometimes twit us of being descended from the refuse of their Goals and from transported convicts. But it is well known that the first setlers of New England were no such persons, but worthy conscientious people who fled from Religious percecution to a New World and planted themselves amidst Savages that they might enjoy their Religion unmolested.

[1] "As the old Gentleman [Col. Edmund Quincy] is still living, I wish Mr. Cranch would question him about it, and know what Hands it went into, and whether there is any probability of its ever being recoverd, and be so good as to ask uncle [Norton] Quincy how our Grandfather came by it, and from whence our Great-granfather came? where he first settled? and take down in writing all you can learn from him, and Mr. Edmund Quincy respecting the family. You will smile at my Zeal, perhaps on this occasion, but can it be wonderd at that I should wish to Trace an Ancestor amongst the Signers of Magna Carta" (AA to Mrs. Cranch, 15 Sept. 1787, MWA).

Went to the Cathedral Church at Winchester. It is a very curious structure. It is said to have been part built by Bishop Walkelyne in the year 1079. In a Chaple belonging to this Edifice Queen Mary was married to King Philip, and the Chair in which she was seated during the ceremony is still to be seen. There is also a Statue of James the 1 and Charles the first. This place since its first foundation has been 3 time[s] nearly destroyd by fire. It has been the residence of many Kings, and this place was the first that obtain a free Charter which King Henry the first Granted. After hearing divine service, we proceeded to South hampton which is bounded by the Sea and is a very pretty Town much resorted to during the Summer Months as a Sea Bathing place, which for the first time in my Life I tried this morning, 24th of July.[1]

[1] Error for 23 July. AA's dates are one day in advance until her entry for 26 July, which is correct because, inadvertently or not, she included two days in the entry she dated 25 July.

### 24 [*i.e.* 23] JULY.

We dinned at South hampton and set out after dinner for Salsbury 22 miles, where we meant to have passt the night and taken a view of the Town, but when we reachd the Inn we found it fully occupied, and not a single Bed to be had neither at the Inn we went to, or any other in Town, the Court of Assize being held there for the week. Tho nine oclock we were obliged to proceed to the next stage eleven miles, which we did not accomplish till eleven oclock. We then put up at an inn in a small thatchd villiage Woodyats by Name. We were neatly accommodated, but not a single Hut in sight. Through a Country as fertile as Eden and cultivated like a Garden you see nothing but misirable low thatchd Huts moulderd by time with a small old fashiond glass window perhaps two in the whole House. A stone floor is very common. One may travell many miles without seeing a House. On some lone Heath a Shepeards Cottage strikes your Eye, who with his trusty dog is the keeper of a vast flock owned by some Lord, or Duke. If poverty, hunger and want should tempt him to slay the poorest Lamb of the flock, the penal Laws of this Land of freedom would take his Life, from thence I presume the old proverb took its rise, one had as goods be hanged for a Sheep as a Lamb, and if the Lord or Duke was murderd the poor man would no more forfeit his life, than for the Sheep or Lamb, yet surely the crime is very different.

### JULY [24–]25.

We left this village and proceeded on our way to Blanford where we put up for the Night. Saw nothing striking in this place and met with poor accommodations oweing chiefly to the Assizes, which were to commence the next Day and the House was nearly occupied when we arrived. We stayd only untill the next morning and then persued our route. Arrived at diner time at Dorchester an other very old Town. It is famous for Beer and Butter. It resembles Dorchester in New England, in the Hills and in the appearence of the Land. About four miles from the middle of the Town on the road to Weymouth is a very Regular entrenchment upon a very high Hill: this must have been the encampment of some Army. Some say it was a Danish encampment, others that it was a Roman. There is an Amphitheatre in the middle of a mile circumference and a castle calld Maiden Castle. Weymouth lies 8 miles from Dorchester, is a Sea port and esteemed a very Healthey Situation, a Noted Bathing place and much resorted to during the Summer Months.[1] The whole Town draws its Support from the company which frequent it. It is a small place and little Land which is not occupied by Buildings for the conveniency of the company. It has no Manufactory of any kind. Some vessels are built here. We tarried here only one Night.

[1] "we . . . went ten miles out of our way in order to visit Weymouth merely for its Name" (AA to Mrs. Cranch, 15 Sept. 1787, MWA).

### JULY 26[–27].

Our next Stage was Bridport a small Sea port but a very bad harbour. No trade only in coal which is carried there by water for the supply of the inhabitants. We dinned there, and then proceeded for Axmister, the first town in the County of Devonshire. Here we put up at the best Inn I ever saw, the George kept by a Mr. Ellis.[1] The appartments were not only neat and convenient, but every thing had an air of Elegance and taste. Here we were visited by Mr. John Cranch a Nephew of my Brother Cranch who is an Attorney and resides here.[2] The Town is a little narrow dirty village, but a great through fare, all the Plimouth, Exeter and many other Stages passing through it. Went with Mr. Cranch to see the Manufactory of carpets for which this place is famous. The building in which this buisness is carried on is by no means equal to an American Barn. The whole Buisness is performd by women and children. The carpets are equally durable with the Turky, but surpass them in coulours and figure.

They are made of coars wool and the best are 24 shillings a square yd., others at fourteen. They have but two prices. From thence we went to a tape manufactory which are the only two manufactories in the Town. Mr. Cranch invited us to drink Tea with him. He is a single man, of a delicate complexion, small features, about 26 or 27 years old. He never looks one in the face and appears as if he had been cramped and cowed in his Youth. He has a good understanding, which he has improved by reading, and appears a virtuous amiable man. He accompanied us to Exeter and Plimouth.[3]

[1] "In obedience to your command about the inns, permit me to acquaint you, that I think you will be accomodated much to your satisfaction at the George, here; and I shall expect to be honor'd in due time with your preparatory commands to the host and hostess (Ellard) as to beds, horses, time, &c., if necessary, that you may suffer no inconvenience which it might have been put into my power to prevent" (John Cranch to AA, Axminster, 17 July 1787, Adams Papers).

[2] Upon learning of JA's presence in London during his first visit there late in 1783, John Cranch had sent him compliments and a present of two hares for his table (Cranch to JA, 17 Jan. 1784, Adams Papers). (The hares had to be eaten by the bookseller John Stockdale, to whose care they were sent, because JA and JQA had left England for Amsterdam; see Stockdale to JA, 20 Jan. 1784, Adams Papers.) Other gifts followed after the Adamses settled in Grosvenor Square. From his letters Cranch appears to have been warmly pro-American in his politics; see especially Cranch to AA, 7 Nov. 1786 (Adams Papers), commenting on Ramsay's *History of the Revolution of South-Carolina*, a copy of which the Adamses had presented to him.

[3] "27th. . . . Mr. C. dined with us, and requested we would take tea at his cottage; he came at six to attend us.

He lives in a small, neat cottage; every thing around him has an air of taste, united with neatness. He has a variety of small prints, the heads of many eminent persons, and the six prints, Hogarth's representation of la marriage a la mode. He has also a painting of Sir Walter Raleigh, which is thought an original picture; it was lately left, by an old gentleman who died, to the British Museum. Mr. C. says he has a great inclination never to deliver it; he thinks it ought to be preserved sacred in this county, because its original was born here in the parish of Baidley, and that Sir Walter's character stands very high throughout the county of Devonshire. Papa observed that his character did not appear unexceptionable; he answered that none of his faults were known here; they believed only in his virtues and excellencies" (AA2, *Jour. and Corr.*, 1:86).

This portrait of Raleigh by the Dutch-English artist "Cornelius Jansen, at Mr. J. Cranch's, Axminster," is also mentioned by JA (entry of July–Aug., below). It appears not to have survived; at any rate it is not entered in Alexander J. Finberg's "A Chronological List of Portraits by Cornelius Johnson, or Jonson," *Walpole Society*, 10 (1921–1922):1–37; and recent searches by museum officials in England have not brought it to light.

**28TH.**

We left Axminster and proceeded to Exeter. Here we put up at the Hotell in the Church yard and opposite to the Cathedral Church. At this place lives Mr. Andrew Cranch the Eldest Brother of Mrs. Palmer and Mr. R. Cranch. We went to visit him. A Mr. Bowering a very Worthy Tradesman came to see us, and as he lives near to Mr. Cranch, he persuaded the old Gentleman to come and drink Tea with him. He is very infirm and about 78 years old, is very poor and past his labour, bears a Good Character as a man of great integrity and industery. His wife is near as old as he, a small woman, but very lively and active and looks like to last many years. Mr. Bowerings Brother married with[1]

[1] Here AA's journal breaks off, but the substance of this incomplete sentence is supplied in her letter to Mrs. Cranch, 15 Sept. 1787 (MWA): "Mr. [Andrew] Cranchs daughter married Mr. Bowerings [John Bowring's] Brother, they have three Sons. She is a sprightly woman like her Mother, and Mr. Bowering's daughter married a Son of Mr. Natll. Cranchs, so that the family is doubly linked together."

The travelers remained in Exeter from Saturday the 28th until Monday the 30th. "From Exeter we went to Plimouth. There we tarried several days [30 July–4 Aug.], and visited the fortifications, Plimouth Dock, and crossed over the Water to Mount Edgcume [Edgcumb Mount, Devon, on the Tamar River, near Saltash]; a Seat belonging to Lord Edgcume" (same).

### [*John Adams' Diary resumes.*]

### [MEMORANDA ON A TOUR FROM LONDON TO PLYMOUTH, JULY–AUGUST 1787.][1]

Michael Sawrey, at Plymouth[2]
Gillies St. Martins Lane. Garthshores
Sastres Edgware Road. No. 20.

fallitur egregio quisquis sub Principe credit,
Servitium: nunquam Libertas, gratior exit [extat]
quam sub Rege pio. Claud. Lib. 3. in Stillic.
quos præfecit ipsi [præficit ipse], regendis rebus, ad arbitrium
Plebis, Patrumque reducit.[3]

Mad. La Marquise de Champsenets au Chateau de Thuilleries.

To Epsom, Guilford, Farnham, Alton, Winchester, Salisbury. Blandford, Dorchester, Bridport, Axminster, Honniton (Valley), Exeter.

Niccolaides. Chambourgs Rhodes.
Gentlemans Pocket Farrier.
Truslers practical Husbandry. Baldwins P[ater] N[oster] Row.
O fair Columbia, hail.
An original Sir. W. Rawleigh, by Cornelius Jansen, at Mr. J.

Cranch's, Axminster.[4] Sir W. was born at Hays in the Parish of Bodley, Devon.—John Bowering. Andrew Cranch.

Ingratitude thou marble hearted fiend, more hideous when thou shewest thee in a Child than a sea Monster. S'pear.

[1] These highly miscellaneous jottings are on a loose folded sheet separated from the Diary and filed under its assigned date in the Adams Papers. On the fourth and last page is a list in JA's hand of six military companies in Boston, with their commanders, beginning "Boston Troop of Horse, Swan." Possibly this list was put down from a newspaper account of forces mustered to deal with the Shays insurgents during the winter of 1786–1787. The notes printed here are mere scraps of information that JA wished to remember and were doubtless mainly taken down during the family excursion to the west of England. But from the fact that the name of Michael Sawrey of Plymouth heads the list they may have been begun in London, for some of the notes that follow pertain to persons and things encountered by JA before he reached Plymouth.

[2] "At Plimouth we were visited by a Mr. and Mrs. Sawry; with whom we drank Tea one afternoon; Mr. Sawry is well known to many Americans, who were prisoners in Plimouth jail during the late war. The money which was raised for their relief, past through his Hands and he was very kind to them, assisting many in their escape" (AA to Mrs. Cranch, 15 Sept. 1787, MWA).

[3] From Claudian's *Consulship of Stilicho*, book 3, lines 113–116, but carelessly copied by JA as usual. Corrections have been inserted from the Loeb Classical Library text of *Claudian* (London and N.Y., 1922). The Loeb translation is as follows: "He errs who thinks that submission to a noble prince is slavery; never does liberty show more fair than beneath a good king. Those he himself appoints to rule he in turn brings before the judgment-seat of people and senate."

[4] See note 3 on entry in AA's Diary for 26[–27] July, above.

## 1787. AUGUST 7 [*i.e.* 6?].[1]

At Kin[gsbridge, the southerly] Point of the County of Dev[onshire, the b]irth Place of my Brother Cranch. [Wen]t Y[ester]day to Church in the Morning, dined with Mr. Burnell, went to the Presbyterian Meeting afternoon, drank Tea with Mr. Trathan,[2] and went to the Baptist Meeting in the Evening.—Lord Petre is the Lord of this mannor.—The Nephew of my Brother Cranch possesses the Family Estate, which I saw, very near the Church, four Lotts of very fine Land in high Cultivation. The Nephews and Nieces are married and settled here, all Tradesmen and Farmers in good Business and comfortable Circumstances and live in a harmony with each other, that is charming.—On Saturday We passed thro Plympton And Modbury. From the last Town emigrated my Brother Cranch with Mr. Palmer. It is a singular Village at the Bottom of a Valley formed by four high and steep hills. On Fryday We went out from Plymouth to Horsham, to see Mr. Palmer, the Nephew of our Acquaintance in America. His sister only was at home. This is a pleasant Situation.[3] We had before seen Mr. Andrew Cranch at Exeter, the aged Brother of my friend, and Mr. William Cranch, another Brother deprived by a Paralytick Stroke of all his faculties.

[Mr. Bowring, at Exe]ter, went with me to see Mr. Towg[ood, the au]thor of the dissenting Gentlemans answer [to] Mr. Whites three Letters, 87 years of age.[4]

Brook is next Door to Swainstone and Strachleigh, near Lee Mill Bridge, about two miles from Ivy Bridge.[5] Strachleigh did belong to the Chudleighs the Dutchess of Kingstons Family.

Haytor Rock is at the Summit of the highest Mountain in Dartmore Forrest. Brentor is said by some to be higher.

[1] Here begin the scraps of JA's Diary, nine paper booklets or folded sheets, of various sizes and shapes, which are collectively designated D/JA/46 in the Adams Papers and which complete the MS of the Diary as JA kept it, very intermittently, from 1787 to 1804.

As to the date of this entry, since JA says he attended church and meeting three times "Yesterday," it can only be supposed that he was writing on Monday, 6 August.

The top edge of this sheet of the MS is charred. Some words and parts of words have been supplied, in brackets, from the text printed by CFA.

[2] Both Burnell and Trathan were connections of the Cranches in Kingsbridge, a village which was so overwhelmingly "the Chief resort of the Cranch family" that bells were set ringing soon after the Adamses' arrival, and no fewer than fifteen members and connections of the family called on the travelers during their first evening there (AA to Mrs. Cranch, 15 Sept. 1787, MWA).

[3] In a letter to her niece Elizabeth Cranch, 1 Oct. 1787 (Dft, Adams Papers), AA furnished a detailed and vivid account of the expedition from Plymouth to Horsham on 3 August. Since "we were the first coach and four that ever attempted Horsham House," the trip was full of difficulties and perils, which John Cranch proved himself a veritable Samson in overcoming.

[4] Michaijah Towgood, a nonconformist clergyman and prolific writer of theological tracts (*DNB*).

[5] These were places in Devon that the Adamses passed through or near on Saturday, 4 Aug., while traveling from Plymouth to Kingsbridge. They dined at Ivybridge, and JA made a side trip of several miles to Brook to visit William Cranch, another of Richard's brothers (AA to Mrs. Cranch, 15 Sept. 1787, MWA). In AA's Diary (M/AA/1) there is an undated, detached note on the final leaf: "Cadleigh, Brook, Strashleigh, Ivey Bridge, visited by Mr. A in company with Mr. J. Cranch."

MONDAY. AUG. 6.[1]

Dined at Totness, thro which the River Dart runs to Dartmouth. Slept at Newton bushell.[2]

[1] This date is evidently correct, being a second entry written this day (see note 1 on preceding entry). On the 7th the Adamses were back in Exeter, for on that day JA recorded receiving a supply of cash at the bank in Exeter (Accounts, 31 May 1785–10 April 1788, Lb/JA/36, Adams Papers, Microfilms, Reel No. 124).

[2] These places were along the road from Kingsbridge to Exeter. By the 12th the tourists were in Bristol, where according to AA2 "We visited Lord Clifford's grounds." On the 15th, probably, they toured the colleges and other sights of Oxford, and they devoted the following day to a very thorough inspection of Blenheim Palace. See AA2, *Jour. and Corr.*, 1:89–94; AA to Lucy Cranch, 3 Oct. 1787, MWA, printed in AA, *Let-*

*ters*, ed. CFA, 1848, p. 336–340. The precise date of their return to London is not known, but it was probably about 20 August.

Thus ends JA's European Diary. His commission to Great Britain, limited to three years, was due to expire on 24 Feb. 1788, and exactly a year and a month before that date he had written to Secretary Jay formally requesting that Congress recall him, not only from the British Court but from his mission to the Netherlands and his joint mission (with Jefferson) to the Barbary Powers, so that he would be able to embark "in the Early Spring Ships in 1788" (24 Jan. 1787, LbC, Adams Papers; *Dipl. Corr., 1783–1789*, 2:691–693). To make certain that his intention would not be doubted, JA addressed a letter next day to the Massachusetts delegates in Congress announcing his "fixed resolution" against remaining longer in Europe even if Congress voted to extend his appointments: "To be explicit I am determined to come home" (25 Jan., LbC, Adams Papers). While the convention to frame a new federal constitution sat, Congress was even more depleted than usual, and it took no action on JA's request (on which Jay had reported favorably on 26 July) until 5 Oct. 1787, when it voted that "the honble. John Adams . . . be permitted agreeably to his request, to return to America at any time after the 24th. day of February . . . 1788," and also that "the thanks of Congress be presented to him for the patriotism, perseverence, integrity and diligence with which he has ably and faithfully served his Country" (JCC, 33:612–613).

Jay's letter of 16 Oct. transmitting this intelligence reached JA in mid-December. The resolves were gratifying to the recipient (who had not, however, waited for them in order to begin winding up his affairs and preparing for his homeward voyage), but Congress' failure to send with them actual letters of recall, as JA had requested, posed a problem of protocol for him, especially with respect to the Dutch government. Without a letter of recall it would be difficult to terminate his mission to The Hague with due politeness except in person, and JA did not relish the prospect of

either another winter's crossing and re-crossing of the North Sea or visiting again a country in which his best friends had been swept out of power, or worse, by the recent counter-revolution in the Dutch Republic. As time grew short he adopted the expedient of writing, so to speak, his own letters of recall, in the form of memorials to the Stadholder and the States General that explained why a personal leave-taking was almost impossible. To his mortification the memorials were returned by Secretary Fagel, who politely but firmly pronounced them unsatisfactory unless accompanied by letters of recall. At first JA thought he would risk the offense of returning to America without taking formal leave, but on second thought he reluctantly decided to pay a last visit to The Hague, and he so informed Jay on the day after he had his final and perfunctory audience with George III. (Jay to JA, 16 Oct. 1787, with enclosed resolves of Congress, Adams Papers; *Dipl. Corr., 1783–1789*, 2:796–800. JA to Jay, 16 Dec., LbC, Adams Papers; same, p. 824. JA to the Prince of Orange and to the States General of the United Provinces, 25 Jan. 1788, enclosed in a letter of the same date to Hendrik Fagel, letterbook copies, Adams Papers; *Works*, 8:470–472. Fagel to JA, 12 Feb., Adams Papers; *Dipl. Corr., 1783–1789*, 2:828–829. JA to Jay, 16, 21 Feb., letterbook copies, Adams Papers; same, p. 827–828, 832. JA, draft of remarks on taking leave of George III, 20 Feb., Adams Papers; *Works*, 8:480, note.)

Though he did not know it when he left London (29 Feb.) for Hellevoetsluis and The Hague (where he arrived on 4 March), JA was to transact much more important business in the Netherlands than his ceremonial leave-takings. A day or two after he completed those ceremonies he wrote AA from Amsterdam to tell her that he "should have been in London at this hour if you had not . . . laid a Plott, which has brought me to this Town.—Mr. Jefferson at the Receipt of your Letter [of 26 Feb., mentioning JA's forthcoming trip to The Hague; Jefferson, *Papers*, ed. Boyd, 12:624], come post to meet me, and he cutts out so much Business for me, to put the Money Matters of the United States upon a sure footing, that I certainly shall not be able to get into the Packet at Helvoet before Saturday.... I thought myself dead, and that it was well with me, as a Public Man: but I think I shall be forced, after my decease, to open an additional Loan. At least this is Mr. Jeffersons opinion, and that of Mr. Vanstaphorst" (11 March, Adams Papers). The fourth and final loan that JA negotiated with the Willinks and Van Staphorsts was in the amount of one million guilders, at 5 per cent interest, to be entirely redeemed in fifteen years; the contract was signed on 13 March, and JA as usual spent the following days in signing obligations, to the number of one thousand. Though undertaken at JA's sole discretion, the loan was promptly ratified by Congress, 2 July (JCC, 34:283; an English text, followed by a signed copy of the ratification, is in DLC:Continental Congress Miscellany). Jefferson's purpose in urging JA to execute a new loan, as he told Jay in a dispatch from Amsterdam, 16 March, had been to secure funds sufficient not only to meet immediate and very pressing needs but to carry the credit of the United States safely through the "trying interval" of the next two years while the new government was establishing itself (*Papers*, ed. Boyd, 12:671–672; see also Jefferson's account in his Autobiography, *Writings*, ed. Ford, 1:114–117; and P. J. van Winter, *Het aandeel van den Amsterdamschen handel aan den opbouw van het Amerikaansche gemeenebest*, The Hague, 1927–1933, vol. 1: ch. 6, esp. p. 179–186).

JA returned to London a few days before the end of March and found that AA had moved to the Bath Hotel in Picadilly so that the furniture and books in the Grosvenor Square legation could be packed for shipping. WSS, AA2, and their infant son had already left for Falmouth, where they were to embark on a vessel bound for New York. On 30 March, just as he was stepping into his carriage to leave for Portsmouth, JA received the official letters of recall from the British and Dutch governments he had so ardently wanted earlier. He posted one to Lord Carmarthen and the other to the new Dutch ambassador in London, Baron van Nagell, and set off. (The original letters of recall, dated 12 Feb. and signed by Pres. Cyrus Griffin and Secretary Jay, are in the Public Record Office, London, F.O. 4, vol. 6, and in the Rijksarchief, The Hague, respectively; letterbook copies of the covering letters are in Adams Papers.)

# Abigail Adams' Diary of her Return Voyage to America, 30 March–1 May 1788 [1]

Sunday London March 30. We took our departure from the Bath Hotell where I had been a Fortnight, and sat out for Portsmouth, which we reachd on Monday Evening. We put up at the Fountain Inn. Here we continued a week waiting for the Ship which was detaind by contrary winds in the River.[2] The wind changing we past over to the Isle of Wight and landed at a place call'd Ryed, where we took post Chaises and proceeded to Newport to dine. From thence to Cows where our Ship was to call for us. Here Mr. Adams, myself and two Servants took up our abode at the Fountain Inn kept by a widow woman whose Name is Symes.[3] Our Lodging room very small, and the drawing room Confind and unpleasent. I found myself on the first Night much disposed to be uneasy and discontented. On the next day I requested the Land Lady to let me have a very large Room from whence we had a fine view of the Harbour, vessels, east Cowes and surrounding Hills. I found my Spirits much relieved. Never before experienced how much pleasure was to be derived from a prospect, but I had been long used to a large House, a large Family and many and various cares. I had now got into an unpleasent place without any occupation for mind or Body. Haveing staid at Portsmouth untill I had read all our Books and done all the Work I had left out, I never before experienced to such a degree what the French term enui. Monday took a walk to the Castle and upon a Hill behind it which commanded a pleasent view of the Harbour and Town which is a small villiage subsisting chiefly by fishing and piloting Vessels. Cowes is a safe and commodious Harbour. Here many Boats ply to take up the oyster which is always found in an Infant State. Small Vessels calld Smacks receive them and carry them to Colchester where they throw them again into water where the Sea only flows up by tides, and there they fatten and are again taken up and carried [to] the London market. The Isle of Wight is taken all together a very fertile agreable place 24 miles Long and 12 Broad. Produces great plenty of Grain, Sheep and Cattle, is a hilly country and a very Healthy Situation. On tuesday we went to Newport in order to visit Carisbrook Castle. This is a very ancient Ruins. The first account of it in English History is in the year 1513. This is the castle where Charles the first was kept a prisoner and they shew you the window from whence he attempted to escape. In this castle is a well of such a depth that the water is drawn from it by an ass walking in a wheel like a turn spit dog. The woman who shew it to us told us it was 300 feet deep. It is Beautifully stoned and in as good order as if finishd but yesterday. She lighted paper and threw [it] down to shew us its depth and dropping in a pin, it resounded as tho a large stone had been thrown in. We went to the Top of the citidal which commands a most extensive prospect. We returnd to Newport to dine. After dinner a Gentleman introduced himself to us by the Name of Sharp. Professed himself a warm and zealous Friend to America. After some little conversation in which it was easy to discover that he was a curious Character he requested that we would do him the Honour to go to his House and drink Tea. We endeavourd [to] excuse ourselves, but he would insist upon it, and we accordingly accepted. He carried us home and introduced to us an aged Father of 90 Years, a very surprizing old Gentleman who tho deaf appeard to retain his understanding perfectly. Mrs. Sharp his Lady appeard to be an amiable woman tho not greatly accustomed to company. The two young Ladies soon made their appeerence, the Youngest about 17 very Beautifull.

The eldest might have been thought Handsome, if she had not quite spoild herself by affectation. By aiming at politeness she overshot her mark, and faild in that Symplicity of manners which is the principal ornament of a Female Character.

This Family were very civil, polite and Friendly to us during our stay at Cowes. We drank Tea with them on the Sunday following and by their most pressing invitation we dined with them the tuesday following. Mr. Sharp is a poet, a man of reading and appears to possess a good mind and Heart and [is] enthusiastick in favor of America. He collected a number of his Friends to dine with us all of whom were equally well disposed to our Country and had always Reprobated the war against us. During our stay at Cowes we made one excursion to Yarmouth about 15 miles distant from Cowes, but the road being Bad it scarcely repaid us for the trouble as we did not meet with any thing curious. After spending a whole fortnight at Cowes the Ship came round and on Sunday the 20 of April we embarked on Board the ship Lucretia Captain Callihan with three Gentlemen passengers viz. Mr. Murry a Clergyman,[4] Mr. Stewart a grandson of old Captain Erwin of Boston who is going out to Bermudas collector of the Customs in that Island, His parents being British subjects, Mr. Boyd of Portsmouth a young Gentleman who received His Education in this Country.

The wind with which we saild scarcely lasted us 5 hours, but we continued our course untill Monday Evening when it blew such a gale that we were driven back and very glad to get into Portland Harbour. Here we have lain ever since, now 8 days,[5] a Situation not to be desired, yet better far than we should have been either at Sea or in the downs. Whenever I am disposed to be uneasy I reflect a moment upon my preferable Situation to the poor Girl my maid, who is very near her Time, in poor Health and distressingly Sea sick, and I am then silent. I Hush every murmer, and tho much of my anxiety is on her account, I think that God will suit the wind to the shorn Lamb, that we may be carried through our difficulties better than my apprehensions. Trust in the Lord, and do good. I will endeavour to practise this precept. My own Health is better than it has been. We fortunately have a Doctor on Board, and I have taken an old woman out of kindness and given her a passage who seems kind, active and cleaver, is not Sea sick and I hope will be usefull to me. I am much better accommodated than when I came and have not sufferd so much by Sea Sickness. Want of Sleep is the greatest inconvenience I have yet sufferd but I shall not escape so. This day 3 weeks Mr. and Mrs. Smith saild and my dear Grandson just one Year old for New York in the Thyne packet.

I fear they will have a bad time as the Westerly Winds have been so strong. God protect them and give us all a happy meeting in our Native Land.[6] We Lie Here near the Town of Weymouth, and our Gentlemen go on shore almost every day which is an amusement to them and really some to me, as they collect something or other to bring Back with them either Mental or Bodily food. This is Sunday 27 April. Mr. Murry preachd us a Sermon. The Sailors made them-selves clean and were admitted into the Cabbin, attended with great decency to His discourse from these words, "Thou shalt not take the Name of the Lord thy God in vain, for the Lord will not hold him Guiltless that taketh His Name in vain." He preachd without Notes and in the same Stile which all the Clergymen I ever heard make use of who practise this method, a sort of familiar talking without any kind of dignity yet perhaps better calculated to do good to such an audience, than a more polishd or elegant Stile, but in general I cannot approve of this method. I like to hear a discourse that would read well. If I live to return to America, how much shall I regreet the loss of good Dr. Prices Sermons. They were always a delightfull entertainment to me. I revered the Character and Loved the Man. Tho far from being an orator, his words came from the Heart and reached the Heart. So Humble, so diffident, so liberal and Benevolent a Character does honour to that Religion which he both professes and practises.

On Sunday Eve the wind changed in our favour, so much as to induce the Captain to come to sail. This is Thursday the first of May, but we have made very small progress, the winds have been so light; yesterday we past Sylla and are now out of sight of Land. The weather is very fine and we only want fresher winds. The confinement of a Ship is tedious and I am fully of the mind I was when I came over that I will never again try the Sea. I provided then for my return in the Resolution I took, but now it is absolute. Indeed I have seen enough of the world, small as [it?] has been, and shall be content to learn what is further to be known from the page of History. I do not think the four years I have past abroad the pleasentest part of my Life. Tis Domestick happiness and Rural felicity in the Bosom of my Native Land, that has charms for me. Yet I do not regreet that I made this excursion since it has only more attached me to America.[7]

[1] This third and last of AA's fragmentary diaries is in M/AA/1 (Adams Papers, Microfilms, Reel No. 197).

[2] The ship was the *Lucretia*, Capt. John Callahan, of Boston, for whose wife the ship was named; the Adamses paid £200 for their passage and the transportation of their furniture, &c., in the *Lucretia* (Thwing Catalogue, MHi, under Callahan's name; Callahan to AA, 31 Jan. 1788, Adams Papers). On 8 April Callahan wrote AA from London

that the weather had been so "Boysterous" that the pilot "Would not venter to moove the Ship, but She is Now in the Downes and will be at Portsmouth the first fair wind" (Adams Papers).

³ AA is casual about dates, but apparently the Adamses left Portsmouth and arrived at Cowes on Sunday, 6 April; they stayed there until Sunday, 20 April, making occasional excursions to points nearby.

⁴ John Murray (1741–1815), a native of England, minister of the Church of Christ in Gloucester, Mass., and the founder of the Universalist denomination in the United States. Murray gave an account of this voyage in his autobiography, *The Life of Rev. John Murray, Preacher of Universal Salvation . . .*, new edn., Boston, 1870, p. 349–350. The other passengers mentioned by AA were, according to the *Massachusetts Centinel*, 18 June, John Stuart and William Boyd.

⁵ Actually seven: from Monday the 21st through Sunday the 27th.

⁶ The Smiths sailed on 5 April from Falmouth in the *Tyne* packet, reached Halifax in one month, and probably disembarked at New York on 13 May (AA2 to AA, 18 [i.e. 13?]–20 May 1788; *Jour. and Corr.*, 2:70–76).

⁷ AA reported part of the rest of the voyage, which was stormy and protracted, in a letter to AA2 written at sea, 29 May. The *Lucretia* aided a dismasted American vessel bound for Baltimore, and on 28 May the Brieslers' child, a daughter, was born (same, p. 76–79).

The ship arrived in Boston Harbor on 17 June. As early as 7 May Gov. John Hancock had placed a letter in the hands of the pilot at Boston Light announcing to JA the arrangements for his public reception (Adams Papers). These were elaborate and, as carried out, were reported fully in the *Massachusetts Centinel* of 18 June:

"Yesterday, after an absence of nine years, arrived in this metropolis, from England, his Excellency JOHN ADAMS, Esq. late Ambassadour from the United States of America, to the Court of Great-Britain—with his lady. His Excellency the Governour having previously ordered, that every mark of respect be paid his Excellency on his arrival, the approach of the ship in which he arrived, was announced by a signal from the Light and a discharge of cannon from the Castle—when off the Castle he was saluted with a federal discharge of cannon from that fortress, and when the ship had arrived at her moorings, the Secretary of the State, by order of his Excellency the Governour repaired in his Excellency's carriage to the end of the pier, from whence, in the State barge, the Secretary waited on the Ambassadour on board, and in his Excellency the Governour's name, congratulated him on his arrival, and invited him and family to his Excellency's seat. The wind being fresh and fair, the ship arrived at town too early to admit our fellow citizens receiving his Excellency in the manner they had previously intended—Notwithstanding, short as the time was, the Pier was crowded—and his Excellency welcomed on shore by three huzzas from several thousand persons. The Secretary of the State accompanied his Excellency in the barge on shore, where his Excellency the Governour's Carriage waited for him—in which he, his lady, the Secretary of the State, and others, rode to the Governour's house, receiving as he passed the compliments and congratulations of his fellow-citizens. The bells in the several churches rang during the remainder of the day—every countenance wore the expressions of joy—and every one testified that approbation of the eminent services his Excellency has rendered his country, in a manner becoming freemen, federalists, and men alive to the sensations of gratitude.

"Mr. ADAMS resides at the House of his Excellency the Governour—where he yesterday received the congratulations of his Honour the Lieutenant-Governour, the Hon. Council and, the heads of the several departments of government, on his safe arrival in his native country."

On the 18th JA was received by the General Court, informed that on the 6th he had been elected a member of the Massachusetts delegation to the First Congress under the Federal Constitution (John Avery Jr., Secretary to the Council, to JA, 6 June, Adams Papers), assigned a chair in the House for his use "whenever he may please to attend the debates" (Order of the House, 18 June, Adams Papers), and tendered an address of welcome and gratitude by both houses, to which he replied in two brief and moving paragraphs (Address in Adams Papers; Answer, in JA's hand, facsimiled in Stan V. Henkels, Catalogue of Sale No. 1372, 19 March 1925; both printed in *Mass. Centinel*, 21 June 1788).

At Newburyport on the 18th JQA learned of his parents' arrival, but could not get accommodations to Boston until the 20th, when he got a horse and rode over to Boston. He found his father gone to Braintree but his mother still at the Governor's house; they went to Braintree together in the afternoon. JQA spent much of the next ten days unpacking books and other goods, which came by

lighters from the *Lucretia*, in the house his parents had bought in preparation for their return (JQA, Diary, 18–30 June; JQA, *Life in a New England Town*, p. 143–146). This was the former John Borland house, which had been briefly owned by Royall Tyler in the 1780's but which reverted to the possession of Leonard Vassall Borland, son of John and Anna Vassall Borland, and was purchased from him by JA for £600 on 26 Sept. 1787 through the agency of Cotton Tufts and Thomas Welsh (Deed recorded in Suffolk co. Registry of Deeds, 161:123, under date of 20 Oct. 1787; see note 1 on the second entry of Jan. 1759, above). For AA's lively impressions of the new house and the difficulties of repairing and settling it, see her letter to AA2 of 7 July (AA2, *Jour. and Corr.*, 2:84–86).

[*John Adams' Diary resumes.*]

[NOTES OF DEBATES IN THE UNITED STATES SENATE]
JULY 15. 1789.[1]

## Power of Removal.

*Mr. Carrol.* The Executive Power is commensurate with the Legislative and Judicial Powers.

The Rule of Construction of Treaties, Statutes and deeds.

The same Power which creates must annihilate.—This is true where the Power is simple, but when compound not.

If a Minister is suspected to betray Secrets to an Ennemy, the Senate not sitting, cannot the President displace, nor suspend.

The States General of France, demanded that offices should be during good behaviour.

It is improbable that a bad President should be chosen—but may not bad Senators be chosen.

Is there a due ballance of Power between the Executive and Legislative, either in the General Government or State Governments.

Montesquieu. English Liberty will be lost, when the Legislative shall be more corrupt, than the Executive.—Have We not been witnesses of corrupt Acts of Legislatures, making depredations? Rhode Island yet perseveres.

*Mr. Elsworth.* We are sworn to support the Constitution.

There is an explicit grant of Power to the President, which contains the Powers of Removal.

The Executive Power is granted—not the Executive Powers hereinafter enumerated and explained.

The President—not the Senate appoint. They only Consent, and Advise.

The Senate is not an Executive Council—has no Executive Power.

The Grant to the President express, not by Implication.

*Mr. Butler.* This Power of Removal would be unhinging the equilibrium of Power in the Constitution.

The Statholder witheld the fleet from going out, to the Anoyance of the Ennemies of the nation.

In Treaties, all Powers not expressly given are reserved.

Treaties to be gone over, Clause by Clause, by the President and Senate together, and modelled.

The other Branches are imbecil.

Disgust and alarm.

The President not sovereign. The U.S. sovereign, or People, or Congress sovereign.

The House of Representatives would not be induced to depart, so well satisfied of the Grounds.

*Elsworth.* The Powers of this Constitution are all vested—parted from the People, from the States, and vested not in Congress but in the President.

The Word Sovereignty is introduced without determinate Ideas.—Power in the last Resort. In this sense the Sovereign Executive is in the president.

The U.S. will be Parties to 1000 Suits. Shall Proscess issue in their Name vs. or for themselves.

The President it is said, may be put to Goal for Debt.

*Lee.* U.S. merely figurative meaning the People.

*Grayson.* The President is not above the Law. An Absurdity to admit this Idea into our Government. Not improbable that the President may be sued. Christina Q. of Sweeden committed Murder. France excused her. The Jurors of our Lord the President, present that the President committed Murder.

A Monarchy by a Sidewind. You make him Vindex Injuriarum. The People will not like The Jurors of our Lord the President—nor the Peace of our Lord the President, nor his Dignity. His Crown will be left out. Do not wish to make the Constitution a more unnatural monstrous Production than it is.—The British Constitution a three legged Stool. If one legg is longer than another, the Stool will not stand.

Unpallatable. The removal of Officers not palatable. We should not risk any Thing for nothing. Come forward like Men, and reason openly, and the People will hear more quietly than if you attempt side Winds. This Measure will do no good and will disgust.

*Mr. Lee.* The Danger to liberty greater from the disunited Opinions and jarring Plans of many, than from the energetic operations of one. Marius, Sylla, Cæsar, Cromwell trampled on Liberty with Armies.

The Power of Pardon—of adjourning the Legislature.

Power of Revision, sufficient to defend himself. He would be supported by the People.

Patronage. Gives great Influence. The Interference more nominal than real.

The greater Part of Power of making Treaties in the President.

The greatest Power is in the President, the less in the Senate.

Cannot see Responsibility, in the President or the great Officers of State.

A masqued Battery of constructive Powers would compleat the destruction of Liberty.

Can the Executive lay Embargoes, establish Fairs, Tolls &c.?

The fœderal Government is limited, the Legislative Power of it is limited, and therefore the Executive and judicial must be limited.

The Executive not punishable but by universal Convulsion, as Charles 1st.

The Legislative in England not so corrupt as the Executive.

There is no Responsibility, in the President, or Ministry.

Blackstone. The Liberties of England owing to Juries. The greatness of England owing to the Genius of that People.

The Crown of England can do what it pleases, nearly.

There is no ballance in America, to such an Executive as that in England.

Does the Executive Arm, mean a standing Army?

Willing to make a Law, that the President, if he sees gross misconduct may suspend pro tempore.

*Mr. Patterson.* Laments that We are obliged to discuss this question. Of great Importance and much difficulty.

The Executive co extensive with the Legislative. Had the Clause stood alone, would not there have been a devolution of all Executive Power?

Exceptions are to be construed strictly. This is an invariable Rule.

*Mr. Grayson.* The P[resident] has not a continental Interest, but is a Citizen of a particular State. A K[ing] of E[ngland] otherwise. K. of E. counteracted by a large, powerful, rich and hereditary aristocracy.—Hyperion to a Satyr.

Where there are not intermediate Powers, an alteration of the Government must be to despotism.

Powers ought not to be inconsiderately given to the Executive, without proper ballances.

Triennial and septenial Parliaments made by Corruption of the Executive.

Bowstring. General Lally. Brutus's Power to put his Sons to death.

The Power creating shall have that of uncreating. The Minister is to hold at Pleasure of the Appointor.

If it is in the Constitution, why insert it, in the Law? Brought in by a Sidewind, inferentially.

There will be every endeavour to increase the consolidatory Powers, to weaken the Senate, and strengthen the President.

No Evil in the Senates participating with the P. in Removal.

*Mr. Reed.* P. is to take care that the Laws be faithfully executed. He is responsible. How can he do his duty or be responsible, if he cannot remove his Instruments.

It is not an equal sharing of the Power of Appointment between the President and senate. The Senate are only a Check to prevent Impositions of the President.

The Minister, an Agent a Deputy to the great Executive.

Difficult to bring great Characters to Punishment or Tryal.

Power of Suspension.

*Mr. Johnson.* Gentlemen convince themselves that it is best the President should have the Power, and then study for Arguments.

Exceptions.

Not a Grant. Vested in the President, would be void for Uncertainty. Executive Power is uncertain. Powers are moral, mechanical, natural. Which of these Powers—what Executive Power? The Land. The Money. Conveys nothing. What Land? What Money.

Unumquodque dissolvitur, eodem modo, quo ligatur.

Meddles not with the question of Expediency.

The Executive wants Power, by its duration and its want of a Negative, and Power to ballance. Fœderalist.

*Mr. Elsworth.* What is the difference between a Grant and a Partition.

*Mr. Izard.* Cujus est instituere ejus est abrogare.

[1] First entry by JA in his Diary since his return from Europe; written, like those that follow, in a small, detached gathering of leaves that the diarist seized for his immediate purpose and that constitutes one of the numerous segments of D/JA/46. Since the story of the first national election in 1788–1789, of JA's own election as Vice-President, and of the first steps in organizing the new government in New York would require a very long summary, and since JA's Diary from this point on is a mere collection of fragments, the editors have made no attempt to fill in this or later gaps in the Diary record. The reader may be referred, however, to the Chronology of JA's life preceding the index in vol. 4, below.

The debate here recorded was upon the House bill organizing a department of foreign affairs. This bill was sent to the Senate on 24 June, and the point at issue in the Senate was whether the President possessed, or should possess, the exclusive power to remove officers whom he had appointed with the advice and consent of the Senate. In a long note on the history of the bill CFA pointed out that JA probably took these minutes "for the sake of guiding his judgment in the contingency which happened of his being called to decide the disputed question by his casting vote" (JA, *Works*, 3:408). According to Senator William Maclay, who was as usual in the minority and who left a characteristically lively and acidulous record of this debate, JA twice cast tie-breaking votes which reserved to the President the unqualified power of removing his appointees from office, as has ever since been the practice (Maclay, *Journal*, 1890, p. 109–121, especially p. 116, 119; see also U.S. Senate, *Jour.*, 1st Cong., 1st sess., under dates of 24–25 June, 14–18 July 1789).

A comparison of JA's notes with Maclay's shows that the former pertain to speeches delivered on more than one day, but systematic assignment of dates to all the speeches is not now possible.

## 1789 SEPTR. 16. WEDNESDAY.

Mr. Elsworth informed me That Governor Randolph of Virginia, opened the Convention at Philadelphia, and offered a Project of a Constitution. After him several other Members proposed Plans, some in Writing, others verbally. A Committee was at length appointed to take them all into Consideration, the Virginia Scheme being the Ground Work. This Committee consisted of Governor Rutledge of S.C., Mr. Wilson of Philadelphia, Mr. Gorham of Massachusetts, and Mr. Elsworth of Connecticut. When the Report of this Committee, had been considered and discussed, in the Convention it was recommitted to Governeur Morris, Mr. Maddison and some others.[1]

[1] Ellsworth's information was substantially correct though incomplete, at least as JA recorded it. Edmund Randolph introduced "the Virginia plan" on 29 May 1787. The Committee of Detail was appointed on 24 July, and besides the four members mentioned here, Randolph was also a member (Farrand, *Records of the Federal Convention*, 2:97). The members of the Committee of Style, appointed 8 Sept., were William Samuel Johnson, Alexander Hamilton, Gouverneur Morris, James Madison, and Rufus King (same, p. 547).

[NOTES OF DEBATES IN THE SENATE ON THE RESIDENCE BILL]
SEPT. 22. 1789.
Permanent Seat.[1]

*Mr. Grayson.* No Census yet taken, by which the Center of Population—

We have Markets, Archives, Houses, Lodgings.—Extreamly hurt at what has passed in the House of Rep[resentative]s. The Money. Is your Army paid? Virginia offered £100,000. towards the federal Buildings. The Buildings may be erected without Expence to the Union. Lands may be granted—these Lands laid out in Lots and sold to Adventurers.

*Mr. Butler....*[2] The recent Instance in France shews that an Attempt to establish a Government vs. Justice and the Will of the People is vain, idle, and chimerical.

[1] After warm debates the House of Representatives sent to the Senate this day a bill to establish the seat of national government at a site ten miles square, to be chosen by commissioners who were to be appointed by the President, "at some convenient place on the banks of the river Susquehannah, in the state of Pennsylvania" (*Penna. Packet,* 28 Sept. 1789). The Pennsylvania delegation in the House, which had carried its objective against a strong Southern bloc that favored a site on the Potomac, had in mind the area surrounding the village of Wright's Ferry, now Columbia, Penna. Thanks to the determination and skill of Senator Robert Morris, the proposed Susquehanna site and an amendment substituting a site on the Potomac were both defeated, and the new site agreed on by the Senate was Germantown and the Northern Liberties of Philadelphia, Vice-President Adams casting the deciding vote. The fullest record of the debate in the Senate, including the bargaining maneuvers that accompanied it and incorporating the usual severities on JA's conduct as presiding officer, is in William Maclay's *Journal,* 1890, p. 158–165; see also Rufus King's notes in King, *Life and Corr.,* 1:370–375; U.S. Senate, *Jour.,* 1st Cong., 1st sess., under 22–24 Sept.; Bryan, *Hist. of the National Capital,* 1:27–35; McMaster, *History,* 1:555–563. Congress adjourned before agreement could be reached between the two houses, and the Residence Act that eventually passed in July 1790 placed the capital at Philadelphia for ten years and then permanently on the Potomac.

[2] Suspension points in MS.

[NOTES OF DEBATES ON THE RESIDENCE BILL, CONTINUED]
SEPT. 23. WEDNESDAY.

*Mr. Lee.* Navigation of the Susquehannah.

*Mr. Grayson.* Antwerp and the Scheld. Reasons of State have influenced the Pensilvanians to prevent the navigation from being opened. The limiting the Seat of Empire to the State of Pen. on the Delaware is a characteristic Mark of Partiality. The Union will think that Pen. governs the Union, and that the general Interest is sacrificed to that of one State.

The Czar Peter took time to enquire and deliberate before he fixed a Place to found his City.

We are about founding a City which will be one of the first in the World, and We are governed by local and partial Motives.

*Mr. Morris* moves to expunge the Proviso.[1]

*Mr. Carrol.* Against the Motion to expunge the Proviso. Considers the Western Country of great Importance. Some Gentlemen in both houses seem to undervalue the Western Country or despair of commanding it. Government on the Potowmack would secure it.

*Mr. Butler.* The question is not whether Pensilvania or Maryland shall be benefited—but how are the United States benefited or injured.

*Mr. Macclay.* Pensilvania has altered the Law this month respecting the navigation of the Susquehannah.

[1] A proviso in the House bill required Pennsylvania and Maryland to consent to improving the navigation of the Susquehanna. Morris opposed this proviso on the ground that it would give commercial advantages to Baltimore over Philadelphia; see his speech and Carroll's and Maclay's replies as reported in King, *Life and Corr.*, 1:371–372, and in Maclay, *Journal*, 1890, p. 159–161.

[NOTES OF DEBATES ON THE RESIDENCE BILL, CONTINUED]
SEPT. 24. THURSDAY.

*Mr. Grayson* moves to strike out the Words, "in the State of Pensilvania."[1]

*Mr. Butler.* The Center of Population the best Criterion. The Center of Wealth and the Center of Territory.

*Mr. Lee.* The Center of Territory is the only permanent Center.

*Mr. Macclay.* See his minutes.[2]

[1] That is, following the words "river Susquehannah" in the House bill, and thus assigning the federal capital to Maryland; all the senators present from the South voted for this amendment, but it lost by ten votes to eight.

[2] Maclay's "minutes" of this day's debate are very full, but it would have been remarkable if he had offered to let JA see them, since they accuse him of grossly unfair conduct in the chair (*Journal*, 1890, p. 162–165).

[NOTES OF DEBATES IN THE SENATE CONCERNING UNFINISHED BUSINESS] 1790 JAN. 25. MONDAY.[1]

It was not the sense of either House, or of any member of either, that the Business pending at the Adjournment should be lost.[2]

Where is the Œconomy of repeating the Expence of Time?

Can this opinion be founded on the Law of Parliament? The K[ing] can prorogue the Parliament. But there is no such Power here.

The Rule of Parliament that Business once acted on, and rejected shall not be brought on again, the same session, is a good Rule, but not applicable to this Case.

*Mr. Elsworth.* In Legislative Assemblies, more to be apprehended from precipitation than from Delay.

[1] Early in the second session the question arose whether business not finished between the two houses in the former session could "now be proceeded in, as if no adjournment had taken place." On 20 Jan. a committee of the Senate was appointed to confer with a committee of the House on this subject, and on the 25th the Senate debated the joint committee's report. JA doubtless took his brief minutes of the debate in anticipation of the possibility of a tie vote. But the Senate voted, ten to eight, to accept the report, in these words: "Resolved, That the business unfinished between the two Houses at the late adjournment, ought to be regarded, as if it had not been passed upon by either"; and next day the House concurred. See U.S. Senate, *Jour.*, 1st Cong., 2d sess., under dates of 20–26 Jan. 1790.

[2] Though JA failed to name this speaker, it was almost certainly Maclay of Pennsylvania, who both in the joint committee and in the Senate had vigorously contested the view that business between the two houses should be begun *de novo* in each session. During the debate on the 25th, Maclay wrote, "I was four times up in all." See his *Journal*, 1890, p. 179–186.

## [1790?][1]

Interest, Corruption, Prejudice, Error, Ignorance. Causes of wrong Judgments.

Have not these Causes, as much Influence in one Assembly as in two? If either or all of these Causes should prevail, over Reason, Justice, and the public good in one Assembly, is not a Revision of the Subject in another a probable means of correcting the false decree?

[1] The notes or reflections which follow were written in pencil on the verso of the Diary leaf which has the entry of 25 Jan. 1790 on its recto. There is no other clue to their date, and their substance is so perfectly typical of JA's political thought that it does not suggest the occasion of his putting them down on paper.

## [NOVEMBER? 1791.][1]

*Williamson.*[2] Great Numbers emigrate to the back parts of North and S.C. and G. for the Sake of living without Trouble. The Woods, such is the mildness of the Climate, produce grass to support horses and Cattle, and Chesnuts, Acorns and other Things for the food of hogs. So that they have only a little corn to raise which is done without much Labour. They call this kind of Life *following the range.* They are very ignorant and hate all Men of Education. They call them Pen and Ink Men.

[1] Written on a detached, folded sheet which JA, probably at a much later date, docketed "Scrap." The only clue to the date when this note of a conversation was written down is the fact that the next entry, precisely dated 11 Nov. 1791, appears overleaf.

[2] Hugh Williamson (1735–1819),

who held an M.D. from the University of Utrecht and had represented North Carolina in the Federal Convention of 1787, was a member of the First and Second Congresses and a writer on scientific and other subjects (*DAB*).

### FRYDAY. NOV. 11. 1791.

Yesterday a No. of the national Gazette was sent to me, by Phillip Freneau, printed by Childs and Swaine. Mr. Freneau, I am told is made Interpreter.[1]

[1] The first number of the *National Gazette*, edited by the poet-journalist Philip Freneau, was published in Philadelphia on 31 Oct. 1791. The aim of Jefferson and Madison in encouraging Freneau in this venture was to offset the influence of John Fenno's "tory" *Gazette of the United States*, which had moved from New York to Philadelphia in Nov. 1790 and to which JA had contributed his "Discourses on Davila," April 1790–April 1791. At the same time that Freneau attacked Administration measures and especially Secretary of the Treasury Alexander Hamilton, he held a small post as clerk for foreign languages in the State Department, presided over by Thomas Jefferson. See Brant, *Madison*, 3:334–336.

### 1795 JUNE 21.

Lime dissolves all vegetable Substances, such as Leaves, Straws, Stalks, Weeds, and converts them into an immediate food for Vegetables. It kills the Eggs of Worms and Seeds of Weeds. The best method is to spread it in your Barn Yard among the Straw and Dung. It succeeds well when spread upon the Ground. Burning Lime Stones or Shells, diminishes their Weight: but slaking the Lime restores that Weight. The German farmers say that Lime makes the father rich, but the Grandson poor—i.e. exhausts the Land. This is all from Mr. Rutherford.[1] Plaister of Paris has a vitriolic Acid in it, which attracts the Water from the Air, and operates like watering Plants. It is good for corn—not useful in wet Land. You sprinkle it by hand as you sow Barley, over the Ground, 5 Bushells powdered to an Acre. Carry it in a Bag as you would grain to sow.

[1] John Rutherfurd, U.S. senator from New Jersey, 1791–1798 (*Biog. Dir. Cong.*); see entry of 3 Aug. 1796, below, and note there.

### 1795.

Mr. Meredith at Mr. Vaughans explained to me his Method.[1] He takes a first Crop of Clover early: then breaks up the Ground, cross ploughs and harrows it. Then plants Potatoes. He only ploughs a furrow, drops the Potatoes a foot a sunder and then covers them with another furrow. He ploughs now and then between these Rows: but never hoes. As soon as the Season comes for sowing his Winter Barley: He diggs the Potatoes, ploughs and harrows the Ground, sows the Winter Barley with Clover Seeds and orchard Grass Seeds: and the next Spring he has a great Crop of Barley and afterwards a great Burthen of Grass.—He prefers Orchard Grass to Herds Grass as much more productive.

[1] JA's informant was doubtless Samuel Meredith, formerly a member of the Continental Congress and from 1789 to 1801 treasurer of the United States (*Biog. Dir. Cong.*). His host was John Vaughan, brother of JA's old friend Benjamin Vaughan. John Vaughan settled in Philadelphia and was perpetual secretary of the American Philosophical Society (Robert Hallowell Gardiner, *Early Recollections*, Hallowell, Maine, 1936, p. 118–120).

### JUNE 20 [1796].[1]

Sullivan Lathrop came for 6 Mo[nths] at 12 1/2.

[1] Here begins a brief revival of JA's Diary, extending through the summer of 1796 and comprising the only regular series of entries he made after his return from Europe in 1788. JA had come home from Philadelphia in mid-May, following the long and highly partisan struggle in Congress over Jay's Treaty, and though there was to be a national election in November in which he was in the highest degree interested, the following entries deal almost entirely with farming activities.

CFA printed the Diary entries for 1796 very selectively and frequently omitted personal names or disguised them by reducing them to their initials.

### JUNE 22.

Thomas Lathrop came for 6 Mo[nths] at 9.

### QUINCY JULY 12. TUESDAY.

Yesterday mow'd all the Grass on Stony field Hill. To day ploughing for Hilling among the Corn over against the House. Brisler laying the foundation of the new Barn which is to be rais'd tomorrow, at the East End of my Fathers barn. Puffer and Sullivan Lathrop ploughing among Potatoes in the lower Garden.

This Journal is commenced, to allure me into the habit of Writing again, long lost. This habit is easily lost but not easily regained. I have, in the Course of Life, lost it several times and regained it as often. So I will now. I can easily credit the Reports I have heard of Dr. Robertson the Scottish Historian, who is said to have lost the Habit of Writing for many Years: but he reacquired it, before his death, and produced his Inquiry into the Knowledge of the Ancients of India.

In the Course of my Walk, this morning to my new Barn, I met Major Miller, who offered to sell me his Cedar Swamp and Woodlot of 20 Acres, beyond Harmans, descended from his Grandfather and

Father. His Price £9 = 30 dollars per Acre. Part of it has never been cutt—Part cutt 20 Years ago and grown up very thick. Billings came home before dinner, but did no Work.

### JULY 13. WEDNESDAY.

My new Barn is to be raised this Afternoon, a Rod or two from my Fathers which he built when I was two or three Years old—about 58 years ago, or 59.

Billings went out to hoe this morning but soon came in. Said he had sprained his Arm and could not work.

Billings soon went out towards Captn. Beales's.[1] Puffer, one of my Workmen from Stoughton, came home late last night. Said Captn. Lindzee had call'd him in and given him a Bottle of Brandy.[2] By what Sympathy do these Tipplers discover one another?

This Day my new Barn was raised near the Spot where the old Barn stood which was taken down by my Father when he raised his new barn in 1737. The Frame is 50 by 30–13 foot Posts.

[1] Capt. Benjamin Beale had built a large house just to the west of JA's property in 1792 (HA2, MS Notes in Adams Papers Editorial Files). This house is still standing.

[2] John Linzee, a former British naval officer who had married a niece of the Boston merchant John Rowe, resigned his commission in 1791 and settled in Milton (Rowe, *Letters and Diary*, p. 10–13 and *passim*).

### JULY 14. 1796 THURSDAY.

The Wind N.W. after a fine rain. A firing of Cannon this morning in the Harbour. I arose by four O Clock and enjoyed the Charm of earliest Birds. Their Songs were never more various, universal, animating or delightful.

My Corn this Year, has been injured by two Species of Worms. One of the Size and Shape of a Catterpillar, but of a mouse Colour, lies at the root, eats off the Stalk and then proceeds to all the other Plants in the Hill, till he frequently kills them all. The other is long and slender as a needle, of a bright yellow Colour. He is found in the Center of the Stalk near the Ground where he eats it off, as the Hessian fly eats the Wheat. My Brother taught me, the Method of finding these Vermin, and destroying them. They lie commonly near the Surface.

I have been to see my Barn, which looks very stately and strong. Rode up to Braintree and saw where Trask has been trimming Red Cedars. He has not much more to do. He was not at Work. He has probably worked two days since I was there last.

It rains at 11. O Clock. The Barley is growing white for the Harvest. My Men are hilling the Corn over the Road. A soft fine rain, in a clock calm is falling as sweetly as I ever saw in April, May or June. It distills as gently as We can wish. Will beat down the grain as little as possible, refresh the Gardens and Pastures, revive the Corn, make the fruit grow rapidly, and lay the foundation of fine Rowen and After feed.

### JULY 15. FRYDAY.

A very heavy Shower of Rain. Thunder in the morning. Billings still unable to work—goes over towards Basses first, then up in Town with Seth.

Went with 3 hands, Puffer, Sullivan Lathrop and Mr. Bass, to Braintree and cutt between 40 and 50 Red Cedars and with a team of five Cattle brought home 22 of them at a Load. We have opened the Prospect so that the Meadows and Western Mountain may be distinctly seen.

Burrell had two hands employed in heaping up Manure in his Barn Yard. The Cattle have broken into his Corn field, through the Gap which We left unfinished in the great Wall, and eaten an hundred hills.

The new Barn is boarded on the Roof, and the underpinning is finished.

### JULY 16. 1796 SATURDAY.

Paid off Puffer, for Eleven Days Works at a Dollar a Day. Trask and Stetson at work in the Garden. Sullivan and Bass gone for another Load of Red Cedar Posts. Billing over at Bass's in the Morning and going up in Town with Seth as usual.

Trask told me he had worked 20 days. This day in the Garden makes 21. Monday he is to cutt the Wood in the Swamp on Pens Hill. We got in two Loads the last of our English Hay, and bro't home a Load of Red Cedars.

### JULY 17. 1796 SUNDAY.

Warm but clear. Billings at home but running down Cellar for Cyder.

We are to have a Mr. Hilliard.

Yesterday Dr. Tufts and Mr. Otis and Family dined with me. Otis was very full of Elections and had many Things to say about Pinckney and Henry, Jefferson and Burr. He says there was a Caucus at Philadelphia, that they agreed to run Jefferson and Burr—that Butler was offended and left them. O. takes it for granted the P. will retire. Pickering has given out publickly that he will. Mrs. W. takes it for granted that he will. Collections, Packages and Removals of Cloaths and furniture of their own have been made. Anecdotes of Dandridge, and Mrs. W.s Negro Woman. Both disappeared—never heard of—know not where they are. When the Electors are chosen the Declaration is to be made.—Q. Is this Arrangement made that the Electors may make him the Compliment of an Election after a Nolo, and thus furnish an Apology for Accepting after all the Talk?[1]

Mr. Otis confirms the Account of the nomination and Appointment of my Son to be Minister Plenipotentiary of the U.S. at the Court of Portugal.[2] He also confirms the Adjournment of Congress to the Constitutional Day, 1. Monday in December. Mrs. W. is not to return to Phil[adelphia] till November.

Mr. Hilliard of Cambridge preached for Us. He is the Son of our old Acquaintance Minister of Barnstable and afterwards at Cambridge. Mr. Quincy and Mr. Sullivan drank Tea with Us.

[1] JA's informant on the political situation was Samuel Allyne Otis, secretary of the U.S. Senate, whose second wife, the former Mary Smith, was AA's first cousin (*Appletons' Cyclo. Amer. Biog.*, 4:607). The maneuvers by both Federalists and Republicans to obtain the succession to the Presidency were in some degree checked by Washington's silence concerning his own intentions until the publication of his advice to his countrymen, ever since known as his "Farewell Address," in *Claypoole's American Daily Advertiser*, 19 Sept. 1796.

CFA omitted two sentences in the foregoing paragraph: (1) that beginning "Anecdotes of Dandridge," and (2) JA's final query to himself. On the sudden disappearance of Bartholomew Dandridge, Mrs. Washington's nephew and one of the President's secretaries, see Washington, *Writings*, ed. Fitzpatrick,

35:77–79, 135–136, 159, 162. The reasons for it were less discreditable than gossip imputed.

[2] JQA, who had been serving as minister resident of the United States at The Hague since 1794, was appointed, with the unanimous consent of the Senate, minister plenipotentiary to Portugal on 30 May 1796 (Commission in Adams Papers under that date; see also AA to JQA, 10 Aug. 1796, Adams Papers). But because of orders from Secretary of State Pickering to remain at The Hague until a replacement could be sent there, JQA never went to Lisbon; instead, he was commissioned in 1797 by his father, now President, to go to Berlin to negotiate a new commercial treaty with Prussia (Commission, 1 June 1797, in Adams Papers; see also Bemis, *JQA*, 1:88–90).

### JULY 18 1796. MONDAY.

Billings is at hoe. The Kitchen Folk say he is steady. A terrible drunken distracted Week he has made of the last. A Beast associating with the worst Beasts in the Neighborhood. Drunk with John Copeland, Seth Bass &c. Hurried as if possessed, like Robert the Coachman, or Turner the Stocking Weaver. Running to all the Shops and private Houses swilling Brandy, Wine and Cyder in quantities enough to destroy him. If the Ancients drank Wine as our People drink rum and Cyder it is no wonder We read of so many possessed with Devils.

Went up to Penns hill. Trask has the Rheumatism in his Arm and is unable to work. He told me that Rattlesnakes began to appear—two on Saturday by Porters and Prays. One kill'd. The other escaped. He told me too of another Event that vex'd, provoked and allarm'd me much more—vizt., That my Horses were Yesterday in such a frenzy at the Church Door, that they frightened the Crowd of People, and frightened a Horse or the People in the Chaise so that they whipp'd their Horse, till he ran over two Children. The children stooped down or fell down, so that the chaise went over them without hurting them. But it must have been almost a Miracle, that they were not kill'd or wounded. I know not when my Indignation has [been] more excited, at the Coachman for his folly and Carelessness: and indeed at others of the Family for the Carriage going to Meeting at all. As Mrs. A. could not go the Coach ought not to have gone. The Coachman and Footman ought to have gone to Meeting—and the Girls to have walk'd. L. Smith has no Pretentions to ride in a Coach more than Nancy Adams or even Polly Howard. It is spoiling her Mind and her Reputation both, to indulge her Vanity in that Manner.[1] I scolded at the Coachman first and afterwards at his Mistress, and I will scold again and again. It is my Duty. There is no greater Insolence or Tyranny, than sporting with Horses and Carriages among Crouds of People.

[1] Louisa Catherine Smith (1773?–1857), who never married, was the daughter of AA's errant brother William Smith of Lincoln; she lived for many years with the Adamses, serving as JA's amanuensis in his old age, and was generously remembered in the wills of both AA and JA (Quincy, First Church, MS Records, 6 June 1857; AA to JA, 3 Jan. 1784, Adams Papers; AA, *New Letters, passim*). "Nancy" was Ann (1773–1818), daughter of Peter Boylston Adams, JA's brother; in Jan. 1797 she married Josiah Bass of Quincy (Quincy, First Church, MS Records, 2 May 1773; A. N. Adams, *Geneal. Hist. of Henry Adams of Braintree*, p. 408). Polly Howard has not been identified.

### JULY 19. 1796. TUESDAY.

A plentifull Shower of Rain with Thunder and Lightning this Morning. Took a Tea spoonful of Bark in Spirit.

Billings steady: but deep in the horrors, gaping, stretching, groaning.

JULY 20. 1796. WEDNESDAY. COMMENCEMENT.

Rode to the Swamp, at the Top of Penns hill. Trask is mowing the Bushes, cutting the Trees, and leaves only the White Oaks which he trims and prunes as high as he can reach. My design is to plough up a Corn field for Burrell, against next Year, in that Inclosure. Walked in the Afternoon over the Hills and across the fields and Meadows, up to the old Plain. The Corn there is as good as any I have seen, excepting two or three Spots. Brisler and Sullivan cutting Sleepers for the Barn. My beautiful Grove, so long preserved by my Father and my Uncle, proves to be all rotten. More than half the Trees We cutt are so defective as to be unfit for any Use but the fire. I shall save the White Oaks, and cutt the rest.

I was overtaken with the Rain, at the End of my Walks and re-turn[ed] home in it. Mrs. Tufts, Mrs. Norton,[1] Mrs. Cranch and Mrs. Smith were here.

[1] AA's niece, the former Elizabeth Cranch (1763–1811); in 1789 she had married Rev. Jacob Norton, Harvard 1785, recently settled as minister of the First Church of Weymouth (Weymouth Hist. Soc., *History of Weymouth, Massachusetts*, Weymouth, 1923, 4:444–445).

JULY 21. THURSDAY.

Sullivan Lathrop and Bass carting earth into the Yard from the Ground which is to be thrown into the High Way over against my House. The old Appletree, probably an hundred Years of Age is to fall.

Billings and Thomas Lathrop mowing in the Meadow.

Six hogsheads of Lime, 50 Gallons each were brought home Yesterday for Manure. I have it of Mr. Brackett, at 15s. the Hdd.

I am reading Dr. Watsons Apology for the Bible in Answer to T. Paines 2d Part of Age of Reason.

That Appletree, over the Way, to which the Beauty and Convenience of the Road has been sacrificed for an hundred Years, has now in its turn, with Apples enough upon it to make two Barrells of Cyder, fallen a Sacrifice to the Beauty and Convenience of the Road. It has been felled this morning, never to rise again and the Road is to be widened and enlarged. The Stump and Roots are to be dug out of the Ground and the Wall to be removed Back and made an Ha! Ha!

Billings had a mind to go upon Wall. I went with him from Place to Place, and could resolve on nothing. I then set him to split and mortise some Posts for the fence vs. Mrs. Veasie. We went up, carried the Posts but when We came there We found that the Wall was too heavy and Stones too large for two hands—four at least were necessary. Billings was wild and We came to some Explanation. He must go off &c. Mrs. Adams paid him off, and then He thought he would not go. After long Conversations Billings came to a Sort of Agreement to stay a Year from this day, at £45. He declared he would not drink Spirit nor Cyder for the whole Year. He reserved however twelve days for himself. We shall see tomorrow Morning how he behaves.

JULY 22. FRYDAY.

Billings sober and steady, persevering in his declaration that he will not drink, these 12 months. Paid Trask in full sixteen Dollars for 24 Days Works. He insisted on 4s. a Day. He has finished clearing the Swamp on Penns Hill this day.

JULY 23. 1796. SATURDAY.

Rode down to the Barley and Black grass at the Beach. The Barley is better than I hoped. The Clover has taken pretty well in general. Parts where the Tide has flowed are kill'd. Weeds very thick round the Margin of the Salt Meadow, or rather Black grass meadow. Twitch Grass scattering and thin. Billings sober, composed as ever. Bass and Brisler mowing with him. James the Coachman, enjoying the Pleasures of a Sportsman, shooting marsh Birds instead of mowing.

I rode up to Burrells in Braintree to tell Sullivan and Thomas that they might stay with the Team till they had got in all Burrells Hay. Billings thinks there will be 30 Bushells of Barley at the Beach and 30 Bushells to an Acre on Stony field Hill.

Burrells Barn is already nearly full of English Hay and fresh. His Salt Hay, he must stack or stow it in his Barn floor. He has collected his Summer Dung into heaps in his Barn Yard, and has a good deal of it. He will have manure enough, from his Cows and young Cattle, to serve a good Cornfield next Year. His Hogs besides will make a good deal.

I have concluded to break up upon Penns Hill a good Corn field on each side of the new Wall, one for Burrell and one for French and Vinton. They may sled or cart the manure in the Winter, and that Land will produce Clover and Herds grass much better than the plain below. I am weary of wasting so much labour and manure upon that dry plain, which is scorched and burnt up in a dry Season.

Still reading Bishop Watsons Apology. Finished.

My Men mowed the Black Grass and Barley at the Beach, came home and split all the Red Cedars into Posts and morticed some of them. Sullivan morticed after having assisted Burrell to get in all his fresh Hay.

Began The Life of Petrarch by Susanna Dobson.

### JULY 24. 1796. SUNDAY.

We are to have for a Preacher a Mr. Whitcomb.

Billings is still cool and steady.

In the 1st. Vol. of the Life of Petrarch page 52. it is said that Pope John the 22d believed that the Souls of the Just would not enjoy The Vision of God till after the Universal Judgment and the Resurrection of their Bodies. This Opinion is Priestleys and Price was much inclin'd to it. This Popes imprudent Endeavours to establish this Doctrine, produced an Insurrection of the Cardinals and Court of Rome—Decisions of the Doctors in Theology at Paris &c. and obliged the Pope to retract. Petrarch appears to have favoured his Opinion concerning The Vision of God.

Went to Church Forenoon and Afternoon, and heard Mr. Whitcomb of Bolton.

### JULY 25. 1796. MONDAY.

Dull Weather but no Rain. The Lathrops with the Team are going to the Swamp on Penns Hill for a Load of Wood that Trask has cutt.

Rode up to the Swamp on Penns hill. Sullivan and Bass loaded up a Cord of Wood and Sullivan drove it home. Bass staid and cutt down and cutt up an old Walnut, murdered: by the Women and Children for their Dye Potts, cutt down and cutt up an old Appletree and a Buttonwood Tree. When Sullivan returned he climbed and trimmed two large Buttonwoods. I then left Bass and Sullivan to load their Waggon with the Wood and came home to dinner.

Brisler, Billings, Thomas, James and Prince, after mowing the Barley on Stoney field Hill, were gone down to the Beech to rake and heap the Barley ready for Sullivan to bring home, after he shall have unloaded his Wood. The Weather is warm and clear. Sullivan came home, unloaded his Wood, went down to the Beech and brought up all the Black Grass and Barley at one Load, which was so heavy however that he could not ascend the Hill to the little Barn. Brisler, Bass and James raked upon Stony field hill.

### JULY 26. 1796. TUESDAY.

Cloudy and begins to rain, the Wind at N.E. The Men gone up the Hill to rake the Barley.

In conformity to the fashion I drank this Morning and Yesterday Morning, about a Jill of Cyder. It seems to do me good, by diluting and dissolving the Phlegm or the Bile in the Stomach.

The Christian Religion is, above all the Religions that ever prevailed or existed in ancient or modern Times, The Religion of Wisdom, Virtue, Equity and Humanity, let the Blackguard Paine say what he will. It is Resignation to God—it is Goodness itself to Man.

### JULY 27. 1796 WEDNESDAY.

Billings and Sullivan making and liming an heap of Manure. They compounded it, of Earth carted in from the Ground opposite the Garden where the Ha! Ha Wall is to be built, of Salt Hay and Seaweed trodden by the Cattle in the Yard, of Horse dung from the Stable, and of Cow dung left by the Cows, over all this Composition they now and then sprinkle a layer of Lime. Bass and Thomas hoeing Potatoes in the lower Garden.

I rode up to The Barn, which Mr. Pratt has almost shingled, and over to the Plain, but found My Tenants were at work in my Fathers old Swamp, which I could not reach without more trouble than I was willing to take.

Dr. Welsh[1] came up, with two young Gentlemen from New York, Mr. John and Mr. Henry Cruger, the youngest of whom studies with my son Charles as a Lawyer, who gives him an excellent Character.[2] They are journeying Eastward as far as Portland and return by Albany. The Eldest of them has lately return'd from the East Indies.

[1] Thomas Welsh (1752?–1831), Harvard 1772, a Boston physician, had in 1777 married Abigail Kent, AA's first cousin. He and his family maintained very close relations with the Adamses over two or three generations, and Welsh's successive residences served frequently as headquarters for members of the Adams family when they were in Boston. See a biographical sketch of Welsh in JQA, *Life in a New England Town*, p. 25, note, and another, which adds further details, in Walter L. Burrage, *A History of the Massachusetts Medical Society* ... 1781–1922, [Boston,] 1923, p. 32–33.

[2] CA had been graduated at Harvard in 1789. He then went to New York to live with his parents and was placed in Alexander Hamilton's law office; but when Hamilton was appointed secretary of the treasury later that year CA was transferred to the office of John Laurance, a Federalist congressman, later a U.S. senator from New York, and a large speculator in wild lands. Upon completing his legal training, CA opened an office of his own in Hanover Square, New York City. In Aug. 1795 he married Sarah, or Sally, Smith, sister of AA2's husband, WSS; two daughters were born of this marriage. For a time things went well with the family, and CA continued his frequent and affectionate correspondence with his father. But CA had, or developed, intemperate habits and died in his thirty-first year after a brief illness, 30 Nov. 1800, adding another bitter draft to that which his father was obliged to swallow at this very time by losing the election for a second term as President. (JA to Hamil-

ton, 21 July 1789, and to John Laurance ["Lawrence"], 19 Sept. 1789, letterbook copies, Adams Papers. CA to AA, 15 Aug., and to JA, 20 Aug. 1792, Adams Papers. AA to Mrs. Cranch, 8 Dec. 1800, MWA; *New Letters,* p. 261–262. JA to F. A. Van der Kemp, 28 Dec. 1800, LbC, Adams Papers; *Works,* 9:576–577. *N.Y. Geneal. and Biog. Record,* 13:87 [April 1882]. Arthur J. Alexander, "Judge John Laurance, Successful Investor in New York State Lands," *New York History,* 42:35–45 [Jan. 1944].)

### JULY 28. 1796. THURSDAY.

Billings and Sullivan are gone to the Beech for a Load of Seaweed to put into their Hill of Compost. Bass and Thomas hoeing still in the lower Garden. James sick of a Surfeit of fruit.

I continue my practice of drinking a Jill of Cyder in the Morning and find no ill but some good Effect.

It is more than forty Years since I read Swifts Comparison of Dryden in his Translation of Virgil to The Lady in a Lobster. But untill this Day I never knew the meaning of it.[1] To Day at Dinner seeing Lobsters at Table I enquired after the Lady, and Mrs. Brisler rose and went into the Kitchen to her Husband who sent in the little Lady herself in the Cradle in which she resides. She must be an old Lady—she looks like Dr. Franklin, i.e. like an Egyptian Mummy. Swifts droll Genius must have been amused with such an Object. It is as proper a Subject or rather allusion or Illustration, for Humour and Satyr as can be imagined. A little old Woman in a spacious Habitation as the Cradle is would be a proper Emblem of a President in the new House at Philadelphia.

Billing and Sullivan brought up in the Morning a good Load of green Seaweed. Billing and Bass have [been] carting Dirt and liming the heap of Compost. Sullivan and Thomas threshing Barley at the little Barn. Billing and Bass brought up a second Load of Seaweed at night.

[1] See Swift's description of the encounter between Virgil and Dryden in *The Battle of the Books* (1710): Dryden's "helmet was nine times too large for the head, which appeared situate far in the hinder part, even like the lady in a lobster, or like a mouse under a canopy of state, or like a shrivelled beau, from within the penthouse of a modern periwig."

### JULY 29. 1796. FRYDAY.

Hot after Thunder, Lightening and an Hours Rain. The two Lathrops threshing. Billing and Bass carting Earth. Lathrops threshing. Billing and Bass brought up a third Load of Seaweed. They go on making the Heap of Compost with Lime, Seaweed, Earth, Horse Dung, Hogs dung &c.

Still reading the Second Volume of Petrarchs Life.

### JULY 30TH. SATURDAY.

All hands carting Earth and making Compost, i.e. 4 hands Billings, Bass and the two Lathrops. Billings is in his Element. Building Wall and making manure are his great delights, he says. He says he will cover all my Clover with green Seaweed. Drop part of a Load on the lower Part and carry the rest up the hill to the Barley Stubble. He will make a heap of Compost too upon the Top of the Hill to dung the Corn in the holes next Year upon the Piece which I propose to break up, and he will make an heap of Compost in the Spring with winter Dung to dung Corn beyond the Ditch. He will get a Scow load of Rockweed, and Scow loads of Seaweed and marsh mud. If he did not execute as well as plann, I should suppose this all Gasconade. But he is the most ingenious, the most laborious, the most resolute and the most indefatigable Man I ever employed.

### JULY 31. 1796. SUNDAY.

A fine N.W. Wind, pure Air, clear Sky, and bright Sun. Reading the second Volume of Petrarchs Life. This singular Character had very wild Notions of the Right of the City of Rome to a Republican Government and the Empire of the World. It is strange that his Infatuation for Rienzi did not expose him to more Resentment and greater Danger. In the Absence of the Pope at Avignon, and the People having no regular Check upon the Nobles, these fell into their usual Dissentions, and oppressed the People till they were ripe to be duped by any single Enthusiast, bold Adventurer, ambitious Usurper, or hypocritical Villain who should, with sufficient Imprudence, promise them Justice, ⟨Humanity⟩ Clemency and Liberty. One or all of these Characters belonged to Rienzi, who was finally murdered by the People whom he had deceived, and who had deceived him.

Tacitus appears to have been as great an Enthusiast as Petrarch for the Revival of the Republic, and universal Empire. He has exerted the Vengeance of History upon the Emperors, but has veiled the Conspiracies against them, and the incorrigible Corruption of the People, which probably provoked their most atrocious Cruelties. Tyranny can scarcely be practiced upon a virtuous and wise People.

Mr. Whitcomb preached and dined with me.

### AUGUST 1. 1796. MONDAY.

Hands all gone to finish our Equinoctial Line of Wall as Billings calls it.—Hot, sultry, muggy last night Muskitoes numerous and busy, poor sleep, up and down all night.

Have my Brothers Oxen to day.

### AUGUST 2. 1796 TUESDAY.

Wrote to Mr. Sullivan by Dr. Tufts an Answer to his Inquiries concerning Mitchels Map and St. Croix River.[1]

My own Hands with Nathaniel Hayden only and my own oxen only, finished the great Wall upon Penn's Hill. Mr. Benjamin Shaw and his Wife, (Charity Smith,) drank Tea with Us. He is a Clerk in the Branch Bank at 600 dollars a Year, and She is opening an Accademy of young Ladies for Painting and Music. They live in his Mothers House, and she boards with them. I took a ride with him in his Chaise to the Top of Penns Hill. If innate Levity is curable, they may be happy. If a soft, sweet Voice, a musical Ear, and melodious Modulations, could feed the hungry and cloath the naked, how happy might some People be. She rattles about Independence and boasts of having earned fifty dollars last Month. But the Foible of the Race is rattle.

[1] Article V of the Anglo-American Treaty of 1794 ("Jay's Treaty") provided for a joint commission to determine "what River was truly intended under the name of the River St. Croix," which had been designated in the Preliminary and Definitive Treaties of 1782 and 1783 as part of the boundary between Canada and the United States (Miller, ed., *Treaties*, 2:249). James Sullivan, attorney general of Massachusetts and president of the Massachusetts Historical Society, was the agent appointed to represent the United States before the Commissioners, and being about to sail to Halifax for a meeting of the tribunal, he wrote to JA, 30 July, to inquire whether the river called the St. Croix on John Mitchell's *Map of . . . North America* was the river that the Peace Commissioners had meant (Adams Papers; JA, *Works*, 8:518–519). A draft or retained fair copy of JA's answer of 2 Aug. is also in Adams Papers; same, p. 519–520. Concerning Mitchell's *Map*, the most important map in American diplomatic history, see the discussion in Miller, ed., *Treaties*, 3:328–351. The proceedings of the St. Croix Commission are printed in Moore, ed., *International Arbitrations*, vol. 1: ch. 1. See also the entries of 10–11 Aug., below.

### AUGUST 3. 1796. WEDNESDAY.

Brisler is going to Squantum and Long Island, for my Twin Oxen who are reprieved for a Year. The Lathrops to threshing and Billings and Bass, to manure.

Answered Mr. Rutherfords Letter of 28. June.[1]

This Day Thomas Lothrop went away to Bridgwater, unwell, and I paid him 9 dollars. Billings brought up a Load of green Seaweed.

¹ See John Rutherfurd to JA, 28 June 1796 (Adams Papers), relative to a work by Robert Somerville entitled *Outlines of the Fifteenth Chapter of the Proposed General Report from the Board of Agriculture. On the Subject of Manures . . .*, London, 1795. JA's answer has not been found; he soon afterward presented a copy of the book to the American Academy of Arts and Sciences (Eliphalet Pearson to JA, 7 Sept. 1796, Adams Papers).

### AUGUST 4. 1796 THURSDAY.

Of all the Summers of my Life, this has been the freest from Care, Anxiety and Vexation to me. The Sickness of Mrs. A. excepted. My Health has been better, the Season fruitful, my farm was conducted. Alas! what may happen to reverse all this? But it is folly to anticipate evils, and madness to create imaginary ones.

Went over to Weymouth with Mrs. A., visited Mr. Norton and dined with Dr. Tufts whose salted Beef and shell beans with a Whortleberry Pudden and his Cyder is a Luxurious Treat. Col. Hubbard and his Wife came and I laid a Plan to plough Penns Hill [by?] Abington Ploughmen.¹

Bass went to Squantum for the oxen—disappointed. The Wind too high to go over to Long Island. Sullivan threshing. Billings and Bass carting Dirt, making Compost with Lime, brought up a Load of Seaweed.

¹ Bottom of page worn away and text only partly legible; but see entry of 8 Aug., below.

### AUGUST 5. 1796. FRYDAY.

A fine day. I have finished Petrarch. Walked up to the new Barn and over to the old Plain. Sullivan and Mr. Sam. Hayward threshing— Billings and Bass carting Earth and Seaweed and liming the Compost. Mr. Wibirt dined with Us. James brought home the twin oxen from Long Island. Trask burning Bushes in the Swamp on Penns Hill.

### AUGUST 6. 1796. SATURDAY.

Billings and Bass off by Day for Seaweed. Twin oxen sent to be shod.

Omnium Rerum Domina, Virtus. Virtue is The Mistress of all Things. Virtue is The Master of all Things. Therefore a Nation that should never do wrong must necessarily govern the World. The Might of Virtue, The Power of Virtue is not a very common Topick, not so common as it should be.

Bass and Billings brought another Load of Seaweed in the Evening for the Swine. Sullivan Lothrop went home. Mrs. A. paid him 15 dollars. Mr. Flynt called at Evening. Tomorrow is the last Sunday of his Engagement at Milton. He then goes a Journey for 3 Weeks after which he returns.[1] Mr. Whitcomb supplies Us in the mean time. Rode up to the burnt Swamp.

[1] Jacob Flint, Harvard 1794, who was afterward for many years minister at Cohasset (E. Victor Bigelow, *A Narrative History of the Town of Cohasset, Mass.*, Cohasset, 1898, p. 367, 506).

### AUGUST 7. 1796. SUNDAY.

I am reading a Work of Cicero that I remember not to have read before. It is intituled M. Tullii Ciceronis Si Deo placet Consolatio.[1] Remarkable for an ardent hope and confident belief of a future State.

Mr. Whitcomb preached and dined with Us. Prince, having provoked beyond bearing by his insolent Contempt of repeated orders, got a gentle flogging, and went off, i.e. run away. Thomas Lothrop return'd from Bridgwater.

[1] Cicero's *Consolatio* is a work of which only fragments, some of them known to be spurious, survive.

### AUGUST 8. 1796. MONDAY.

Billing and Bass gone to mowing Salt Grass at the Beach Meadow. T. Lothrop unloading the Sea weed. No Negro but James, who shall be the last.—Agreed with Mr. Reed of Abington to plough for me next Monday &c. Trask half a day mowing bushes.

### AUGUST 9. 1796. TUESDAY.

4 hands mowing Salt Grass. Finished the Beach Meadow. Trask mowing Bushes to make room for the plough upon Penns hill. T. Lothrop, threshing Corn—Brisler winnowing Barley.

### AUGUST 10. 1796 WEDNESDAY.

Billing and Bass collecting Compost. Brought up two Loads of Seaweed and carted several Loads of Earth from behind the Outhouse.

Mr. Howell of Rhode Island came up to see me and conversed the whole Evening concerning St. Croix and his Commission for settling that Boundary.[1]

[1] David Howell, a lawyer and a former member of the Continental Congress, was one of the commissioners appointed to arbitrate the disputed boundary between the United States and Canada under Article V of Jay's Treaty (*DAB*; see also entry of 2 Aug., above, and note there).

### AUGUST 11. 1796. THURSDAY.

Mr. Howell lodged with Us and spent the whole Morning in Conversation concerning the Affairs of his Mission. He said by way of Episode that the President would resign, and that there was one Thing which would make R. Island unanimous in his Successor and that was the funding System. He said they wanted Hamilton for V.P.—I was wholly silent.

Billing and Bass brought up a Load of Dulce and Eelgrass and are carting Earth from below the Outhouse. The Lothrops threshing.

Mr. Thomas Johnson, only son of Joshua Johnson of London, Consul, came to visit Us and spent the day and night with Us.[1] I carried him to the Pinnacle of Penns Hill to show him the Prospect.

[1] Thomas Baker Johnson (1779?–1843), only brother of Louisa Catherine Johnson whom JQA was to marry in July 1797 and who is designated in the present work as LCA. T. B. Johnson seems to have lived an obscure and wandering life. In 1808 he arrived in New Orleans and for some years served as postmaster there, but his diaries for 1807–1838 (now in the Adams Papers, Microfilms, Reel Nos. 332–339) show that he spent his later years as a valetudinarian in Europe.

### AUGUST 12. 1796. FRYDAY.

Billing, Bass and Sullivan carting Salt Hay from the Beech Marsh. Tirell and Th. Lothrop threshing and winnowing Barley.

### AUGUST 13. 1796 SATURDAY.

Three Load of Salt Hay Yesterday from the Beach Marsh. Got in 51 Bushells of Barley winnowed and raddled. Billing, Bass, Sullivan Lothrop and E. Belcher with Brisler poling off and carting Salt Hay. Tirrell and T. Lothrop threshing. Trask burning Bushes on Penns Hill.

Reading Tullys Offices. It is a Treatise on moral obligation. Our Word Obligation answers nearer and better than Duty, to Ciceros Word, officium.

Our Men have brought up 3 loads of Salt Hay and left a 4th. stacked upon the Ground. The Barley not all threshed. Prince return'd from Boston.

Read much in Tullys Offices.

### AUGUST 14. 1796. SUNDAY.

The Weather hot and dry.

One great Advantage of the Christian Religion is that it brings the great Principle of the Law of Nature and Nations, Love your Neighbour as yourself, and do to others as you would that others should do to you, to the Knowledge, Belief and Veneration of the whole People. Children, Servants, Women and Men are all Professors in the science of public as well as private Morality. No other Institution for Education, no kind of political Discipline, could diffuse this kind of necessary Information, so universally among all Ranks and Descriptions of Citizens. The Duties and Rights of The Man and the Citizen are thus taught, from early Infancy to every Creature. The Sanctions of a future Life are thus added to the Observance of civil and political as well as domestic and private Duties. Prudence, Justice, Temperance and Fortitude, are thus taught to be the means and Conditions of future as well as present Happiness.

### AUGUST 15. 1796. MONDAY.

My Team met the Abington Team at the Bars, and plough'd the Baulk between Burrells Corn and the great Wall, with the great Plough.

Ploughed on the North Side of the Wall from the Road to the rocky Vally with the small breaking up plough. Trask mowing Bushes and burning. At Night both Teams came home with both Ploughs.

Mrs. Adams went with Mrs. Otis to Situate and Plymouth.

### AUGUST 16. 1796. TUESDAY.

Mr. Reed and Mr. Gurney with Billings ploughing below the lower Garden with 9 Cattle, and the small breaking up plough. It took a long time to fix the Plough with a Wheel &c. In the Afternoon ploughed upon Stony field Hill.

Sullivan with one Yoke of oxen, the Steers and Mare gone to cart Salt Hay for my Tenants French and Vinton.

Tirrell and Thomas still threshing. James and Prince, idle as usual.

### AUGUST 17. 1796. WEDNESDAY.

Seven Yoke of Oxen and a Horse, Mr. Reed, Mr. Gurney, Mr. Billings, Mr. Brisler, Sullivan and Thomas Lothrop and black James, Seven hands ploughing with the great Plough in the Meadow below the lower Garden. Prince gone to Mill. The Weather dry, fair and cool. The Wind Easterly.

### AUGUST 18. 1796. THURSDAY.

Ten Yoke of Oxen and ten Men ploughing in the Meadow below my House.

AUGUST 19. 1769 [*i.e.* 1796]. FRYDAY.

Ten Yoke of Oxen and twelve hands ploughing in the meadow. It is astonishing that such a Meadow should have lain so long in such a State. Brakes, Hassock Grass, Cramberry Vines, Poke or Skunk Cabbage, Button Bushes, alder Bushes, old Stumps and Roots, Rocks, Turtles, Eels, Frogs, were the Chief Things to be found in it. But I presume it may be made to produce Indian and English Grain, and English Grass, especially Herdsgrass in Abundance. At least the Beauty of the Meadow and the Sweetness of it and the Air over it will be improved. Brackets, Vintons and My Brothers oxen added to mine and those from Abington.

AUGUST 20. 1796. SATURDAY.

Bracket and Vinton left me. We procured Captn. Baxters Oxen and William Field Junr. and went on with Eight Yoke including my red Steers, and ploughed as well as ever.

Paid Reed £11. 2s. in full for the Weeks Work of two Men, three Yoke of Oxen and a Horse.

The Men I allowed 6s. a day, tho I found them,[1] being one Shilling more than the Agreement. The Oxen I allowed 7s. 6d. a Day, as they found them, which was according to Agreement. The Horse I allowed four shillings a Day for the Days he worked, or rather danced, which were three, and I allowed them one shilling a Day for his Keeping, when he was idle. Making in the whole £11 2s: od.

The[y] left a miserable Dogs Ear in the Meadow unploughed, which mortifies me. In other Respects I am satisfied. I allowed them however a very extravagant sum for keeping their Cattle, and a shilling a Man a Day more than they asked for their Labour.

Mrs. Adams returned with Mr. and Mrs. Otis and Miss Harriot about 9 O Clock at night.

[1] That is, furnished them with food; see *OED* under Find, verb, 18.

AUGUST 21. 1796. SUNDAY.

The hottest day. Unwell.

AUGUST 22. 1796 MONDAY.

Mr. Otis and Family went to Boston. Mr. C. Storer and Mr. Storrow breakfasted.

Billings and Sullivan began the Wall against the Road opposite the Corner of the Garden.

Very hot but the Wind springs up. Unwell.

### AUGUST 23. 1796 TUESDAY.

All hands and Tirrell, upon the Wall—carting Stones and Earth &c.

Went down to Mr. Quincys and up to our Tenants with Mrs. Adams. Unwell. Brisler and the two black Boys picking Apples.

### AUGUST 24. 1796. WEDNESDAY.

Billings, Bass and the Lothrops upon the Wall. The blacks going to pick Apples. I took Rhubarb and Salt of Wormwood.

Bathing my Feet and drinking balm Tea, last night composed me somewhat, and I hope the Rhubarb and Salt of Wormwood I took this Morning will carry off my Complaints: but the Pain in my head and the burnings in my hands and feet were so like the Commencement of my Fevers of 1781 at Amsterdam and of 1783 at Paris and Auteuil, that I began to be allarmed.

Mr. and Mrs. Norton dined with Us.

Old Mr. Thomas Adams of Medfield, the Father of Hannah Adams, the Author of The View of Religions, came in to return a Volume he borrowed last Spring of Bryants Analysis of the ancient Mythology, and to borrow the other two Volumes which I lent him.[1]

Brisler and the black Boys picking Apples.

[1] Thomas Adams of Medfield was a distant cousin of JA; considered eccentric because he doted on books, he acquired the name "Book Adams." However, he returned all three volumes of Jacob Bryant's *New System, or an Analysis of Ancient Mythology,* 2d edn., London, 1775–1776, for they may be found among JA's books in the Boston Public Library.

His daughter Hannah Adams (1755–1831) was "probably the first woman in America to make writing a profession" (*DAB*), and was accordingly much patronized by literary Boston. Her *View of Religions, in Two Parts,* an enlargement of an earlier work, was published in Boston, 1791, and was dedicated to JA, who subscribed for three copies. Though a mere compilation, this is still a useful book. See Hannah Adams to JA, 21 Feb. 1791, Adams Papers; and JA's reply, 10 March, LbC, Adams Papers; also the engaging *Memoir of Miss Hannah Adams, Written by Herself. With Additional Notices, by a Friend,* Boston, 1832.

### AUGUST 25. 1796. THURSDAY.

Billings, Bass and the two Lothrops all this Week upon the Wall over the Way. They make about a Rod and a half a day. Captn. Beale began Yesterday to clear his Brook. So much for the Exemplary Influence of ploughing my Meadow.

The Benediction of Ulysses to The Pheacians, B. 13. l. 60. "Sure fix'd on Virtue may your nation stand and public Evil never touch the Land" comprehends the Essence and Summary of Politicks. A Nation can stand on no other Basis, and standing on this it is founded on a Rock. Standing on any other Ground it will be washed away by the Rains or blown down by the Winds.

This Day has been intolerably hot. But about 9 O Clock in the Evening it began to rain with Thunder and Lightening and continued to rain very steadily for an hour or two.

My Men complained of the heat more than at any time, they accomplished never the less about a rod and an half of the Wall.

### AUGUST 26. 1796. FRYDAY.

Cloudy. Wind. N.E. but not rainy. The shower last night has refreshed Us. The Corn, the Gardens, the Pastures, The After feed, the Fruit trees all feel it.

Sullivan gone for a Load of Seaweed. The other Men upon the Wall. In digging a Trench for the Wall We find Stones enough, in Addition to the old Wall to compleat the New one. Four hands with a Yoke of Oxen have done Six Rods in four days Monday, Tuesday, Wednesday and Thursday.

Brisler went Yesterday a plovering with a Party who killed about an hundred.

"Inflexible to preserve, virtuous to pursue, and intelligent to discern the true Interests of his Country." Flattering expressions of a Toast, the more remarkable as they originated in N. York.—God grant they may never be belied, never disproved.

Mr. Sedgwick and Mr. Barrell came up to see me, and gives a sanguine Account of the future Elections of Senators and Representatives.

Sullivan brought up a Load of Seaweed for the Swine. Trask at Work the 3d day mowing Bushes in the old Plain.

### AUGUST 27. 1796. SATURDAY.

Sullivan carting Seaweed, spread one Load among the red Loam in the Cavity in the Yard. Trask mowing Bushes in the meadow below the Garden. James cutting the Trees. Billings, Bass and Thomas, about the Wall. Brisler absent on Account of his sick Child.

The Wall, the Alterations of the Road, and the Carting of the Earth, Soil, Loam, Gravel and Stones, out of the Way, whether We spread them on the Meadow, lay them in heaps for Compost in the Yard, or deposit them in Parts of the Road where they may be wanted, will in the most frugal Course We can take consume much labour at a great Expence.

### AUGUST 28. 1796. SUNDAY.

Hot. Went not out. Mr. Strong preached. Reading Bryants Analysis of ancient Mythology.

### AUGUST 29. MONDAY. 1796.

Warm. Billings, Bass and two Sullivans[1] with James on the Wall. Carted 9 or 10 Load of excellent Soil into an heap, below the lower Garden Wall, and put it to two Loads of Seaweed and some Lime, for manure for the Corn in the Meadow next Year. Carted besides, 3 Loads into the Hollow in the Cowyard. An extream hot day. Reading Bryant. Wrote to Phila. to Wolcot and Pickering.[2]

[1] Probably an error for the "two Lathrops" (or Lothrops).
[2] The letter to Oliver Wolcott Jr., secretary of the treasury (CtHi), requested "a Quarters Salary." The letter to Timothy Pickering has not been found, but Pickering's reply of 5 Sept. (Adams Papers) shows that JA had inquired about the health of TBA, secretary of legation to his brother JQA at The Hague.

### AUGUST 30. TUESDAY. 1796.

Prospect of another hot day. Pursuing the Wall. Tirrell worked with our Men. Trask cutting Bushes on the ploughed Meadow at the other Place. Wind shifted to the North and then to the N.E. and the Air became very cold. Rode up to see Trask. Carted Mould into the Yard all Day.

### AUGUST 31. 1796. WEDNESDAY.

Wind north and Air cold. Working on the high Ways. Carried a great Part of my gravel and spread it on the Road to the Meeting House.

### SEPTEMBER 1. 1796. THURSDAY.

The Summer is ended and the first day of Autumn commenced. The Morning is cold tho the Wind is West. To Work again on the high Ways. Billings out upon his Wall a little after Sunrise. Captn. Hall Surveyor of High Ways finished the Road between my Garden and new Wall.

### SEPTEMBER 2. 1796. FRYDAY.

To work again on the high Ways. They have taxed me this Year between forty nine and fifty days Works on the Roads besides the other Farm in Quincy and the farm in Braintree. This is unjust, more than my Proportion, more than Mr. Black or Mr. Beale.[1]

Stumbled over a Wheelbarrow in the dark and hurt my Shin.

[1] Moses Black, an Irishman who had acquired the house and farm formerly owned by Col. Edmund Quincy (the "Dorothy Q." house), and Squire Benjamin Beale were both at this time prominent in town affairs and among the largest property owners in Quincy. See the tax list for 1792, when Quincy was taken off from Braintree, in Pattee, *Old Braintree and Quincy*, p. 623 ff., and numerous references to both men in the same work.

### SEPTEMBER 3. 1796. SATURDAY.

Pursuing the Wall. Tirrell is here and We expect French with his Team. Some soft warm Showers in the night and this morning. French came not, because it rained.

Anniversary of Peace, which has lasted 13 Years.

### SEPTEMBER 4. 1796. SUNDAY.

Fair. No Clergyman to day.

### SEPTEMBER 5. 1796. MONDAY.

The Anniversary of The Congress in 1774.

Sullivan brought a good Load of green Seaweed, with six Cattle, which We spread and limed upon the heap of Compost in the Meadow. Carted Earth from the Wall to the same heap. Tirrell here. Stetson opening the Brook three feet wider, Two feet on one Side and three feet on the other, at 9d. Pr. rod. Billings has never laid up more than a Rod and a half a day, of the Wall, till Yesterday when he thinks he laid up 28 feet.

### SEPT. 6. 1796. TUESDAY.

Walked up to Trask mowing Bushes.

### SEPT. 7. 1796. WEDNESDAY.

Belcher, Bass and Sullivan gone to mow the Marsh and get out the Thatch at Penny ferry.[1]

Billings laying Wall. Thomas, carting Earth. Stetson, widening the Brook to seven feet at 9d. Pr. Rod and a dinner. Brisler and James preparing, Yesterday and to day, the Cyder Mill, Press, and Casks.

Yesterday Jackson Field came to offer me Mount Arrarat at Three hundred Dollars. I could not agree. He fell to 275. I could not agree. He fell to 250 reserving the Right to work in Stone with one hand, for Life. I agreed at length to this extravagant Price and have drawn the Deed this Morning.

This Afternoon He came and took the Deed to execute and acknowledge.[2]

[1] "In 1823, ex-President John Adams was asked whether Judge Edmund Quincy of Braintree, went to Boston over Milton Hill? He replied, 'No, Judge Quincy would have thought it unsafe to venture as far inland as Milton Hill, for fear of the Indians; he was accustomed to go to Boston by the way of Penny's Ferry;'—a ferry so called because passengers paid a penny a piece to be rowed over the Neponset" (*Quincy Patriot*, 25 Dec. 1875, as quoted in Pattee, *Old Braintree and Quincy*, p. 69, note).

[2] Mount Arrarat was part of the old Braintree North Commons (now in West Quincy), divided and sold as lots in 1765 under the management of a town committee of which JA was a member (*Braintree Town Records*, p.

406–407). On 9 June of the present year JA had acquired from Neddie Curtis 20 acres of this land, which was to prove valuable for its granite quarries, and he now acquired 20 more (information from Mr. Ezekiel S. Sargent, Quincy, Mass., in a letter to the editors from Mr. H. Hobart Holly, president of the Quincy Historical Society, 13 March 1960). In 1822 JA held still more granite-producing land in this neighborhood, and one of his gifts to the town toward building a new church and an academy comprised "fifty four acres more or less, commonly known by the name of the Lane's Pasture, or the Mount Ararat Pasture, near the seat of the Hon. Thomas Greenleaf" ([Quincy, Mass.,] *Deeds and Other Documents . . .*, Cambridge, 1823, p. 3–5).

### SEPTR. 8. 1796. THURSDAY.

Sullivan gone for Seaweed. Bass and Thomas carting Manure from the Hill of Compost in the Yard. Billings and Prince laying Wall. Brisler and James picking Apples and making Cyder. Stetson widening the Brook.

I think to christen my Place by the Name of Peace field, in commemoration of the Peace which I assisted in making in 1783, of the thirteen Years Peace and Neutrality which I have contributed to preserve, and of the constant Peace and Tranquility which I have enjoyed in this Residence.[1]

Carted 6 Loads of slimy Mud from the Brook to the heap of Compost.

Jackson Field brought me his Deed of Mount Arrarat executed by himself and his Wife and acknowledged before Major Miller. I received it, and gave him my Note for 250 dollars. I then gave him my Consent, without his asking it, to pasture his Cow as usual the Remainder of this Season, for which he expressed Gratitude, and engaged to keep off Geese, Sheep, Hogs and Cattle. Received Letters from my Son at the Hague as late as 24. June.[2]

[1] "Peacefield" (variously written) was the first of several names JA used for his Quincy homestead; they varied according to his mood. Following his unhappy return from Washington in March 1801, he headed his letters "Stony Field, Quincy," a name he drew from Stony Field Hill, the eminence that he owned and farmed across the road from his house and that later acquired the more elegant name Presidents Hill. After resuming his correspondence with Jefferson in 1812, JA whimsically adopted an Italianate name, "Montezillo," which he cryptically explained to Richard Rush as follows: "Mr. Jefferson lives at Monticello the lofty Mountain. I live at *Montezillo* a little Hill" (24 Nov. 1814, PHi:Gratz Coll.). This name persisted

until JA's last years, though he used it irregularly, and occasionally varied it by employing the English form, "Little Hill."

[2] At the end of May JQA had returned to The Hague after a stay of nearly seven months in London. He had gone there on what turned out to be a superfluous diplomatic errand, but in the course of his visit he had become engaged to Louisa Catherine Johnson; see his Diary, 11 Nov. 1795–31 May 1796; JQA to AA, 5 May 1796, Adams Papers; Bemis, *JQA*, 1:68–69. The letters JA mentions as receiving were doubtless those dated 6 and 24 June 1796, both in Adams Papers and both in large part printed in JQA's *Writings*, 1:490–493, 497–508.

SEPTR. 9. 1796. FRYDAY.

Appearances of Rain.

SEPTEMBER 10. 1796. SATURDAY.

Walked, with my Brother to Mount Arrarat, and find upon Inquiry that Jo. Arnold's Fence against the New Lane begins at the Road by the Nine mile Stone. My half is towards Neddy Curtis's Land lately Wm. Fields. The Western Half of the Fence against Josiah Bass, or in other Words that Part nearest to Neddy Curtis's is mine. Against Dr. Greenleaf my half is nearest to Josiah Bass's Land.[1]

[1] The tempo of electioneering increased rapidly after the publication of Washington's Farewell Address on 19 Sept., but JA stayed quietly on at Quincy for two months longer, pushing his program of farm improvements into severely cold weather. On 23 Nov. he left for Philadelphia, passing a day on the way with his daughter in East Chester and another with CA in New York (JA to AA, 27 Nov., 1 Dec., both in Adams Papers). He arrived in Philadelphia on 2 Dec., in ample time for the opening of the second session of the Fourth Congress three days later. The city was seething with politics on the eve of the voting by Presidential electors in the sixteen states, and so indeed was the

country; but JA wrote much more calmly of the prospects of both himself and his rivals, not to mention the maneuvers of party understrappers and the libels of journalists, than AA could. "I look upon the Event as the throw of a Die, a mere Chance, a miserable, meagre Tryumph to either Party," he told JQA in a letter of 5 Dec. (Adams Papers). What he meant was that, since the contest was bound to be very close, the new President, whoever he might be, would have so small a majority that he would "be very apt to stagger and stumble" in discharging his duties (to AA, 7 Dec., Adams Papers). The result of the electors' balloting was not perfectly certain until late that month. By the 27th JA could write his wife: "71 is the Ne plus ultra—it is now certain that no Man can have more and but one so many"; and though he did not yet know beyond all doubt whether Jefferson or Thomas Pinckney would be Vice-President he discussed with AA their imminent problems respecting "House, Furniture, Equipage, Servants," and the like (Adams Papers). At length, on 8 Feb., as he was bound to do, he presided over a joint meeting of the two houses in which the votes were unsealed and counted, and announced the result as 71 votes for himself (one more than the necessary majority of 70), 68 for Jefferson, 59 for Pinckney, and the rest scattered among ten others, so that John Adams and Thomas Jefferson were elected President and Vice-President respectively, to serve for four years beginning on 4 March 1797 (*Annals of Congress*, 4th Cong., 2d sess., col. 2095–2098).

Four years later, on 11 Feb. 1801, Vice-President Jefferson found himself obliged to perform a similar duty and announced that Jefferson and Burr had each received 73 electoral votes, JA 65, Charles Cotesworth Pinckney 64, and John Jay 1 vote (same, 6th Cong., 2d sess., col. 743–744). The tie vote for the two Democratic-Republican candidates led to complications, but JA was out of the running, and early on the day of his successor's inauguration he left the new seat of government in Washington, and public life, for good.

## [JULY–AUGUST] 1804.[1]

| | | | |
|---|---|---|---|
| July | 2d. | Mowed, over vs. Yard and Garden | |
| | 3 | One Load, from the road to the ditch and from the cart path to the pasture Lane | 1 |
| | 4 | Four Loads, over the Way and between the ditch and orchard | 4 |
| | 5 | One Load from Chris Webbs House Lott | 1 |
| | 6 | One from the 10 Acre Lot on the hill | 1 |
| | 7 | Two in Cranchs Barn and two from the 10 Acre Lott | 4 |
| Sunday | 8 | | |
| | 9 | Two load one from Mr. Cranchs and 1 from 10 Acre Lot | 2 |
| Wed. | 11. | 4 Load from about the Hancock Cellar | 4 |
| T. | 12. | 6 Load five from about Hancocks Cellar and one from the Walnut Lot | 6 |
| F. | 13 | 6 Load. 3 from Walnut Lot and three from about Hancocks Cellar and one Jag[2] | 7 |
| S. | 14. | Six Loads from Chris. Webbs farm | 6 |
| Sunday | 15 | | |
| Monday | 16 | | |
| Tuesday | 17 | | |
| Wednesday | 18 | Seven Loads 3 from the orchard and 4 into Mr. Cranches Barn of Clover—Jaggs **all.** | 7 |

| | | | |
|---|---|---|---|
| Thursday | 19 | | |
| F. | 20 | | |
| S. | 21 | 5 Load from the Wire Grass Hill | 5 |
| Sunday | 22 | | |
| Monday | 23 | Three Loads from the ten Acre hill | 3 |
| Tuesday | 24 | Three Loads from the orchard and beyond it | 3 |
| Wednesday | 25 | Two Loads from the Ditch | 2 |
| Thursday | 26 | Three Loads in Mr. Cranchs Barn | 3 |
| Fryday | 27 | Three, fresh and all into Mr. C. Barn | 3 |
| Saturday | 28 | One Load from the Beech Meadow part black grass | 1 |
| | | | 63 |
| Sunday | 29 | | |
| Monday | 30 | One Load Salt [hay] from the Coves | 1 |
| August | 17 | Fryday 5 loads of Salt Hay from the Coves | 5 |
| Saturday | 18 | 3 loads, one from the Coves and two from Mount Wollaston at the Salt pond | 3 |
| Sunday | 19 | | |
| Monday | 20 | 3 Loads from the Meadows on this and the other side the Causey | 3 |
| Tuesday | 21 | 2 Loads from the Causey at Mount Wollaston | 2 |
| Wednesday | 22 | Four loads from the beach | 4 |
| Thursday | 23 | Two loads from the Beach Salt Hay | 2 |
| | | | 20 |

[1] This tabular record of JA's haying operations and the homely entry immediately following, the final scraps of JA's Diary, were not printed by CFA.

[2] Jag, substantive, 2 (origin unknown): "*dial.* and *U.S.* . . . 1. A load (usually a small cart-load) of hay, wood, etc." (*OED*).

## 1784 [*i.e.* 1804]. AUG.

The last Week in August We ploughed a ditch and brought the Earth into the Yard and 32 loads of Mud from the Cove.

*Autobiography of John Adams*

# Autobiography of John Adams

## Part One: To October 1776

### JOHN ADAMS.[1]

Begun Oct. 5. 1802.

As the Lives of Phylosophers, Statesmen or Historians written by them selves have generally been suspected of Vanity, and therefore few People have been able to read them without disgust; there is no reason to expect that any Sketches I may leave of my own Times would be received by the Public with any favour, or read by individuals with much interest. The many great Examples of this practice will not be alledged as a justification, because they were Men of extraordinary Fame, to which I have no pretensions.[2] My Excuse is, that having been the Object of much Misrepresentation, some of my Posterity may probably wish to see in my own hand Writing a proof of the falsehood of that Mass of odious Abuse of my Character, with which News Papers, private Letters and public Pamphlets and Histories have been disgraced for thirty Years. It is not for the Public but for my Children that I commit these Memoirs to writing: and to them and their Posterity I recommend, not the public Course, which the times and the Country in which I was born and the Circumstances which surrounded me compelled me to pursue: but those Moral Sentiments and Sacred Prin-

[1] This is JA's own title for the first part of his Autobiography, dealing with his life up to the beginning of Oct. 1776. For a description of the MS as a whole, an account of its composition, and the editorial treatment now given it, see the Introduction to the present work. As preserved by the family, the MS of the Autobiography is preceded by two undated holograph fragments. The first, entitled "The Life of John Adams," is a two-page folio MS that was undoubtedly composed earlier than the Autobiography as it now stands; it is a false start or rough draft, much crossed out and interlined, that summarizes the early history of the Adams family in America and breaks off after a paragraph or two on JA's boyhood; see notes 2 and 3 immediately below. The second fragment, entitled "Sketch," consists of three quarto pages in JA's later hand, and is a very condensed summary of JA's whole life, ending: "On the        day of blank in the Year        he died, and is buried ⟨on Shepards Hill heretofore called Mount Wollaston. What Fortune had he pray? His own and his Fathers.⟩"

[2] In the rough draft this sentence begins: "The Examples of De Thou, Clarendon, Hume, Gibbon &c., will not be alledged. . . ." The entire sentence was subsequently crossed out.

ciples, which at all hazards and by every Sacrifice I have endeavoured to preserve through Life.

The Customs of Biography require that something should be said of my origin.[3] Early in the Settlement of the Colony of Massachusetts, a Gentleman from England arriving in America with Eight Sons, settled near Mount Wollaston and not far from the ancient Stone Building erected for the double Purpose of Public Worship and Fortification against the Indians. His House, Malthouse and the Lands belonging to them still remain in the Possession of his Posterity.[4]

Of the Eight Sons, one returned to England: four removed to Medfield: two are said to have removed to Chelmsford: One only Joseph remained at Braintree.[5] He had three sons Joseph, Peter and John. Joseph and Peter remained in Braintree: John removed to Boston and

[3] In the rough draft JA added here the following sentences: "Although this Investigation will present nothing on the one hand to excite the pride of my Successors or the Envy of others, Yet on the other, it will discover no causes for blushes or regret. My Father, Grandfather, Great Grandfather, and Great Great Grandfather all lived and died in this Town of Quincy, for so many Years the First Parish in the Ancient Town of Braintree, and are buried in the Congregational Church Yard. They were all in the middle rank of People in Society: all sober, industrious, frugal and religious: all possessed of landed Estates, always unincumbered with debts, and as independent as human nature is, or ought to be in the World."

[4] The immigrant was Henry Adams (ca. 1583–1646), a farmer and maltster of Barton St. David and Kingweston, Somersetshire, who married Edith Squire in 1609 and came with a numerous family to Massachusetts Bay in 1638 (Bartlett, *Henry Adams of Somersetshire*, p. 46–72). In an epitaph composed for the progenitor of his line in America, JA said that Henry Adams "took his flight from the Dragon persecution in Devonshire" (Wilson, *Where Amer. Independence Began*, p. 301). He was mistaken about Henry Adams' place of origin (though it was not until the publication of Bartlett's researches in 1927 that the true place of origin was known), and there is only family tradition to support the belief that the Adamses were

driven from Somersetshire to the Bay Colony by "the Dragon persecution." On 24 Feb. 1639/40 Henry Adams was granted forty acres, for a family of ten heads, "at the mount" (Mount Wollaston), and he settled there in what became in 1640 the town of Braintree (Boston Record Commissioners, *2d Report*, p. 49). The site of his farm and malthouse is on the north side of present Elm Street about opposite the head of South Street in modern Quincy, which was taken off from Braintree in 1792 (HA2, *Birthplaces*, p. 1). The occupation and the property stayed with the family into the 19th century; for JA's recollections of boyhood visits to his "Great Uncle, Captain and Deacon Peter Adams," at the malthouse, see JA to Benjamin Rush, 19 July 1812 (MB; Biddle, *Old Family Letters*, p. 413). Henry Adams' highly revealing will and inventory are printed from the Suffolk co. Probate Records in Bartlett, *Henry Adams of Somersetshire*, p. 67–68.

[5] Joseph Adams (1626–1694), seventh son of Henry Adams and great-grandfather of JA, inherited his father's property and trade in Braintree, married in 1650 Abigail Baxter of Roxbury, and served from time to time as selectman, constable, and surveyor of highways (Bartlett, *Henry Adams of Somersetshire*, p. 80, 90–93; *Braintree Town Records*, p. 13, 14, 27, 28). A copy of his will, 18 July 1694, with comments by JA, is in the Adams Papers, Wills and Deeds (Microfilms, Reel No. 607).

was the Father of Samuel Adams and Grandfather of the late Governor of the State of Massachusetts.

Joseph my Grandfather had ten Children, five sons and five daughters, all named in his Will which I now have in my Possession.[6]

John my Father had three Sons, John, Peter Boylston, and Elihu. Peter Boylston is still living my Neighbour, my Friend and beloved Brother.[7] Elihu died at an early Age in 1775. His Life was a Sacrifice to the Cause of his Country, having taken, in our Army at Cambridge in which he commanded a Company of Volunteers from the Militia, a contagious distemper, which brought him to his Grave leaving three young Children John, Susanna and Elisha.

In 1629 October the twentieth, a Choice was made, at a General Court of the Company in London, of Governor and Assistants, consisting of such Persons as had determined to go over to America, with the Patent of the Massachusetts Colony, and Thomas Adams was chosen as one of the Assistants. By this it appears that Thomas Adams had declared his intention of removing to the new World, and We are informed in Mr. Prince's Chronology, that this Gentleman was one of the most active and zealous in promoting the design to transport the Patent across the Seas: Yet it does not appear that he ever arrived in America. It is not improbable that his Brother, or some other Relation, with his numerous Family, might be sent over, to reconnoitre the Country and prepare a Situation: and that death, or some unfavourable report brought back by the Eighth Son who returned to England, might prevent his pursuing his former intention of following the Charter to this Country. But this is mere Conjecture.[8]

[...][9] engaged and while [...] him in his Writings learned his

[6] The second Joseph Adams of Braintree (1654–1737), eldest son and second child of the first Joseph, married three times; his second wife was Hannah Bass of Braintree, a granddaughter of John and Priscilla Alden of Plymouth, whom he married in 1688 and by whom he had eight of his eleven children, including Deacon John, father of JA (Bartlett, *Henry Adams of Somersetshire*, p. 93, 94–95). He served in the same town offices his father had held (*Braintree Town Records*, p. 39, 46, 83, 87, 90, 99). A copy of a draft of his will dated 23 July 1731, with comments by JA, is in the Adams Papers, Wills and Deeds (Microfilms, Reel No. 607).

[7] Born in 1738, Peter Boylston Adams

died in 1823 (Quincy, First Church, MS Records).

[8] No evidence is known indicating that the Thomas Adams who was one of the proprietors of the Massachusetts Bay Company under its royal charter of 4 March 1629, but who did not come to America, was connected with the Henry Adams of Somersetshire who came to Boston in 1638.

[9] At least half a line of text is missing here. The missing matter occurs at the top of a second folded sheet of the MS which is larger than the preceding and following sheets and has thus become brittle and is worn away. Several other oversize sheets in the Autobiography have suffered similar damage, but the

Trade. My Father by his Industry and Enterprize soon became a Person of more Property and Consideration in the Town than his Patron had been. He became a Select Man, a Militia Officer and a Deacon in the Church. He was the honestest Man I ever knew. In Wisdom, Piety, Benevolence and Charity In proportion to his Education and Sphere of Life, I have never seen his Superiour. My Grandmother was a Bass of Braintree: but as she died many Years before I was born, I know little of her History except that I have been told by an ancient Lady the Relict of our ancient Minister Mr. Marsh a Daughter of our more ancient Minister Mr. Fiske, that she was a Person possessed of more Litterature than was common in Persons of her Sex and Station, a dilligent Reader and a most exemplary Woman in all the Relations of Life. She died of a Consumption and had Leisure to draw up advice to her Children, which I have read in her handwriting in my Infancy, but which is now lost. I know not that I have seen it for si[x]ty Years, and the Judgment of a Boy of seven Years old is not ⟨worth much⟩ to be recollected, but it appeared to me then wonderfully fine. From his Mother probably my Father received an Admiration of Learning as he called it, which remained with him, through Life, and which prompted him to his unchangeable determination to give his first son a liberal Education.

My Mother was Suzanna Boylston a Daughter of Peter Boylston of Brooklyne, the oldest son of Thomas Boylston a Surgeon and Apothecary who came from London in 1656, and married a Woman by the Name of Gardner of that Town, by whom he had Issue Peter my Grandfather, Zabdiel the Physician, who first introduced into the British Empire the Practice of Inocculation for the Small Pox, Richard, Thomas and Dudley and several Daughters.[1]

[My Grand]father married Ann [White, a daughter of Benjamin] White who lived on the South Side of the Hill in Brooklyne as you go to little Cambridge, known by the name of Whites Hill, which he owned.[2] My Grandmother was the Sister of Edward White Esqr. the

present passage is the only one the text of which is not wholly recoverable by one means or another.

[1] For a brief genealogy of the Boylston family of Muddy River (later Brookline) and Boston, see *NEHGR*, 7 (1853): 145–150.

[2] By "little Cambridge" JA meant what is now Brighton (formerly part of Cambridge). The house on White's Hill, built before 1736, rebuilt by Dr. Zabdiel Boylston after he purchased it in 1737, and owned successively by Boylstons, Hyslops, Lees, and Richardsons, still stands on Boylston Street in Brookline, overlooking the Reservoir; see Nina Fletcher Little, *Some Old Brookline Houses*, Brookline, 1949, p. 115–118; Frances R. Morse, *Henry and Mary Lee: Letters and Journals*, Boston, 1926, p. 297 ff.). In a letter to Ward Nicholas Boylston, 15 Sept. 1820 (Tr, Adams Papers), JA recalled his childhood visits to his mother's Brookline homestead.

9. THE AMERICAN COMMISSIONERS AT THE PRELIMINARY PEACE
NEGOTIATION WITH GREAT BRITAIN, PARIS, 1782

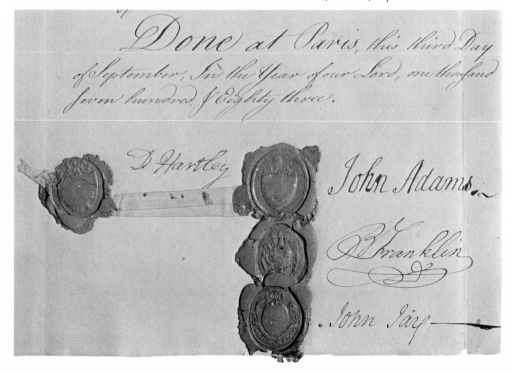

10. SIGNATURES AND SEALS ON THE DEFINITIVE TREATY OF PEACE
WITH GREAT BRITAIN, SIGNED AT PARIS IN SEPTEMBER 1783

11. THE ADAMS FAMILY'S RESIDENCE IN AUTEUIL, 1784–1785

12. DU SIMITIÈRE'S DESIGNS FOR A MEDAL TO COMMEMORATE THE
EVACUATION OF BOSTON, 1776

Father of Benjamin White, a Councillor and Representative for several Years, both of whom possessed in succession the Family Estate. She had several Sisters, one of whom married a Minister of Rochester of the name of Ruggles, by whom she had Timothy Ruggles a Lawyer, Judge, Member of the Legislature and a Brigadier General in the Army in the War with the French of 1755 in which he conducted with Reputation. Another of her Sisters married a Mr. Sharp and was the Mother of Mrs. Sumner of Roxbury the Mother of the late Governor Sumner, whose praises are justly celebrated in this State.

My Father married Susanna Boylston in October 1734, and on the 19th of October 1735 [3] I was born. As my Parents were both fond of reading, and my father had destined his first born, long before his birth to a public Education I was very early taught to read at home and at a School of Mrs. Belcher the Mother of Deacon Moses Belcher, who lived in the next house on the opposite side of the Road. I shall not consume much paper in relating the Anecdotes of my Youth. I was sent to the public School close by the Stone Church, then kept by Mr. Joseph Cleverly, who died this Year 1802 at the Age of Ninety. Mr. Cleverly was through his whole Life the most indolent Man I ever knew ⟨*excepting Mr. Wibirt*⟩ though a tolerable Schollar and a Gentleman. His inattention to his Schollars was such as gave me a disgust to Schools, to books and to study and I spent my time as idle Children do in making and sailing boats and Ships upon the Ponds and Brooks, in making and flying Kites, in driving hoops, playing marbles, playing Quoits, Wrestling, Swimming, Skaiting and above all in shooting, to which Diversion I was addicted to a degree of Ardor which I know not that I ever felt for any other Business, Study or Amusement. [4]

My Enthusiasm for Sports and Inattention to Books, allarmed my Father, and he frequently entered into conversation with me upon the Subject. I told him [I did not?] love Books and wished he would lay aside the thoughts of sending me to Colledge. What would you do Child? Be a Farmer. A Farmer? Well I will shew you what it is to be a Farmer. You shall go with me to Penny ferry tomorrow Morning and help me get Thatch. I shall be very glad to go Sir.—Accordingly next morning he took me with him, and with great good humour kept me all

[3] According to the "old style" calendar. According to the "new style," his birth date was 30 Oct. 1735, which, after the adoption of the Gregorian calendar in England in 1752, JA always regarded as his birthday. See his Diary entry of 19 Oct. 1772.

[4] This sentence and that which follows are partly worn away in the MS, but the missing matter has been supplied from JA's rough draft, which has virtually identical phraseology (and ends at this point).

day with him at Work. At night at home he said Well John are you satisfied with being a Farmer. Though the Labour had been very hard and very muddy I answered I like it very well Sir. Ay but I dont like it so well: so you shall go to School to day. I went but was not so happy as among the Creek Thatch. My School master neglected to put me into Arithmetick longer than I thought was right, and I resented it. I procured me Cockers [5] I believe and applyd myself to it at home alone and went through the whole Course, overtook and passed by all the Schollars at School, without any master. I dared not ask my fathers Assistance because he would have disliked my Inattention to my Latin. In this idle Way I passed on till fourteen and upwards, when I said to my Father very seriously I wished he would take me from School and let me go to work upon the Farm. You know said my father I have set my heart upon your Education at Colledge and why will you not comply with my desire. Sir I dont like my Schoolmaster. He is so negligent and so cross that I never can learn any thing under him. If you will be so good as to perswade Mr. Marsh to take me, I will apply myself to my Studies as closely as my nature will admit, and go to Colledge as soon as I can be prepared. Next Morning the first I heard was John I have perswaded Mr. Marsh to take you, and you must go to school there to day. This Mr. Marsh was a Son of our former Minister of that name, who kept a private Boarding School but two doors from my Fathers. To this School I went, where I was kindly treated, and I began to study in Earnest. [6] My Father soon observed the relaxation of my Zeal for

[5] JA's own copy of (Edward) *Cocker's Decimal Arithmetick* . . . , 3d edn., London, 1703, has survived and is among his books in the Boston Public Library. It bears the marks of hard use, if not abuse, and its magnificently descriptive titlepage is reproduced as an illustration in the present volume.

[6] Fragments of the text now worn away in the two preceding sentences have been restored from the text of JA's narrative of his entrance to Harvard contributed by CFA2 to MHS, *Procs.*, 2d ser., 14 (1900–1901):200–201.

Some fragmentary notes taken down by Harriet Welsh from JA's conversations in 1823 slightly amplify JA's recollections of his school days. (The Welsh notes survive chiefly in the form of a copy by CFA in his literary miscellany, Adams Papers, Microfilms, Reel No. 327. Suspension points in the pas-

sages quoted below indicate omissions by the present editors.)

"JA loquitur. . . . I was about nine or ten years old at that time and soon learn'd the use of the gun and became strong enough to lift it. I used to take it to school and leave it in the entry and the moment it was over went into the field to kill crows and squirrels and I tried to see how many I could kill: at last Mr. Cleverly found this out and gave me a most dreadful scolding and after that I left the gun at an old woman's in the neighborhood. I soon became large enough to go on the marshes to kill wild fowl and to swim and used to beg so hard of my father and mother to let me go that they at last consented and many a cold boisterous day have I pass'd on the beach without food waiting for wild fowl to go over—often *lying* in wait for them on the cold ground—

my Fowling Piece, and my daily encreasing Attention to my Books. In a little more than a Year Mr. Marsh pronounced me fitted for Colledge. On the day appointed at Cambridge for the Examination of Candidates for Admission I mounted my horse and called upon Mr. Marsh, who was to go with me. The Weather was dull and threatened rain. Mr. Marsh said he was unwell and afraid to go out. I must therefore go alone. Thunder struck at this unforeseen disappointment, And terrified at the Thought of introducing myself to such great Men as the President and fellows of a Colledge, I at first resolved to return home: but foreseeing the Grief of my father and apprehending he would not only be offended with me, but my Master too whom I sincerely loved, I arroused my self, and collected Resolution enough to proceed. Although Mr. Marsh had assured me that he had seen one of the Tutors the last Week and had said to him, all that was proper for him to say if he should go to Cambridge; that he was not afraid to trust me to an Examination and was confident I should acquit my self well and be honourably admitted; yet I had not the same confidence in my self, and suffered a very melancholly Journey. Arrived at Cambridge I presented myself according to my directions and underwent the usual Examination by the President Mr. Holyoke and the Tutors Flint, Hancock, Mayhew and Marsh.[7] Mr. Mayhew into whose Class We were to be admitted, presented me a Passage of English to translate into Latin. It was long and casting my Eye over it I found several Words the latin for which did not occur to my memory. Thinking that I must translate it without a dictionary, I was in a great fright and expected to be turned by, an Event that I dreaded above all things. Mr. Mayhew went into his Study and bid me follow him. There Child, said he is a dictionary, there a Gramar, and there Paper, Pen and Ink, and you may take your

---

to hide myself from them. I cared not what I did if I could but get away from school, and confess to my shame that I sometimes play'd truant. At last I got to be thirteen years of age and my life had been wasted. I told my father if I must go to College I must have some other master for I detested the one I had and should not be fitted ever if I staid with him but if he would put me to Mr. Marsh's school I would endeavor to get my lessons and make every exertion to go. He said I knew it was an invariable rule with Mr. M. not to take any boys belonging to the town—he only took eight or ten to live with him. However I said so much to him that he said he would try, and after a great deal of persuasion Master Marsh consented. The next day after he did so I took my books and went to him. I fulfill'd my promise and work'd diligently and in eighteen months was fitted for college. He lived where Hardwicke now keeps a shop opposite to where the Cleverlys live.... Mr. Marsh was a good instructor and a man of learning. The house I learn'd my letters in was opposite my father's nearly and I have pulled it down within this twenty years."

[7] Edward Holyoke, Henry Flynt, Belcher Hancock, Joseph Mayhew, Thomas Marsh.

own time.[8] This was joyfull news to me and I then thought my Admission safe. The Latin was soon made, I was declared Admitted and a Theme given me, to write on in the Vacation. I was as light when I came home as I had been heavy when I went: my Master was well pleased and my Parents very happy. I spent the Vacation not very profitably chiefly in reading Magazines and a British Apollo. I went to Colledge at the End of it and took the Chamber assigned me and my place in the Class under Mr. Mayhew. I found some better Schollars than myself, particularly Lock, Hemmenway and Tisdale.[9] The last left Colledge before the End of the first Year, and what became of him I know not. Hemmenway still lives a great divine, and Lock has been President of Harvard Colledge a Station for which no Man was better qualified. With these I ever lived in friendship, without Jealousy or Envy. I soon became intimate with them, and began to feel a desire to equal them in Science and Literature. In the Sciences especially Mathematicks, I soon surpassed them, mainly because, intending to go into the Pulpit, they thought Divinity and the Classicks of more Importance to them. In Litterature I never overtook them.

Here it may be proper to recollect something which makes an Article of great importance in the Life of every Man. I was of an amorous disposition and very early from ten or eleven Years of Age, was very fond of the Society of females. I had my favorites among the young Women and spent many of my Evenings in their Company and this disposition although controlled for seven Years after my Entrance into College returned and engaged me too much till I was married. I shall draw no Characters nor give any enumeration of my youthfull flames.[1] It would be considered as no compliment to the dead or the living: This I will say—they were all modest and virtuous Girls and always maintained this Character through Life. No Virgin or Matron ever had cause to blush at the sight of me, or to regret her Acquaintance with me. No Father, Brother, Son or Friend ever had cause of Grief or Resentment for any Intercourse between me and any Daughter,

---

[8] Several words now missing in the MS have been supplied in this sentence from CFA2's text cited in note 6, just above.

[9] All members of the class of 1755: Rev. Samuel Locke, president of Harvard, 1770–1773; Rev. Moses Hemmenway, minister at Wells, Maine, for many years; William Tisdale of Lebanon, Conn., who stayed in college only a year and then dropped from sight (Weis,

*Colonial Clergy of N.E.; Harvard Quinquennial Cat.;* information from Harvard University Archives).

[1] Several words now missing from the MS have been supplied in this sentence from CFA's text in JA's *Works,* 2:145. The present paragraph, with some omissions, is the earliest passage printed by CFA in his combined edition of the Diary and Autobiography.

Sister, Mother, or any other Relation of the female Sex. My Children may be assured that no illegitimate Brother or Sister exists or ever existed. These Reflections, to me consolatory beyond all expression, I am able to make with truth and sincerity and I presume I am indebted for this blessing to my Education. My Parents held every Species of Libertinage in such Contempt and horror, and held up constantly to view such pictures of disgrace, of baseness and of Ruin, that my natural temperament was always overawed by my Principles and Sense of decorum. This Blessing has been rendered the more prescious to me, as I have seen enough of the Effects of a different practice. Corroding Reflections through Life are the never failing consequence of illicit amours, in old as well as in new Countries. The Happiness of Life depends more upon Innocence in this respect, than upon all the Philosophy of Epicurus, or of Zeno without it. I could write Romances, or Histories as wonderfull as Romances of what I have known or heard in France, Holland and England, and all would serve to confirm what I learned in my Youth in America, that Happiness is lost forever if Innocence is lost, at least untill a Repentance is undergone so severe as to be an overballance to all the gratifications of Licentiousness. Repentance itself cannot restore the Happiness of Innocence, at least in this Life.

Continued November 30. 1804.

In my own class at Collidge, there were several others, for whom I had a strong affection—Wentworth, Brown, Livingston, Sewall and Dalton all of whom have been eminent in Life, excepting Livingston an amiable and ingenious Youth who died within a Year or two after his first degree.[2] In the Class before me I had several Friends, Treadwell the greatest Schollar, of my time, whose early death in the Professorship of Mathematicks and natural Phylosophy at New York American Science has still reason to deplore,[3] West the eminent Divine of New Bedford,[4] and Samuel Quincy, the easy, social and benevolent Companion, not without Genius, Elegance and Taste.

I soon perceived a growing Curiosity, a Love of Books and a fondness for Study, which dissipated all my Inclination for Sports, and

[2] John Wentworth, last royal governor of New Hampshire; William Browne of Salem, a justice of the Superior Court of Judicature and a loyalist; Philip Livingston, reported dead in 1756; David Sewall of York, Maine, a state and federal judge and long a good friend of JA; Tristram Dalton of Newburyport, U.S. senator and correspondent of JA (*Harvard Quinquennial Cat.*).

[3] Daniel Treadwell; see JA's Diary, Summer 1759, and note 9 there.

[4] Samuel West, D.D., minister at New Bedford, 1761–1803 (Weis, *Colonial Clergy of N.E.*).

even for the Society of the Ladies. I read forever, but without much method, and with very little Choice. I got my Lessons regularly and performed my recitations without Censure. Mathematicks and natural Phylosophy attracted the most of my Attention, which I have since regretted, because I was destined to a Course of Life, in which these Sciences have been of little Use, and the Classicks would have been of great Importance. I owe to this however perhaps some degree of Patience of Investigation, which I might not otherwise have obtained. Another Advantage ought not to be omitted. It is too near my heart. My Smattering of Mathematicks enabled me afterwards at Auteuil in France to go, with my eldest Son, through a Course of Geometry, Algebra and several Branches of the Sciences, with a degree of pleasure that amply rewarded me for all my time and pains.

Between the Years 1751 when I entered, and 1754 [*i.e.* 1755] when I left Colledge a Controversy was carried on between Mr. Bryant the Minister of our Parish and some of his People, partly on Account of his Principles which were called Arminian and partly on Account of his Conduct, which was too gay and light if not immoral.[5] Ecclesiastical Councils were called and sat at my Fathers House. Parties and their Accrimonies arose in the Church and Congregation, and Controversies from the Press between Mr. Bryant, Mr. Niles, Mr. Porter, Mr. Bass, concerning the five Points. I read all these Pamphlets and many other Writings on the same Subject and found myself involved in difficulties beyond my Powers of decision. At the same time, I saw such a Spirit of Dogmatism and Bigotry in Clergy and Laity, that if I should be a Priest I must take my side, and pronounce as positively as any of them, or never get a Parish, or getting it must soon leave it. Very strong doubts arose in my mind, whether I was made for a Pulpit in such times, and I began to think of other Professions. I perceived very clearly, as I thought, that the Study of Theology and the pursuit of it as a Profession would involve me in endless Altercations and make my Life miserable, without any prospect of doing any good to my fellow Men.

The two last years of my Residence at Colledge, produced a Clubb of Students, I never knew the History of the first rise of it, who invited me to become one of them. Their plan was to spend their Evenings together, in reading any new publications, or any Poetry or Dramatic

[5] Lemuel Briant (1722–1754), Harvard 1739, was minister of the First or North Church of Braintree, 1745–1753. Like his famous friend Jonathan Mayhew, he was unorthodox in his theology, and his position as a controversialist was not strengthened by his wife's "eloping from him," either because "she [was] distracted" or because "he did not use her well," or both (Sibley-Shipton, *Harvard Graduates*, 10:345).

Compositions, that might fall in their Way. I was as often requested to read as any other, especially Tragedies, and it was whispered to me and circulated among others that I had some faculty for public Speaking and that I should make a better Lawyer than Divine. This last Idea was easily understood and embraced by me. My Inclination was soon fixed upon the Law: But my Judgment was not so easily determined. There were many difficulties in the Way. Although my Fathers general Expectation was that I should be a Divine, I knew him to be a Man of so thoughtful and considerate a turn of mind, to be possessed of so much Candor and moderation, that it would not be difficult to remove any objections he might make to my pursuit of Physick or Law or any other reasonable Course. My Mother although a pious Woman I knew had no partiality for the Life of a Clergyman. But I had Uncles and other relations, full of the most illiberal Prejudices against the Law. I had indeed a proper Affection and veneration for them, but as I was under no Obligation of Gratitude to them, which could give them any colour of Authority to prescribe a course of Life to me, I thought little of their Opinions. Other Obstacles more serious than these presented themselves. A Lawyer must have a Fee, for taking me into his Office. I must be boarded and cloathed for several Years: I had no Money; and my Father having three Sons, had done as much for me, in the Expences of my Education as his Estate and Circumstances could justify and as my Reason or my honor would allow me to ask. I therefore gave out that I would take a School, and took my Degree at Colledge undetermined whether I should study Divinity, Law or Physick. In the publick Exercises at Commencement, I was somewhat remarked as a Respondent, and Mr. Maccarty of Worcester who was empowered by the Select Men of that Town to procure them a Latin Master for their Grammar School engaged me to undertake it. About three Weeks after commencement in 1755, when I was not yet twenty Years of Age, a horse was sent me from Worcester and a Man to attend me. We made the Journey about Sixty miles in one day and I entered on my Office. For three months I boarded with one Green at the Expence of the Town and by the Arrangement of the Select Men. Here I found Morgans Moral Phylosopher,[6] which I was informed had circulated, with some freedom, in that Town and that the Principles of Deism had made a considerable progress among several Persons, in that and other Towns in the County. Three months after this the

---

[6] [Thomas Morgan,] *The Moral Philosopher. In a Dialogue between Philalethes a Christian Deist, and Theophanes a Christian Jew* ..., London, 1737–1740; 3 vols. (*Catalogue of JA's Library*).

Select Men procured Lodgings for me at Dr. Nahum Willards. This Physician had a large Practice, a good reputation for Skill, and a pretty Library. Here were Dr. Cheynes Works, Sydenham and others and Van Sweetens Commentaries on Boerhave. I read a good deal in these Books and entertained many thoughts of Becoming a Physician and a Surgeon: But the Law attracted my Attention more and more, and Attending the Courts of Justice, where I heard Worthington, Hawley, Trowbridge, Putnam and others, I felt myself irresistably impelled to make some Effort to accomplish my Wishes. I made a Visit to Mr. Putnam, and offered myself to him: He received me with politeness and even Kindness, took a few days to consider of it, and then informed me that Mrs. Putnam had consented that I should board in his House, that I should pay no more, than the Town allowed for my Lodgings, and that I should pay him an hundred dollars, when I should find it convenient. I agreed to his proposals without hesitation and immediately took Possession of his Office. His Library at that time was not large: but he had all the most essential Law Books: immediately after I entered with him however he sent to England for a handsome Addition of Law Books and for Lord Bacons Works. I carried with me to Worcester, Lord Bolingbrokes Study and Use of History, and his Patriot King. These I had lent him, and he was so well pleased with them that he Added Bolingbrokes Works to his List, which gave me an Opportunity of reading the Posthumous Works of that Writer in five Volumes. Mr. Burke once asked, who ever read him through? I can answer that I read him through, before the Year 1758 and that I have read him through at least twice since that time: But I confess without much good or harm. His Ideas of the English Constitution are correct and his Political Writings are worth something: but in a great part of them there is more of Faction than of Truth: His Religion is a pompous Folly: and his Abuse of the Christian Religion is as superficial as it is impious. His Style is original and inimitable: it resembles more the oratory of the Ancients, than any Writings or Speeches I ever read in English.

In this Situation I remained, for about two Years Reading Law in the night and keeping School in the day. At Breakfast, Dinner, and Tea, Mr. Putnam was commonly disputing with me upon some question of Religion: He had been intimate with one Peasley Collins, the Son of a Quaker in Boston, who had been to Europe and came back, a Disbeliever of Every Thing: fully satisfied that all Religion was a cheat, a cunning invention of Priests and Politicians: That there would be no future State, any more than there is at present any moral Government. Putnam could not go these whole Lengths with him. Although he would argue to the extent of his Learning and Ingenuity, to destroy or invalidate the Evidences of a future State, and the Principles of natural and revealed Religion, Yet I could plainly perceive that he could not convince himself, that Death was an endless Sleep. Indeed he has sometimes said to me, that he fully believed in a future Existence, and that good Conduct in this Life, would fare better in the next World than its contrary. My Arguments in favor of natural and revealed Religion, and a future State of Rewards and Punishments, were nothing more than the common Arguments and his against them may all be found in Lucretius, together with many more.

There were two other Persons in the Neighbourhood, Doolittle and Baldwin, who were great Readers of Deistical Books, and very great Talkers.[7] These were very fond of conversing with me. They were great Sticklers for Equality as well as Deism: and all the Nonsense of these last twenty Years, were as familiar to them as they were to Condorcet or Brissot. They were never rude however or insolent to those who differed from them. Another excentric Character was Joseph Dyer, who had removed from Boston and lived on a Farm of Mr. Thomas Handcock, Uncle of the late Governor, and kept a Shop.[8] He had Wit and learning of some Sorts, but being very sarcastic, and very bitter against almost every body, but especially the Clergy, he was extreamly unpopular. An Arian by profession, he was far more odious among the People than the Deists. He had written many Manuscripts especially upon the Athanasian Doctrine of the Trinity, which he lent me: but though I read them all, having previously read Dr. Clark and Emlin as well as Dr. Waterland, I found nothing new. He was also a very profound Student in the Prophecies, and had a System of his own. According to him Antichrist signified all Tyranny and Injustice through the World. He carried his Doctrine of Equality, to a greater Extremity, or at least as great as any of the wild Men of the French Revolution. A perfect Equality of Suffrage was essential to Liberty. I stated to him the Cases of Women, of Children, of Ideots, of Madmen, of Criminals, of Prisoners for Debt or for Crimes. He could not give me any sensible Answer to these Objections: but still every limitation of the right of

[7] Ephraim Doolittle, a merchant and military officer; Nathan Baldwin, register of deeds, "an ardent politician, and the author of many of the addresses and documents of our revolutionary annals" (Lincoln, *Worcester*, p. 176, note).

[8] Dyer mixed trade and an irregular practice as an attorney, and was the town crank. In 1759 he was jailed for refusing to pay a fine, spent his three years in jail compiling a dictionary, and had to be forcibly ejected when friends collected the sum necessary to release him; his first act thereafter was to sue the keeper for false imprisonment (Lincoln, *Worcester*, p. 226-227).

Suffrage, every qualification of freehold or any other property, was Antichrist. An entire Levell of Power, Property, Consideration were essential to Liberty and would be introduced and established in the Millenium. I spent the more Evenings with these Men, as they were readers and thinking Men, though I differed from them all in Religion and Government, because there were no others in Town who were possessed of so much litterature, Mr. Maccarty and Mr. Putnam excepted. With Mr. Maccarty I lived in Harmony and social Conversation. The Family of the Chandlers, were well bred and agreable People and I as often visited them as my School and my Studies in the Lawyers office would Admit, especially Colonel Gardiner Chandler with whom I was the most intimate. The Family of the Willards of Lancaster, were often at Worcester, and I formed an Acquaintance with them, especially Abel Willard who had been one Year with me at Colledge, who had studied the Law under Mr. Pratt in Boston. With him I lived in Friendship and once made him a Visit in Lancaster in the Lifetime of his venerable Mother, with whom he then lived. The Family of the Greens in Boston, connected with the Chandlers, were often at Worcester where I became acquainted with many of them of both Sexes. They were then a Family of considerable Wealth and agreable manners. Their descendants, who have generally pursued the same mercantile Employments are now become numerous, have formed powerful connections and have accumulated Riches.

While I was at Worcester, three great Personages from England passed through that Town: Lord Loudoun was one. He travelled in the Winter from New York to Boston and lodged at Worcester in his Way. The Relations We had of his manners and Conduct on the Road gave Us no great Esteem of his Lordships qualifications to conduct the War and excited gloomy Apprehensions. The Young Lord Howe, who passed from Boston to New York, was the very reverse and spread every where the most sanguine hopes, which however were too soon disappointed by his melancholly but Heroic Death. The third was Sir Geoffery Amherst, afterward Lord Amherst and Commander in Chief of the English Army. Amherst who had arrived at Boston from the Conquest of Louisbourg, marched with his Army of four thousand Men, across the Country, and halted a few days at Worcester, having encamped his Army on the hill behind the present Court house. Here We had an opportunity of seeing him, his officers and Army. The officers were very social, spent their Evenings and took their Suppers with such of the Inhabitants as were able to invite, and entertained Us with their Music and their dances. Many of them were Scotchmen in their plaids and their Music was delightfull; Even the Bagpipe was not disagreable. The General Lodged with Coll. Chandler the elder and was very inquisitive concerning his farm insisting on rambling over the whole of it. The excellent order and discipline observed by these Troops, revived the hopes of the Country, which were ultimately fully satisfied by the entire conquest of Canada, with the help of the Militia of the Country, which was sent on to their Assistance with great confidence.

At the time when Fort William Henry was besieged,[9] there came down almost every day dispatches from the General to the New England Collonies urging for Troops and Assistance. Col. Chandler the Younger had sent so many Expresses that he found it difficult to get Persons to undertake the Journeys. Complaining of this Embarrassment one Evening, in company, I told him, I had so long led a sedendary Life that my health began to fail me, and that I had an inclination to take a Journey on Horseback. The next Morning by Day break he was at my Chamber Door, with Dispatches for the Governor of Rhode Island. He said a Horse was ready. Without hesitation I arose and was soon mounted. Too much dispatch was necessary for my comfort and I believe for my health, for a Journey so fatiguing, to a Man who was not on horseback more than once a Year on a short visit to his Parents, I cannot think callculated to relieve a valetudinarian. Arrived at Providence I was informed that the Governor Mr. Green [William Greene] was at Newport with the General Assembly. I had then to ride through the Narragansett Country and to cross over Conannicutt to Rhode Island. In the Woods of Narragansett I met two Gentlemen on Horse back, of whom I took the Liberty to enquire whether The Governor was still at Newport? One of them answered he was not: but the Gentleman with him was the Governor. My Dispatches were delivered to him and he broke the Seals and read them on the Spot. He said he believed the French were determined to have the Country: asked many questions, gave me many polite Invitations to return with him to his home, which as he said he had no answer to return by me, and as I was determined to see Newport I civilly declined. Pursuing my Journey I found a great difficulty to get over the Water, As the boat and Men were gone upon their usual Employment. One was found after a

---

[9] Fort William Henry, on Lake George, fell to the French after a siege in Aug. 1757. In his recollections in old age recorded by Harriet Welsh, JA had more to say about the alarms in Massachusetts over the French victories during the early years of the war; he also said that he tried unsuccessfully to obtain a captain's commission for himself in 1755 or 1756 (M/CFA/31, Adams Papers, Microfilms, Reel No. 327).

time very tedious to me and I landed on the Island, and had a good opportunity to see the whole of it as my road to Bristol lay through the whole length of it. To Me, the whole Island appeared a most beautifull Garden: an ornamented Farm: but hostile Armies have since degarnished it of a principal Embellishment, the noble rows and plantations of Trees. Crossing over the Ferry to Bristol I spent a night with Col. Green whose Lady was a Church and Sister to Mrs. John Chandler. Here I was happy and felt myself at home. Next Morning I pursued my Journey by Land to Worcester. The whole Journey was accomplished in four days, one of which was Sunday. As I was obliged to ride all that day I had an opportunity of observing the manners of Rhode Island, much more gay and social than our Sundays in Massachusetts. At Angells in Providence I met a relation and a Neighbour Mr. John Bass, who had lost his Parish at Ashford, by the Intollerance of ⟨orthodoxy at that time⟩ the times and had removed his Family to Providence and begun the Practice of Physick.[1] I met another Clergyman and a sensible Man at Bristol. At the Inns as usual there were Scænes and Characters, for the Amusement of Swift or even Shakespeare.

Another Journey had well nigh proved fatal to me. Mr. Joshua Willard of Petersham, who had married Miss Ward a Niece of General Ward of Shrewsbury, invited me with many other Gentlemen of Worcester, to escort home his Wife.[2] I procured the only horse that could be found to be lett. Gay and active enough but the hardest both upon the Trott and Canter, I ever mounted. We went through a Wilderness of old Rutland and New Rutland, now a garden, spent a day or two at Petersham where I conversed much and with great pleasure with Mr. [Aaron] Whitney, a very sensible, entertaining and good humoured Clergyman, the Grandfather of Mr. [Peter] Whitney the amiable, ingenious, eloquent and pious Minister of Quincy and Father of Mr. [Peter] Whitney of Northborough. On our return we rode through Number Six and other Numbers to Number two since called Westminster, a perfect Wilderness and the thickest I ever saw, but now a well cultivated and thick settled Country. We spent a night with Mr. Marsh a Clergyman at the foot of the Wachusett, a Mountain which We ascended to the Top the next morning. From this hight the whole World appeared on a level below Us excepting the Monad-

[1] On the short and unhappy career of Rev. John Bass, Harvard 1737, of Braintree, Ashford, and Providence, see Sibley-Shipton, *Harvard Graduates*, 10: 114–120.

[2] Joshua Willard married Lucretia Ward at Shrewsbury, 28 Feb. 1757 (Charles Martyn, *The William Ward Genealogy*, N.Y., 1925, p. 154).

nocks. Even the blue hills, which I have since seen very distinct from Mr. Gills house, were scarce discernible. The Wind was so high and the Air so cold that We had little Inclination to remain long upon it. Descending to the foot We found it as uncomfortably warm. We mounted our Horses and returned home by the Way of Lunenbourg and Lancaster. After this Journey, whatever was the cause, whether the fatigue in general or the rude Motions of my horse in particular I know not, I found myself in very ill health. The Physicians told me that close Application to a School and to Studies by night and by Day had [thickened?] and corrupted the whole Mass of my blood and Juices, and that I must have recourse to a Milk Diet according to the Theory and Practice of Dr. Cheyne, at that time the height of the Fassion in Medicine. I had read the Writings of Dr. Cheyne and now read them again, renounced all Meat and Spirits and lived upon Bread and milk, Vegetables and Water. I found my head more at Ease and thought I pursued my Studies to more Advantage: but was tormented with a heart burn every afternoon, which nothing but large potions of Tea at Evening could extinguish. I pursued this course for Eighteen months, six or seven of which passed at my fathers house, with the Advice of Dr. Savil and Dr. Hearsey [Hersey], who were both unqualified Admirers of Cheyne's in Theory, though not in their own practice. My excellent Father at last by his tender Advice at sometimes and a little good humoured ridicule at others converted me again to the Use of a little meat and more comforting Drink, but in both of these I was extreamly sparing for many Years after, and indeed untill I became a Member of Congress and a Traveller, when long Journeys and Voyages made a more generous Regimen essential to my being.

In 1758 my Period with Mr. Putnam expired. Doolittle and Baldwin visited me in the office, and invited me to settle in Worcester. They said as there were two Sides to a question and two Lawyers were always wanted where there was one, I might depend upon Business in my profession, they were pleased to add that my Character was fair and well esteemed by all Sorts of People in the Town and through the County: that they wished to get me chosen at the next Election which was very near, Register of Deeds, which would procure me something handsome for the present, and insure me Employment at the Bar. That as the Chandler Family had engrossed almost all the public offices and Employment in the Town and County, they wished to select some Person qualified to share with them in these honors and Emoluments. My Answer was that as the Chandlers were worthy People and discharged the Duties of their offices very well I envied not their felicity and had no desire to sett myself in Opposition to them, and especially to Mr. Putnam who had married a beautifull Daughter of that Family and had treated me with Civility and Kindness. But there was one Motive with me, which was decisive. I was in very ill health and the Air of Worcester appeared to be unfriendly to me, to such a degree that I panted for want of the Breezes from the Sea and the pure Zephirs from the rocky mountains of my native Town: that my Father and Mother invited me to live with them, and as there never had been a Lawyer in any Country Part of the then County of Suffolk, I was determined at least to look into it and see if there was any chance for me. They replied that the Town of Boston was full of Lawyers and many of them of established Characters for long Experience, great Abilities and extensive Fame, who might be jealous of such a Novelty as a Lawyer in the Country part of their County, and might be induced to obstruct me. I returned that I was not wholly unknown to some of the most celebrated of those Gentlemen, that I believed they had too much candour and Generosity to injure a young Man, and at all Events I could but try the experiment, and if I should find no hope of Success I should then think of some other place or some other course.

An Error was committed at this time by Mr. Putnam or me or both, which I thought not of much consequence at the time, and have never been able to account for since. Mr. Putnam should have presented me, to the Court of Common Pleas in Worcester, and a Certificate of my Oath and Admission, before that Court would have been a sufficient Ground, to justify the Court of Common Pleas in Suffolk, on receiving me there. This was however omitted, and I removed to Braintree without it. Here I passed a few Weeks not without much Anxiety and Apprehension. When the October term arrived I went to Boston and attended the Tryals, full of doubts about the most prudent Steps for me to take. I determined at last to know what my fate was to be, and one Morning went early to Mr. Gridleys Office and was fortunate enough to find him alone.[3] I opened to him with much frankness my Situation and my Views. He said Mr. Putnam had mentioned me to him, and he had seen me before in several Companies at Worcester: but have you been sworn? I have not Sir. You must be sworn, before you can practice. As my Master is not here, I have no One to present me to the Court.—How long have you studied Law? How long have

---

[3] JA obviously recorded the following interview wholly from memory, and it differs materially from the record in his Diary (entry of 25 Oct. 1758, q.v.). Nearly every author and title mentioned in the conversation will be found in the *Catalogue of JA's Library* as that collection survives in the Boston Public Library.

[you] served in your Clerkship, with Mr. Putnam? Between two and three Years? What Books have you read? Many more I fear than have done me any good. I have read too fast, much faster than I understood or remembered as I ought. I was directed to begin with Woods Institutes, and then to Hawkins's Abridgment of Coke upon Littleton, then to the Work at large, and the second, third and fourth Institute: then to Salkelds Reports and Ld. Raymonds Reports, Bacons Abridgment, &c., then to Instructor Clericalis and Rastalls and Cokes Entries. The former We used dayly for Precedent, the two latter consulted occasionally. The last Book I had read and with most pleasure, because I thought I understood it best was Hawkins's Pleas of the Crown. I mentioned also Hale's History of the Common Law, Doctor and Student [4] and an Institute of the common Law in imitation of Justinians Institute.... [5] Do you read Latin? A little sometimes. What Books have you lately read? Cicero's Orations and Epistles, and the last Latin I read was Justinians Institute with Vinnius's Notes. Where did you find that Work? Mr. Putnam had it not I believe, and I know of no other Copy than my own, in the Country. I borrowed it, Sir, from Harvard Colledge Library, by the Aid of a Friend. Oh? I conjecture it was among the Books that Sir Harry Franklin lately presented to the Colledge. But Vinius is a Commentator more suitable for Persons, of more advanced Age and longer research, than yours: I can lend you Books better adapted to youth: follow me and I will shew you something: He lead me up a pair of Stairs into a Chamber in which he had a very handsome library of the civil and Cannon Laws and Writers in the Law of Nature and Nations. Shewing me a Number of small manuals and Compendiums of the civil Law he put one of them into my hand, and said put that in your Pocket and when you return that I will lend you any other you cho[o]se. I thanked him for his Kindness, and returned with him down Stairs, after I had taken down and looked into a number of Books he pointed out to me. When below he said what have you read upon the Law of Nature and Nations? Burlamaqui Sir and Heineccius in Turnbulls Translation, and Turnbulls Moral Phylosophy. These are good Books, said Mr. Gridley. Turnbull was a correct thinker, but a bad Writer. Have you read Grotius and Puffendorf? I cannot say I have Sir. Mr. Putnam read them, when I was with him, and as his Book lay on the Desk in the office for the most part when

[4] [Christopher Saint German,] *Doctor and Student: or Dialogues between a Doctor of Divinity and a Student in the Laws of England,* a 16th-century work which went through innumerable editions (LC, *Catalog*).

[5] Suspension points, here and below in the record of this conversation, are in the MS.

he had it not in his hand, I had generally followed him in a cursory manner, so that I had some very imperfect Idea of their Contents: but it was my intention to read them both as soon as possible. You will do well to do so: they are great Writers. Indeed a Lawyer through his whole Life ought to have some Book on Ethicks or the Law of Nations always on his Table. They are all Treatises of individual or national Morality and ought to be the Study of our whole Lives. A pause ensued: after which Mr. Gridley turned towards me with the benignity of a parent in his Countenance, and said Mr. Adams permit me to give you a little Advice: I could scarcely refrain from tears when I said I shall certainly receive it as a great honor and felicity. In the first place pursue the Law itself, rather than the gain of it. Attend enough to the profits, to keep yourself out of the Briars: but the Law itself should be your great Object. In the next place, I advize you not to marry early. This was so unexpected to me that it struck up a smile in my face, that I could not conceal. Perceiving it he said Are you engaged? I assure you Sir, I am at present perfectly disengaged: but I am afraid I cannot be answerable how long I shall remain so. At this Mr. Gridley smiled in his turn, and Added, An early marriage will probably put an End to your Studies, and will certainly involve you in expence.... Looking at his Watch, You have detained me here the whole forenoon, and I must go to Court. The Court will adjourn to the last Fryday in this month, (October). Do you attend in the Morning, and I will present you to the Court to be sworn. With some expressions of gratitude I took my Leave. His Advice made so deep an Impression on my mind that I believe no Lawyer in America ever did so much Business as I did afterwards in the seventeen Years that I passed in the Practice at the Bar, for so little profit: and although my Propensity to marriage, was ardent enough, I determined I would not indulge it, till I saw a clear prospect of Business and profit enough to support a family without Embarrassment. I afterwards waited on Mr. Pratt, Mr. Thatcher and Mr. Otis. Mr. Pratt asked if I had been sworn at Worcester. This allarmed me, but I was relieved when he said that Mr. Putnam had given me a good Character.[6] Mr. Thatcher, as it was Evening when I waited on him, invited me to Tea and then made me smoke Bridgwater tobacco with him, till after ten O Clock. He said nothing about Law, but examined me more severely in Metaphysicks. We had Clark and Leibnitz, Descartes, Malbranche and Lock, Baxter, Bolinbroke and Berkley, with many others on the Carpet, and Fate, foreknowledge,

[6] See the more detailed and quite different account of this interview in JA's Diary entry of 26 Oct. 1758.

Eternity, Immensity, Infinity, Matter and Spirit, Essence and Attribute, Vacuum and plenum, Space, and duration, Subjects which neither of Us understood, and which I have long been convinced, will never be intelligible to human Understanding. I had read at Colledge and afterwards a great deal on these Subjects: but would not advise any one to study longer than to convince him, that he may devote his time to more satisfactory and more usefull pursuits. We may know more in a future State: but many of these Subjects may be well suspected to be comprehensible only by the Supream Intelligence. Mr. Otis received me more like a Brother than a father, and began to descant on Homer and Horace and Latin and Greek Prosody. He was then composing a Treatise on Prosody. In answer to my request for his Countenance at the Bar, he said Mr. Putnam had mentioned me to him, and asked whether I had seen Mr. Gridley and Mr. Pratt. There were so many Lawyers in Boston he said that it was not worth my while to call upon more than three or four of them. I listened too willingly to this opinion: for I afterwards found there were several others well entitled to this respect from me: and some little offence was taken. Mr. Pratt was made Chief Justice of New York a few years after this: but with him, Mr. Gridley, Mr. Otis and Mr. Thatcher, I lived in entire Friendship till their deaths.

When the last Fryday of October arrived, I was in Boston very early and at Court before it was opened.[7] Mr. Pratt presented my Friend Mr. Samuel Quincy and Mr. Gridley presented me. Some Gentleman asked, whether any one knew enough of me to satisfy the Court. Mr. Gridley said he had known me some Years, but that he had lately spent half a day in examining me, and he could say that I had made a very considerable nay "I must say to your honours" a great Proficiency in the Principles of the Law. This was a higher Character than I expected from so great a Man as Mr. Gridley: but I heard it with no small Comfort, as I had been very dubious, whether his examination of me, had not lessened me in his Esteem. Mr. Pratt, Mr. Otis and Mr. Thatcher said I had served a regular Clerkship with Mr. Putnam at Worcester, who had recommended me to them. The Court ordered the Oath to be administered to Mr. Quincy and Mr. Adams, which was done accordingly, and at night I returned to Braintree in good Spirits.

At this Time October 1758 the Study of the Law was a dreary Ramble, in comparison of what it is at this day. The Name of Blackstone had not been heard, whose Commentaries together with Sullivans

---

[7] The date was probably 6 Nov. 1758; see the entry assigned to that date in JA's Diary, and note 1 there.

Lectures and Reeves's History of the Law, have smoothed the path of the Student, while the long Career of Lord Mansfield, his many investigations and Decisions, the great Number [of] modern Reporters in his time and a great Number of Writers on particular Branches of the Science have greatly facilitated the Acquisition of it. I know not whether a sett of the Statutes at large or of the State Tryals was in the Country. I was desirous of seeking the Law as well as I could in its fountains and I obtained as much Knowledge as I could of Bracton, Britton, Fleta and Glanville, but I suffered very much for Want of Books, which determined me to furnish myself, at any Sacrifice, with a proper Library: and Accordingly by degrees I procured the best Library of Law in the State.

Looking about me in the Country, I found the practice of Law was grasped into the hands of Deputy Sheriffs, Pettyfoggers and even Constables, who filled all the Writts upon Bonds, promissory notes and Accounts, received the Fees established for Lawyers and stirred up many unnecessary Suits. I mentioned these Things to some of the Gentlemen in Boston, who disapproved and even resented them very highly. I asked them whether some measures might not be agreed upon at the Bar and sanctioned by the Court, which might remedy the Evil? They thought it not only practicable but highly expedient and proposed Meetings of the Bar to deliberate upon it. A Meeting was called and a great Number of regulations proposed not only for confining the practice of Law to those who were educated to it and sworn to fidelity in it, but to introduce more regularity, Urbanity, Candour and Politeness as well as honor, Equity and Humanity, among the regular Professors. Many of these Meetings were the most delightfull Entertainments, I ever enjoyed. The Spirit that reigned was that of Solid Sense, Generosity, Honor and Integrity: and the Consequences were most happy, for the Courts and the Bar instead of Scenes of Wrangling, Chicanery, Quibbling and ill manners, were soon converted to order, Decency, Truth and Candor. Mr. Pratt was so delighted with these Meetings and their Effects, that when We all waited on him to Dedham in his Way to New York to take his Seat as Chief Justice of that State, when We took leave of him after Dinner, the last Words he said to Us, were, "Brethren above all things forsake not the Assembling of yourselves together." [8]

[8] Benjamin Prat was appointed chief justice of New York Province in March 1761 and left for his new post about the beginning of November (Sibley-Shipton, *Harvard Graduates*, 10:233– 235). A fuller version of his parting injunction to his colleagues at the bar is quoted in a letter from Oxenbridge Thacher to Prat evidently written in 1762 (MHS, *Procs.*, 1st ser., 20 [1882–

The next Year after I was sworn, was the memorable Year 1759 when the Conquest of Canada was compleated by the surrender of Montreal to General Amherst. This Event, which was so joyfull to Us and so important to England if she had seen her true Interest, inspired her with a Jealousy, which ultimately lost her thirteen Colonies and made many of Us at the time regret that Canada had ever been conquered. The King sent Instructions to his Custom house officers to carry the Acts of Trade and Navigation into strict Execution. An inferiour Officer of the Customs in Salem whose Name was Cockle petitioned the Justices of the Superiour Court, at their Session in November for the County of Essex, to grant him Writs of Assistants, according to some provisions in one of the Acts of Trade, which had not been executed, to authorize him to break open Ships, Shops, Cellars, Houses &c. to search for prohibited Goods, and merchandizes on which Duties had not been paid.[9] Some Objection was made to this Motion, and Mr. Stephen Sewall, who was then Chief Justice of that Court, and a zealous Friend of Liberty, expressed some doubts of the Legality and Constitutionality of the Writ, and of the Power of the Court to grant it. The Court ordered the question to be argued at Boston, in February term 1761. In the mean time Mr. Sewall died and Mr. Hutchinson then Lt. Governor, a Councillor, and Judge of Probate for the County of Suffolk &c. was appointed in his Stead, Chief Justice. The first Vacancy on that Bench, had been promised, in two former Administrations, to Colonel James Otis of Barnstable. This Event produced a Dissention between Hutchinson and Otis which had Consequences of great moment. In February Mr. James Otis Junr. a Lawyer of Boston, and a Son of Colonel Otis of Barnstable, appeared at the request of the Merchants in Boston, in Opposition to the Writ. This Gentlemans reputation as a Schollar, a Lawyer, a Reasoner, and a Man of Spirit was then very high. Mr. Putnam while I was with him had often said to me, that Otis was by far the most able, manly and commanding Character of his Age at the Bar, and this appeared to me in Boston to be the universal opinion of Judges, Lawyers and the public. Mr. Oxenbridge Thatcher whose amiable manners and pure principles, united to a very easy and musical Eloquence, made him very popular, was united with Otis, and Mr. Gridley alone appeared for Cockle the

---

1883]:48). The records of this early Boston law association have not been found, although JA himself was ordered in Jan. 1770 by the organization that succeeded it to "wait on Judge Auchmuty and request of him, the Records of a former Society of the Bar, in this County" (Suffolk Bar Book, MS, MHi).

[9] On this famous case and JA's record of the arguments therein, see his Diary entry of 3 April 1761 and note 6 there.

Petitioner, in Support of his Writ. The Argument continued several days in the Council Chamber, and the question was analized with great Acuteness and all the learning, which could be connected with the Subject. I took a few minutes, in a very careless manner, which by some means fell into the hands of Mr. Minot, who has inserted them in his history. I was much more attentive to the Information and the Eloquence of the Speakers, than to my minutes, and too much allarmed at the prospect that was opened before me, to care much about writing a report of the Controversy. The Views of the English Government towards the Collonies and the Views of the Collonies towards the English Government, from the first of our History to that time, appeared to me to have been directly in Opposition to each other, and were now by the imprudence of Administration, brought to a Collision. England proud of its power and holding Us in Contempt would never give up its pretentions. The Americans devoutly attached to their Liberties, would never submit, at least without an entire devastation of the Country and a general destruction of their Lives. A Contest appeared to me to be opened, to which I could foresee no End, and which would render my Life a Burden and Property, Industry and every Thing insecure. There was no Alternative left, but to take the Side, which appeared to be just, to march intrepidly forward in the right path, to trust in providence for the Protection of Truth and right, and to die with a good Conscience and a decent grace, if that Tryal should become indispensible.

About this time, the Project was conceived, I suppose by the Chief Justice Mr. Hutchinson, of cloathing the Judges and Lawyers with Robes. Mr. Quincy and I were directed to prepare our Gowns and Bands and Tye Wiggs, and were admitted Barristers having practiced three Years at the Inferiour Courts, according to one of our new Rules.[1]

On the 25 of May in this Year 1761, my venerable Father died in his 71st Year, beloved, esteemed and revered by all who knew him. Nothing that I can say or do, can sufficiently express my Gratitude for his parental Kindness to me, or the exalted Opinion I have of his Wisdom and Virtue. It was a melancholly House. My Father and Mother were seized at the same time with the violent Fever, a kind of Influenza, or an Epidemick which carried off Seventeen Aged People in our Neighbourhood. My Mother remained ill in bed at my Fathers

---

[1] JA has here merged two separate events. He was admitted to practice in the Superior Court of Judicature on 14 Nov. 1761 (see his Diary under that date), and admitted barrister, with numerous others, in August term, 1762 (Superior Court of Judicature, Minute Book 79; see also JA, *Works*, 10:233, 245, and Quincy, *Reports*, p. 35).

Funeral, but being younger than my Father and possessed of a stronger constitution, she happily recovered and lived to my inexpressible Comfort, till the Year 1797, when she died at almost ninety Years of Age....[2] My Father by his Will left me, what he estimated one third of his Real State, which third consisted in a House and Barn such as they were and forty Acres of Land. He also left me one third of his personal Estate.[3] My house humble as it was, with a few repairs and a very trifling Addition served for a comfortable habitation for me and my family, when We lived out of Boston, till our return from Europe in 1788. The Uncertainty of Life as well as of Property, which then appeared to me, in the prospect of futurity, suppressed all thought of a more commodious Establishment. If I should fall which was very probable in a Contest which appeared to me inevitable, I thought it would be an Addition to the Misery of my Wife and Children to be turned out of a more envyable Situation. I continued to live with my Mother and my Brothers, for the first Year, when my youngest Brother, Elihu, removed to the South Parish in Braintree, now Randolph, to a Farm which my father left him, which he cultivated to Advantage, and is now possessed by his oldest Son. I continued with my Mother and my oldest Brother Peter Boylston, till my Marriage in 1764 with Miss Abigail Smith, Second Daughter of the Reverend Mr. William Smith of Weymouth and Grand Daughter of Colonel John Quincy of Mount Wollaston. Sometime after this my Brother married Miss Crosby a Daughter of Major Joseph Crosbey, sold me the House and Farm which my father left to him and went to live in a House of his Wife's.[4] Sometime before this,[5] in pursuance of my plan of reforming the practice of Sherriffs and Pettyfoggers in the Country I procured of all the Justices in Braintree, John Quincy, Edmund Quincy, Josiah Quincy and Joseph Crosbey a recommendation of my Brother to Stephen Greenleaf Sherriff of the County, and a Certificate of his Character, upon receiving which Mr. Greenleaff readily gave him a Deputation. He was young, loved riding and discharged his Duties

[2] Suspension points in MS.

[3] Actually Deacon John Adams' will, proved 10 July 1761, divided his property more or less equally among his three sons after one third was devised to their mother, but JA's share was somewhat smaller than his brothers' because his father had provided for him "a Libberal Education" (Tr, Adams Papers, Wills and Deeds, Microfilms, Reel No. 607). A copy of the inventory of Deacon John Adams' estate, attested by JA as one of the executors before Probate Judge Thomas Hutchinson, 9 Oct. 1761, is with the will.

[4] Peter Boylston Adams married Mary Crosby in Aug. 1768 and sold the house now known as the John Adams Birthplace to JA early in 1774.

[5] In 1761; see Diary entry of 11 June 1761 and note 1 there.

with Skill and Fidelity but his disposition was so tender, that he often assisted his Debtors, with his own Purse and Credit, and upon the whole to say the least was nothing the richer for his Office.

Sometime in 1761 or two [6] Mr. Samuel Quincy with whom I sometimes corresponded, shewed to Mr. Jonathan Sewall, a Lawyer somewhat advanced before Us at the Bar, some juvenile Letters of mine of no consequence, which however Sewall thought discovered a Mind awake to the love of Litterature and Law and insisted on being acquainted with me and writing to me. His Acquaintance and Correspondence were readily embraced by me, and continued for many Years, till political disputes grew so warm as to seperate Us, a little before the War was commenced. His Courtship of Miss Esther Quincy, a Daughter of Edmund Quincy, brought him to Braintree commonly on Saturdays where he remained till Monday, and gave Us frequent Opportunities of Meeting, besides those at Court in Boston, Charlestown and Cambridge. He possessed a lively Wit, a pleasing humour, a brilliant Imagination, great Sub[t]lety of Reasoning and an insinuating Eloquence. His Sentiments of public Affairs were for several Years conformable to mine, and he once proposed to me, to write in concert in the public Prints to stir up the People to militia Duty and military Ardor and was fully of my Opinion that the British Ministry and Parliament would force Us to an Appeal to Arms: but he was poor, and Mr. Trowbridge and Governor Hutchinson contrived to excite him to a quarrell with Mr. Otis, because in the General Court, Col. Otis and his Son had not very warmly supported a Petition for a Grant to discharge the Debt of his Uncle the late Chief Justice who died insolvent. To this Artifice they added another which wholly converted him, by giving him the office of Solicitor General. I know not that I have ever delighted more in the friendship of any Man, or more deeply regretted an irreconcileable difference in Judgment in public Opinions. He had Virtues to be esteemed, qualities to be loved and Talents to be admired. But political Principles were to me in that State of the Country, Sacred. I could not follow him, and he could not follow me.

Now become a Freeholder I attended the Town Meetings, as a Member, as I had usually attended them before, from a Boy as a Spectator. In March [7] when I had no suspicion, I heard my name pronounced in a Nomination of Surveyors of Highways. I was very wroth, because I

---

[6] A mistake for, presumably, 1759, since JA's surviving correspondence with Jonathan Sewall begins in that year.

[7] Presumably in 1761, but see the Diary entry of 3 March 1761 and note 1 there, which applies also to the next paragraph in the Autobiography.

knew no better, but said Nothing. My Friend Dr. Savil came to me and told me, that he had nominated me to prevent me from being nominated as a Constable: for said the Doctor, they make it a rule to compell every Man to serve either as Constable or Surveyor, or to pay a fine. I said they might as well have chosen any Boy in School, for I knew nothing of the Business: but since they had chosen me, at a venture, I would accept it in the same manner and find out my Duty as I could. Accordingly I went to ploughing and ditching and blowing Rocks upon Penn's Hill, and building an entire new Bridge of Stone below Dr. Millars and above Mr. Wibirts. The best Workmen in Town were employed in laying the foundation and placing the Bridge but the next Spring brought down a flood, that threw my Bridge all into Ruins. The Materials remained and were afterwards relaid in a more durable manner: and the blame fell upon the Workmen not upon me, for all agreed that I had executed my Office with impartiality, Diligence and Spirit.

There had been a controversy in Town for many Years, concerning the mode of repairing the Roads. A Party had long struggled, to obtain a Vote that the High Ways should be repaired by a Tax, but never had been able to carry their point. The Roads were very bad, and much neglected, and I thought a Tax a more equitable Method and more likely to be effectual, and therefore joined this party in a public Speech, carried a Vote by a large Majority and was appointed [to] prepare a By Law to be enacted at the next Meeting. Upon Inquiry I found that Roxbury and after them Weymouth had adopted this Course: I procured a Copy of their Law and prepared a Plan for Braintree, as nearly as possible conformable to their Model, reported it to the Town and it was adopted by a great Majority.[8] Under this Law the Roads have been repaired to this day, and the Effects of it are visible to every Eye.

In 1763 or 1764, The Town voted to sell their Common Lands.[9] This had been a Subject of Contention for many Years. The South Parish was zealous and the middle Parish much inclined to the Sale, the North Parish was against it. The Lands in their common Situation, appeared to me of very little Utility to the Public or to Individuals: Under the care of Proprietors when they should become private Property, they would probably be better managed And more productive. My Opinion was in favour of the Sale: The Town now adopted the

---

[8] This report, adopted 21 May 1764, is printed in *Braintree Town Records*, p. 397.

[9] Actually 5 March 1765 (*Braintree Town Records*, p. 400). For the reports and proceedings of the committee see same, p. 401–402, 406–407.

Measure, appointed [Mr.] Niles, Mr. Bass and me, to survey the Lands, divide them into Lots to sell them by Auction and execute deeds of them in Behalf of the Town. This was no small Task. We procured our Surveyors and Chainmen and rambled with them over Rocks and Mountains and through Swamps and thicketts for three or four Weeks. Having made the Division and prepared the Plans, a day was appointed for the Vendue. We handled the Mallett ourselves as Vendue Masters and finished all the Sales in one Night: the Deeds were made out, the Bonds for the Money executed and the whole reported to the Town at the next Meeting. Of the original Purchasers I bought two Woodlotts in one of which is Hemlock Swamp and a Pasture in which is Rocky Run, and I should have bought much more, if the awfull Prospect of publick affairs had not discouraged me.

In the Winter of 1764 the Small Pox prevailing in Boston, I went with my Brother into Town and was innoculated under the Direction of Dr. Nathaniel Perkins and Dr. Joseph Warren.[1] This Distemper was very terrible even by Innocculation at that time. My Physicians dreaded it, and prepared me, by a milk Diet and a Course of Mercurial Preparations, till they reduced me very low before they performed the operation. They continued to feed me with Milk and Mercury through the whole Course of it, and salivated me to such a degree, that every tooth in my head became so loose that I believe I could have pulled them all with my Thumb and finger. By such means they conquered the Small Pox, which I had very lightly, but they rendered me incapable with the Aid of another fever at Amsterdam of speaking or eating in my old Age, in short they brought me into the same Situation with my Friend Washington, who attributed his misfortune to cracking of Walnuts in his Youth. I should not have mentioned this, if I had not been reproached with this personal Defect, with so much politeness in the Aurora. Recovered of the Small Pox, I passed the summer of 1764 in Attending Court and pursuing my Studies with some Amusement on my little farm to which I was frequently making Additions, till the Fall when on the 25th of October 1784 [*i.e.* 1764] I was married to Miss Smith a Daughter of the Reverend Mr. William Smith a Minister of Weymouth, Grand daughter of the Honourable John Quincy Esquire of Braintree, a Connection which has been the Source of all my felicity, Although a Sense of Duty which forced me away from her and my

[1] This medical incident occurred in April–May 1764. Perkins inoculated JA, and Warren inoculated JA's brother, but which of his two brothers this was is uncertain. JA's letters at this period give abundant details on the method and regimen of smallpox inoculation before Jenner's discovery of vaccination. to his fiancée, Abigail Smith (Adams Papers), give abundant details on the method and regimen of smallpox inoculation before Jenner's discovery of vaccination.

Children for so many Years has produced all the Griefs of my heart and all that I esteem real Afflictions in Life. The Town of Braintree had chosen me, one of the Select Men, Overseers of the Poor and Assessors,[2] which occasioned much Business, of which I had enough before: but I accepted the Choice and attended diligently to the functions of the Office, in which humble as it was I took a great deal of Pleasure. The Courts at Plymouth Tau[n]ton, Midd[l]esex and sometimes at Barnstable and Worcester, I generally attended. In the Spring of 1765, Major Noble of Boston had an Action at Pownalborough, on Kennebeck River. Mr. Thatcher, who had been his Council, recommended him to me, and I engaged in his cause, and undertook the Journey. I was taken ill on the Road and had a very unpleasant Excursion. It is unnecessary to enlarge upon the fatigue and disgust of this Journey. It was the only time in my Life, when I really suffered for want of Provisions. From Falmouth now Portland in Casco Bay, to Pounalborough There was an entire Wilderness, except North Yarmouth, New Brunswick and Long reach, at each of which places were a few Houses. In general it was a Wilderness, incumbered with the greatest Number of Trees, of the largest Size, the tallest height, I have ever seen. So great a Weight of Wood and timber, has never fallen in my Way. Birches, Beaches, a few Oaks, and all the Varieties of the Fir, i.e. Pines, Hemlocks, Spruces and Firs. I once asked Judge Cushing his Opinion of their hight upon an Avaradge, he said an hundred feet. I believe his estimation was not exaggerated. An Hemlock had been blown down across the Road. They had cutt out a logg as long as the road was wide. I measured the Butt at the Road and found it seven feet in Diameter, twenty one feet in circumference. We measured 90 feet from the Road to the first Limb, the Branches at Top were thick: We could measure no farther but estimated the Top to be about fifteen feet, from the Butt at the Road to the Root we did not measure: but the Tree must have been in the whole at least an hundred and ⟨thirty⟩ twenty feet. The Roads, where a Wheel had never rolled from the Creation, were miry and founderous, incumbered with long Sloughs of Water. The Stumps of the Trees which had been cutt to make the road all remaining fresh and the Roots crossing the path some above ground and some beneath so that my Horses feet would frequently get between the Roots and he would flounce and blunder, in danger of breaking his own Limbs as well as mine. This whole Country, then so rough, is now beautifully cultivated,

[2] On 3 March 1766; see Diary entry of that date, and *Braintree Town Records*, p. 408.

Handsome Houses, Orchards, Fields of Grain and Grass, and the Roads as fine as any except the Turnpikes, in the State. I reached Pownalborough alive, gained my Cause much to the Satisfaction of my Client and returned home. This Journey, painfull as it was, proved much for my Interest and Reputation, as it induced the Plymouth Company to engage me in all their Causes, which were numerous and called me annually to Falmouth Superiour Court for ten years.

This Year 1765 was the Epocha of the Stamp Act....[3] I drew up a Petition to the Select Men of Braintree, and procured it to be signed by a Number of the respectable Inhabitants, to call a Meeting of the Town to instruct their Representatives in Relation to the Stamps.[4] The public Attention of the whole Continent was alarmed, and my Principles and political Connections were well known.... I prepared a Draught of Instructions, at home and carried them with me: the cause of the Meeting was explained, at some length and the state and danger of the Country pointed out, a Committee was appointed to prepare Instructions of which I was nominated as one. We retired to Mr. Niles House, my Draught was produced, and unanimously adopted without Amendment, reported to the Town and Accepted without a dissenting Voice. These were published in Drapers Paper, as that Printer first applied to me for a Copy.[5] They were decided and spirited enough. They rung thro the State, and were adopted, in so many Words, As I was informed by the Representatives of that Year, by forty Towns, as Instructions to their Representatives. They were honoured sufficiently, by the Friends of Government with the Epithets of inflammatory &c. I have not seen them now for almost forty Years and remember very little of them. I presume they would now appear a poor trifle: but at that time they Met with such strong feelings in the Readers, that their Effect was astonishing to me and excited some serious Reflections. I thought a Man ought to be very cautious what kinds of fewell he throws into a fire when it is thus glowing in the Community. Although it is a certain Expedient to acquire a momentary Celebrity: Yet it may produce future Evils which may excite serious Repentance. I have seen so many fire brands, thrown into the flames, ⟨especially⟩ not only in the worthless and unprincipled Writings of the

[3] Here and below in JA's account of the Stamp Act crisis, the suspension points are in the MS.

[4] No text of such a petition has been found.

[5] Adopted in town meeting on 24 Sept. (*Braintree Town Records*, p. 404–406), the Braintree Instructions were first printed in Draper's *Massachusetts Gazette and Boston News Letter*, 10 Oct. 1765, and later elsewhere; see note on Diary entry of 18 Dec. 1765. JA's rough draft (Adams Papers) has never been printed, and the Instructions as a whole deserve closer textual study than they have yet received.

profligate and impious Thomas Paine and in the French Revolution, but in many others, that I think, every Man ought to take Warning. In the Braintree Instructions however, If I recollect any reprehensible fault in them, it was that they conceeded too much to the Adversary, not to say Enemy. About this time I called upon my Friend Samuel Adams and found him at his Desk. He told me the Town of Boston had employed him to draw Instructions for their Representatives: that he felt an Ambition, which was very apt to mislead a Man, that of doing something extraordinary and he wanted to consult a Friend who might suggest some thoughts to his mind. I read his Instructions and shewed him a Copy of mine. I told him I thought his very well as far as they went, but he had not gone far enough. Upon reading mine he said he was of my Opinion and accordingly took into his, some paragraphs from mine.[6]

On the fourteenth of August this Year, The People in Boston rose, and carried Mr. Oliver who had been appointed Distributor of Stamps, to Liberty Tree where they obliged him to take an Oath, that he would not exercise the office.[7] The Merchants of Boston could not collect their debts, without Courts of Justice. They called a Town Meeting, chose a Committee of thirty Gentlemen to present a Petition to the Governor and Council, to order the Courts of Justice to proceed without Stamped Papers, upon the principle that the Stamp Act was null because unconstitutional. This Principle was so congenial to my Judgment that I would have staked my Life on the question: but had no suspicion that I should have any thing to do with it, before the Council, till a Courier arrived with a Certificate from the Town Clerk that I was elected by the Town, with Mr. Gridley and Mr. Otis, to argue the Point the next morning. With so little preparation and with

[6] Samuel Adams' biographer pointed out that this was a mistaken claim, since Boston had adopted its instructions to its representatives on 18 Sept. and published them on the 23d, whereas the Braintree Instructions were not even adopted until the 24th (Wells, *Samuel Adams,* 1:65, note; see also Samuel Adams, *Writings,* 1:7–12; Boston Record Commissioners, *16th Report,* p. 155–156). Despite the argument from chronology it is perfectly possible that the cousins conferred together on this occasion. It would have been characteristic of them both to do so, and especially characteristic of JA to have been ready with a public paper, or at least well-

formed ideas for it, in the expectation of being asked to write it. A comparison of the texts of the two sets of instructions shows no identical paragraphs, but the arguments and occasionally the phrasing of the Boston Instructions are enough like those from Braintree to give some color to JA's claim.

[7] Andrew Oliver's house had been mobbed on 14 Aug. 1765, but it was not until the following 17 Dec. that he was forced to renounce his post as stamp distributor. On these and subsequent events alluded to here, see JA's Diary entries of 15 Aug. 1765 (and note 2 there), 19 Dec. 1765 and following.

no time to look into any books for analogous Cases, I went and introduced the Argument but made a very poor figure. Mr. Gridley and Mr. Otis more than supplied all my defects. But the Governor and Council would do nothing. The Court of Common Pleas, however were persuaded to proceed and the Superiour Court postponed and continued the Question till the Act was repealed. At an Inferiour Court in Plymouth, Mr. Paine and I called a Meeting of the Bar, and We laboured so successfully with our Brothers that We brought them all to agree in an Application to the Court to proceed without Stamps, in which We succeeded.

On the 14 day of July of this Year 1765, Mrs. Adams presented me with a Daughter and in her confinement in her Chamber, I was much alone in ⟨the Parlour below⟩ my Office of Evenings and Mornings. The Uneasy State of the public Mind, and my own gloomy Apprehensions, turned my Thoughts to writing. Without any particular Subject to write on, my Mind turned I know not how into a Speculation or rather a Rhapsody which I sent to the Boston Gazette, and was there published without Title or Signature, but which was afterwards reprinted in London under the Title of a dissertation on the Cannon and Feudal Law. It might as well have been called an Essay upon Forefathers Rock. Writings which appear mean enough at the present day, were then highly applauded, in proportion to their Zeal rather than their Merit, and this little production had its full Share of praise.[8]

After the 14 of August this Year 1765, I went on a Journey to Martha's Vineyard, on the Tryal of a Cause before Referees, between Jerusha Mayhew and her Relations. The keen Understanding of this Woman, and the uncontroulable Violence of her irascible Passions, had excited a quarrel of the most invidious, inveterate and irreconcileable nature between the several Branches of the Mayhew Family, which had divided the whole Island into Parties. The Rancour of that fiend the Spirit of Party had never appeared to me, in so odious and dreadfull a Light, though I had heard much of it, in a Contest between Roland Cotton and Parson Jackson at Woburne: and had remarked enough of it in the Tryal between Hopkins and Ward at Worcester.[9]

[8] An early, fragmentary draft of this essay appears in JA's Diary and is printed there under the assigned date of Feb. 1765, q.v., with the notes and references there.

[9] The political, religious, and personal feud between Rev. Edward Jackson of Woburn and his Harvard classmate and parishioner Roland Cotton during the 1740's was long regarded as "the classic example of New England cantankerousness," to give it no worse a name; see Sibley-Shipton, *Harvard Graduates*, 6: 301, 322–323. On the Hopkins-Ward feud in the neighboring province of Rhode Island, see JA's Diary entry of 1 Jan. 1766 and note 3 there.

In all these cases it seemed to have wrought an entire metamorphosis of the human Character. It destroyed all sense and Understanding, all Equity and Humanity, all Memory and regard to Truth, all Virtue, Honor, Decorum and Veracity. Never in my Life was I so grieved and disgusted with my Species. More than a Week I think was spent in the Examination of Witnesses and the Arguments of Council, Mr. Paine on one Side and I on the other. We endeavoured to argue the cause on both Sides, as well as We could, but which of Us got the cause I have forgot. It was indeed no matter: for it was impossible for human Sagacity to discover on which Side Justice lay. We were pretty free with our Vituperations on both Sides and the Inhabitants appeared to feel the Justice of them. I think the Cause was compromised.[1] —I forgot to mention that while We were at Falmouth waiting to be ferried over to the Island the News arrived from Boston of the Riots on the twenty fifth of August in which Lt. Governor Hutchinsons House was so much injured.

The Stamp Act was repealed, and the Declaratory Act passed: but as We expected it would not be executed, good humour was in some measure restored. In the year 1766 [1767][2] Mr. Gridley died, and to his last moment retained his kindness for me, recommending his Clients to me, with expressions of confidence and Esteem too flattering for me to repeat. For several Years before, he had insisted on my Meeting him in a little Clubb once a Week, for the Sake of Sociability, litterary Conversation and reading new publications as well as the Classicks in concert. Many Things were produced and some were read: but his

[1] This passage alludes to a whole complex of cases which were in litigation for years and divided the great Mayhew clan on the island of Martha's Vineyard into warring camps. One side was endeavoring to recover a boy whose father, Abel Chase, and mother, Mercy (Mayhew) Chase, had separated; the boy himself had been put out by indenture, until he reached a certain age, to his grandmother, Bethiah (Wadsworth) Mayhew. The grandmother, her Amazonian daughter Jerusha, and others in the household succeeded for some time in foiling all attempts by the sheriff and other officers to recover the boy. But the administration of justice on the island was also in the hands of Mayhews, and Jerusha was in Oct. 1762 seized and carried off to jail, though not before numerous scuffles and some actual shooting had taken place. Jerusha now sued one of her captors for assault and battery and false imprisonment, and thus the suits multiplied almost unendingly. Jerusha finally prevailed and won a judgment for damages against JA's clients, the law-enforcing officers, in May 1766. A statement of the facts and minutes of the testimony and of R. T. Paine's arguments in two of the cases (Jerusha Mayhew v. Robert Allen; Cornelius Bassett v. Wadsworth Mayhew et al.) are among JA's legal papers (M/JA/6, Adams Papers, Microfilms, Reel No. 185). See also Suffolk co. Court House, Early Court Files, &c., Nos. 83471, 85247, 86474, 144133, 144145, 144187, 144233; Quincy, *Reports*, p. 93 and note; R. T. Paine, Diary (MHi), 27–31 Aug. 1765.

[2] The correct year, here bracketed, was inserted in the MS by JQA.

Conversation was too amusing and instructive to leave Us any very earnest Wishes for Books. He had frequently invited me to visit him at his Country Seat in Brooklyne, on Saturdays, and to remain with him till Monday. I went but once, though he urged so much and so often that I was afraid he would take offence at my Negligence. On that Visit he produced to me, the first Copy of Blackstones Inaugural oration and Analysis, which ever appeared in America I believe. Mr. Thomas Oliver had received it, very early from a Friend in England, and lent it to Mr. Gridley. It was much admired and great hopes were conceived of what was to follow, which when the History of Magna Charta and especially the Commentaries made their Appearance were not disappointed. Mr. Gridley thought the Analosis excellent, as great an Improvement on Hales, as his had been upon Noy's. The Day was spent, partly at Church, partly in conversation, and partly in Reading some passages in Puffendorf, with Barbeyrac's Notes, after We had read Blackstone. He was a great Admirer of Barbeyrac: thought him a much more sensible and learned Man than Puffendorf. I admired the facility with which he translated and criticised the Greek Passages in the Notes.[3]

This Year[4] also died Dr. Mayhew, whose Loss I deplored, as I had but lately commenced an Acquaintance with him, which was likely to become a lasting and intimate Friendship.

In the Years 1766 and 1767 my Business increased, as my Reputation spread, I got Money and bought Books and Land. I had heard my father say that he never knew a Piece of Land run away or break, and I was too much enamoured with Books, to spend many thoughts upon Speculation on Money. I was often solicited to lend Money and sometimes complied upon Land Security: but I was more intent on my Business than on my Profits, or I should have laid the foundation of a better Estate.

In the Beginning of the Year 1768 My Friends in Boston, were very urgent with me to remove into Town. I was afraid of my health: but they urged so many Reasons and insisted on it so much that being determined at last to hazard the Experiment, I wrote a Letter to the Town of Braintree declining an Election as one of their Select Men, and removed in a Week or two, with my Family into the White House as it was called in Brattle Square, which several of the old People told

[3] JA's copy of Pufendorf, *Of the Law of Nature and Nations .... To Which Are Added All the Large Notes of Mr. Barbeyrac ...*, 4th edn., London, 1729, folio, remains among his books in the Boston Public Library (*Catalogue of JA's Library*).

[4] 1766.

me was a good omen as Mr. Bollan had lived formerly in the same house for many Years. The Year before this, i.e. in 1767 My Son John Quincy Adams was born on the [eleventh] day of August [July],[5] at Braintree, and at the request of his Grandmother Smith christened by the Name of ⟨her Father⟩ John Quincy on the day of the Death of his Great Grandfather, John Quincy of Mount Wollaston.

In the Course of this Year 1768 My Friend Mr. Jonathan Sewall who was then Attorney General called on me in Brattle Street, and told me he was come to dine with me. This was always an acceptable favour from him, for although We were at Antipodes in Politicks We had never abated in mutual Esteem or cooled in the Warmth of our Friendship. After Dinner Mr. Sewall desired to have some Conversation with me alone and proposed adjourning to the office. Mrs. Adams arose and chose to Adjourn to her Chamber. We were accordingly left alone. Mr. Sewall then said he waited on me at that time at the request of the Governor Mr. Bernard, who had sent for him a few days before and charged him with a Message to me. The Office of Advocate General in the Court of Admiralty was then vacant, and the Governor had made Enquiry of Gentlemen the best qualified to give him information, and particularly of one of great Authority ⟨meaning Lt. Governor and Chief Justice Hutchinson⟩, and although he was not particularly acquainted with me himself the Result of his Inquiries was that in point of Talents, Integrity, Reputation and consequence at the Bar, Mr. Adams was the best entitled to the Office and he had determined Accordingly, to give it to me. It was true he had not Power to give me more than a temporary Appointment, till his Majestys Pleasure should be known: but that he would give immediately all the Appointment in his Power, and would write an immediate Recommendation of me to his Majesty and transmitt it to his Ministers and there was no doubt I should receive the Kings Commission, as soon as an Answer could be returned from England: for there had been no Instance of a refusal to confirm the Appointment of a Governor in such Cases.

Although this Offer was unexpected to me, I was in an instant prepared for an Answer. The Office was lucrative in itself, and a sure introduction to the most profitable Business in the Province: and what was of more consequence still, it was a first Step in the Ladder of Royal Favour and promotion. But I had long weighed this Subject in my own Mind. For seven Years I had been solicited by some of my friends and Relations, as well as others, and Offers had been made me

[5] The day of the month was left blank in the MS by JA and was filled in by JQA, who also corrected the month from August to July.

by Persons who had Influence, to apply to the Governor or to the Lieutenant Governor, to procure me a Commission for the Peace. Such an Officer was wanted in the Country where I had lived and it would have been of very considerable Advantage to me. But I had always rejected these proposals, on Account of the unsettled State of the Country, and my Scruples about laying myself under any restraints, or Obligations of Gratitude to the Government for any of their favours. The new Statutes had been passed in Parliament laying Duties on Glass, Paint &c. and a Board of Commissioners of the Revenue was expected, which must excite a great fermentation in the Country, of the Consequences of which I could see no End.

My Answer to Mr. Sewall was very prompt, that I was sensible of the honor done me by the Governor: but must be excused from Accepting his Offer. Mr. Sewall enquired why, what was my Objection. I answered that he knew very well my political Principles, the System I had adopted and the Connections and Friendships I had formed in Consequence of them: He also knew that the British Government, including the King, his Ministers and Parliament, apparently supported by a great Majority of the Nation, were persevereing in a System, wholly inconsistent with all my Ideas of Right, Justice and Policy, and therefore I could not place myself in a Situation in which my Duty and my Inclination would be so much at Variance. To this Mr. Sewall returned that he was instructed by the Governor to say that he knew my political Sentiments very well: but they should be no Objection with him. I should be at full Liberty to entertain my own Opinions, which he did not wish to influence by this office. He had offered it to me, merely because he believed I was the best qualified for it and because he relied on my Integrity. I replied This was going as far in the generosity and Liberality of his sentiments as the Governor could go or as I could desire, if I could Accept the Office: but that I knew it would lay me under restraints and Obligations that I could not submit to and therefore I could not in honor or Conscience Accept it.

Mr. Sewall paused, and then resuming the Subject asked, why are you so quick, and sudden in your determination? You had better take it into consideration, and give me an Answer at some future day. I told him my Answer had been ready because my mind was clear and my determination decided and unalterable. That my Advice would be that Mr. Fitch should be appointed, to whose Views the Office would be perfectly agreable. Mr. Sewal said he should certainly give me time to think of it: I said that time would produce no change and he had better make his report immediately. We parted, and about three

13. GROSVENOR SQUARE, LONDON, IN 1789

14. THE FIRST AMERICAN LEGATION BUILDING IN LONDON, CORNER OF
DUKE AND BROOK STREETS, GROSVENOR SQUARE

# COCKER's
## DECIMAL ARITHMETICK,

Wherein is shewed the Nature and Use of Decimal Fractions in the usual Rules of Arithmetick, and the Mensuration of Plains and Solids.

Together with Tables of Interest and Rebate for the valuation of Leases and Annuities, Present, or in Reversion, and Rules for Calculating those Tables.

Whereunto is added

His Artificial Arithmetick, shewing the Genesis or Fabrick of the Logarithms, and their use in the Extraction of Roots, the solving of Questions in Anatocism, and in other Arithmetical Rules in a Method not usually practised.

### ALSO

His Algebraical Arithmetick, containing the Doctrine of Composing and Resolving an Equation ; with all other Rules requisite for the understanding of that mysterious Art, according to the Method used by Mr. *John Kersey* in his Incomparable Treatise of *ALGEBRA*.

Composed by *EDWARD COCKER*, late Practitioner in the Arts of Writing, Arithmetick and Engraving.

Perused, Corrected and Published
By *JOHN HAWKINS*, Writing Master at St. *Georges-Church* in *Southwark*.

*Cum tua non edas cur bæc mea Zoile Carpis,*
*Carpere vel noli nostra, vel eda tua.*
*Μωμήσεται ράν ράδιον, μιμήσεται δὲ χαλεπόν.*

### The Third Edition.

*LONDON,*

Printed for George Sawbridge, at the *Three Flower de Luces* in *Little-Britain :* And *Richard Wellington,* at the *Dolphin* and *Crown* at the West end of *St. Paul's Church-Yard.* 1703.

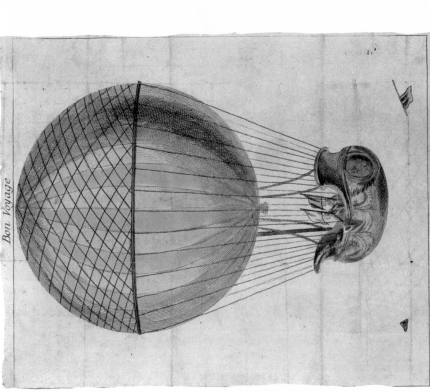

*Bon Voyage*

*Nouveau Globe Aerostatique inventée par Mrs Charles et Robert ; enlevé devant la Famille Royale le lundi 1er. Decembre 1783. à 1 heure 40 minutes.*

*Ces Messieurs on descendue à 3. heures 3. quarts entre Nesle et Hedouville dans la Prairie de Nesle à 9. lieues Nord-Ouest de Paris près la Ville de Beaumont sur l'Oise . Mr. Charles a remonté seule dans la même Machine en présence de Mrs. les Ducs de Chartres et de Fitz-de -James. et nombres de Spectateurs.*

Weeks afterwards he came to me again and hoped I had thought more favourably on the Subject: that the Governor had sent for him and told him the public Business suffered and the office must be filled. I told him my Judgment and Inclination and determination were unalterably fixed, and that I had hoped that Mr. Fitch would have been appointed before that time. Mr. Fitch however never was appointed. He acted for the Crown, by the Appointment of the Judge from day to day, but never had any Commission from the Crown or Appointment of the Governor.[6]

This Year 1768 I attended the Superiour Court at Worcester, and the next Week proceeded on to Sprin[g]field in the County of Hampshire, where I was accidentally engaged in a Cause between a Negro and his Master,[7] which was argued by me, I know not how, but it seems it was in such a manner as engaged the Attention of Major Hawley, and introduced an Acquaintance which was soon after strengthened into a Friendship, which continued till his Death. During my Absence on this Circuit, a Convention sat in Boston.[8] The Commissioners of the Customs had arrived and an Army Landed.[9] On my Return I found the Town of Boston full of Troops, and as Dr. Byles of punning Memory express'd it, our grievances reddressed. Through the whole succeeding fall and Winter a Regiment was excercised, by Major Small, in Brattle Square directly in Front of my house. The Spirit Stirring

[6] A very different version of what must be the same incident was recorded by Thomas Hutchinson:

"Mr. John Adams . . . is said to have been at a loss which side to take. Mr. Sewall, who was on the side of government, would have persuaded him to be on the same side, and promised him to desire governor Bernard to make him a justice of peace. The governor took time to consider of it, and having, as Mr. Adams conceived, not taken proper notice of him, or having given him offence on some former occasion, he no longer deliberated, and ever after joined in opposition" (*Massachusetts Bay*, ed. Mayo, 3:213–214).

It is curious that Hutchinson seems to have first heard these details in London in 1778 from the Boston loyalists Samuel Quincy and Richard Clarke, who "agreed" with each other that they were true. (Hutchinson, *Diary and Letters*, 2:220). By recording them in his *History* Hutchinson accepted at least their plausibility and thus concurred in the view that JA opposed the royal government because it had not provided him with an office.

Sewall himself held the post of advocate general (as well as that of attorney general) at the time he transmitted this offer to JA, but having been appointed judge of the Halifax Court of Vice-Admiralty he was looking for a successor. The successor proved to be Samuel Fitch, at first by a temporary appointment, then permanently. See Carl Ubbelohde, *The Vice-Admiralty Courts and the American Revolution*, Chapel Hill, 1960, p. 139, 161.

[7] Newport *v.* Billing, a case in the Superior Court of Judicature during its September term at Springfield. JA acted (and won) for the defendant, who was being sued by his slave (Superior Court of Judicature, Minute Book 83). Brief notes on the arguments are in JA's legal papers (M/JA/6, Adams Papers, Microfilms, Reel No. 185).

[8] 22–29 Sept. 1768.

[9] 1 Oct. 1768.

Drum, and the Earpiercing fife arroused me and my family early enough every morning, and the Indignation they excited, though somewhat soothed was not allayed by the sweet Songs, Violins and flutes of the serenading Sons of Liberty, under my Windows in the Evening. In this Way and a thousand others I had sufficient Intimations that the hopes and Confidence of the People, were placed on me, as one of their Friends: and I was determined, that as far as depended on me they should not be disappointed: and that if I could render them no positive Assistance, at least I would never take any part against them. My daily Reflections for two Years, at the Sight of those Soldiers before my door were serious enough. Their very Appearance in Boston was a strong proof to me, that the determination in Great Britain to subjugate Us, was too deep and inveterate ever to be altered by Us: For every thing We could do, was misrepresent[ed], and Nothing We could say was credited.

On the other hand, I had read enough in History to be well aware of the Errors to which the public opinions of the People, were liable in times of great heat and danger, as well as of the Extravagances of which the Populace of Cities were capable, when artfully excited to Passion, and even when justly provoked by Oppression. In ecclesiastical Controversies to which I had been a Witness; in the Contest at Woburn and on Marthas Vinyard, and especially in the Tryal of Hopkins and Ward, which I had heard at Worcester, I had learned enough to shew me, in all their dismal Colours, the deceptions to which the People in their passion, are liable, and the totall Suppression of Equity and humanity in the human Breast when thoroughly heated and hardened by Party Spirit.

The danger I was in appeared in full View before me: and I very deliberately, and indeed very solemnly determined, at all Events to adhere to my Principles in favour of my native Country, which indeed was all the Country I knew, or which had been known by my father, Grandfather or Great Grandfather: but on the other hand I never would deceive the People, conceal from them any essential truth, nor especially make myself subservient to any of their Crimes, Follies or Excentricities. These Rules to the Utmost of my capacity and Power, I have invariably and religiously observed to this day 21. Feb. 1805. and I hope I shall obey them till I shall be gathered to the Dust of my Ancestors, a Period which cannot be far off. They have however cost me the torment of a perpetual Vulcano of Slander, pouring on my flesh all my life time.

I was solicited to go to the Town Meetings and harrangue there.

This I constantly refused. My Friend Dr. Warren the most frequently urged me to this: My Answer to him always was "That way madness lies." The Symptoms of our great Friend Otis, at that time, suggested to Warren, a sufficient comment on these Words, at which he always smiled and said "it was true." Although I had never attended a Meeting the Town was pleased to choose me upon their Committee to draw up Instructions to their Representatives, this Year 1768 and the next 1769 or in the year 1769 and the Year 1770, I am not certain which two of these Years.[1] The Committee always insisted on my preparing the Draught, which I did and the Instructions were adopted without Alteration by the Town; they will be found in the Boston Gazette for those Years, and although there is nothing extraordinary in them of matter or Style, they will sufficiently shew the sense of the Public at that time.

In 1769 The House I lived in, was to be sold: I had not sufficient confidence in the Stability of any Thing, to purchase it, and I therefore removed to a house in cold Lane:[2] where I lost a Child a Daughter, whose name was Susana, and where in 1770 my Son Charles was born.

The Year 1770 was memorable enough, in these little Annals of my Pilgrimage. The Evening of the fifth of March, I spent at Mr. Henderson Inches's House at the South End of Boston, in Company with a Clubb, with whom I had been associated for several Years. About nine O Clock We were allarmed with the ringing of Bells, and supposing it to be the Signal of fire, We snatched our Hats and Cloaks, broke up the Clubb, and went out to assist in quenching the fire or aiding our friends who might be in danger. In the Street We were informed that the British Soldiers had fired on the Inhabitants, killed some and wounded others near the Town house. A Croud of People was flowing down the Street, to the Scene of Action. When We arrived We saw nothing but some field Pieces placed before the south door of the Town house and some Engineers and Grenadiers drawn up to protect them. Mrs. Adams was in Circumstances, and I was apprehensive of the Effect of the Surprise upon her, who [was] alone, excepting her Maids and a Boy in the House. Having therefore surveyed round the Town house and seeing all quiet, I walked down Boylstons Alley into Brattle Square, where a Company or two of

---

[1] 1768 and 1769. They were printed in the *Boston Gazette,* 20 June 1768, 15 May 1769, and reprinted in JA's *Works,* 3:501–510.

[2] This street ran northward from Han-over Street to the Mill Pond and was indiscriminately called Cold and Cole Lane (*Boston Streets, &c.,* 1910, p. 121; see also JA's Diary, second entry of 21 Nov. 1772).

regular Soldiers were drawn up in Front of Dr. Coopers old Church with their Musquets all shouldered and their Bayonetts all fixed. I had no other way to proceed but along the whole front in a very narrow Space which they had left for foot passengers. Pursuing my Way, without taking the least notice of them or they of me, any more than if they had been marble Statues, I went directly home to Cold Lane. My Wife having heard that the Town was still and likely to continue so, had recovered from her first Apprehensions, and We had nothing but our Reflections to interrupt our Repose. These Reflections were to me, disquieting enough. Endeavours had been systematically pursued for many Months, by certain busy Characters, to excite Quarrells, Rencounters and Combats single or compound in the night between the Inhabitants of the lower Class and the Soldiers, and at all risques to inkindle an immortal hatred between them. I suspected that this was the Explosion, which had been intentionally wrought up by designing Men, who knew what they were aiming at better than the Instrument employed. If these poor Tools should be prosecuted for any of their illegal Conduct they must be punished. If the Soldiers in self defence should kill any of them they must be tryed, and if Truth was respected and the Law prevailed must be acquitted. To depend upon the perversion of Law and the Corruption or partiality of Juries, would insensibly disgrace the Jurisprudence of the Country and corrupt the Morals of the People. It would be better for the whole People to rise in their Majesty, and insist on the removal of the Army, and take upon themselves the Consequences, than to excite such Passions between the People and the Soldiers [as] [3] would expose both to continual prosecution civil or criminal and keep the Town boiling in a continual fermentation. The real and full Intentions of the British Government and Nation were not yet developed: and We knew not whether the Town would be supported by the Country: whether the Province would be supported by even our neighbouring States of New England; nor whether New England would be supported by the Continent. These were my Meditations in the night. The next Morning I think it was, sitting in my Office, near the Steps of the Town house Stairs, Mr. Forrest came in, who was then called the Irish Infant.[4] I had some Acquaintance with him. With tears streaming from his Eyes, he said I am come with a very solemn Message from a very unfortunate Man,

[3] MS: "and."
[4] James Forrest, a native of Ireland and a prosperous Boston merchant; he became an ardent loyalist and left Boston with the British troops in 1776 (Jones, *Loyalists of Mass.*, p. 136–137; Rowe, *Letters and Diary, passim*).

Captain Preston in Prison. He wishes for Council, and can get none. I have waited on Mr. Quincy, who says he will engage if you will give him your Assistance: without it possitively he will not. Even Mr. Auchmuty declines unless you will engage....[5] I had no hesitation in answering that Council ought to be the very last thing that an accused Person should want in a free Country. That the Bar ought in my opinion to be independent and impartial at all Times And in every Circumstance. And that Persons whose Lives were at Stake ought to have the Council they preferred: But he must be sensible this would be as important a Cause as ever was tryed in any Court or Country of the World: and that every Lawyer must hold himself responsible not only to his Country, but to the highest and most infallible of all Try-bunals for the Part he should Act. He must therefore expect from me no Art or Address, No Sophistry or Prevarication in such a Cause; nor any thing more than Fact, Evidence and Law would justify. Captain Preston he said requested and desired no more: and that he had such an Opinion, from all he had heard from all Parties of me, that he could chearfully trust his Life with me, upon those Principles. And said Forrest, as God almighty is my Judge I believe him an innocent Man. I replied that must be ascertained by his Tryal, and if he thinks he cannot have a fair Tryal of that Issue without my Assistance, without hesitation he shall have it. Upon this, Forrest offered me a single Guinea as a retaining fee and I readily accepted it. From first to last I never said a Word about fees, in any of those Cases, and I should have said nothing about them here, if Calumnies and Insinuations had not been propagated that I was tempted by great fees and enormous sums of Money. Before or after the Tryal, Preston sent me ten Guineas and at the Tryal of the Soldiers afterwards Eight Guineas more, which were all the fees I ever received or were offered to me, and I should not have said any thing on the subject to my Clients if they had never offered me any Thing.[6] This was all the pecuniary Reward I ever had for fourteen or fifteen days labour, in the most exhausting and fatiguing Causes I ever tried: for hazarding a Popularity very general and very

[5] Suspension points in MS.

[6] This statement cannot be readily squared with the entries for legal fees in a bill of costs of the trials forwarded by Lt. Col. William Dalrymple in a letter to Gen. Gage, 17 Dec. 1770:

"To a retaining fee to C:
    Prestons Lawyers    £10–10
To–Do.–to the mens–Do.    10–10
To a fee for pleading at the
tryal to C: Prestons Lawyers  63
To–Do.–to the Mens–Do.    42"

(Printed from the Gage Papers in Randolph G. Adams, "New Light on the Boston Massacre," *Amer. Antiq. Soc., Procs.*, 47 [1937]:354.)

There were three lawyers for the defense in each trial; see note on Diary entry of 10 Jan. 1771.

hardly earned: and for incurring a Clamour and popular Suspicions and prejudices, which are not yet worn out and never will be forgotten as long as History of this Period is read. For the Experience of all my Life has proved to me, that the Memory of Malice is faithfull, and more, it continually adds to its Stock; while that of Kindness and Friendship is not only frail but treacherous. It was immediately bruited abroad that I had engaged for Preston and the Soldiers, and occasioned a great clamour which the Friends of Government delighted to hear, and slyly and secretly fomented with all their Art. The Tryal of the Soldiers was continued for one Term, and in the Mean time an Election came on, for a Representative of Boston. Mr. Otis had resigned: Mr. Bowdoin was chosen in his Stead: at the general Election Mr. Bowdoin was chosen into the Council and Mr. Hutchinson then Governor did not negative him. A Town Meeting was called for the Choice of a Successor to Mr. Bowdoin; Mr. Ruddock a very respectable Justice of the Peace, who had risen to Wealth and Consequence, by a long Course of Industry as a Master Shipwright, was sett up in Opposition to me. Notwithstanding the late Clamour against me, and although Mr. Ruddock was very popular among all the Tradesmen and Mechanicks in Town, I was chosen by a large Majority.[7] I had never been at a Boston Town Meeting, and was not at this, till Messengers were sent to me, to inform me that I was chosen. I went down to Phanuel Hall and in a few Words expressive of my sense of the difficulty and danger of the Times; of the importance of the Trust, and of my own Insuffi[ci]ency to fulfill the Expectations of the People, I accepted the Choice. Many Congratulations were offered, which I received civilly, but they gave no Joy to me. I considered the Step as a devotion of my family to ruin and myself to death, for I could scarce perceive a possibility that I should ever go through the Thorns and leap all the Precipices before me, and escape with my Life. At this time I had more Business at the Bar, than any Man in the Province: My health was feeble: I was throwing away as bright prospects [as] any Man ever had before him: and had devoted myself to endless labour and Anxiety if not to infamy and to death, and that for nothing, except, what indeed was and ought to be all in all, a sense of duty. In the Evening I expressed to Mrs. Adams all my Apprehensions: That excellent Lady, who has always encouraged me, burst into a flood of Tears, but said she was very sensible of all the Danger to her and to our Children as well as to me, but she thought I had done as I ought, she was very

[7] JA was elected on 6 June 1770 by 418 out of 536 votes cast (Boston Record Commissioners, *18th Report*, p. 33).

willing to share in all that was to come and place her trust in Providence. I immediately attended the General Court at Cambridge, to which place the Governor had removed it, to punish the Town of Boston, in Obedience however, as he said I suppose truly to an Instruction he had received from the King. The Proceedings of the Legislature, at that time and place may be seen in their Journals, if they are not lost. Among other Things will be found a laboured controversy between the House and the Governor, concerning these Words "In general Court assembled and by the Authority of the same." I mention this merely on Account of an Anecdote which the friends of Government circulated with diligence, of Governor Shirley who then lived in retirement at his Seat in Roxbury. Having read this dispute in the public Prints, he asked who has revived these old Words. They were expressed during my Administration. He was answered the Boston Seat. "And who are the Boston Seat?" Mr. Cushing, Mr. Hancock, Mr. Samuel Adams and Mr. John Adams. Mr. Cushing I know and Mr. Hancok [I] know, replied the old Governor, but where the Devil this brace of Adams's came from, I know not. This was archly circulated by the Ministerialists, to impress the People, with the Obscurity of the original, of the par nobile fratrum, as the Friends of the Country used to call Us, by way of Retaliation.[8] This was to me a fatiguing Session, for they put me upon all the Drudgery of managing all the disputes, and an executive Court had a long Session which obliged me to attend, allmost constantly there upon a Number of very disagreable Causes. Not long after the Adjournment of the General Court came on the Tryals of Preston and the Soldiers. I shall say little of these Cases. Prestons Tryal was taken down in short hand and sent to England but was never printed here.[9] I told the Court and Jury in both Causes, that as I was no Authority, I would propose to them no Law from my own memory: but would read to them, all I had to say of that Nature, from Books, which the Court knew and the Council on the other Side must acknowledge to be indisputable Authorities. This Rule was carefully

[8] See Diary entry of 9 Feb. 1772 and notes there.

[9] It was never printed anywhere, and JA's assertion that Preston's trial was recorded, sent to England, and suppressed by the government (see his letter to Morse, quoted below) cannot be verified and is very doubtful indeed. The trial of the soldiers was, however, recorded and printed. Before publication "The Court allowed [the reporter] to shew his Manuscript to the Council [counsel]. He brought it to me. Upon reading it over, I found so much inaccuracy, and so many errors, that I scratched out everything, but the legal Authorities, and the testimonies of the Witnesses. Mr. Quincy and Mr. Paine were consulted, and the results of their deliberations appear in the printed trial" (JA to Jedidiah Morse, 5 Jan. 1816, LbC, Adams Papers). This was *The Trial of William Wemms . . . Taken in Short-Hand by John Hodgson*, Boston, 1770.

observed but the Authorities were so clear and full that no question of Law was made. The Juries in both Cases, in my Opinion gave correct Verdicts. It appeared to me, that the greatest Service which could be rendered to the People of the Town, was to lay before them, the Law as it stood that the[y] might be fully apprized of the Dangers of various kinds, which must arise from intemperate heats and irregular commotions. Although the Clamour was very loud, among some Sorts of People, it has been a great Consolation to me through Life, that I acted in this Business with steady impartiality, and conducted it to so happy an Issue.

The complicated Cares of my legal and political Engagements, the slender Diet to which I was obliged to confine myself, the Air of the Town of Boston which was not favourable to me who had been born and passed allmost all my life in the Country; but especially the constant Obligation to speak in public almost every day for many hours, had exhausted my health, brought on a Pain in my Breast and a complaint in my Lungs, which seriously threatened my Life, and compelled me, to throw off a great part of the Load of Business both public and private, and return to my farm in the Country. Early in the Spring of 1771 I removed my family to Braintree, still holding however an office in Boston.[1] The Air of my native Spot, and the fine Breezes from the Sea on one Side and the rocky Mountains of Pine and Savin on the other, together with daily rides on horse back and the Amusements of Agriculture always delightfull to me soon restored my health in a considerable degree. I was advised to take a Journey to the Stafford Springs in Connecticutt, then in as much Vogue as any mineral Springs have been since. I spent a few days in drinking the Waters and made an Excursion, through Somers and Windsor down to Hartford and the Journey was of Use to me, whether the Waters were or not.[2] On my Return I had my Annual Journey to make on the Eastern Circuit at Ipswich, York and Falmouth, now Portland, and this Exercise continued to improve my health.

Finding my health much improved, and finding great Inconvenience in conducting my Business in Boston, in my Office there, while my family was in the Country, I began to entertain thoughts of returning. Having found it very troublesome to hire houses and be often obliged to remove, I determined to purchase a house, and Mr. Hunt offering me one in Court Street near the Scæne of my Business, opposite the Court house, I bought it and inconvenient and contracted as it was I

---

[1] See Diary entry of 16 April 1771.
[2] See Diary entries of 30 May 1771 and following.

made it answer both for a Dwelling and an Office, till a few Weeks before the 19th of Appril 1775 when the War commenced.[3]

During my last Residence in Boston, two Causes occurred, of an extraordinary Character, in which I was engaged and which cost me no small Portion of Anxiety. That of the four Sailors, who killed Lieutenant Panton of the Rose Frigate. These were both before Special Courts of Admiralty held in Consequence of the Statute. The four Sailors were acquitted as their Conduct was adjudged to be in Self Defence, and the Actions justifiable Homicide.[4] The other was the Tryal of Ansell Nicholson [Nickerson], for the Murder of three or four Men, on board a Vessell. This was and remains still a misterious Transaction. I know not to this day what Judgment to form of his Guilt or Innocence. And this doubt I presume was the Principle of Acquittal. He requested my Assistance and it was given. He had nothing to give me, but his promissory Note, for a very moderate Fee. But I have heard nothing of him, nor received any Thing for his note, which has been lost with many other Notes and Accounts to a large Amount, in the distraction of the times and my Absence from my Business.[5]

In the Year 1773 arose a Controversy concerning the Independence of the Judges. The King had granted a Salary to the Judges of our Superiour Court and forbidden them to receive their Salaries as usual from the Grants of the House of Representatives, and the Council and Governor, as had been practiced till this time. This as the Judges Commissions were during pleasure made them entirely dependent on the Crown for Bread [as] well as office. The Friends of Government were anxious to perswade the People, that their Commissions were during good Behaviour. Brigadier General Brattle, who had been a Prac[ti]tioner of Law, and was at this time in his Majestys Council, after some time, came out with his name in one of the Gazettes, with a formal Attempt to prove that the Judges held their offices for Life. Perhaps I should not have taken any public Notice of this, if it had not been industriously circulated among the People, that the General had at a Town Meeting in Cambridge the Week before advanced this doctrine And challenged me by name, to dispute the point with him. His Challenge I should have disregarded, but as his Appeal to me was public, if I should remain silent it would be presumed that my Opinion coincided with his. It was of great Importance that the People should form a correct Opinion on this Subject: and therefore I sent

[3] See Diary entry of 22 Sept. 1772 and note 2 there.
[4] See Diary entry of 23 Dec. 1769 and note.
[5] See Diary entry of 28 [i.e. 27?] Nov. 1772 and note 4 there.

to the press a Letter in Answer, which drew me on to the Number of Eight Letters, which may be seen in the Boston Gazette for this Year.[6] The Doctrine and the History of the Independence of Judges was detailed and explained as well as my time, Avocations and Information enabled me: imperfect and unpollished as they were they were well timed. The Minds of all Men were awake and every thing was eagerly read by every one, who could read. These papers Accordingly, contributed to spread correct Opinions concerning the Importance of the Independence of the Judges to Liberty and Safety, and enabled the Convention of Massachusetts in 1779 to adopt them into the Constitution of the Commonwealth, as the State of New York had done before, partially, and as the Constitution of the United States did afterwards [in] 1787. The Principles develloped in these Papers have been very generally, indeed almost universally prevalent among the People of America, from that time, till the Administration of Mr. Jefferson, during which they have been infringed and are now in danger of being lost. In such a Case, as the Ballance in our national Legislature is imperfect and very difficult to be preserved, We shall have no ballance at all of Interests or Passions, and our Lives, Liberties, Reputations and Estates will lie at the mercy of a Majority, and of a tryumphant Party.

At this Period,[7] the Universal Cry, among the Friends of their Country was "What shall We do to be saved?" It was by all Agreed, As the Governor was entirely dependent on the Crown, and the Council in danger of becoming so if the Judges were made so too, the Liberties of the Country would be totally lost, and every Man at the Mercy of a few Slaves of the Governor. But no Man presumed to say what ought to be done, or what could be done. Intimations were frequently given, that this Arrangement should not be submitted to.—I understood very well what was meant, and I fully expected that if no Expedient could be suggested, that the Judges would be obliged to go where Secretary Oliver had gone to Liberty Tree, and compelled to take an Oath to renounce the Royal Salaries. Some of these Judges were men of Resolution and the Chief Justice in particular, piqued himself so much upon it and had so often gloried in it on the Bench, that I shuddered at the expectation that the Mob might put on him a Coat of Tar and Feathers, if not put him to death. I had a real respect

[6] Actually seven letters; see Diary entry of 4 March 1773 and note 2 there.

[7] That is, during the winter of 1773–1774. The attempt by the House to impeach Chief Justice Peter Oliver because he would not renounce salary grants from the crown occurred in Feb. 1774; see Diary entry of 2 March 1774 and note.

for the Judges. Three of them Trowbridge, Cushing and Brown[8] I could call my Friends. Oliver and Ropes abstracted from their politicks were amiable Men, and all of them were very respectable and virtuous Characters. I dreaded the Effect upon the Morals and temper of the People, which must be produced, by any violence offered to the Persons of those who wore the Robes and bore the sacred Characters of Judges, and moreover I felt a strong Aversion to such partial and irregular Recurrences to original Power. The poor People themselves who by secret manœuvres are excited to insurrection are seldom aware of the purposes for which they are set in motion: or of the Consequences which may happen to themselves: and when once heated and in full Career, they can neither manage themselves, nor be regulated by others. Full of these Reflections, I happened to dine with Mr. Samuel Winthrop at New Bost[on], who was then Clerk of the Superiour Court, in company with several Members of the General Court of both Houses and with several other Gentlemen of the Town. Dr. John Winthrop Phylosophical Professor at Colledge and Dr. Cooper of Boston both of them very much my Friends, were of the Company. The Conversation turned wholly on the Topic of the Day—the Case of the Judges. All agreed that it was a fatal Measure and would be the Ruin of the Liberties of the Country: But what was the Remedy? It seemed to be a measure that would execute itself. There was no imaginable Way of resisting or eluding it. There was lamentation and mourning enough: but no light and no hope. The Storm was terrible and no blue Sky to be discovered. I had been entirely silent, and in the midst of all this gloom, Dr. Winthrop, addressing himself to me, said Mr. Adams We have not heard your Sentiments on this Subject, how do you consider it? I answered that my Sentiments accorded perfectly with all which had been expressed. The Measure had created a Crisis, and if it could not be defeated, the Liberties of the Province would be lost. The Stroke was levelled at the Essence of the Constitution, and nothing was too dear to be hazarded in warding it off. It levelled the Axe at the Root, and if not opposed the Tree would be overthrown from the foundation. It appeared so to me at that time and I have seen no reason, to suspect that I was in an Error, to this day. But said Dr. Winthrop, What can be done? I answered, that I knew not whether any one would approve of my Opinion but I believed there was one constitutional Resource, but I knew not whether it would be

[8] William Browne was not appointed to the Superior Court until June 1774, when he succeeded Nathaniel Ropes, who had died in March (Whitmore, *Mass. Civil List*, p. 70).

possible to persuade the proper Authority to have recourse to it. Several Voices at once cryed out, a constitutional Resource! what can it be? I said it was nothing more nor less than an Impeachment of the Judges by the House of Representatives before the Council. An Impeachment! Why such a thing is without Precedent. I believed it was, in this Province: but there had been precedents enough, and by much too many in England: It was a dangerous Experiment at all times: but it was essential to the preservation of the Constitution in some Cases, that could be reached by no other Power, but that of Impeachment. But whence can We pretend to derive such a Power? From our Charter, which gives Us, in Words as express, as clear and as strong as the Language affords, all the Rights and Priviledges of Englishmen: and if the House of Commons in England is the grand Inquest of the Nation, the House of Representatives is the Grand Inquest of this Province, and the Council must have the Powers of Judicature of the House of Lords in Great Britain. This Doctrine was said by the Company to be wholly new. They knew not how far it could be supported, but it deserved to be considered and examined. After all if it should be approved by the House, the Council would not convict the Judges.—That, I said, was an after consideration, if the House was convinced that they had the Power, and that it was their duty to exercise it, they ought to do it, and oblige the Council to enquire into their Rights and Powers and Duties. If the Council would not hearken to Law or Evidence, they must be responsible for the consequences, and the Guilt and blame must lie at their door. The Company seperated, and I knew that the Governor and the Judges would soon have Information of this Conversation, and as several Members of both Houses were present, and several Gentlemen of the Town, I was sensible that it would soon become the Talk of the Legislatures as well as of the Town. The next day, I believe, Major Hawley came to my House and told me, he heard I had broached a strange Doctrine. He hardly knew what an Impeachment was, he had never read any one and never had thought on the Subject. I told him he might read as many of them as he pleased. There stood the State Tryals on the Shelf which were full of them, of all sorts good and bad. I shewed him Seldens Works in which is a Treatise on Judicature in Parliament, and gave it him to read.[9] That Judicature in Parliament was as ancient as common Law and as Parlia-

---

[9] The authorities referred to were, presumably, Thomas Salmon, *A New Abridgement and Critical Review of the State Trials and Impeachments for High Treason . . .* , London, 1738, folio; and John Selden's *Opera Omnia,* ed. David Wilkins, London, 1726, 3 vols., folio, both of which remain among JA's books in the Boston Public Library (*Catalogue of JA's Library*).

ment itself; that without this high Jurisdiction it was thought impossible to defend the Constitution against Princes and Nobles and great Ministers, who might commit high Crimes and Misdemeanors which no other Authority would be powerfull enough to prevent or punish. That our Constitution was a Miniature of the British: that the Charter had given Us every Power, Jurisdiction and right within our Limits which could be claimed by the People or Government of England, with no other exceptions than those in the Charter expressed. We looked into the Charter together, and after a long conversation and a considerable Research he said he knew not how to get rid of it. In a Day or two another Lawyer in the House came to me, full of doubts and difficulties, He said he heard I had shown Major Hawley some Books relative to the Subject and desired to see them. I shewed them to him and made nearly the same comment upon them. It soon became the common Topick and research of the Bar. Major Hawley had a long Friendship for Judge Trowbridge and a high Opinion of his Knowledge of Law which was indeed extensive: he determined to converse with the Judge upon the Subject, went to Cambridge on Saturday and staid till monday. On this Visit he introduced this subject, and appealed to Lord Coke and Selden, as well as to the Charter, and advanced all the Arguments which occurred to him. The Judge although he had renounced the Salary We may suppose was not much delighted with the Subject, on Account of his Brothers. He did however declare to the Major that he could not deny, that the Constitution had given the Power to the House of Representatives, the Charter was so full and express, but that the Exercise of it, in this Case would be vain as the Council would undoubtedly acquit the Judges even if they heard and tryed the Impeachment. Hawley was not so much concerned about that as he was to ascertain the Law. The first time I saw Judge Trowbridge, he said to me, I see Mr. Adams you are determined to explore the Constitution and bring to Life all its dormant and latent Powers, in defence of your Liberties as you understand them. I answered I should be very happy if the Constitution could carry Us safely through all our difficulties without having recourse to higher Powers not written. The Members of the House, becoming soon convinced that there was something for them to do, appointed a Committee to draw up Articles of Impeachment against the Chief Justice Oliver.[1] Major Hawley who was one of this Committee, would do nothing without me, and insisted on bringing them to my house, to examine and discuss

[1] Adopted on 24 Feb. 1774 by a vote of 92 to 8 (Mass., *House Jour.*, 1773–1774, p. 194–201).

the Articles paragraph by Paragraph, which was readily consented to by the Committee. Several Evenings were spent in my Office, upon this Business, till very late at night. One Morning, meeting Ben. Gridley, he said to me Brother Adams you keep late Hours at your House: as I passed it last night long after midnight, I saw your Street door vomit forth a Crowd of Senators. The Articles when prepared were reported to the House of Representatives, adopted by them and sent up to the Council Board. The Council would do nothing and there they rested. The Friends of Administration thought they had obtained a Tryumph but they were mistaken. The Articles were printed in the Journals of the House and in the Newspapers, and the People meditated on them at their Leisure. When the Superiour Court came to sit in Boston, the Grand Jurors and Petit Jurors as their names were called over refused to take the Oaths. When examined and demanded their reasons for this extraordinary Conduct, they answered to a Man, that the Chief Justice of that Court stood impeached of high Crimes and Misdemeanors, before his Majestys Council, and they would not sit as Jurors while that Accusation was depending.[2] Att the Charlestown Court the Jurors unanimously refused in the same manner: They did so at Worcester and all the other Counties. The Court never sat again untill a new one was appointed by the Council exercising the Powers of a Governor under the Charter after the Battle of Lexington on the 19 of April 1775.

In the Fall of the Year 1773, The General Court appointed Mr. Bowdoin and me to draw a State of the Claim of this Province to the Lands to the Westward of New York. Mr. Bowdoin left it wholly to me: and I spent all my Leisure time in the Fall, Winter and Spring in Collecting all the Evidence and Documents: I went to Mr. John Moffat, who had made a large Collection of Records, Pamphlets and Papers, and examined his Treasures: then to Dr. Samuel Mathers Library which descended to him from his Ancestors Dr. Increase Mather, and Dr. Cotton Mather who had been Agent of the Province: and then to the Balcony of Dr. Sewalls Church, where Mr. Prince had deposited the amplest Collection of Books, Pamphlets, Records and Manuscripts relative to this Country which I ever saw, and which as I presume ever was made, Mr. Prince having pursued thro his whole Life a plan which he began at Colledge. I spent much time in

---

[2] Graphic accounts of the closing of the Superior Court of Judicature in Boston at the end of August and beginning of September 1774 were furnished to JA in letters from two of the young men in his office, William Tudor, 3 Sept., and Edward Hill, 8 Aug. [i.e. Sept.] 1774 (both in Adams Papers).

that elevated Situation, and found some things of Use in my Investigation, but I found a greater Gratification to my Curiosity, and cannot but lament that this invaluable Treasure was dispersed and ruined by the British Army, when they afterwards converted this venerable Temple into a Stable and a riding School. Having compleated my State of the Claim of the Province, and confuted the Pretensions of New York, I reported it to Mr. Bowdoin who after taking Time to read it, for it was very long, told me, that he approved it, and thought it wanted no Addition or correction. He Accordingly reported it to the Senate where it was read and sent down to the House, where it was read again. Mr. Samuel Adams was then Clerk of the House, and in the Confusion which soon afterwards happened at Salem, when the Governor dissolved the General Court for choosing Members to go to Congress, he lost it. But several Years afterwards it was found, and delivered to the Agents for Massachusetts, who attended the Settlement of the dispute with New York. Mr. King has repeatedly told me, that without that Statement, none of them would have understood any Thing of the Subject, and the Claim would have been lost.[3] The

[3] This is one of at least three accounts by JA of this interesting episode, all differing in details that are not easily reconcilable because the principal document in question has not been found.

The earliest account, in a letter from JA to Elbridge Gerry, Braintree, 17 Oct. 1779 (LbC, Adams Papers), is doubtless the most reliable. It states that "the General Court in 1774 appointed Mr. Bowdoin and me a Committee to state our Claim to those Lands" now called Vermont but then usually spoken of as the New Hampshire Grants, meaning the territory between the Connecticut River and the New York lakes north of a western projection of New Hampshire's present southern boundary. The date of this appointment, 1 March 1774 (rather than the fall of 1773), is confirmed by copies of the votes of both houses of the General Court among JA's papers relating to his work for this committee that are now in the Huntington Library (see below in this note). JA went on to say in his letter to Gerry that after spending "most of the Winter [i.e. spring] in rummaging" through books and documents, he "wrote a very lengthy, I cannot say a very accurate State of the Massachusetts Claim to those Lands, a particular Examination, and an Attempt at a Refutation of the Claim of New York, and a similar Discussion of that of New Hampshire.—Mr. Bowdoin revised it and reported it, a few days before Gen. Gage removed the General Court to Salem" in May 1774. At Salem (as told also in the Autobiography) the report was lost in the shuffle. "There is no other Copy that I know of—the first rough blotted Draught, was left in my Table drawer in my Office in Boston, when the Regulars shut up the Town. The Table, Papers and all were carried off, when they left the Town."

Thus far JA in 1779. The statement in his Autobiography that his report of 1774 reappeared and proved useful a decade later when Massachusetts' western claims were reasserted and eventually settled on the one hand by a cession to the United States and on the other by a compromise with New York, seems to be clearly confirmed by a letter from Tristram Dalton to JA, Newburyport, 6 April 1784 (Adams Papers). (The connection between Massachusetts' claim to Vermont and its claim to lands "to the Westward of New York" was owing to the sea-to-sea grant in the 1629 Charter of the Massa-

Decision was much less favourable to Massachusetts than it ought to have been, and the State have very unœconomically alienated all the Land since that time for a very inadequate sum of Money. I wish they had first given me a Township of the Land. It would have been much more prudently disposed of than any of the rest of it was, and more justly. I never had any thing for my half Years service, not even Credit nor Thanks.

As I have written hitherto, wholly from my memory, without recurring to any Books or Papers, I am sensible I have made several Anachronisms, and particularly in some things immediately preceeding. It was I believe in 1772 [4] that Governor Hutchinson, in an elaborate Speech to both Houses of Congress endeavoured to convince them, their Constituents and the World that Parliament was our Sovereign Legislature, and had a Right to make Laws for Us in all Cases whatso-

---

chusetts Bay Company; see Paullin, *Atlas*, pl. 42, 47E, 97A-B, and p. 26, 36, 72–73.)

Only fragments of the once voluminous record of JA's investigation of Massachusetts' territorial claims have survived. These include some dozen folio pages of notes and drafts among his miscellaneous papers (M/JA/17, Adams Papers, Microfilms, Reel No. 191), one page captioned "An Examination of the Claim of New York," a six-page draft entitled "A State of the Title of the Massachusetts-Bay, to Lands between Connecticutt & Hudsons Rivers, at the North West Corner of the Province," and three pages of "Additions to be made to the Title of the Massachusetts." These, at least, were not carried off by the British from JA's Boston office. In the present century a further and very miscellaneous mass of papers assembled by JA during his work for the committee of 1774 came into the autograph market. They are listed and inaccurately described in *The Library of Henry F. De Puy* (*Part One*), Anderson Galleries, N.Y., Catalogue of Sale No. 1440, 17–18 Nov. 1919, lot 8 (now in CSmH). They consist of nearly 50 pages in various hands, including JA's, but the principal paper, which is identified in the auction catalogue as JA's "brief" for Massachusetts' claims (to Vermont), is actually, according to both internal evidence and JA's own endorsement there-

on, a copy by JA of "Charles Phelps's State of this Case." Phelps was "an Inhabitant of the [New Hampshire] Grants" who favored Massachusetts' claims; see JA to Gerry, 17 Oct. 1779, cited above. Among the other papers in CSmH is a copy of James Bowdoin's report to the Massachusetts Council on the petition of Charles Phelps, undated but followed immediately by copies of the votes of the Council and House, 25, 28 Feb., 1 March 1774, appointing Bowdoin and JA "to prepare a full and clear State of the Province's Title" (JA's endorsement)—the action that led to JA's undertaking his laborious researches.

Whatever the fate of JA's elaborate but apparently irrecoverable report may have been, his interest in Massachusetts' northern and western territorial claims remained strong, and his early investigation of them later proved extremely useful in the struggle over the northeastern boundary of the United States in the preliminary peace negotiations at Paris; see his Diary entry of 10 Nov. 1782 and note 1 there; also his letters printed in the *Boston Patriot*, Oct.–Nov. 1811 (partly reprinted in JA, *Works*, 1:667–668), in which he told once more the story of his defense of Massachusetts' title to Vermont under the Charter of 1629.

[4] Jan. 1773. On the contest alluded to here and JA's part in it, see Diary entry of 4 March 1773 and note 1 there.

ever, to Lay Taxes on all things external and internal, on Land as well as on Trade. The House appointed a Committee to answer this Speech. An Answer was drawn prettily written, I never knew certainly by whom, whether Mr. Samuel Adams or Dr. Joseph Warren ⟨or both together⟩ or Dr. Church, or all three together. Major Hawley was pleased with the Composition but was not satisfied with all the Principles, nor with all the Reasoning. Major Hawley would do nothing without me, and without Major Hawley the Committee could do nothing. I must be invited and must be present at every Meeting. This Attachment of the Major to me, I soon perceived and often afterwards perceived was an Eye Sore to some Gentlemen. I have seen at Antwerp, an admirable Picture by one of the flemish Masters of the Saviour and his Disciples. The Saviour is represented as shewing to the beloved Disciple John, some peculiar marks of his tender Affection and Friendship for him. The Eyes of all the Disciples are turned to those two principal figures, and these Partialities are observed by them all. The Artist understood human Nature so well, that he had stamped a Jealousy on every Countenance, especially on that of St. Peter whose Eyes allmost start out of his head with it. The Painter knew that the holiest Men were Men still. I must declare that my Experience has been conformable to that of the Painter. I have never known in the Course of my whole Life any Man however exalted in Rank, Genius, Talents, Fame, Fortune or Virtue, in whom I have not seen disgusting Instances and proofs of this Passion. I will not say that I have never felt them in myself, but I will say I have been always on my guard against them and always endeavoured to suppress them and that I never took one Step to supplant any Man from such Motives. I had reason to make this Observation at the time. I saw in Mr. Hancock and Mr. Samuel Adams very visible marks of Jealousy and Envy too at this superiour Attachment of Major Hawley to me. I regarded it very little and it made no Alteration in my respectfull and friendly behaviour to them. The Draught of a Report was full of very popular Talk and with those democratical Principles which have since done so much mischief in this Country. I objected to them all and got them all expunged which I thought exceptionable, and furnished the committee with the Law Authorities, and the legal and constitutional Reasonings that are to be seen on the part of the House in that Controversy. How these Papers would appear to me or to others, at this day I know not, having never seen them since their first publication: but they appeared to me, at that time to be correct.

In the fall of the Year 1773, a great Uproar was raised in Boston, on Account of the Unlading in the Night of a Cargo of Wines from the Sloop Liberty from Madeira, belonging to Mr. Hancock, without paying the Customs. Mr. Hancock was prosecuted upon a great Number of Libells for Penalties, upon Acts of Parliament, amounting to Ninety or an hundred thousand Pounds Sterling. He thought fit to engage me as his Counsell and Advocate; and a painfull Drudgery I had of his cause. There were few days through the whole Winter, when I was not summoned to attend the Court of Admiralty. It seemed as if the Officers of the Crown were determined to examine the whole Town as Witnesses. Almost every day a fresh Witness was to be examined upon Interrogatories. They interrogated many of his near Relations and most intimate Friends and threatened to summons his amiable and venerable Aunt, the Relict of his Uncle Thomas Hancock, who had left the greatest Part of his Fortune to him. I was thoroughly weary and disgusted with the Court, the Officers of the Crown, the Cause, and even with the tyrannical Bell that dongled me out of my House every Morning; and this odious Cause was suspended at last only by the Battle of Lexington, which put an End for ever to all such Prosecutions.[5]

[5] Here JA's memory seriously misled him. This protracted admiralty case, Advocate General Jonathan Sewall *v.* John Hancock, occurred in 1768–1769. It followed the seizure in Boston harbor of Hancock's sloop *Liberty,* 10 June 1768, by members of the crew of the *Romney* man-of-war at the instance of the new board of customs commissioners, not for smuggling but for failing to obtain a permit for a cargo it had loaded. The *Liberty* was condemned in August and sold in September. The following month, after British troops had garrisoned Boston (also at the behest of the customs commissioners), a suit was filed against Hancock, not by a grand jury indictment but by an "information" and an admiralty court order, for the enormous sum of £9,000. The charge was for smuggling wine that had been brought in earlier by the *Liberty.* JA's notes on this case are in his "Admiralty Book" (Adams Papers, Microfilms, Reel No. 184) and are printed, with introductory commentary and valuable references, in Quincy, *Reports,* p. 456–463.

In his stubborn and eloquent defense before Judge Auchmuty, JA questioned the validity of the legislation under which the case was tried, because it denied his client the right of a jury trial and thus, by repealing "Magna Charta, as far as America is concerned," "degraded [Hancock] below the Rank of an Englishman." The defense was successful. At the end of the record appears this notation, dated 25 March 1769: "The Advocate General prays leave to Retract this Information and says our Sovereign Lord the King will prosecute no further hereon. Allow'd" (Suffolk co. Court House, Records, Court of Vice Admiralty, Province of Massachusetts Bay, 1765–1772).

See also George G. Wolkins, "The Seizure of John Hancock's Sloop 'Liberty,'" MHS, *Procs.,* 55 (1921–1922):239–284; Oliver M. Dickerson, *The Navigation Acts and the American Revolution,* Phila., 1951, p. 231–246, 260–265; and David S. Lovejoy, "Rights Imply Equality: The Case against Admiralty Jurisdiction in America, 1764–1776," WMQ, 3d ser., 16: 459–484 (Oct. 1959), especially p. 478–482.

It is well known that in June 1774 The General Court at Cambridge appointed Members to meet with others from the other States in Congress on the fifth of August.[6] Mr. Bowdoin, Mr. Cushing, Mr. Samuel Adams, Mr. John Adams and Mr. Robert Treat Paine were appointed. After this Election I went for the tenth and last time on the Eastern Circuit: At York at Dinner with the Court, happening to sit at Table next to Mr. Justice Seward,[7] a Representative of York, but of the unpopular Side, We entered very sociably and pleasantly into conversation, and among other Things he said to me, Mr. Adams you are going to Congress, and great Things are in Agitation. I recommend to you the Doctrine of my former Minister Mr. Moody.[8] Upon an Occasion of some gloomy prospect for the Country, he preached a Sermon from this text "And they know not what to do." After a customary introduction, he raised this Doctrine from his Text, that "in times of great difficulty and danger, when Men know not what to do, it is the Duty of a Person or a People to be very careful that they do not do, they know not what." This oracular Jingle of Words, which seemed, however to contain some good Sense, made Us all very gay. But I thought the venerable Preacher when he had beat the Drum ecclesiastic to animate the Country to undertake the Expedition to Louisbourg in 1745, and had gone himself with it as a Chaplain, had ventured to do he knew not what, as much as I was likely to do in the Expedition to Congress. I told the Deacon that I must trust Providence as Mr. Moody had done, when he did his duty though he could not foresee the Consequences.

To prepare myself as well as I could, for the Storm that was coming on, I removed my Family to Braintree. They could not indeed have remained in Safety in Boston, and when the time arrived Mr. Bowdoin having declined the Appointment Mr. Cushing, Mr. Adams, Mr. Paine and myself, satt out on our Journey together in one Coach. The Anxiety and Expectation of the Country was very great, and all the Gentlemen on the Road assembled from place to place to escort Us all the Way to Philadelphia, especially in Connecticutt, New York, the Jersies and Pensilvania. On the 5th of August [September] Congress assembled in Carpenters Hall. The Day before, I dined with Mr. Lynch a Delegate

[6] This session of the General Court took place at Salem, and the time set for convening the Continental Congress was 1 Sept.; see Diary entry of 20 June 1774 and note.

[7] Jonathan Sayward (Whitmore, *Mass. Civil List*, p. 111).

[8] Samuel Moody, Harvard 1697, for many years minister at York and a famous eccentric. JA reported this conversation and other anecdotes of Moody in a letter to AA from York, 30 June (Adams Papers; JA-AA, *Familiar Letters*, p. 5–6).

from South Carolina, who, in conversation on the Unhappy State of Boston and its inhabitants, after some Observations had been made on the Eloquence of Mr. Patrick Henry and Mr. Richard Henry Lee, which had been very loudly celebrated by the Virginians, said that the most eloquent Speech that had ever been made in Virginia or any where else, upon American Affairs had been made by Colonel Washington. This was the first time I had ever heard the Name of Washington, as a Patriot in our present Controversy, I asked who is Colonel Washington and what was his Speech? Colonel Washington he said was the officer who had been famous in the late french War and in the Battle in which Braddock fell. His Speech was that if the Bostonians should be involved in Hostilities with the British Army he would march to their relief at the head of a Thousand Men at his own expence. This Sentence Mr. Lynch said, had more Oratory in it, in his Judgment, than all that he had ever heard or read. We all agreed that it was both sublime, pathetic and beautifull.[9]

The more We conversed with the Gentlemen of the Country, and with the Members of Congress the more We were encouraged to hope for a general Union of the Continent. As the Proceedings of this Congress are in Print, I shall have Occasion to say little of them. A few Observations may not be amiss. After some days of general discussions, two Committees were appointed of twelve members each, one from each State, Georgia not having yet come in.[1] The first Committee was instructed to prepare a Bill of Rights as it was called or a Declaration of the Rights of the Colonies: the second, a List of Infringements or Violations of those Rights. Congress was pleased to appoint me, on the first Committee, as the Member for Massachusetts. It would be endless to attempt even an Abridgment of the Discussions in this Committee, which met regularly every Morning, for many days

[9] Thomas Lynch Sr. told this apparently apocryphal anecdote to JA on 31 Aug. 1774; see Diary entry of that date and note 2 there.

[1] The summary in this paragraph and the next of the work of the first Continental Congress was written by JA without consulting either the record in his own Diary of the debates in that Congress or its proceedings as printed in the *Journals of Congress*, of which he owned several sets of the original edition and early reprints; see *Catalogue of JA's Library*, p. 60–61; also note 4 at p. 338, below. With some charity CFA described JA's present summary as "sub-stantially" consonant with official records but not "precisely accurate in the details." In a footnote extending over several pages CFA then corrected and clarified JA's narrative, which is misleading in many if not most of its details. Pending the publication in Series III of *The Adams Papers* of JA's writings as a member of the first Continental Congress, the reader may be referred to CFA's careful note (JA, *Works*, 2:375–377) and, of course, to JA's Diary entries and notes of debates, with the editorial notes there, for the period 8 Sept. — 17? Oct. 1774.

successively, till it became an Object of Jealousy to all the other Members of Congress. It was indeed very much against my Judgment, that the Committee was so soon appointed, as I wished to hear all the great Topicks handled in Congress at large in the first Place. They were very deliberately considered and debated in the Committee however. The two Points which laboured the most, were 1. Whether We should recur to the Law of Nature, as well as to the British Constitution and our American Charters and Grants. Mr. Galloway and Mr. Duane were for excluding the Law of Nature. I was very strenuous for retaining and insisting on it, as a Resource to which We might be driven, by Parliament much sooner than We were aware. The other great question was what Authority We should conceed to Parliament: whether We should deny the Authority of Parliament in all Cases: whether We should allow any Authority to it, in our internal Affairs: or whether We should allow it to regulate the Trade of the Empire, with or without any restrictions. These discussions spun into great Length, and nothing was decided. After many fruitless Essays, The Committee determined to appoint a Sub committee, to make a draught of a Sett of Articles, that might be laid in Writing before the grand Committee and become the foundation of a more regular debate and final decision. I was appointed on the Subcommittee, in which after going over the ground again, a Sett of Articles were drawn and debated one by one. After several days deliberation, We agreed upon all the Articles excepting one, and that was the Authority of Parliament, which was indeed the Essence of the whole Controversy. Some were for a flatt denial of all Authority: others for denying the Power of Taxation only. Some for denying internal but admitting [ex]ternal Taxation. After a multitude of Motions had [been] made, discussed [and] negatived, it seems as if We should never agree upon any Thing. Mr. John Rutledge of South Carolina, one of the Committee, addressing himself to me, was pleased to say "Adams We must agree upon Something: You appear to be as familiar with the Subject as any of Us, and I like your Expressions *the necessity of the Case* and *excluding all Ideas of Taxation external and internal.*[2] I have a great Opinion of that same Idea of the Necessity of the Case and I am determined against all taxation for revenue. Come take the Pen and see if you cant produce something that will unite Us." Some others of the Committee seconding Mr. Rutledge, I took a sheet of paper and drew up an Article. When it was read I believe not one of the Committee

[2] In the fourth article of the Declaration of Rights as finally adopted (JA, *Works*, 2:538–539; JCC, 1:68–69).

were fully satisfied with it, but they all soon acknowledged that there was no hope of hitting on any thing, in which We could all agree with more Satisfaction. All therefore agreed to this, and upon this depended the Union of the Colonies. The Sub Committee reported their draught to the grand Committee, and another long debate ensued especially on this Article, and various changes and modifications of it were Attempted, but none adopted. The Articles were then reported to Congress, and debated Paragraph by Paragraph. The difficult Article was again attacked and defended. Congress rejected all Amendments to it, and the general Sense of the Members was that the Article demanded as little as could be demanded, and conceeded as much as could be conceeded with Safety, and certainly as little as would be accepted by Great Britain: and that the Country must take its fate, in consequence of it. When Congress had gone through the Articles, I was appointed to put them into form and report a fair Draught for their final Acceptance. This was done and they were finally accepted.

The Committee of Violations of Rights reported a sett of Articles which were drawn by Mr. John Sullivan of New Hampshire: and These two Declarations, the one of Rights and the other of Violations, which are printed in the Journal of Congress for 1774, were two Years afterwards recapitulated in the Declaration of Independence on the fourth of July 1776. The Results of the Procedings of Congress for this Year remain in the Journals: and I shall not attempt any Account of the debates, nor of any thing of the share I took in them. I never wrote a Speech beforehand, either at the Bar or in any public Assembly, nor committed one to writing after it was delivered, and it would be idle to attempt a Recollection, of Arguments from day to day, through a whole session, at the distance of thirty Years. The Delegates from Massachusetts, representing the State in most immediate danger, were much visited, not only by the members of Congress but by all the Gentlemen in Phyladelphia and its neighbourhood, as well as Strangers and Occasional Travellers. We took Lodgings all together at the Stone House opposite the City Tavern then held by Mrs. Yard, which was by some Complimented with the Title of Head Quarters, but by Mr. Richard Henry Lee, more decently called Liberty Hall. We were much caressed and feasted by all the principal People, for the Allens, and Penns and others were then with Us, though afterwards some of them cooled and fell off, on the declaration of Independence. We were invited to Visit all the public Buildings and places of resort, and became pretty well acquainted with Men and things in Philadelphia.

There is an Anecdote, which ought not to be omitted, because it had Consequences of some moment, at the time, which have continued to operate for many Years and indeed are not yet worn out, though the cause is forgotten or rather was never generally known.[3] Governor Hopkins and Governor Ward of Rhode Island came to our Lodgings, and said to Us, that President Manning of Rhode Island Colledge and Mr. Bachus [Backus] of Massachusetts were in Town, and had conversed with some Gentlemen in Philadelphia who wished to communicate to Us a little Business, and wished We would meet them at Six in the Evening at Carpenters Hall. Whether they explained their Affairs more particularly to any of my Colleagues I know not, but I had no Idea of the design. We all went at the hour, and to my great Surprize found the Hall almost full of People, and a great Number of Quakers seated at the long Table with their broad brimmed Beavers on their Heads. We were invited to Seats among them: and informed that they had received Complaints from some Anabaptists and some Friends in Massachusetts against certain Laws of that Province, restrictive of the Liberty of Conscience: and some Instances were mentioned in the General Court and in the Courts of Justice, in which Friends and Baptists had been grievously oppressed. I know not how my Colleagues felt, but I own I was greatly surprized and somewhat indignant, being like my Friend Chase of a temper naturally quick and warm, at seeing our State and her Delegates thus summoned before a self created Trybunal, which was neither legal nor Constitutional.

Israel Pemberton a Quaker of large Property and more intrigue began to speak and said that Congress were here, endeavouring to form a Union of the Colonies: but there were difficulties in the Way, and none of more importance than Liberty of Conscience. The Laws of New England and particularly of Massachusets, were inconsistent with it, for they not only compelled Men to pay to the Building of Churches and Support of Ministers but to go to some known Religious Assembly on first days &c. and that he and his friends were desirous of engaging Us, to assure them that our State would repeal all those Laws, and place things as they were in Pennsylvania. A Suspicion instantly arose in my Mind, which I have ever believed to have been well founded, that this artfull Jesuit, for I had been before apprized of his Character, was endeavouring to avail himself of this opportunity, to break up the Congress, or at least to withdraw the Quakers

[3] On the background and aftermath of the dramatic incident related here, see Diary entry of 14 Oct. 1774 and note 3 there.

and the Governing Part of Pensilvania from Us: for at that time by means of a most unequal Representation, the Quakers had a Majority in their House of Assembly and by Consequence the whole Power of the State in their hands. I arose and spoke in Answer to him. The Substance of what I said was, that We had no Authority to bind our Constituents to any such Proposals: that the Laws of Massachusetts, were the most mild and equitable Establishment of Religion that was known in the World, if indeed they could be called an Establishment: that it would be in vain for Us to enter into any Conferences on such a Subject, for We knew before hand our Constituents would disavow all We could do or say, for the Satisfaction of those who invited Us to this meeting. That the People of Massachusetts were as religious and Consciencious as the People of Pensylvania: that their Consciences dictated to them that it was their duty to support those Laws and therefore the very Liberty of Conscience which Mr. Pemberton invoked, would demand indulgence for the tender Consciences of the People of Massachusetts, and allow them to preserve their Laws. That it might be depended on, this was a Point that could not be carried: that I would not deceive them by insinuating the faintest hope, for I knew they might as well turn the heavenly Bodies out of their annual And diurnal Courses as the People of Massachusetts at the present day from their Meeting House and Sunday Laws.—Pemberton made no Reply but this, Oh! Sir pray dont urge Liberty of Conscience in favour of such Laws!—If I had known the particular complaints, which were to be alledged, and if Pemberton had not broke irregularly into the Midst of Things, it might have been better perhaps to have postponed this declaration. However the Gentlemen proceeded and stated the particular Cases of Oppression, which were alledged in our General and executive Courts. It happened that Mr. Cushing and Mr. Samuel Adams had been present in the General Court, when the Petitions had been under deliberation, and they explained the whole so clearly that every reasonable Man must have been satisfied. Mr. Paine and myself had been concerned at the Bar in every Action in the executive Courts which was complained of, and We explained them all to the entire Satisfaction of impartial Men: and shewed that there had been no Oppression or injustice in any of them. The Quakers were not generally and heartily in our Cause, they were jealous of Independence, they were then suspicious and soon afterwards became assured, that the Massachusetts Delegates and especially John Adams, were Advocates for that Ob[no]xious Measure, and they conceived prejudices, which were soon increased and artfully inflamed, and are not yet worn out. In some of the late Elections for President, some of the Quakers were heard to say "Friend, the[e] must know that We dont much affect the Name of Adams." This Sentiment was not however Universal nor General, for I have had Opportunities to know that great Numbers of the Friends in all parts of the Continent, were warmly attached to me, both when I was Vice President and President. I left Congress and Philadelphia in October 1774, with a Reputation, much higher than ever I enjoyed before or since.

Upon our Return to Massachusetts, I found myself elected by the Town of Braintree into the provincial Congress, and attended that Service as long as it sat. About this time, Drapers Paper in Boston swarmed with Writers, and among an immense quantity of meaner productions appeared a Writer under the Signature of Massachusettensis, suspected but never that I knew ascertained to be written by two of my old Friends Jonathan Sewall and Daniel Leonard.[4] These Papers were well written, abounded with Wit, discovered good Information, and were conducted with a Subtlety of Art and Address, wonderfully calculated to keep Up the Spirits of their Party, to depress ours, to spread intimidation and to make Proselytes among those, whose Principles and Judgment give Way to their fears, and these compose at least one third of Mankind. Week after Week passed away, and these Papers made a very visible impression on many Mind[s]. No Answer appeared, and indeed, some who were capable, were too busy and others too timorous. I began at length to think seriously of the Consequences and began to write, under the Signature of Novanglus, and continued every Week, in the Boston Gazette, till the 19th. of April 1775. The last Number was prevented from impression, by the Commencement of Hostilities, and Mr. Gill gave it to Judge William Cushing, who now has it in Manuscript.[5] An Abridgment of the printed Numbers was made by some one in England unknown to me, and published in a Supplement to Almons Remembrancer for the Year 1775 under the Title of Prior Documents, and afterwards reprinted in a Pamphlet in 1783 under the Title of History of the Dispute with America.[6] In New England they had the Effect of an Antidote to the

[4] That is, by one or the other of these two loyalist lawyers. They were actually by Leonard; see Diary entry of 30 April 1775, note 1.

[5] A copy of this final, unpublished number, in the hand of William Cushing, is in MHi:Paine Papers.

[6] The abridged version of the "Novanglus" letters printed by John Almon is not in the so-called "Prior Documents" (*A Collection of Interesting, Authentic Papers, ... 1764 to 1775*, London, 1777), but in the first volume of Almon's *Remembrancer, or Impartial Repository of Public Events*, London, 1775, p. 24–32, 45–54. And the "Pamphlet" edition to which JA refers was issued by John Stockdale, London, 1784,

Poison of Massachusettinsis: and the Battle of Lexington on the 19th of April, changed the Instruments of Warfare from the Penn to the Sword. A few days after this Event I rode to Cambridge where I saw General Ward, General Heath, General Joseph Warren, and the New England Army. There was great Confusion and much distress: Artillery, Arms, Cloathing were wanting and a sufficient Supply of Provisions not easily obtained. Neither the officers nor Men however wanted Spirits or Resolution. I rode from thence to Lexington and along the Scene of Action for many miles and enquired of the Inhabitants, the Circumstances. These were not calculated to diminish my Ardour in the Cause. They on the Contrary convinced me that the Die was cast, the Rubicon passed, and as Lord Mansfield expressed it in Parliament, if We did not defend ourselves they would kill Us. On my Return home I was seized with a fever, attended with allarming Symptoms: but the time was come to repair to Philadelphia to Congress which was to meet on the fifth [7] of May. I was determined to go as far as I could, and instead [of] venturing on horseback as I had intended, I got into a Sulkey attended by a Servant on horseback and proceeded on the Journey. This Year Mr. Hancock was added to our Number: I overtook my Colleagues before they reached New York.[8] At Kingsbridge We were met by a great Number of Gentlemen in Carriages and on horseback, and all the Way their Numbers increased till I thought the whole City was come out to meet Us. The same Ardour was continued all the Way to Philadelphia.

Congress assembled and proceeded to Business, and the Members appeared to me to be of one Mind, and that mind after my own heart. I dreaded the danger of disunion and divisions among Us, and much more among the People. It appeared to me, that all Petitions, Remonstrances and Negotiations, for the future would be fruitless and only occasion a Loss of time and give Opportunity to the Ennemy to sow divisions among the States and the People. My heart bled for the poor People of Boston, imprisoned within the Walls of their City by a British Army, and We knew not to what Plunder or Massacres or

with the title *History of the Dispute with America; from Its Origin in 1754. Written in the Year 1774. By John Adams, Esq.* (A copy inscribed by JA to Count Sarsfield is in MHi.) JA does not mention here the Dutch edition, *Geschiedenis van het geschil tusschen Groot-Britannie en Amerika, zedert deszelfs oorsprong, in den jaare 1754, tot op den tegenwoordigen tijd. Door ...* John Adams, Amsterdam: W. Holtrop, 1782.

[7] An error for the 10th, and an indication that JA was still writing wholly from memory.

[8] See Diary entry of 30 April 1775 and note 1 there; also JA's Account with Massachusetts, April–Aug. 1775, which is included in the present edition of his Diary.

Cruelties they might be exposed. I thought the first Step ought to be, to recommend to the People of every State in the Union, to Seize on all the Crown Officers, and hold them with civility, Humanity and Generosity, as Hostages for the Security of the People of Boston and to be exchanged for them as soon as the British Army would release them. That We ought to recommend to the People of all the States to institute Governments for themselves, under their own Authority, and that, without Loss of Time. That We ought to declare the Colonies, free, Sovereign and independent States, and then to inform Great Britain We were willing to enter into Negotiations with them for the redress of all Grievances, and a restoration of Harmony between the two Countries, upon permanent Principles. All this I thought might be done before We entered into any Connections, Alliances or Negotiations with forreign Powers. I was also for informing Great Britain very frankly that hitherto we were free but if the War should be continued, We were determined to seek Alliances with France, Spain and any other Power of Europe, that would contract with Us. That We ought immediately to adopt the Army in Cambridge as a Continental Army, to Appoint a General and all other Officers, take upon ourselves the Pay, Subsistence, Cloathing, Armour and Munitions of the Troops. This is a concise Sketch of the Plan, which I thought the only reasonable one, and from Conversation with the Members of Congress, I was then convinced, and have been ever since convinced, that it was the General Sense, at least of a considerable Majority of that Body. This System of Measures I publicly and privately avowed, without Reserve.

The Gentlemen in Pensilvania, who had been attached to the Proprietary Interest and owed their Wealth and Honours to it, and the Great Body of the Quakers, had hitherto acquiesced in the Measures of the Colonies, or at least had made no professed opposition to them; many of both descriptions had declared themselves with Us and had been as explicit and as ardent as We were....[9] But now these People began to see that Independence was approaching they started back. In some of my public Harrangues in which I had freely and explicitly laid open my Thoughts, on looking round the Assembly, I have seen horror, terror and detestation, strongly marked on the Countenances of some of the Members, whose names I could readily recollect, but as some of them have been good Citizens since and others went over afterwards to the English I think it unnecessary to record

[9] Suspension points, here and below in the discussion of sentiment concerning independence and JA's intercepted letters, are in the MS.

them here. There is One Gentleman however whom I must mention in Self Defence, I mean Mr. John Dickinson then of Philadelphia, now of Delaware. This Gentleman had been appointed a Member of Congress by the Legislature of Pensilvania about a Week before the Close of the Congress of 1774 and now in 1775 made his Appearance again at the Opening of the Congress of 1775. The Quaker and Proprietary Interests in Pennsilvania now addressed themselves to Mr. Dickinson, who as well as his Wife were Quakers, and in various Ways stimulated him to oppose my designs and the Independence of the Country: and they succeeded so well that although they could not finally prevent any one of my Measures from being carried into compleat Execution, they made him and his Cousin Charles Thompson, and many others of their Friends, my Ennemies from that time to this 2 April 1805. Hence one of the most considerable Causes of Mr. Jeffersons Success in 1801. In some of the earlier deliberations in Congress in May 1775, after I had reasoned at some Length on my own Plan, Mr. John Rutledge in more than one public Speech, approved of my Sentiments and the other Delegates from that State Mr. Lynch, Mr. Gadsden and Mr. Edward Rutledge appeared to me to be of the same Mind. Mr. Dickinson himself told me afterwards, that when We first came together, the Ballance lay with South Carolina. Accordingly all their Efforts were employed, to convert the Delegates from that State. Mr. Charles Thompson, who was then rather inclined [to] our Side of the Question, told me, that the Quakers had intimidated Mr. Dickinsons Mother, and his Wife, who were continually distressing him with their remonstrances. His Mother said to him "Johnny you will be hanged, your Estate will be forfeited and confiscated, you will leave your Excellent Wife a Widow and your charming Children Orphans, Beggars and infamous." From my Soul I pitied Mr. Dickinson. I made his case my own. If my Mother and my Wife had expressed such Sentiments to me, I was certain, that if they did not wholly unman me and make me an Apostate, they would make me the most miserable Man alive. I was very happy that my Mother and my Wife and my Brothers, My Wifes Father and Mother, and Grandfather Col. John Quincy and his Lady, Mr. Norton Quincy, Dr. Tufts, Mr. Cranch and all her near Relations as well as mine, had uniformly been of my Mind, so that I always enjoyed perfect Peace at home.... The Proprietary Gentlemen, Israel Pemberton and other principal Quakers, now united with Mr. Dickenson, addressed themselves with great Art and Assiduity to all the Members of Congress whom they could influence, even to some of the Delegates of Massachusetts: but most of all to the Delegates from South Carolina. Mr. Lynch had been an old Acquaintance of the Penn Family particularly of the Governor. Mr. Edward Rutledge had brought his Lady with him, a Daughter of our former President Middleton. Mr. Arthur Middleton her Brother was now a Delegate in place of his Father.[1] The Lady and the Gentlemen were invited to all Parties and were visited perpetually by the Party, and We soon began to find that Mr. Lynch, Mr. Arthur Middleton, and even the two Rutledges, began to waver and to clamour about Independence. Mr. Gadsden was either, from despair of success, never attempted: or if he was he received no impression from them. I became the dread and terror and Abhorrence of the Party. But all this I held in great contempt. Arthur Middleton became the Hero of Quaker and Proprietary Politicks in Congress. He had little Information and less Argument: in rudeness and Sarcasm his fort lay, and he played off this Artillery without reserve. I made it a rule to return him a Rowland for every Oliver, so that he never got and I never lost any thing from these Rencounters. We soon parted never to see each other more, I believe without a Spark of malice on either Side: for he was an honest and generous fellow with all his Zeal in this cause. The Party made me as unpopular as they could, among all their connections, but I regarded none of these Things. I knew and lamented that many of these Gentlemen, of great Property, high in Office, and of good Accomplishments, were laying the foundations, not of any Injury to me, but of their own ruin, and it was not in my Power to prevent it. When the Party had prepared the Members of Congress, for their purpose, and indeed had made no small impression on three of my own Colleagues, Mr. Dickinson made or procured to be made a Motion for a second ⟨Address⟩ Petition to the King to be sent by Mr. Richard Penn, who was then bound on a Voyage to England. The Motion was introduced and supported by long Speeches. I was opposed to it, of course; and made an Opposition to it, in as long a Speech as I commonly made, not having ever been remarkable for very long Harrangues, in Answer to all the Arguments which had been urged. When I satt down, Mr. John Sullivan arose, and began to argue on the same side with me, in a strain of Wit, Reasoning and fluency which allthough he was

---

[1] Edward Rutledge's wife was Henrietta, daughter of Henry Middleton, who had served as president of Congress during the last few days of the session of 1774. Henry Middleton's son Arthur did not succeed his father in the Continental Congress until the spring of 1776 (Burnett, ed., *Letters of Members,* 1:lxiii)—a circumstance suggesting that in the present account of opinions for and against independence in 1775 JA is to some extent anticipating the events and opinions of early 1776.

always fluent, exceeded every Thing I had ever heard from him before. I was much delighted and Mr. Dickinson very much terrified at what he said and began to tremble for his Cause. At this moment I was called out to the State house Yard, very much to my regret, to some one who had business with me. I took my hat and went out of the Door of Congress Hall: Mr. Dickinson observed me and darted out after me. He broke out upon me in a most abrupt and extraordinary manner.[2] In as violent a passion as he was capable of feeling, and with an Air, Countenance and Gestures as rough and haughty as if I had been a School Boy and he the Master, he vociferated out, "What is the Reason Mr. Adams, that you New Englandmen oppose our Measures of Reconciliation. There now is Sullivan in a long Harrangue following you, in a determined Opposition to our Petition to the King. Look Ye! If you dont concur with Us, in our pacific System, I, and a Number of Us, will break off, from you in New England, and We will carry on the Opposition by ourselves in our own Way." I own I was shocked with this Magisterial Salutation. I knew of no Pretensions Mr. Dickenson had, to dictate to me more that I had to catechise him. I was however as it happened, at that moment, in a very happy temper, and I answered him very coolly. "Mr. Dickenson, there are many Things that I can very chearfully sacrifice to Harmony and even to Unanimity: but I am not to be threatened into an express Adoption or Approbation of Measures which my Judgment reprobates. Congress must judge, and if they pronounce against me, I must submit, as if they determine against You, You ought to acquiesce."—These were the last Words which ever passed between Mr. Dickinson and me in private. We continued to debate in Congress upon all questions publickly, with all our usual Candor and good humour. But the Friendship and Acquaintance was lost forever by an unfortunate Accident, which must now be explained. The more I reflected on Mr. Dickinsons rude Lecture in the State house Yard the more I was vexed with it, and the determination of Congress, in favour of the Petition, did not allay the irritation. A young Gentleman from Boston, Mr. Hitchbourne, whom I had known as a Clerk in Mr. Fitch's office, but with whom I had no Particular connection or Acquaintance, had been for some days soliciting me, to give him Letters to my Friends in the Massachusetts. I was so much engaged in the Business of Congress in the day time and in consultations with the Members on Evenings and Mornings that I could not find time to write a Line. He came to me

---

[2] On the quarrel between Dickinson and JA and its spectacular consequences in the summer of 1775, see Diary entry of 16 Sept. 1775 and note 1 there.

at last and said he was immediately to sett off, on his Journey home, and begged I would give him some Letters. I told him I had not been able to write any. He prayed I would write if it were only a Line to my Family, for he said, as he had served his Clerkship with Mr. Fitch he was suspected and represented as a Tory, and this Reputation would be his ruin, if it could not [be] corrected, for nobody would employ him at the Bar. If I would only give him, the slightest Letters to any of my Friends, it would give him the Appearance of having my Confidence, and would assist him in acquiring what he truly deserved the Character of a Whigg. To get rid of his importunity, I took my Penn, and wrote a very few Lines to my Wife and about an equal Number to General James Warren. Irritated with the Unpoliteness of Mr. Dickinson and more mortified with his Success in Congress, I wrote something like what has been published. But not exactly. The British Printers made it worse, than it was in the Original. Mr. Hitchbourne was intercepted in crossing Hudsons River by the Boats from a British Man of War, and my Letters, instead of being destroyed, fell into the hands of the Ennemy, and [were] immediately printed, with a little garbling.[3] They thought them a great Prize. The Ideas of Independence, to be sure were glaring enough, and they thought they should produce quarrells among the Members of Congress, and a division of the Colonies. Me they expected utterly to ruin because, as they represented, I had explicitly avowed my designs of Independence. I cared nothing for this. I had made no secret in or out of Congress of my Opinion that Independence was become indispensable; and I was perfectly sure, that in a little time the whole Continent would be of my Mind. I rather rejoiced in this as a fortunate Circumstance, that the Idea was held up to the whole World, and that the People could not avoid contemplating it and reasoning about it. Accordingly from this time at least if not earlier, and not from the publication of "Common Sense" did the People in all parts of the Continent turn their Attention to this Subject. It was, I know, considered in the same Light by others.

---

[3] Hichborn was captured at Conanicut Ferry in Narragansett Bay, not on the Hudson. It cannot be shown that the British or anyone else doctored the texts of the intercepted letters unless the original letters (both dated 24 July 1775) can be found and compared with the newspaper versions. So far they have eluded searches in all likely repositories. A letter from Benjamin Harrison in Congress to George Washington in camp, also captured on Hichborn's person, *was* doctored when printed; see Allen French, "The First George Washington Scandal," MHS, *Procs.*, 65 (1932–1936): 460–474. But JA never pointed out any specific passage that was tampered with, and seems to have accepted unhesitatingly those passages in his letters that raised the greatest outcry.

I met Colonel Reed soon afterwards, who was then General Washingtons Secretary, who mentioned those Letters to me and said, that Providence seemed to have thrown these Letters before the Public for our good: for Independence was certainly inevitable and it was happy that the whole Country had been compelled to turn their Thoughts upon it, that it might not come upon them presently by Surprize....[4] There were a few Expressions which hurt me, when I found the Ennemy either misunderstood them or willfully misrepresented them. The Expressions were Will your Judiciary Whip and hang without Scruple. This they construed to mean to excite Cruelty against the Tories, and get some of them punished with Severity. Nothing was farther from my Thoughts. I had no reference to Tories in this. But as the Exercise of Judicial Powers without Authority from the Crown, would be probably the most offensive Act of Government to Great Britain and the least willingly pardoned, my Question meant no more than "Will your Judges have fortitude enough to inflict the severe punishments when necessary as Death upon Murderers and other capital Criminals, and flaggellation upon such as deserve it."[5] Nothing could be more false and injurious to me, than the imputation of any sanguinary Zeal against the Tories, for I can truly declare that through the whole Revolution and from that time to this I never committed one Act of Severity against the Tories. On the contrary I was a constant Advocate for all the Mercy and Indulgence consistent with our Safety. Some Acts of Treachery as well as Hostility, were combined together in so atrocious a manner that Pardon could not be indulged. But, as it happened, in none of these had I any particular concern.... In a very short time after the Publication of these Letters I received one from General Charles Lee, then in the Army in the neighbourhood of Boston, in which, after expressing the most obliging Sentiments of my Character, he said some Gentlemen had hinted to him, that I might possibly apprehend that he would take Offence at them: But he assured me he was highly pleased with what was said of him in them. The Acknowledgement from me, that he was a Soldier and a Schollar, he esteemed as an honor done to him:

[4] For approving comments by Reed in letters to others at the time, see William B. Reed, *Life and Correspondence of Joseph Reed*, Phila., 1847, 1:118, 120). But Reed agreed with JA because he believed a firm stand was the only possible means of attaining "peace and reconciliation"; he was far from an advocate of independence in the summer of 1775; and the present passage is thus another example of JA's habitual anachronism.

[5] Considerations of this kind had marked bearing on JA's acceptance of the post of chief justice of Massachusetts later this year; see p. 359–363, below.

and as to his Attachment to his Dogs, when he should discover in Men as much Fidelity, Honesty and Gratitude as he daily experienced in his Dogs, he promised to love Men as well as Dogs.[6] Accordingly the Cordiality between him and me continued, till his Death.

This Measure of Imbecility, the second Petition to the King embarrassed every Exertion of Congress: it occasioned Motions and debates without End for appointing Committees to draw up a declaration of the Causes, Motives, and Objects of taking Arms, with a view to obtain decisive declarations against Independence &c.[7] In the Mean time the New England Army investing Boston, the New England Legislatures, Congresses and Conventions, and the whole Body of the People, were left, without Munitions of War, without Arms, Cloathing, Pay or even Countenance and Encouragement. Every Post brought me Letters, from my Friends Dr. Winthrop, Dr. Cooper, General James Warren: and sometimes from General Ward and his Aids and General Heath and many others, urging in pathetic terms, the impossibility of keeping their Men together, without the Assistance of Congress. I was daily urging all these Things but We were embarassed with more than one Difficulty. Not only the Party in favour of the Petition to the King, and the Party who were jealous of Independence, but a third Party, which was a Southern Party against a Northern and a Jealousy against a New England Army under the Command of a New England General. Whether this Jealousy was sincere, or whether it was mere pride and a haughty Ambition, of furnishing a Southern General to command the northern Army. But the Intention was very visible to me, that Col. Washington was their Object, and so many of our staunchest Men were in the Plan that We could carry nothing without conceeding to it. Another Embarrassment which was never publickly known, and which was carefully concealed by those who knew it. The Massachusetts Delegates and other New England Delegates were divided. Mr. Hancock and Mr. Cushing hung back. Mr. Paine did not come forward, and even Mr. Samuel Adams was irresolute. Mr. Hancock himself had an Ambition to be appointed Commander in Chief. Whether he thought, An Election, a Compliment due to him and intended to have the honor of declining it or whether he would have accepted I know not. To the Compliment he had some Pretensions, for at that time his Exertions, Sacrifices and general Merit in the Cause of his Country, had been incomparably

---

[6] See Lee to JA, 5 Oct. 1775 (Adams Papers; JA, *Works*, 2:414, note).
[7] For the papers alluded to here, adopted by Congress in July 1775, see the texts and commentary in Jefferson, *Papers*, ed. Boyd, 1:187–223.

greater than those of Colonel Washington. But the Delicacy of his health, and his entire Want of Experience in actual Service, though an excellent Militia Officer, were decisive Objections to him in my Mind. In canvassing this Subject out of Doors, I found too that even among the Delegates of Virginia there were difficulties. The Apostolical Reasonings among themselves which should be greatest, were not less energetic Among the Saints of the Ancient dominion, than they were among Us of New England. In several Conversations I found more than one very cool about the Appointment of Washington, and particularly Mr. Pendleton was very clear and full against.[8] Full of Anxieties concerning these Confusions, and apprehending daily that We should he[a]r very distressing News from Boston, I walked with Mr. Samuel Adams in the State house Yard, for a little Exercise and fresh Air, before the hour of Congress, and there represented to him the various dangers that surrounded Us. He agreed to them all, but said what shall We do? I answered him, that he knew I had taken great pains to get our Colleagues to agree upon some plan that We might be unanimous: but he knew that they would pledge themselves to nothing: but I was determined to take a Step, which should compell them and all the other Members of Congress, to declare themselves for or against something. I am determined this Morning to make a direct Motion that Congress should adopt the Army before Boston and appoint Colonel Washington Commander of it. Mr. Adams seemed to think very seriously of it, but said Nothing.—Accordingly When congress had assembled I rose in my place and in as short a Speech as the Subject would admit, represented the State of the Colonies, the Uncertainty in the Minds of the People, their great Expectations and Anxiety, the distresses of the Army, the danger of its dissolution, the difficulty of collecting another, and the probability that the British Army would take Advantage of our delays, march out of Boston and spread desolation as far as they could go.[9] I concluded with a Motion in form that Congress would Adopt the Army at Cambridge and appoint a General, that though this was not the proper time to nominate a General, yet as I had reason to believe this was a point of the greatest difficulty, I had no hesitation to declare that I had but

[8] No evidence confirming this statement about Pendleton is known to the editors.

[9] This speech and the motion that followed it must have been made on 14 June or a day or two earlier. Since they were made in a committee of the whole on "the state of America," which had been deliberating some days, there is no record of them in the Journal. But on the 14th Congress did, in effect, "adopt the Army before Boston" (*JCC*, 2:89–90). On the following day "George Washington, Esq. was unanimously elected" commander in chief (same, p. 91).

one Gentleman in my Mind for that important command, and that was a Gentleman from Virginia who was among Us and very well known to all of Us, a Gentleman whose Skill and Experience as an Officer, whose independent fortune, great Talents and excellent universal Character, would command the Approbation of all America, and unite the cordial Exertions of all the Colonies better than any other Person in the Union. Mr. Washington, who happened to sit near the Door, as soon as he heard me allude to him, from his Usual Modesty darted into the Library Room. Mr. Hancock, who was our President, which gave me an Opportunity to observe his Countenance, while I was speaking on the State of the Colonies, the Army at Cambridge and the Ennemy, heard me with visible pleasure, but when I came to describe Washington for the Commander, I never remarked a more sudden and sinking Change of Countenance. Mortification and resentment were expressed as forcibly as his Face could exhibit them. Mr. Samuel Adams Seconded the Motion, and that did not soften the Presidents Phisiognomy at all. The Subject came under debate and several Gentlemen declared themselves against the Appointment of Mr. Washington, not on Account of any personal Objection against him: but because the Army was all from New England, had a General of their own, appeared to be satisfied with him and had proved themselves able to imprison the British Army in Boston, which was all they expected or desired at that time. Mr. Pendleton of Virginia [and] Mr. Sherman of Connecticutt were very explicit in declaring this Opinion, Mr. Cushing and several others more faintly expressed their Opposition and their fears of discontent in the Army and in New England. Mr. Paine expressed a great Opinion of General Ward and a strong friendship for him, having been his Classmate at Colledge, or at least his contemporary: but gave no Opinion upon the question. The Subject was postponed to a future day. In the mean time, pains were taken out of doors to obtain a Unanimity, and the Voices were generally so clearly in favour of Washington that the dissentient Members were persuaded to withdraw their Opposition, and Mr. Washington was nominated, I believe by Mr. Thomas Johnson of Maryland, unanimously elected, and the Army adopted. The next Question was who should be the Second Officer. General Lee was nominated, and most strenuously Urged by many, particularly Mr. Mifflin who said that General Lee would serve chearfully under Washington, but considering his Rank, Character and Experience could not be expected to serve under any other. That Lee must be aut secundus, aut nullus.— To this I as strenuously objected. That it would be a great deal to expect of General Ward that he should serve under any Man, but that under a stranger he ought not to serve. That though I had as high an Opinion of General Lees Learning, general Information and especially of his Science and experience in War, I could not advize General Ward to humiliate himself and his Country so far as to serve under him.—General Ward was elected the second and Lee the third. Gates and Mifflin, I believe had some Appointments, and General Washington took with him Mr. Reed of Philadelphia, a Lawyer of some Eminence for his private Secretary. And the Gentlemen all sett off for the Camp. They had not proceeded twenty miles from Philadelphia before they met a Courier with the News of the Battle of Bunkers Hill, the Death of General Warren, the Slaughter among the British Officers and Men as well as among ours and the burning of Charlestown. Mr. Hancock however never loved me so well after this Event as he had done before, and he made me feel at times the Effects of his resentment and of his Jealousy in many Ways and at diverse times, as long as he lived, though at other times according to his variable feelings, he even overacted his part in professing his regard and respect to me. Hitherto no Jealousy had ever appeared between Mr. Samuel Adams and me. But many Years had not passed away before some Symptoms of it appeared in him, particularly when I was first chosen to go to Europe, a distinction that neither he nor Mr. Hancock could bear. Mr. Adams however disguised it under a pretence that I could not be spared from Congress and the State. More of this Spirit appeared afterwards, when I had drawn up at his and Mr. Bowdoins desire a Constitution for Massachusetts, and it was about to be reported in my hand Writing. But after the Coalition between Mr. Hancock and him in 1788, both these Gentlemen indulged their Jealousy so far as to cooperate in dissiminating Prejudices against me, as a Monarchy Man and a Friend to England, for which I hope they have been forgiven, in Heaven as I have constantly forgiven them on Earth, though they both knew the insinuations were groundless.

I have always imputed the Loss of Charleston, and of the brave Officers and Men who fell there, and the Loss of an Hero of more Worth than all the Town, I mean General Warren, to Mr. Dickinsons petition to the King, and the Loss of Quebec and Mongomery to his subsequent unceasing though finally unavailing Efforts against Independence. These impeded and parrallized all our Enterprizes. Had our Army been acknowledged in Season, which Acknowledgement ought to have been our first Step, and the measures taken to comfort and encourage it, which ought to have been taken by Congress, We should not have lost Charleston, and if every Measure for the Service in Canady, from the first Projection of it to the final Loss of the Province, had not been opposed, and obstinately disputed by the same party, so that We could finally carry no measure but by a bare Majority.[1] And every Measure was delayed, till it became ineffectual. In the fall of the Year Congress were much fatigued with the Incessant Labours, Debates, Intrigues, and heats of the Summer and agreed on a short Adjournment.[2] The Delegates from Massachusetts returned home, and as the two Houses of the Legislature had chosen Us all into the Council we went to Watertown and took our Seats: for such times as We could spare before our return to Congress. I had been chosen before, two Years sucessively, that is in 1773 and 1774 and been negatived by the Governor, the first time by Hutchinson and the second by Gage. My Friend Dr. Cooper attempted to console me under the first Negative, which he called a Check: but I told him I considered it not as a Check but as a Boost, a Word of John Bunyan which the Dr. understood. These negatives were indeed no mortification to me for knowing that neither honor nor profit were to be obtained, nor good to be done in that Body in these times I had not a wish to sit there. When a Person came running to my Office to tell me of the first of them, I cryed out laughing Now I believe in my Soul I am a clever fellow, since I have the Attestation of the three Branches of the Legislature. This vulgar, familiar little Sally was caught as if it had been a prize, and immediately scattered all over the Province.

Mr. Hancock came home, but would not call upon General Washington. Dr. Cooper told me, he was so offended, that Washington was appointed instead of himself, that his friends had the utmost difficulty to appease him. I went to head Quarters and had much Conversation with General Washington, Ward, Lee, Putnam, Gates, Mifflin and others, and went with General Lee to visit the Outposts and the Centinells, nearest the Ennemy at Charleston. Here Lee found his Dogs inconvenient, for they were so attached to him that they insisted on keeping close about him, and he expected he should be known by them to the British officers in the Fort, and he expected every moment a discharge of Balls, Grape or Langredge[3] about our Ears. After visiting

[1] This fragmentary sentence requires some such concluding clause as "we would not have lost Canada."

[2] Congress adjourned on 1 or 2 Aug., to meet again on 5 Sept. (JCC, 2:239; see also note on Diary entry of 1 Aug.

1775 [Mrs. Yard's Bill]).

[3] Langrage: "Case-shot loaded with pieces of iron of irregular shape, formerly used in naval warfare to damage the rigging and sails of the enemy" (OED).

my friends, and the General Court, the Army and the Country, I returned to Philadelphia, but not till I had followed My youngest Brother to the Grave. He had commanded a Company of Militia all Summer at Cambridge, and there taken a fatal Dissentary then epidemic in the Camp of which he died leaving a young Widow and three Young Children, who are all still living. My Brother died greatly lamented by all who knew him and by none more than by me, who knew the excellence of his heart and the purity of his Principles and Conduct. He died as Mr. Taft, his Minister informed me exulting, as his Father had done, in the exalted hopes of [a] Christian.[4]

An Event of the most trifling nature in Appearance, and fit only to excite Laughter, in other Times, struck me into a profound Reverie, if not a fit of Melancholly. I met a Man who had sometimes been my Client, and sometimes I had been against him. He, though a common Horse Jockey, was sometimes in the right, and I had commonly been successfull in his favour in our Courts of Law. He was always in the Law, and had been sued in many Actions, at almost every Court. As soon as he saw me, he came up to me, and his first Salutation to me was "Oh! Mr. Adams what great Things have you and your Colleagues done for Us! We can never be gratefull enough to you. There are no Courts of Justice now in this Province, and I hope there never will be another!" ...[5] Is this the Object for which I have been contending? said I to myself, for I rode along without any Answer to this Wretch. Are these the Sentiments of such People? And how many of them are there in the Country? Half the Nation for what I know: for half the Nation are Debtors if not more, and these have been in all Countries, the Sentiments of Debtors. If the Power of the Country should get into such hands, and there is great danger that it will, to what purpose have We sacrificed our Time, health and every Thing else? Surely We must guard against this Spirit and these Principles or We shall repent of all our Conduct. However The good Sense and Integrity of the Majority of the great Body of the People, came in to my thoughts for my relief, and the last resource was after all in a good Providence. — How much reason there was for these melancholly reflections, the subsequent times have too fully shewn. Opportunities enough had been presented to me to convince me that a very great Portion of the People of America were debtors: but that enormous Gulf of debt to Great

---

[4] Elihu Adams had marched from Braintree as a captain in Col. Benjamin Lincoln's company during the alarm of 19 April 1775, had participated in the action at Grape Island, off Weymouth, in May, and died on 10 or 11 Aug. (*Mass. Soldiers and Sailors*, 1:45; CFA2, *Three Episodes*, 2:857; AA to JA, 10–11 Aug. 1775, Adams Papers).
[5] Suspension points in MS.

Britain from Virginia and some other States, which have since swallowed up the Harmony of all our Councils, and produced the Tryumph of Principles too nearly resembling those of my Client, was not known to me at that time in a tenth part of its extent. When the Consequences will terminate No Man can say.

At the appointed time, We returned to Philadelphia and Congress were reassembled.[6] Mr. Richard Penn had sailed for England, and carried the Petition, from which Mr. Dickenson and his party expected Relief. I expected none, and was wholly occupied in measures to support the Army and the Expedition into Canada. Every important Step was opposed, and carried by bare Majorities, which obliged me to be almost constantly engaged in debate: but I was not content with all that was done, and almost every day, I had something to say about Advizing the States to institute Governments, to express my total despair of any good from the Petition or any of those Things which were called conciliatory measures. I constantly insisted that all such measures, instead of having any tendency to produce a Reconciliation, would only be considered as proofs of our Timidity and want of Confidence in the Ground We stood on, and would only encourage our Ennemies to greater Exertions against Us. That We should be driven to the Necessity of Declaring ourselves independent States, and that We ought now to be employed in preparing a Plan of Confe[de]ration for the Colonies, and Treaties to be proposed to foreign Powers particularly to France and Spain, that all these Measures ought to be maturely considered, and carefully prepared, together with a declaration of Independence. That these three Measures, Independence, Confederation and Negotiations with foreign Powers, particularly France, ought to go hand in hand, and be adopted all together. That foreign Powers could not be expected to acknowledge Us, till We had acknowledged ourselves and taken our Station, among them as a sovereign Power, and Independent Nation. That now We were distressed for Want of Artillery, Arms, Ammunition, Cloathing and even for Flynts. That the People had no Marketts for their Produce, wanted Cloathing and many other things, which foreign Com-

[6] JA and Samuel Adams traveled together from Watertown and arrived in Philadelphia on 12 Sept.; with a quorum present, Congress resumed its proceedings on the 13th (JCC, 2:240). In the present paragraph JA blended inextricably together measures that were proposed and debated in Congress from Sept. through Dec. 1775 and others that were dealt with after his return to Congress early in Feb. 1776 following a two-month leave of absence. See the Diary entries for the corresponding periods and especially JA's Memorandum of Measures to Be Pursued in Congress, printed in his Diary under date of Feb.? 1776, with the editorial notes there.

merce alone could fully supply, and We could not expect Commerce till We were independent. That the People were wonderfully well united and extreamly Ardent: their was no danger of our wanting Support from them, if We did not discourage them by checking and quenching their Zeal. That there was no doubt, of our Ability to defend the Country, to support the War, and maintain our Independence. We had Men enough, our People were brave and every day improving in all the Exercises and Discipline of War. That we ought immediately to give Permission to our Merchants to fit out Privateers and make reprisals on the Ennemy. That Congress ought to Arm[7] Ships and Commission Officers and lay the foundations of a Navy. That immense Advantages might be derived from this resource. That not only West India Articles, in great Abundance, and British Manufactures of all kinds might be obtained but Artillery, Ammunitions and all kinds of Supplies for the Army. That a System of Measures taken with unanimity and pursued with resolution, would insure Us the Friendship and Assistance of France. Some Gentlemen doubted of the Sentiments of France, thought She would frown upon Us as Rebells and be afraid to countenance the Example. I replied to these Gentlemen, that I apprehended they had not attended to the relative Situation of France and England. That it was the unquestionable Interest of France that the British continental Colonies should be independent. That Britain by the Conquest of Canada and their naval Tryumphs during the last War, and by her vast Possessions in America and the East Indies, was exalted to a height of Power and Preeminence that France must envy and could not endure. But there was much more than pride and Jealousy in the Case. Her Rank, her Consideration in Europe, and even her Safety and Independence was at stake. The Navy of Great Britain was now Mistress of the Seas all over the Globe. The Navy of France almost annihilated. Its Inferiority was so great and obvious, that all the Dominions of France in the West Indies and in the East Indies lay at the Mercy of Great Britain, and must remain so as long as North America belonged to Great Britain, and afforded them so many harbours abounding with Naval Stores and Resources of all kinds and so many Men and Seamen ready to assist them and Man their Ships. That Interest could not lie, that the Interest of France was so obvious, and her Motives so cogent, that nothing but a judicial Infatuation of her Councils could restrain her from embracing Us. That our Negotiations with France ought however, to be conducted with great caution and with all the foresight We

[7] MS: "Arms."

could possibly obtain. That We ought not to enter into any Alliance with her, which should entangle Us in any future Wars in Europe, that We ought to lay it down as a first principle and a Maxim never to be forgotten, to maintain an entire Neutrality in all future European Wars. That it never could be our Interest to unite with France, in the destruction of England, or in any measures to break her Spirit or reduce her to a situation in which she could not support her Independence. On the other hand it could never be our Duty to unite with Britain in too great a humiliation of France. That our real if not our nominal Independence would consist in our Neutrality. If We united with either Nation, in any future War, We must become too subordinate and dependent on that nation, and should be involved in all European Wars as We had been hitherto. That foreign Powers would find means to corrupt our People to influence our Councils, and in fine We should be little better than Puppetts danced on the Wires of the Cabinetts of Europe. We should be the Sport of European Intrigues and Politicks. That therefore in preparing Treaties to be proposed to foreign Powers and in the Instructions to be given to our Ministers, We ought to confine ourselves strictly to a Treaty of Commerce. That such a Treaty would be an ample Compensation to France, for all the Aid We should want from her. The Opening of American Trade, to her would be a vast resource for her Commerce and Naval Power, and a great Assistance to her in protecting her East and West India Possessions as well as her Fisheries: but that the bare dismemberment of the British Empire, would be to her an incalculable Security and Benefit, worth more than all the Exertions We should require of her even if it should draw her into another Eight or ten Years War.—When I first made these Observations in Congress I never saw a greater Impression made upon that Assembly or any other. Attention and Approbation was marked on every Countenance. Several Gentlemen came to me afterwards to thank me for that Speech, particularly Mr. Cæsar Rodney of Delaware and Mr. Duane of New York. I remember those two Gentlemen in particular because both of them said, that I had considered the Subject of foreign Connections more maturely than any Man they had ever heard in America, that I had perfectly digested the Subject, and had removed, Mr. Rodney said all, and Mr. Duane said, the greatest part of his objections to foreign Negotiations. Even Mr. Dickinson said to Gentlemen out of Doors, that I had thrown great light on the subject.

These and such as these were my constant and daily Topicks, sometimes of Reasoning and no doubt often of declamation, from the Meeting of Congress in the Autumn of 1775, through the whole Winter and Spring of 1776.

Many Motions were made, and after tedious discussions lost. I received little Assistance from my Colleagues in all these Contests: three of them, were either inclined to lean towards Mr. Dickinsons System, or at least chose to be silent, and the fourth spoke but rarely in Congress, and never entered into any extensive Arguments, though when he did speak, his Sentiments were clear and pertinent, and neatly expressed. Mr. Richard Henry Lee of Virginia, Mr. Sherman of Connecticutt, and Mr. Gadsden of South Carolina, were always on my Side; and Mr. Chase of Maryland, when he did speak at all, was always powerfull, and generally with Us. Mr. Johnson of Maryland was the most frequent Speaker from that State and while he remained with Us, was inclined to Mr. Dickinson, for some time, but eer long he and all his State came cordially into our System. In the fall of 1776 his State appointed him General of Militia, and he marched to the Relief of General Washington in the Jerseys. He was afterwards chosen Governor of Maryland and he came no more to Congress.

In the Course of this Winter appeared a Phenomenon in Philadelphia *a Star of Disaster* (Disastrous Meteor),[8] I mean Thomas Paine. He came from England, and got into such company as would converse with him, and ran about picking up what Information he could, concerning our Affairs, and finding the great Question was concerning Independence, he gleaned from those he saw the common place Arguments concerning Independence: such as the Necessity of Independence, at some time or other, the peculiar fitness at this time: the Justice of it: the Provocation to it: the necessity of it: our Ability to maintain it &c. &c. Dr. Rush put him upon Writing on the Subject, furnished him with the Arguments which had been urged in Congress an hundred times, and gave him his title of common Sense.[9] In the latter part of Winter, or early in the Spring he came out, with his Pamphlet. The Arguments in favour of Independence I liked very well: but one third of the Book was filled with Arguments from the old Testament, to prove the Unlawfulness of Monarchy, and another Third, in planning a form of Government, for the seperate States in One Assembly, and for the United States, in a Congress. His Arguments from the

[8] Parentheses supplied. JA interlined these two words but did not cross out the words they may have been intended to replace.

[9] For Benjamin Rush's connection with *Common Sense* see Rush's *Autobiography*, p. 113–114, 323, and his *Letters*, 1:95–96; 2:1008. *Common Sense* was first advertised for sale on 9 Jan. 1776 (Richard Gimbel, *Thomas Paine: A Bibliographical Check List of Common Sense*, New Haven, 1956, p. 21).

old Testiment, were ridiculous, but whether they proceeded from honest Ignorance, or foolish Supersti[ti]on on one hand, or from will-full Sophistry and knavish Hypocricy on the other I know not. The other third part relative to a form of Government I considered as flowing from simple Ignorance, and a mere desire to please the demo-cratic Party in Philadelphia, at whose head were Mr. Matlock, Mr. Cannon and Dr. Young.[1] I regretted however, to see so foolish a plan recommended to the People of the United States, who were all waiting only for the Countenance of Congress, to institute their State Gov-ernments. I dreaded the Effect so popular a pamphlet might have, among the People, and determined to do all in my Power, to counter Act the Effect of it. My continued Occupations in Congress, allowed me no time to write any thing of any Length: but I found moments to write a small pamphlet which Mr. Richard Henry Lee, to whom I shewed it, liked[2] so well that he insisted on my permitting him to publish it: He accordingly got Mr. Dunlap to print it, under the Tittle of Thoughts on Government in a Letter from a Gentleman to his Friend.[3] Common Sense was published without a Name: and I

---

[1] Timothy Matlack, James Cannon, and Thomas Young, leaders of the radical party in Pennsylvania during the Revolution; see J. Paul Selsam, *The Pennsylvania Constitution of 1776*, Phila., 1936, *passim*.

[2] MS: "liked it."

[3] *Thoughts on Government: Applicable to the Present State of the American Colonies. In a Letter from a Gentleman to His Friend*, Phila.: John Dunlap, 1776; also a reprint, Boston: John Gill, 1776. Owing to the multiple versions of this production that JA furnished in MS form to friends engaged in constitution-making in several colonies, and owing also to discrepancies in the author's own accounts of it, the facts about its genesis are still imperfectly known. What *is* known is merely summarized here. Fuller discussion must await the publication of *Thoughts on Government* and related writings in Series III of *The Adams Papers*.

The starting point for any inquiry is JA's letter to James Warren, 20 April 1776 (MHi; *Warren-Adams Letters*, 1:230–231), which originally enclosed a copy of the pamphlet as printed in Philadelphia and thus fixes the date of publication as before that date and

probably very shortly before it. JA told Warren, in brief, that two delegates from North Carolina, William Hooper and John Penn, being about to go south to take their seats in a state constitutional convention, had applied separately to him for his advice on a proper constitution. JA "concluded to borrow a little Time from his Sleep and accordingly wrote with his own Hand, a Sketch, which he copied, giving the original to Mr. Hooper and a Copy to Mr. Penn, which they carried to Carolina. Mr. Wythe getting a sight of it, desired a Copy which [JA] made out from his Memory as nearly as he could. Afterwards Mr. Serjeant of New Jersey requested another, which [JA] made out again from Memory, and in this he enlarged and amplified a good deal, and sent it to Princetown. After this Coll. Lee requested the same Favour, but [JA] having written amidst all his Engagements five Copies, or rather five sketches, for no one of them was a Copy of the other, ... was quite weary of the office. To avoid the Trouble of writing any more he borrowed Mr. Wythe's Copy and lent it to Coll. Lee, who has put it under Types and thrown it into the shape you see. It is a Pity it had not thought it best to suppress my name too: but as common Sense when it first appeared was generally by the public ascribed to me or Mr. Samuel Adams, I soon regretted that my name did not appear. Afterward I had a new Edition of it printed with my name and the name of Mr. Wythe of Virginia to whom the Letter was at first intended to have been addressed.[4] The Gentlemen of New York availed themselves of the Ideas in this Morsell in the formation of the Constitution

---

been Mr. Serjeant's Copy, for that is larger and more compleat, perhaps more correct."

JA speaks here of five versions, but he enumerates only four, and the order of their composition clearly was: that for Hooper, that for Penn, that for George Wythe of Virginia, and that for Jonathan Dickinson Sergeant of New Jersey. The only MS version in JA's hand that is now known is the one he wrote for Penn, which later came into the possession of Penn's son-in-law, John Taylor of Caroline, and is now in MHi:Washburn Coll. The date on which the North Carolinians left Philadelphia is well established as 27 March (see Burnett, ed., *Letters of Members*, 1:lviii), so that the two earliest versions must have been prepared before that date. The Wythe and Sergeant versions, both "made out . . . from Memory," must almost certainly have been written after 27 March and probably in the first week or ten days of April, since on the one hand JA sent Sergeant's copy to him in Princeton, where Sergeant arrived about 5 April (same, p. li), and on the other hand Richard Henry Lee had caused the Wythe version to be printed by 20 April (which rendered any more copying superfluous). In later reminiscences JA inverted the order of the several versions he remembered and, as so often when he reminisced, advanced the date of the event in question. See his letter to John Taylor, 9 April 1814, in which he assigned the genesis of the whole series of papers to a conversation with George Wythe one evening in "January 1776, six months before the declaration of Independence," and, curiously, spoke of all the other versions as having been written *after* the letter to Wythe was put into print by Lee

(MHi:Washburn Coll.; JA, *Works*, 10:94–96).

There is a very strong presumption that *no* version of this series of letters on state constitution-making was composed until within a few days of Hooper's and Penn's departure for North Carolina (27 March), for in a letter to AA of 19 March, alluding to the reception of Paine's *Common Sense*, JA said: "It has been very generally propagated through the Continent that I wrote this Pamphlet. But altho I could not have written any Thing in so manly and striking a style, I flatter myself I should have made a more respectable Figure as an Architect, if I had undertaken such a Work. This Writer seems to have very inadequate Ideas of what is proper and necessary to be done in order to form Constitutions for single Colonies, as well as a great Model of Union for the whole" (Adams Papers). The implication is almost overwhelming that JA was about to sit down to do better what he thought Paine had done badly.

The most easily available printed text of *Thoughts on Government* (that is to say, the "Wythe version") is in JA's *Works*, 4:193–200, apparently based on the Philadelphia edition of 1776, with silent corrections by the editor of printer's errors. It is followed (p. 203–209) by a text of the "Penn version," taken from its earliest publication, in John Taylor of Caroline's *Inquiry into the Principles and Policy of the Government of the United States*, Fredericksburg, 1814. A printing of what can only be supposed the "Hooper version" is also known, in the *Southern Literary Messenger*, 13:42–47 (Jan. 1847); it varies markedly from the "Penn version" and helps confirm JA's statement that "no one of them was a Copy of the other."

[4] No such edition has been found.

of that State. And Mr. Lee sent it to the Convention of Virginia when they met to form their Government and it went to North Carolina, New Jersey and other States. Matlock, Cannon, Young and Paine had influence enough however, to get their plan adopted in substance in Georgia and Vermont as well as Pennsilvania. These three States have since found them, such Systems of Anarchy, if that Expression is not a contradiction in terms, that they have altered them and made them more conformable to my plan.—Paine soon after the Appearance of my Pamphlet hurried away to my Lodgings and spent an Evening with me. His Business was to reprehend me for publishing my Pamphlet. Said he was afraid it would do hurt, and that it was repugnant to the plan he had proposed in his Common Sense. I told him it was true it was repugnant and for that reason, I had written it and consented to the publication of it: for I was as much afraid of his Work [as] [5] he was of mine. His plan was so democratical, without any restraint or even an Attempt at any Equilibrium or Counterpoise, that it must produce confusion and every Evil Work. I told him further, that his Reasoning from the Old Testament was ridiculous, and I could hardly think him sincere. At this he laughed, and said he had taken his Ideas in that part from Milton: and then expressed a Contempt of the Old Testament and indeed of the Bible at large, which surprized me. He saw that I did not relish this, and soon check'd himself, with these Words "However I have some thoughts of publishing my Thoughts on Religion, but I believe it will be best to postpone it, to the latter part of Life." This Conversation passed in good humour, without any harshness on either Side: but I perceived in him a conceit of himself, and a daring Impudence, which have been developed more and more to this day...." [6] The third part of Common Sense which relates wholly to the Question of Independence, was clearly written and contained a tollerable Summary of the Arguments which I had been repeating again and again in Congress for nine months. But I am bold to say there is not a Fact nor a Reason stated in it, which had not been frequently urged in Congress. The Temper and Wishes of the People, supplied every thing at that time: and the Phrases, suitable for an Emigrant from New Gate, or one who had chiefly associated with such Company, such as "The Royal Brute of England," "The Blood upon his Soul," and a few others of equal delicacy, had as much Weight with the People as his Arguments. It has been a general Opinion, that this Pamphlet was of great Importance in the Revolution. I doubted it at the time and have

[5] MS: "and."           [6] Suspension points in MS.

doubted it to this day. It probably converted some to the Doctrine of Independence, and gave others an Excuse for declaring in favour of it. But these would all have followed Congress, with Zeal: and on the other hand it excited many Writers against it, particularly plain Truth,[7] who contributed very largely to fortify and inflame the Party against Independence, and finally lost us the Allens, Penns, and many other Persons of Weight in the Community. Notwithstanding these doubts I felt myself obliged to Paine for the Pains he had taken and for his good Intentions to serve Us which I then had no doubt of. I saw he had a capacity and a ready Pen, and understanding he was poor and destitute, I thought We might put him into some Employment, where he might be usefull and earn a Living. Congress appointed a Committee of foreign affairs not long after and they wanted a Clerk. I nominated Thomas Paine, supposing him a ready Writer and an industrious Man. Dr. Witherspoon the President of New Jersey Colledge and then a Delegate from that State rose and objected to it, with an Earnestness that surprized me. The Dr. said he would give his reasons; he knew the Man and his Communications: When he first came over, he was on the other Side and had written pieces against the American Cause: that he had afterwards been employed by his Friend Robert Aitkin, and finding the Tide of Popularity run ⟨pretty strong⟩ rapidly, he had turned about: that he was very intemperate and could not write untill he had quickened his Thoughts with large draughts of Rum and Water: that he was in short a bad Character and not fit to be placed in such a Situation.— General Roberdeau spoke in his favour: no one confirmed Witherspoons Account, though the truth of it has since been sufficiently established. Congress appointed him: but he was soon obnoxious by his Manners, and dismissed.

There was one Circumstance, in his conversation with me about the pamphlets, which I could not Account for. He was extreamly earnest to convince me, that common Sense was his first born: declared again and again that he had never written a Line nor a Word that had been printed before Common Sense. I cared nothing for this but said nothing: but Dr. Witherspoons Account of his Writing against Us, brought doubts into my mind of his Veracity, which the subsequent histories of his Writings and publications in England when he was in the Custom house, did not remove.

[7] *Plain Truth; Addressed to the Inhabitants of America* . . . , Phila., 1776, a reply to *Common Sense* by "Candidus," a pseudonym for James Chalmers (Richard Gimbel, *Thomas Paine: A Bibliographical Check List of Common Sense*, New Haven, 1956, p. 116).

At this day it would be ridiculous to ask any questions about Tom Paines Veracity, Integrity or any other Virtue.

I was incessantly employed, through the whole Fall, Winter and Spring of 1775 and 1776 in Congress during their Sittings and on Committees on mornings and Evenings, and unquestionably did more business than any other Member of that house. In the Beginning of May I procured the Appointment of a Committee, to prepare a resolution recommending to the People of the States to institute Governments. The Committee of whom I was one requested me to draught a resolve which I did and by their Direction reported it. Opposition was made to it, and Mr. Duane called it a Machine to fabricate independence but on the 15th of May 1776 it passed. It was indeed on all hands considered by Men of Understanding as equivalent to a declaration of Independence: tho a formal declaration of it was still opposed by Mr. Dickinson and his Party.[8]

Not long after this the three greatest Measures of all, were carried. Three Committees were appointed, One for preparing a Declaration of Independence, another for reporting a Plan of a Treaty to be proposed to France, and a third to digest a System of Articles of Confederation to be proposed to the States.—I was appointed on the Committee of Independence, and on that for preparing the form of a Treaty with France: on the Committee of Confederation Mr. Samuel Adams was appointed. The Committee of Independence, were Thomas Jefferson, John Adams, Benjamin Franklin, Roger Sherman and Robert R. Livingston. Mr. Jefferson had been now about a Year a Member of Congress, but had attended his Duty in the House but a very small part of the time and when there had never spoken in public: and during the whole Time I satt with him in Congress, I never heard him utter three Sentences together. The most of a Speech he ever made in my hearing was a gross insult on Religion, in one or two Sentences, for which I gave him immediately the Reprehension, which he richly merited.[9] It will naturally be enquired, how it happened that he was appointed on a Committee of such importance. There were more reasons than one. Mr. Jefferson had the Reputation of a masterly Pen. He had been chosen a Delegate in Virginia, in consequence of a very handsome public Paper which he had written for the House of Burgesses, which had given him the Character of a

[8] See Diary entries (Notes of Debates), 13–15 May 1776, and editorial notes there; also the entries in the Autobiography dated 10, 11, 14, 15 May 1776, below.

[9] CFA omitted this sentence from his text of the Autobiography. Nothing beyond what JA says here is known to the present editors concerning such an incident.

fine Writer. Another reason was that Mr. Richard Henry Lee was not beloved by the most of his Colleagues from Virginia and Mr. Jefferson was sett up to rival and supplant him. This could be done only by the Pen, for Mr. Jefferson could stand no competition with him or any one else in Elocution and public debate. Here I will interrupt the narration for a moment to observe that from all I have read of the History of Greece and Rome, England and France, and all I have observed at home, and abroad, that Eloquence in public Assemblies is not the surest road, to Fame and Preferment, at least unless it be used with great caution, very rarely, and with great Reserve. The Examples of Washington, Franklin and Jefferson are enough to shew that Silence and reserve in public are more Efficacious than Argumentation or Oratory. A public Speaker who inserts himself, or is urged by others into the Conduct of Affairs, by daily Exertions to justify his measures, and answer the Objections of Opponents, makes himself too familiar with the public, and unavoidably makes himself Ennemies. Few Persons can bare to be outdone in Reasoning or declamation or Wit, or Sarcasm or Repartee, or Satyr, and all these things are very apt to grow out of public debate. In this Way in a Course of Years, a Nation becomes full of a Mans Ennemies, or at least of such as have been galled in some Controversy, and take a secret pleasure in assisting to humble and mortify him. So much for this digression. We will now return to our Memoirs. The Committee had several meetings, in which were proposed the Articles of which the Declaration was to consist, and minutes made of them. The Committee then appointed Mr. Jefferson and me, to draw them up in form, and cloath them in a proper Dress. The Sub Committee met, and considered the Minutes, making such Observations on them as then occurred: when Mr. Jefferson desired me to take them to my Lodgings and make the Draught. This I declined and gave several reasons for declining. 1 That he was a Virginian and I a Massachusettensian. 2. that he was a southern Man and I a northern one. 3. That I had been so obnoxious for my early and constant Zeal in promoting the Measure, that any draught of mine, would undergo a more severe Scrutiny and Criticism in Congress, than one of his composition. 4thly and lastly and that would be reason enough if there were no other, I had a great Opinion of the Elegance of his pen and none at all of my own. I therefore insisted that no hesitation should be made on his part. He accordingly took the Minutes and in a day or two produced to me his Draught. Whether I made or suggested any corrections I remember not. The Report was made to the Committee of five, by them examined, but whether altered or corrected in any thing I cannot recollect. But in substance at least it was reported to Congress where, after a severe Criticism, and striking out several of the most oratorical Paragraphs it was adopted on the fourth of July 1776, and published to the World.[1]

The Committee for preparing the Model of a Treaty to be proposed to France consisted of[2]                     When We met to deliberate on the Subject, I contended for the same Principles, which I had before avowed and defended in Congress, viz. That We should avoid all Alliance, which might embarrass Us in after times and involve Us in future European Wars. That a Treaty of commerce, which would opperate as a Repeal of the British Acts of Navigation as far as respected Us and Admit France into an equal participation of the benefits of our commerce; would encourage her Manufactures, increase her Exports of the Produce of her Soil and Agriculture, extend her navigation and Trade, augment her resources of naval Power, raise her from her present deep humiliation, distress and decay, and place her on a more equal footing with England, for the protection of her foreign Possessions, and maintaining her Independence at Sea, would be an ample Compensation to France for Acknowledging our

[1] This casual account of the drafting and adoption of the Declaration of Independence, 11 June – 4 July 1776, was elaborated, though not contradicted in any essential way, by JA in a letter to Timothy Pickering written at the latter's request and dated 6 Aug. 1822 (LbC, Adams Papers; *Works*, 2:512, note). Pickering quoted passages from JA's letter in remarks he made at a Fourth of July celebration in Salem the following year; they were printed in *Col. Pickering's Observations Introductory to Reading the Declaration of Independence ...*, Salem, 1823, and thus soon came to Jefferson's attention (Pickering and Upham, *Pickering*, 4:335, 463–469). In a letter to Madison, 30 Aug. 1823, Jefferson gave a very different account of the composition of his great state paper from that which JA had furnished Pickering. He denied both that there had been any subcommittee and that it was JA who had urged him to draft the document. It was rather, said Jefferson, the committee of five as a whole that "unanimously pressed on myself alone to undertake the draught," though before reporting back to the full committee, Jefferson added, he com-

municated the text separately to both Franklin and JA, "because they were the two members of whose judgments and amendments I wished most to have the benefit" (Jefferson, *Writings*, ed. Ford, 10:267). Exhaustive textual study and the discovery of further documents have greatly amplified both JA's and Jefferson's accounts and corrected them in some respects, but the principal points on which they disagreed have not been and may never be resolved.

See, further, the entries in JA's Autobiography dated 7, 11 June, 1 July 1776, below.

[2] Here two-thirds of a line was left blank in the MS, doubtless indicating that JA intended to consult the *Journals of Congress* (which were on his shelves) and fill in the names. The members of "the committee to prepare a plan of treaties to be proposed to foreign powers," appointed on 12 June, were Dickinson, Franklin, JA, Harrison, and Robert Morris (JCC, 5:433). JA himself listed the names of the committee members when he went over this ground later in his Autobiography with the *Journals* in hand; see a later entry under 12 June 1776, below.

Independence, and for furnishing Us for our money or upon Credit for a Time, with such Supplies of Necessaries as We should want, even if this Conduct should involve her in a War. If a War should ensue, which did not necessarily follow, for a bare Acknowledgement of our Independence after We had asserted it, was not by the Law of Nations an Act of Hostility, which would be a legitimate cause of War. Franklin although he was commonly as silent on committees as in Congress, upon this Occasion, ventured so far as to intimate his concurrence with me in these Sentiments, though as will be seen hereafter he shifted them as easily as the Wind ever shifted: and assumed a dogmatical Tone, in favour of an Opposite System. The Committee after as much deliberation upon the Subject as they chose to employ, appointed me, to draw up a Plan and Report. Franklin had made some marks with a Pencil against some Articles in a printed Volume of Treaties, which he put into my hand. Some of these were judiciously selected, and I took them with others which I found necessary into the Draught and made my report to the Committee at large, who after a reasonable Examination of it, agreed to report it. When it came before Congress, it occupied the Attention of that Body for several days. Many Motions were made, to insert in it Articles of entangling Alliance, of exclusive Priviledges, and of Warrantees of Possessions: and it was argued that the present Plan reported by the Committee held out no sufficient temptation to France, who would despize it and refuse to receive our Ambassador. It was chiefly left to me to defend my report, though I had some able Assistance, and We did defend it with so much Success, that the Treaty passed without one Particle of Alliance, exclusive Priviledge, or Warranty.[3]

I have omitted some things in 1775 which must be inserted.[4] On

[3] JA's draft of the "Plan of Treaties," a document which "furnished the model for all, except one, of the eighteenth-century treaties of the United States, and may be regarded as a charter document of early American maritime practice" (Bemis, *Diplomacy of the Amer. Revolution*, p. 46), is in PCC, No. 47, and is printed, with appended forms of passports, &c., also drafted by JA, in JCC, 5:576–589, under date of 18 July 1776, when it was reported to Congress. On 20 July Congress ordered it printed for the use of the members; on 22 and 27 Aug. it was debated in committee of the whole and on the latter date, after amendments, referred back to the original committee for the purpose of drawing up instructions to agents to be sent to France. On 17 Sept. it was adopted in its final form as a "plan of a treaty [to] be proposed to His Most Christian Majesty" (same, p. 768–779; see also p. 594, 696, 709–710, 718, and entry No. 121 in "Bibliographical Notes," same, 6:1124). JA's present summary of his arguments for the Plan probably pertains to the debates in committee of the whole late in August.

[4] JA was reminded of these omissions by picking up a copy of the *Journals of Congress. Containing the Proceedings from Sept. 5. 1774. to Jan. 1. 1776*

the 18th of September 1775. It was resolved in Congress, that a Secret Committee be appointed to contract for the Importation and delivery of any quantity of Gunpowder, not exceeding five hundred Tons. That in case such a quantity of Gunpowder cannot be procured to contract for the Importation of so much Saltpetre, with a proportionable quantity of Sulphur, as with the Powder procured will make five hundred tons. That the Committee be impowered to contract for the importation of forty brass field Pieces, six pounders, for 10,000 Stand of Arms and twenty thousand good plain double bridle musket Locks. That the said Committee be impowered to draw on the Treasurers to answer the said Contract. That the said Committee consist of nine members, any five of whom to be a quorum. The Members chosen Mr. Willing, Mr. Franklin, Mr. Livingston, Mr. Alsop, Mr. Deane, Mr. Dickinson, Mr. Langdon, Mr. McKean and Mr. Ward. On the Eig[h]th of November 1775. On Motion resolved That the Secret Committee appointed to contract for the Importation of Arms, Ammunition &c. be impowered to export to the foreign West Indies, on Account and risque of the Continent, as much provision, or any other produce (except horned Cattle, Sheep, hogs and Poultry) as they may deem necessary for the Importation of Arms, Ammunition, Sulphur and Saltpetre. See the Journals of Congress for 1775. Page 238. Wednesday November 8. 1775 and the Note.

On Wednesday November 29. 1775. (See Journals of Congress for the Year 1775 page 272. and 273.) It was resolved that a Committee of five be appointed for the sole purpose of corresponding with our Friends in Great Britain, Ireland and other parts of the World, and that they lay their Correspondence before Congress when directed. Resolved that Congress will make provision to defray all such Expenses as may arise by carrying on such a Correspondence and for the payment of such Agents as they may send on this Service. The Members chosen Mr. Harrison, Dr. Franklin, Mr. Johnson, Mr. Dickinson and Mr. Jay.

---

. . . . *Volume I*, Phila.: R. Aitken, 1777, which he had long owned but until now had not consulted for autobiographical purposes. From this point through his departure from Congress in Oct. 1776, the Autobiography consists almost entirely of a series of extracts from the *Journals*, chosen rather unsystematically but with emphasis on JA's own activities, copied without benefit of quotation marks, and amplified by a running commentary. CFA in his edition distinguished matter drawn from the *Journals* by a smaller size of type (JA, *Works*, 3:3–88), but direct quotations, paraphrased passages, and comments are so inextricably woven together that CFA sometimes erred in trying to disentangle them and thus proved his method unfeasible. The present editors follow JA's MS.

This last provision for an Agent was contrived I presume for Mr. Deane who had been left out of the Delegation by the State, but instead of returning home to Connecticutt, remained in Philadelphia, soliciting an Appointment under the two foregoing Committees, as an Agent of theirs first in the West Indies and then in France. Unfortunately Mr. Deane was not well established at home. The good People of Connecticutt thought him a Man of Talents and Enterprize, but of more Ambition than Principle. He possessed not their Esteem or Confidence. He procured his first Appointment in 1774 to Congress by an Intrigue. Under the pretext of avoiding to committ the Legislature of the State in any Act of Rebellion, he got a Committee ⟨of three⟩ appointed with some discretionary Powers, under which they undertook to appoint the Members to Congress. Mr. Deane being one ⟨of the three⟩ was obliged to Vote for himself, to obtain a Majority of the Committee. On the 3 of November 1774 The Representatives indeed chose Mr. Deane among others, to attend Congress the next May. But on the second Thursday of October 1775 The General Assembly of Governor and Company left him out. On the 16. of Jan. 1776 The New Delegates appeared in Congress. See the Journal Vol. 2. page 24 and 25.[5] To the two Secret Committees, that of Commerce and that of Correspondence, Mr. Deane applied, and obtained of them Appointments as their Agent. Dr. Franklin also gave him private Letters one to Dr. Dubourg of Paris a Physician who had translated his Works into French and Mr. Dumas at the Hague, who had seen him in England. With these Credentials, Mr. Deane went first to the West Indies and then to France. The Use he made of his Powers We shall hereafter see. He was a person of a plausible readiness and Volubility with his Tongue and his Pen, much addicted to Ostentation and Expence in Dress and Living but without any deliberate forecast or reflection or solidity of Judgment, or real Information. The manner in which he made Use of his Powers We shall see hereafter. I had hitherto, however, thought well of his Intentions and had acted with him on terms of entire Civility.

Within a day or two after the Appointment in Congress of the Committee of Correspondence, Mr. Jay came to my Chamber to spend an Evening with me. I was alone, and Mr. Jay opened himself to me, with great frankness. His Object seemed to be, an Apology to me, for my being omitted in the Choice of the two great Secret Com-

[5] This reference is to *Journals of Congress. Containing the Proceedings from January 1, 1776, to January 1, 1777. . . . Volume II*, York-Town [York, Penna.]: John Dunlap, 1778.

mittees of Commerce and Correspondence. He said in express terms, "that my Character stood very high with the Members, and he knew there was but one Thing which prevented me from being universally acknowledged to be the first Man in Congress, and that was this, there was a great Division in the House, and two Men had effected it, Samuel Adams and Richard Henry Lee, and as I was known to be very intimate with those two Gentlemen, many others were jealous of me.".…[6] My Answer to all this was, that I had thought it very strange, and had imputed it to some secret Intrigue out of Doors, that no Member from Massachusetts had been elected on either of those Committees. That I had no Pretensions to the distinction of the first Man in Congress: and that if I had a clear title to it, I should be very far from assuming it, or wishing for it. It was a Station of too much responsibility and danger in the times and Circumstances in which We lived and were destined to live. That I was a Friend very much Attached to Mr. Lee and Mr. Adams, because I knew them to be able Men and inflexible in the cause of their Country. I could not therefore become cool in my friendship for them, for the sake of any distinctions that Congress could bestow. That I believed that too many commercial Projects and private Speculations were in contemplation by the composition of those Committees: but even those had not contributed so much to it, as the great division in the House on the Subject of Independence and the mode of carrying on the War. Mr. Jay and I however parted good Friends and have continued such without interruption to this day 8 of March 1805. There is a Secret in this Business, that ought to be explained. Mr. Arthur Lee in London, had heard some insinuations against Mr. Jay as a suspicious Character, and had written to his Brother Richard Henry Lee or to Mr. Samuel Adams or both: and although they were groundless and injurious, as I have no doubt, my Friends had communicated them too indiscreetly, and had spoken of Mr. Jay too lightly. Mr. Lee had expressed doubts whether Mr. Jay had composed the Address to the People of Great Britain and ascribed it to his Father in Law Mr. Livingston afterwards Governor of New Jersey. These Things had occasioned some Words, and Animosities which Uniting with the great Questions in Congress, had some disagreable Effects. Mr. Jays great Superiority to Mr. Livingston in the Art of Composition would now be sufficient to decide the question if the latter had [not] expressly denied having any share in that Address.[7]

[6] Suspension points in MS.
[7] The negative in this sentence was inadvertently omitted by the diarist. Thirteen years later JA exchanged let-

On Wednesday June 12. 1776 Congress resolved, That a Committee of Congress be appointed by the name of a board of War and Ordinance to consist of five members, with a secretary, Clerks &c. and their extensive Powers are stated, Vol. 2. page 209 of the Journals.[8] On the 13th. Congress having proceeded to the Election of a Committee to form the board of War and ordinance, the following Members were chosen Mr. J. Adams, Mr. Sherman, Mr. Harrison, Mr. Wilson and Mr. E. Rutledge, and Richard Peters Esq. was elected Secretary. The Duties of this Board kept me in continual Employment, not to say Drudgery from this 12 of June 1776 till the Eleventh of November 1777 when I left Congress forever. Not only my Mornings and Evenings were filled up with the Croud of Business before the Board, but a great Part of my time in Congress was engaged in making, explaining and justifying our Reports and Proceedings. It is said there are Lawyers in the United States who receive five thousand Guineas a Year and many are named who are said to receive to the Amount of ten thousand dollars. However this may be I dont believe there is one of them who goes through so much Business, for all his Emoluments as I did for a Year and a half nearly that I was loaded with that office. Other Gentlemen attended as they pleased, but as I was Chairman, or as they were pleased to call it President, I must never be absent.

On Thursday October 5. 1775. See the Journals. Sundry Letters from London were laid before Congress and read, and a motion was made, that it be resolved that a Committee of three be appointed to prepare a Plan for intercepting two Vessells which are on their Way to Canada, laden with Arms and Powder, and that the Committee proceed on this Business immediately. The Secretary has omitted to insert the Names of this Committee on the Journals. But as my Memory has recorded them, they were Mr. Deane, Mr. Langdon and myself, three Members who had expressed much Zeal, in favour of the Motion. As a considerable part of my time, in the Course of my profession, had been spent upon the Sea coast of Massachusetts, in Attending the Courts and Law Suits at Plymouth, Barnstable,

---

ters with John Jay on the authorship of the Address to the People of Great Britain, written by Jay and issued by Congress in Oct. 1774; see JA to Jay, 9 Jan. 1818, LbC, Adams Papers; Jay to JA, 31 Jan. 1818, Adams Papers; both printed in Jay, *Correspondence and Public Papers*, 4:395–402.

[8] Farther on in his Autobiography, in a more intensive review of the record in the *Journals*, JA copied "the Constitution, Powers and Duties of this Board" into his narrative *in extenso;* see a later entry dated 12 June 1776, below.

Marthas Vineyard, to the Southward and in the Counties of Essex, York and Cumberland to the Eastward, I had conversed much with the Gentlemen, who conducted our Cod and Whale Fisheries, as well as the other Navigation of the Country, and had heard much of the Activity, Enterprize, Patience, Perseverance, and daring Intrepidity of our Seamen, I had formed a confident Opinion that if they were once let loose upon the Ocean, they would contribute greatly to the relief of our Wants as well as to the distress of the Ennemy. I became therefore at once, an Ardent Advocate for this motion, which We carried, not without great difficulty. The Opposition to it was very loud and vehement. Some of my own Colleagues, appeared greatly allarmed at it: and Mr. Edward Rutledge never displayed so much Eloquence as against it. He never appeared to me to discover so much Information and Sagacity, which convinced me that he had been instructed out of Doors, by some of the most knowing Merchants and Statesmen in Philadelphia. It would require too much time and space to give this debate at large, if any memory could Attempt it. Mine cannot. It was however represented as the most wild, visionary mad project that ever had been imagined. It was an Infant, taking a mad Bull by his horns. And what was more profound and remote, it was said it would ruin the Character, and corrupt the morals of all our Seamen. It would make them selfish, piratical, mercenary, bent wholly upon plunder, &c. &c. &c. These formidable Arguments and this terrible Rhetoric, were answered by Us by the best Reasons We could alledge, and the great Advantages of distressing the Ennemy, supplying ourselves, and beginning a System of maritime and naval Opperations, were represented in colours as glowing and animating. The Vote was carried, the Committee went out, and returned very soon,[9] brought in the Report, in these Words, The Committee appointed to prepare a plan for intercepting the two Vessells bound to Canada, brought in a Report which was taken into Consideration; whereupon

Resolved, That a Letter be sent to General Washington to inform him that Congress having received certain Intelligence of the Sailing of two north Country built Briggs, of no force, from England, on the eleventh of August last, loaded with Arms, Powder and other Stores for Quebec, without Convoy, which, it being of importance to intercept, desire that he apply to the Council of Massachusetts Bay

[9] On the very same day (5 Oct.). Concerning this and the succeeding actions that JA records here and that initiated the Continental Navy, see his Diary entry (Notes of Debates) of 7 Oct. 1775 and note 1 there.

for the two armed Vessells in their service, and dispatch the same, with a sufficient number of People, Stores &c. particularly a number of Oars, in order, if possible, to intercept the two Briggs and their Cargoes, and secure the same for the Use of the Continent; also any other Transports, laden with Ammunition, Cloathing, or other Stores, for the Use of the Ministerial Army or Navy in America, and secure them in the most convenient places for the purpose abovementioned; that he give the Commander or Commanders such Instructions as are necessary, as also proper Encouragement to the marines and Seamen, that shall be sent on this Enterprize, which Instructions are to be delivered to the Commander or Commanders sealed up, with orders not to open the same, untill out of sight of Land on Account of Secrecy.

That a Letter be written to the said honourable Council, to put the said Vessells under the Generals Command and Direction, and to furnish him instantly with every necessary in their Power, at the Expence of the Continent.

That the General be directed to employ the said Vessells and others, if he judge necessary, to effect the purposes aforesaid; and that he be informed that the Rhode Island and Connecticutt Vessells of Force, will be sent directly to their Assistance.

That a Letter be written to Governor Cooke, informing him of the above, desiring him to dispatch one or both the Armed Vessells of the Colony of Rhode Island on the same Service, and that he Use the Precautions above mentioned.

That a Letter be written to Governor Trumbull, requesting of him the largest Vessell in the Service of the Colony of Connecticutt, to be sent on the Enterprize aforesaid, acquainting him with the above particulars, and recommending the same precautions.

That the said Ships and Vessells of War be on the Continental Risque and pay, during their being so employed.

Fryday October 6. 1775. The Committee appointed to prepare a Plan &c. brought in a further report which was read. Ordered to lie on the Table for the Perusal of the Members.

Fryday October 13. 1775. The Congress taking into Consideration the report of the Committee appointed to prepare a Plan &c. after some debate

Resolved That a swift sailing Vessell to carry ten Carriage Guns, and a proportionable Number of Swivells, with Eighty Men, be fitted with all possible dispatch, for a Cruize of three months, and that the Commander be instructed to cruize eastward, for intercepting such

Transports as may be laden with warlike Stores, and other Supplies for our Ennemies, and for such other purposes as the Congress shall direct. That a Committee of three be appointed to prepare an Estimate of the Expence, and lay the same before Congress, and to contract with proper Persons to fit out the Vessell.

Resolved that another Vessell be fitted out for the same purpose, and that the said Committee report their Opinion of a proper Vessel, and also an Estimate of the Expence. The following Members were chosen to compose the Committee. Mr. Deane, Mr. Langdon and Mr. Gadsden.

Resolved that the further consideration of the Report be referred to Monday next.

Monday October 30th. 1775. The Committee appointed to prepare an Estimate, and to fit out the Vessells, brought in their report, which being taken into Consideration. Resolved that the second Vessell ordered to be fitted out on the 13th. instant, be of such a Size as to carry fourteen Guns, and a proportionate number of Swivels and Men. Resolved that two more Vessels be fitted out with all expedition; the one to carry not exceeding twenty Guns and the other not exceeding thirty six Guns, with a proportionable number of Swivells and Men, to be employed in such manner for the protection and defence of the United Colonies, as the Congress shall direct. Resolved that four Members be chosen and added to the former Committee of three, and that these seven be a Committee to carry into Execution, with all possible Expedition, as well the Resolutions of Congress passed the thirteenth Instant, as those passed this day for fitting our armed Vessells. The Members chosen, Mr. Hopkins, Mr. Hewes, Mr. Richard Henry Lee and Mr. John Adams. This Committee immediately procured a Room in a public house in the City, and agreed to meet every Evening at six o Clock in order to dispatch this Business with all possible celerity.

On Thursday November 2. 1775 Congress resolved that the Committee appointed to carry into Execution the Resolves of Congress for fitting out four armed Vessells, be authorized to draw on the Continental Treasurers from time to time, for as much cash as shall be necessary for the above Purpose, not exceeding the Sum of one hundred thousand dollars, and that the said Committee have Power to agree, with such Officers and Seamen as are proper to man and command said Vessells, and that the Encouragement to such Officers and Seamen be, One half of all Ships of War made prize of by them, and one third of all transport Vessels, exclusive of Wages.

On the 8th of November 1775 Congress resolved, that the Bills of Sale of the Vessells ordered to be purchased, be made to the Continental Treasurers, or those who shall succeed them in that Office, in trust never the less for the Use of the Continent or their Representatives, in Congress met.

On the 10th of November 1775 Congress resolved that two Battalions of Marines be raised, consisting of one Colonel, two Lieutenant Colonels, two Majors, and other Officers as usual in other regiments; that they consist of an equal Number of privates with other Battalions; that particular care be taken, that no Person be appointed to Officers, or inlisted into said Battalion[s], but such as are good Seamen or so acquainted with maritime Affairs, as to be able to serve to Advantage by Sea when required: that they be inlisted and commissioned to serve for and during the present War between Great Britain and the Colonies, unless dismissed by order of Congress; that they be distinguished by the names of the first and second Battalions of American Marines, and that they be considered as part of the number which the Continental Army before Boston is ordered to consist of. Ordered that a Copy of the above, be transmitted to the General.

On the 17th of November 1775. A Letter from Gen. Washington, inclosing a Letter and Journal of Colonel Arnold, and sundry papers being received, the same were read, whereupon

Resolved that a Committee of seven be appointed to take into Consideration so much of the Generals Letter, as relates to the disposal of such Vessells and Cargoes belonging to the Ennemy, as shall fall into the hands of, or be taken by the Inhabitants of the United Colonies. The Members chosen Mr. Wythe, Mr. E. Rutledge, Mr. J. Adams, Mr. W. Livingston, Dr. Franklin, Mr. Wilson and Mr. Johnson.[1]

Thursday. November 23. 1775. The Committee for fitting out armed Vessells laid before Congress, a draught of Rules for the Government of the American Navy and Articles to be signed by the Officers and Men employed in that Service, which were read and ordered to lie on the Table for the Perusal of the Members.[2]

[1] Washington's letter, 8 Nov. 1775, is printed in his *Writings*, ed. Fitzpatrick, 4:71–75. The report of this committee, recommending the establishment of prize courts, was brought in on 23 Nov., debated the next day, and adopted on the next (JCC, 3:364–365, 368–369, 371–375). JA copied it into his Autobiography under 25 Nov. but did not assert his authorship.

[2] This "draught" was the work of JA. It was debated, probably amended, and adopted by Congress on 28 Nov., and was printed (with some last-minute changes) as *Rules for the Regulation of the Navy of the United Colonies of North-America* ..., Phila.: William and Thomas Bradford, 1775. See JCC, 3:364, 375–376, 378–387, 393, 513. A facsimile reprint of this exceedingly

Saturday November 25. 1775. Congress resumed the consideration of the report of the Committee on General Washingtons Letter, and the same being debated by Paragraphs, was agreed to as follows:

Whereas it appears from undoubted information, that many Vessells which had cleared at the respective Custom houses in these Colonies, agreable to the regulations established by Acts of the British Parliament, have in a lawless manner, without even the semblance of just Authority, been seized by his Majestys Ships of War, and carried into the harbour of Boston and other Ports where they have been rifled of their Cargoes, by orders of his Majestys naval and military officers there commanding, without the said Vessells having been proceeded against, by any form of Tryal, and without the charge of having offended against any Law.

And whereas orders have been issued in his Majestys name, to the Commanders of his Ships of War, "to proceed as in the case of actual rebellion, against such of the Sea port Towns and places being accessible to the Kings Ships, in which any Troops shall be raised, or military Works erected," under colour of which said orders the Commanders of his Majesty's said Ships of War have already burned and destroyed the flourishing and populous Town of Falmouth, and have fired upon and much injured several other Towns within the United Colonies, and dispersed, at a late Season of the Year, hundreds of helpless Women and Children, with a savage hope that those may perish under the approaching rigours of the Season, who may chance to escape destruction from Fire and Sword, a mode of Warfare long exploded among civilized Nations.

And whereas the good People of these Colonies, sensibly affected by the destruction of their property, and other unprovoked Injuries, have at last determined to prevent as much as possible a repetition thereof, and to procure some reparation for the same, by fitting out armed Vessels and Ships of Force; in the Execution of which commendable designs it is possible that those, who have not been instrumental in the unwarrantable violences abovementioned may suffer, unless some Laws be made to regulate, and Trybunals erected competent to determine the Propriety of Captures. Therefor Resolved.

1. That all such Ships of War, Frigates, Sloops, Cutters, and armed Vessels as are or shall be employed in the present cruel and unjust War against the united Colonies, and shall fall into the

---

rare founding document of the United States Navy was issued by the Naval Historical Foundation, Washington, 1944.

hands of, or be taken by the Inhabitants thereof, be seized and forfeited to and for the purposes herein after mentioned.

2. Resolved, That all Transport Vessels in the same Service, having on board any Troops, Arms, Ammunition, Cloathing, Provisions, or military or naval stores of what kindsoever, and all Vessels to whomsoever belonging, that shall be employed in carrying provisions or other necessaries to the British Army or Armies, or navy, that now are or hereafter may be, within any of the United Colonies, or any Goods, Wares, or Merchandizes for the Use of such fleet or Army, shall be liable to seizure, and with their Cargoes shall be confiscated.

3. That no Master or commander of any Vessel shall be intitled to cruize for, or make prize of any Vessel or cargo before he shall have obtained a Commission from the Congress, or from such Person or Persons as shall be for that purpose appointed in some one of the United Colonies.

4. That it be, and is hereby recommended to the several Legislatures in the United Colonies as soon as possible, to erect Courts of Justice, or give Jurisdiction to the Courts now in being, for the purpose of determining concerning the Captures to be made as aforesaid, and to provide that all Tryals in such case be had by a Jury under such qualifications as to the respective Legislatures shall seem expedient.

5. That all Prosecutions shall be commenced in the Court of that Colony in which the Captures shall be made, but if no such Court be, at that time erected in the said Colony, or if the Capture be made on open Sea, then the prosecution shall be in the Court of such Colony as the Captor may find most convenient, provided that nothing contained in this resolution shall be construed so as to enable the Captor to remove his prize from any Colony competent to determine concerning the Seizure, after he shall have carried the Vessel so seized, within any harbour of the same.

6. That in all Cases an Appeal shall be allowed to the Congress, or such Person or Persons as they shall appoint for the Tryal of Appeals, provided the Appeal be demanded within five days after definitive Sentence, and such Appeal be lodged with the Secretary of Congress, within forty days afterwards, and provided the Party appealing shall give Security to prosecute the said Appeal to effect, and in case of the death of the Secretary during the Recess of Congress, then the said Appeal to be lodged in Congress within twenty days after the meeting thereof.

7. That when any Vessel or Vessels shall be fitted out at the Expence of any private Person or Persons, then the Captures made, shall be to the Use of the owner or owners of the said Vessel or Vessels; and where the Vessels employed in the capture shall be fitted out at the Expence of any of the United Colonies, then one third of the Prize taken shall be to the Use of the Captors, and the remaining two thirds to the Use of the said Colony, and where the Vessel so employed, shall be fitted out at the continental charge, then one third shall go to the Captors, and the remaining two thirds to the Use of the United Colonies, provided nevertheless, that if the Capture be a Vessel of War, then the Captors shall be entitled to one half of the Value, and the Remainder shall go to the Colony or Continent as the case may be, the necessary charges of the condemnation of all Prizes, being deducted before distribution made.

8. That the Captures heretofore made by Vessels fitted out at the Continental Charge were justifiable, and that the distribution of the Captors Share of the Prizes by General Washington be confirmed, which is as follows. A Captain or Commander 6 shares. First Lieutenant 5. Second Lieutenant 4. Surgeon 4. Master 3. Steward 2. Mate one and a half. Gunner, Boatswain, Gunners Mate, Serjeant, one and a half each. Privates one Share.

Resolved that, that Part of General Washingtons Letter of the 11th. instant respecting the capture of a Vessell by the Inhabitants of New Hampshire be referred to the committee, who brought in the forgoing Report.[3] Congress next took into Consideration the Rules and Orders for the Fleet of the United Colonies, but not having Time to finish them Resolved that the farther consideration of them be deferred till Monday next. I have been particular in transcribing the Proceedings of this day 25. of November 1775, because, the[y] contain the true Origin and Formation of the American Navy, and as I had at least as great a share in producing them as any Man living or dead, they will shew that my Zeal and Exertions afterwards in 1798. 1799. and 1800, at every hazard and in Opposition to a more powerfull Party than that against me in 1775, was but a perseverance in the same Principles, Systems and Views of the public Interest.

On Tuesday November 28. 1775. The Congress resumed the Consideration of the Rules and Orders for the Navy of the United Colonies,

---

[3] Washington's letter of 11 Nov. is printed in his *Writings*, ed. Fitzpatrick, 4: 81–84. Congress did not act on it until 20 Dec., after JA had taken leave of absence (JCC, 3:439).

and the same being debated by Paragraphs were agreed to as follows: These Regulations are to be found in the 262. 3. 4. 5. 6. 7. 8. 9. 10. 11th. Pages of the Journals of Congress for 1775. They are too long to transcribe. They were drawn up in the Marine Committee[4] and by my hand, but examined, discussed and corrected by the Committee. In this place I will take the Opportunity to observe, that the pleasantest part of my Labours for the four Years I spent in Congress from 1774 to 1778 [*i.e.* 1777] was in this naval Committee. Mr. Lee, Mr. Gadsden, were sensible Men, and very chearful: But Governor Hopkins of Rhode Island, above seventy Years of Age kept us all alive. Upon Business his Experience and Judgment were very Usefull. But when the Business of the Evening was over, he kept Us in Conversation till Eleven and sometimes twelve O Clock. His Custom was to drink nothing all day nor till Eight O Clock, in the Evening, and then his Beveredge was Jamaica Spirit and Water. It gave him Wit, Humour, Anecdotes, Science and Learning. He had read Greek, Roman and British History: and was familiar with English Poetry particularly Pope, Tompson [Thomson] and Milton. And the flow of his Soul made all his reading our own, and seemed to bring to recollection in all of Us all We had ever read. I could neither eat nor drink in those days. The other Gentlemen were very temperate. Hopkins never drank to excess, but all he drank was immediately not only converted into Wit, Sense, Knowledge and good humour, but inspired Us all with similar qualities.

This Committee soon purchased and filled five Vessells. The first We named Alfred in honor of the founder of the greatest Navy that ever existed. The second Columbus after the Discover[er] of this quarter of the Globe. The third Cabot, for the Discoverer of this northern Part of the Continent. The fourth Andrew Doria in memory of the Great Genoese Admiral and the fifth Providence, for the Town where she was purchased, the Residence of Governor Hopkins and his Brother Eseck whom We appointed first Captain. We appointed all the officers of all the Ships. At the Solicitation of Mr. Deane We appointed his Brother in Law Captain Saltonstall.[5]

Sometime in December, worn down with long and uninterrupted Labour I asked and obtained Leave to visit my State and my Family. Mr. Langdon did the same, Mr. Deane was left out of the Delegation

[4] More correctly, the Naval Committee, which was absorbed and replaced by the standing Marine Committee early in 1776.

[5] See the Journal, 30 Oct. (*JCC*, 3:311–312); JA's Diary entry (Notes of Debates) of the same date and note; and his List of Persons Suitable for Naval Commands, printed in the Diary under date of Nov. 1775.

by his State and some others of the naval Committee were dispersed, when Congress appointed a Committee of twelve one from each State, for naval Affairs,[6] so that I had no longer any particular Charge relative to them: but as long as I continued a Member of Congress I never failed to support all reasonable measures reported by the new Committee.

It is necessary that I should be a little more particular, in relating the Rise and Progress of the new Governments of the States.

On Fryday June 2. 1775. Journals of Congress, page 112. The President laid before Congress a Letter from the Provincial Convention of Massachusetts Bay dated May 16. which was read, setting forth the difficulties they labour under, for want of a regular form of Government, and as they and the other Colonies are now compelled to raise an Army to defend themselves from the Butcheries and devastations of their implacable Enemies, which renders it still more necessary to have a regular established Government, requesting the Congress to favour them with explicit Advice respecting the taking up and exercising the Powers of civil Government, and declaring their readiness to submit to such a general Plan as the Congress may direct for the Colonies, or make it their great Study to establish such a form of Government there, as shall not only promote their Advantage but the Union and Interest of all America.

This Subject had engaged much of my Attention before I left Massachusetts, and had been frequently the Subject of Conversation between me and many of my Friends Dr. Winthrop, Dr. Cooper, Colonel Otis, the two Warrens, Major Hawley and others besides my Colleagues in Congress and lay with great Weight upon my Mind as the most difficult and dangerous Business that We had to do, (for from the Beginning I always expected We should have more difficulty and danger, in our Attempts to govern ourselves and in our Negotiations and connections with foreign Powers, than from all the Fleets and Armies of Great Britain). It lay therefore with great Weight upon my mind: and when this Letter was read, I embraced the Opportunity to open myself in Congress, and most earnestly to intreat the serious Attention of all the Members and of all the Continent to the measures which the times demanded. For my Part I thought there was great Wisdom in the Adage when the Sword is drawn throw away the Scabbard. Whether We threw it away voluntarily or not, it was useless now and

---

[6] Appointed 14 Dec. (JA having left Philadelphia on the 9th), this became the permanent Marine Committee (JCC, 3:428; Charles O. Paullin, *The Navy of the American Revolution*, Cleveland, 1906, p. 86–87).

would be useless forever. The Pride of Britain, flushed with late Tryumphs and Conquests, their infinite Contempt of all the Power of America, with an insolent, arbitrary Scotch Faction with a Bute and Mansfield at their head for a Ministry, We might depend upon it, would force Us to call forth every Energy and resource of the Country, to seek the friendship of Englands Enemies, and We had no rational hope but from the Ratio Ultima Regum et Rerum publicarum. These Efforts could not be made without Government, and as I supposed no Man would think of consolidating this vast Continent under one national Government, We should probably after the Example of the Greeks, the Dutch and the Swiss, form a Confederacy of States, each of which must have a seperate Government. That the Case of Massachusetts was the most urgent, but that it could not be long before every other Colony must follow her Example. That with a View to this Subject I had looked into the Ancient and modern Confederacies for Examples: but they all appeared to me to have been huddled up in a hurry by a few Chiefs. But We had a People of more Intelligence, Curiosity and Enterprize, who must be all consulted, and We must reallize the Theories of the Wisest Writers and invite the People, to erect the whole Building with their own hands upon the broadest foundation. That this could be done only by Conventions of Representatives chosen by the People in the several Colonies, in the most exact proportions. That it was my Opinion, that Congress ought now to recommend to the People of every Colony to call such Conventions immediately and set up Governments of their own, under their own Authority: for the People were the Source of all Authority and Original of all Power. These were new, strange and terrible Doctrines, to the greatest Part of the Members, but not a very small Number heard them with apparent Pleasure, and none more than Mr. John Rutledge of South Carolina and Mr. John Sullivan of New Hampshire.

Congress however ordered the Letter to lie ⟨under⟩ on the Table for farther Consideration. On Saturday June the 3d 1775. The Letter from the Convention of the Massachusetts Bay dated the 16th. of May, being again read, the Subject was again discussed, and then Resolved That a Committee of five Persons be chosen, to consider the same and report what in their Opinion is the proper Advice to be given to that Convention. The following Persons were chosen by ballot, to compose that Committee, viz. Mr. J. Rutledge, Mr. Johnson, Mr. Jay, Mr. Wilson and Mr. Lee. These Gentlemen had several Conferences with the Delegates from our State, in the course of which I suppose the hint was suggested that they adopted in their report.

On Wednesday June 7. 1775. On motion resolved, that Thursday the 20th. of July next be observed throughout the twelve united Colonies, as a Day of Humiliation, Fasting and Prayer; and that Mr. Hooper, Mr. J. Adams and Mr. Paine, be a Committee to bring in a resolve for that purpose.[7]

The Committee appointed to prepare Advice in Answer to the Letter from the Convention of Massachusetts Bay, brought in their report, which was read and ordered to lie on the Table for Consideration.

On Fryday June 9th. 1775. The report of the Committee on the Letter from the Convention of Massachusetts Bay being again read, the Congress came into the following Resolution:

Resolved, That no Obedience being due to the Act of Parliament, for altering the Charter of the Colony of Massachusetts Bay, nor to a Governor or Lieutenant Governor who will not observe the directions of, but endeavour to subvert that Charter, the Governor and Lieutenant Governor of that Colony are to be considered as absent and their Offices vacant; and as there is no Council there and the Inconveniences arising from the Suspension of the Powers of Government are intollerable, especially at a time when General Gage hath actually levyed War, and is carrying on Hostilities against his Majestys peaceable and loyal Subjects of that Colony; that in order to conform as near as may be to the Spirit and Substance of the Charter, it be recommended to the provincial Convention to write Letters to the Inhabitants of the several Places, which are intituled to representation in Assembly, requesting them to chuse such Representatives, and that the Assembly when chosen, do elect Councillors; and that such Assembly or Council exercise the Powers of Government, untill a Governor of his Majestys Appointment will consent to govern the Colony according to its Charter.

Ordered That the President transmit a Copy of the Above to the Convention of Massachusetts Bay.

Although this Advice was in a great degree conformable, to the New York and Pensilvania System, or in other Words to the System of Mr. Dickinson and Mr. Duane, I thought it an Acquisition, for it was a Precedent of Advice to the seperate States to institute Gov-

---

[7] This committee reported a proclamation on 12 June, which was adopted (apparently with some changes) and ordered to be "published in the newspapers, and in hand bills" (JCC, 2:87–88; 3:507 ["Bibliographical Notes," Nos. 47–48]). A draft, perhaps but not certainly in the hand of William Hooper, is in the Adams Papers under date of June 1775; it contains some but not much of the language eventually used.

ernments, and I doubted not We should soon have more Occasions to follow this Example. Mr. John Rutledge and Mr. Sullivan had frequent Conversations with me upon this subject. Mr. Rutledge asked me my Opinion of a proper form of Government for a State. I answered him that any form, that our People would consent to institute would be better than none. Even if they placed all Power in a House of Representatives, and they should appoint Governors and Judges: but I hoped they would be wiser, and preserve the English Constitution in its Spirit and Substance, as far as the Circumstances of this Country required or would Admit. That no hereditary Powers ever had existed in America, nor would they or ought they to be introduced or proposed. But that I hoped the three Branches of a Legislature would be preserved, an Executive, independent of the Senate or Council and the House and above all things the Independence of the Judges. Mr. Sullivan was fully agreed with me in the necessity of instituting Governments and he seconded me very handsomely in supporting the Argument in Congress. Mr. Samuel Adams was with Us in the Opinion of the Necessity and was industrious in Conversation with the Members out of Doors: but he very rarely spoke much in Congress, and he was perfectly unsettled in any Plan to be recommended to a State, always inclining to the most democratical forms, and even to a single Sovereign Assembly: untill his Constituents, afterwards in Boston compelled him to vote for three branches. Mr. Cushing was also for one Sovereign Assembly, and Mr. Paine were [8] silent and reserved upon the Subject at least to me.

Not long after this Mr. John Rutledge returned to South Carolina, and Mr. Sullivan went with General Washington to Cambridge: so that I lost two of my able Coadjutors. But We soon found the Benefit of their Co-operations at a distance.

On Wednesday October 18. 1775. The Delegates from New Hampshire laid before the Congress a part of the Instructions delivered to them by their Colony, in these Words:

"We would have you immediately Use your utmost Endeavours, to obtain the Advice and direction of the Congress, with respect to a Method for our Administering Justice, and regulating our civil Police. We press you not to delay this matter, as its being done speedily will probably prevent the greatest confusion among Us."

This Instruction might have been obtained by Mr. Langdon or Mr. Whipple but I always supposed it was General Sullivan, who suggested the measure because he left Congress with a stronger im-

[8] Thus in MS.

pression upon his mind of the importance of it, than I ever observed in either of the others. Be this however as it may have been, I embraced with Joy the opportunity of harranguing on the Subject at large, and of urging Congress to resolve on a general recommendation to all the States to call Conventions and institute regular Governments. I reasoned from various Topicks, many of which perhaps I could not now recollect. Some I remember as 1. The danger of the Morals of the People, from the present loose State of Things and general relaxation of Laws and Government through the Union. 2. The danger of Insurrections in some of the most disaffected parts of the Colonies, in favour of the Enemy or as they called them, the Mother Country, an expression that I thought it high time to erase out of our Language. 3. Communications and Intercourse with the Ennemy, from various parts of the Continent could not be wholly prevented, while any of the Powers of Government remained, in the hands of the Kings servants. 4. It could not well be considered as a Crime to communicate Intelligence, or to Act as Spies or Guides to the Ennemy, without assuming all the Powers of Government. 5. The People of America, would never consider our Union as compleat, but our Friends would always suspect divisions among Us, and our Ennemies who were scattered in larger or smaller Numbers not only in every State and City, but in every Village through the whole Union, would forever represent Congress as divided, and ready to break to pieces, and in this Way would intimidate and discourage multitudes of our People who wished Us well. 6. The Absurdity of carrying on War, against a King, When so many Persons were daily taking Oaths and Affirmations of Allegeance to him. 7. We could not expect that our Friends in Great Britain would believe Us United and in earnest, or exert themselves very strenuously in our favour, while We acted such a wavering hesitating Part. 8. Foreign Nations particularly France and Spain would not think Us worthy of their Attention, while We appeared to be deceived by such fallacious hopes of redress of Grievances, of pardon for our Offences, and of Reconciliation with our Enemies. 9. We could not command the natural Resources of our own Country; We could not establish Manufactories of Arms, Cannon, Salt Petre, Powder, Ships &c. Without the Powers of Government, and all these and many other preparations ought to be going on in every State or Colony, if you will, in the Country.

Although the Opposition was still inveterate, many Members of Congress began to hear me with more Patience, and some began to ask me civil questions. How can the People institute Governments?

My Answer was by Conventions of Representatives, freely, fairly and proportionally chosen.—When the Convention has fabricated a Government, or a Constitution rather, how do We know the People will submit to it? If there is any doubt of that, the Convention may send out their Project of a Constitution, to the People in their several Towns, Counties or districts, and the People may make the Acceptance of it their own Act. But the People know nothing about Constitutions. I believe you are much mistaken in that Supposition: if you are not, they will not oppose a Plan prepared by their own chosen Friends: but I believe that in every considerable portion of the People, there will be found some Men, who will understand the Subject as well as their representatives, and these will assist in enlightening the rest. . . .[9] But what Plan of a Government, would you advise? A Plan as nearly resembling the Governments under which We were born and have lived as the Circumstances of the Country will admit. Kings We never had among Us, Nobles We never had. Nothing hereditary ever existed in the Country: Nor will the Country require or admit of any such Thing: but Governors, and Councils We have always had as Well as Representatives. A Legislature in three Branches ought to be preserved, and independent Judges. Where and how will you get your Governors and Councils? By Elections. How, who shall elect? The Representatives of the People in a Convention will be the best qualified to contrive a Mode.

After all these discussions and interrogations, Congress was not prepared nor disposed to do any thing as yet. The[y] must consider farther.

Resolved that the Consideration of this matter be referred to Monday next. Monday arrived and Tuesday and Wednesday passed over, and Congress not yet willing to do any thing.

On Thursday October 26. 1775. The Subject again brought on the Carpet, and the same discussions repeated, for very little new was produced. After a long discussion in which Mr. John Rutledge, Mr. Ward, Mr. Lee, Mr. Sherman, Mr. Gadsden, Mr. Dyer, and some others had spoken on the same Side with me, Congress resolved that a Committee of five members be appointed to take into Consideration, the Instructions given to the Delegates of New Hampshire, and report their Opinion thereon. The Members chosen Mr. John Rutledge, Mr. J. Adams, Mr. Ward, Mr. Lee and Mr. Sherman.

Although this Committee was entirely composed of Members, as well disposed to encourage the Enterprize as could have been found

[9] Suspension points in MS.

in Congress, yet they could not be brought to agree upon a Report, and to bring it forward in Congress till Fryday November 3. 1775. When Congress taking into Consideration the Report of the Committee on the New Hampshire Instructions, after another long deliberation and debate, Resolved That it be recommended to the provincial Convention of New Hampshire, to call a full and free representation of the People, and that the Representatives if they think it necessary, establish such a form of Government, as in their Judgment will best produce the happiness of the People, and most effectually secure Peace and good Order in the Province, during the Continuance of the present dispute between Great Britain and the Colonies.

By this Time I mortally hated the Words "Province" "Colonies" and Mother Country and strove to get them out of the Report. The last was indeed left out, but the other two were retained even by this Committee who were all as high Americans, as any in the House, unless Mr. Gadsden should be excepted. Nevertheless I thought this resolution a Tryumph and a most important Point gained.[1]

Mr. John Rutledge was now compleatly with Us, in our desire of revolutionizing all the Governments, and he brought forward immediately, some representations from his own State, when Congress then taking into consideration, the State of South Carolina, and sundry papers relative thereto, being read and considered

Resolved that a Committee of five be appointed to take the same into Consideration and report what in their Opinion is necessary to be done. The Members chosen Mr. Harrison, Mr. Bullock, Mr. Hooper, Mr. Chase and Mr. S. Adams.[2]

On November 4th. 1775 The Committee appointed to take into Consideration the State of South Carolina, brought in their report, which being read a number of Resolves were passed, the last of which will be found in page 235 of the Journals at the bottom.

Resolved that if the Convention of South Carolina, shall find it necessary to establish a form of Government in that Colony, it be recommended to that Convention to call a full and free Representation of the People, and that the said Representatives, if they think

[1] The authorship of the report on the New Hampshire Instructions is unknown. JA's account of the debates on the subject must have been drawn entirely from his own memory, for there is no known contemporary record of those debates in Congress or in committee. But in forwarding the resolution of Congress to the New Hampshire Provincial Congress, the delegates of that colony said: "The arguments on this matter ... were truly Ciceronial, the eminent Speakers did honour to themselves and the Continent; carried by a very great majority" (Burnett, ed., *Letters of Members*, 1:246).

[2] This was also on 3 Nov.; see JCC, 3:319.

it necessary, shall establish such a form of Government as in their Judgment will produce the happiness of the People, and most effectually secure Peace And good Order in the Colony, during the continuance of the present dispute between Great Britain and the Colonies.

Although Mr. John Rutledge united with me and others in persuading the Committee to report this Resolution, and the distance of Carolina made it convenient to furnish them with this discretionary Recommendation, I doubt whether Mr. Harrison or Mr. Hooper were as yet, sufficiently advanced to agree to it.—Mr. Bullock, Mr. Chace and Mr. Samuel Adams were very ready for it. When it was under Consideration, I laboured afresh to expunge the Word Colony and Colonies, and insert the Words States and State, and the Word Dispute to make Way for that of War, and the Word Colonies for the Word America or States. But the Child was not yet weaned.—I laboured also to get the Resolution enlarged and extended into a Recommendation to the People of all the States to institute Governments, and this Occasioned more Interrogations from one part and another of the House. What Plan of Government would you recommend? &c. Here it would have been the most natural to have made a Motion that Congress should appoint a Committee to prepare a Plan of Government, to be reported to Congress and there discussed Paragraph by Paragraph, and that which should be adopted, should be recommended to all the States: but I dared not make such a Motion, because I knew that if such a Plan was adopted it would be if not permanent, yet of long duration: and it would be extreamly difficult to get rid of it. And I knew that every one of my friends, and all those who were the most zealous for assuming Government, had at that time no Idea of any other Government but a Contemptible Legislature in one assembly, with Committees for Executive Magistrates and Judges. These Questions therefore I answered by Sporting off hand, a variety of short Sketches of Plans, which might be adopted by the Conventions, and as this Subject was brought into View in some Way or other, almost every day and these Interrogations were frequently repeated, I had in my head and at my Tongues End, as many Projects of Government as Mr. Burke says the Abby Seieyes [Sieyès] had in his Pidgeon holes, not however constructed at such Length nor laboured with his metaphysical Refinements. I took care however always to bear my Testimony against every plan of an unballanced Government.

I had read Harrington, Sydney, Hobbs, Nedham and Lock, but with very little Application to any particular Views: till these Debates in Congress and these Interrogations in public and private, turned my thoughts to those Researches, which produced the Thoughts on Government, the Constitution of Massachusetts, and at length the Defence of the Constitutions of the United States and the Discourses on Davila, Writings which have never done any good to me though some of them undoubtedly contributed to produce the Constitution of New York, the Constitution of the United States, and the last Constitutions of Pensylvania and Georgia. They undoubtedly also contributed to the Writings of Publius, called the Federalist, which were all Written after the Publication of my Work in Philadelphia, New York and Boston. Whether the People will permit any of these Constitutions to stand upon their Pedestals, or whether they will throw them all down I know not. Appearances at present are unfavourable and threatening. I have done all in my Power, according to what I thought my Duty. I can do no more.

About the sixth of December 1775, I obtained Leave of Congress to visit my Family and returned home.[3] The General Court satt at Watertown, Our Army was at Cambridge and the British in Boston. Having a seat in Council, I had opportunity to Converse with the Members of both Houses, to know their Sentiments and to communicate mine. The Council had unanimously appointed me, in my Absence, without any Solicitation or desire on my Part, Chief Justice of the State. I had accepted the Office, because it was a Post of danger, but much against my Inclination. I expected to go no more to Congress, but to take my Seat on the Bench.[4] But the General Court would not

---

[3] JA asked for leave on 8 Dec. and departed on the following day for Braintree, where he arrived on 21 Dec.; see Diary entry of 9 Dec. 1775. The principal reason for his requesting leave—his need to know whether he was expected to stay on in Congress at this critical time or to assume the duties of chief justice of Massachusetts (see the following note)—is ably discussed by CFA (JA, *Works*, 1:191–192).

[4] On 11 Oct. 1775 the new Massachusetts Council, acting on the legal fiction that the governor was "absent," nominated JA "a Justice of the Superior Court of Judicature" (M-Ar: Council Records, 17:128), and on 28 Oct. Deputy Secretary Perez Morton notified him that he had been elected "first or Chief Justice," to serve with William Cushing, William Read, Robert Treat

Paine, and Nathaniel Peaslee Sargeant, "who are to hold their Seats in the Order therein arranged," as associate justices (Adams Papers; see also James Warren to JA, 5 Nov. 1775, Adams Papers, printed in *Warren-Adams Letters*, 1:178). After some deliberation JA accepted, stating that in view of the "Hazards and Embarrassments" of such a post at such a time he dared not decline it and would return to take his seat "as soon as the Circumstances of the Colonies will admit of an Adjournment of the Congress" (to Perez Morton, 24 Nov., Dft, Adams Papers; *Works*, 3:23, note). As for the "Hazards" of the post, see JA's defense of a much criticized passage in his intercepted letter to James Warren of 24 July 1775, p. 320, above.

excuse me from again attending Congress and again chose me a Member with all my former Colleagues except Mr. Cushing who I believe declined, and in his room Mr. Gerry was chosen, who went with me to Philadelphia, and We took our Seats in Congress on Fryday 9. February 1776. In this Gentleman I found a faithfull Friend, and an ardent persevering Lover of his Country, who never hesitated to promote with all his Abilities and Industry the boldest measures reconcileable with prudence. Mr. Samuel Adams, Mr. Gerry and myself, now composed a Majority of the Massachusetts Delegation, and We were no longer vexed or enfeebled by divisions among ourselves, or by indecision or Indolence. On the 29 of Feb. 1776 William Whipple Esq. appeared as one of the Delegates from New Hampshire, another excellent Member in Principle and Disposition, as well as Understanding.

I returned to my daily routine of Service in the Board of War,[5] and a punctual Attendance on Congress, every day, in all their hours. I returned also to my almost dayley exhortations to the Institutions of Governments in the States and a declaration of Independence. I soon found there was a Whispering among the Partisans in Opposition to Independence, that I was interested, that I held an office under the New Government of Massachusetts, and that I was afraid of loosing it, if We did not declare Independence; and that I consequently ought not to be attended to. This they circulated so successfully that they got it insinuated among the Members of the Legislature in Maryland where their Friends were powerfull enough to give an Instruction to their Delegates in Congress, warning them against listening to the Advice of Interested Persons, and manifestly pointing me out, to the Understanding of every one. This Instruction was read in Congress.[6]

[5] A mistake of memory. The Board of War and Ordnance was not established until 12 June 1776, and JA was appointed chairman of it next day (JCC, 5:434, 438).

[6] On 11 Jan. 1776 the Maryland Convention sitting at Annapolis voted instructions to its delegates in Congress of a very conservative character. They declared that the sole purpose for which the Colonies were "associated" was "the redress of *American* grievances," that reconciliation should therefore be aimed at, and that no proposition looking toward independence, foreign alliances, or confederation should be assented to by the delegates of that colony before recurring to the Convention itself. All this ran directly counter to the program of JA and the independence party in Congress. And a further instruction required the Maryland delegates to move and try to obtain "a resolve of Congress, that no person who holds any military command, . . . nor any person who holds or enjoys any office of profit under the Continental Congress, or any Government assumed since the present controversy with *Great Britain* began, . . . or who directly or indirectly receives the profits of such command or office, shall, during the time of his

It produced no other effect upon me than a laughing Letter to my Friend Mr. Chace, who regarded it no more than I did.[7] These Chuckles I was informed of and witnessed for many Weeks, and at length they broke out in a very extraordinary Manner. When I had been speaking one day on the Subject of Independence, or the Institution of Governments which I always considered as the same thing, a Gentleman of great Fortune and high Rank arose and said he should move, that No Person who held any Office under a new Government should be admitted to vote, on any such Question as they were interested Persons. I wondered at the Simplicity of this motion: but knew very well what to do with it. I rose from my Seat with great coolness and deliberation: So far from expressing or feeling any resentment, I really felt gay, though as it happened I preserved an unusual Gravity in my countenance and Air, and said Mr. President I will second the Gentlemans Motion, and I recommend it to the Honourable Gentleman to second another, which I should make, vizt. that No Gentleman who holds any Office under the Old or present Government, should be admitted to vote on any such question, as they were interested Persons. The moment when this was pronounced, it flew like an Electric Stroke through every Countenance in the Room: for the Gentleman who made the Motion, held as high an Office under the old Government, as I did under the new, and many other Members present held Offices under the Royal Government. My Friends accordingly were delighted with my retaliation, and The

---

holding or receiving the same, be eligible to sit in Congress" (Force, *Archives,* 4th ser., 4:653–654).

On 30 Jan. Robert Alexander, a member of the Maryland delegation, acknowledged these instructions, declared himself "much pleased with them," and reported that "the Farmer [i.e. John Dickinson] and some others to whom in Confidence they were shown" also highly approved of them (Burnett, ed., *Letters of Members,* 1:334). Just when the instruction that JA believed was aimed at him personally was read in Congress is unknown. But a motion to prohibit members from holding lucrative offices was introduced late in April; see William Whipple to John Langdon, 29 April (same, p. 434–435 and notes). The immediate occasion of it was the nomination of John Langdon, a New Hampshire delegate

in Congress, as a naval agent of Congress, and although it was undoubtedly the same motion that JA says below he seconded and foiled (and so prevented its being entered in the Journal), it could have been only indirectly aimed at him. JA's sensitivity being what it was (he had been a very vocal critic of the Hutchinsons' and Olivers' pluralism in office), he immediately resigned his seat on the Massachusetts Council (JA to James Otis Sr., 29 April 1776, printed, from a MS not found, in *Works,* 9:374; see also JA to James Warren, 12 May 1776, MHi, printed in *Warren-Adams Letters,* 1:242–243).

[7] JA to Samuel Chase, 14 June 1776, which briefly relates JA's brush with an unidentified Maryland delegate in terms similar to those in the following account (LbC, Adams Papers; JA, *Works,* 9: 396–398).

Friends of my Antagonist were mortified at his Indiscretion in exposing himself to such a retort. Finding the house in a good disposition to hear me, I added I would go farther and chearfully consent to a Self denying Ordinance, that every Member of Congress before We proceeded to any question respecting Independence should take a solemn Oath never to accept or hold any Office of any kind in America, after the Revolution. Mr. Wythe of Virginia rose here and said Congress had no Right to exclude any of their Members from voting on these questions. Their constituents only had a right to restrain them. And that no Member had a right to take, nor Congress to prescribe any Engagement not to hold Offices after the Revolution or before. Again I replied that whether the Gentlemans Opinion was well or ill founded, I had only said that I was willing to consent to such an Arrangement. That I knew very well what these Things meant. They were personal Attacks upon me, and I was glad that at length they had been made publickly where I could defend myself. That I knew very well, that they had been made secretly, and circulated in Whispers not only in the City of Philadelphia and State of Pensilvania, but in the Neighbouring States particularly Maryland, and very probably in private Letters throughout the Union. I now took the Opportunity to declare in Public, that it was very true, the unmerited and unsolicited, though unanimous good Will of the Council of Massachusetts had appointed me to an important Office, that of Chief Justice. That as this Office was a very conspicuous station and consequently a dangerous one, I had not dared to refuse it, because it was a Post of Danger, though by the Acceptance of it, I was obliged to relinquish another Office, meaning my Barristers Office which was more than four times so profitable. That it was a Sense of Duty, and a full conviction of an honest cause, and not any motives of Ambition or hopes of honor or profit which had drawn me into my present course. That I had seen enough already in the course of my own Experience, to know that the American Cause was not the most promising road, to Profits, honours, Power or Pleasure. That on the Contrary a man must renounce all these and devote himself to labour, danger and death, and very possibly to disgrace and Infamy, before he was fit, in my Judgment in the present State and future prospect of the Country, for a Seat in that Congress. This whole Scæne was a Comedy to Charles Thompson whose countenance was in raptures all the time. When all was over he told me he had been highly delighted with it, because he had been witness to many of their Conversations in which they had endeavoured to excite and propagate Prejudices against me, on Account of my Office of Chief Justice. But he said I had cleared and explained the thing in such a manner that he would be bound I should never hear any more Reflections on that head. No more indeed were made in my presence, but the Party did not cease to abuse me in their secret Circles, on this Account as I was well informed.

Not long afterwards, hearing that the Supream Court in Massachusetts was organized and proceeding very well on the Business of their Circuits, I wrote my Resignation of the Office of Chief Justice to the Council, very happy to get fairly rid of an Office that I knew to be burthensome, and whose Emoluments with my small fortune would not support my family.[8]

On the 9th. of Feb. 1776 The day on which Mr. Gerry and I took our Seats for this Year, sundry Letters from General Washington, General Schuyler, Governor Trumbull, with Papers enclosed were read, and referred to Mr. Chase, Mr. J. Adams, Mr. Penn, Mr. Wythe and Mr. Rutledge.[9]

On the 14th. of Feb. 1776 sundry Letters from General Schuyler, General Wooster and General Arnold were read and referred with the Papers enclosed, to Mr. Wythe, Mr. J. Adams and Mr. Chase.[1] On the same day Congress resolved itself into a Committee of the whole House, to take into Consideration the Report of the Committee on the regulations and Restrictions, under which the Ports should

[8] As JA predicted, it proved extremely difficult to find persons willing to serve on the Superior Court of Judicature. But at length in June 1776 the Court held a session in Ipswich with three justices (William Cushing, Jedidiah Foster, James Sullivan) on the bench; in September it sat in Braintree to try Suffolk cases; and at the beginning of 1777 a fourth justice, Nathaniel Peaslee Sargeant, who had previously declined to serve, joined the others (Quincy, *Reports*, p. 340, note; AA to JA, 15 Sept. 1776, printed in JA-AA, *Familiar Letters*, p. 227). On 10 Feb. JA submitted his resignation as chief justice in a letter to the Massachusetts Council, appending the following note to his retained copy: "Wrote another Letter the same day to Portia [i.e. his wife], . . . informed her of the above Resignation [and] that I was determined that whilst I was ruining my Constitution both of Mind and Body, and running daily Risques of Life and Fortune in defence of the Independency of my Country, I would not knowingly resign my own" (JA to Deputy Secretary Avery, enclosing a letter to the Council, both dated 10 Feb. 1777, letterbook copies, Adams Papers; enclosure printed in JA, *Works*, 3:25).

[9] For these letters see JCC, 4:123 and note. The committee reported on 16 Feb.; the report is in Samuel Chase's hand and was tabled (same, p. 154–155). On 5 and 6 March further letters from Washington were referred to the same committee; see under those dates below.

[1] For these letters see JCC, 4:147 and note. Next day further letters from general officers were referred to the same committee of three (see the following paragraph), which reported on 17 Feb., and Congress thereupon adopted a number of resolutions (same, p. 151, 157–159). The authorship of this report is not known.

be opened after the first day of March next, and after some time spent thereon the President resumed the Chair and Mr. Ward reported that the Committee had taken into consideration the matter referred to them, but not having come to a conclusion desired leave to sit again, which was granted for tomorrow.

On the 15th of Feb. 1776. Sundry other Letters from General Lee, General Schuyler and General Wooster were referred to the Committee to whom the Letters received Yesterday were referred. On the same day Congress took into Consideration the Report from the Committee of the whole house, and after debate resolved that it be recommitted. Resolved that Congress will tomorrow morning resolve itself into a Committee of the whole, to take into Consideration, the Propriety of Opening the Ports, and the Restrictions and regulations of Trade of these Colonies after the first of March next.

Fryday Feb. 16. 1776. Agreable to the order of the day, the Congress resolved itself into a Committee of the whole, to take into consideration the Propriety of Opening the Ports &c. After some time spent Mr. Ward reported, that not having come to a conclusion, The Committee asked leave to sit again. Granted.[2]

Saturday Feb. 17. 1776. The Committee to whom the Letters from Generals Arnold, Wooster, Schuyler and Lee were referred brought in their report, which was agreed to in the several Resolutions detailed in page 67. and 68 of this Volume of the Journals.

Same day Resolved that Mr. J. Adams, Mr. Wythe and Mr. Sherman be a Committee to prepare Instructions for the Committee appointed to go to Canada.[3]

Resolved that Congress will on Tuesday next resolve itself into a Committee of the whole, to take into Consideration the Propriety of Opening the Ports &c.

This Measure of Opening the Ports, &c. laboured exceedingly, because it was considered as a bold step to Independence. Indeed I urged it expressly with that View and as connected with the Institutions of Government in all the States and a Declaration of National Independence. The Party against me had Art and Influence as yet,

[2] See Diary entry (Notes of Debates), 16 Feb. 1776.

[3] See Diary entry of Feb.? 1776 (3d under that date) and note; also the entries in JA's Autobiography, 9, 11, 12, and 20 March below. According to Richard Smith's Diary, 23 Feb., "J. Adams presented a Sett of Instructions for [the commissioners going to Canada] which were recom[itte]d that some Matter may be added" (Burnett, ed., *Letters of Members*, 1:361); but this action does not appear in the Journal. The text of these important instructions, as adopted on 20 March after debate and amendment, is in JCC, 4:215–219.

to evade, retard and delay every Motion that We made. Many Motions were made and argued at great Length and with great Spirit on both Sides, which are not to be found in the Journals. When Motions were made and debates ensued, in a Committee of the whole house, no record of them was made by the Secretary, unless the Motion prevailed and was reported to Congress and there adopted. This Arrangement was convenient for the Party in Opposition to Us, who by this means evaded the Appearance on the Journals, of any Subject they disliked.[4]

On Monday Feb. 19. 1776 Congress attended an Oration in honour of General Montgomery, and the Officers and Soldiers who fell with him.

'JA frequently complained in his Autobiography (as historians have later) of the meagerness of the record in the MS Journals of Congress, and consequently in the published *Journals.* But his charges that Secretary Thomson's omissions (or, as JA thought them, "suppressions") sprang from his partiality for the anti-independence party in Congress cannot be substantiated: Thomson simply confined the Journal record to motions that "prevailed," i.e. resolutions actually adopted. This practice (in force until 2 Aug. 1777; see below) excluded the names of movers and seconders of motions, the texts of all motions eventually negatived, all debates on and amendments (as such) to motions and reports, all enumeration of votes, and all business done in committees, including committees of the whole house—except committee reports or recommendations that were ultimately adopted, and then always *in the form agreed on by Congress,* which was of course by no means always the form reported. It hardly needs to be said that the Secretary's method bore precisely as hard on one faction in Congress as it did on another. But it should be pointed out that Thomson's docketings on the motions and committee reports that have been preserved are usually much more revealing than the bare entries of action recorded in the Journal, the latter being considered from the outset a record that would be made public.

From time to time members complained that the proceedings were too secret and that, for instance, they had no way of making their dissents on measures they disapproved known to their constituents; see especially Thomas Burke's Abstract of Debates, 27 Feb. 1777 (Burnett, ed., *Letters of Members,* 2:285), and Samuel Chase's motion of the same date, which, since it failed, was not entered in the Journal (*JCC,* 7:164). But Thomson's narrow interpretation of his duties as secretary persisted until 2 Aug. 1777, when Congress resolved "That all proceedings of Congress, and all questions agitated and determined by Congress, be entered on the journal, and that the yeas or nays of each member, if required by any State, be taken on every question as stated and determined by the house" (same, 8:599).

Thomson's engaging justification of his practice will be found in recollections attributed to him by an anonymous writer in 1827. It concludes: "what congress adopted, I committed to writing; with what they rejected, I had nothing farther to do; and even this method led to some squabbles with the members, who were desirous of having their speeches and resolutions, however put to rest by the majority, still preserved upon the minutes" (*Amer. Quart. Rev.,* 1:31). Thomson's statement is printed in full in Burnett, ed., *Letters of Members,* 1:10, note.

See, further, entries below dated 23 March, 2, 6 April, 10 May, 7 June, 20 Aug., and 17 Sept. 1776, and notes thereunder.

On Tuesday Feb. 20. 1776. and on Wednesday Feb. 21. Means were contrived to elude the Committee of the whole House.

Thursday Feb. 22. 1776. Two Letters from General Washington, were referred to a Committee of the whole house. Accordingly Congress resolved itself into a Committee of the whole, and after some time, Mr. Ward reported that the Committee had come to no Conclusion, and Congress resolved that Tomorrow they would again resolve themselves into a Committee of the whole, to take into their farther consideration the Letters from General Washington.

Fryday Feb. 23. 1776. Resolved that Congress will on Monday next resolve itself into a Committee of the whole, to take into Consideration the Letters from General Washington.

Monday Feb. 26. 1776 arrived, and a Letter from General Lee, was referred to Mr. McKean, Mr. John Adams and Mr. Lewis Morris,[5] but no Resolution of Congress into a Committee of the whole.

On Tuesday Feb. 27. 1776. The order of the day was renewed, but nothing done.

Wednesday Feb. 28. 1776. The Committee to whom the Letters from General Lee &c. were referred brought in their report. Resolved that the Consideration of it be postponed till tomorrow.

Mr. William Whipple from New Hampshire appeared: an excellent Member and a valuable Addition to our Phalanx.[6]

A Letter of the 14th. from General Washington, inclosing a Letter from Lord Drummond to General Robinson,[7] and sundry other Papers were read. Agreable to the order of the day, the Congress resolved itself into a Committee of the whole, to take into consideration the Letter from General Washington of the 9th. instant and the Trade of the Colonies after the first of March. After some time Mr. Ward reported that the Committee not having come to a conclusion desired leave to sit again. Granted. Resolved That this Congress will, tomorrow, resolve itself into a Committee of the whole to take into farther con-

[5] Lee's letter, dated 22 Feb., is in PCC, No. 158. A "Report [thereon] was delivered in by J Adams" on 28 Feb.; action was deferred until 1 March and then quashed (Richard Smith, Diary, Burnett, ed., *Letters of Members*, 1:367, 371).

[6] JA here overlooked a date heading in the *Journals* he was abstracting. Whipple took his seat on 29 Feb., and the proceedings recorded in the next paragraph of JA's narrative also occurred on that day.

[7] That is, Brig. Gen. James Robertson (the error is in the printed *Journals*). Washington's letter is printed in his *Writings*, ed. Fitzpatrick, 4:330–332. On the conciliatory schemes of Thomas, Lord Drummond, which so aroused JA's indignation, see the documents printed in an appendix to Washington's *Writings*, ed. Sparks, 3:525–529.

sideration, the Letter from General Washington and the Trade of the Colonies.

The very short Sketch, which is here traced, is enough to show that Postponement was the Object of our Antagonists, and the Journals for these days will shew the frivolus importance of the Business transacted in them, in comparison of the great Concerns which were before the Committees of the whole House. There was however still a Majority of Members who were either determined against all Measures preparatory to Independence, or yet too timorous and wavering to venture on any decisive Steps. We therefore could do nothing but keep our Eyes fixed on the great Objects of free Trade, new Governments and Independence of the United States: and seize every Opening Opportunity of advancing Step by Step in our progress. Our Opponents were not less vigilant in seizing on every excuse for delay. The Letter from Lord Drummond, which seemed to derive Importance from the transmission of it, by General Washington, was a fine Engine to play cold Water on the fire of Independence. They set it in Operation with great Zeal and Activity. It was indeed a very airy Phantom, and ought not to have been sent Us by the General who should only have referred Lord Drummond to Congress. But there were about head Quarters some who were as weak and wavering as our Members and the General himself had chosen for his private confidential Correspondent a Member from Virginia, Harrison, who was still counted among the cold Party. This was an indolent, luxurious, heavy Gentleman, of no Use in Congress or Committees, but a great Embarrassment to both. He was represented to be a kind of Nexus utriusque Mundi, a corner Stone in which the two Walls of Party met in Virginia. He was descended from one of the most ancient, wealthy and respectable Families in the ancient dominion, and seemed to be set up in Opposition to Mr. Richard Henry Lee. Jealousies and divisions appeared among the Delegates of no State more remarkably, than among those of Virginia. Mr. Wythe told me, that Thomas Lee the elder Brother of Richard Henry was the delight of the Eyes of Virginia and by far the most popular Man they had. But Richard Henry was not. I asked the reason, for Mr. Lee appeared a Schollar, a Gentleman, a Man of uncommon Eloquence, and an agreable Man. Mr. Wythe said this was all true but Mr. Lee had when he was very young and when he first came into the House of Burgesses moved and urged on an Inquiry into the State of the Treasury which was found deficient in a large Sum, which had been lent by the Treasurer to many of the most influential Families of the Country, who found themselves exposed, and had never forgiven Mr. Lee.[8] This he said had made him so many Enemies, that he never had recovered his Reputation, but was still heartily hated by great Numbers. These feelings among the Virginia Delegates, were a great Injury to Us. Mr. Samuel Adams and myself were very intimate with Mr. Lee, and he agreed perfectly with Us in the great System of our Policy, and by his means We kept a Majority of the Delegates of Virginia with Us, but Harrison, Pendleton and some others, shewed their Jealousy of this Intimacy plainly enough, at times. Harrison consequently courted Mr. Hancock and some others of our Colleagues: but We had now a Majority, and gave ourselves no trouble about their little Intrigues. This is all necessary to shew the Operation of Lord Drummonds communication. I have forgotten the particulars: but He pretended to have had conversation with Lord North, talked warmly of Lord Norths good Will and desire of Reconciliation: but had no Authority to shew and no distinct proposition to make. In short it was so flimsy a veil, that the purblind might see through it. But yet it was made instrumental of much delay and Amusement to numbers.

Fryday March 1. 1776. Resolved that this Congress will tomorrow resolve itself into a Committee of the whole, to take into Consideration the Letter of General Washington of the 14th with the Papers inclosed.

Resolved That the Memorial from the Merchants of Montreal be referred to a Committee of five Mr. Wilson, Mr. J. Adams, Mr. W. Livingston, Mr. L. Morris and Mr. Tilghman.[9]

Tuesday March 5. 1776. Congress resolved itself into a Committee of the whole to take into their consideration the Letter from General Washington of the 14th of Feb. and the Papers enclosed and after some time the President resumed the Chair and Mr. Harrison reported, that the Committee have had under their consideration the Letters and Papers to them referred, but have come to no resolution thereon.

Resolved that the Letter from General Washington, so far as it has not been considered by the Committee of the whole be referred to the Committee to whom his other Letters, of the 24. and 30th of January were referred.[1]

[8] This is a garbled allusion to "The Robinson Affair," concerning which see a chapter with that title in David J. Mays, *Edmund Pendleton,* Cambridge, 1952, 2:174–208.

[9] JA here again overlooked a date heading in the *Journals.* This committee was appointed on 4 March; it reported on the 13th (report not found), and on the 20th Congress voted "That the memorial from the Indian traders, residing at Montreal, be delivered to the Commissioners going to Canada" (JCC, 4:182, 200, 219).

[1] Washington's letter is printed in his *Writings,* ed. Fitzpatrick, 4:330–332. See entries of 9 Feb., above, and 6, 13 March, below.

Wednesday March 6. 1776. A Letter from General Washington of the 26. of Feb. was read. Resolved that it be referred to the Committee to whom his other Letters are referred.[2] The order of the day renewed.

Thursday March 7. 1776. The order of the day was renewed.

Fryday March 8. No order of the day. The Committee to whom the Letters from Generals Schuyler, Wooster and Arnold were referred brought in their report.[3]

Saturday March 9. 1776. The Committee appointed to prepare Instructions for the Commissioners going to Canada, brought in a draught which was read.

Monday March 11. 1776. Congress took into Consideration the Instructions to the Commissioners going to Canada. Postponed.

Tuesday March 12. 1776. Postponed again.

Wednesday March 13. 1776. Although the System had been so long pursued to postpone all the great Political Questions, and take up any other Business of however trifling Consequence; Yet We were daily urging on the order of the day: and on this day We succeeded.

Congress resolved itself into a Committee of the whole to take into Consideration the Memorial of the Merchants &c. of Philadelphia &c., The Letters from General Washington, the State of the Trade of the Colonies &c. Mr. Ward reported no Resolution. Leave to sit again.

Thursday March 14. 1776. The State of the Country so obviously called for independent Governments, and a total Extinction of the Royal Authority, and We were so earnestly urging this measure from day to day, and the Opposition to it was growing so unpopular, that a kind of Evasion was contrived in the following Resolution, which I considered as an important Step, and therefore would not oppose it, though I urged with several others, that We ought to make the

---

[2] Washington's letter is printed in his *Writings*, ed. Fitzpatrick, 4:348–350. See the preceding entry and the references cited in the note there. No separate report on these further letters has been found.

[3] These letters had been read in Congress on 4 March and referred that day to the committee (of which JA was a member) appointed to prepare instructions for the commissioners going to Canada (JCC, 4:182–183; see entry of 17 Feb., above), but JA overlooked the entry of 4 March when abstracting the

*Journals,* and he also forgot the wrangle evoked by his report on the 8th. According to Richard Smith's Diary, 8 March, "a long Altercation followed on the first Article of a Report made by John Adams for reconciling the Differences between the Generals Schuyler and Wooster. the Article was at last voted out and other Parts of the Report adopted" (Burnett, ed., *Letters of Members,* 1:382–383, and see note at p. 383). The report has not been found, but the resolutions adopted are in JCC, 4:190–192.

Resolution more general, and Advize the People to assume all the Powers of Government. The Proposition that passed was

Resolved That it be recommended to the several Assemblies, Conventions and Committees or Councils of Safety, of the United Colonies, immediately to cause all Persons to be disarmed, within their respective Colonies, who are notoriously disaffected to the cause of America, or who have not associated, and shall refuse to associate to defend by Arms these united Colonies, against the hostile Attempts of the British Fleets and Armies, and to apply the Arms taken from such Persons in each respective Colony, in the first place, to the Arming the continental Troops raised in said Colony, in the next, to the arming such Troops as are raised by the Colony for its own defence, and the Residue to be applied to the arming the Associators; that the Arms when taken be appraised by indifferent Persons, and such as are applied to the Arming the Continental Troops, be paid for by the Congress and the Residue by the respective Assemblies, Conventions, or Councils or Committees of Safety.

Ordered that a Copy of the foregoing resolution be transmitted by the Delegates of each Colony, to their respective Assemblies, Conventions, or Councils or Committees of Safety.

This Resolution and Order was indeed assuming the Powers of Government in a manner as offensive, as the Measures We proposed could have been: But it left all the Powers of Government in the hands of Assemblies, Conventions and Committees, which composed a Scæne of much Confusion and Injustice the Continuance of which was much dreaded by me, as tending to injure the Morals of the People and destroy their habits of order, and Attachment to regular Government. However I could do nothing but represent and remonstrate: The Vote as yet was against me.

Fryday March 15. 1776. Congress resolved itself into a Committee of the whole to take into Consideration the State of New York, and after some time the President resumed the Chair and Mr. Harrison reported, that the Committee have come to certain Resolutions. These may be seen in the Journal and relate wholly to the defence of New York.[4]

This is the first Appearance of Mr. Harrison as Chairman of the Committee of the whole. The President Mr. Hancock had hitherto nominated Governor Ward of Rhode Island to that conspicuous distinction. Mr. Harrison had courted Mr. Hancock, and Mr. Hancock had courted Mr. Duane, Mr. Dickenson and their Party, and leaned

[4] JCC, 4:206–207.

so partially in their favour, that Mr. Samuel Adams had become very bitter against Mr. Hancock and spoke of him with great Asperity, in private Circles, and this Alienation between them continued from this time till the Year 1789, thirteen Years, when they were again reconciled. Governor Ward was become extreamly Obnoxious to Mr. Hancocks Party by his zealous Attachment to Mr. Samuel Adams and Mr. Richard Henry Lee. Such I supposed were the motives which excited Mr. Hancock, to bring forward Mr. Harrison.[5]

Although Harrison was another Sir John Falstaff, excepting in his Larcenies and Robberies, his Conversation disgusting to every Man of Delicacy or decorum, Obscæne, profane, impious, perpetually ridiculing the Bible, calling it the Worst Book in the World, yet as I saw he was to be often nominated with Us in Business, I took no notice of his Vices or Follies, but treated him and Mr. Hancock too with uniform Politeness. I was however, too intimate with Mr. Lee, Mr. Adams, Mr. Ward &c. to escape the Jealousy and Malignity of their Adversaries. Hence I suppose the Calumnies that were written or otherwise insinuated into the Minds of the Army that I was an Enemy to Washington, in favour of an annual Election of a General, against Enlisting Troops during the War &c. &c. all utterly false and groundless.[6]

Saturday March 16 1776. Mr. W. Livingston brought in a Proclamation for a Fast on the 17th of May.

Congress resolved itself into a Committee of the whole, according to the standing order of the Day. Mr. Harrison reported no Resolution.

Monday March 18. Order of the Day again. Mr. Harrison reported no Resolution.

Tuesday March 19. The order of the Day again. Mr. Harrison reported that the Committee have come to sundry Resolutions,[7] which

[5] Ward may have already been ill with smallpox, of which he died on 26 March; see the entry of that date below. But JA's own extracts above show that Harrison had been named chairman of a committee of the whole as early as 5 March.

[6] An adequate explanation of these allusions would require a short monograph on the relations of JA and Washington and particularly on the charges sometimes encountered that JA participated in what has come to be called "the Conway Cabal." For the worst of the allegations against JA see John C. Fitzpatrick, *George Washington Himself*, Indianapolis, 1933, ch. 48; and for a refutation see Bernhard Knollenberg, *Washington and the Revolution: A Reappraisal*, N.Y., 1940, ch. 7, including the important appendix thereto. In an appendix on "Rush and Washington," in Benjamin Rush's *Letters*, 2:1197–1208, L. H. Butterfield has dealt with aspects of the JA–Washington relationship and concluded that Fitzpatrick's delineation of JA as Washington's spiteful rival during the Revolution is caricature rather than history.

[7] Authorizing and regulating priva-

they directed him to lay before Congress. The Report of the Committee being read Resolved that a Committee of three be appointed to draw a Declaration pursuant to said Report and lay the same before Congress. The Members chosen Mr. Wythe, Mr. Jay and Mr. Wilson.

Mr. Wythe was one of our best Men, but Mr. Jay and Mr. Wilson, tho excellent Members when present, had been hitherto generally in favour of the dilatory System.

Resolved that it be an instruction to the said Committee to receive and insert a Clause or Clauses, that all Seamen and Mariners on board of Merchant Ships and Vessells taken and condemned as Prizes, shall be entitled to their pay, according to the Terms of their contracts, untill the time of condemnation.

Wednesday March 20. 1776. Congress resumed the Consideration of the Instruction and Commission to the Deputies or Commissioners going to Canada, and agreed to them as they appear in the Journal. In these We obtained one Step more towards our great Object, a General Recommendation to the States to institute Governments. Congress recommended to the People of Canada to set up such a form of Government, as will be most likely in their Judgment to produce their happiness. And pressed them to have a compleat Representation of the People assembled in Convention, with all possible Expedition to deliberate concerning the Establishment of a Form of Government, and a Union with the United Colonies.—It will readily be supposed that a great part of these Instructions were opposed by our Antagonists with great Zeal: but they were supported on our Side with equal Ardour, and the Acceptance of them afforded a strong proof of the real determination of a Majority of Congress to go with Us to the final Consummation of our Wishes.

Thursday March 21. 1776. There are three Resolutions, which I claim

Resolved That it be recommended to the several Assemblies &c. that they exert their Utmost Endeavours to promote the Culture of Hemp, Flax and Cotton and the grouth of Wool.

Resolved that it be recommended to the said Assemblies &c. that they take the earliest measures for erecting and establishing in each and every Colony, a Society for the Improvement of Agriculture, Arts, Manufactures and commerce, and to maintain a Correspondence between such Societies, that the rich and numerous natural Advantages of this Country for supporting its Inhabitants may not be neglected.

---

teers. See the Memorandum in JA's Diary under date of Feb.? 1776 and note 10   there; also his Autobiography under 22, 23 March, below.

Resolved that it be recommended to the said Assemblies &c. that they forthwith consider of Ways and means of introducing the Manufactures of Duck, Sail Cloth and Steel, where they are not now understood, and of encouraging, encreasing and improving them, where they are.

These Resolutions I introduced and supported, not only for their Intrinsic Utility, which I thought would be very considerable: but because they held up to the view of the Nation the Air of Independence.[8]

Fryday March 22. 1776. Congress took into Consideration the Declaration brought in by the Committee, and after debate, the further Consideration of it, at the request of a Colony was postponed till tomorrow.

Saturday March 23. 1776. The Congress resumed the Consideration of the Declaration, which was agreed to as follows.

Whereas the Petitions of the United Colonies to the King, for the redress of great and manifold grievances, have not only been rejected, but treated with Scorn and contempt, and the Opposition to designs evidently formed to reduce them to servile Submission, and their necessary defence against hostile forces, actually employed to subdue them, declared Rebellion, and whereas an unjust War hath been commenced against them, which the Commanders of the British Fleets and Armies have prosecuted, and still continue to prosecute, with their Utmost vigour, and in a cruel manner, wasting, spoiling and destroying the Country, burning Houses and defenceless Towns, and exposing the helpless Inhabitants to every Misery from the Inclemency of the Winter, and not only urging Savages to invade the Country, but instigating Negroes to murder their Masters; and Whereas the Parliament of Great Britain hath lately passed an Act, affirming these Colonies to be in open Rebellion, forbidding all trade and commerce with the Inhabitants of them, untill they shall accept Pardons, and submit to despotic Rule, declaring their property, wherever found upon the Water, liable to seizure and confiscation, and enacting that what had been done there, by Virtue of the Royal Authority had been just and lawfull Acts, and shall be so deemed; from all which it is manifest, that the iniquitous Scheme, concerted to deprive them of the Liberty they have a right to by the Laws of Nature and the English Constitution, will be pertinaciously pursued: It being therefore neces-

---

[8] For these resolutions as originally drafted, and a related one that Congress did not accept, see an entry in JA's Diary under the assigned date of Feb.–March 1776.

sary to provide for their defence and Security, and justifiable to make Reprisals upon their Enemies, and otherwise to annoy them according to the Laws and Usages of Nations, the Congress, trusting that such of their Friends in Great Britain (of whom it is confessed there are many intitled to applause and gratitude for their Patriotism and Benevolence, and in whose favour a discrimination of Property cannot be made) as shall suffer by Captures, will impute it to the Authors of our common Calamities, do declare and resolve as followeth to Wit

Resolved That the Inhabitants of these Colonies be permitted to fit out armed Vessells to cruise on the Enemies of these United Colonies.

Resolved That all Ships and other Vessells, their Tackle, Apparell and Furniture, and all Goods, Wares and Merchandizes, belonging to any Inhabitant or Inhabitants of Great Britain, taken on the high Seas or between high and low Water mark, by any Armed Vessell, fitted out by any private Person or Persons, and to whom Commissions shall be granted, and being libelled and prosecuted in any Court erected for the Tryal of maritime Affairs in any of these Colonies, shall be deemed and adjudged to be lawfull Prize; and after deducting and paying the Wages which the Seamen and Mariners on board of such captures as are Merchant Ships and Vessels, shall be entitled to, according to the terms of their contracts, untill the time of the Adjudication, shall be condemned to and for the Use of the Owner or Owners, and the Officers, Marines and Mariners of such Armed Vessel, according to such Rules and proportions as they shall agree on; provided always that this Resolution shall not extend to any Vessel bringing Settlers, Arms, Ammunition and warlike Stores to and for the Use of these Colonies, or any of the Inhabitants thereof, who are Friends to the American Cause, or to such Warlike Stores, or to the Effects of such Settlers.

Resolved That all Ships &c. belonging to any Inhabitant of Great Britain as aforesaid, which shall be taken by any of the Vessells of War of these united Colonies, shall be deemed forfeited; one third after deducting and paying the Wages of Seamen and Mariners as aforesaid to the Officers and Men on board, and two thirds to the Use of the United Colonies.

Resolved that all Ships &c. belonging to any Inhabitants of Great Britain as aforesaid, which shall be taken by any Vessell of War, fitted out by and at the Expence of any of the United ⟨*States*⟩ Colonies, shall be deemed forfeited, and divided, after deducting and paying the Wages of Seamen and Mariners as aforesaid, in such manner and proportions as the Assembly or Convention of such Colony shall direct.

Resolved that all Vessells &c. and Cargoes, belonging to the Inhabitants of Great Britain as aforesaid, and all Vessells which may be employed in carrying Supplies to the ministerial Armies, which shall happen to be taken near the Shores of any of these Colonies, by the People of the Country, or detachments from the Army, shall be deemed lawful Prize; and the Court of Admiralty within the said Colony is required on condemnation thereof, to adjudge that all Charges and Expences which may attend the Capture and Tryal, be first paid out of the monies arising from the Sales of the Prize, and the Remainder equally among all those who shall have been actually engaged and employed in taking the said Prize. Provided, that where any detachments of the Army shall have been employed as aforesaid, their part of the Prize Money, shall be distributed among them in proportion to the Pay of the Officers and Soldiers so employed.

Resolved that a Committee of five be appointed to consider of the fortifying one or more ports on the American Coast, in the strongest manner for the Protection of our Cruisers, and the reception of their Prizes; that they take the Opinion of the best Engineers on the manner and Expence and report thereon to Congress. The Members chosen Mr. Harrison, Mr. J. Adams, Mr. Hewes, Mr. R. Morris and Mr. Whipple.[9]

Resolved that this Congress will on Monday next resolve itself into a committee of the whole to take into Consideration the Trade of the United Colonies; and that sundry Motions offered by the Members from Massachusetts Bay, Maryland, and Virginia be referred to said Committee.

Here is an Instance, in addition to many others, of an extraordinary Liberty taken by the Secretary, I suppose at the Instigation of the Party against Independence, to suppress, by omitting on the Journals the many Motions that were made disagreable to that sett. These motions ought to have been inserted verbatim on the Journals, with the names of those who made them.

On Monday the 25 of March 1776 I made a Motion and laid it in Writing on the Table in these Words

Resolved That the Thanks of this Congress, in their own Names and in the Name of the thirteen United Colonies, whom they repre-

---

[9] This resolution was the final, "secret" paragraph in the resolves or "Declaration" authorizing the fitting out of privateers (JCC, 4:233). The committee submitted a report on 24 June, the original of which, in JA's hand, is in PCC, No. 28; it is printed in JCC, 5:476.

sent be presented to his Excellency General Washington and the Officers and Soldiers under his Command, for their wise and spirited Conduct in the Seige and Acquisition of Boston; and that a Medal of Gold be struck in Commemoration of this great Event, and presented to his Excellency; and that a Committee of three be appointed to prepare a Letter of Thanks, and a proper device for the Medal. The Members chosen Mr. J. Adams, Mr. Jay and Mr. Hopkins.[1]

Tuesday March 26, 1776. Congress were informed of the Death of Governor Ward and on

Wednesday March 27 1776 they attended his Funeral in mourning for a Month. In this Gentleman who died of the Small Pox, We lost an honourable, a conscientious, a benevolent and inflexible Patriot.[2]

Thursday March 28. 1776 a Multitude of details but no Committee of the whole house.

Friday March 29. 1776. More Trifles but no Committee of the whole.

Saturday March 30. 1776. Ditto.

Monday April 1st. A Measure of Great Importance was adopted—a Treasury Office with an Auditor and a sufficient Number of Clerks. On the 17th. of February 1776 Congress had Resolved that a standing Committee of five be appointed for superintending the Treasury. Their duties pointed out and Mr. Duane, Mr. Nelson, Mr. Gerry, Mr. Smith and Mr. Willing were chosen on the Committee.

On this day April 1. 1776. The Treasury was much improved in its System. No order of the day.

April 2. 1776. The Committee appointed to prepare a Letter of Thanks to General Washington, and the Officers and Soldiers under his command brought in a draught which was read and agreed to: Ordered that it be transcribed, signed by the President and forwarded.

[1] On 2 April this committee "brought in a draught [of a letter], which being read, was agreed to: *Ordered,* That it be transcribed, signed by the president, and forwarded" (JCC, 4:248, followed by the text of the letter from the original in DLC:Washington Papers; see also entry on 2 April and note, below). As for "a proper device for the Medal," JA waited on Pierre Eugène Du Simitière, the Swiss-born artist and antiquarian then living in Philadelphia, and described Du Simitière's idea for it in a letter to AA, 14 Aug. (Adams Papers; JA–AA, *Familiar Letters,* p. 210–211). Du Simitière executed sketches, which remain among his papers in the Library Company of Philadelphia, and Congress on 29 Nov. authorized payment to him in the amount of $32, but his design was not used, and the commission was finally executed after the war by the French artist Duvivier (JCC, 6:991; *PMHB,* 13 [1889–1890]:357, 482–483; 69 [1945]:322). See illustrations in this volume.

[2] See also JA to AA, 29 March (Adams Papers; JA–AA, *Familiar Letters,* p. 147–148); Dr. Thomas Young to Henry Ward, 27 [26] March (Samuel Ward, *Correspondence,* ed. Bernhard Knollenberg, Providence, 1952, p. 201–203).

—But the Letter a great part of the Compliment of which would have lain in the Insertion of it in the Journal, was carefully secluded. Perhaps the Secretary or the President or both, chose rather to conceal the Compliment to the General than make one to the Member who made the motion and the Committee who prepared it. I never troubled myself about the Journals, and should never have known the Letter was not there, if I had not been called to peruse them, now after twenty nine Years have rolled away.[3]

April 3. 1776 great Things were done. The Naval System made great Progress.[4]

April 4. 1776. We did great Things again.

Agreable to the order of the Day, the Congress resolved itself into a Committee of the whole to take into Consideration the Trade of the United Colonies, and after some time spent thereon, the President resumed the Chair and Mr. Harrison reported that the Committee had taken into Consideration the matters referred to them and had come to sundry Resolutions, which he was ordered to deliver in. The Resolutions agreed to by the Committee of the whole Congress being read, Ordered to lie on the Table.

April 5. 1776. Good Fryday.

April 6. 1776. Congress resumed the consideration of the Report, from the Committee of the whole, and the same being twice read, and debated by paragraphs, was agreed to. These Resolutions are on the Journal, and amount to something.[5] They opened the Ports and sett our Commerce at Liberty: But they were far short of what had been moved by Members from Massachusetts, Maryland and Virginia. There is one Resolution I will not omit.

Resolved that no Slaves be imported into any of the thirteen Colonies.

I will not omit to remark here, the manifest Artifice, in concealing in the Journal the Motions which were made and the Names of the Members who made them, in these daily Committees of the whole. The Spirit of a Party which has been before exposed can alone Account, for this Unfairness.

Resolved that the Remainder of the report be postponed.

---

[3] The omission from the Journal of the text of the congratulatory letter to Washington was surely a dereliction on Thomson's part, and the sole case among many cited by JA that appears indefensible (see p. 365, above, and note 4 there). But oversight is far more likely to have been the cause of this lapse than the insidious motive assigned by JA.

[4] See *JCC,* 4:251–254.

[5] See same, p. 257–259.

A Letter from General Washington of the 27th. of March. And a Letter from Brigadier General Heath being received and read,

Resolved that the Letter from General Washington, with the Papers inclosed, be referred to a Committee of the whole Congress.

Tuesday April 9th. 1776. No Committee of the whole.

Wednesday April 10. 1776. Resolved that the Letters from General Washington be referred to a Committee of the whole Congress.[6]

April 11. 1776. Resolved that a Committee of three be appointed to enquire into the Truth of the Report respecting Governor Tryons exacting an Oath from Persons going by the Packet, and to ascertain the Fact, by Affidavits taken before a Chief Justice, or other Chief Magistrate. The Members chosen Mr. Jay, Mr. Wythe and Mr. Wilson. This helped forward our designs a little.

Resolved That it be recommended to the several Assemblies, Conventions and Committees or Councils of Safety of the United Colonies, to Use their best Endeavours in communicating to foreign nations, the Resolutions of Congress relative to Trade.—This also was a considerable Advance. But it would now be scarcely credited if I were to relate the Struggle it cost Us to obtain every one of these Resolutions.

April 12th. 1776. No Committee of the whole.

April 13. 1776. No Committee of the whole. April 15. No Committee of the whole.

Tuesday April 16. 1776. Whereas Information has been this day laid before Congress, from which there is great reason to believe that Robert Eden Esq. Governor of Maryland, has lately carried on a Correspondence with the British Ministry highly dangerous to the Liberties of America:

Resolved therefore that the Council of Safety of Maryland be earnestly requested immediately to cause the Person and Papers of Governor Eden to be seized and secured, and such of the Papers as relate to the American dispute, without delay conveyed safely to Congress: and that Copies of the intercepted Letters from the Secretary of State be inclosed to the said council of Safety. A similar Resolution relative to Alexander Ross and his Papers. No Committee of the whole.

Wednesday April 17. 1776. Thursday April 18. No Committee of the whole.

Fryday April 19. Resolved that a Committee of seven be appointed to examine and ascertain the Value of the several Species of Gold and

---

[6] These were two additional letters, both dated 1 April (JCC, 4:266); they are printed in Washington, *Writings*, ed. Fitzpatrick, 4:456–457.

Silver Coins current in these Colonies, and the Proportions they ought to bear to Spanish milled Dollars. Members chosen Mr. Duane, Mr. Wythe, Mr. John Adams, Mr. Sherman, Mr. Hewes, Mr. Johnson and Mr. Whipple.[7]

The Committee to whom General Washingtons Letter of the 15th. instant, as well as other Letters were referred brought in their report, which being taken into Consideration, was agreed to whereupon resolved—See the Journal.[8]

One Resolution was that the Resignation of James Warren, as Paymaster General of the Army be Accepted.—This Gentleman had been appointed at my Solicitation. Mr. Samuel Adams and Mr. Gerry concurring. Our other Colleagues notwithstanding.

The Committee to whom were referred the Letter from General Washington of the 4th and the Letter from General Schuyler of the second of this month, brought in their report. Adjourned to Monday.

Monday April 22. 1776. A Letter from the Canada Commissioners, one from General Washington of the 19th, one from General Schuyler, inclosing sundry Letters and Papers from Canada, and one from the Committee of Inspection of West Augusta with sundry Papers inclosed, were referred to Mr. R. H. Lee, Mr. J. Adams, Mr. Jay, Mr. Braxton and Mr. Johnson.[9]

Tuesday April 23. 1776. The Committee to whom the Letters from General Washington, General Schuyler and the Letters from Canada &c. were referred brought in their report.

Wednesday April 24. Thomas Heywood [Heyward] Junr. Esqr. a new Member from Carolina, and an excellent one, appeared in Congress from South Carolina. On him We could always depend for sound Measures, though he seldom spoke in public. Thomas Lynch Junr. Esqr. also appeared.

Congress resolved itself into a Committee of the whole, but came to no resolutions.

[7] This committee brought in a report, written by Wythe, on 22 May; on 24 July the report was recommitted and Jefferson added to the committee; a new report, by Jefferson, was submitted on 2 Sept. and tabled (JCC, 4:293–294, 381–383; 5:608, 724–728; Jefferson, *Papers*, ed. Boyd, 1:511–518). It does not appear that JA had any hand in either report.

[8] JCC, 4:295–297. JA was not a member of this committee.

[9] For these letters see JCC, 4:298, note. Washington's letter is printed in his *Writings*, ed. Fitzpatrick, 4:492–494. The committee brought in a report, prepared by John Jay, on the 23d, and Congress adopted several resolutions thereon; on the 29th it adopted further resolutions; and on 3 May "after some debate the farther consideration [of the report] was postponed" (JCC, 4:301, 318, 324).

Thursday April 25. 1776. Two Letters from General Washington of the 22 and 23 were referred to Mr. R. H. L[ee,] Mr. J. Adams and Mr. Hewes.[1] Congress resolved itself into a Committee of the whole, to take into their farther consideration the Letter from General Washington of the 27th. of March last and the Papers therein enclosed, Mr. Harrison reported that the Committee had come to a Resolution, on the matters referred to them, which he read and delivered in. Report read again and postponed.

Fryday April 26. Postponed. Saturday April 27. Ditto.

Monday April 29 1776. Congress resumed the Consideration of the Report of the Committee on General Washingtons Letter of the 19 and came to sundry Resolutions which may be seen in the Journal.

Tuesday April 30. 1776. Congress took into Consideration the Report of the Committee on General Washingtons Letter of the 24 of March, whereupon resolved as in the Journal.[2] Of some importance but nothing to the great Objects still kept out of Sight.

The Delegates from New Jersey having laid before Congress a number of Bills counterfeited to imitate the continental Bills of Credit

Resolved that a Committee of six be appointed to consider of this matter and report thereon to Congress.

The Members chosen Mr. W. Livingston, Mr. McKean, Mr. Sherman, Mr. J. Adams, Mr. Braxton and Mr. Duane.[3] Adjourned to Thursday.

Thursday May 2. 1776. Congress resumed the Consideration of the Report of the Committee on General Washingtons Letter of the 24 of March last and after debate

Resolved That it be recommitted; and as the members of the former committee are Absent, that a new committee be appointed. The Members chosen Mr. Dickinson, Mr. W. Livingston and Mr. Rutledge. The Recommitment and the names of the new Committee shew the design.

Fryday May 3. 1776. A Petition from Peter Simon was presented to Congress and read. Ordered that it be referred to a Committee of three. The Members chosen Mr. McKean, Mr. Wythe and Mr. J. Adams.[4]

The Committee to whom the Report on General Washingtons Letter

[1] Washington's letters are printed in his *Writings,* ed. Fitzpatrick, 4:500–504, 505–507. No report has been found.

[2] JCC, 4:320–321.

[3] This committee brought in a report, written by William Livingston, on 7 June, and it was tabled (JCC, 5:426 and note).

[4] This committee reported on 22 May, and Congress acted on its recommendations (JCC, 4:374). The report itself has not been found.

of the 24. of March last was recommitted, brought in their report which was read. Ordered to lie on the Table.

Monday May 6. 1776. Congress resumed the Consideration of the Report on General Washingtons Letter of the 24th. of March, and thereupon came to the following resolution:

Whereas General Washington has requested directions concerning the Conduct that should be observed towards Commissioners said to be coming from Great Britain to America

Resolved That General Washington be informed that Congress suppose if commissioners are intended to be sent from Great Britain to treat of peace, that the practice usual in such cases will be observed, by making previous Application for the necessary Passports or Safe Conduct, and on such Application being made, Congress will then direct the proper measures for the Reception of such Commissioners.

It will be observed how long this trifling Business had been depending, but it cannot be known from the Journal how much debate it had occasioned, or how much time it had consumed. It was one of those delusive Contrivances by which the Party in Opposition to Us endeavoured, by lulling the People with idle hopes of Reconciliation, into Security, to turn their hearts and thoughts from Independence. They endeavoured to insert in the Resolution, Ideas of Reconciliation, We carried our point for inserting Peace. They wanted Powers to be given to the General to receive the Commissioners in Ceremony. We ordered nothing to be done till We were solicited for Pasports. Upon the whole We avoided the Snare and brought the Controversy to a close, with some dignity. But it will never be known how much labour it cost Us, to accomplish it.

Then a Committee of the whole on the State of the Colonies: Mr. Harrison reported sundry Resolutions, which as they stand on the Journal will shew the Art and Skill with which the Generals Letters, Indian Affairs, Revenue Matters, Naval Arrangements and twenty other Things, many of them very trivial, were mixed, in these Committees of the whole, with the Great Subjects of Government, Independence and Commerce. Little Things were designedly thrown in the Way of Great Ones. And the Time consumed upon trifles which ought to have been consecrated to higher Interests. We could only harrangue against the misapplication of time, and harrangues consumed more time: so that We could only now and then snatch a transient Glance at the promised Land.

Wednesday May 8. 1776. The Instructions from the Naval Committee to Commodore Hopkins being laid before Congress and read:

Ordered That they be referred to a Committee of seven, and that it be an Instruction to that Committee to enquire how far Commodore Hopkins has complied with the said Instructions, and if upon Inquiry they shall find that he has departed therefrom, to examine into the Occasion thereof; also to inquire into the Situation of the Governor and Lieutenant Governor of Providence and the other Officers brought from thence, and report what in their Opinion is proper to be done with them. That the said Committee have power to send for Witnesses and Papers. The Members chosen Mr. Harrison Mr. J. Adams, Mr. McKean, Mr. Duane, Mr. Lynch, Mr. Sherman and Mr. W. Livingston.[5]

There were three Persons at this time, who were a standing Subject of Altercation in Congress. General Wooster, Commodore Hopkins and a Mr. Wrixon. I never could discover any reason for the Bitterness against Wooster, but his being a New England man: nor for that against Hopkins but that he had done too much: nor for that against Wrixon, but his being patronized by Mr. Samuel Adams and Mr. R. H. Lee. Be it as it may, these three consumed an immense quantity of time and kept up the Passions of the Parties to a great hight. One design was to divert us from our main Object.[6]

A Committee of the whole, Mr. Harrison report[ed] no resolution. Leave to sit again.

Thursday May 9. 1776. A Committee of the whole:—Mr. Harrison reported a Resolution, which he read and delivered in.

The Resolution of the Committee of the whole was again read, and the determination thereof, at the Request of a Colony was postponed till tomorrow.

Fryday May 10. 1776. Congress resumed the Consideration of the Resolution reported from the Committee of the whole, and the same was agreed to as follows:

Resolved, That it be recommended to the respective Assemblies and Conventions of the United Colonies, where no Government sufficient to the Exigencies of their Affairs, hath been hitherto established, to adopt such Government as shall in the Opinion of the Representatives

[5] A part of these instructions to the committee was not adopted until 22 May; on 31 May other papers were referred to the same committee, which on 7 June brought in a report, written by JA (in PCC, No. 19, III), on which Congress acted; but on 12 July the committee was discharged and super-seded by the Marine Committee (JCC, 4:375, 407; 5:424–425, 545). See also the entries in JA's Autobiography under 12, 15–17, 19 Aug., below.

[6] On these controversies see the very full references in Burnett, ed., *Letters of Members*, 1:441, note.

of the People best conduce to the Happiness and Safety of their Constituents in particular, and America in general.

Resolved that a Committee of three be appointed to prepare a Preamble to the foregoing Resolution. The Members chosen Mr. J. Adams, Mr. Rutledge and Mr. Richard Henry Lee.[7]

Marshall in his Life of Washington says this Resolution was moved by R. H. Lee and seconded by J. Adams.[8] It was brought before the Committee of the whole House, in concert between Mr. R. H. Lee and me, and I suppose General Washington was informed of it by Mr. Harrison the Chairman or some other of his Correspondents: but nothing of this Appears upon the Journal. It is carefully concealed like many other Things relative to the greatest Affairs of the Nation which were before Congress in that Year.

This Resolution I considered as an Epocha, a decisive Event. It was a measure which I had invariably pursued for a whole Year, and contended for, through a Scæne and a Series of Anxiety, labour, Study, Argument, and Obloquy, which was then little known and is now forgotten, by all but Dr. Rush and a very few who like him survive. Millions of Curses were poured out upon me, for these Exertions and for these Tryumphs over them, by the Essex Juntoes, for there were such at that time and have continued to this day in every State in the Union; who whatever their pretences may have been have never forgotten nor cordially forgiven me. By this Term which is now become vulgarly and politically technical, I mean, not the Tories, for from them I received always more candour, but a class of People who thought proper and convenient to themselves to go along with the Public Opinion in Appearance, though in their hearts they detested it. Although they might think the public opinion was right in General, in its difference with G. Britain, yet they secretly regretted the Seperation, and above all Things the Connection with France. Such a Party has always existed and was the final Ruin of the Federal Administration as will hereafter very plainly appear.

A Committee of the whole again. Mr. Harrison reported no Resolution. I mention these Committees to shew how all these great ques-

[7] On this momentous step toward independence, and JA's part in it, see not only what follows in the Autobiography but an earlier passage at p. 335, above, and JA's Diary (Notes of Debates), 13–15 May 1776, with the editorial notes there.

[8] A mistake, as CFA pointed out in a note on this passage (JA, *Works*, 3:

44). Marshall's account of the adoption of the resolve and its preamble recommending the establishment of new governments is correct, but JA evidently confused it with Marshall's passage on the resolution of independence, introduced on 7 June. See John Marshall, *Life of George Washington*, Phila., 1804–1807, 2:402–403, 409–410.

tions laboured. Day after day consumed in debates without any Conclusion.

Saturday May 11. 1776. A Petition from John Jacobs in behalf of himself and others was presented to Congress and read. Ordered that it be referred to a Committee of three. The Members chosen Mr. John Adams, Mr. Lee and Mr. Rutledge.[9]

A Committee of the whole. Mr. Harrison reported no Resolution. This days Journal of this Committee shews, with what Art other matters were referred to these Committees of the whole, in order to retard and embarrass the great questions.

Monday May 13. 1776. Sundry Petitions were presented to Congress and read, viz. one from Dr. Benjamin Church, and one from Benjamin, Samuel and Edward Church, with a Certificate from three Physicians respecting the health of Dr. B. Church. Here I am compelled, much against my Inclination to record a Fact, which if it were not necessary to explain some things I should rather have concealed. When this Petition was before Congress, Mr. Samuel Adams said something, which I thought I confess too favourable to Dr. Church. I cannot recollect that I said any Thing against him. As it lies upon my Mind I was silent. Mr. Hancock was President, and Mr. Harrison Chairman of the Committee of the whole and a constant confidential Correspondent of General Washington. Neither of them friendly to me. I cannot suspect Mr. Samuel Adams of writing or insinuating any Thing against me to the Friends of Dr. Church, at that time. But Mr. Samuel Adams told me that Dr. Church and Dr. Warren, had composed Mr. Hancocks oration on the fifth of March, which was so celebrated, more than two thirds of it at least. Mr. Hancock was most certainly not friendly to me at that time, and he might think himself in the Power of Dr. Church. When Mr. Edward Church printed his poetical Libel against me at New York in 1789 or 1790, I was told by an Acquaintance of his that he was full of Prejudices against me on Account of Dr. Church his Brother. I leave others to conjecture how he came by them. I know of no other Way to account for his Virulence, and his Cousin Dr. Jarvis's Virulence against me, having never injured or offended any of them. Misrepresentation at that day was a Pestilence that walked in darkness. In more modern times it has stalked abroad with more impudence at Noon day.[1]

[9] This petition is not clearly identifiable, and no action by this committee is recorded in the Journal.

[1] This entire paragraph was omitted by CFA. When Hancock's oration on the Boston Massacre was delivered, JA thought it a splendid performance and voiced no suspicion that the speaker was not the writer; see his Diary under 5 March 1774. In 1776 Dr. Benjamin

Tuesday May 14. 1776. A Letter of the 11th. from General Washington inclosing sundry Papers; a Letter of the 3d from General Schuyler; and a Letter of the 9th. from Daniel Robertson were laid before Congress and read. Resolved that they be referred to a Committee of three. The Members chosen Mr. W. Livingston, Mr. Jefferson and Mr. John Adams.[2]

William Ellery Esqr. appeared a Delegate from Rhode Island, in the place of Governor Ward, and being an excellent Member, fully supplied his place.

The Committee appointed to prepare a Preamble, thought it not necessary to be very elaborate, and Mr. Lee and Mr. Rutledge desired me as Chairman to draw something very short which I did and with their Approbation.[3]

On Wednesday May 15. 1776 reported the following which was agreed to

Whereas his Britannic Majesty, in conjunction with the Lords and Commons of Great Britain, has, by a late Act of Parliament, excluded the Inhabitants of these united Colonies from the Protection of his Crown; and whereas no Answer whatever to the humble Petitions of the Colonies for redress of Grievances and reconciliation with Great Britain has been or is likely to be given, but the whole force

---

Church, who had secretly defected to the enemy and been caught, was in jail in Norwich, Conn.; on 14 May Congress voted that he be allowed to return to Massachusetts, under sureties, pending his trial, and he afterward sailed for the West Indies and was lost at sea (*JCC,* 4:350, 352; *DAB*). His brother Edward Church's "poetical Libel" against JA was an anonymous satire in heroic couplets entitled *The Dangerous Vice ———. A Fragment. Addressed to All Whom It May Concern. By a Gentleman formerly of Boston,* Columbia [i.e. New York?], 1789 (Evans 21736). Its theme was that, while Washington could safely be entrusted with executive power, JA, "Tainted with foreign vices, and his own," hankered for the attributes and perquisites of royalty. On Charles Jarvis, Harvard 1766, Boston physician and political disciple of Jefferson, see Thacher, *Amer. Medical Biog.,* 1:313–316. His attacks on JA may have been in newspaper articles as yet unidentified.

[2] For the letters in question see *JCC,* 4:352, note. Washington's letter is printed in his *Writings,* ed. Fitzpatrick, 5:32–37. Further letters were referred to this committee on 16 and again on 18 May, all relative to the northern campaign, and on the latter date the committee was enlarged. Its tangled history is summarized, with full references, in an editorial note in Jefferson, *Papers,* ed. Boyd, 1:295–296. A portion of its report of 21 May is in JA's hand (PCC, No. 19, VI; *JCC,* 4:377).

[3] This had been brought in as a "draught" on 13 May and postponed (*JCC,* 4:351), though curiously JA overlooked the relevant passage in the *Journals* under that date and thus mistakenly says below that it was "reported" (he should have said "taken into consideration") on the 15th. No MS version of the famous preamble has been found except that which was spread on the Journal as finally adopted; it was printed, with the resolution of 10 May, in the *Pennsylvania Gazette,* 22 May.

of that Kingdom aided by foreign Mercenaries is to be exerted for the destruction of the good People of these Colonies; and whereas it appears absolutely irreconcileable to reason, and good Conscience, for the People of these Colonies now to take the Oaths and Affirmations necessary for the support of any Government under the Crown of Great Britain, and it is necessary that the Exercise of every kind of Authority under the said Crown should be totally suppressed, and all the Powers of Government exerted under the Authority of the People of the Colonies, for the preservation of internal peace, Virtue and good order, as well as for the defence of their Lives, Liberties and Properties against the hostile Invasions and cruel depredations of their Ennemies; therefore

Resolved That it be recommended to the respective Assemblies and Conventions of the United Colonies, where no Government sufficient to the Exigencies of their affairs hath been hitherto established, to adopt such Government as shall in the Opinion of the Representatives of the People best conduce to the happiness and Safety of their Constituents in particular and America in General.

Ordered that the said Preamble, with the Resolution passed the 10th. instant, be published.—Mr. Duane called it, to me, a Machine for the fabrication of Independence. I said, smiling, I thought it was independence itself: but We must have it with more formality yet.

May 16. 1776. Thursday. The following Letters were laid before Congress and read. One of the first from the Commissioners of Congress in Canada: one of the 10th from General Schuyler, and one without date from General Washington, inclosing a Letter to him from Dr. Stringer.

Resolved That the Letter from Dr. Stringer to General Washington be referred to the Committee appointed to prepare medicine Chests: that the other Letters be referred to Mr. W. Livingston, Mr. Jefferson and Mr. J. Adams.[4]

Resolved that the President write to General Washington requesting him to repair to Philadelphia as soon as he can conveniently, in order to consult with Congress upon such measures as may be necessary for the carrying on the ensuing Campaign.

Horatio Gates Esqr. was elected a Major General and Thomas Mifflin Esqr. Brigadier General.

I take Notice of this Appointment of Gates, because it had great Influence on my future fortunes. It soon Occasioned a Competition

---

[4] For these letters see JCC, 4:358, note. Washington's letter (of 15 May) is printed in his *Writings*, ed. Fitzpatrick, 5:44–46.

between him and Schuyler, in which I always contended for Gates, and as the Rivalry occasioned great Animosities among the Friends of the two Generals, the consequences of which are not yet spent. Indeed they have affected the Essential Interests of the United States and will influence their ultimate Destiny. They effected an Enmity between Gates and Mr. Jay who always supported Schuyler, and a dislike in Gates of Hamilton who married Schuylers daughter, with which Mr. Burr wrought so skillfully as to turn the Elections in New York not only against Hamilton but against the Federalists, and whatever Hamilton may have pretended, I am persuaded that the decided part I had acted and the free Speeches I had made in Congress against Schuyler and in favour of Gates, had been rankling in Hamiltons heart from 1776 till he wrote his Libel against me in 1799.[5] Gates's Resentment against Jay, Schuyler and Hamilton made him turn in 1799 against me, who had been the best Friend and the most efficacious Supporter he ever had in America. I had never in my Life any personal Prejudice or dislike against General Schuyler: on the contrary I knew him to [be] industrious, studious and intelligent: But the New England Officers, Soldiers and Inhabitants, knew Gates in the Camp at Cambridge. Schuyler was not known to many and the few who had heard of him were prejudiced against him from the former french War. The New England Soldiers would not enlist to serve under him and the Militia would not turn out. I was therefore under a Necessity of supporting Gates. Mr. Duane, Mr. Jay, Colonel Harrison &c. supported Schuyler. There is no difficulty therefore in Accounting for Hamiltons ancient any more than his modern Malice against me.

On this same May 16 it was resolved that it be recommended to the general Assemblies of Massachusetts Bay and Connecticutt, to endeavour to have the battallions inlisted for two Years, unless sooner discharged by Congress; in which case the Men to be allowed one Months pay on their discharge; but if the Men cannot be prevailed on to inlist for two Years, that they be inlisted for one; and that they be ordered as soon as raised and armed, to march immediately to Boston.

Here it is proper for me, to obviate some Aspersions in Hamiltons

---

[5] *Letter from Alexander Hamilton, concerning the Public Conduct and Character of John Adams, Esq....,* N.Y., 1800. CFA omitted from his text the preceding lines beginning "and whatever Hamilton may have pretended." He also omitted the final sentence in the present paragraph, and in the next paragraph but one below he made a few slight alterations in order to suppress Hamilton's name.

Libell against me, which is not the less malicious for being silly. I will not here charge him with willfull falshood, because I can readily believe that among the Correspondents with the Army and the Connections of my Opponents he may have heard insinuations and misrepresentations, that he too easily credited. The Truth is I never opposed the raising of Men during the War.[6] I was always willing the General might obtain as many Men as he possibly could, to enlist during the War, or during the longest Period, they could be persuaded to inlist for. And I always declared myself so. But I contended that I knew the Number to be obtained in this manner would be very small in New England, from whence almost the whole Army was derived. A Regiment might possibly be obtained, of the meanest, idlest, most intemperate and worthless: but no more. A Regiment was no Army to defend this Country. We must have tradesmens Sons and farmers Sons, or We should be without defence. And such Men certainly would not inlist during the War or for long Periods as yet. The Service was too new, they had not yet become attached to it by habit. Was it credible that Men who could get at home better living, more comfortable Lodgings, more than double the Wages, in Safety, not exposed to the Sicknesses of the Camp, would bind themselves during the War? I knew it to be impossible. In the Middle States, where they had imported from Ireland and Germany so many transported Convicts and Redemptioners, it was possible they might obtain some. Let them try. I had no Objection: But I warned them against depending on so improbable a Resource, for the defence of the Country. Congress confessed the unanswerable force of this reasoning. Mr. McKean I remember said in Congress, Mr. John Adams has convinced me that you will get no Army, upon such terms. Even in Pensylvania, the most desperate of imported Labourers cannot be obtained in any Numbers upon such terms. Farmers and Tradesmen give much more Encouragement to Labourers and Journeymen. Mr. McKeans Opinion was well founded and proved to be true in Experience for Pensylvania never was able to obtain half the Compliment of New England in Proportion.

Monday. May. 20. 1776. Lyman Hall and Button Gwinnet appear as Delegates from Georgia: both intelligent and spirited Men, who made a powerful Addition to our Phalanx.

[6] Or, as would be said today, for the duration of the war. For Hamilton's charge against JA on this score, see his *Letter* (cited in the preceding note), p. 4. For JA's advocacy of long-term enlistments see p. 434, 448, below; also James Duane's Notes of Debates in Congress, 22 Feb. 1776 (Burnett, ed., *Letters of Members*, 1:360).

Certain Resolutions of the Convention of South Carolina, respecting the Battalions to be [7] raised in that Colony; also certain resolutions passed by the General Assembly of the said Colony, respecting the manner in [which] Commissioners coming from England are to be received and treated in that Colony, were laid before Congress and read.

Resolved that the Resolutions respecting the Battalions be referred to a Committee of five.

The Members chosen Mr. John Adams, Mr. Sherman, Mr. Floyd, Mr. W. Livingston and Mr. Morton.[8]

A Committee of the whole: Mr. Harrison reported no Resolution.

Tuesday May 21. 1776. Three Letters from General Washington, inclosing Letters and Papers of Intelligence from England, and a Copy of the Treaties made by his Britannic Majesty with the Duke of Brunswick for 4084 of his Troops; and with the Landgrave of Hesse Cassel for 12,000 of his Troops; and with the Count of Hanau for 668 of his Troops.

A Letter from William Palfrey with a Copy of his Weekly Account,

A Letter from John Langdon to General Washington

A Petition from Samuel Austin, John Rowe, S. Patridge [Partridge], Samuel Dashwood and John Scollay of Boston:

Resolved that the said Letters and Papers and Petition be referred to a Committee of five; that the said Committee be directed to extract and publish the Treaties, and such parts of the Intelligence as they think proper: also to consider of an Adequate reward for the Person who brought the Intelligence; and that they prepare an Address to the foreign Mercenaries, who are coming to invade America.

The Members chosen Mr. John Adams, Mr. William Livingston, Mr. Jefferson, Mr. R. H. Lee and Mr. Sherman.[9]

The Committee to whom the Letter of the 10th from General

---

[7] JA mistakenly inserted the two preceding words when copying; they are not in the *Journals*.

[8] This committee reported on 25 May; on 7 June, after debate, Congress recommitted the report; and on 18 June a new report was brought in and a long series of resolutions was adopted (JCC, 4:393; 5:425, 461–463). No texts of the reports as submitted have been found.

[9] For the letters in question see JCC, 4:369, note. Those of Washington (18, 19, 20 May) are printed in his *Writings*, ed. Fitzpatrick, 5:56–57, 58, 62. The publication by the committee is in the *Pennsylvania Gazette*, 22 May, and later in other papers. The committee reported to Congress on 30 May and 4 and 17 June, its third report being in JA's hand (PCC, No. 22; see JCC, 4:405, 415; 5:458–459). These did not complete the duties assigned to the committee; for example, it issued no address to the German mercenaries; but JA was later to have a part in such an address; see under 26, 27 Aug., below.

Lee was referred brought in their report, which was read, and after some Debate

Resolved that the farther Consideration thereof be postponed till the Arrival of General Washington.

The Committee to whom the Letters from General Washington, Major General Schuyler, and the Commissioners in Canada were referred, brought in their report which was read.

Resolved that the Consideration thereof be postponed till tomorrow.

Thursday May 23 1776. Resolved That a Committee of five be appointed to confer with General Washington, Major General Gates, and Brigadier General Mifflin, upon the most speedy and effectual means of supporting the American Cause in Canada. The Members chosen, Mr. Harrison, Mr. R. H. Lee and Mr. J. Adams, Mr. Wilson and Mr. Rutledge.[1]

Fryday May 24. 1776. The Committee appointed to confer with his Excellency General Washington, Major General Gates and Brigadier General Mifflin brought in their report. The Resolutions reported and adopted may be seen on the Journal.

Agreable to order, General Washington attended in Congress, and after some Conference with him, Resolved that he be directed to attend again tomorrow.

Saturday May 25. 1776. Resolved that a Committee be appointed to confer with his Excellency General Washington, Major General Gates, and Brigadier General Mifflin, and to concert a Plan of military Operations for the ensuing Campaign. The Members appointed Mr. Harrison, Mr. R. H. Lee, Mr. J. Adams, Mr. Wilson, Mr. R. R. Livingston, Mr. Whipple, Mr. Sherman, Mr. Hopkins, Mr. W. Livingston, Mr. Read, Mr. Tilghman, Mr. Hewes, Mr. Middleton and Mr. Hall.[2]

Congress took into Consideration the Report of the Committee on the Letter from General Washington of 11 May, the Letter from

---

[1] This "committee of conference" brought in a report next day which had been prepared by Benjamin Harrison and which was approved by Congress; at the same time Robert R. Livingston was added to the committee and it was given further duties; on the 25th it brought in a report written by Edward Rutledge (*JCC*, 4:387–388, 394–396).

[2] The history of this larger committee of conference is too complex to warrant a detailed account here. Its successive reports in the last days of May and early days of June (none of them, so far as the inadequate records show, written by JA) were taken up almost simultaneously in committees of the whole, and on 15 June Congress appointed a committee (of which JA was not a member) "to digest and arrange the several resolutions reported" as a result of recommendations by these and other committees that had been concurrently at work during the preceding crucial weeks in the military as well as political history of the Revolution (*JCC*, 5:446). See the draft reports prepared by Jefferson for the committee of review, in Jefferson, *Papers*, ed. Boyd, 1:389–396, and the editorial notes there.

Gen. Schuyler of the third &c. which was in part agreed to, as may be seen on the Journal.[3]

Resolved that the Consideration of the first Paragraph in said report be postponed, and that the third and fifth Paragraphs be referred to the Committee appointed to confer with the Generals.

Resolved that the several Reports on General Washingtons Letters, not yet considered, and the Generals Letters, which were referred to a Committee of the whole Congress, be committed to the Committee appointed to confer with the Generals.

Thus as Postponement and Embarassment had been for Many Months, the Object, We now had all our Business to go over again.

A Number of Deputies from four of the six Nations of Indians, having Arrived in Town and notified Congress, that they are desirous of an Audience.

Resolved That they be admitted to an Audience on Monday next at Eleven O Clock.

Monday May 27. 1776. Agreable to order, the Indians were admitted to an Audience.

Wednesday May 29. 1776. The Committee appointed to confer with the Generals brought in a Report which was read and considered, Resolved that the farther Consideration of the Report be postponed till tomorrow.

Thursday May 30. 1776. Congress took into Consideration the Report of the Committee appointed to confer with the Generals. Resolved that it be referred to a Committee of the whole Congress. Mr. Harrison reported one Resolution, relative to the defence of New York. Leave to sit again.

Fryday May 31. The Committee of Conference brought in a farther report which was read. Resolved that it be referred to the Committee of the whole Congress. Mr. Harrison reported a request to sit again. Granted.

Saturday June 1. 1776. Colonel Joseph Read resigned his Office of Secretary to General Washington.

Committee of the whole again. Mr. Harrison reported some resolutions. Leave to sit again.

Monday June 3. 1776 Committee of the whole. Mr. Harrison reported sundry resolutions. Leave to sit again.

Tuesday June 4th. 1776. Committee of the whole. Mr. Harrison reported more resolutions. Leave to sit again. Resolutions reported postponed.

[3] JCC, 4:391–392.

Wednesday June 5th. 1776. Congress took into Consideration the report of the Committee of the whole; whereupon resolved, That a Committee of five be appointed to consider what is proper to be done with Persons giving Intelligence to the Ennemy or supplying them with provisions.

The Members chosen Mr. J. Adams, Mr. Jefferson, Mr. Rutledge, Mr. Wilson and Mr. R. Livingston.[4]

Resolved that Robert Hanson Harrison Esq. have the Rank of Lieutenant Colonel in the Continental Army. The Generals Secretary as I suppose. Joseph Reed Esqr. was elected Adjutant General.

Fryday June 7th. 1776. Certain Resolutions respecting Independency being moved and seconded. Resolved That the Consideration of them be referred till tomorrow morning; and that the members be enjoyned to attend punctually at ten O Clock, in order to take the same into their consideration.

It will naturally be enquired why these Resolutions and the Names of the Gentlemen who moved and seconded them, were not inserted in the Journals? To this question I can give no other Answer than this. Mr. Hancock was President, Mr. Harrison Chairman of the Committee of the whole House. Mr. Thompson the Secretary was cousin to Mr. Dickinson. And Mr. R. H. Lee, Mr. John Adams[5] were no favourites of either.[6]

Saturday June 8. 1776. Resolved that the Resolutions respecting Independency be referred to a Committee of the whole Congress. Mr. Harrison reported no Resolution. Leave to sit again.

Monday June 10. 1776. Committee of the whole. Mr. Harrison reported a Resolution. The Resolution agreed to in the Committee of the whole Congress being read,

Resolved that the Consideration of the first resolution be postponed to the first day of July next; and in the mean while, that no time be lost in Case the Congress agree thereto, that a Committee be appointed to prepare a declaration to the effect of the first Resolution, which is in these Words, "That these United Colonies are, and of right ought to be free and independent States; that they are absolved, from all Allegiance to the British Crown; and that all political connection be-

[4] Later called "the Committee on Spies." It reported on 24 June and again on 29 July (JCC, 5:475, 616), but its most important action was the revision of the Articles of War, assigned to it on 14 June and dealt with in Congress during August and September; see the entries of 19 Aug., 20 Sept. in JA's Autobiography, below.

[5] Here several words follow which have been heavily inked out, doubtless by the diarist. The best guess for them is "and Mr. Adams Principles," but the last word is utterly conjectural.

[6] But see p. 365, note 4, above.

tween them and the State of Great Britain, is and ought to be totally dissolved."

June 11. 1776. Tuesday. Resolved that a Committee of three be appointed to consider of a Compensation to the Secretary for his services. The Members chosen Mr. J. Adams, Mr. Rutledge and Mr. Hewes.[7]

Resolved that the Committee for preparing the declaration consist of five. The Members chosen Mr. Jefferson, Mr. John Adams, Mr. Franklin, Mr. Sherman and Mr. R. R. Livingston. Jefferson was chairman because he had most votes, and he had most votes because We united in him, to the Exclusion of R. H. Lee in order to keep out Harrison.[8]

Resolved that a Committee be appointed to prepare and digest the form of a Confederation to be entered into between these Colonies.

That a Committee be appointed to prepare a plan of Treaties to be proposed to foreign Powers.[9]

Wednesday June 12. 1776. Resolved that the Committee to prepare and digest the form of a confederation, to be entered into between these Colonies, consist of a Member from each Colony. The Members appointed Mr. Bartlet, Mr. S. Adams, Mr. Hopkins, Mr. Sherman, Mr. R. R. Livingston, Mr. Dickenson, Mr. McKean, Mr. Stone, Mr. Nelson, Mr. Hewes, Mr. E. Rutledge and Mr. Gwinnet.

Resolved that the Committee to prepare a Plan of Treaties to be proposed to foreign Powers consist of five.

The Members chosen Mr. Dickenson, Mr. Franklin, Mr. J. Adams, Mr. Harrison and Mr. R. Morris.

Congress took into Consideration the Report of the Committee on the War Office, whereupon

Resolved That a Committee of Congress be appointed by the Name of a board of War and Ordinance, to consist of five Members.

[7] This committee brought in a report on 14 June, and Congress acted thereon (JCC, 5:442). The original report has not been found.

[8] This sentence was interlined in the MS after the following paragraph was written. It is at least partly an invention of JA's memory. The real reason why R. H. Lee did not serve on the committee to prepare a declaration of independence was that he wished to be in Williamsburg during "the formation of our new Government" (the Virginia Constitution), and he left Philadelphia

for that purpose on 13 June (R. H. Lee, *Letters,* ed. Ballagh, 1:201, 203). For JA's accounts of the drafting of the Declaration see p. 335 ff. and p. 337, note 1, above.

[9] As JA records below, he was named a member of this committee next day. See also JA's earlier discussion of this subject in his Autobiography, p. 337–338, above, and notes there, which, taken together, summarize the history of this important measure and JA's part in it. See also p. 432, below.

In order to shew the insupportable Burthen of Business, that was thrown upon me, by this Congress, it is necessary to transcribe from the Journal an Account of the Constitution, Powers and Duties of this Board.

It was resolved that a Secretary and one or more Clerks be appointed by Congress, with competent Salaries, to assist the said Board, in executing the Business of their department.

That it shall be the duty of the said Board to obtain and keep an Alphabeticall and accurate Register of the Names of all Officers of the Land Forces in the Service of the United Colonies, with their Rank and the dates of their respective Commissions; and also regular Accounts of the State and distribution of the Troops in the respective Colonies, for which purpose the Generals and Officers commanding the different Departments and Posts, are to cause regular returns to be made into the said War Office.

That they shall obtain and keep exact Accounts of all the Artillery, Arms, Ammunition and warlike Stores, belonging to the United Colonies and of the manner in which, and the Places where the same shall from time to time be lodged and employed; and that they shall have the immediate Care of all such Artillery, Arms, Ammunition and Warlike Stores, as shall not be employed in actual Service; for preserving whereof, they shall have Power to hire proper Magazines at the public Expence:

That they shall have the care of forwarding all dispatches from Congress to the Colonies and Armies, and all Monies to be transmitted for the public Service by order of Congress; and of providing suitable Escorts and Guards for the safe Conveyance of such dispatches and Monies, when it shall appear to them to be necessary.

That they shall superintend the raising, fitting out, and dispatching all such Land Forces as may be ordered for the Service of the United Colonies.

That they shall have the Care and direction of all Prisoners of War, agreable to the orders and directions of Congress;

That they shall keep and preserve in the said Office in regular Order, all original Letters and papers, which shall come into said Office by Order of Congress or otherwise, and shall also cause all draughts of Letters and dispatches to be made or transcribed in books to be set apart for that purpose and shall cause fair Entries in like manner to be made and registers preserved of all other business, which shall be transacted in said Office.

That before the Secretary of any Clerk of the War Office shall enter on his Office, they shall respectively take and subscribe the following Oath, a Certificate whereof shall be filed in the said Office.

I, A.B. do solemnly swear, that I will not directly or indirectly divulge any matter or Thing, which shall come to my Knowledge as Secretary of the Board of War and Ordinance, (or Clerk of the Board of War and Ordinance) established by Congress, without the Leave of the said Board of War and Ordinance, and that I will faithfully execute my said Office, according to the best of my Skill and Judgment. So help me God.

That the said Board of War be authorised to hire suitable Appartments and provide Books, Papers and other Necessaries at the Continental Expence, for carrying on the Business of the said Office.

Thursday June 15. 1776. Congress having proceeded to the Election of a Committee to form the Board of War and Ordinance, the following Members were chosen

Mr. J. Adams, Mr. Sherman, Mr. Harrison, Mr. Wilson and Mr. E. Rutledge.

Richard Peters Esqr. was elected Secretary of the said Board.

From this time, We find in Almost every days Journal References of various Business to the Board of War, or their Reports upon such Things as were referred to them.

Fryday June 28. 1776 a new Delegation appeared from New Jersey. Mr. William Livingston and all others who had hitherto resisted Independence were left out. Richard Stockton, Francis Hopkinson and Dr. John Witherspoon were new Members.

Monday July 1. 1776. A Resolution of the Convention of Maryland, passed the 28th. of June was laid before Congress and read: as follows: That the Instructions given to their Deputies in December last, be recalled, and the restrictions therein contained, removed, and that their Deputies be authorised to concur with the other Colonies, or a Majority of them, in declaring the United Colonies free and independent States: in forming a Compact between them; and in making foreign Alliances &c.

Resolved that Congress will resolve itself into a Committee of the whole to take into Consideration the Resolution respecting Independency.

That the Declaration be referred to said Committee.

The Congress resolved itself into a Committee of the whole. After some time The President resumed the Chair and Mr. Harrison reported, that the Committee had come to a Resolution, which they desired him to report and to move for leave to sit again.

The Resolution agreed to by the Committee of the whole being read, the determination thereof, was at the Request of a Colony[1] postponed till tomorrow.

I am not able to recollect, whether it was on this, or some preceeding day, that the greatest and most solemn debate was had on the question of Independence. The Subject had been in Contemplation for more than a Year and frequent discussions had been had concerning it. At one time and another, all the Arguments for it and against it had been exhausted and were become familiar. I expected no more would be said in public but that the question would be put and decided. Mr. Dickinson however was determined to bear his Testimony against it with more formality. He had prepared himself apparently with great Labour and ardent Zeal, and in a Speech of great Length, and all his Eloquence, he combined together all that had before been written in Pamphlets and News papers and all that had from time to time been said in Congress by himself and others.[2] He conducted the debate, not only with great Ingenuity and Eloquence, but with equal Politeness and Candour: and was answered in the same Spirit.

No Member rose to answer him: and after waiting some time, in hopes that some one less obnoxious than myself, who had been all along for a Year before, and still was represented and believed to be the Author of all the Mischief, I determined to speak.

It has been said by some of our Historians, that I began by an Invocation to the God of Eloquence. This is a Misrepresentation.[3] Nothing so puerile as this fell from me. I began by saying that this was the first time of my Life that I had ever wished for the Talents and Eloquence of the ancient Orators of Greece and Rome, for I was very

[1] South Carolina; see Jefferson's Notes of Proceedings (*Papers*, ed. Boyd, 1: 314).

[2] Dickinson's very able speech of 1 July, long unknown to historians, survives in the form of a partial rough draft extended by notes, the whole entitled "Arguments agt. the Independance of these Colonies—in Congress," now in PHi. It has been edited, or reconstructed, with valuable introductory comment by J. H. Powell, in *PMHB*, 65: 458–481 (Oct. 1941). The burden of it was that separation from Great Britain was at this time premature: the colonists should settle their own differences and obtain the approval of the Bourbon powers before taking such an irrevocable and possibly fatal step.

[3] Whether or not "a Misrepresentation," the notion that JA began in this fashion can be traced to Benjamin Rush, who wrote a memorandum on this debate a few years after it took place; see Powell's article (cited in the preceding note), p. 462. The memorandum might be characterized as well-informed hearsay; it represents Dickinson as answering JA rather than the other way around; and its version of the debate was followed by a number of the earliest historians of the Revolution. For testimony regarding the effect of JA's speech see a long note by CFA in JA's *Works*, 3:55 ff.; also John H. Hazelton, *The Declaration of Independence: Its History*, N.Y., 1906, p. 161–162.

sure that none of them ever had before him a question of more Importance to his Country and to the World. They would probably upon less Occasions than this have begun by solemn Invocations to their Divinities for Assistance but the Question before me appeared so simple, that I had confidence enough in the plain Understanding and common Sense that had been given me, to believe that I could answer to the Satisfaction of the House all the Arguments which had been produced, notwithstanding the Abilities which had been displayed and the Eloquence with which they had been enforced. Mr. Dickinson, some years afterwards published his Speech. I had made no Preparation beforehand and never committed any minutes of mine to writing. But if I had a Copy of Mr. Dickinsons before me I would now after Nine and twenty Years have elapsed, endeavour to recollect mine.[4]

Before the final Question was put, the new Delegates from New Jersey came in, and Mr. Stockton, Dr. Witherspoon and Mr. Hopkinson, very respectable Characters,[5] expressed a great desire to hear the Arguments. All was Silence: No one would speak: all Eyes were turned upon me. Mr. Edward Rutledge came to me and said laughing, Nobody will speak but you, upon this Subject. You have all the Topicks so ready, that you must satisfy the Gentlemen from New Jersey. I answered him laughing, that it had so much the Air of exhibiting like an Actor or Gladiator for the Entertainment of the Audience, that I was ashamed to repeat what I had said twenty times before, and I thought nothing new could be advanced by me. The New Jersey Gentlemen however still insisting on hearing at least a Recapitulation of the Arguments and no other Gentleman being willing to speak, I summed up the Reasons, Objections and Answers, in as concise a manner as I could, till at length the Jersey Gentlemen said they were fully satisfied and ready for the Question, which was then put and determined in the Affirmative.[6]

---

[4] Dickinson never published his speech of 1 July 1776, but he wrote a recapitulation and exegesis of it in newspaper articles that were published in 1783 (reprinted in Stillé, *Dickinson*, p. 364–414; see especially p. 367–374). JA may have known of this "Vindication," as it is usually called, without having seen it.

[5] The words "Dr. Witherspoon and Mr. Hopkinson" are inserted above the line in the MS. As first written this passage read: "... and Mr. Stockton, one of them, a very respectable Character."

[6] That is, in the committee of the whole house; Congress adopted the resolution of independence on 2 July. See JA to Samuel Chase, 1 July, LbC, Adams Papers, printed in JA, *Works*, 9:415–416; *JCC*, 5:506–507; Jefferson, Notes of Proceedings, in his *Papers*, ed. Boyd, 1:314. Two years after writing the present passage JA furnished another account of the final debate on independence which varies in important details from that above—most importantly in limiting his own contribution to a single speech on 1 July, not two speeches go-

Mr. Jay, Mr. Duane and Mr. William Livingston of New Jersey were not present. But they all acquiesced in the Declaration and steadily supported it ever afterwards.

July [4]. 1776. Resolved that Dr. Franklin, Mr. J. Adams and Mr. Jefferson be a Committee to prepare a device for a Seal for the United States of America.[7]

Monday July 15. 1776. A Letter from Mr. Jay and two Letters from the Convention of New York of the 11th with sundry Papers inclosed, among which were the following Resolutions

In Convention of the Representatives of the State of New York White Plains July 9. 1776

Resolved Unanimously, that the Reasons assigned by the Continental Congress for declaring the United Colonies free and independent States, are cogent and conclusive, and that while We lament the cruel Necessity, which has rendered that Measure unavoidable, We approve the same and will at the Risque of our Lives and fortunes join with the other Colonies in supporting it.

Resolved Unanimously, That the Delegates of this State, in the Continental Congress, be and they hereby are authorised to concert and adopt all such measures as they may deem conducive to the happiness and Welfare of America.

Extract from the Minutes    Robert Benson Secretary

This was the Convention, which formed the Constitution of New York, and Mr. Jay and Mr. Duane had Attended it as I suppose for the Purpose of getting a Plan adopted conformable to my Ideas, in the Letter to Mr. Wythe which had been published in the Spring before. I presume this was the Fact, because Mr. Duane after his return to Congress, asked me if I had seen the Constitution of New York? I answered him, that I had. He then asked me if it was not agreable to my Ideas, as I had published them in my Letter to Mr. Wythe. I said I thought it by far the best Constitution that had yet been adopted.

The dayly references to the Board of War, rendered it necessary

---

ing over much the same ground, as seems to be implied in the present account (JA to Mercy Warren [17 Aug.] 1807, MHi; MHS, *Colls.,* 5th ser., 4 [1878]:465–469).

[7] This paragraph is interlined in the MS and mistakenly placed between the last two paragraphs of the entry dated 1 July. The editors have placed it where JA no doubt intended to put it. This committee reported on 20 Aug., but its report was tabled, and no device for a Great Seal of the United States was adopted until 1782. See the proposals and report of 1776 and a summary of later developments in Jefferson, *Papers,* ed. Boyd, 1:494–497; also JA to AA, 14 Aug. 1776 (Adams Papers; JA–AA, *Familiar Letters,* p. 211). In his abstract of Congress' proceedings on 20 Aug. JA overlooked the report of this committee.

for me to spend almost my whole time in it, on Mornings till Congress met and on Evenings, till late at night. The Journals will shew some of the results of the tedious details. There is one Report, which may be mentioned here.

Wednesday July 17. 1776. The Board of War to whom the Letter from General Washington of the 14th was referred brought in their report which was taken into consideration; whereupon

Resolved That General Washington, in refusing to receive a Letter, said to be sent from Lord Howe, addressed to George Washington Esqr., acted with a Dignity becoming his Station; and therefore the Congress do highly approve the same; and do direct, that no Letter or Message be received on any Occasion whatsoever from the Enemy, by the Commander in Chief or others the Commanders of the American Army but such as shall be directed to them in the Characters they respectively sustain.

Resolved that Mr. J. Adams, Mr. Harrison and Mr. Morris be a Committee to bring in a Resolution for subjecting to Confiscation, the Property of the Subjects of the Crown of Great Britain, and particularly of the Inhabitants of the British West Indies taken on the high Seas or between high and low Water Mark.[8]

Thursday July 18. 1776. Resolved that a Member be added to the Board of War. The Member chosen Mr. Carrol, an excellent Member, whose Education, Manners and Application to Business and to Study did honour to his Fortune, the first in America.

The Committee appointed to prepare a Plan of Treaties to be entered into, with foreign States and Kingdoms, brought in their report, which was read. Ordered to lie on the Table.

Fryday July 19. 1776. The Board of War brought in a report, which was taken into Consideration whereupon Resolved. See the Resolutions in the Journal.[9]

The Committee appointed to prepare a Resolution for subjecting to Confiscation the property of the Subjects of Great Britain &c. brought in the same which was read: Ordered to lie on the Table, and that the same be taken into consideration on Monday next.

The committee to whom the Letters from Lord Howe to Mr.

[8] This committee brought in a report on 19 July which was tabled for later consideration; on the 24th Congress adopted a preamble and resolution relative thereto, but two days later expunged the preamble and the final sentence of the report. The amended resolution appears in JA's Autobiography under 24 July, below. See JCC, 5:591, 605–606; Hancock to Washington, 26 July, in Burnett, ed., *Letters of Members*, 2:26. The authorship of the report and preamble is not known.

[9] JCC, 5:591. This concerned complaints and jealousies among the officers and troops in Gen. Schuyler's command.

Franklin &c. were referred, brought in a report, which was taken into Consideration whereupon

Resolved That a Copy of the Circular Letters, and the declaration inclosed from Lord Howe to Mr. William Franklin, Mr. Penn, Mr. Eden, Lord Dunmore, Mr. Martin, and Sir James Wright, which were sent to Amboy by a flagg, and forwarded to Congress by General Washington, be published in the several Gazettes, that the good People of these United States may be informed, of what nature are the Commissioners, and what the terms, with expectation of which the insidious court of Britain has endeavoured to amuse and disarm them, And that the few, who still remain suspended by a hope founded either in the justice or moderation of their late King, may now, at length be convinced, that the valour alone of their Country, is to save its Liberties.

Saturday July 20. 1776. Resolved that the Letter from General Lee with the papers inclosed, which were received and read Yesterday be referred to the Board of War.

A Petition and memorial of Monsieur Pellissier was presented to Congress and read.

Resolved that it be referred to the Board of War.

Resolved that the Plan of Treaties be printed for the Use of the Members, under the Rest[r]ictions and regulations prescribed for printing the Plan of Confederation; and that, in the printed copy, the names of Persons, places and States be omitted.

The Board of War, brought in a report, which was taken into Consideration; whereupon Resolved, as in the Journal.[1]

The Delegates of Pennsylvania produced Credentials of a new Appointment made on the 20th. of July 1776. See their names in the Journal. Among them are those of Franklin, Clymer, Morris, Wilson, and Rush.

Resolved, that Dr. Franklin may, if he thinks proper, return an Answer to the Letter, he received from Lord Howe.

Monday July 22. 1776.

The Congress resolved itself into a Committee of the whole, to take into consideration the Articles of confederation, and after some time the President resumed the Chair, and Mr. Harrison reported, that the Committee have made some progress in the matter to them referred, but not having come to a conclusion, desire leave to sit again.

Resolved that this Congress will tomorrow again resolve itself into

[1] JCC, 5:595. This concerned commissions for combat and medical officers.

a Committee of the whole to take into their further Consideration, the Articles of Confederation.[2]

Tuesday July 23. 1776 was employed in making Referrences to the Board of War, and in receiving, considering and adopting their reports, as may be seen in the Journal.[3]

Also in a Committee of the whole on the Articles of Confederation.

Wednesday. July 24. 1776. A Letter from Lieutenant Colonel William Allen was laid before Congress and read; requesting Leave to resign his Commission. Resolved that Leave be granted.

About this time it was that, the Gentlemen in the Pennsilvania Proprietary Interest generally left Us.

A Petition from George Kills [Kitts] was presented to Congress and read.

Resolved that it be referred to the Board of War.

The Congress took into Consideration the Report of the Committee appointed to prepare a resolution for confiscating the Property of the Subjects of Great Britain. Whereupon

Resolved That all the Resolutions of Congress passed on the twenty third day of March last, and on the third day of April last, relating to Ships and other Vessels, their tackle, Apparel and furniture, and all goods, Wares and Merchandizes, belonging to any inhabitant or inhabitants of Great Britain taken on the high Seas, or between high and low Water mark, be extended to all Ships and other Vessels, their Tackle, Apparel and furniture, and to all goods, Wares and Merchandizes, belonging to any Subject or Subjects of the King of Great Britain; except the Inhabitants of the Bermudas, and Providence or Bahama Islands.

The Board of War brought in their report, which was taken into Consideration whereupon resolved, as in the Journal.[4] Among the number I select with great pleasure, the two following, vizt.

Resolved that Colonel Knox's plan for raising another battalion of Artillery be approved and carried into Execution as soon as possible.

Resolved That General Washington be impowered to agree to the exchange of Governor Skene for Mr. James Lovell.

A Committee of the whole on the Articles of Confederation but no progress.

[2] See JA's Diary entry for 25 July 1776 (Notes of Debates) and the editorial notes there. Several entries that follow in the Diary continue JA's minutes of debates in committee of the whole on the Articles of Confederation; but it is obvious here, as everywhere else in this section of the Autobiography, that JA did not look back at his private and very illuminating records of what went on in Congress.

[3] JCC, 5:601–603.

[4] Same, p. 606–607.

Then a List of Letters from General Washington and others, referred to the Board of War.

Thursday July 25. 1776. A memorial from sundry Officers, who served in Canada, referred to the Board of War.

Committee of the whole on the Articles of Confederation.

Letter from General Washington inclosing Letters from Governor Trumbull, and [the] Committee of Safety of New Hampshire, referred to the board of War.

Fryday July 26. 1776. A Committee of the whole, on the Articles of the Confederation, Mr. Morton in the Chair.

Monday July 29. 1776. A long List of Refferences to the Board of War of Letters from Washington, Schuyler, Reed, Trumbull, Convention of New Jersey, Council of Massachusetts &c. &c.[5]

The Board of War brought in a report, which was taken into Consideration, whereupon resolved as in the Journal.[6]

Committee of the whole on the Articles of Confederation, Mr. Morton in the Chair.

Tuesday July 30. 1776. Two reports from the Board of War, with Resolutions in consequence of them as in the Journal.[7]

Committee [of the whole] on the Articles of Confederation, Mr. Morton in the Chair.

Wednesday July 31. 1776. The Board of War brought in a report, which was taken into Consideration: whereupon Resolved as in the Journal.[8]

A Committee of the whole on the Articles of Confederation Mr. Morton in the Chair.

Thursday August 1. 1776. Letters from General Mercer and General Roberdeau referred to the Board of War.

Committee of the whole on the Articles of Confederation, Mr. Morton in the Chair.

Letters from General Washington, General Schuyler and Col. Dubois referred to the Board of War.

---

[5] Only a portion of these letters was referred to the Board of War; see JCC, 5:613.

[6] JCC, 5:614–615. This chiefly concerned appointments and assignments of officers.

[7] JCC, 5:620–621. These concerned fees to officers for obtaining recruits, Gen. Mercer's proposal for building boats, cannon for Mercer's post at Am-

boy, publication of a recent treaty with the Six Nations, &c., &c.—a miscellany typical of the varied and unending chores of the Board of War.

[8] JCC, 5:623. Concerning "musquet powder" for Washington's troops, and rations and pay for Massachusetts militia replacing Continental troops withdrawn from that state.

The Board of War brought in two Reports, which were accepted as in the Journal.[9]

Fryday August 2. 1776. The Board of War brought in a report, which was accepted as in the Journal.[1]

The Marine Committee brought in a report, on the Conduct of Commodore Hopkins.

Committee of the whole on the Articles of Confederation, Mr. Morton in the Chair.

Saturday August 3. 1776. A Letter from Neil McLean, referred to the Board of War.

Monday August 5. 1776. Two Letters from General Washington; one from the Council of Virginia, with sundry Copies of Letters from North Carolina And South Carolina inclosed; one from E. Anderson; and sundry Resolutions passed by the Convention of Pennsylvania, were laid before Congress and read. Referred to the Board of War.

The Board of War brought in a report; which was taken into consideration: whereupon

Resolved, that the Commanders of all Ships of War, and armed Vessels in the Service of these States, or any of them, and all Letters of Marque and Privateers, be permitted to inlist into Service on board the said Ships and Vessels, any Seaman who may be taken on board any of the Ships and Vessels of our Ennemies, and that no such Seamen be intitled to receive the Wages due to them, out of the said Prizes, but such as will so inlist and that all other Seamen so taken, be held as prisoners of War, and exchanged for others taken by the Enemy, whether on board Vessels of War, or Merchantmen, as there may be Opportunity.

[That] Lieutenant Colonel Rufus Putnam be appointed an Engineer with the Rank of Colonel and pay of sixty dollars a month.

A Petition from Commodore Hopkins, for a hearing &c.

Ordered that the Board of War furnish the Committee of Treasury, with the names of the British Officers and other Prisoners, who are entitled to the Allowance made by Congress of two dollars a Week, with the times of their Captivity and the places where they are quartered.

[9] JCC, 5:625–626. These reported the draft of a letter to Washington relative to vacancies in the army, and miscellaneous recommendations on small matters.

[1] JCC, 5:627–628. This concerned funds for the paymaster of the northern department, the employment of Stockbridge Indians in the army, the repair of old arms, a plan for weekly returns from commissaries and quartermasters, &c.

Resolved that the Pay of an Assistant Clerk to the Board of War be 266 dollars and two thirds a Year.

A Petition from Lewis de Linkensdorf, referred to the Board of War.

Tuesday August 6. 1776. A Letter of the 5th. from General Washington, enclosing copies of Letters between him and General Howe, respecting the Exchange of Prisoners, and sundry other Letters and Papers: Also one from Brigadier General Mercer of the 4th. were laid before Congress and read:

Resolved that they be referred to the Board of War.

A Committee of the whole on the Articles of Confederation, Mr. Morton in the Chair.

Wednesday August 7th. 1776. A Letter from George Measam referred to the Board of War.

A Report from the Board of War, as in the Journal.[2]

A Committee of the whole on the Articles of Confederation, Mr. Morton in the Chair.

Thursday August 8. The Board of War directed to see certain Resolutions carried into Effect.[3]

Resolved that the Board of War be directed to take into immediate Consideration, the State of the Army in the Northern department, and our naval force on the Lakes; and that Mr. Chace be directed to attend the said Board, and give them all the Information in his Power; and that Mr. Williams be desired to furnish the said Board with an Extract of the Letter he has received from Governor Trumbull, relative to the said Army and naval force; and that the said Board report thereon as soon as possible.

Resolved that tomorrow be assigned for electing four Major Generals And six Brigadier Generals.

A Committee of the whole on the Articles of Confederation, Mr. Morton in the Chair.

Fryday August 9th. 1776. The Board of War, brought in a report. Ordered to lie on the Table.

Resolved that the Secret Committee be directed to deliver to the order of the Board of War such Articles in their possession, belonging to the Continent, as, in the Opinion of the said Board of War, are Necessary for the Deleware Battalion.

William Heath, Joseph Spencer, John Sullivan, Nathaniel Green Esqrs. chosen Major Generals.

[2] *JCC*, 5:636. This ordered payment for the board and lodging of certain Canadian prisoners at Bristol.

[3] The Board was to see that the militia troops in Philadelphia marched immediately to the "flying camp" at Amboy (*JCC*, 5:637).

James Read, John Nixon, Arthur St. Clair, Alexander McDougal, Samuel Holden Parsons and James Clinton Esqrs., Brigadiers.

Resolved that the hearing of Commodore Hopkins be postponed to Monday next at Eleven O Clock, and that Captain Jones be directed to attend at the same time.

Saturday August 10th. 1776.

The Board of War brought in a Report, which was taken into Consideration: Whereupon

Resolved, That Commissions be made out, and sent to General Washington to be delivered to the several Officers recommended in the List exhibited by the said Board, to fill the Vacancies mentioned in the said List, excepting those Persons recommended to fill the Vacancies occasioned by Officers being in Captivity; which ought not to be filled, but to be left open, untill those Officers shall be redeemed, and excepting the Case of Lieutenant Colonel Tyler, who is to have a Commission for Colonel of the Regiment lately commanded by Colonel Parsons, promoted: and that Lieutenant Colonel Durkee have a Commission of Colonel of the 20th. Regiment and that Major Prentice be made Lieutenant Colonel of the Regiment in which he is now Major; and Major Knolton Lieutenant Colonel of the 20th. Regiment.

Resolved that William Tudor, Judge Advocate General, have the rank of Lieutenant Colonel in the Army of the United States; and that he be ordered immediately to repair to the discharge of his duty at New York.

Monday August 12. 1776. A Letter from General Washington of the 8th. with sundry Papers enclosed, and one from General Mercer, with one inclosed to him from Colonel Dickinson, were read:

Resolved that the Letter from General Washington, with the Papers inclosed, be referred to the Board of War.

Commodore Hopkins had his hearing, as in the Journal. On this Occasion I had a very laborious task, against all the Prejudices of the Gentlemen from the southern and middle States, and of many from New England....[4] I thought, however that Hopkins had done great Service and made an important beginning of Naval Operations.

The Record in the Journal stands as follows.

Agreable to the order of the day, Commodore Hopkins attended and was admitted, when the examination taken before the marine Committee, and the report of the said Committee in consequence thereof, were read to him; and the Commodore being heard in his

[4] Suspension points in MS.

own defence, and having delivered in some farther answers to the questions asked him by the marine Committee and two Witnesses being at his request introduced and examined, he withdrew.

Congress then took into Consideration, the Instructions given to Commodore Hopkins, his examination and Answers to the Marine Committee and the report of the marine Committee thereupon; also the farther defence by him made, and the Testimony of the Witnesses; and after some debate the farther Consideration thereof was postponed.

It appeared to me, that the Commodore was pursued and persecuted by that Anti New England Spirit, which haunted Congress in many other of their proceedings, as well as in this Case and that of General Wooster. I saw nothing in the Conduct of Hopkins, which indicated Corruption or Want of Integrity. Experience and Skill might have been deficient, in several Particulars: But where could We find greater Experience or Skill? I knew of none to be found. The other Captains had not so much, and it was afterwards found, they had not more Success.

I therefore entered into a full and candid Investigation of the whole Subject, considered all the Charges and all the Evidence: as well as his Answers and proofs: and exerted all the Talents and Eloquence I had, in justifying him where he was justifiable, and excusing him where he was excusable.[5] When the Tryal was over Mr. Ellery of Newport, came to me and said you have made the old Man your Friend for Life. He will hear of your Defence of him, and he never forgets a Kindness. More than twenty Years afterwards, the Old Gentleman hobbled on his Crutches to the Inn in Providence, at four score Years of Age, one half of him dead in consequence of a paralytic Stroke, with his Eyes overflowing with tears to express his Gratitude to me. He said He knew not for what End he was continued in Life, unless it were to punish his Friends or to teach his Children and Grand Children to respect me. The President of Rhode Island Colledge who had married his Daughter, and all his Family shewed me the same affectionate Attachment.[6]

Tuesday August 13. 1776. The Board of War brought in a Report, which was taken into Consideration; whereupon Resolved as in the Journal.[7]

[5] Hopkins was, nevertheless, formally censured by Congress; see entries of 15, 16 Aug., below, and JA to Samuel Adams, 18 Aug. (NN; Burnett, ed., *Letters of Members*, 2:53–54).

[6] Jonathan Maxcy, acting president of Rhode Island College (Brown University), from 1792, and president, 1797–1802, had married Susan, daughter of Esek Hopkins, in 1791 (*DAB*).

[7] JCC, 5:651. This concerned a variety of routine matters.

A Letter of the twelf[th] from Brigadier General Mercer was read. Resolved that it be referred to the Board of War.

Congress took into Consideration the Articles of War, and after some time spent thereon, the farther Consideration thereof was postponed till tomorrow.

Wednesday. August 14. 1776. A Letter of the 12th from General Washington with a return of the Army at New York, and sundry other Papers inclosed, being received was read. Also sundry Letters from England were read.

Resolved That the Letter from General Washington with the Papers inclosed be referred to the Board of War.

The Board of War brought in a report, which was taken into Consideration, whereupon Resolved, as in the Journal.[8]

Thursday. August 15. 1776. The Board of War brought in a report, which was taken into Consideration: whereupon Resolved as in the Journal.[9]

A Petition from Return Jonathan Meigs in behalf of himself and others was presented to Congress and read.

Resolved that it be referred to the Board of War.

Congress resumed the Consideration of the Instructions given to Commodore Hopkins &c.

Resolved That the said Commodore Hopkins, during his Cruise to the southward, did not pay due regard to the Tenor of his Instructions, whereby he was expressly directed to annoy the Ennemy's Ships upon the Coasts of the southern States; and that his reasons for not going from Providence immediately to the Carolinas, are by no means satisfactory. At the request of the delegates of Pennsylvania the farther Consideration of the report was postponed till tomorrow.

Fryday August 16. 1776.

Resolved that a Member be added to the Committee to whom were referred the Letters and Papers respecting the murder of Mr. Parsons. The Member chosen Mr. J. Adams.[1]

[8] JCC, 5:656–657. The portion of this report dealing with the appointment and perquisites of a general officer to command the militia troops replacing Continental troops withdrawn from Massachusetts, is in JA's hand (PCC, No. 147, I).

[9] JCC, 5:657–658. This concerned the commissioning of certain officers.

[1] This episode remains a mystery. Samuel Holden Parsons of Lyme, Conn., a lawyer and recently promoted Conti-nental brigadier general, had been at Harvard with JA and they maintained a friendly correspondence. On 24 July 1776 Parsons wrote JA about "The Unhappy Fate of my B[rothe]r about 4 Years ago," allegedly robbed and murdered by one Basil Bouderot in Nova Scotia (Adams Papers). Apparently Bouderot had now been captured in Canada (Washington, *Writings*, ed. Fitzpatrick, 5:173). The full story was in a memorial Parsons sent to Congress, but this has

Resolved that the Letters received Yesterday from General Washington, General Schuyler and General Gates be referred to the Board of War.

Congress resumed the consideration of the Instructions given to Commodore Hopkins &c. and thereupon came to the following Resolution.

Resolved that the said Conduct of Commodore Hopkins deserves the Censure of this House and this House does accordingly censure him.

Ordered that a Copy of the Resolutions passed against Commodore Hopkins be transmitted to him.

Although this Resolution of Censure was not, in my Opinion demanded by Justice and consequently was inconsistent with good Policy, as it tended to discourage an Officer and diminish his Authority by tarnishing his reputation; Yet as it went not so far as to cashier him, which had been the Object intended by the Spirit that dictated the Prosecution, I had the Satisfaction to think that I had not laboured wholly in vain, in his defence.

Saturday August 17. 1776. Congress resumed the Consideration of the Report of the Committee, to whom was referred Brigadier General Woosters Letter requesting an Inquiry into his Conduct, while he had the honor of commanding the Continental forces in Canada, which was read as follows:

That Brigadier General Wooster produced Copies of a Number of Letters, which passed between him and General Schuyler, and of his Letters to Congress, from which it appears, that he from time to time, gave seasonable and due notice of the State of the Army under his Command, and what Supplies were in his Opinion necessary to render the Enterprize successful; that a number of Officers and other Gentlemen from Canada, who were acquainted with his Conduct there, and who happened to be occasionally in this City, were examined before the Committee; to which Letters, and the minutes of the examination of the Witnesses herewith exhibited, the Committee beg leave to refer Congress for further Information, and report, as the Opinion of the Committee upon the whole of the Evidence that was before them, that nothing censurable or blame worthy appears against Brigadier General Wooster.

---

not been found, and the ponderous *Life and Letters of Samuel Holden Parsons* by Charles S. Hall, Binghamton, 1905, does not even mention the matter. For Congress' action see JCC, 5:609, 661, 692–693; see also JA to Parsons, 3 Aug. 1776 (LbC, Adams Papers).

The Report being read again, was agreed to.

But not, however, without a great Struggle.—In this Instance again as in many others, when the same anti New England Spirit which pursued Commodore Hopkins, persecuted General Wooster, I had to contend with the whole Host of their Ennemies, and with the Utmost Anxiety and most arduous Efforts, was scarcely able to preserve them from disgrace and Ruin, which Wooster had merited even less than Hopkins. In Woosters case there was a manifest Endeavour to lay upon him the blame of their own misconduct in Congress in embarrassing and starving the War in Canada. Wooster was calumniated for Incapacity, Want of Application and even for Cowardice, with[out] a Colour of Proof of either. The Charge of Cowardice he soon confut[ed][2] by a glorious and voluntary Sacrifice of his Life, which compelled his Ennemies to confess he was a Hero.

The Board of War brought in a report which was taken into Consideration; whereupon Resolved, as in all the rest of the Journal.[3]

Monday August 19. 1776. Letters from General Washington referred to the Board of War.

A Letter of the 14th. from Commodore Hopkins was read; whereupon Resolved That Commodore Hopkins be directed to repair to Rhode Island, and take the Command of the Fleet formerly put under his Care.

Congress resumed the consideration of the Articles of War as revised by the Committee for that Purpose appointed, and after some time spent thereon, the farther Consideration thereof was postponed.

This Report was made by me and Mr. Jefferson, in Consequence of a Letter from General Washington, sent by Colonel Tudor, Judge Advocate General, representing the Insufficiency of the Articles of War and requesting a Revision of them. Mr. John Adams and Mr. Jefferson were appointed a Committee, to hear Tudor and revise the Articles....[4] It was a very difficult and unpopular Subject: and I observed to Jefferson, that Whatever Alteration We should report with the least Ennergy in it, or the least tendency to a necessary discipline of the Army, would be opposed with as much Vehemence as if it were the most perfect: We might as well therefore report a compleat System at once and let it meet its fate. Some thing perhaps might be gained. There was extant one System of Articles of War, which had carried two Empires to the head of Mankind, the Roman And the British:

---

[2] MS: "confuting."
[3] *JCC,* 5:665–666. This report embodied a great variety of recommendations, a number of them relating to the exchange of prisoners.
[4] Suspension points in MS.

for the British Articles of War were only a litteral Translation of the Roman: it would be in vain for Us to seek, in our own Inventions or the Records of Warlike nations for a more compleat System of military discipline: it was an Observation founded in undoubted facts that the Prosperity of Nations had been in proportion to the discipline of their forces by Sea and Land: I was therefore for reporting the British Articles of War, totidem Verbis. Jefferson in those days never failed to agree with me, in every Thing of a political nature, and he very cordially concurred in this. The British Articles of War were Accordingly reported and defended in Congress, by me Assisted by some others, and finally carried. They laid the foundation of a discipline, which in time brought our Troops to a Capacity of contending with British Veterans, and a rivalry with the best Troops of France.[5]

Tuesday August 20 1776. A Letter of the 18th. from General Washington, with sundry Papers inclosed, was laid before Congress and read.

Resolved that the same be referred to a Committee of five: the Members chosen, Mr. Jefferson, Mr. Franklin, Mr. Rutledge, Mr. J. Adams and Mr. Hooper.[6]

A Committee of the whole on the Articles of Confederation. Mr. Morton reported that the Committee had gone through the same, and agreed to sundry Articles which he was ordered to submit to Congress.

Ordered that Eighty Copies of the Articles of Confederation, as reported from the Committee of the whole, be printed under the same Injunctions as the former Articles, and delivered to the Members under the like Injunctions as formerly.

Thus We see the whole Record of this momentous Transaction. No

[5] Though probably substantially correct, this account is inaccurate in details. On 14 June Congress assigned to the "Committee on Spies" (JA, Jefferson, Rutledge, Wilson, and R. R. Livingston) the duty of revising "the rules and articles of war" (JCC, 5:442). On 7 Aug. the committee brought in a report which was debated on 19 Aug. and again on 19 and 20 Sept.; on the last of these dates the revised Articles were adopted and recorded in the Journal (same, p. 636, 670, 787, 788–807). The MS of the revised Articles (in PCC, No. 27) is mainly in the hand of Timothy Pickering (who was not in Congress) and gives no clue to the actual authorship of this document by which JA set so much store. For contemporary printings see JCC, 6:1125–1126 ("Bibliographical Notes," Nos. 127–130). See also JA's comments in the entries dated 19, 20 Sept., below.

[6] Washington's letter enclosed a recent exchange of correspondence with Thomas, Lord Drummond. Jefferson drafted a report for the committee, which was slightly amended by JA, and brought in, 22 Aug., in the expectation that Congress would publish it. Instead, it was tabled, though on 17 Sept. Congress ordered the Washington-Drummond correspondence published. See Washington, *Writings*, ed. Fitzpatrick, 5:451–452; JCC, 5:672, 696, 767; Jefferson, *Papers*, ed. Boyd, 1:501–502; Burnett, ed., *Letters of Members*, 2:60.

Motions recorded. No Yeas and Nays taken down. No Alterations proposed. No debates preserved. No Names mentioned. All in profound Secrecy. Nothing suffered to transpire: No Opportunity to consult Constituents. No room for Advice or Criticisms in Pamphlets, Papers or private Conversation. I was very uneasy under all this but could not avoid it. In the Course of this Confederation, a few others were as anxious as myself. Mr. Wilson of Pennsylvania, upon one Occasion moved that the debates should [be] public, the Doors opened, galleries erected, or an Adjournment made to some public Building where the People might be accommodated. Mr. John Adams seconded the Motion and supported it, with Zeal. But No: Neither Party were willing: some were afraid of divisions among the People: but more were afraid to let the People see the insignificant figures they made in that Assembly. Nothing indeed was less understood, abroad among the People, than the real Constitution of Congress and the Characters of those who conducted the Business of it. The Truth is, the Motions, Plans, debates, Amendments, which were every day brought forward in those Committees of the whole House, if committed to Writing, would be very voluminous: but they are lost forever. The Preservation of them indeed, might for any thing I recollect be of more Curiosity than Use.[7]

Wednesday August 21. 1776. A Petition from Prudehome La Junesse was read and referred to the Board of War.

The Committee to whom part of the Report from the Committee on Spies was recommitted, having brought in a report, the same was taken into Consideration whereupon

Resolved, That all Persons, not Members of, nor owing Allegiance to any of the United States of America, as described in a Resolution of Congress of the 24th. of June last, who shall be found lurking as Spies, in or about the fortifications or Encampments of the Armies of the United States, or of any of them, shall suffer death, according

---

[7] The publication of the *Secret Journals of the Acts and Proceedings of Congress*, Boston, 1820, 4 vols., under the supervision of JQA as secretary of state, in part obviated the criticisms voiced here. The first volume of that edition (p. 267 ff.) printed for the first time, from the MS Secret Journal of the Continental Congress, the texts of the Articles of Confederation successively proposed in July 1775 and in July and Aug. 1776.

No motion by James Wilson proposing that "the debates should [be] public" has been traced. In his Abstract of Debates, 27 Feb. 1777, Thomas Burke of North Carolina reported that Samuel Chase made such a motion that day and that Burke himself seconded it, but Chase's motion as preserved in the Papers of the Continental Congress falls well short of this (Burnett, ed., *Letters of Members*, 2:285; JCC, 7:164, note).

to the Law and Usage of Nations by Sentence of a Court Marshall, or such other punishment as a Court martial shall direct.

Ordered that the Above resolution be printed at the End of the Rules and Articles of War.

The Board of War brought in a report, which was taken into Consideration whereupon resolved as in the Journal.[8]

Resolved that the Letter from General Washington read Yesterday, and that of the 12th, with the Papers inclosed, be referred to the Board of War.

Resolved that a Committee of three be appointed to revise the Resolutions of Congress, respecting the place where Prizes are to be carried into, and to bring in such farther resolutions as to them shall seem proper: the Members chosen Mr. Jefferson, Mr. Morris and Mr. J. Adams.[9]

Thursday August 22. 1776. Letters from Generals Washington and Schuyler with Papers inclosed, referred to the Board of War.

The Board of War brought in a Report, which was read: ordered to lie on the Table.

The Committee to whom the Letter from General Washington of the 18th was referred, brought in a report which was read: ordered to lie on the Table.

A Committee of the whole on the Form of a Treaty: Mr. Nelson in the Chair.

A Letter from Brigadier General Lewis: also a letter from the Committee of Carlisle, in Pennsylvania, inclosing a memorial from the Officers Prisoners there, were read and referred to the Board of War.

Fryday August 23. 1776. A Letter of the 21. from General Washington inclosing a Copy of a Letter from him to Lord Howe, together with his Lordships Answer was read:

Resolved That the same be referred to the Board of War, with orders to publish the General's Letter to Lord Howe, and his Lordships Answer.

Monday August 26. 1776. Three Letters of the 22 and 23 from General Washington with sundry Papers inclosed; a Letter from William Finnie, deputy Quarter Master general of the southern department, were read, and referred to the Board of War.

---

[8] *JCC*, 5:693–694. These resolves concerned the casting of cannon, the retention of Gen. Ward in command of the eastern department, &c.
[9] The report of this committee has not been found.

A Letter of the 22d. from Colonel James Wilson, was read, and referred to Mr. Jefferson, Mr. Franklin and Mr. John Adams.[1]

Tuesday August 27. 1776. A Letter of the 23d from General Mercer, was read and referred to the Board of War.

The Board of War brought in a report, which was taken into Consideration; whereupon Resolved. See the several Resolutions in the Journal.[2]

The Committee to whom the Letter from Colonel Wilson was referred brought in a Report, which was taken into Consideration; whereupon Congress came to the following resolutions: which see in the Journal.[3]

A Committee of the whole, on the Plan of foreign Treaties. Mr. Nelson reported that the Committee had gone through the same and reported sundry Amendments.

Resolved that the Plan of Treaties, with the Amendments, be referred to the Committee who brought in the original Plan, in order to draw up Instructions, pursuant to the Amendments made by the Committee of the whole. That two Members be added to that Committee. The Members chosen Mr. Richard Henry Lee and Mr. Wilson.

A Petition from the deputy Commissary General was read, and referred to the Board of War.

Delegates from Virginia produced new Credentials. George Wythe, Thomas Nelson, Richard Henry Lee, Thomas Jefferson, and Francis Lightfoot Lee, Esqrs.[4]

Thursday August 29. 1776. A Letter of the 27th. from R. H. Harrison, the Generals Secretary, and one of the 28th. from General Mercer, both giving an Account of an Action on Long Island on the 27th. were read and referred to the Board of War.

[1] See the following entry (27 Aug.) and note 3, below.

[2] JCC, 5:706. These resolves provided for clothing the Continental troops raised in Virginia, &c.

[3] Col. James Wilson, an officer in the "flying camp" at Amboy, had written to Pres. Hancock, 22 Aug. 1776, proposing that Congress offer rewards to the officers of the German mercenary troops encamped on Staten Island if they would desert the British service (Force, *Archives*, 5th ser., 1:1110). The first proposal of this kind had been made in Congress on 21 May (see under that date in JA's Autobiography, above), and Congress had more recently put into effect an ingenious scheme to suborn the Ger-

man troops themselves (JCC, 5:640, 653–655). The report of the present committee, written by Jefferson and brought in on 27 Aug., recommended that free land be offered to officers on a graduated scale according to their rank; it is printed in Jefferson's *Papers*, ed. Boyd, 1:509–510. On this whole curious episode see L. H. Butterfield, "Psychological Warfare in 1776: The Jefferson-Franklin Plan to Cause Hessian Desertions," Amer. Philos. Soc., *Procs.*, 94 (1950):233–241.

[4] The Virginia delegates' new credentials were produced on 28, not 27, Aug., JA having once again overlooked a date caption in the *Journals*.

The Board of War brought in a report, which was taken into Consideration, whereupon Resolved. See the several Resolutions in the Journal.[5]

Resolved That the Committee, to whom the Plan of Treaties with the Amendments, was recommitted, be impowered to prepare such farther Instructions as to them shall seem proper, and make report thereof to Congress.

Fryday August 30. 1776. A Memorial from Mr. Kosciusko was read and referred to the Board of War.

Monday. September 2. 1776. A Letter of the 31. of August from General Washington, inclosing the determination of a Council of War, and the reasons for quitting Long Island, and a Copy of a Letter from Lord Sterling: Also, one of the 23d from General Gates, with sundry Papers inclosed: one from sundry field Officers in the Army at Ticonderoga, dated the 19th of August, with the Proceedings between a Court Martial and brigadier General Arnold.

Also a Letter of the 23d, from Captain John Nelson, and one from Benjamin Harrison Junior, deputy Pay master General, with his Weekly Account, were read and referred to the Board of War.

Congress being informed, that General Sullivan was come to Philadelphia, with a design to communicate a Message from Lord Howe:

Ordered that he be admitted and heard before Congress.

A petition from Michael Fitzgerald; one from John Weitzell and one from James Paul Govert, were read and referred to the Board of War.

General Sullivan being admitted, delivered a Verbal Message he had in Charge from Lord Howe, which he was desired to reduce to Writing and then he withdrew.

Resolved that the board of War be directed to prepare and bring in a plan of military Operations for the next Campaign.

Tuesday September 3. 1776.

General Sullivan, having reduced to Writing the verbal message from Lord Howe, the same was read as follows:

"The following is the purport of the message of Lord Howe to Congress by General Sullivan.

That, though he could not at present treat with Congress as such, yet he was very desirous of having a Conference, with some of the members, whom he would consider for the present only as private

---

[5] JCC, 5:717. This appears to be a single resolve, continuing George Measam as commissary of stores for the northern army and fixing his pay.

Gentlemen, and meet them himself as such, at such place as they should appoint.

That he in conjunction with General Howe, had full Powers, to compromise the dispute between Great Britain and America upon terms Advantageous to both; the Obtaining of which delayed him near two months in England, and prevented his Arrival at this place, before the declaration of Independancy took place:

That he wished a compact might be settled at this time, when no decisive blow was struck, and neither party could say they were compelled to enter into such Agreement.

That in case Congress were disposed to treat, many Things, which they had not as yet asked, might and ought to be granted them; and that, if, upon the Conference, they found any probable ground of Accommodation, the Authority of Congress must be afterwards Acknowledged, otherwise the Compact would not be compleat."

In this written Statement of the Message it ought to be observed that General Sullivan has not inserted, what he had reported verbally, that Lord Howe had told him "he would sett the Act of Parliament wholly aside, and that Parliament had no right to tax America or meddle with her internal Polity." [6]

The Board of War brought in a report, which was read, and a number of Resolutions adopted upon it, which see in the Journal.[7]

Wednesday September 4. 1776.

Resolved that the board of War be directed to call in the several Recruiting Parties of the German Battalions, and to have them formed and armed with all possible Expedition, and forwarded to New York, taking measures, and giving proper directions to have the battalion recruited to the full Compliment as soon as the same can conveniently be done.

Resolved, that the proposal made by General Howe, as delivered by General Sullivan, of exchanging General Sullivan for General

[6] JA's feelings of repugnance toward Lord Howe's proposal and Sullivan's willingness to convey it are very fully expressed in several letters JA copied into his Autobiography at p. 424 ff., below. According to Benjamin Rush's recollections, JA turned to him (Rush) while Sullivan was delivering Howe's request to Congress and "whispered to me a wish 'that the first ball that had been fired on the day of the defeat of our army [on Long Island], had gone through [Sullivan's] head.' When he rose to speak against the proposed interview, he called Genl. Sullivan 'a decoy duck, whom Lord Howe has sent among us to seduce us into a renunciation of our independance'" (Rush, *Autobiography*, p. 140; see also p. 119–120).

[7] JCC, 5:732. This concerned establishing a post route between Philadelphia and Ticonderoga.

Prescott, and Lord Sterling for Brigadier General McDonald be complied with.

Congress took into Consideration, the Report of the Board of War, and after some time spent thereon

Resolved that the farther Consideration thereof be postponed, till tomorrow.

Thursday September 5. 1776. A Petition referred to the Board of War.

Resolved That General Prescot, and Brigadier General McDonald be sent by the Board of War, under an Escort, to General Washington, to be exchanged for General Sullivan and Lord Sterling.

Congress resumed the Consideration of the Report of the Board of War, whereupon

Resolved, That General Sullivan be requested to inform Lord Howe that, this Congress, being the Representatives of the free and independent States of America, cannot with propriety send any of its members, to confer with his Lordship in their private Characters, but that, ever desirous of establishing peace, on reasonable terms, they will send a Committee of their body, to know whether he has any Authority to treat with persons, authorized by Congress for that purpose in behalf of America, and what that Authority is, and to hear such propositions as he shall think fit to make respecting the same:

That the President be desired to write to General Washington and Acquaint him, that it is the Opinion of Congress, no proposals for making peace between Great Britain and the United States of America ought to be received or attended to, unless the same be made in Writing and Addressed to the Representatives of the said States in Congress, or persons authorized by them: And if application be made to him, by any of the Commanders of the British forces on that Subject, that he inform them, that these United States, who entered into the War, only for the defence of their Lives and Liberties, will chearfully agree to peace on reasonable terms, whenever such shall be proposed to them in manner aforesaid.

Resolved That a Copy of the first of the two foregoing resolutions, be delivered to General Sullivan, and that he be directed to repair immediately to Lord Howe.

Resolved That tomorrow be assigned for electing the Committee.

Fryday September 6. 1776.

Resolved that General Sullivan be requested to deliver to Lord Howe, the Copy of the Resolution given to him.

Resolved that the Committee, "to be sent to know whether Lord Howe has any Authority to treat with persons authorized by Congress for that purpose in behalf of America, and what that Authority is, and to hear such propositions as he shall think fit to make respecting the same" consist of three:

Congress then proceeded to the Elections, and the ballots being taken, Mr. Franklin, Mr. John Adams, and Mr. Rutledge were elected.

Letters from Generals Washington, Schuyler, Gates and Mercer, referred to the Board of War.

The Board of War brought in a Report—Resolutions upon it.[8]

Saturday September 7. 1776.

A Letter of the 5th. from Charles Preston, Major of the 26th. Regiment a Prisoner, was read and referred to the Board of War.

Resolved, that a Copy of the Resolutions passed by Congress, on the Message brought by General Sullivan, and the names of the Committee appointed, be sent to General Washington.

Congress resumed the Consideration of the Report of the Board of War whereupon

Resolved, that all Letters to and from the Board of War and ordinance or the Secretary of the same, be free of all Expence in the Post office of the United States. &c.

Monday September 9, 1776.

Resolved, that in all Continental Commissions, and other Instruments where heretofore the Words, "United Colonies," have been used, the Stile be altered for the future to the United States.

The Board of War brought in a report, which was read.

On this day, Mr. Franklin, Mr. Edward Rutledge and Mr. John Adams proceeded on their Journey to Lord Howe on Staten Island, the two former in Chairs and the last on Horseback; the first night We lodged at an Inn, in New Brunswick.[9] On the Road and at all the public Houses, We saw such Numbers of Officers and Soldiers, straggling and loytering, as gave me at least, but a poor Opinion of the Discipline of our forces and excited as much indignation as anxiety. Such thoughtless dissipation at a time so critical, was not calculated to inspire very sanguine hopes or give great Courage to Ambassadors: I was nevertheless determined that it should not dishearten me. I saw

---

[8] *JCC*, 5:740. A single routine resolution was adopted and the rest of the report postponed.

[9] On this dramatic but fruitless mission see JA's Diary entry of 10 Sept. 1776 and note there; also JA's letters copied into his Autobiography, p. 425 ff., below, and the frequent and animated discussion of it in letters and other documents, 2–17 Sept., printed in Burnett, ed., *Letters of Members*, 2:65–93.

that We must and had no doubt but We should be chastised into order in time.

The Taverns were so full We could with difficulty obtain Entertainment. At Brunswick, but one bed could be procured for Dr. Franklin and me, in a Chamber little larger than the bed, without a Chimney and with only one small Window. The Window was open, and I, who was an invalid and afraid of the Air in the night ⟨*blowing upon me*⟩, shut it close. Oh! says Franklin dont shut the Window. We shall be suffocated. I answered I was afraid of the Evening Air. Dr. Franklin replied, the Air within this Chamber will soon be, and indeed is now worse than that without Doors: come! open the Window and come to bed, and I will convince you: I believe you are not acquainted with my Theory of Colds. Opening the Window and leaping into Bed, I said I had read his Letters to Dr. Cooper in which he had advanced, that Nobody ever got cold by going into a cold Church, or any other cold Air: but the Theory was so little consistent with my experience, that I thought it a Paradox: However I had so much curiosity to hear his reasons, that I would run the risque of a cold. The Doctor then began an harrangue, upon Air and cold and Respiration and Perspiration, with which I was so much amused that I soon fell asleep, and left him and his Philosophy together: but I believe they were equally sound and insensible, within a few minutes after me, for the last Words I heard were pronounced as if he was more than half asleep. . . .[1] I remember little of the Lecture, except, that the human Body, by Respiration and Perspiration, destroys a gallon of Air in a minute: that two such Persons, as were now in that Chamber, would consume all the Air in it, in an hour or two: that by breathing over again the matter thrown off, by the Lungs and the Skin, We should imbibe the real Cause of Colds, not from abroad but from within. I am not inclined to introduce here a dissertation on this Subject. There is much Truth I believe, in some things he advanced: but they warrant not the assertion that a Cold is never taken from cold air. I have often conversed with him since on the same subject: and I believe with him that Colds are often taken in foul Air, in close Rooms: but they are often taken from cold Air, abroad too. I have often asked him, whether a Person heated with Exercise, going suddenly into cold Air, or standing still in a current of it, might not have his Pores suddenly contracted, his Perspiration stopped, and that matter thrown into the Circulations or cast upon the Lungs which he acknowledged was the Cause of Colds. To this he never could give me a satisfactory Answer.

[1] Suspension points in MS.

And I have heard that in the Opinion of his own able Physician Dr. Jones he fell a Sacrifice at last, not to the Stone but to his own Theory; having caught the violent Cold, which finally choaked him, by sitting for some hours at a Window, with the cool Air blowing upon him.[2]

The next Morning We proceeded on our Journey, and the Remainder of this Negotiation, will be related from the Journals of Congress, and from a few familiar Letters, which I wrote to my most intimate Friends before and after my Journey. The abrupt uncouth freedom of these, and all others of my Letters, in those days require an Apology. Nothing was farther from my Thoughts, than that they would ever appear before the Public. Oppressed with a Load of Business, without ⟨a Clerk⟩ an Amanuensis, or any Assistance, I was obliged to do every Thing myself. For seven Years before this I had never been without three Clerks in my Office as a Barrister: but now I had no Secretary nor servant whom I could trust to write: and every thing must be copied by myself, or be hazarded without any. The few that I wrote upon this Occasion I copied; merely to assist my memory as Occasion might demand.

There were a few Circumstances which appear neither in the Journals of Congress nor in my Letters, which may be thought by some worth preserving. Lord How had sent over an Officer as an Hostage for our Security. I said to Dr. Franklin, it would be childish in Us to depend upon such a Pledge and insisted on taking him over with Us, and keeping our Surety on the same side of the Water with Us. My Colleagues exulted in the Proposition and agreed to it instantly. We told the Officer, if he held himself under our direction he must go back with Us. He bowed Assent, and We all embarked in his Lordships Barge. As We approached the Shore his Lordship, observing Us, came down to the Waters Edge to receive Us, and looking at the Officer, he said, Gentlemen, you make me a very high Compliment, and you may depend upon it, I will consider it as the most sacred of Things. We walked up to the House between Lines of Guards of Grenadiers, looking as fierce as ten furies, and making all the Grimaces and Gestures and motions of their Musquets with Bayonets fixed, which I suppose military Ettiquette requires but which We neither understood nor regarded.

The House had been the Habitation of military Guards, and was

---

[2] Franklin was long and deeply interested in the causes of common colds and projected a treatise on the subject; see his *Writings*, ed. Smyth, index, under "Colds"; see also Benjamin Rush to Franklin, 1 May 1773 (Rush, *Letters,* 1:78–80). For an advance in JA's views on fresh air, see his Diary entry of 21 May 1783.

as dirty as a stable: but his Lordship had prepared a large handsome Room, by spreading a Carpet of Moss and green Spriggs from Bushes and Shrubbs in the Neighbourhood, till he had made it not only wholesome but romantically elegant, and he entertained Us with good Claret, good Bread, cold Ham, Tongues and Mutton.

I will now proceed to relate the Sequel of this Conference, 1st from the Journal of Congress. 2d from the Letters written to some of my friends at the time: and 3dly a Circumstance or two which are not preserved in the Journals or Letters.

Fryday September 13. 1776. The Committee appointed to confer with Lord Howe, having returned made a verbal Report.

Ordered that they make a report in Writing as soon as conveniently they can.

Tuesday. September 17th. 1776. The Committee appointed to confer with Lord Howe, agreable to the order of Congress, brought in a report in Writing, which was read as follows:

In Obedience to the orders of Congress, We have had a meeting with Lord Howe. It was on Wednesday last upon Staten Island, opposite to Amboy, where his Lordship received and entertained Us, with the Utmost politeness.

His Lordship opened the Conversation by Acquainting Us, that, tho' he could not treat with Us as a Committee of Congress, yet, as his Powers enabled him to confer and consult with any private Gentlemen of Influence in the Colonies, on the means of restoring Peace, between the two Countries, he was glad of this Opportunity of conferring with Us, on that Subject, if We thought ourselves at Liberty to enter into a Conference with him in that Character. We observed to his Lordship, that, as our Business was to hear, he might consider Us, in what Light he pleased, and communicate to Us, any propositions he might be authorised to make, for the purpose mentioned; but that We could consider Ourselves in no other Character than that, in which We were placed, by order of Congress. His Lordship then entered into a discourse of considerable Length, which contained no explicit proposition of Peace, except one, namely, That the Colonies should return to their Allegiance and Obedience to the Government of Great Britain. The rest consisted principally of Assurances, that there was an exceeding good disposition in the King and his Ministers, to make that Government easy to Us, with intimations, that, in case of our Submission, they would cause the Offensive Acts of Parliament to be revised, and the Instructions to Ministers to be re–considered; that so, if any just causes of complaint were found in the

Acts, or any Errors in Government were perceived to have crept into the Instructions, they might be amended or withdrawn.

We gave it, as our Opinion to his Lordship, that a return to the domination of Great Britain, was not now to be expected. We mentioned the repeated humble petitions of the Colonies to the King and Parliament, which had been treated with Contempt, and answered only by additional Injuries; the Unexampled Patience We had shewn, under their tyrannical Government, and that it was not till the late Act of Parliament, which denounced War against Us, and put Us out of the Kings Protection, that We declared our Independence; that this declaration had been called for, by the People of the Colonies in general; that every colony had approved of it, when made, and all now considered themselves as independent States, and were settling or had settled their Governments accordingly; so that it was not in the Power of Congress to agree for them, that they should return to their former dependent State; that there was no doubt of their Inclination for peace, and their Willingness to enter into a treaty with Britain, that might be advantageous to both Countries; that, though his Lordship had at present, no power to treat with them as independent States, he might, if there was the same good disposition in Britain, much sooner obtain fresh Powers from thence, for that purpose, than powers could be obtained by Congress, from the several Colonies to consent to a Submission.

His Lordship then saying, that he was sorry to find, that no Accommodation was like to take place, put an End to the Conference.

Upon the whole, it did not appear to your Committee, that his Lordships commission contained any other Authority, than that expressed in the Act of Parliament, namely, that of granting Pardons, with such exceptions as the Commissioners shall think proper to make, and of declaring America or any part of it, to be in the Kings Peace, upon Submission: for as to the Power of enquiring into the State of America, which his Lordship mentioned to Us, and of conferring and consulting with any Persons the Commissioners might think proper, and representing the result of such conversation to the Ministry, who, provided the Colonies would subject themselves, might, after all, or might not at their pleasure, make any Alterations in the former Instructions to Governors, or propose in Parliament any Amendment of the Acts complained of, We apprehended any expectations from the Effects of such a Power would have been too uncertain and precarious to be relied on by America, had she still continued in her State of dependence.

Ordered that the foregoing Report, and also the Message from Lord Howe as delivered by General Sullivan, and the Resolution of Congress, in consequence thereof, be published by the Committee, who brought in the foregoing report.[3]

Ordered that the said Committee publish Lord Drummonds Letters to General Washington and the Generals Answers.

Two or three Circumstances, which are omitted in this report, and indeed not thought worth notice in any of my private Letters, I afterwards found circulated in Europe, and oftener repeated than any other Part of this whole Transaction. Lord How was profuse in his Expressions of Gratitude to the State of Massachusetts, for erecting a marble Monument in Westminster Abbey to his Elder Brother Lord How who was killed in America in the last French War, saying "he esteemed that Honour to his Family, *above all Things in this World. That such was his gratitude and affection to this Country, on that Account, that he felt for America, as for a Brother, and if America should fall, he should feel and lament it, like the Loss of a Brother." Dr. Franklin, with an easy Air and a collected Countenance, a Bow, a Smile and all that Naivetee which sometimes appeared in his Conversation and is often observed in his Writings, replied "My Lord, We will do our Utmost Endeavours, to save your Lordship that mortification." His Lordship appeared to feel this, with more Sensibility, than I could expect: but he only returned "I suppose you will endeavour to give Us employment in Europe." To this Observation, not a Word nor a look from which he could draw any Inference, escaped any of the Committee.

Another Circumstance, of no more importance than the former, was so much celebrated in Europe, that it has often reminded me of the Question of Phocion to his Fellow Citizen, when something he had said in Public was received by the People of Athens with a clamorous Applause, "Have I said any foolish Thing?"—When his Lordship observed to Us, that he could not confer with Us as Members of Congress, or public Characters, but only as private Persons and British Subjects, Mr. John Adams answered somewhat quickly, "Your Lordship may consider me, in what light you please; and indeed I should be willing to consider myself, for a few moments, in any Character which would be agreable to your Lordship, *except that of a British Subject.*" His Lordship at these Words turn'd to Dr. Franklin

[3] They were published in the *Pennsylvania Gazette*, 18 Sept. 1776. The authorship of the report is not known, but the language of JA's letter to Samuel Adams, 14 Sept. (p. 426–429, below), contains marked parallels with the language of the report as submitted and printed.

and Mr. Rutledge and said "Mr. Adams is a decided Character:" with so much gravity and solemnity: that I now believe it meant more, than either of my Colleagues or myself understood at the time. In our report to Congress We supposed that the Commissioners, Lord and General Howe, had by their Commission Power to [except]⁴ from Pardon all that they should think proper. But I was informed in England, afterwards, that a Number were expressly excepted by Name from Pardon, by the privy Council, and that John Adams was one of them, and that this List of Exceptions was given as an Instruction to the two Howes, with their Commission. When I was afterwards a Minister Plenipotentiary, at the Court of St. James's The King and the Ministry, were often insulted, ridiculed and reproached in the Newspapers, for having conducted with so much folly as to be reduced to the humiliating Necessity of receiving as an Ambassador a Man who stood recorded by the privy Council as a Rebell expressly excepted from Pardon. If this is true it will account for his Lordships gloomy denunciation of me, as "a decided Character."—Some years afterwards, when I resided in England as a public Minister, his Lordship recollected and alluded to this Conversation with great politeness and much good humour. Att the Ball, on the Queens Birthnight, I was at a Loss for the Seats assigned to the foreign Ambassadors and their Ladies. Fortunately meeting Lord How at the Door I asked his Lordship, where were the Ambassadors Seats. His Lordship with his usual politeness, and an unusual Smile of good humour, pointed to the Seats, and manifestly alluding to the Conversation on Staten Island said, "Aye! Now, We must turn you away among the foreigners."

The Conduct of General Sullivan, in consenting to come to Philadelphia, upon so confused an Errand from Lord Howe, though his Situation as a Prisoner was a temptation and may be considered as some Apology for it, appeared to me to betray such Want of Penetration and fortitude, and there was so little precision in the Information he communicated that I felt much resentment and more contempt upon the Occasion than was perhaps just. The time was extreamly critical. The Attention of Congress, the Army, the States and the People ought to have been wholly directed to the Defence of the Country. To have it diverted and relaxed by such a poor Artifice and confused tale, appeared very reprehensible. To a few of my most confidential friends, I expressed my feelings, in a very few Words, which I found time to write: and all the Letters, of which I find

---

⁴ MS: "accept."

Copies, in my Letter Book, are here subjoined, relative to this Transaction from its Beginning to its End.[5]

Extract of a Letter from John Adams to Colonel William Tudor, dated Philadelphia August 29. and continued to September 2, 1776.

"So! The Fishers have set a Seine, and a whole Schull,[6] a whole Shoal of Fishes, have swam into it and been caught. The Fowlers have set a Net, and a whole flock of Pidgeons have alighted on the bed, and the Net has been drawn over them.... But the most insolent Thing of all, is sending one of those very Pidgeons, as a Flutterer to Philadelphia, in order to decoy the great flock of all.... Did you ever see a decoy-Duck? or a Decoy Brant?"...

Extract of a Letter from John Adams to Colonel James Warren, dated Philadelphia September 4th. 1776.

"Before this time, the Secretary, (Mr. Samuel Adams) has arrived and will give you, all the Information you can wish, concerning the State of Things here.... Mr. Gerry got in, the day before Yesterday very well.... There has been a change, in our Affairs at New York.— What effects it will produce, I cannot pretend to foretell. I confess I do not clearly foresee. Lord Howe is surrounded with disaffected Americans, Machiavilian Exiles from Boston and elsewhere, who are instigating him, to mingle Art with Force.... He has sent Sullivan here, upon his parole, with the most insidious, 'tho ridiculous message which you can conceive.... It has put Us, rather in a delicate Situation, and gives Us much trouble.

"Before this day, no doubt, you have appointed some other Persons to come here and I shall embrace the first Opportunity, after our Affairs shall get into a more settled train, to return.... It is high time, for me, I assure you: Yet I will not go, while the present fermentation

---

[5] The letters and extracts of letters that follow were omitted by CFA when editing the Diary and Autobiography; most but not all of them he printed elsewhere in JA's *Works* or in JA–AA, *Familiar Letters*. The texts given here, including their punctuation, are according to the copies in the Autobiography, but though all differences of any significance between the copies and the versions in the letterbook have been noted, trifling mistakes have been silently corrected. (The texts from which JA copied are in Adams Papers, Microfilms, Reel Nos. 89–90.) JA's chief idiosyncrasy as a copyist was a frequent use of series of curled dashes, resembling tildes, between sentences. These have been rendered here as suspension points, but the reader must be advised that they rarely indicate omissions; they are, rather, JA's random equivalents of dashes, periods, and sometimes new paragraphs in the letterbook texts he was copying.

[6] LbC: "School."

lasts.—I will stay and watch the Crisis; and assist Nature, like an honest Physician, in throwing off the morbific matter."

Another Letter from [John Adams] [7] to Colonel James Warren, dated Phyladelphia September 8, 1776.

"I am going tomorrow Morning, on an Errand to Lord Howe; not to beg [a] Pardon, I assure you, but to hear what he has to say.... He sent Sullivan here, to let Us know, that he wanted a Conversation with some members of Congress.... We are going to hear him; but as Congress have voted, that they cannot send Members to talk with him, in their private Capacities, but will send a Committee of their Body as Representatives of the free and independent States of America; I presume his Lordship cannot see Us, and I hope he will not; but, if he should, the whole will terminate in nothing. Some think it will occasion a delay of military Operations, which they say, We much want.—I am not of this mind.... Some think, it will clearly throw the Odium of continuing this War, on his Lordship and his Master.— I wish it may.... Others think it will silence the Tories and establish the timid Whigs.—I wish this also: but dont expect it. But all these Arguments and twenty others, as weighty, would not have convinced me of the Necessity, Propriety or Utility of this Embassy, if Congress had not determined [on] it.... I was totis Viribus, against it, from first to last. But, upon this Occasion, New Hampshire, Connecticut and even Virginia, gave Way.... All Sides agreed in sending me. The staunch and intrepid, such as were Ennimies as much as myself to the measure, pushed for me, I suppose, that as little Evil might come of it, as possible.... Others agreed to vote for me, in order to entice some of our Inflexibles, to vote for the Measure.—You will hear more of this Embassy.—It will be famous enough. Your Secretary, (Mr. Samuel Adams) will rip, about this measure, and well he may. Nothing I assure you but the Unanimous Vote of Congress, the pressing Solicitation of the firmest Men in Congress, and the particular Advice of my own Colleagues, at least of Mr. Hancock and Mr. Gerry, would have induced me to have accepted this Trust."

A Letter from John Adams to Samuel Adams, (then in Boston) dated Philadelphia September 8, 1776.

"Dear Sir  Tomorrow Morning Dr. Franklin, Mr. Edward [Rutledge and your humble servant sett off to see that rare] [8] Curiosity,

---

[7] Words missing at top of leaf, worn away.
[8] Words missing at top of leaf, worn away, supplied from LbC.

Lord Howe.... Dont imagine from this that a Panick has spread in[9] Philadelphia.... By no means.... This is only refinement in Policy! ... It has a deep, profound reach, no doubt! So deep that you cannot see to the bottom of it, I dare say!... I am sure I cannot.... Dont however be concerned. When you see the whole, as you will e'er long, you will not find it very bad.... I will write you, the particulars, as soon as I shall be at Liberty to do it."

A Letter from John Adams to Samuel Adams, then in Boston, dated Philadelphia September 14, 1776.

"In a few Lines of the 8th. instant, I promised you, a more particular Account of the Conference.

"On Monday last, the Committee satt off, from Philadelphia, and reached Brunswick on Tuesday night.... Wednesday Morning they proceeded to Amboy, and from thence to Staten Island, where they met the Lord Howe, by whom they were politely received and entertained.

"His Lordship opened the Conference, by giving Us an Account of the motive which first induced him to attend to the dispute with America, which he said was the honor which had been done to his Family by the Massachusetts Bay, which he prized very highly.... From whence, I concluded in my own mind, that his Lordship had not attended to the Controversy, earlier than the Port Bill and Charter Bill, and consequently must have a very inadequate Idea of the Nature, as well as of the rise and progress of the Contest.

"His Lordship then observed that he had requested this Interview that he might satisfy himself, whether there was any probability, that America would return to her Allegiance: but he must observe to Us, that he could not acknowledge Us, as Members of Congress or a Committee of that Body, but that he only desired this Conversation with Us, as private Gentlemen, in hopes, that it might prepare the Way, for the Peoples returning to their Allegiance, and to an Accommodation of the Disputes between the two Countries. That he had no Power to treat with Us, as independent States or in any other C[haracter than as British Subjects and][1] private Gentlemen. But that upon our Acknowledging ourselves to be British Subjects, he had Power to consult with Us. That the Act of Parliament had given Power to the King, upon certain Conditions, of declaring the Colonies to be at peace: and his Commission gave him Power to confer, advise and

[9] LbC: "to."
[1] Words missing at top of leaf, worn away, supplied from LbC.

426

consult, with any number or description of Persons concerning the Complaints of the People in America. That the King and Ministry, had very good Dispositions to redress the Grievances of the People and reform the Errors of the Administration in America. That his Commission gave him Power to converse with any Persons whatever in America concerning the former Instructions to Governors, and the Acts of Parliament complain'd of. That the King and Ministry were very willing to have all these revised and reconsidered, and if any Errors had crept in, if they could be pointed out, they were very willing they should be rectified.

"One of the Committee, Mr. Rutledge, mentioned to his Lordship, what General Sullivan had said, that his Lordship told him, he would sett the Act of Parliament wholly aside, and that Parliament had no right to tax America, or meddle with her internal Polity. His Lordship answered Mr. Rutledge, that General Sullivan had misunderstood him, and extended his Words much beyond their import.

"His Lordship gave Us, a long Account of his Negotiations, in order to obtain Powers sufficiently ample for his Purpose. He said, he had told them (the Ministry, I suppose he meant) that those Persons whom you call Rebells, are the most proper to confer with, of any, because they are the Persons who complain of Grievances. The others, those who are not in Arms, and are not, according to your Ideas in Rebellion, have no Complaints or Grievances. They are satisfied, and therefore it would be to no purpose to converse with them. So that, his Lordship said he would not accept the Commission, or Command, untill he had full Power to confer, with any Persons whom he should think proper, who had the most Abilities and Influence. But having obtained those Powers, he intended to have gone directly to Philadelphia, not to have treated with Congress as such, or to have acknowledged that Body, but to have consulted with Gentlemen of that Body, in their private Capacities, upon the Subjects in his Commission.

"His Lordship did not incline to give Us any farther Account of his Powers or to make any other Propositions to Us,[2] than those which are contained in Substance in the foregoing lines.

"I have the pleasure to assure you, that there was no disagrement in Opinion, among the members of the Committee, upon any one point. They were perfectly united in Sentiment, and in language, as they are in the Result of the whole, which is, that his Lordships Powers are fully expressed in the late Act of Parliament: and that his Commission contains no other Authority, than that of granting Pardons,

[2] LbC has an added phrase at this point: "in one Capacity or another."

with such Exceptions as the Commissioners shall think proper to make: and of declaring America, or any part of it, to be at Peace upon Submission: and of enquiring into the State of America, of any Persons, with whom, they might think proper to confer, advize, converse and consult, even although they should be Officers of the Army, or Members of Congress; and then representing the Result of their Inquiries to the Ministry, who, after all, might or might not, at their pleasure, make any Alterations in the former Instructions to Governors, or propose in Parliament any Alterations in the Acts complained of.

"The whole Affair of the Commission appears to me, as it ever did, to be a bubble, an Ambuscade, a mere insidious Maneuvre, calculated only to decoy and deceive:—And it is so gross, that they must have a wretched Opinion of our Generalship, to suppose that We can fall into it.

"The Committee assured his Lordship, that they had no Authority, to wait upon him, or to treat or converse with him, in any other Character, but that of a Committee of Congress, and as Members of independent States. That the Vote, which was their Commission, clearly ascertained their Character. That the Declaration which had been made, of Independence, was the Result of long and cool deliberation. That it had been made by Congress, after long and great Reluctance, in Obedience to the possitive Instructions of their Constituents; every Assembly upon the Continent, having instructed their Delegates to this [Purpose, and since the Dec]laration[3] has been made And published, it has been solemnly ratified and confirmed by the Assemblies: so that neither this Committee, nor that Congress, which sent it here, have Authority to treat in any other Character, than as independent States.... One of the Committee Dr. Franklin, assured his Lordship, that in his private Opinion, America would not again come under the domination of Great Britain: and therefore it was the Duty of every good Man, on both sides the Water, to promote Peace, and an Acknowledgment of American Independency, and a Treaty of Friendship and Alliance, between the two Countries. Another of the Committee, Mr. John Adams, assured his Lordship that in his private Opinion, America would never treat, in any other Character, than as independent States.... The other Member Mr. Rutledge concurred in the same Opinion.... His Lordship said he had no Powers nor Instructions, upon that Subject: it was entirely new.—Mr. Rutledge observed to his Lordship that most of the Colonies, had submitted, for two Years, to all the Inconveniences of Anarchy, and to

[3] Words missing at top of leaf, worn away, supplied from LbC.

live without Governments in hopes of Reconciliation: But now had instituted Governments. Mr. John Adams observed, that all the Colonies had gone compleatly through a Revolution. That they had taken all Authority from the Officers of the Crown, and had appointed Officers of their own, which his Lordship would easily conceive had cost great Struggles: and that they could not easily go back. And that Americans had too much understanding, not to know that after such a declaration as they had made, the Government of Great Britain never would have any Confidence in them or could govern them but by Force of Arms."

A Letter from John Adams to a Friend[4] in Massachusetts dated Philadelphia, Fryday September 6, 1776.

"This Day, I think has been the most remarkable of all.... Sullivan came here, from Lord Howe, five days ago, with a Message, that his Lordship desired a half an Hours Conversation, with some of the Members of Congress, in their private Capacities.... We have spent three or four days, in debating, whether We should take any notice of it.... I have to the Utmost of my Abilities, during the whole Time, opposed our taking any notice of it.... But at last it was determined by a Majority, 'That the Congress, being the Representatives of the free and independent States of America, it was improper to appoint any of their Members to confer in their private Characters with his Lordship. But they would appoint a Committee of their Body, to wait on him to know whether he had Power to treat with Congress upon Terms of Peace, and to hear any Propositions that his Lordship may think proper to make.'[5]

"When the Committee came to be balloted for, Dr. Franklin and your humble Servant, were unanimously chosen.... Mr. Rutledge and Colonel Lee (Richard Henry Lee) had an equal Number: but upon a second Vote, Mr. Rutledge was chosen. I requested to be excused, but was desired to consider of it, till tomorrow.[6] My Friends here advize me to go.... All the staunch and intrepid, are very earnest with me to go.... And all the timid and wavering agree in the request: So I believe I shall undertake the Journey. I doubt whether His Lordship will see Us: but the same Committee will be directed to inquire

[4] His wife, AA.
[5] This is a close paraphrase, rather than a precise text, of the resolution adopted on 5 Sept.; see JCC, 5:737.
[6] See a canceled entry in the Journal: "Mr. J. Adams requesting to be excused, the question whether he shall be excused from this service was postponed till to morrow" (JCC, 5:738). R. H. Lee said he would not serve and refused to be voted for a second time (same, note).

429

into the State of the Army, at New York,[7] so that there will be business enough, if his Lordship makes none. It would fill this Letter Book to give you all the Arguments, for and against this measure, if I had Liberty to attempt it.... His Lordship seems to have been playing off a Number of Machiavillian Maneuvres, in order to throw upon Us the Odium of continuing this War. Those, who have been Advocates for the Appointment of this Committee, are for opposing Maneuvre to Maneuvre, and are confident that the Consequence will be, that the Odium will lie upon him.... However this may be, my Lesson is plain, to ask a few Questions and take his Answers. I can think of but one Reason for their putting me, upon this Embassy, and that is this. An Idea has crept into many minds here, that his Lordship is such another as Mr. Hutchinson: and they may possibly think, that a Man who has been accustomed to Penetrate into the mazy Windings of Hutchinsons heart, and the serpentine Wiles of his head, may be tolerably qualified to converse with his Lordship.

"Sunday. September 8. Yesterdays Post brought me, yours of Aug. 29. The Report you mentioned 'that I was poisoned upon my return at New York,' I suppose will be thought to be a Prophecy, delivered by the oracle in mystic Language: and meant only that I should be politically or morally poisoned by Lord Howe.... But the Prophecy shall be a false one."

Extract of another Letter to a Friend,[8] dated Philadelphia September 14th, 1776.

"Yesterday Morning I returned with Dr. Franklin and Mr. Rutledge from Staten Island, where We met Lord Howe, and had about three hours Conversation with him. The Result of this Interview will do no disservice to Us. It is now plain, that his Lordship has no Power, but what is given him in the Act of Parliament. His Commission authorizes him to grant Pardons upon Submission: and to converse, confer, consult and advize, with such Persons as he may think proper, upon American Grievances, Upon the Instructions to Governors and the Acts of Parliament, and if any Errors should be found to have crept in, his Majesty and the Ministers were willing they should be rectified.

"My ride has been of Service to me. We were absent but four days.

[7] This does not appear in the resolutions adopted on 5 and 6 Sept. (JCC, 5:737, 738), nor did the committee to confer with Lord Howe carry out such an assignment. A different committee reported to Congress on this subject on 3 Oct. (same, p. 842–844).

[8] AA.

It was an agreable Excursion. His Lordship is about fifty Years of Age. He is a well bred Man but his Address is not so irresistable, as it has been represented. I could name you many Americans in your own Neighbourhood, whose Art, Address and Abilities are greatly superiour."

I return to the Journal of Congress.

Fryday September 13. 1776. Two Letters of the 7th. and 11. from General Washington, one of the Eighth from General Green, and a resolution of the Committee of Safety of Pennsilvania of the 13th were read, and referred to the Board of War.

Two Letters of the 8th, from General Schuyler, with sundry Papers enclosed; one of the 7th. from Walter Livingston, and one of the 12th. from Brigadier General Armstrong were read—referred to the Board of War.

A Committee of the whole to take into Consideration, a report of the Board of War. Mr. Nelson reported no resolution.

Saturday September 14. 1776.

A Letter from R. H. Harrison, Secretary to General Washington, was read. Four French Officers, who arrived in the Reprisal Captain Weeks, being recommended to Congress, Resolved that they be referred to the Board of War.

The Board of War brought in a Report, which was taken into Consideration, whereupon Nine Resolutions were adopted. See the Journal.[9]

A Letter of the 9th. from General Lee to the Board of War, was laid before Congress and read.

Monday September 16. 1776.

A Letter of the 14th. from General Washington, One of the 9th. from General Schuyler, inclosing a copy of one from General Gates, dated the 6th., and one of the 2d, from General Gates with sundry Papers inclosed, were read, and referred to the Board of War.

A Committee of the whole, on a report of the Board of War. Mr. Nelson reported sundry Amendments and Congress adopted the Resolutions with the Amendments. The Resolutions, which may be seen in the Journal, contain the whole Plan of an Army of Eighty Eight Battalions, to be inlisted as soon as possible, to serve during the War.[1]

[9] JCC, 5:757–758. These concerned rations for militia officers, winter quarters for the northern army, settlement of the accounts of certain officers, powder and flints for Gates' army, measures to enforce the surrender of arms and ammunition by troops leaving the service, &c.

[1] JCC, 5:762–763. The Board of War's plan for an army of 88 battalions, probably introduced on 9 Sept., had

Resolved that tomorrow be assigned for taking into Consideration the Articles of War.

Tuesday September 17. 1776.

Sundry Resolutions being moved and seconded, in Addition to those passed Yesterday, relative to the New Army. After debate, Resolved that they be referred to the Board of War.

A Letter of the 10th. from Brigadier General Lewis, was read: Also a Letter from James Forrest was read, and referred to the Board of War.

Congress took into Consideration the Plan of treaties to be proposed to foreign nations, with the Amendments agreed to by the Committee of the whole, and the same was agreed to.

This is all that I can find in the public Journal relative to this one of the most important Transactions, that ever came before Congress. A Secret Journal was prepared, in which all the Proceedings on this Business, were entered, which has never been published. If that Journal was honestly and faithfully kept, the progress of the Plan of Treaties and the Persons chiefly concerned with it, will there appear.[2]

Wednesday September 18. 1776.

The Board of War, brought in a report, which was taken into Consideration and six resolutions adopted, from it, which appear on the Journal. The Remainder of the Report postponed.[3]

Resolved that the Board of War be directed to prepare a resolution for enforceing and perfecting Discipline in the Army.

Congress took into Consideration the Instructions to the Commissioners &c.

---

been debated in Congress and in a committee of the whole every day from 10 through 13 Sept. (same, p. 747, 749, 751, 754, 756–757). (JA was absent on his mission to Staten Island, 9–12 Sept.) As amended and adopted it was spread on the Journal of the 16th, and after further amendment next day it was on the 20th ordered to be printed (same, p. 762–763, 768, 807). In its final form it appeared in the *Pennsylvania Gazette* on 25 Sept. No version has been found in the Reports of the Board of War and Ordnance, PCC, No. 147. In his comments in the entry of 20 Sept. below, JA implies that he had a large part in initiating this plan for a large and permanent army.

[2] The "Plan of a Treaty with France,"

with appended forms of sea letters and passports, and the instructions (adopted on 24 Sept.) to the commissioners about to be appointed to negotiate a treaty, were printed in the *Secret Journals . . . of Congress*, Boston, 1820, 2:7–30 (in JCC, 5:768–779). On JA's role in the preparation and adoption of these important papers, see p. 337–338, 393, above.

[3] JCC, 5:780–781. The recommendations adopted were highly miscellaneous. Those postponed concerned disputes among officers in the northern army and included a resolution of thanks to Gen. Gates for his "Vigilance Prudence and Activity" with respect to these disputes, &c.

These I suppose, were the Ministers to France, and other Courts in Europe.

Thursday September 19. 1776.

The Board of War brought in a report, which was taken into Consideration, and five Resolutions adopted from it, which see in the Journal.[4] The last of these, is in these Words.

That the Commander in Chief of the forces of these States in the several departments, be directed to give possitive orders, to the Brigadier Generals and Colonels, and all other Officers in their several Armies, that the Troops under their command may every day be called together, and trained in Arms, in order that Officers and Men may be perfected in the manual Exercises and Manœuvres, and inured to the most exemplary discipline, and that all Officers be assured, that the Congress will consider Activity and Success, in introducing discipline into the Army, among the best recommendations for promotion.

This Resolution was the Effect of my late Journey, through the Jersies to Staten Island. I had observed such dissipation and Idleness, such Confusion and distraction, among Officers and Soldiers, in various parts of the Country as astonished, grieved and allarmed me. Discipline, Discipline had become my constant topick of discourse and even declamation in and out of Congress and especially in the Board of War. I saw very clearly that the Ruin of our Cause and Country must be the Consequence if a thoughrough Reformation and strict Discipline could not be introduced. My Zeal on this Occasion was no doubt represented, by my faithfull Ennemies, in great Secrecy however, to their friends in the Army, and although it might recommend me to the Esteem of a very few, yet, it will be easily believed that it contributed nothing to my Popularity, among the many.

A Memorial from the Chevalier Dorre was read. Ordered that it be referred to the Board of War.

Congress resumed the Consideration of the Articles of War, and, after some time, the farther Consideration thereof was postponed.

This was another Measure, that I constantly urged on with all the Zeal and Industry possible: convinced that nothing short of the Roman and British Discipline could possible save Us. Yet the Upright Hamilton with his usual Veracity, charges me, with being an Ennemy to a regular Army.[5]

Fryday September 20th. 1776.

[4] JCC, 5:784.
[5] CFA omitted the final sentence of this paragraph. For JA's part in revising the Articles of War see entries of 5 June, 19 Aug., and notes, above; 20 Sept., below.

Congress resumed the Consideration of the Articles of War, which being debated in Paragraphs, were agreed to as follows.

Resolved that from and after the publication of the following Articles, in the respective Armies of the United States, the Rules and Articles, by which the said Armies have heretofore been governed, shall be, and they are hereby repealed. The Articles are inserted in the Journal of this day, and need not be transcribed, they are the System which I persuaded Jefferson to agree with me in reporting to Congress. They fill about sixteen Pages of the Journal.[6]—In Congress Jefferson never spoke, and all the labour of the debate on these Articles, Paragraph by Paragraph, was thrown upon me, and such was the Opposition, and so indigested were the notions of Liberty prevalent among the Majority of the Members most zealously attached to the public Cause, that to this day I scarcely know how it was possible, that these Articles could be carried. They were Adopted however, and have governed our Armies, with little variation to this day, the 7th. of June 1805.

Ordered that the foregoing Articles of War be immediately published.

Ordered that the Resolutions for raising the new Army be published, and copies thereof sent to the Commanding Officers in the several departments, and to the Assemblies and Conventions of the several States.

These were for raising Eighty Eight Battalions, with a Bounty for inlisting the Men during the War, granting Lands &c. which may be seen page 357 and 358 of the Journal of 1776.[7]

Here again the Honesty of Hamilton appears. The Articles of War and the Institution of the Army during the War, were all my Work, and yet he represents me as an Ennemy to a regular Army. Although I have long since forgiven this Arch Ennemy, yet Vice, Folly and Villany are not to be forgotten, because the guilty Wretch repented, in his dying Moments. Although David repented, We are no where commanded to forget the Affair of Uriah: though the Magdalene reformed, We are not obliged to forget her former *Vocation*:[8] though the Thief on the cross was converted, his Felony is still upon Record. The Prodigal Son repented and was forgiven, yet his Harlots and riotous living, and even the Swine and the husks that brought him

[6] JCC, 5:788-807.
[7] Under date of 16 Sept., when the resolutions were reported out of a committee of the whole and adopted; see entry of that date, above, and note 1

there.
[8] In the MS the word "frailty" is written above "*Vocation*," but the latter word is not deleted.

to consideration, cannot be forgotten. Nor am I obliged by any Principles of Morality or Religion to suffer my Character to lie under infamous Calumnies, because the Author of them, with a Pistol Bullet through his Spinal Marrow, died a Penitent. Charity requires that We should hope and believe that his humiliation was sincere, and I ⟨sincerely⟩ hope he was forgiven: but I will not conceal his former Character at the Expence of so much Injustice to my own, as this Scottish Creolion Bolingbroke in the days of his disappointed Ambition and unbridled Malice and revenge, was pleased falsely to attempt against it. Born on a Speck more obscure than Corsica, from an Original not only contemptible but infamous, with infinitely less courage and Capacity than Bonaparte, he would in my Opinion, if I had not controuled the fury of his Vanity, instead of relieving this Country from Confusion as Bonaparte did France, he would have involved it in all the Bloodshed and distractions of foreign and civil War at once.[9]

Monday September 23. 1776. A Letter of the 20 and 21st. from General Washington; two of the 19th. from J. Trumbull; one of the 21st. from the Convention of Delaware; one of the 14th from R. Varick; one of the 19th. from Governor Livingston; also, one of the 14th. from General Schuyler and one of the 19th from Colonel Van Schaick, and one from Dr. William Shippen were read:

Ordered that the Letter from Dr. Shippen be referred to the medical Committee, and the rest to the Board of War.

Two Petitions, one from Colonel J. Stark, and the other from Mons. Devourouy, were read and referred to the Board of War.

Tuesday September 24. 1776.

The Board of War brought in a report, which was read. Ordered to lie on the Table.

The Board of War brought in a farther report. Ordered to lie on the Table.

Congress resumed the Consideration of the Instructions to the Commissioners and the same being debated by Paragraphs and amended, were agreed to.

These Instructions were recorded only on the Secret Journal, and are not therefore, in my Power. They may be found, no doubt, at the Seat of Government, in the Office of the Secretary of State.

Wednesday, September 25. 1776. Two Letters from General Lee; one of the 24th. of August to the President, the other of the 27 of

---

[9] The whole of the foregoing paragraph was omitted by CFA.

the same Month to the board of War, both dated at Savannah, being received, were read.

Congress took into Consideration the Report of the Board of War, whereupon Resolved &c. These Resolutions fill two Pages of the Journal.[1]

Fryday. September 27. 1776. Two Letters of the 24th. and 25th from General Washington, with sundry Papers inclosed; one of the 20th. from the Convention of New York; one of the 22d. from Joseph Trumbull; one of the 25th. from Colonel John Shee inclosing his Commission; and one of the 25th. from Jon. B. Smith requesting Leave to resign his office of Deputy Muster Master general were laid before Congress and read. Ordered that the Letters from General Washington, be referred to a Committee of five. The Members chosen Mr. Wythe, Mr. Hopkinson, Mr. Rutledge, Mr. J. Adams, and Mr. Stone.[2]

Ordered that the Secret Committee deliver to the Board of War, the Care And Custody of all Arms, Ammunition and other warlike Stores now under their care, or that may hereafter be imported or purchased by them for Account of the United States of America.

Saturday September 28. 1776.

The Board of War, to whom the Petition of William McCue was referred, brought in a report, whereupon Resolved, as in the Journal.[3]

Monday September 30. 1776.

Resolved that the Board of War be impowered and directed, on requisition of the General, or commanding Officers in the several departments, to send such Articles of Military Stores, and other necessaries, which they may have in their Possession, or can procure.

Resolved that the Board of War be directed to order the three Virginia Battalions, now on their March to New York, to be lodged in the Barracks at Wilmington; there to remain till further orders.

The Committee to whom were referred the Letters from General Washington of the 24th. and 25th instant, and the Papers inclosed therein, brought in their report, which was taken into Consideration;

[1] *JCC,* 5:823–825. There are twelve resolutions on a great variety of routine matters.

[2] Washington's letters are printed in his *Writings,* ed. Fitzpatrick, 6:105–118. The committee brought in a report on 30 Sept., which was acted on in part that day and in part on 7 Oct., the rest being postponed and thereafter merged with action on the report of the committee that had visited the army in New York (*JCC,* 5:836, 853, 855 ff.). The resolutions passed on the 30th were chiefly directed to improving army medical personnel and care; those passed on the 7th increased the pay of officers engaging to serve throughout the war. The authorship of the report is not known.

[3] *JCC,* 5:833.

whereupon many Resolutions were passed, which appear in the Journal, and the Remainder of the Report postponed.

Tuesday October 1. 1776.

Resolved that a Committee of four be appointed to confer with Brigadier General Mifflin. The Members chosen, Mr. R. H. Lee, Mr. Sherman, Mr. J. Adams and Mr. Gerry.[4]

Resolved that a Committee of five be appointed to prepare and bring in a Plan of a military Accademy at the Army: The Members chosen Mr. Hooper, Mr. Lynch, Mr. Wythe, Mr. Williams and Mr. J. Adams.[5]

On this same day, I wrote to Colonel Knox in these Words. "This day I had the honour of making a motion for the Appointment of a Committee to consider of a Plan for the Establishment of a military Accademy, in the Army. The Committee was appointed and your Servant was one. Write me your Sentiments upon the Subject."[6]

As this was, in my Opinion the most critical and dangerous Period of the whole revolutionary War, as all that I had seen and heard and read of the State of our Army made a great impression [upon] my Mind, and arroused the most allarming Apprehension, I will conceal nothing from Posterity. My own private Letters, to confidential Friends, will shew my Opinion at the time of the State of facts, and the measures that were necessary, to retrieve our disgraces. Like Mr. Gifford, I look back, with a sort of Scepticism, on the Application of those days and cannot account for the possibility of finding time amidst all my Employments in Congress and the Board of War, to write and copy the Letters I find in my Books.[7] I had no Secretary or Clerk and all appears in my hand Writing. I wrote to Colonel Tudor

Dr. Sir                                   Philadelphia September 26. 1776

Your obliging favours of September 6 from New York and that of the 23d from the Plains of Haarlem, are now before me.[8] The Picture you draw of the Army, and the disorders which prevail in it, is shock-

[4] Mifflin was about to resume his post as Continental quartermaster general. On 2 Oct. this committee brought in recommendations concerning supplies, employees, pay, appropriations, &c., for the quartermaster's department, on which Congress acted (JCC, 5:839–840). The authorship of the report is not known.

[5] The history of this project is obscure, but nothing came of it at the time. See a note on it in Burnett, ed., *Letters of Members*, 2:108.

[6] This is the postscript to JA's letter to Knox of 29 Sept. (LbC, Adams Papers), which JA copied in full into his Autobiography a few pages farther on.

[7] The letters that follow were omitted by CFA in his text of the Diary and Autobiography, though he printed several of them elsewhere in JA's *Works*. In the present edition they have been treated like those inserted earlier; see p. 424, above, and note 5 there.

[8] Both in Adams Papers.

ing: but I believe it is just. But We often find, that in the variagated Scæne of human life, that much good grows out of great Evil.... A few disgraces and defeats have done more, towards convincing the Congress, than the Rhetorick of many months, assisted by frequent Letters from the General, and many other Officers of the Army, was able to effect. Before this time you have been informed, that the Articles of War, are passed and printed, and a new Plan for the formation of a permanent and regular Army, is adopted. I wish it may have Success.—Pray give me your Opinion of it.

The late Events at New York have almost overcome my Utmost Patience. I can bear the Conflagration of Towns, nay almost any thing else, public or private, better than disgrace. The Cowardice of New England men is an unexpected discovery to me, and I confess has put my Philosophy to the Tryal. If I had heard, that Parsons's and Fellows's Brigades had been cutt to Pieces, and had my Father, my Brother and Son been among the Slain, I sincerely believe, upon a cool examination of my own heart, it would not have given me so much grief as the shamefull flight of the 15th. instant.... I hope that God will forgive the guilty in the next World: but, should any question concerning this transaction, come into any place where I have a Vote, I should think it my duty to be inexorable, in this. We have none of the particulars, but I conclude, that such detestable Behaviour of whole Brigades, could not have happened, without the worst Examples, in some Officers of Rank.—These, if any such there are, shall never want my Voice, for sending them to another World. If the best Friend I have, should prove to be one of them, I should think myself guilty of his Crime, and that I deserved his Punishment, if I interposed one Word, between him and death.

I lament the Fall of the young Hero, Henly. But I wish you had been more particular, in your narration of the Enterprize, which proved so glorious and so fatal to him. You are much mistaken in your Apprehension, that We are minutely informed of such Events. We suffer great Anxiety, and the Public suffers many Misfortunes, for Want of Information. The Post Office, which has been in fault, is now beginning to do its duty. Dont you neglect yours.
Colonel Tudor.

Another Letter to Colonel Tudor, without a date, but about the same time.[9]

[9] JA was mistaken; this is actually a continuation of the letter to Tudor of 26 Sept. The evidence in JA's letter-book is confusing, but a copy of the

My young Friend.

I pity the Situation of the General, because it is a difficult, a dangerous and a most important one. I make it my Rule to cover all Imperfections in the Generals, and other Officers of inferiour rank as well as I can, and to make full and ample Allowances for all their Virtues, Merits, and Services.

I recollect that Polybius, who was as great a Judge of War as any of his Age, was loud in his Praises of the Roman Troops. He never imputed any defeat, to the fault of the men, but, universally to the folly and incapacity, of their Commanders. Our Generals and other Officers must learn the same Justice and Policy. General imputations of Cowardice and impatience of discipline to the Men, are false, or, if true, it is the fault of the Officers: it is owing to their ignorance, incapacity or indolence: and farther, if it was true, concealing is the Way to cure it, not publishing of it. The frequent Surprizes, by which our Officers and Men are taken, in the most palpable trapps, convince me, that there is a dearth of Genius among them.

There never was perhaps, a Crisis, in which a Coincidence of Circumstances, offered a fairer Opportunity for some great mind, to shew and exert itself.

And perhaps there is not in all Antiquity, if there is in universal History, an Example, more apposite to our Situation, than that of Thebes, or a Character more deserving of imitation, than that of Epaminondas.

The Bœotians were remarkable, even to a proverb, for their dullness, and untill the Age of Epaminondas, made no figure in War. By the Peace of Antalcidas, the honor and interest of Greece, was prostituted to the Pride of Sparta. The Thebans were compelled to acceed to that Treaty, although it deprived them of the dominion of Bœotia, and the Spartans by tampering with a perfidious Aristocratick faction at last got possession of their citadel, and reduced the Thebans to unconditional Subjugation. From this wretched State both of foreign and domestic Slavery, they were delivered, by the Virtue and Ability of Epaminondas, and raised to power superiour to the other Grecian States. The honest Citizens, enraged to see their Country, thus cheated into Servitude, determined to set her free. The project was well laid, and boldly executed by Pelopidas, who entered the City with a small number of resolute men in disguise, destroyed Leontidas and Archias,

letter made by Tudor (MHi: Tudor Papers) contains the text of both parts and an additional paragraph that was evidently appended to the (missing) recipient's copy.

the two Traytors and Tyrants, and with the assistance of Epaminondas and his friends, together with a body of Athenians, regained the Citadel. The Spartans hearing of this revolution, entered the territories of the Thebans with a powerful Army, to take vengeance of the Rebells, and reduce the City to its former Subjection. The timorous Athenians, dreading the formidable Power of Sparta, renounced all Friendship for the Thebans, and punished with great Severity, such of their Citizens as favoured them. The Thebans, destitute of Friends, and deserted by their Allies, appeared to the rest of the World to be devoted to inevitable destruction. In such a desperate conjuncture of Affairs, the Genius and Virtue of two great Men shone forth to the Astonishment of all Mankind.

But what means did they Use?... Their Men were raw Militia, fresh recruits, new raised Citizens and husbandmen, unexperienced, undisciplined, unused to Subordination, having been born and educated under the most democratical government in all Greece, and, what is worse, from a natural or habitual hebetude, not very adroit, at learning any Thing.

They began by training their Men, inspiring them with a Contempt and hatred of Servitude, and the noble resolution of dying in defence of the Liberty and glory of their Country. They judged it rash, to hazard a decisive battle, with their new raised Militia, against the best troops in Greece: but chose rather to harrass the Spartans, with frequent Skirmishes, to instruct their men in military discipline and the manœuvres of War. The minds of their Soldiers were thus animated with the desire of glory, and their Bodies hardened to the fatigues of War, whilst they gained Experience, Confidence and Courage by daily Rencounters.

These great Generals, like all others in similar Circumstances, never engaging presumptuously, but carefully watching for favourable Opportunities, let loose the Thebans, like young hounds upon their Enemies, and rendered them alert and brave, by tasting the Sweets of Victory. By bringing them off, in Safety, they made them fond of the Sport and eager after the most dangerous Enterprizes. By this skilfull Conduct, they brought their forces, to defeat the Spartans at Platea, Thespia, Tenagra and Tegyra. These Actions were only preludes to the decisive Battle of Leuctra: for, flushed with these Successes, the Thebans dreaded no Enemy, however superior in number. Greece saw with Astonishment, the Spartans defeated by inferiour numbers of Men, who had always been held in Contempt. This train of Successes elated the Thebans, but only enraged the Spartans. They negotiated

a Peace with Athens and all the other Grecian States, and Thebes was devoted to Spartan revenge. The largest Army, they ever sent into the field entered Bœotia, but Epaminondas, with six thousand Men only, by his admirable disposition of them and their bravery, engaged and defeated three times their number, and soon afterwards marched to the Gates of Sparta, and exhibited to that haughty People a Sight they had never before beheld.
Coll. Tudor.

### John Adams to Henry Knox

Dear Sir                                   Philadelphia September 29. 1776
   This Evening I had the Pleasure of your's, of the 25th.... I have only to ask you, whether it would be agreable to you, to have Austin made your Lieutenant Colonel? Let me know sincerely, for I will never propose it without your Approbation.
   I agree with you that there is nothing of the vast, in the Characters of the Ennemy's General or Admiral.... But I differ in Opinion from you, when you think, that if there had been, they would have Annihilated your Army.... It is very true, that a silly Panick has been spread in your Army and from thence even to Philadelphia. But Hannibal spread as great a Panick, once, at Rome, without daring to take Advantage of it.... If he had, his own Army would have been annihilated: and he knew it. A Panick in an Army when pushed to desperation, becomes Heroism.
   However, I despize that Panick and those who have been infected with it, and I could almost consent that the good old Roman fashion of decimation should be introduced. The Legion, which ran away, had the name of every Man in it, put into a Box, and then drawn out, and every tenth Man was put to death. The terror of this Uncertainty, whose Lot it would be to die, restrained the whole in the time of danger from indulging their fears.
   Pray tell me, Colonel Knox, does every Man to the Southward of Hudsons River, behave like an Hero, and every Man to the Northward of it, like a Poltroon, or not? The Rumours, Reports and Letters which come here upon every Occasion, represent the New England Troops, as Cowards, running away perpetually, and the Southern Troops as standing bravely. I wish I could know, whether it is true. I want to know for the Government of my own Conduct, because, if the New Englandmen are a Pack of Cowards, I would resign my place in Congress, where I should not choose to represent Poltroons, and re-

move to some Southern Colony, where I could enjoy the Society of Heros, and have a chance of learning some time or other, to be part of an Hero myself.... I must say, that your Amiable General gives too much Occasion for these reports by his Letters, in which he often mentions things to the disadvantage of some part of New England, but seldom any thing of the Kind about any other Part of the Continent.[1]

You complain of the popular Plan of raising the new Army. But if you make the plan as unpopular, as you please, you will not mend the matter. If you leave the Appointment of Officers to the General, or to the Congress, it will not be so well done, as if left to the Assemblies. The true cause of the Want of good Officers in the Army is not, because the Appointment is left to the Assemblies, but because such officers in sufficient Numbers are not in America. Without materials the best Workmen can do nothing. Time, Study and Experience alone, must make a sufficient number of able Officers.

I wish We had a military Accademy, and should be obliged to you for a Plan of such an Institution. The Expence would be a trifle, no object at all, with me.[2]

### John Adams to Colonel Hitchcock[3]

Dear Sir           Philadelphia October 1. 1776 Tuesday.

Yours of September the 9th. was duely received.[4] The measure of a Standing Army, is at length resolved on. You have seen the plan. How do you like it? I wish it was liable to fewer Exceptions, but We must be content to crawl into the right Way, by degrees. This was the best that We could obtain, at present.

I am extreamly sorry, to learn, that the Troops have been disheartened. But this despondency of Spirit, was the natural Effect, of the Retreats you have made, one after another. When the Men saw your General Officers, taken in a trap, upon Long Island, and the Army obliged to abandon that important Post, in consequence of that

---

[1] In LbC this sentence was amended by interlineation, doubtless before the (missing) recipient's copy was sent to Knox. It first read: "I must say that your *amiable* General gives too much Occasion for these Reports by his Letters, in which he is eternally throwing some Slur or other upon some Part of New England, but never one Word of the Kind about any other Part of the Continent."

[2] Here follows a postscript dated 1 Oct. which JA had already copied into his Autobiography, p. 437, above, and which is therefore omitted here.

[3] Daniel Hitchcock of Rhode Island; colonel, 11th Continental regiment; died Jan. 1777 (Heitman, *Register Continental Army*).

[4] From "Harlem Camp" (in Adams Papers).

Ambuscade, and the City of New York, evacuated in Consequence of the Retreat from Long Island, the firmest Army in the World, would have been seized, in similar Circumstances, with more or less of a Panick. But your men will now recover their Spirits in a short time.

There is a Way, of introducing Discipline into the most irregular Army, and of inspiring Courage into the most pusillanimous Collection of Men.

Your Army, Sir, give me leave to say, has been ill managed in two most essential points. The first is, in neglecting to train your Regiments and Brigades to the manual Exercises and the Manœuvres. Nothing inspires the Men with military pride and Ambition (for even the Men must have Ambition) like calling them together every day, and making them appear as well as they can. By living much together, and moving in concert, they acquire a confidence in themselves, and in each other. By being exposed to the Inspection, and Observations of each other, they become ambitious of appearing as clean and neat as they can, which as well as the Exercise preserves their health and hardens their Bodies against diseases. But instead of these martial, manly and elegant Exercises, they have been kept constantly at Work in digging Trenches in the Earth; which keeps them constantly dirty, and not having Wives, Mothers, Sisters or Daughters, as they used to have at home to take care of them and keep them clean, they gradually loose their Perspiration and their health.

Another particular, which is absolutely necessary to introduce military Ardour into a new raised Army, has been totally neglected. Such an Army should be governed with caution and circumspection, I agree. It should act chiefly upon the defensive, and no decisive Battle should be hazarded. But still an enterprizing Spirit should be encouraged. Favourable Opportunities should be watched, and Parties should be ordered out upon little excursions and expeditions: and in this manner Officers and Men should be permitted to acquire fame and honor in the Army, which will soon give them a real fondness for fighting. They will love the Sport. But instead of this, every Spark of an enterprizing Spirit in the Army, seems to have been carefully extinguished.

Our inevitable destruction will be the Consequence, if these faults are not amended. I rejoiced to hear of the Attempt, upon Montresors Island: but am vexed and mortified, at its shameful Issue. I am more humiliated still to learn, that the Enterprize was not renewed. If there had been Officers or Men, who would have undertaken the Expedition, a second, a third or a fiftieth time, I would have had that Island, if it had cost me, half my Army. Pray inform me what Officers and Men were sent upon that Attempt. It is said, there was shameful Cowardice. If any Officer was guilty of it, I sincerely hope he will be punished with death. This most infamous and detestable Crime, must never be forgiven in an Officer. Punishments as well as rewards will be necessary to Government, as long as fear, as well as hope, is a natural Passion in the human Breast.

Colonel Hitchcock.

### John Adams to General Parsons

My dear Sir          Philadelphia October 2. 1776. Wednesday

Your Letter from Long Island of the 29th. of August,[5] has not been answered. I was very much obliged to You, for it: because it contained Intelligence of a transaction, about which, We were left very much in the dark, at that time, and indeed to this hour, are not so well informed as We should be. I think, Sir, that the Enemy, by landing upon that Island, put it compleatly in our Power to have broke their plans, for this Campaign, and to have defended New York. But there are strong Marks of Negligence, Indolence, Presumption, and Incapacity on our Side, by which scandalous Attributes We lost that Island wholly, and Manhattan Island nearly. I am happy to hear your Behaviour commended. But, Sir, it is manifest that our Officers were not acquainted with the Ground; that they had never reconnoitred the Enemy; that they had neither Spies, Sentries, nor Guards placed as they ought to have been; and that they had been shamefully remiss in Obtaining Intelligence, of the Numbers and Motions of the Enemy, as well as of the nature of the Ground.

I have read, somewhere or other that a Commander, who is surprized in the night, though guilty of an egregious fault, may yet plead something in Excuse: but, in point of discipline, for a General to be surprized by an Enemy, just under his nose, in open day and caught in a State of wanton Security, from an overweening presumption in his own Strength, is a crime of so capital a nature, as to admit of neither Alleviation nor Pardon.[6] Ancient Generals have been nailed to Gibbets alive, for such crimes.

[5] Mainly concerning the action on Long Island, 27 Aug. (in Adams Papers).

[6] In LbC this sentence, beginning with the words "a Commander," is in quotation marks, and at the end of the paragraph JA parenthetically noted his source: "E. W. Montagues Reflections on the Rise and fall of the ancient Republicks. p. 203." JA's copy of this popular work by Edward Wortley Montagu, 2d edn., London, 1760, remains among his books in the Boston Public Library.

Be this as it may, I think the Enemy have reached their Ne plus, for this Year. I have drawn this Conclusion from the Example of Hannibal, whose Conquests changed the face and fortune of the War. According to Montesquieu, so long as he kept his whole Army together, he always defeated the Romans: but when he was obliged to put Garrisons into Cities, to defend his Allies, to besiege Strong holds, or prevent their being besieged, he then found himself too weak, and lost a great part of his Army by piece meal. Conquests are easily made, because We atchieve them with our whole force: they are retained with difficulty because We defend them, with only a part of our forces.

Howe, with his whole Army could easily take Possession of Staten Island, where there was nothing to oppose him. With the same Army, he found no great difficulty, in getting Long Island, where even *his* Talent at Strategem, which is very far from Eminent, was superiour to the Capacity of his Antagonist. After this it was easy to take New York which was wisely abandoned to him. But, Sir, the Case is altered. A Garrison is left at Staten Island, another at Long Island, a little one at Montresor's Island, another at Paulus Hook, a large Body in the City of New York and a larger still to man the Lines, across the Island, between the Seventh and the Eighth mile Stone. After such a division and distribution of his forces, I think he has nearly reached the End of his *tether* for this Year.

The Ennemies Forces are now in a Situation peculiarly happy, for Us to take Advantage of.... If an enterprizing Spirit should be indulged and encouraged, by our Commanders, in little Expeditions to Staten Island, Long Island, Montresors Island and elsewhere, you would gradually form your Soldiers for great Exploits and you would weaken, harrass and dispirit your Enemy.

Thus you see I scribble my Opinions with great Assurance, upon Subjects, which I understand not. If they are right, it is well, if wrong they will not mislead you.
General Parsons.

If these Papers should hereafter be read by disinterested Persons, they will perhaps think that I took too much upon me, in assuming the Office of Preceptor to the Army. To this Objection I can only reply, by asserting that it was high time, that the Army had some Instructor, or other. It was a Scæne of Indiscipline, Insubordination and Confusion. Colonel Tudor had been my Pupil, as a Clerk in my Office as a Barrister at Law. Colonel Knox had been a Youth, who had attracted my notice by his pleasing manners and inquisitive turn of Mind, when I was a Man in Business in Boston. General Parsons had been my junior for three Years at Colledge, and upon terms of familiarity. I had therefore no reason to suppose that either of them would take offence, at any thing I should write. Again I had formed an Opinion, that Courage and reading were all that were necessary to the formation of an Officer. Of the Courage of these Gentlemen and the Officers in general I had no doubt. But I was too well informed, that most of the Officers were deficient in reading: and I wished to turn the Minds of such as were capable of it, to that great Source of Information. I had met with an Observation among regular Officers, that Mankind were naturally divided into three Sorts. One third of them are animated at the first appearance of danger, and will press forward to meet it and examine it; another third are allarmed at it: but will neither advance nor retreat, till they know the nature of it: but stand to meet it: the remaining third will run or fly upon the first thought of it. If this Remark is just, as I believed it was, it appeared to me that the only Way to form an Army to be confided in, was a systematic discipline: by which means all Men may be made Heroes. In this manner, in time our American Army was made equal to the Veterans of France and England: and in this Way the Armies of France have been made invincible hitherto: and in the same Way, they will be ultimately conquered or at least successfully resisted by their Ennemies.

All the Powers of Government, Legislative, Executive and judiciary, were at that time collected in one Centre and that Centre was the Congress. As a Member of that Body I had contributed my Share towards the Creation of the Army, and the Appointment of all the Officers: and as President of the Board of War it was my peculiar Province to superintend every thing relating to the Army. I will add without Vanity, I had read as much on the military Art and much more of the History of War than any American Officer of that Army, General Lee excepted. If all these Considerations are not a sufficient Apology, for my Interference, I submit to censure. Certain it is, that these Letters and many more that I wrote, without preserving Copies, were not callculated to procure me popularity in the Army: but on the contrary contributed to produce those misrepresentations which were diffused from that Source against me as well my Friend Samuel Adams and others. The Generals Secretaries and Aids, all from the Southward, Reed, Harrison &c. &c. were young Gentlemen of Letters, and thought full as highly of themselves as they ought to think, and much more disrespectfully of New England and even of Congress, than they ought to have thought, dictated Letters, which were not well calculated to preserve the Subordination of the military Power, to the civil Authority, which the Spirit of Liberty will always require and enforce. Of Hamilton, when he came into the Generals Family I need say nothing. For my Part I never heard of him till after the Peace, and the Evacuation of the City of New York. The World has heard enough of him since. His Petulance, Impertinence and Impudence, will make too great a figure in these memoires hereafter.[7]

October 1st. 1776.

Resolved that a Committee of four be appointed to confer with Brigadier General Mifflin. The Members chosen Mr. R. H. Lee, Mr. Sherman, Mr. J. Adams and Mr. Gerry.[8]

Some time in the month of October 1776, I cannot from the Journals ascertain the day, worn down with continual Application, through all the heats of a Summer in Philadelphia, anxious for the State of my family and desirous of conferring with my Constituents on the critical and dangerous State of Affairs at home, I asked Leave of Congress to be absent, which they readily granted.[9]

However, before I proceed to relate the Occurrences of this Journey, I will copy some other Letters which ought to be inserted in this place, or perhaps they would be better thrown into an Appendix all together.[1]

### John Adams to General Parsons

Dear Sir                                    Philadelphia August 19. 1776

Your favours of the 13th and 15th are before me.[2] The Gentlemen you recommend for Majors, Chapman and Dier [Dyer], will be recommended by the Board of War, and I hope agreed to in Congress.

I thank you for your Observations upon certain Field Officers. Patterson, Shepherd and Brooks, make the best figure, I think, upon paper. If it is my misfortune, that I have not the least Acquaintance with any of those Gentlemen, having never seen any one of them, or heard his name, till lately. This is a little remarkable. Few Persons

[7] Preceding four sentences omitted by CFA in his text.

[8] This entry is repeated from p. 437, above; see note 4 there.

[9] JA left Philadelphia for Braintree on 13 Oct.; see Diary entry of that date and note there.

[1] JA never did "relate the Occurrences of this Journey," nor did he copy more than the single letter, to Samuel Holden Parsons, which follows. When, after a year and a half, he resumed his autobiographical narrative, he simply disregarded the thirteen-month period Oct. 1776 – Nov. 1777.

[2] Both from New York and largely concerned with recommendations of officers for promotion (in Adams Papers).

in the Province, ever travelled over the whole of it more than I have, or had better opportunities to know every conspicuous character. But I dont so much as know, from what Parts of the Province Shepherd and Brooks come; of what families they are; their Educations, or Employments.... Should be very glad to be informed.

Lt. Coll. Henshaw has been recommended to me by Coll. Reed for Promotion, as a usefull Officer.... But upon the whole, I think the List you have given me, dont shine.... I am very much ashamed of it.... I am so vexed, sometimes as almost to resolve to make Interest to be a Collonel, myself. I have almost Vanity enough to think, that I could make a figure in such a group. But a treacherous shattered Constitution, is an eternal Objection against my aspiring at military Command. If it were not for this insuperable Difficulty, I should certainly imitate Old Noll Cromwell, in one particular, that is, in launching into military Life, after forty, as much as I dislike his Character and Example in others. But enough of this.

I wish I could find materials, any where in sufficient quantities, to make good Officers. A brave and able Man, wherever he is, shall never want my Vote, for his Advancement: nor shall an ignorant awkward dastard, ever want it, for his dismission. Congress must assume an higher tone of discipline over Officers, as well as these over the Men.

*With regard to Encouragements in Money and in land, for Soldiers to inlist during the War, I have ever been in favour of it as the best Œconomy and the best policy: and I have no doubt, that rewards in Land, will be given after the War is over. But the Majority are not of my mind, for promising, of it, now.*[3] ... I am the less anxious about it, for a reason, which does not seem to have much weight, however, with the majority: Although, it may cost us more, and We may put now and then, a battle, to a hazard, by the method We are in, Yet We shall be less in danger of Corruption and Violence, from a Standing Army, and our Militia will acquire Courage, Experience, Discipline and hardiness in actual Service. I wish every Man upon the Continent was a Soldier, and obliged upon Occasion to fight, and determined to conquer or to die.

Flight was unknown to the Romans.... I wish it was to Americans. There was a flight from Quebec, and worse than a flight from the Cædars. If We dont attone for these disgraces, We are undone.

A more exalted Love of their Country; a more enthusiastic Ardor

---

[3] JA added the emphasis by underlining this passage when he copied the letter into his Autobiography.

for military Glory; a deeper detestation, disdain, and horror of martial disgrace must be excited among our People, or We shall perish in infamy.... I will certainly give my Voice for devoting to the infernal Gods, every man, high or low, who shall be convicted of bashfulness, in the day of battle.
Gen. Parsons.

P.S. Since the above was written, Congress has accepted the Report of the Board of War, and appointed Dier and Chapman, Majors. I had much pleasure in promoting Dier, not only from his own excellent Character, but from respect to my good friend his father.